W9-DCW-690

United States History

United States History
A Selective Guide to
Information Sources

Ron Blazek
Professor
Florida State University

and

Anna H. Perrault
Librarian Emeritus
Louisiana State University

1994
Libraries Unlimited, Inc.
Englewood, Colorado

To our families with love for their support and encouragement

Genevieve Blazek	*Joseph Perrault*
David Blazek	*Jean-Paul Perrault*
Daniel Blazek	*Andre Perrault*

LIBRARIES UNLIMITED, INC.
P.O. Box 6633
Englewood, CO 80155-6633
1-800-237-6124

Library of Congress Cataloging-in-Publication Data

Blazek, Ron.
    United States history : a selective guide to information sources /
Ron Blazek and Anna H. Perrault.
    xxviii, 411 p. 17x25 cm.
    Includes bibliographical references and index.
    ISBN 0-87287-984-4
    1. United States--History--Bibliography. 2. Reference books-
-United States--History--Bibliography. 3. United States--History-
-Data bases--Catalogs. 4. CD-ROM books--United States-
-Bibliography. I. Perrault, Anna H., 1944-   . II. Title.
Z1236.B57   1994
[E178]
016.973--dc20   93-41174
                                                             CIP

Contents

PART II
U.S. HISTORY—TOPICS AND ISSUES

List of Abbreviations and Symbols

ann.	annual
ann. cum.	annual cumulation
bi.	bimonthly
bienn.	biennial
bienn. cum.	biennial cumulation
col.	columns
comp.	compiler, compiled
corr.	corrected
ed.	edition, editor, edited
enl.	enlarged
et al.	additional (names) elsewhere
exp.	expanded
irreg.	irregular
mo.	monthly
n	minor entry or co-entry in annotations
quart.	quarterly
quin. cum.	quinquennial cumulation
repr.	reprint, reprinted
rev.	revised
semiann.	semiannual
supp.	supplement, supplemented
wk.	weekly
*	available online or in CD-ROM

Preface

PURPOSE AND SCOPE

This guide to the reference literature of U.S. history is designed for a wide spectrum of users: sophisticated researchers and practicing historians; students, both graduate and undergraduate; librarians; and the general public. It represents a selective but thorough coverage of both bibliographic and informational materials, as compared to the focus on bibliographic and biographical sources presented by Prucha in 1987 (entry 25). In addition to printed reference books, coverage is given to online databases and CD-ROM titles, as well as those in microform; publication dates range from the nineteenth century, in the case of certain standard and classic works, to spring 1993, when the searching and annotating was completed. To assure a historical perspective, it was decided to use 1975 or thereabouts, the close of the Vietnam period, as the cutoff date in terms of content.

In keeping with the recent emphasis on the "New History" described in the introduction, our work offers a social science perspective and emphasizes social history in its thorough treatment of multicultural and gender influences and its recognition of various societal systems, institutions, and issues (education, religion, the law, crime, etc.). Indeed, it is the first guide of its kind to consider the gay influence and to treat genealogy in a serious manner. Chapter 5 represents the bulk of the text and contains 421 of the 947 major entries.

Our work hardly ignores the titles associated with the study of history in a more traditional fashion, however, as a glance at the table of contents will indicate. Political history, military history, regional history, and so forth, are treated to a degree commensurate with their available resources. Excluded from coverage are the visual arts, music, and literature from the humanities and psychology and sociology from the social sciences. It is recommended that the searcher use other literature guides more specific to those areas.

METHOD OF SELECTION AND
USEFUL SOURCES

As indicated above, both standard tools and new reference materials are included, although emphasis is given to more recent titles. Selections were made either on the basis of favorable reviews or firsthand knowledge, the rationale being to offer the very best titles for any of the intended user groups. Certain helpful sources that did not receive separate entries should be identified, beginning with the standard, *International Bibliography of Historical Sciences*, which has appeared annually since 1926 and is now available from K. G. Saur with the cooperation of the International Committee of the Historical Sciences. Although its appearance is marked by a lack of promptness, its listings of books and periodical articles furnish an international perspective that at times is useful, especially to the study of diplomatic history of this country.

Most helpful for its provision of excellent reviews in history as well as other subjects is *American Reference Books Annual,* which has appeared each year since 1970 and is now in its 24th volume (1993) from Libraries Unlimited. Useful review journals are *Booklist* ("Reference Books Bulletin" section), *Choice, Library Journal,* and *Reference Services Review (RSR).*

More specialized to the social sciences are the following three annotated guides, all of which address both history in general and U.S. history in particular: *Sources of Information in the Social Sciences: A Guide to the Literature,* 3rd edition, by William H. Webb, et al. (American Library Association, 1986); *The Social Sciences: A Cross Disciplinary Guide to Selected Sources,* edited by Nancy L. Herron (Libraries Unlimited, 1989); and *Social Science Reference Sources: A Practical Guide,* 2nd edition, revised and enlarged by Tze-Chung Li (Greenwood, 1990).

The authors cannot overlook the utility of several general purpose tools in identifying important associations/societies and periodicals, respectively. **Encyclopedia of Associations* is an annual multivolume effort that has been issued since 1956 and is now published by Gale Research Company, which also publishes the *Gale Directory of Publications and Broadcast Media,* now in its 123rd edition and useful for both current and historical information. **Ulrich's International Periodicals Directory* has been issued by Bowker since 1932 and is also a yearly publication.

Finally, there are three especially useful titles that did receive coverage in our work, two of which are described within a single entry: *Guide to Reference Books,* 10th edition, edited by Eugene Sheehy, and its supplement, *Guide to Reference Books Covering Materials from 1985–1990,* edited by Robert Balay (entry 23). The third is *Handbook for Research in American History: A Guide to Bibliographies and Other Reference Works* by Francis P. Prucha (entry 25).

COMPOSITION AND ORGANIZATION

The introduction furnishes perspective regarding the nature of historical research and inquiry, along with the conditions of reference publishing. The section on "Electronic Reference Sources" offers suggestions for searching the literature as well as exposition of the computer environment.

The guide is then divided into two major parts: part I covers the general sources (Chapter 1), whereas part II covers specific topics and issues of U.S. history (Chapters 2–7).

Introductory notes are furnished for each chapter and for many sections and even subsections. These notes are likely to provide historical summaries of events and/or publishing developments relevant to the topic, as well as descriptions of relevant associations and their publications not covered in the section on "Historical Organizations and Publications" in chapter 1. Also treated in many of these passages are relevant general indexes which cover historical writings to some degree. In certain segments, such as "Genealogy and Immigration" in chapter 5 and

"Government Publications" in chapter 1, suggestions and recommendations are given for searching the literature.

Arrangement of major sections and some subsections is topical in nature, and form divisions are utilized when there are more than ten entries for the segment. Most frequently used are the four categories below:

1. *Library Resources*, which embrace library catalogs and directories of archival and library collections;

2. *Bibliographic Sources*, which identify the complement of relevant bibliographic apparatus, specialized bibliographies both current and retrospective, and specialized indexes and abstracting services;

3. *Information Sources*, which cite all types of reference tools that furnish exposition or description (dictionaries, atlases, encyclopedias, handbooks, chronologies, source books, etc.); and

4. *Biographical Sources*, a topical category that includes both bibliographic and information sources dealing with the lives or careers of people.

In general, in making decisions regarding placement of entries within sections, racial considerations are considered uppermost, followed by gender influences— e.g., a tool on African-American women is placed within "The Black Experience," and a source on women in politics is placed within "The Female Experience." An attempt was made to capture alternative categories through the indexes and through cross-references in the introductory segments to each topic.

ENTRIES AND ANNOTATIONS

There are 947 major entries, as well as hundreds of co-entries and minor entries that appear within the body of the annotation of the major entries. Major entries are given full bibliographic coverage in cases of single and dual authorship; in cases of more than two authors, only the first author is named, followed by "et al." International Standard Book Numbers (ISBNs) are given for major entries only. Minor entries and co-entries are identified in the indexes through "n" designations following the entry numbers.

Annotations tend to be lengthy, ranging from 85 to over 250 words, and describe scope and coverage of the tool. Description may also include information on authorship, publication history, topical (historical) analysis, value to particular audience, and search strategies, as well as co-entries and minor entries. Availability in online database or CD-ROM format is noted by an asterisk (*), an indicator also used in the indexes.

Acknowledgments

It is important that bibliographers receive the cooperation and assistance of others in doing their work. We were fortunate to benefit from the generosity of our respective employers—the Florida State University School of Library and Information Studies and the Middleton Library of Louisiana State University—in gaining access to much-needed personnel and technology in order to complete this project.

At Florida State University no less than four graduate assistants participated in the project over its two-and-a-half-year duration. David Hartman began the search of the literature using guides and bibliographies when this work was still in its formative and less-focused stage, then passed the torch to Zhen-Mei (Mae) Wang, who prepared a comprehensive database of citations. Once the selections were made, it was left to Kristine Tardiff to furnish yeoman service in finding reviews, then doing the bulk of the word processing of the annotated entries. John Hatton completed the task, which involved a combination of searching and word processing; he also offered sound advice on suitable additional entries for certain areas, and was responsible for the detailed author-title index.

Thanks are owed to Ms. Sherry Stafford of the school's secretarial staff, who cheerfully participated in the work at the word processing stages when such demands mounted and threatened delay. Finally, a great debt is acknowledged to the manager of the computer laboratory at the school, David Miner. His can-do attitude coupled with his extensive expertise was heartening when the authors were unsure of the possibilities of the various systems employed.

Several graduate assistants at the Middleton Library of the Louisiana State University Reference Services Division searched entries in the book review indexes—Alberta Songe, Jeffrey Faust, Marc Wellman, Rebecca Plunkett, and Scott Allen. Two library associates in Reference Services, Paula Bryars and Scott Campbell, were also particularly helpful in searching for book reviews and performing miscellaneous small tasks. Trish Cruse of the Business Administration/ Government Documents department served as a reader.

Without all of these contributors, the effort would have taken far longer, and might not have come to fruition.

Introduction

NATURE OF SCHOLARSHIP AND
RESEARCH TRADITIONS

Historical inquiry and its writing have passed through different stages representing different philosophical traditions through time. One of the earliest positions, espoused initially by the ancient Greeks, favored the belief in recurrent conditions or historical cycles. Subsequently, St. Augustine placed an emphasis on God and Christianity, which was followed by a growing belief in the elevation of man and his progress toward a noble future, a view characteristic of the eighteenth and nineteenth centuries. In all these philosophical orientations, the intent has been to give a complete picture of the past as a comprehensible, logical progression of events.

These attempts to depict the universality of the historical record and the presence of a guiding principle are embodied in what has now come to be called traditionalist theory. The writing of history in the traditionalist sense presents historical narrative to explain the large sweep of the past. As a discipline, history in this framework originated as part of the humanities. As such, it emphasized the importance of the high and mighty decisionmakers during the various chronological periods and gave little thought to the sentiments and activity of the common people or their impact on societal development.

During the nineteenth century, historians and philosophers in Europe, especially in Germany, began to question the theoretical and methodological assumptions upon which historical scholarship was based. The developing trend favored a more scientific and critical approach to the use of records, with more care given to their selection and to the nature of documentary evidence. It was at this time that history began to emerge as a professional discipline and theories of historical writing were developed.

Such writing remained largely within the humanistic frame and focused primarily on politics and political figures. It was not until the end of the nineteenth century and beginning of the twentieth that traditional history was challenged as being too narrow and exclusive. The need for inclusion of cultural, social, and economic factors in order to fully comprehend political developments was gradually accepted by modern historians in their desire to furnish an accurate picture of the past.

The influence of German scholarship diminished during the twentieth century for a number of reasons (not the least of which were the two world wars). The "New History" emerged as a challenge to the large-scale historical narrative of the past. It was given impetus by World War II, which inspired the behavioral or psychosocial approach and study of comparative relationships between people and events. Since the 1960s, this new approach has been linked to the social sciences, which encourage investigators to ask precise questions or even formulate hypotheses and then to seek answers in appropriate documents.

This process requires a certain precision of operation in enumerating assumptions, defining terms, refining strategies, and most importantly in defining the problems to be investigated. These problems relate closely to everyday life and the experience of the common man and woman. As studies embrace the social, cultural, and economic context through which political history is developed, such elements as urban history, business history, legal history, family history, women's studies, ethnic studies, popular culture, and so forth take on added significance. Indeed, the study of U.S. history has achieved primacy at the expense of the more traditional emphasis on ancient or medieval Europe.

In this climate, the study of history has become highly diversified. The basic areas of inquiry, such as political history, social history, and intellectual history, still remain, but they now are aided by the knowledge generated through psychology, sociology, and demography. The recent emphasis on statistics has given birth to the "cliometrician," or statistical historian, who applies rigorous social science principles to the collection of quantifiable historical data.

Thus, history remains an exciting and fertile field of inquiry. Today it embodies a number of possible approaches with a mix of research orientations ranging from exclusively quantitative to wholly qualitative in nature. Cliometricians and traditionalists do agree on the nature of the historian's role in revealing truth about the past and the need for historical honesty in seeking to understand it. They understand the fundamental complexity of their task but seem to revel in their adoptive roles. Through it all, the search for meaning remains the universal rationale for all historical inquiry.

THE REFERENCE LITERATURE—
MATERIALS AND ACCESS

In a recent master's thesis, Sally Ann Shurtz revealed a 55 percent increase in the publication of reference works in U.S. history between 1970 and 1990. This figure reflects the 50 percent increase in the number of both reference and trade publications in all historical subdisciplines since 1980.[1] Clearly, the matter of bibliographic control of the historical literature presents a major problem when viewed within the rather disparate levels of sophistication of potential users.

One of the more useful reference aids from the periodical literature of recent years has been the annual review of reference sources in U.S. history by Gary Barber and Carol Burroughs. The series began with the April/June 1978 issue of *Reference Services Review* (*RSR*) and seems to have ended abruptly with the Winter 1989 issue. The authors noted that there is a dearth of new information tools in the field, despite vigorous publishing activity with regard to retrospective indexing. Also, new microform sources had broadened access. Serial indexes were seen as an increasingly important element in bibliographic control. Barber and Burroughs chose to organize their annual surveys using only three simple but adequate categories; 1) "Revision of Standard Sources and New Titles in Series"; 2) "Micrographics"; and 3) "New Works."[2]

Charles Osburn identified several trends in historical research for the past two to three decades that corresponded closely to our observations after having studied the field in preparation of this guide. There is widening availability of data in varied formats and more and more use of computerized information. This trend, of course, aids the growing body of cliometricians immeasurably; it also opens up new avenues of inquiry to the more traditional social historians. It is important that traditionalists seize the day in this regard, for Osburn reports a shrinking proportion of research produced in the traditional manner and dealing with traditional subjects.[3]

With the emergence and growth of the "New History" has come an availability of reference tools in ethnic and black history, women's history, family history, and so forth, all of which have become important areas of inquiry. Although the historian's dependence upon primary source material for purposes of research has not changed through the years, the types of records consulted have undergone some transformation in the recent past. Archives, research libraries, museums, and repositories more frequently are being asked to provide church records, probates, tax rolls, voting and election records, and the like.

In response to this need, reference sources have been developed that make it possible for the new social historian to operate effectively. Greater use of micro-graphics and the development of oral history collections are salient characteristics of new information trends. Through both audio and video tapes, it is possible to gain unprecedented insight and perspective in detecting nuances of meaning from players and eyewitnesses, dimensions not offered by print transcripts.

Recently, Donald O. Case reported the results of a study examining the collection and use of information by a select group of historians concerned with U.S. history. He was able to confirm the continuing primacy of archival holdings and primary source material and the secondary role of reference sources in the conduct of research. All types of materials were used to some degree, however, although there was a surprising lack of use of bibliographic databases by historians in his study.[4]

Case did point out the importance of covering historical materials by *topic* in guides and bibliographies, as opposed to subdividing a large body of knowledge by time and place. Topical categories are perceived to be more useful to the historian than are chronological categories; the topics he identified represent the subject matter of the New History and include gender, ethnicity, crime, popular culture, the Depression, and so forth.[5]

That print material remains an important staple in the life of the historian cannot be disputed. Bibliographies, cumulative indexes, and documentary sources continue to appear in print or in micrographic form. More than likely, however, they are also issued in computer readable format or will be in the future. It is essential that the historian become aware of the advantages of computerized products in terms of both timeliness and searching efficiency in order to derive full benefit from the available reference literature.

ELECTRONIC REFERENCE SOURCES

Since the mid-1980s there has been an explosion in electronic resources for research. Even though library computer databases were begun in the 1970s, they were used mainly by library staff and not by individual researchers. In the 1980s researchers in all fields began to utilize personal computers instead of typewriters for the production of manuscripts. Although some inveterate journalists and historians still use their typewriters, the younger generation of students and scholars are all computer literate.

Up until the mid-1980s, most libraries had only a few electronic databases available for use by the public, offering access to remote bibliographic and information databases through mediated searching, usually for a fee. During the same time frame, many libraries were beginning to build an online catalog to replace the manually maintained card catalog. Some libraries allowed interested users to search the remote cataloging databases. Those who were disposed to shun computers could avoid having to use them. The introduction of CD-ROM indexing products in the mid-1980s completely changed the nature of reference work and research. It has become impossible to maintain a current list of CD-ROM databases because new products are entering the market every day.

Besides the currency of information in electronic databases, one major advantage of printed indexes and catalogs over manual searches is the ability to tailor search strategies by including more than one term. With printed materials it is necessary to go singly from one term or access point to another. In electronic searching, the use of Boolean search logic enables the user to precisely define a subject area through the use of multiple terms and to search several terms simultaneously. The Boolean logic capability has convinced users of the superiority of electronic databases over manual searching methods.

For many years bibliographic information in machine-readable format was also produced in printed format. Although the majority of the periodical databases and reference tools are still available in printed form, many datafiles and bibliographic records are now available only through electronic access. The U.S. Censuses for 1980 and 1990, for example, were only partially produced in printed form, with the vast quantity of information only available on machine-readable tapes. Other examples are the Library of Congress current cataloging MARC (Machine-Readable Cataloging) records and the ESTC (Eighteenth Century Short-Title Catalogue), both of which are available in electronic form or in computer-output microfiche.

This section introduces electronic reference sources first to suggest an order in which library users should approach the search for materials. Whether the terminology is "online database," "CD-ROM index," "machine-readable datafiles," "OPAC" (online public access catalog), or the name of a network database or vendor, the most effective search for materials frequently begins with some type of electronic reference source.

One caveat for the historical researcher is that although one cannot afford to ignore the up-to-date electronic resources, many library and archival holdings do not appear in these databases. Thus, the historical researcher must master not only the new technology but also the old idiosyncrasies of card catalogs and the printed bibliographies, microforms, and finding aids that make up the majority of the reference sources in this guide.

Library Network Databases and Services

OCLC

The first large library database, OCLC (Online Computer Library Center), was formed in 1967 by a group of academic libraries in Ohio. From a modest beginning as a statewide online union catalog, by 1992 OCLC had become an international bibliographic utility with over 28 million records from nearly 15,000 libraries of all types worldwide which have access to the database. The bibliographic records are for book and journal titles, government documents, musical scores, and audio-visual materials. Some archival cataloging is present. Not until the 1980s did OCLC regard this vast database of bibliographic records with the holdings of libraries indicated as anything other than a source of cataloging records for libraries and an auxiliary interlibrary loan module made possible by the locations. Subject searching was not possible.

In the mid-1980s OCLC began to develop a new marketing strategy aimed at the end user—the individual researcher—rather than libraries and library staff. By the early 1990s search strategies and protocols that had been developed for catalog-ing were revamped, and menu systems to guide the uninitiated were put in place. Many libraries encourage users to search the OCLC database in the reference areas through dedicated terminals. It is now also possible for individuals to access the entire OCLC bibliographic database (World Cat) from office or home via PCs to search for specific subject terms. "FirstSearch" is the service that offers this type of access. In addition to covering the OCLC bibliographic database, the FirstSearch service includes subject periodical indexes such as the *Humanities Index* (entry 55), the *Social Sciences Index* (entry 55), and *Biography Index* (entry 138). Another feature is a document delivery option. The researcher beginning to prepare a bibliography can search the database and download the machine-readable records to a personal computer file without having to rekey the bibliographic records. Although there is much retrospective material in the OCLC bibliographic database, some older works of use to the historian may not be included.

Arrangements for searching can be made through libraries or by contacting the OCLC Online Computer Library Center, Inc., 6565 Frantz Road, Dublin, OH, 430017-3395, (800) 848-8286.

RLIN

Another large bibliographic database was begun in the late 1960s at Stanford University. The Research Libraries Group (RLG), a consortium of large research libraries formed in the early 1970s, used the Stanford University library database as the foundation for the Research Libraries Information Network (RLIN). The RLIN database contains more than 52 million items—bibliographic records to books, serials, archives and manuscripts, maps, music scores, sound recordings, films, and photographs—held by over 110 academic and special research libraries.

The main bibliographic catalog is noted for its strong retrospective research holdings. Of particular interest to the historical researcher are a number of separate files and databases within RLIN. The foremost of these is the Archives and

Manuscripts file, to which many research library archival collections have been contributing cataloging since the network was founded (see entry 87). The majority of these records do not appear in any published source, and it has become impossible to do archival research, especially for major U.S. collections, without consulting this database.

Another RLIN database of use to U.S. historians is the Eighteenth Century Short-Title Catalogue. The holdings of the American Antiquarian Society, as well as the eighteenth-century American imprints owned by British and North American libraries, are included in this ongoing project. Because of the overwhelming number of eighteenth-century imprints in English that exist worldwide, there will never be a printed catalog of the ESTC; it is available only in microfiche and through the RLIN database. (Research Publications, Inc. has an ongoing microfilming project based on the ESTC to film at least one copy of the text of the titles.)

Other specialized files in the RLIN database are musical recordings and scores and machine-readable data files. A number of other specialized databases (such as the Avery architectural index, the History of Technology, and periodical and newspaper indexing) are offered through a separate service, CitaDel, which also includes a document delivery component. Although almost all sizes and types of libraries are OCLC users, a smaller number of academic and special research libraries are RLG members, and access policies may vary. RLG also encourages direct access to the database by individuals. Personal search accounts for access through the Internet can be purchased from RLG (Research Libraries Group), 1200 Villa St., Mountain View, CA, 94041-1100, (800) 537-7546.

Other Library Networks

In addition to the two largest library online databases (OCLC and RLIN), there are a number of other networks and utilities. The Washington Library Network (WLN) is based in the northwest and has member libraries in the United States and Canada. Another network is CARL, the Colorado Alliance of Research Libraries, which in 1991 incorporated UTLAS, the University of Toronto system. CARL offers access to groups of databases, including library catalogs, periodical indexes and tables of contents (UNCOVER), information databases, and the Internet Resources Guide.

In the 1990s, library networks began to offer table of contents databases and electronic indexing services for online searching combined with document delivery services. CARL was the first network to offer a large database of tables of contents from journals and the capability to order article photocopies through the online database. All of these end-user services allow the researcher to order and receive material directly, with billing by credit card.

Internet

A vast array of library catalogs and databases is now available to individual researchers at universities and colleges through the Internet, a system of computers communicating with each other using a uniform addressing format. The Internet was formed through federal funding in the 1970s by the National Science Foundation. It is the backbone of a telecommunications network that affords scholars and researchers in the United States national and international electronic communications capability. Two basic services of the Internet are electronic mail (e-mail) and file transfer (FTP). Using electronic mail, colleagues around the world may converse directly with each other in pairs or in groups. They also may receive news through focused interest groups (listservs). Using the file transfer capability, researchers working together can send data or text electronically. Individuals having accounts that allow them to connect to a local institutional computer facility can use electronic mail to get into library catalogs throughout the world, most of them available without search fees.

A guide for those who have not yet used computer e-mail is *Directory of Fulltext Online Resources, 1992* by Jack Kessler (Meckler, 1992). This guide explains in nontechnical language the basics of becoming an Internet user. One chapter explains library online catalogs (OPACS) and has a listing of over 100 library catalogs that can be accessed free of charge through the Internet. The directory also covers CD-ROM products, bulletin boards, commercial fulltext databases, and information on electronic journals. There is a bibliography of references on the use of electronic communication in research. The best feature of the directory is that e-mail addresses are generously supplied.

A guide suitable for the novice is *The Internet Companion: A Beginner's Guide to Global Networking* (Addison-Wesley, 1992) by Tracy LaQuey. Much more in-depth and comprehensive is *The Whole Internet: User's Guide & Catalog* (O'Reilly & Associates, 1992), by Ed Krol. Another well-known guide is *Crossing the Internet Threshold: An Instructional Handbook* (Library Solutions Press, 1993), which has helpful fact sheets on various Internet tools from FTP and telnet to Archie, Gopher, WAIS, and World Wide Web. One of the first and most popular guides to the Internet is *Zen and the Art of the Internet: A Beginner's Guide to the Internet* by Brendan P. Kehoe (Prentice Hall, 1993).

The Association of Research Libraries publishes both print and online versions of *Directory of Electronic Journals, Newsletters, and Discussion Lists* (ARL, 1991–). Instructions for subscribing to these directories and guides and many other services and databases are in the *Directory of Fulltext Online Resources*. Most academic libraries and computer centers have programs and personnel to assist users in obtaining accounts and accessing the Internet.

CD-ROM Indexes and Information Databases

For over a decade the dominant method for accessing indexing and information databases was the online search conducted through commercial vendors such as DIALOG, BRS, WESTLAW, LEXIS, and WILSONLINE. The library bibliographic networks—OCLC, RLIN, CARL, and others—now also offer online database searching for many of the same indexing and full-text databases as the commercial vendors but with different charging structures.

In the last years of the 1980s CD-ROM became the dominant electronic medium for reference services. The number of databases in CD-ROM format continues to grow at a fast pace. The availability of individual CD-ROM and other information databases will vary from library to library according to research priorities and funding. Throughout this guide, printed reference tools and indexes that are also available in electronic formats are indicated by an asterisk (*) in front of the entry number, and with the phrase.

A number of directories of computer-readable databases are published. Two for CD-ROM products are *The CD-ROM Directory* (7th ed., Omnigraphics, 1992) and *CD-ROMs in Print, 1992: An International Guide to CD-ROM, CD-I, CDTV, & Electronic Book Products* (5th ed., Meckler, 1991). *Computer-Readable Databases: A Directory and Data Sourcebook* (Gale Research, 1976–) is also available as Dialog file 230. This database is very comprehensive, with detailed descriptions on nearly 6,800 databases available throughout the world. The online file has the advantage of being more up to date than any print source.

The Government Printing Office and many federal agencies have increasingly been producing information in electronic formats, much of it not available in printed form. Until recently, much of the information was available on tape or disks as raw data, with no user-friendly programming to assist in retrieval and manipulation of the contents. An ever-growing number of CD-ROM products with federal information is now becoming available from the GPO. Users will need to be informed and guided by a knowledgeable librarian as to the availability of specific information in electronic formats. A current listing of electronic products from federal agencies is published periodically in *Administrative Notes,* produced by the Library Program Office of the Government Printing Office. The U.S. Department of Commerce produces a *Directory of Computerized Data Files: A Guide to U.S. Government Information in Machine-Readable Format* (NTIS, 1988). Another guide to government datafiles is by William Evinger, *Federal Statistical Databases* (see entry 114). Information on specific reference sources of use in historical research is incorporated in the "Bibliographic Sources" section of this guide on "Government Publications" and "Statistical and Demographic Sources" and in Chapter 3 on "Politics and Government." A gateway for dial-up access to much government information in electronic form has been proposed in congressional legislation for several years. When provision is finally made by Congress, the public will have access to a large body of government information through the Internet or National Research and Education Network (NREN). In the near future, it appears that most government information will exist only in electronic form and that only the information needed will be accessed and downloaded or printed out.

Another source of statistical and numeric data is the Inter-University Consortium for Political and Social Research (entry 115). The ICPSR has been collecting statistical data for over 30 years. The use of machine-readable datafiles is widespread in the social sciences among sociologists, political scientists, and economists. Statistical information gathered by the federal government is used by government employees and researchers in the academic and private sectors. As current information ages, historians will find much useful unpublished statistical and demographic information in numeric datafiles.

Database sources for the study of U.S. history are being compiled abroad as well as in the United States. The Centre d'Etude et de Recherche sur la Culture Anglo-Americaine, at the Universite d'Orleans (CERCA), incorporates materials for the study of American literature and culture since 1945 into its European bibliographic database. The intent is to make sure that scholarly information seldom included in U.S. bibliographies is made available to U.S. and foreign scholars.

Historical materials are particularly suited to multimedia databases, which combine printed sources, visual materials, sounds, and animation. The *Grolier Multimedia Encyclopedia* and *Compton's Family Encyclopedia* are examples of products that contain the complete encyclopedia on one CD-ROM disk. The Bureau of Electronic Publishing offers a *History of the World, Countries of the World,* and

U.S. History on CD-ROM (see entry 101). There are CD-ROMS on the U.S. Constitution (see entry 165) and wars (see entries 382 and 412 and p. 162).

The American Memory Project of the Library of Congress is a multimedia electronic imaging project that concentrates on the 1880–1945 period in U.S. history. Archival materials are stored on CD-ROM and laser videodisk. Varying media, including photographs, motion pictures, speeches, cartoons, and printed journal articles are included. A wide range of subjects from U.S. life and culture are covered.

As more libraries use multimedia technology for preservation and to improve access to historical materials, more research materials will become available. Multimedia products, which are both easy and fun to use, are bringing the study of history to large numbers of students and the general public.

Historians and archivists have joined with librarians in voicing concern about the preservation of data and resources that exist only in electronic formats. The fast pace of changing technologies continues to render hardware and software obsolete, presenting preservation challenges not experienced with paper materials. The National Academy of Public Administration (NAPA) performed a study at the request of the National Archives to address the concerns of historians, archivists, and researchers about preserving government information that is created, maintained and used in electronic form. The recommendations in the report, titled *Archives of the Future; Archival Strategies for the Treatment of Electronic Databases: A Study of Major Automated Databases Maintained by Agencies of the U.S. Government* (NAPA, 1991), apply to electronic information in general, not just to government information.

Although an often-repeated fact is that much of the information in CD-ROM and other electronic formats is current information—more current than printed sources—more and more information is becoming available only in electronic form. As years pass, a greater share of historical research will have to be conducted through database access. The problems of preserving manuscript drafts, data maintained only in electronic form, and government information of all types have come to the forefront, as these are the future materials for historical research. The computer revolution has changed the nature of all research and scholarship. This reference guide attempts to look to the future as well as describe the reference tools produced in recent years.

NOTES

1. Sally Ann Shurtz, "A Content Analysis of Reference Social Science Materials as Reviewed in *American Reference Books Annual, 1970-1990*" (Master's thesis, Louisiana State University, 1992), 41.

2. The annual surveys appeared a total of 10 times with titles that varied slightly but generally approximated "Current Survey of American History Reference Sources" over a period of 11 years from 1978 to 1989. It was not issued in 1988, and compensated with a two-year coverage (1986-1987) in 1989. Although the column was to continue as an annual feature, thereafter, it has not appeared since.

3. Charles B. Osburn, *Academic Research and Library Resources: Changing Patterns in America,* Westport, CT: Greenwood, 1979, 76-77.

4. Donald O. Case, "The Collection and Use of Information by Some American Historians: A Study of Motives and Methods," *Library Quarterly*, 61 (January 1991), 73-74.

5. Ibid., 68-79.

PART I

U.S. HISTORY
GENERAL SOURCES

Chapter 1

Sources of General Importance to U.S. History

HISTORICAL ORGANIZATIONS AND PUBLICATIONS

History is not just an academic pursuit. Even though historical research is the expectation of college and university professors, history is a professional practice, and historical studies are conducted in museums and libraries, federal and local governmental agencies, schools, and the private sector.

Preservation has become a subfield of history, as well as of library, museum, and archival work. Historical sites are among the biggest tourist attractions. Since World War II, preservation efforts in the United States have increased at all levels, with governmental and private funding supporting these efforts.

Historical societies and organizations are numerous, especially on the regional and local level. Only national organizations focusing primarily on U.S. history, study, research, preservation, and writing are listed in this section. Societies with a specialized focus are mentioned in appropriate sections throughout the guide. A full array of historical associations can be found in the *Directory of Historical Organizations in the United States and Canada* (entry 18). Historical organizations are also listed in the *Encyclopedia of Associations* published annually by Gale Research. Because directory information is subject to change, this reference guide only gives addresses and telephone numbers, with no information on personnel. Editorial information for journals and newsletters is also not given. The current volumes of sources such as the *Encyclopedia of Associations*, Bill Katz's *Magazines for Libraries*, or *Ulrich's International Periodicals Directory* should be consulted for accurate directory information. Editorial information for the submission of manuscripts can be found in the directories of historical publications described below (entries 19, 20).

This section is divided into two parts. The first lists major historical organizations and societies; the second lists directories of journals, organizations, or institutions of interest to the historian.

Organizations

1. **American Antiquarian Society.** Founded 1812. 185 Salisbury St., Worcester, MA 01609-1634. (508) 755-5221.

The American Antiquarian Society (AAS) is an organization focused on research and preservation in the history and culture of America up to the year 1876. The organization maintains a library of nearly 5 million titles, one of the nation's richest collections for the study of American history. The AAS sponsors educational programs, research, and fellow-ships for research in the American Antiquarian Society Library.

The American Antiquarian Society publishes the *American Antiquarian Society Proceedings*, a semiannual scholarly publication that contains bibliographies and edited primary documents for the study of U.S. history. The *American Antiquarian Society Newsletter*, also semiannual, covers news of exhibitions, society activities, grants, and other special programs.

2. **American Association for State and Local History.** Founded 1940. 172 2nd Ave., Ste. 202, Nashville, TN 37201. (615) 255-2971.

An organization with over 6,000 members, the AASLH promotes the study of state and local history. Educators, historians, writers, state and local historical societies, and other agencies and individuals interested in this field are members. The association conducts seminars and workshops and bestows awards.

Publications include the bimonthly *History News* and the monthly *History News Dispatch*. The association also publishes the *Directory of Historical Organizations in the United States and Canada* (entry 18), as well as a series of technical pamphlets and books, *Bicentennial State Histories Series*.

3. **American Historical Association.** Founded 1884. 400 A St. SE, Washington, DC. (202) 544-2422.

The AHA membership (14,000) is made up of professional historians, educators, and others interested in historical research and preservation. The organization is involved with historical studies in general and is not focused on a particular geographical area or time period. The AHA sponsors a number of fellowships, grants, prizes, and awards.

The AHA publishes *Grants and Fellowships of Interest to Historians*, updated every few years. This title lists in one place government, private sector, and university and nonprofit foundation funding sources for historical study. Information necessary to prepare applications is given, including submission date, the amount of the funding offered, and addresses and telephone numbers. The guide also lists awards and prizes, as well as educational departments offering degrees in history.

The AHA's scholarly journal, the *American Historical Review*, includes book reviews and bibliographies. The AHA also publishes a newsletter, *American Historical Association—Perspectives*, an annual *Directory of History Departments and Organizations in the United States and Canada*, and an annual *Proceedings*.

4. **American Studies Association.** Founded 1951. 2140 Taliaferro Bldg., University of Maryland, College Park, MD 20742-7711. (301) 405-1364.

The ASA is a professional society of 3,500 members concerned with any field of study relating to U.S. life and culture. The membership is drawn from persons interested in U.S. history, literature, philosophy, anthropology, political science, sociology, and the arts and those employed in libraries, cultural institutions, and government. The association promotes interdisciplinary research and teaching in U.S. culture both past and present.

The ASA publishes the journal *American Quarterly* and a newsletter that includes employment opportunities and research updates. The journal contains articles on the study of U.S. life and culture.

5. **Association for the Bibliography of History.** Founded 1978. Lockwood Memorial Library, SUNY at Buffalo, Amherst, NY 14260. (716) 645-2817.

The 300 members of the Association for the Bibliography of History actively support the development of bibliographical tools to aid in the study of history. The association also promotes the learning of bibliographical skills and the application of high standards in bibliographical practice. The ABH is affiliated with the American Historical Association. It publishes the semiannual *ABH Bulletin*, a newsletter.

6. **Bibliographical Society of America.** Founded 1904. P.O. Box 397, Grand Central Station, New York, NY 10163. (212) 995-9151.

The Bibliographical Society of America (BSA) (membership approximately 1,000) is made up of book dealers, bibliophiles, printers, publishers, historians, and others interested in bibliographical problems and projects. The society sponsors short-term fellowships to encourage scholarship in bibliography.

In 1937 the society completed publication of Joseph Sabin's monumental nineteenth-century enterprise, *A Dictionary of Books Relating to America* (entry 41), as well as *American Newspapers: A Union List* (entry 62n). Recent publications dealing with Americana include Richard J. Wolfe's *Early American Music Engraving and Printing: A History of Music Publishing in America from 1787 to 1825* and Thomas R. Adams's *The American Contro-versy: A Bibliographical Study of the British Pamphlets About the American Disputes, 1764–1783* (published jointly with Brown University) (entry 340). Currently the BSA is supervising publication of the great *Bibliography of American Literature.*

Aside from carrying out various bibliographic projects and joint ventures with other learned societies, the BSA publishes its papers on a quarterly basis.

7. **Institute of Early American History and Culture.** Founded 1943. PO Box 220, Williamsburg, VA 23187. (804) 253-5117.

The Institute for Early American History and Culture focuses on research in North American history from the European origins up to 1815. The institute sponsors various awards, among them a two-year postdoctoral research fellowship. It maintains a library of microfilm including an extensive collection of pre-1800 U.S. newspapers.

The institute publishes the *William and Mary Quarterly,* plus monographs of documen-tary materials, secondary works, biographies, bibliographies, and reprints.

8. **National Council on Public History.** Founded 1979. 301 Cavanaugh, 425 University Blvd., Indianapolis, IN 46202. (317) 274-2716.

The National Council on Public History was formed to stimulate interest in public history and broaden interest in professional history. It serves as an information clearinghouse, sponsors workshops and training programs, and offers advice to other historical associations and agencies. The council maintains an online database on continuing education opportunities and contract services in history.

The major publication of the NCPH is its quarterly journal, *The Public Historian,* which covers all aspects of public history—archives, education, business history, management of museums and cultural resources, and policy issues. The council also publishes *Public History News,* which deals with issues, problems, and trends in the field. Monographs published include *The Craft of Public History* (entry 47), *Guide to Continuing Education for Public Historians*, *A Guide to Graduate Programs in History*, and *Careers for Students of History* (with the AHA).

9. **National Trust for Historic Preservation.** Founded 1949. 1785 Massachusetts Ave. NW, Washington, DC 20036. (202) 673-4000.

The National Trust for Historic Preservation is a national private organization of over 236,000 members chartered by the U.S. Congress. The purpose of the organization is to foster the preservation of historic buildings, sites, and objects significant to the history and culture of the United States. The organization actively promotes preservation by maintaining historic sites, engaging in legal action, acting as a clearinghouse for information on state, local, federal and private preservation programs, sponsoring seminars and workshops, and monitoring legislation. The trust gives awards, grants and loans.

The major publication of the trust is the bimonthly *Historic Preservation*. The magazine includes articles on developments in the preservation field, people and projects, book reviews, and the *Historic House and Museum Directory*. Other publications are a newsletter, a quarterly journal, *Preservation Forum,* and *Preservation Law Reporter*, and *Preservation News*.

10. **Oral History Association.** Founded 1966. 1093 Broxton Ave., No. 720, Los Angeles, CA 90024. (213) 825-0597.

The OHA membership (1,400) is made up of archivists, historians, librarians, medical scholars, authors, editors, interviewers, and institutions. The association was founded to exchange information, to promote the field of oral history, and to improve techniques.

The semiannual journal *Oral History Review* is published by the OHA, as is *Oral History Association—Newsletter,* which includes book reviews and research news. The association issues the *OHA Annual Report and Membership Directory*. A number of publications about oral history research and the use of oral history techniques have been published, including *Oral History Evaluation Guidelines*; *Oral History: An Interdisciplinary Anthology*; *Oral History and the Law*; and *Oral History for Community History Projects*.

11. **Organization of American Historians.** Founded 1907. 112 N. Bryan St., Bloomington, IN 47408. (812) 855-7311. OAH@UCS.INDIANA.EDU.

Formerly the Mississippi Valley Historical Association, the OAH primarily focuses on U.S. history. Membership (12,000) includes professional historians, academics, secondary school teachers, graduate students, and other individuals concerned with U.S. history as a profession and an educational curriculum. Institutional members of the OAH include historical agencies and libraries—public, academic, and school. The organization sponsors educational programs, promotes historical research and study, sponsors 11 prize programs for historical writing, bestows other awards, and maintains a speaker's bureau.

The quarterly *Journal of American History*, which contains book reviews and dissertation lists as well as scholarly articles, is published by the OAH. The OAH's quarterly *Magazine of History* carries news, lesson plans, and articles for teachers. The *OAH Newsletter* is a quarterly about the activities of the organization.

12. **Society of American Archivists.** Founded 1936. 600 S. Federal St., Ste. 504, Chicago, IL 60605. (312) 922-0140.

The SAA is an organization for professionals in the field of archival and records administration and preservation. Approximately 4,500 individuals and institutions are members of the SAA, which publishes a membership directory and the *SAA Newsletter*.

The SAA publishes *The American Archivist*, a quarterly journal that contains books reviews, research reports, and articles devoted to the theory and practice of the profession. The journal includes news and information on the latest technology and techniques in archival administration.

13. **Society of American Historians.** Founded 1939. 603 Fayerweather Hall, Columbia University, New York, NY 10027. (212) 854-2221.

Membership in the Society of American Historians is by invitation only. All 350 members are authors who have at least one book of literary and scholarly distinction in the field of U.S. history. The society's purpose is to encourage literary excellence in the writing of historical and biographical works. The society annually awards the Francis Parkman Prize for the best book in U.S. history; the Alan Nevis Prize for the best Ph.D. dissertation in U.S. history; and the Bruce Catton Prize for lifetime achievement in historical writing.

14. **Society for Historians of American Foreign Relations.** Founded 1967. c/o Alan Spetter, Department of History, Wright State University, Dayton, OH 45435. (513) 873-3110.

The Society for Historians of American Foreign Relations membership (1,200) is composed of academics and others interested in U.S. diplomatic history and the study of foreign relations in general. The society sponsors programs at meetings, fosters cooperation with the National Archives and other federal agencies, and bestows awards and prizes.

SHAFR publishes the quarterly *Diplomatic History*, devoted to U.S. foreign relations. The society also publishes a newsletter, the biennial *Roster and Research List*, and the *Guide to American Foreign Relations*.

15. **Society for Military History.** Founded 1933. PO Box 5576, Friendship Station, Washington, DC 20016. (301) 353-5431.

Membership in the Society for Military History is open to persons interested in the study, research, and writing of military history and the preservation of archival materials and relics. The society awards several prizes and annual awards for the best books in military history.

The quarterly *Journal of Military History* is published by the society. Other publications are a quarterly newsletter, *Headquarters Gazette*, and bibliographies and indexes.

Directories and Handbooks

16. **The American History Sourcebook.** Joel Makower, ed. New York: Prentice-Hall, 1988. 548p. ISBN 0-13-027491-7.

The major portion of this work is a directory listing over 3,000 museums, historical societies, and libraries. Each entry gives the institution's address, phone number, and hours, plus a brief description of the collection and access policies. An appendix contains a chronology of key dates in U.S. history. A bibliography lists bibliographies, manuals, and guides. Indexes are by organization name and by subject. This is a general guide useful to the student or the public. Researchers using libraries may need to consult other directories or collection guides that give more specific information about holdings.

17. **Directory of Historical Consultants.** Philip C. Cockrell, comp. and ed. [Massachusetts]: National Council on Public History, 1988. 61p. ISSN 1950-2662.

Primarily a directory of historians, conservators, archivists, and firms, this work gives name and address, names of staff, and previous experience for each entry. The individuals and firms listed perform contract work in a wide range of historical and preservation activities, including cultural resources management, oral history projects, historical-legal research, grant and proposal design, architectural building surveys, and policy analysis. Indexes are by service category, geographic name, and consultant name. Most useful for agencies seeking to engage individuals or consulting firms.

18. **Directory of Historical Organizations in the United States and Canada.** 14th ed. Mary Bray Wheeler. Nashville, TN: American Association for State and Local History, 1990. 1,108p. ISBN 0-94206-305-8.

Previous editions of this directory have been published under slightly varying titles. The 13th edition was entitled *Directory: Historical Agencies in North America*. The 14th edition contains approximately 13,000 listings. The first section lists historical organizations by state. The second section is the "Quick Reference Guide to State History Offices," which has state organization charts. The third section is devoted to historical organizations in Canada. Part IV is a listing of product/service vendors. The quick reference index to major program areas is essentially a subject listing of organizations according to categories such as living history, maritime organizations, historic preservation, genealogy, and oral history. The index is by title of organization or institution. This is the standard and definitive directory for state and local history. Its purpose is to facilitate communication and assist preservation efforts among history groups and organizations.

19. **Historical Journals: A Handbook for Writers and Reviewers.** Dale R. Steiner. Santa Barbara, CA: ABC-Clio, 1981. 213p. ISBN 0-87436-312-8.

Publication and editorial information on the major journals in the field of history are included in this handbook. In addition to providing the standard bibliographic and publication information, the book lists such factors as whether or not the journal is refereed; whether or not it accepts unsolicited book reviews; the time taken to consider manuscripts; and other useful information. Two handy prose sections are devoted to historical writing, "Advice on Articles" and "Advice on Book Reviewing." Each of these sections has a bibliography of additional sources. This handbook is for students and researchers who plan to submit manuscripts for publication in historical journals.

Publication information for historical journals can also be found in *Historical Periodicals Directory* (ABC-Clio, 1981). This five volume set is divided geographically, with the United States and Canada in the first volume. The information is brief, with only address, frequency, volumes published, and scope noted. Editorial information is not given.

20. **History Journals and Serials: An Analytical Guide.** Janet Fyfe. New York: Greenwood, 1986. 351p. (Annotated Bibliographies of Serials: A Subject Approach, no.8). ISBN 0-313-23999-1.

The guide by Fyfe is very similar to the Steiner work (entry 19). Only English-language journals with an international reputation are included, along with selected local history and specialized journals. The work is divided into geographical or subject sections. Entries include full publication information and are annotated for contents. There are geographical and title indexes. The guide is aimed at librarians and historians seeking manuscript submission information.

21. **The Living History Sourcebook.** Jay Anderson. Nashville, TN: American Association for State and Local History, 1985. 460p. ISBN 0-910050-75-9.

The topic makes this reference work unique. "Living history" is defined as the simulation of life in another time, making history come alive. The author is of the opinion that the living history movement is a significant and growing area of history. This sourcebook lists museums, historic sites, events, films, publications, organizations and even games that provide living history or an historical simulation. Each of the 361 entries is annotated. The entries are selective, and no attempt has been made to compile an exhaustive listing. There is a 49-entry glossary and an index to the book. This sourcebook is useful for planning vacations, just browsing, or for more serious work.

BIBLIOGRAPHICAL SOURCES

Research Guides and General Reference Works

The titles in this section are all basic reference works used frequently by librarians and researchers to identify appropriate sources for historical research. A number of different types of reference works are described. The most general works, such as the *Guide to Reference Books* (entry 23) and *Reference Sources in History* (entry 29), are not specifically focused on U.S. history, but they are of use in identifying reference materials for study and research. Other general reference works are guides for researchers to microform collections (entry 28) and subject collections (entry 30). Also included are a number of guides specifically for research in U.S. history (entries 24, 25, 26). The titles described in this section are useful to the beginning researcher who needs to learn the methods and types of source materials used in conducting historical research and are also of value to the scholar.

22.   **Guide to Historical Literature.** American Historical Association. New York: Macmillan, 1961. 962p.

The AHA guide has been considered a basic source in the field of history for many years. Now, over 30 years after the last revision, the usefulness of the guide is limited. For example, the chapter on general reference sources, compiled by Constance Winchell and Shepard Clough, should not be used without consulting the latest edition of the *Guide to Reference Books* and its supplement (entry 23). International in scope, with each section compiled by experts in the field, the AHA bibliography contains selective coverage of significant sources in each area. It is divided both geographically and chronologically by historical period. The annotations are very brief. A revision has been in process for many years and is projected for publication in 1994. The *Guide to Historical Literature* is still useful for the overview it provides of publications in history prior to 1960 and as an adjunct to bibliographies that concentrate on more recent source materials.

23.   **Guide to Reference Books.** 10th ed. Eugene P. Sheehy. Chicago: American Library Association, 1986. 1,560p. ISBN 0-8389-0390-8. **Guide to Reference Books: Covering Materials from 1985–1990. Supplement to the Tenth Edition.** Robert Balay, ed. Chicago: American Library Association, 1992. 624p. ISBN 0-8389-0588-9.

For reference librarians, the *Guide to Reference Books* has long been the standard and most frequently consulted bibliographical work. It has been known and referred to for many years by the chief editors' names, first Winchell (Constance) and then Sheehy. The 10th edition is the last to be edited by Sheehy, the 1992 supplement having been compiled by a different editorial team. A completely revised edition is planned for publication in the mid-1990s. Library users can count on the availability of the *Guide to Reference Books* in all types and sizes of libraries and archival repositories. The emphasis is on reference materials for scholarly research. The guide lists reference materials in all subfields and a wide variety of foreign languages. It is organized into five major subject sections and 48 subsections. Within the subsections, the organization is by the format of materials and by country, when appropriate to the subject area. Introductory material for each section describes the nature and scope of reference materials available. The annotations vary in length according to the complexity and importance of a title. For many works, there is a description of the organization and contents. The bibliographic history of each reference tool listed is given in full, making the guide an authoritative source to consult for the publication history of a title. The guide is factual rather than evaluative and does not aim to be comprehensive. It is recommended that any student or researcher needing to make frequent use of reference tools, guides, and finding aids in locating material for research become familiar with and a regular user of the *Guide to Reference Books.*

24. **Guide to the Study of United States History Outside the U.S., 1945–1980.** Lewis Hanke, gen. ed. White Plains, NY: Kraus International Publications, 1985. 5v. ISBN 0-527-36717-6.

Sponsored by the American Historical Association and the University of Massachusetts at Amherst, this five-volume set accomplishes several different purposes in one work. It is first of all a historiography of U.S. history outside the United States—that is, it contains essays on the teaching of U.S. history in 48 of the world's major countries and research trends in those countries. Archival sources for U.S. history in those nations are incorporated into many of the sections. Volumes 4 and 5 are bibliographical volumes. Coverage is international and not limited to English-language sources, although the annotations are in English. Sources covered are monographs, foreign dissertations, and periodical articles. The bibliography first treats foreign relations and social and economic history in essay chapters. Sections organized by chronological period follow. One of the chief values of the bibliography is that the periodicals indexed are predominantly foreign-language publications, so this bibliography covers sources not typically indexed for U.S. history. Because a large number of people contributed to the work, essay sections are uneven in their scope and coverage of sources.

25. **Handbook for Research in American History: A Guide to Bibliographies and Other Reference Works.** Francis Paul Prucha. Lincoln: University of Nebraska Press, 1987. 289p. ISBN 0-8032-8719-4.

The Prucha work is an excellent guide to research in U.S. history written for graduate students and other beginning researchers. The work is divided into two parts. One of the volume's strongest features is the first part, which is organized by type and format of source material, explicated in a bibliographical essay. The beginning researcher is guided through the use of library catalogs, book review and periodical indexes, manuscripts, government and archival guides and catalogs, biographical and geographical guides, and other reference sources. The section on the use of federal government documents is excellent, one of the strengths of this work. The section on databases is minimal but still accurate. The second part has a topical organization that covers reference sources for political, social, economic, and military history; foreign affairs; and ethnic groups. Education, religion, the sciences, regional material, and travel accounts are also included. The introductory prose is minimal in the second section, and the sources are listed uncritically, without annotation. The lists are extensive for bibliographies compiled in the 1970s and the first half of the 1980s. This guide is an essential reference work for anyone conducting research in U.S. history.

26. **Harvard Guide to American History.** Rev. ed. Frank Freidel. Cambridge: Belknap Press of Harvard University Press. 1974. 2v. 1,290 p. ISBN 0-674-37560-2.

When the revised and expanded edition of the *Harvard Guide* was published in 1974, it updated the first edition of 20 years earlier. The revised edition is now itself 20 years old but still regarded as one of the standard reference tools for U.S. history research. The first volume covers in condensed fashion the mechanics of research, writing, and publication. Research materials and reference sources are arranged according to format. The first volume also topically covers economic, social, cultural, and constitutional history. The second volume is arranged by chronological period and covers political and diplomatic history. There are no annotations. The strength of this guide is in its thorough coverage of the field up to the publication year of 1970. It remains one of the basic sources to consult. Students are advised to use more current research guides to complete their research.

27. **Historiography: An Annotated Bibliography of Journal Articles, Books, and Dissertations.** Susan K. Kinnell. Santa Barbara, CA: ABC-Clio, 1987. 2v. (Clio Bibliography Series). ISBN 0-87436-490-6 (v.1); ISBN 0-87436-491-4 (v.2).

This compilation of over 8,000 citations produced from the ABC-Clio history databases forms the most recent and most comprehensive general bibliography in historiography. The two volumes have separate author, title, and subject indexes so that the volumes may be used individually or together. The first volume covers bibliographies, books, dissertations, and individual historians in separate sections. The next sections cover subfields of history and historical methodologies. Volume 2 is organized according to a geographic classification encompassing every region of the world. There is a section on the United States and Canada. A foreword by George G. Iggers covers the origins, theories, and changes in historiography. The bibliography is useful for historiography classes and scholars in the field.

28. **Microform Research Collections: A Guide.** 2nd ed. Suzanne Cates Dodson. Westport, CT: Meckler, 1984. (Meckler Publishing Series in Library Micrographics Management, no. 9). ISBN 0-930466-7.

Over 370 microform collections are listed alphabetically and described in this guide. The title, publisher, format, scope and content of the collections are given, as well as price, citations to reviews, arrangement, and bibliographic control. Bibliographies and indexes upon which the collections were based or that accompany the collections are cited and described. The index refers to reviews, bibliographic citations, authors and titles. The compiler attempted to make the subject references numerous and complete, making this guide useful for researchers wanting to know if resources in a particular subject or printing era have been filmed. Beginning and advanced researchers will find the guide helpful for identifying collections that might contain primary sources and other useful materials for their research.

Another microforms reference tool is *An Index to Microform Collections,* edited by Ann Niles (Meckler, 1984, 2v.). This work lists the contents of 44 microform collections and provides an author and title index to each collection. The listings in this index are faster and easier to use than many reel guides, which are not always arranged alphabetically by author and title. The 44 collections contain over 20,000 titles. Many of the collections are not well known and are not analyzed in the cataloging databases. Collections of interest for U.S. history include *Books About North American Indians on Microfilm* (Microfilming Corporation of America), *Western Americana* (University Microfilms), and *Religion in America* (University Microfilms). It is often difficult to find out the contents of microform collections that are not available on site. This index provides the contents of these 44 collections for on-site use and for interlibrary loan requests.

Another useful tool for identifying microfilm copies of older monographs is *The National Register of Microform Masters,* which has now ceased publication. Libraries throughout the United State and Canada reported titles that had been locally microfilmed to the *National Register.* The bibliographic records in this publication of the Library of Congress are being converted into machine-readable form. A large percentage of the printed records are now in both the OCLC and RLIN databases. The conversion project should be completed in 1994. The availability of single microfilm copies owned by libraries can now be determined by searching the OCLC and RLIN databases. The work is continued by the *Bibliographic Guide to Microform Publications.*

29.   **Reference Sources in History: An Introductory Guide.** Ronald H. Fritze, Brian E. Coutts, and Louis A. Vyhnanek. Santa Barbara, CA: ABC-Clio, 1990. 319p. ISBN 0-87436-164-8.

This is an excellent, recent guide to major historical reference materials. The organization is by format of reference sources. The guide is general, covering all geographic areas and time periods. The annotations are well written and informative. The sections on newspaper sources and microform collections are particularly useful. Although the focus is not specifically U.S. history, many of the major reference sources in U.S. history are included. It is most useful for students and researchers needing an overview of the reference literature in history and not seeking specialized subject sources.

30.   **Subject Collections.** 7th ed. Lee Ash and William G. Miller, comps. New York: Bowker, 1993. c.2,500p. ISBN 00-8352-3141-0.

The standard reference work for locating collections in all types of library and museums is *Subject Collections.* The seventh edition has entries for more than 18,000 collections in over 11,000 academic, public, and special libraries and museums in the United States and Canada. The organization is alphabetical by Library of Congress subject headings and then geographical within those categories. The descriptions of the contents of the collections are very brief, mainly a list of names or topics. Loan policies and photocopy facilities are not given. One exclusion is local history collections. This reference work is useful in the first stages of research for locating major collections.

A similar but less comprehensive directory is *Special Collections in College and University Libraries* (Macmillan, 1989), compiled by Leona Rostenberg and Madeleine B. Stern. Special collections at 1,805 institutions are briefly described in an alphabetical arrangement by state. Information on the institution includes address, telephone number, and general library holdings. An index of personal and institutional names and subjects is provided.

Library Resources

Published catalogs of library collections aid the researcher in several ways. They serve to provide information on the specific holdings of a library, special collection, or archival repository. They aid in the compilation of bibliographies by bringing new sources to the attention of the researcher. They can assist in defining the boundaries or subtopics for subjects of research.

In the 1960s and 1970s, a large number of library catalogs were published. The majority of these were compiled by photographing the card catalogs or shelflists of libraries and archival institutions. For many of the catalogs, several supplements were subsequently published to update the base set. As the national cataloging databases grew in retrospective depth and as individual libraries converted to machine-readable cataloging, the publication of printed catalogs diminished. This section lists only a few of the major library catalogs relevant to study and research in U.S. history. There are many others for special and rare collections. The first guide described in the section is a source that lists published library catalogs.

31.   **Guide to Published Library Catalogs.** Bonnie R. Nelson. Metuchen, NJ: Scarecrow, 1982. 342p. ISBN 0-1808-1477-3.

This guide lists 429 published library catalogs according to 33 subject categories. Topics include ancient and classical studies, the U.S. West, women's studies, business, labor, English and American literature, the performing arts, and medical sciences. The description for each catalog includes the organization, types of publications included, article analytics, languages, types of subject headings, and classification scheme utilized. The guide is useful for researchers seeking special collections or definitive bibliographical sources.

Library catalogs and collection guides are listed below, with the exception of catalogs for specific subjects, which are listed in the appropriate subject section in this reference guide.

32. **Bibliotheca Americana: Catalogue of the John Carter Brown Library in Brown University; Books Printed 1675–1700.** Providence: Brown University Press, 1973. 484p. ISBN 0-87057-141-9. **Short-Title List of Additions, Books Printed 1471–1700.** Providence: Brown University, 1973. 67p. ISBN 0-87057-141-9.

The scope of the collection begun by John Carter Brown was anything "printed during the colonial period, that reflects what happened as a result of the discovery and settlement of the New World." The original *Bibliotheca Americana: A Catalog of Books Relating to North and South America in the Library of the Late John Carter Brown of Providence, R.I* was published by the library between 1865 and 1871. Later catalogs published by Brown University Press largely supercede the earlier editions, which were reprinted by Kraus between 1961 and 1965. The Kraus reprint incorporates corrections and annotations by Wilberforce Eames from the New York Public Library copy of *Biblioteca Americana*. So rich are the collections that it has been estimated that roughly half of the works in the published catalogs for the fifteenth through seventeenth centuries are not listed in any other bibliography. There is a particularly high proportion of English sermons and theological titles. The catalogue for 1675–1700 is arranged alphabetically, with indexes by title and subject. Many of the entries give references to other bibliographies that have more detailed descriptions of the work. The John Carter Brown Library collections are a rich resource for research in colonial U.S. history. The printed catalogs provide remote bibliographic access to these resources.

33. **The Center for Research Libraries Handbook.** Chicago: Center for Research Libraries, 1990. 134p. ISBN 0-932486-36-3.

The Center for Research Libraries is a nonprofit organization founded as the Midwest Library Center in 1949 by a group of 10 research libraries for the purpose of increasing research resources available to their users. Over 180 institutions are members of CRL, participating in cooperative purchasing and storage of archival and research collections. Materials housed at CRL in Chicago are loaned to member libraries for use by researchers. The handbook describes the collecting and loan policies of the center. The major collections of newspapers, microforms, government publications, archival materials, foreign dissertations, and periodicals are described. The four area-studies collecting programs and cooperative microfilming programs for African, East Asian, South Asian, and Southeast Asian materials are also described.

CRL began contributing cataloging records to the OCLC online catalog in 1981. Prior to 1981 printed catalogs for monographs (1969–1978), serials (1972–), and newspapers (entry 63) were issued by the center. In 1982 CRL issued a microfiche catalog of holdings up through 1981. Cataloging records since 1981 and many retrospective cataloging records from CRL are accessible through the OCLC and RLIN databases. A number of research libraries also load cataloging tapes from CRL into their local online catalogs. Although the center in Chicago is not a library per se, on-site access to the collections is permitted. Most major research libraries are members of the Center for Research Libraries, and the resources are used through interlibrary loan in those libraries.

34. **A Dictionary Catalog of American Books Pertaining to the 17th Through 19th Centuries.** American Antiquarian Society Library, Worcester, Mass. Westport, CT: Greenwood, 1971. 20v. ISBN 0-83713265-7.

The American Antiquarian Society Library is one of the premiere collections of Americana in the world. The collecting parameters are confined to the "territories that became the United States of America and to the former French and English parts of North America from the period of settlement by Europeans through the year 1876." The library was conceived and built to be a research library. It is the headquarters for the cataloging of American imprints included in the Eighteenth Century Short-Title Catalog, a large number of which are in the society's collections. The *Dictionary Catalog* lists the American imprints prior to 1821 and literary publications of nineteenth-century authors. It is useful for the identification and verification of scarce publications and in preparation for a site visit. The AAS's recent guide, *The Collections and Programs of the American Antiquarian Society: A 175th Anniversary Guide* (American Antiquarian Society, 1987), describes the more remarkable holdings. Among these are maps and atlases, sheet music, engravings and lithographs, manuscript and archival collections, pamphlets, broadsides, newspapers, hymnals, and dime novels. Together, the catalog and the guide give a fairly complete overview of the contents of the collections. All researchers in the history of the United States prior to the twentieth century will need to use this catalog as a resource. The American Antiquarian Society offers fellowships to support scholars' use of the library for research.

35. **Dictionary Catalog of the Edward E. Ayer Collection of Americana and American Indians in the Newberry Library.** Boston: G. K. Hall, 1961. 16v. **First Supp.** 1970. 3v. ISBN 0-8161-0810-2. **Second Supp.** 1980. 4v. ISBN 0-8161-0325-9.

This catalog with supplements contains bibliographic information for approximately 100,000 items in the Newberry Library's Edward E. Ayer and the Everett D. Graff collections. The dictionary catalog includes author, title, and subject entries in one alphabetical arrangement. Library of Congress subject headings are used. The publication formats include monographs, serials, periodical articles, Indian newspapers, and government documents. The Ayer collection spans the history of the Western Hemisphere. It is rich in pre-Columbian material, the archaeology and ethnology of the Indian tribes of the Americas, Arctic voyages, and the exploration and colonization of the New World.

36. **Dictionary Catalog of the Research Libraries of the New York Public Library, 1911–1971.** New York: New York Public Library Astor, Lenox, and Tilden Foundations; Boston: distr. by G. K. Hall, 1979. 800v. ISBN 0-8161-0320-8.

The collections of the New York Public Research Libraries are rich in materials on the history of New York, the theater, natural history and technology, local history and genealogy, tobacco, the growth of U.S. business, and cartographic materials, to mention only a few prominent subjects. The 800-volume dictionary catalog was published after the NYPL closed its card catalog and implemented an online catalog. Two supplements have been published to the original 800-volume edition: one for the years 1972–1980, published in 1980 in 64 volumes, and a second for the years 1981–1988 published in 1988 in 73 volumes.

The *Dictionary Catalog* includes the three largest collections for general research—history and the humanities; economics and public affairs; and science and technology. The catalog also includes the American History and the Local History and Genealogy collections. It is especially valuable for the subject approach made possible by the dictionary arrangement. There are also many analytic entries for journal articles, a feature not found in most library catalogs. Because of the comprehensiveness of the catalog and the depth of the NYPL collections, researchers who have access to this catalog should make it an essential part of their research strategy. There are a number of other catalogs of distinct collections of the NYPL included in this reference guide in the appropriate subject areas. One of these special subject catalogs is the *Dictionary Catalog of the History of the Americas* (G. K. Hall, 1961, 28v.), covers the history of the Western Hemisphere from the prehistory and archaeology of the Indians through the period of exploration and discovery of the New World, settlement and contact with the white man, and down to the modern period. The collection is strong in cartography from the fifteenth through the eighteenth centuries. There is even material on Hawaii, the Philippines, and Oceania. As is the case with all New York Public Library dictionary catalogs, there are helpful analytics provided for periodical articles and chapters in books.

37.   **A Guide to Americana: The American Collections in the British Library.** Gregory Palmer. New York: K. G. Saur, 1988. 252p. ISBN 0-86291-475-2.

The most significant collections outside of the United States of interest to the researcher in U.S. history are in Great Britain. Palmer's guide is divided into two distinct sections, each accomplishing a different purpose. The first section is really a history of the British Museum, now the British Library. In tracing the history of the collections that contain significant materials relating to the Americas and the United States, Palmer in effect reviews the history of the British Library with an emphasis on the collecting of Americana. The role of U.S. publishers in the development of the U.S. collections in the British Library in the nineteenth century is covered in some depth. The second section of the book guides researchers in the techniques and procedures for locating the various collections and identifying materials of use. Part 2 is arranged by format, with chapters on microfilms, newspapers, maps, music, manuscripts, and so on. The index includes personal names. Given the wealth of unique material relating to the history of the United States in the British Library, this book is a real service to historians.

Broader in scope than Palmer's guide, both in subject matter and in the number of libraries, is *The United States, a Guide to Library Holdings in the UK,* compiled by Peter Snow (British Library Lending Division in association with SCONUL; Meckler, 1982). The holdings of over 350 libraries throughout the United Kingdom are described in Snow's guide. Subject matter encompasses the arts, humanities, social sciences, and sciences. All formats are covered, including audiovisual materials. The guide covers large collections of Americana as well as collections on specific subjects, individuals, or periods. Information about the services of each library, including photocopying services, is given. There is an index listing over 1,800 microform and multivolume works with library locations. Anyone planning to conduct research in Great Britain or researchers seeking additional sources will find this guide useful.

38.   **National Union Catalog, pre-1956 Imprints. A Cumulative Author List Representing Library of Congress Printed Cards and Titles Reported by Other American Libraries.** London: Mansell, 1968–1980. 685v. ISBN 0-7201-1562-0. **Supp.** 1980–1981. v.686–754. ISBN 0-7201-1947-2.

The Library of Congress is one of the largest libraries in the world. It was founded to be exactly what it is named, a library for the Congress of the United States. Although it has never been designated as the national library, it is the U.S. library of copyright and receives every copyrighted publication. Throughout the nineteenth and twentieth centuries the library has grown into one of the foremost research libraries in the world, collecting in all subject areas except the agricultural and medical sciences.

The Library of Congress began publishing a book catalog in 1942. In 1952 the title was changed to the *National Union Catalog*, signifying that records and location symbols for other libraries had been incorporated into the work. Since 1983 the *NUC* has been published only on microfiche. The set known as "pre-1956," or "Mansell," is the most useful to historians because it contains works published before 1956 that were cataloged by the Library of Congress and other major U.S. research libraries. The arrangement is alphabetical by author or main entry. There is no subject approach in the main catalogs. *Library of Congress Catalog, Books, Subjects*, a series of catalogs organized by Library of Congress subject headings, provides the only subject approach. A number of cumulative sets for the Library of Congress catalogs have been published by trade publishers. *Library of Congress National Union Catalog Author Lists, 1942–1962* (Detroit: Gale, 1969–1971. 152v.) is one such cumulation.

Because the main entry is the only access point in the Library of Congress author catalogs, it is often difficult to locate anonymous, corporate, governmental, or other works not having a personal author. A service to all who have struggled to locate materials in the Library of Congress catalogs was performed by the Carrollton Press when it published the *Cumulative Title Index to the Library of Congress Shelflist* (1983, 158v.). This bibliographic aid makes locating and verifying titles for which the complete bibliographic information is not known much easier.

Bibliographies and Catalogs

The classic bibliographies are known by the names of the principal compilers and editors. As the publication universe grew throughout the nineteenth and twentieth centuries, it became impossible for any one person and difficult for a team to perform the labors of love the early bibliographers accomplished. This section is divided into two parts: The first part lists the classic bibliographies of Americana of which every historian should be aware on historical principle; the second section lists modern works, a few of which have superceded the classics. The second section also lists serial publications that describe new publications related to U.S. history research.

Classic Bibliographies

39. **American Bibliography: A Chronological Dictionary of all Books, Pamphlets and Periodical Publications Printed in the United States of America from the Genesis of Printing in 1639 down to the Year 1800; with Bibliographical and Biographical Notes.** Charles Evans. Worcester, MA: American Antiquarian Society, 1903–1959. Repr. 1941–1967. 14v. ISBN 0-8446-1175-1.

It was Evans's ambition to bring under bibliographical control all of the titles printed in the United States from 1639 to 1800. Although his work did not achieve this goal, it is one of the monuments of early bibliography, listing almost 36,000 titles. The arrangement is chronological by date, with each title successively numbered. The number assigned to each book is referred to as the "Evans" number, and until the publication by Shipton and Mooney (entry 49) it was the means of access to the microcard/microfiche collection, *Early American Imprints, 1689–1800* (Readex, 1955–1983), based on the bibliography. In addition to providing the bibliographical citation, Evans's work lists library locations, according to abbreviations of the bibliographer's own devising. Evans died before the last volume was completed, and his work was finished by Shipton. The fourteenth volume of the set is an author-title index in one alphabetical arrangement compiled by Bristol.

As bibliographers and historians worked with the Evans bibliography, omissions were discovered. In 1970 a supplement was published that was compiled by Roger Bristol from the systematic combing of many bibliographies and lists. The *Supplement to Charles Evans'*

American Bibliography (Charlottesville, VA: Published for the Bibliographic Society of Virginia by the University Press of Virginia, 1970) includes over 11,000 additional entries to the original bibliography by Evans. An index compiled by Bristol to accompany the supplement was published separately in 1971. The *Index to Supplement to Charles Evans' American Bibliography* (University Press of Virginia, 1971) includes one listing for authors and titles and another for printers, publishers, and booksellers. Bristol had previously compiled an *Index of Printers, Publishers, and Booksellers Indicated by Charles Evans in His American Bibliography* (Bibliographical Society of the University of Virginia, 1961).

40. **Bibliotheca Americana: A Catalogue of American Publications, Including Reprints and Original Works from 1820 to 1861.** Orville Augustus Roorbach. New York: Roorbach, 1852–1861. Repr., 1939. 4v.

Until the *American Bibliography* series by Scarecrow Press (entry 42) is complete through 1875, Roorbach will remain one of the few sources for the 1840–1861 imprint years. Roorbach does contain periodical as well as monograph titles and prices.

The compilation by Roorbach is continued by the *American Catalogue of Books (Original and Reprints). Published in the United States from Jan. 1861 to Jan. 1871, with Date of Publication, Size, Price, and Publisher's Name* (New York: Wiley, 1866–1871. Repr., 1938. 2v.) The *American Catalogue of Books* contains the same basic publication information as Roorbach's. It also contains a list of societies with their publications. Because it covers the time period of the Civil War, the *American Catalogue* is a useful research tool for pamphlets, sermons, and addresses from the war years.

A second, almost identical title is the *American Catalogue founded by F. Leypoldt, 1876–1910* (New York: Publishers Weekly, 1880–1911. Repr., 1941. 8v. in 13 pts.). This second *American Catalogue* is a trade tool and can be regarded as the earliest *Books in Print* for U.S. publishing, as its coverage was all books published in the United States for sale at the time. It is more reliable than its two predecessors, Roorbach and the first *American Catalogue*.

41. **Bibliotheca Americana: A Dictionary of Books Relating to America, from Its Discovery to the Present Time.** Joseph Sabin, Wilberforce Eames, and R.W.G. Vail. New York: Bibliographical Society of America (and others), 1862–1892, 1928–1936. 29v.

Sabin's objective was to list all books published in the United States and those published abroad relating to the history of the entire Western Hemisphere. He combed a number of major European bibliographies and listed anything that came to his attention from publishers flyers to company reports. The monumental dictionary began in the 1860s, and compilation was continued by several others after Sabin's death. The publication eventually reached 29 volumes with 106,413 entries before its completion in 1936. One of the felicitous aspects of Sabin's *Dictionary* is the sheer pleasure one interested in U.S. history can derive from simply browsing through the work. Fugitive publications such as by-laws of organizations, railroad company reports, and excursion trip brochures abound. Many South American and European publications are listed, as are issues of serial publications. For use in conducting a systematic search, the set is much more frustrating. There is one alphabetical arrangement that spans the entire length of the publication period. The entries are mostly by author, although many books are entered under city, state, corporate entry, or title. Full bibliographic information is given, often including contents listings and notes with references to other works. In some cases reviews are cited or library locations given. Later work by others has revealed that there were many duplicate listings among the 106,000 entries.

The maddening aspects of using Sabin were greatly alleviated with the publication of J. E. Molnar's *Author-Title Index to Joseph Sabin's Dictionary of Books Relating to America*

(Scarecrow, 1974, 3v.). Molnar's index is a reference work in itself, for he made an effort to identify anonymous authors. Categories indexed include editors, compilers, publishers, engravers, illustrators and cartographers, corporate authors and government agencies, main titles, half-titles, and series titles. Molnar even indexed the works mentioned in the notes. The index is referenced to Sabin entry numbers. Molnar's index makes it possible to identify and use the wealth of information in the Sabin bibliography.

The Sabin Collection is a microfiche collection being published by Research Publications. The filming of selected works listed in Sabin is an ongoing project, with approximately 12 percent of the works listed available by 1992. Printed guides arranged alphabetically by main entry accompany the microfiche collection.

Recent and Supplementary Works

42. **American Bibliography: A Preliminary Checklist for 1801–1819.** Ralph Shaw and Richard H. Shoemaker. New York: Scarecrow, 1958–1963. 14v. **Addenda, List of Sources, Library Symbols**, v.20. Scarecrow, 1965. **Title Index**, v.21. Scarecrow, 1965. **Corrections, Author Index**, v.22. Scarecrow, 1966.

The names of Ralph Shaw and Richard Shoemaker are associated with the series they inaugurated and compiled for many years. Designed to begin where Evans (entry 39) left off, with the same root title, the series consists of one volume for each imprint year, beginning in 1801. Richard Shoemaker continued the *American Bibliography* series under the title *A Checklist of American Imprints for 1820–1929* (Scarecrow, 1964–1971, 10v.). After the death of Richard Shoemaker, the series was continued for a few years by Gayle Cooper. Beginning with the 1831 imprint year (Scarecrow, 1972– .), Carol Rinderknecht and Scott Bruntjen assumed the compilation of the series. The volumes for the 1840 decade began publication in 1990. The publisher plans to extend the series through the 1875 imprint year.

The 1801–1819 series was largely compiled by combing other printed works. Beginning with the volume for 1821, locations for the books were added to the bibliographical information, and the compilers examined actual copies rather than depending upon secondary sources for information. The organization is alphabetical by main entry, with title and imprint information included. The usefulness of the volumes for each imprint year have been greatly enhanced by the publication of cumulated author and title indexes. An additional index for the first decade is *Printers, Publishers, and Book Sellers Index, Geographical Index* by Frances P. Newton (Scarecrow, 1983). This index is especially valuable to historians of U.S. printing and publishing.

Beginning with the series for the 1840s there is a new entry-numbering system that gives each entry sequential numbering, with the imprint year as the prefix. For previous series the entries were sequentially numbered in each volume but did not contain the imprint year to indicate in which volume the item appeared. All series have *NUC* library location symbols added to the bibliographical information. The *American Bibliography* series is much more comprehensive and accurate than earlier bibliographical catalogs such as Roorbach's (entry 40) and the *American Catalogue of Books* (entry 40n).

The microprint collection *Early American Imprints, Second Series, 1801–1819* (New York: Readex Microprint, 1964–) contains the full text of works listed in *American Bibliography, 1801–1819*. The collection is arranged in chronological and numerical order according to the Shaw/Shoemaker numbers. Bibliographic records for the titles in this series are available in both the OCLC and RLIN cataloging databases.

A new reference work beginning publication in 1993 is *Bibliography of American Imprints to 1901*. K. G. Saur plans to publish a bibliography in 92 volumes that would constitute the only complete record of U.S. publishing from the beginning of book printing through 1900. The bibliography is projected to have 400,000 books, pamphlets, broadsheets, journals, and music indexed by title, author, subject, date, and place. The bibliography will be compiled from the databases of the Research Libraries Group and the American Antiquarian Society.

43. **American History: A Bibliographic Review.** Westport, CT: Meckler Publishing, 1985– . Ann. ISSN 0748-6731

The contents of this annual publication combine some elements of a journal—bibliographic essays and book reviews—with sections of informational matter of a reference nature. A recurring section is the "National Registry for the Bibliography of History." Some issues have contained listings of publishing prizes in U.S. history. Reviews of the annual have commented that the information found in it is already covered in standard indexes and reference tools. It can be useful as a survey of recent bibliographical publications in U.S. history, but it is not an indispensable source.

44. **American Studies: An Annotated Bibliography, 1900–1983.** Jack Salzman, ed. New York: Cambridge University Press, 1986. 3v. ISBN 0-521-32555-2 (set). **Supp.** 1984–1988, 1990. 1,085p. ISBN 0-521-36559-7.

The American Studies Association sponsored this extensive bibliography, which expands and updates an earlier work published by the U.S. Information Agency in 1982, *American Studies: An Annotated Bibliography of Works on the Civilization of the United States.* The Salzman bibliography contains 6,000 annotated entries for publications between 1900 and 1983. The 1990 supplement covers 1984–1988 and contains an additional 3,000 entries. The main work is divided into broad topical chapters, each with an introductory bibliographic essay of reference sources. The citations are further subdivided under subject headings, and the source materials are described. The supplement follows the topical organization of the main set. Many topics in modern social and cultural history are covered, examples being folklore and folklife, popular culture, music, religion, and political science. There are author, title, and subject indexes in volume 3 and at the end of the supplement. This general bibliography is useful to students and researchers of all levels for any topic relevant to the study of U.S. history, life, and culture.

45. **Bibliographic Guide to North American History, 1978– .** Boston: G. K. Hall, 1979– . Ann. ISSN 1470-6491.

One of a number of bibliographic guides that were begun after the closing of the New York Public Library card catalog, this annual is compiled from the cataloging of the New York Public Library and the Library of Congress. The information is presented in "catalog card" format. Although there are other bibliographic guides and indexes in the field, this one is organized according to the Library of Congress classification system, covering mainly the "E" and "F" classifications. Titles of value to U.S. history from other classification areas are not included, although all languages and formats are included for the two classifications. If one is familiar with the Library of Congress call number ranges for the subjects one is interested in, this guide can be easily used to discover recent publications in those areas.

46. **Bibliographies in American History: Guide to Materials for Research.** Henry Putney Beers. New York: Wilson, 1942. Repr., Octagon Books, 1973. ISBN 0-3749-0515-0.

The first bibliography by Beers published in 1938 and revised in 1942 was a standard reference work in U.S. history for many years. It has been reprinted twice, the last time more than 30 years after the first publication. A two-volume update to the first edition was published in 1982, *Bibliographies in American History, 1942–1978: Guide to Materials for Research*

(Research Publications, 1982). Even though 1978 is the last imprint date for inclusion, these two works by Beers provide a very comprehensive listing of bibliographies for research in U.S. history. The two editions form a continuum, with the second edition adding to the listings of the first edition. The organization is mainly by broad subject category, with some sections in history chronologically organized. Full bibliographic information is given, but the listings are not annotated, and the rationale for inclusion is very broad. Even if this reference work is uncritical, it is useful for the sheer number of bibliographies listed—nearly 18,000 in both editions combined. Both separately published bibliographies and those that are articles or subsets of another work are included. Government documents are not excluded, and there are a large number of entries for state histories. For the time period covered, the two Beers editions are useful to consult along with more recent reference compilations. The broad subject coverage also makes them useful for any type of research in the history of a variety of subjects, not just U.S. history per se.

A more recent and more general work is *Bibliographies in History* (ABC-Clio, 1988), edited by Eric Boehm. The first volume of this two-volume work is an index to bibliographies in history journals and dissertations covering the United States and Canada. The work was compiled from the *America: History and Life* (entry 51) database and forms an update to the bibliographies by Beers.

47. The Craft of Public History: An Annotated Select Bibliography. David F. Trask and Robert W. Pomeroy. Westport, CT: Greenwood, 1983. 481p. ISBN 0-313-23687-9.

Public history is defined broadly as the practice of history outside of the academic research setting. The scope of this unique work, the first devoted to this topic, includes both established types of field research, such as genealogy and archaeology, and the newer aspects of history meant to influence governmental and social policies. The work is made up of 11 individual chapters, each compiled by an authority in the field. The practice of history within an institutional setting is covered in chapters on library science; archives, records, and information management; business management; and media and history. Historical research, writing and editing, training, and preservation are also covered. There are 1,700 citations concisely annotated from both monographic and periodical sources, including government publications. Although the bibliography is selective, the coverage of topics is thorough. The section on computer databases and online searching is of both practical and research value. Although it concentrates on the practice of history outside of academe, this work provides useful source material for both academic and nonacademic historical research.

48. European Americana: A Chronological Guide to Works Printed in Europe Relating to the Americas, 1493–1776. John Alden, ed., with Dennis C. Landis. New York: Readex Books, 1980–1988. ISBN 0-918414-03-2 (v.1) 1980; 0-918414-09-1 (v.2) 1982; 0-317-59108-8 (v.5) 1987; 0-918414-02-4 (v.6) 1988. 0-918414-00-8 (series).

The quincentenary of the discovery of America was the impetus for the compilation of this bibliographical work. The objective of the set is to document, year by year, the growing impact of the New World on the old European consciousness. Whereas Sabin's dictionary is arranged by author (or main entry), this bibliography, which covers the same time period and many of the same works, is arranged chronologically by imprint year. This alternative approach enables researchers to focus on publications that reflect the social and political milieu of a particular time period.

The purpose of this bibliography is to list those books that were printed in Europe and reflect the European view of the Americas. The chronological listing makes it possible to know what contemporaries were reading at the time. Many works not listed in Sabin are identified in this bibliography, which broadly covers subject areas in the sciences and literature as well as political and cultural texts. The entries in the main chronological listing contain full bibliographic information, with all editions of a work listed. Other bibliographical references are also cited, and Library of Congress locations symbols are given. There is a separate index of printers and booksellers by geographical location, with chronological listings of their publications. There is also an alphabetical index of printers and booksellers, giving their geographical location. The final index is an author, title, and subject index. This is a key bibliography for historians of the exploration and colonial period of the Americas. The indexes for printers and booksellers make it indispensable for those researching the history of the printing and publishing trades as well.

49. **National Index of American Imprints Through 1800: The Short-Title Evans.** Clifford Kenyon Shipton and James E. Mooney. Worcester, MA: American Antiquarian Society, 1969. 2v. ISBN 8271-6908-6.

Although the index by Shipton and Mooney is entitled the "Short-Title Evans," it is actually an alphabetic guide to the Readex microprint collection *Early American Imprints, First Series (Evans), 1639–1800.* A more fitting title would be the *Shortcut to the Microform Collection,* for until the publication of this index it was necessary to obtain the Evans number in order to locate a title in the microform collection. Shipton and Mooney include in one alphabetical sequence all of the entries in Evans, along with the Evans number of each. The index also includes all of the items in Bristol's supplement to Evans. Much more than a short-title index, this work further indicates errors and ghosts in the previous bibliographies. Because of its cumulative and comprehensive nature, the *National Index* replaces Evans for most research purposes. Anyone seeking the full text of pre-1800 U.S. publications should first consult this index. In addition to being listed in the *National Index,* the bibliographic records for works in the *Early American Imprints First Series* (Evans) microform collection are in the RLIN database.

50. **The New Sabin: Books Described by Joseph Sabin and His Successors, Now Described Again on the Basis of Examination of Original and Fully Indexed by Title, Subject, Joint Authors, and Institutions and Agencies.** 10v. Lawrence S. Thompson. Troy, NY: Whitson Publishing Co., 1974–1986. **Cumulative Index. Volumes I–X.,** 1986. 497p. ISBN 0-87875-330-3.

Although entitled *The New Sabin,* the work by Thompson is not a revised edition of Sabin's *Dictionary of Books.* Many of the works listed in the original Sabin are included in the Thompson work, and many others from the same time period were added. The bibliographical information includes author, title, size, and volume/page numbers. The original Sabin number is not given, nor are LC card numbers or library locations. The entries are numbered consecutively within the 10 volumes. The *New Sabin* is an additional source for publications on the exploration of America from the sixteenth to the nineteenth centuries.

A worthy successor to the eclectic original Sabin is *U.S. Reference-iana (1481–1899): A Concise Guide to Over 4000 Books and Articles...* published by Thomas Truxtun Moebs in 1989. The antique style of the title of this work almost obviates the need for further elaboration. Moebs, who is an antiquarian bookseller, has compiled a very useful annotated listing of reference works and bibliographies by subject categories. This work is primarily focused on information sources about collectibles of all types and formats. Although Moebs does not specifically mention historians or researchers in his title, many of the 4,000 items listed in *U.S. Reference-iana* may be of value in a comprehensive scholarly search.

Book Review and Periodical Indexes

The book has long reigned as the paramount format for the reporting and transmission of historical information and analysis. The essay-length book review is a service to the field, and one of the major journals is *Reviews in American History,* published quarterly by Johns Hopkins University Press (1973–). Essay reviews in historical publications are evaluative and comparative articles, placing the work being reviewed in its intellectual milieu alongside other scholarly works on the same subject. Hence, book review indexes are an important reference tool to those engaged in research and teaching in historical fields. The two general book reviewing services, *Book Review Index* (Gale, 1965–) and *Book Review Digest* (H. W. Wilson, 1905–), are not annotated here. They serve popular as well as scholarly needs in all fields and are available in printed and electronic formats. Only book review indexes specifically oriented toward scholarly works are described in this section.

Although the monograph is still the most respected publication form in historical research, the journal article has come into increased prominence as the field has become more oriented toward the social sciences. Only those periodical indexes that are most directly related to research in U.S. history are listed in this section. A number of subject indexes specific to other fields are described in other sections in this reference guide.

*51. **America: History and Life. A Guide to Periodical Literature.** Santa Barbara, CA: ABC-Clio, 1964– . Quart. ISSN 0002-7065. Available online and as a CD-ROM product from the publisher.

The main index for the field of U.S. history is *America: History and Life,* which began publication in 1964. This publication broadly covers U.S. and Canadian history, area studies, interdisciplinary studies of historical interest, and history-related topics in the social sciences and humanities. In 1974, beginning with volume 11, *America: History and Life* became a computer product, with additional augmentation by human indexers. The computer-assisted indexing method, "Subject Profile Index," assigns four different descriptors to each citation: geographic, subject, biographical, and chronological, with the article appearing under each of these descriptors when applicable. The index is divided into four sections: Part A, "Article Abstracts and Citations"; part B, "Index to Book Reviews"; part C, "American History Index," containing a bibliography of articles cited in part A, new books from part B, and dissertations; and part D, the annual index, which cumulates the indexes for all sections into one volume. The years 1954–1963 have been retrospectively indexed in volume 0 (zero). Cumulations are issued every five years. The organization of the index is somewhat complicated and occasions the multiple listing of articles. In the case of the different descriptor categories, this is an asset ensuring that articles will be found by whatever approach the searcher is utilizing. Part B is the major current book review index for the field of U.S. history. It indexes over 100 U.S. and Canadian journals, including state historical society journals. There is, however, no coverage of journals published outside of North America that include book reviews in U.S. history.

America: History and Life is available for online searching from 1964 to the present and also from the publisher in a CD-ROM format. The capacity to combine two or more terms or descriptors makes searching in the electronic versions superior to using printed index volumes. The publisher has issued a guide, *Searching America: History and Life* and *Historical Abstracts in Dialog* (rev. 1987), which contains a list of the journals covered by both indexes.

*52. **CCI: Cumulative Contents Index.** Alexandria, VA: Chadwyck-Healey, 1993– .
Available in CD-ROM or magnetic tape format.

This index is an electronic product that will not appear in printed format. Segment 1
indexes 300 journal titles in the humanities and social sciences published in the United States
and Canada between 1900–1960. The scholarly journals indexed are those titles most widely
held by U.S. libraries. The indexing is based on the table of contents of the journal issues.
The CCI provides cumulative indexing to titles that have been indexed in 45 different
periodical indexes. Searching provides bibliographic access at the article and issue levels as
well as author-title and keyword access to the table of contents pages. The development of
ideas and trends can be seen from a historical perspective by browsing the CCI.

53. **CRIS: Combined Retrospective Index Set to Journals in History, 1838–1974.**
Washington: Carrollton Press, 1977–1978. 11v. ISBN 0-8408-0175-0.

Both world history and U.S. history are covered in this retrospective index. The indexing
approach is two-pronged in that it utilizes both keyword and subject category indexing. There
are also two author-index volumes. Volume 5 is the first U.S. history volume of the set. Part
1 of this volume is organized by chronological period, and part 2 begins the subject
categorization, which continues through volume 9. The entire CRIS history set indexes
articles from 243 English-language periodicals. Researchers are advised to read the user's
guide at the front of all of the *Combined Retrospective Index* volumes before beginning a
search. All of the sets offer indexing not previously available in other sources in the
convenience of one cumulated set. The print in this particular index is small computer output
typeface, but it is one of the major periodical indexes for U.S. history.

54. **Combined Retrospective Index to Book Reviews in Scholarly Journals, 1886–
1974.** Evan Ira Farber, exec. ed. Arlington, VA: Carrollton Press, 1979–1982. ISBN 0-89-
23506-1-X.

This set was designed to provide retrospective indexing for book reviews in 459 scholarly
journals for the fields of history, political science, and sociology. The journals covered are
international in imprint, but most are English-language titles. Indexing is by author so that
all of an author's works are together. There are separate title index volumes that refer to the
main author entries. The reviews and publications covered in this set are not indexed in the
trade book review tools such as *Book Review Digest*, which focus on fiction, popular, and
trade publications. Another advantage of this set is that it provides a cumulation to indexing
tools such as *Writings in American History* (entry 61) that were published over a long period
of time in annual volumes. Given the importance of the scholarly book review/essay in the
field of history and the nearly 100 years of cumulated coverage, this tool is a valuable one
for research in the social sciences.

A closely related publication with a similar title, which causes confusion, is the *Combined Retrospective Index to Book Reviews in Humanities Journals, 1892–1974* (Research
Publications, 1982–1984, 10v.). This set complements but does not overlap or duplicate the
CRI to Book Reviews in Scholarly Journals. The CRI in humanities covers a broader subject
range, a longer time span, and more European journals. It indexes over 500,000 book reviews
in 150 periodicals. Because the authors of many of the book reviews are well-known literary
figures, they are identified. Thus, this set is a source of indexing for reviews by certain authors
as well as to citations to reviews about books. The broader coverage of the humanities and
the different journals indexed make this set a useful tool for the historian in addition to the
Combined Retrospective Index to Book Reviews in Scholarly Journals.

In 1974 the *Index to Book Reviews in Historical Periodicals* (Scarecrow, 1974–1979)
was inaugurated to continue on an annual basis the coverage provided by the *Combined*

Retrospective indexes. It follows the same author arrangement approach as those two indexes. The *Index to Book Reviews in Historical Periodicals* overlapped with the book review section of *America: History and Life* (entry 51). The only volumes published covered the years 1972–1977. The title then ceased publication.

*55. **Humanities Index.** New York: H. W. Wilson, June 1974– . Quart. with annual cumulations. ISSN 0095-5981. Available as a WILSONLINE database and in a CD-ROM format.

　　Social Sciences Index. New York: H. W. Wilson, 1974– . Quart. with annual cumulations. ISSN 0094-4920. Available as a WILSONLINE database and in a CD-ROM format.

　　These two indexing services grew out of the *International Index,* published from 1907–1965. The *International Index* became the combined *Humanities and Social Sciences Index,* and in 1974 the title was split into the separate *Humanities Index* and the *Social Sciences Index.* Because of the interdisciplinary nature of much historical research, students and scholars may need to use one or the other or both of these two indexes. The *Humanities Index* covers 345 English-language journals in area studies, literature and languages, folklore, history, music, theater, and religion. The *Social Sciences Index* covers 342 international English-language periodicals in the fields of anthropology, economics, geography, international relations, political science, law, minority studies, public administration, sociology, and urban studies. Book reviews are in a separate section in both indexes.

*56. **Index to American Periodicals of the 1700s and 1800s.** Indianapolis, IN: Computer Indexed Systems, 1992– . (CD-ROM).

　　Two printed indexes were begun in 1986 and 1989—*Index to American Periodicals of the 1700s* and *Index to American Periodicals of the 1800s.* Both are keyed to the University Microfilms series, *American Periodicals I,* 1741–1800, and *American Periodicals II,* 1800–1850. The first microfilm series contains 89 titles such as Benjamin Franklin's *General Magazine* and Tom Paine's *Pennsylvania Magazine.* The 911 titles in the second series cover the issue of slavery and events leading up to the Civil War. There are more than 20 women's magazines and children's magazines. These periodicals had never been indexed before the initiation of the *Index to American Periodicals of the 1700s and 1800s.* The CD-ROM database is divided into files of 25-year increments. Descriptions of the periodical titles for the 1800s are included, giving information about the periodical and why it was important. These indexes, both the printed and the CD-ROM versions, provide access to primary sources for research in U.S. social, cultural, and intellectual history of the eighteenth and nineteenth centuries.

57. **The New York Times Book Review Index, 1896–1970.** New York: New York Times and Arno Press, 1973. 5 vols.

　　This set indexes the *New York Times Book Review* comprehensively—that is, not only are the reviews indexed, but so are other essays, biographical sketches, letters to the editor, and so on. The five-volume set was produced as an index to a 125-volume set that reprinted the entire *New York Times Book Review* from 1896–1970. The *Index* can be used with either the reprint set or the newspaper microfilm. Each volume provides a different access point. Volume 1 is the author index (the author of the book being reviewed). Volume 2 is the title index. Volume 3 is a byline index that includes the authors of the reviews and the authors of the nonreview pieces. Volume 4 is a subject index that uses the *Times Thesaurus of Descriptors* as the subject authority. The fifth volume is labeled a "Category Index," in which works are classed into genre categories such as children's fiction, nature and wildlife books, and poetry. This set is a major reference work, not only for the access it provides to individual books reviews but also because of the importance of *The New York Times Book Review* itself in its coverage of the cultural, literary, artistic, social, and political life of the United States.

The *New York Times Book Review* is indexed in several online databases and CD-ROM products, which index the *New York Times* (entry 66).

*58. **Readers' Guide to Periodical Literature.** New York: H. W. Wilson, 1900– Monthly. ISSN 0034-0464. Available as a WILSONLINE database and in CD-ROM format.

Although the *Readers' Guide* is regarded as a general interest and a popular rather than scholarly resource, it is one of the few periodical indexes to cover the early years of the twentieth century. All of the major general interest magazines and many more specialized subject periodicals are indexed in the *Readers' Guide. Scientific American*, the *Atlantic Monthly*, and the Harper's titles—in short, many titles of social, cultural, and intellectual prominence—are indexed. Some years include a few government documents such as the Bureau of Labor Statistics bulletin. The *Readers' Guide* is an excellent source for contemporary accounts and attitudes—social, popular, and political—or for tracing trends over a period of time. Although there are many sophisticated reference tools available for recent years, in many instances there is no substitute for the subject coverage of the *Readers' Guide.*

The *Nineteenth Century Periodical Index,* also published by H. W. Wilson, covers the last decade of the century, 1890–1899. The main periodical index for the nineteenth century is *Poole's Index to Periodical Literature* (Boston: Houghton, 1891. Rev. ed, 2v.; Supp. 1881–January 1, 1907, pub. 1887–1898 in 5v.). The set was reprinted in 1938 and in 1963 by Peter Smith. Poole's index covers 105 years of U.S. and English periodicals. The user is advised to consult the *Guide to Reference Books* (entry 23) for a detailed explanation of the organization and those elements lacking in the *Periodical Index*. A *Cumulative Author Index for Poole's Index to Periodical Literature , 1802–1906* was compiled by C. Edward Wall and others (Ann Arbor, MI: Pierian Press, 1971). Because Poole's original work is a subject index, it has no authors entries. The *Cumulative Index* greatly facilitates use of Poole's, but as many of the entries in the original are of questionable accuracy, the *Cumulative Index* must be used with caution. Another aid to use is *Poole's Index, Date and Volume Key,* compiled by Marion V. Bell and Jean C. Bacon (Chicago: American Library Association, 1957). Researchers seeking contemporary periodical literature from the nineteenth century will need to consult Poole's index.

*59. **Scholarly Book Reviews on CD-ROM.** University Publications of America, 1992– ISSN 1060-1910.

The full text of book reviews in the humanities and social sciences from more than 100 scholarly journals are available on CD-ROM from University Publications of America. *Scholarly Book Reviews on CD-ROM* has book reviews in history, sociology and anthropology, political science and international relations, and languages and literature. An estimated 18,000 reviews from 1991 and 1992 were included in the first year of CD-ROM production, with an additional 11,000 to be added each year. The Boolean search capability makes it possible to search by subject words, and the full text provides reviews for journals to which the user's library does not subscribe. The *Scholarly Book Reviews on CD-ROM* is useful for students and researchers alike.

*60. **Social Sciences Citation Index.** Philadelphia: Institute for Scientific Information, 1973– . ISSN 0091-3707. Available online and as a CD-ROM product from the publisher.
Arts & Humanities Citation Index. Philadelphia: Institute for Scientific Information, 1977– . ISSN 0162-8445. Available online and as a CD-ROM product from the publisher.

Many topics for current historical research are broader than the indexing provided for U.S. history in *America: History and Life* (entry 51). Two indexing tools produced by the Institute for Scientific Information both cover history and subject areas central to historical research. The *Social Sciences Citation Index* broadly covers all of the fields in the social sciences, fully indexing 1,400 journals and selectively indexing another 3,300. Subjects covered include anthropology, area studies, demography and geography, economics, ethnic group studies, international relations, political science, sociology, statistics, urban planning, and women's studies. The *Arts & Humanities Citation Index* fully covers 1,000 journals, with 5,100 selectively covered. Subjects range from archaeology and the arts, Asian studies, film, TV & radio, folklore and history, through literature, linguistics, theology, and religious studies. Both indexes include articles, book reviews, letters, editorials, notes, meeting abstracts, excerpts from books, hardware, software, and database reviews. The indexes are arranged in four sections: the source index, which is an author index; the citation index; a corporate index; and the Permuterm subject index. The corporate index lists institutions, along with the authors affiliated with those institutions. The subject indexing is computer-produced from key words in the title of the work being indexed. Thus, the subject approach is by terms or concepts rather than an assigned subject descriptor. The most unique feature of the citation indexes produced by ISI is that both the references cited in a work and other works that cite the original work are included in the indexing. Thus, it is possible to get a list of references cited in an article that is not obtainable locally. It is also possible to trace the pattern of other works citing an individual article.

ISI also produces an *Index to Social Sciences and Humanities Proceedings,* which indexes conference proceedings published as monographs, journal articles or issues, or preprints. The conference proceedings are indexed by meeting location, Permuterm subject, sponsoring agency, author/editor, and a corporate index. Researchers will find that the ISI citation indexes provide unique information and a different range of information than other periodical indexes, which include historical topics.

61. **Writings on American History.** Washington: American Historical Association, 1902–1961; Millwood, NJ: Kraus-Thomson. 1902–1961.

Writings on American History is a title with a rather tangled history. The American Historical Association began publishing *Writings on American History* in 1902. For a number of years the title was published as part of the association's annual report. It was not published during the years 1904–1905 and 1941–1947. When publication resumed in 1948, the scope was narrowed to include only books and articles directly on the subject of United States history, and reviews for the entries were no longer cited. The organization is a classified subject arrangement with titles in chronological order according to date of the subject matter with author, title, and subject indexes. This series ceased publication in 1961. Until it ceased, *Writings on American History* was the only indexing tool for U.S. history and still must be used for the years 1902–1954, when coverage by *America: History and Life* (entry 51) begins.

A new series annual with the same title, *Writings on American History,* began in 1973–1974 as a publication of the American Historical Association's bibliographical series. The basis for this annual bibliography was *Recently Published Articles,* which, until 1975, was a section of the quarterly *American Historical Review. Recently Published Articles* ceased publication in 1990, and *Writings on American History* ceased with the 1989/1990 volume.

The second series *Writings* is organized into a general section, a chronological section, a geographical section, and a subject section. Articles are listed under all applicable headings. Over 4,000 journals were consulted in compiling the 1989/90 volume, including many foreign journal titles. Although, it was somewhat easier to use, *Writings* overlapped with the larger, more comprehensive *America: History and Life* (entry 51), which began publication in 1964.

A retrospective cumulation, *Writings on American History, 1962-73: A Subject Bibliography of Articles,* was published by KTO Press in 1975. This set was compiled by James J. Dougherty and sponsored by the American Historical Association. A companion set, *Writings on American History 1962-73, a Subject Bibliography of Books and Monographs...,* was also published by Kraus in 1985. Both of these publications fill in the years between the old and new series of *Writings on American History.* Although these retrospective sets overlap with *America: History and Life* (entry 51), they are valuable as cumulations and for the difference in subject classifications they offer.

Newspapers: Bibliographies, Indexes, and Location Tools

Because of their immediacy, newspaper accounts have been central to the historical research process. Contemporary newspaper stories and the publication in that format of official governmental records have made newspapers essential in historical research. In direct juxtaposition to their importance, the stock on which newspapers are produced, newsprint, is one of the most impermanent of materials. Moreover, indexing for individual newspapers has not been available on any large scale until the advent of the computer age. Thus, newspapers have been both the boon and the bane of an historical researcher's existence.

It was not until the advent of microfilming technology in the 1930s that newspaper files became widely available. Large research libraries began converting stacks of newsprint to the more permanent medium of microfilm. Location tools were compiled to aid the researcher in finding the files of microfilm.

This chapter is divided into two sections. The first section describes bibliographic and location tools. The second section lists newspaper indexing tools.

Bibliographical and Location Tools

The classic bibliographies for U.S. and Canadian newspapers, as well as the most current computerized cataloging and location databases, are described in detail in this section.

62. History and Bibliography of American Newspapers, 1690-1820. Clarence S. Brigham. Worcester, MA: American Antiquarian Society, 1947. 2v. Repr. Greenwood, 1975. ISBN 0-8371-8677-3.

This work, originally published in the *Proceedings of the American Antiquarian Society* 1913–1927, was revised, augmented, and published as a monograph in 1947. A further supplemental revision, *Additions and Corrections to History and Bibliography of American Newspapers, 1690–1820,* was published by the American Antiquarian Society in 1961. The work has been reprinted several times, the latest by Greenwood Press in 1975. It is still the most comprehensive printed source for the history of the 2,120 U.S. newspapers it lists for the time period before 1820, arranged alphabetically by state and then by city. The information given includes beginning dates and all changes of title with exact dates, editors, and publishers. Indexes of titles and publishers are included. Although other tools provide location information for microfilmed newspapers, the locations in Brigham are given for original copies in newsprint as well as microfilm. It is still a necessary location tool for issues that have never been filmed.

Another work covering the same time period and to be used in conjunction with Brigham's history is *Chronological Tables of American Newspapers, 1690–1820*, compiled by Edward Latham (American Antiquarian Society, 1972). Latham's work provides locations by date of issues for the newspapers listed in Brigham's history.

The continuation of the history of U.S. newspapers beyond 1820 can be found in *American Newspapers, 1821–1936: A Union List of Files Available in the United States and Canada*, edited by Winifred Gregory and published under the sponsorship of the Bibliographical Society of America by H. W. Wilson in 1937. The emphasis in Gregory's *American Newspapers* is locational rather than historical. The purpose of the work is to locate and list holdings of U.S. and Canadian newspapers in those countries. The organizational pattern is the same one used in Brigham: alphabetical by state and then city, with title, frequencies, and changes of titles. Library of Congress *National Union Catalog* symbols are used to indicate holdings. As with Brigham, the locations for issues that have not been microfilmed can be found in Gregory.

The problem of locating newspaper files for research has been greatly alleviated by commercial microform companies. There are two microfilm collections entitled *Early American Newspapers*. The first one was begun in 1962 by Readex Microprint Corporation to publish on microprint all 2,000 newspapers listed in Brigham. The collection was completed in 1970, and the company began converting the microprint format to microfilm in 1979, a project that is still ongoing. University Microfilms International also has a series entitled *Early American Newspapers, 1789–1949*, which includes papers of journalistic and historical importance from the eighteenth, nineteenth, and early twentieth centuries.

63. The Center for Research Libraries Catalogue: Newspapers. Chicago: Center for Research Libraries, 1969. 176p.

The Center for Research Libraries has collections of U.S. and foreign newspapers in newsprint and on microfilm. Over 500 newspapers published in the United States from the mid-1800s to the present, primarily for specific ethnic groups, are housed at the center. In a series of projects, the center filmed its unique holdings of newspapers and worked with historical societies, libraries, and ethnic organizations to complete runs. The center has retrospective holdings of hundreds of ethnic titles and maintains current subscriptions to either newsprint or microfilm editions. In 1965 the center began subscribing to about 20 papers intended primarily for black communities in major U.S. cities. In addition, the center acquires microfilm editions of general circulation newspapers published in major metropolitan areas in the United States and has retrospective holdings of many U.S. newspapers in original format and in microform. It also holds several hundred foreign newspaper titles. Cataloging records for newspapers are in the center's printed catalog and have been entered into the OCLC and RLIN databases since 1981. Many of the newspaper holdings are not cataloged, but researchers may inquire for any title being sought.

64. Newspapers in Microform. United States, 1948–1983. Washington: Library of Congress, 1984. 2v. ISSN 0097-9627.

The Library of Congress began to gather information on the location of microfilmed newspaper files from libraries and publishers in 1948. The publication of this union list of microform holdings began in 1948 and has been updated and cumulated in several editions, the latest through 1983. Arrangement is by state and then city. There are separate U.S./Canadian and foreign newspaper sections. Publication information is provided for each title with dates and changes of title. Locations for microform files are indicated by Library of Congress *NUC* symbol.

Newspapers in Microform is the most comprehensive source for the location of micro-form holdings of U.S. newspapers from the colonial period to 1983. It is the first and most indispensable reference source for verifying titles and dates and determining the location of holdings for U.S. and foreign newspapers. It is one of a handful of reference tools no historical researcher can manage without.

*65. **United States Newspaper Program National Union List.** 3rd ed. Dublin OH: OCLC, 1989. 55 microfiche in binder with booklet. ISBN 0-555653-074-9 (microfiche).

The United States Newspaper Program began in 1976 with a grant from the National Endowment for the Humanities (NEH). It is an ambitious project that has as its goal the identification and cataloging of all U.S. newspapers and the microfilming for preservation of those titles considered important for research. From its inception, the objective of the project has been to compile within the OCLC database an online union catalog of holdings of U.S. newspapers. A printed union list was first issued in 1985 in eight volumes. The second edition was issued in microfiche in 1987, and a third microfiche edition in 1989. Organization is alphabetical by masthead title rather than the customary geographic arrangement of other compilations of newspaper holdings. A guide that accompanies the microfiche editions includes a preface, overview of the set, list of intended-audience terms, and a key to institution codes. The codes are OCLC location symbols, not the Library of Congress *NUC* symbols. The microfiche sets include four indexes: a beginning/ending date index; an intended-audience index; a language index; and a place of publication/printing index. The NEH has funded a number of state newspaper program projects; for those states the information in the *Newspaper Program National Union List* is very comprehensive. Any researcher making extensive use of U.S. newspapers is advised to become proficient at searching the OCLC online newspaper union list, which is being updated on a daily basis and is preferable to using the microfiche editions. The online union list does not totally replace *Newspapers in Micro-form* (entry 64). For those newspapers in the database, the holdings and location information are more up-to-date, but *NIM* still has information not in the online list. Most researchers will have to use both sources.

Newspaper Indexes

Until the 1970s only the *London Times,* the *New York Times* and a very few other newspapers had their own published indexes. In the 1970s commercial indexing was begun for major U.S. newspapers. Separate printed indexes are published for the *Christian Science Monitor,* the *Wall Street Journal,* the *Washington Post,* the *Chicago Tribune,* and newspapers from other major cities.

The availability of newspaper indexes has greatly increased, first in online databases and now in the popular CD-ROM formats. For researchers needing newspaper references for recent history of the last 10 to 20 years, the availability of newspaper indexing is much greater than for the history of the U.S. prior to the 1970s. In the mid-1980s DataTimes began an online database of newspaper indexing. There are now over 110 U.S. and international newspapers available. Another newspaper indexing service is produced by Newsbank Inc., selectively indexing over 300 U.S. newspapers, with the text in microfiche. The Newsbank index is also available in CD-ROM format, along with CD-ROM indexes for individual newspapers extracted from the DataTimes online database.

The printed indexes begun in the 1970s for major city and nationally distributed newspapers are now available in database formats. *Newspaper Abstracts,* produced by UMI/Data Courier, provides citations, abstracts, and indexing to more than 20 national, regional, and international newspapers from 1984 to present, including the *New York Times,*

USA Today, the *Wall Street Journal*, the *Washington Post,* and ethnic newspapers. *Newspaper Abstracts* is available online and in a CD-ROM version, *Newspaper Abstracts Ondisc*.

Although the newspaper indexes have not been extended retrospectively to the years in which they began, databases are being built to provide historical indexing.

*66.   **New York Times Index**, 1851– . New York: New York Times, 1913–. ISSN 0147-538X.

The most well-known and comprehensive newspaper index in existence is that of the *New York Times*. The index matches the reputation and caliber of the newspaper it indexes. Publication of the index began in 1913, with annual cumulations beginning in 1930. Its present frequency is semimonthly, with quarterly and annual cumulations. A "Prior Series" index of 15 volumes covering the time period 1851–1912 was published by Bowker, 1966–1977. The Prior Series is compiled from a combination of in-house indexing already in existence and retrospective indexing. The handwritten in-house index for 1851–1858 is reproduced in facsimile. Although the indexes for the pre-1912 time period form a set, the indexing is not cumulative but is simply produced as it existed year by year. There is also a microfilm version of the Prior Series that was filmed before the series was printed.

The *New York Times Index* is very thorough in the information given. Exact references are provided for date, page, and column, including a brief indication of the contents of the article. The references are to the edition of the newspaper that was microfilmed. The *New York Times* has its own established subject headings, and there are many cross-references.

Guide to the Incomparable New York Times Index (NY: Fleet Academic Editions, 1980) by Grant W. Morse leads the user through the intricacies of the index and the microfilm. This handy pamphlet gives a brief history of the index and explanations of all the elements of the citations and the parts of the newspaper.

In addition to the long-running main index to the *New York Times,* several complementary indexes have been published. One of the areas for which the newspaper has always been renowned is book reviews. These are included in the main index under the heading "Book Reviews." The separate publication, the *New York Times Book Review Index*, is described in entry 58.

The *Personal Name Index, 1851–1974* was published by Roxbury Data Interface in 22 volumes from 1976–1983. This finding aid was compiled from the *New York Times Index* volumes and not directly from the newspaper. Additional names were added. A supplement for the years 1875–1989 was published in 1990–1991 in five volumes.

The *New York Times Biographical File* has been produced by the New York Times Company since June 1980 and is available online from Mead Data Central. The *Biographical File* contains the full text of selected articles, interviews, and obituaries.

The *New York Times Index* is a major research tool, useful not only for the primary indexing of the newspaper but also for establishing dates for which to consult other newspaper sources. It is remarkable as an index for its coverage of the political, intellectual, and social life of the United States for nearly 150 years.

Indexing for the *New York Times* is available in several online databases offered by Dialog and Nexis, a number with full text, and in a number of CD-ROM indexing services, including *Infotrac* (Information Access) and the University Microfilms *Proquest* newspaper database (full text). A separate product, the *New York Times Ondisc*, is also produced by University Microfilms.

67. **Newspaper Indexes: A Location and Subject Guide for Researchers.** Anita Cheek Milner. Metuchen, NJ: Scarecrow, 1977–1982. 3v. ISBN 0-8108-1244-4.

Until the advent of computerized indexing, only a small number of newspapers with national or international reputations had their own separately published indexes. For many newspapers, however, there is unpublished indexing available through locally maintained indexes or clipping files. The Milner work is a compilation of information on locally available indexing obtained through questionnaires sent to public, college, and society libraries. The publication follows a geographic arrangement by state and then by city. There are separate listings of the institutions included in the index, which give information on services provided and photocopy rates. Although this publication did not continue, it is valuable for its identification and listing of existing newspaper indexes at the local level.

A similar guide is the *Lathrop Report on Newspaper Indexes: An Illustrated Guide to Published and Unpublished Newspaper Indexes in the United States and Canada* (Wooster, OH: Lathrop Enterprises, 1979). This loose-leaf service was short-lived, but it listed over 500 indexes and clipping files, most of which would still be in existence and valuable for historical research.

Government Publications

One of the most difficult areas for the researcher to master is that of government publications. The phenomenal growth of the federal bureaucracy in the twentieth century has produced a voluminous array of publications to identify, classify, and index. Bibliographical control of U.S. federal government publications has not been comprehensive until very recent years. State and local government publications have usually been even more difficult for the researcher to identify and locate. The earlier catalogs and indexes that list historically significant documents have been, for the most part, very inadequate. First microform and then computer technology have aided in bibliographic control of both historical and current government publications.

Only the broad, general indexes to federal publications are described in this section. For statistical information sources, see the section in this chapter headed "Statistical and Demographic Sources." Guides and indexes for specific branches of the federal government and for state and local government are in chapter 3, "Politics and Government." The resources described in this chapter give an overview of the reference tools with which to locate U.S. government publications. This reference guide is not a substitute for the research guides described in the first section below. Any researcher who must constantly use documents is advised to acquire a guide to federal publications for in-depth and step-by-step guidance.

Research Guides and Handbooks

Because of the difficulty government publications present to the lay person, there have been a number of guides to their use published. Only a few of the best and most recent guides are described in this section.

68. **How to Use the Major Indexes to U.S. Government Publications.** John M. Ross. Chicago: American Library Association, 1990. 64p. ISBN 0-8389-0509-9.

The six most frequently used indexes to U.S. government publications are explained in this pamphlet—the *Monthly Catalog* (entry 76), the *Index to U.S. Government Periodicals* (entry 76n), the *Congressional Record Index* (entry 209), the *American Statistics Index* (entry 111), and *Legislative Histories of U.S. Public Laws.* Each index is treated separately, and the emphasis is on searching by subject. Given the complexity of these indexes and the reluctance of many researchers to attempt to use them, this is a handy guide for all researchers.

69. **Introduction to United States Government Information Sources.** 4th ed. Joe Morehead and Mary Fetzer. Englewood, CO: Libraries Unlimited, 1992. 474p. (Library Science Text Series). ISBN 0-87287-909-7.

One of the best introductory works for librarians and researchers alike is this library science text, now in its fourth edition. The work begins with a brief overview of the structure of government and the processes and issues in access to government information. Detailed chapters on the Government Printing Office (GPO), the Office of the Superintendent of Documents, and the Depository Library System introduce the student and researcher to the complicated apparatus and procedures of the government publications system. The next section is devoted to the general catalogues, indexes, and bibliographies produced for accessing federal publications. The legislative, administrative law, and executive departments and agencies are covered in separate chapters, with a fourth on the presidency. The chapter on the executive departments and independent agencies is much longer here than in the third edition, as is the section on technical report literature, both chapters reflecting the growth in these sectors of government information. This guide is very thorough in its explication of the organization and bibliographic apparatus of the federal publication universe. Those conducting extensive research using U.S. government publications would do well to own this complete handbook.

70. **Tapping the Government Grapevine: The User-friendly Guide to U.S. Government Information Sources.** Judith Schiek Robinson. Phoenix: Oryx Press, 1993. 227p. ISBN 0-89774-712-7.

As its title implies, this guide is meant for the ordinary library user and beginning researcher. It is an excellent introduction to the use of government publications, covering the organization of government agencies; the publication, distribution, and servicing of government publications; and how-to instructions for common uses of government information. This guide makes an excellent place to begin for anyone who has a need for government information. The writing style is as lively as the title suggests, and it accomplishes the purpose of simplifying the complex organization and bibliographic apparatus of government publications. Visual explanations in the form of charts, illustrations, and summary tables further aid in the simplification process. Students and researchers who find library organization and terminology bewildering will be enthusiastic about this publication, which makes it all so easy to understand.

71. **Using Government Information Sources: Print and Electronic.** 2d ed. Jean L. Sears and Marilyn K. Moody. Phoenix: Oryx Press, 1993. 544p. ISBN 0-89774-670-8.

The first edition of this work, titled *Using Government Publications*, became known for its approach, which emphasized search strategies. Although the second edition has been somewhat reorganized and is in one volume instead of two, the sources are still explained in the context of research strategies. After the introduction there are two sections on "Search Strategy and Government Information Sources" and the "Basics of Searching." There are three large sections organized around the subject search, the agency search, and the statistical search. Among the subjects covered are tax and copyright information, audiovisual information, climate, elections, maps, genealogy, agriculture, education, health, the environment, and travel information. In the second edition research sources for astronomy and space, transportation statistics, and judicial reports have been added. A fourth section on "Special Techniques" covers legislative histories, technical reports, patents and trademarks, standards and specifications, and other difficult materials. Electronic resources for government information have been incorporated including online databases, CD-ROM, electronic bulletin boards, and telephone hotline numbers. Two appendices include addresses for government agencies and commercial firms. There are indexes by author, title, and SuDoc classification numbers. This source is extremely useful for anyone who needs to be guided through the steps involved in searching for specific types of information. The chapters can be utilized separately as the need arises.

Catalogs and Indexes

Only general catalogs and indexes are described in this section. Indexes and catalogs for congressional publications and other specific guides are found in the appropriate section in chapter 3, "Politics and Government." This section lists the general catalogs and indexes for U.S. government documents in roughly chronological rather than alphabetical order so that the relationships and overlap between the various catalogs can be understood.

72. **A Descriptive Catalogue of the Government Publications of the United States, September 5, 1774–March 4, 1881.** Benjamin Perley Poore, comp. Washington: Government Printing Office, 1885. 1,392p.

The earliest bibliographical compilation attempting to list all federal documents is Poore's catalogue. The arrangement of the 60,000 entries is chronological, with a very inadequate index to the publications. The Serial Set number is not given, making it necessary to use another finding aid to locate the documents, but until the publication of the *CIS U.S. Serial Set Index* (entry 196), Poore was the main source for the period it covers.

73. **Comprehensive Index to the Publications of the United States Government, 1881–1893.** John G. Ames. Washington: U.S. Department of the Interior, Division of Documents, 1905. 2v.

Filling in the interim period between Poore's catalogue (entry 72) and the beginning of the *Document Catalog* (entry 74) is the *Comprehensive Index to the Publications of the United States Government, 1881–1893* by John Griffith Ames. Neither Poore's nor Ames's work succeeded in listing all of the government publications for their respective time periods, but both are still useful for finding documents. Ames is organized alphabetically by subject. Serial Set volume numbers were developed by Ames and are given in a separate table. There is also a separate name index. Both Poore and Ames are still useful for finding documents from the eighteenth and nineteenth centuries.

74. **Catalog of the Public Documents of Congress and of Other Departments of the Government of the United States for the Period March 4, 1893–December 31, 1940.** Washington: U.S. Superintendent of Documents, 1896–1945. 25v.

The *Document Catalog*, spanning the time period 1893–1940, was discontinued in 1947. Its coverage spanned the 53rd to 76th Congresses, and it is marvelously complete for those years. It has a dictionary catalog arrangement that includes entries under personal and government agency names, subject, and title. It indexes periodicals with regular frequencies, as well as proclamations and executive orders. The Serial Set number is included from the 56th Congress forward.

75. **United States Government Publications: A Monthly Catalogue, 1885–1894.** John H. Hickcox. Arlington, VA: Carrollton Press, 1978. 10v. in 6.

The period 1885–1894 was covered by John H. Hickcox's *Monthly Catalogue* of U.S. government publications, issued by Hickcox in ten annual volumes, which were for the most part not indexed. Hickcox's catalogue included both congressional and executive department publications in one alphabetical author and subject arrangement. A six-volume reprint by Carollton Press in 1978 included SuDocs numbers, added to the entries by Mary Elizabeth Poole.

Carrollton Press also produced the three-volume *Cumulative Index to Hickcox's Monthly Catalog* (1981) compiled by Edna Kanely. The index has both author and subject access to the publications. There was also some revision to the original indexing, with additional entries and access points provided. The cumulated index does not include many of the personal names listed in House and Senate reports for pensioners and so on, but these are included in the *CIS U.S. Serial Set Index* (entry 196).

*76. **Monthly Catalog of United States Government Publications.** Washington: Government Printing Office, January 1895– . ISSN 0362-6830.

Although the bibliography of U.S. government publications did not begin with the *Monthly Catalog*, its comprehensiveness and long publication history make it the core resource to which others relate. The *Monthly Catalog* began in 1895 and has undergone several title changes since then. The most sweeping change in its bibliographical history came in 1976, when it was converted to AACR2 cataloging rules and machine-readable format in order to be entered into the OCLC online catalog database. Prior to 1976 the *MC* was arranged· alphabetically by government agency, with one index for authors, titles, and subjects. Since 1976, the *MC* has been arranged by SuDocs. There are also separate indexes by author, title, subjects (LC subject headings), title key word, series/report numbers, and GPO stock numbers. A SuDocs classification number is included in the semiannual and annual indexes. The *MC* also includes information on ordering government publications and lists of GPO bookstores and regional depository libraries. The annual *Serials Supplement* lists current periodical titles.

The *Monthly Catalog* is available for online searching through major database vendors and as a CD-ROM database from Autographics, Brodart, and Marcive. Magnetic tapes for loading into local online catalogs can be purchased from the Library of Congress or Marcive. The *Monthly Catalog* does not contain periodical indexing. Many periodical indexes, such as the *Readers' Guide* (entry 59), *Infotrac* and *PAIS International,* include a small number of government periodicals. The *American Statistics Index* (entry 111) covers U.S. government serial titles for statistical data. The most comprehensive article indexing is provided by the *Index to U.S. Government Periodicals (IUSGP)* (Chicago: Infodata International, Inc., 1974–). Nearly 200 government periodicals are indexed by author and subject from 1970 forward. The IUSGP is available online. The index, unfortunately, has not maintained a current schedule and is several years behind.

77. **Checklist of United States Public Documents, 1789–1976.** Daniel W. Lester and Marilyn A. Lester. Arlington, VA: U.S. Historical Documents Institute, 1976. 118 microfilm reels. Printed **Index**, 1978. 5v. ISBN 0-88222-000-(1-5).

The microfilming of the shelflist of the Public Documents Department Library provides one listing for U.S. documents in SuDocs classification order. The comprehensive "dual media" listing of U.S. government publications, sometimes referred to as "Checklist 76," supercedes an earlier checklist that ended with the 1909 imprint year. The checklist also includes the materials in the *Documents Catalog* (entry 74) and the *Monthly Catalog* (entry

76). In addition, it lists many publications in the Public Documents Department Library that had never been listed in any previous catalog. The 118 microfilm reels contain 1,300,000 bibliographic entries for over 2,000,000 publications. A five-volume printed index by government author/organization accompanies the microfilm set.

A separate index to the microfilm checklist is the *Cumulative Title Index to U.S. Government Publications, 1789–1976* (U.S. Historical Documents Institute, 1979–1982), compiled by Daniel Lester, Sandra Faull, and Lorraine E. Lester. This 16-volume printed index lists all titles in the microfilm set, along with the SuDocs number, date, and microfilm reel location. Because the checklist is organized in shelflist order, this title index makes the location of known titles much faster than was possible before its publication. Serial Set volumes are not included in this index.

Bibliographical Guides

78. **Bibliographic Guide to Government Publications—U.S.** Boston: G. K. Hall, 1975– . Ann. ISSN 0360-2796.

This annual subject bibliography published since 1975 includes publications from federal, state, and local governmental sources. It is compiled from the cataloging of the New York Public Research Libraries and entries from the Library of Congress MARC tapes. Thus, the publications listed were not necessarily published in the imprint year of the annual; anything cataloged within that particular year may be listed. It is particularly useful for nonfederal government publications, many of which are hard to verify. The subject organization makes it an excellent source for finding new citations, and those publications owned by the New York Public Library are identified.

79. **Government Reference Books: A Biennial Guide to U.S Government Publications.** Leroy Schwarzkopf, comp. Englewood, CO: Libraries Unlimited, 1969– . Bien. ISSN 0072-5185.

The first volume of *Government Reference Books*, covering the period 1968–1969, included books and serials. It was published in 1970 and was compiled by Sally Wynkoop. Since the 1986–1987 volume, serial publications have been covered in a separate, complementary volume *Government Reference Serials* (Libraries Unlimited, 1988–), with both titles being compiled by LeRoy C. Schwarzkopf. These two guides are both arranged by subject into four broad categories of general reference, social sciences, science and engineering, and humanities, with subdivisions under each. Entries are annotated with complete bibliographic information, including LC and Dewey call numbers, OCLC number, SuDocs classification number, item number, and shipping list number. When coverage of serials was placed in a separate publication, more detail was incorporated into the bibliographic entries. The history of the serial is given, including title changes and changes in SuDocs number. There are separate indexes by title, corporate author, subject, and SuDocs class number. Both guides list only publications distributed through the depository library program during the two-year period covered by each volume. Both printed and microformat publications are included. These guides are useful for library reference and collection development. Researchers will find them useful on a current basis to become aware of reference tools that would aid in their research.

80. **Guide to U.S. Government Publications.** John L. Andriot. McLean, VA: Documents Index, 1973– . Ann. ISSN 0092-3168.

The publication history of this title, referred to as "Andriot," is rather complicated, but it is one of the best-known and relied-upon sources among government documents librarians.

It began as a loose-leaf publication in 1975 with the title *Guide to U.S. Serials and Periodicals* and became an annual in 1981. It is valued for its completeness in the listing of government serial publications, including historical and bibliographic information. It lists titles that have ceased as well as those currently being published. There are indexes by agency and by publication title. One of the most valuable features for historical research is the "Agency Class Chronology," which lists the changes undergone through the years in SuDocs classification numbers for each agency. Once a researcher learns to utilize the unique features of this guide, it becomes an indispensable resource.

81. **Subject Guide to U.S. Government Reference Sources.** Judith Schiek Robinson. Littleton, CO: Libraries Unlimited, 1985. 333p. ISBN 0-87287-496-6.

This guide is a revision of an earlier work of the same title by Sally Wynkoop published by Libraries Unlimited in 1972. A broad range of reference sources is included from bibliographies to numeric databases. The 1,324 annotated entries are arranged into the four broad subject categories of general, social sciences, humanities, and science and technology. For those using the guide as an acquisition tool, GPO stock number, LC card number, and OCLC numbers are given. For research use, this subject guide lists SuDocs classification and is indexed by title, topic, and place name. There are a large number of bibliographies available for the myriad agency publications, making it necessary to consult a guide such as this one when first approaching a research topic using government publications.

A similar but more selective publication is the *Subject Guide to Major United States Government Publications* by Wiley J. Williams (American Library Association, 1987, 2nd ed.). Also a revision of an earlier (1968) guide, this work lists sources under a much more detailed subject breakdown than that used in the Robinson guide. In the main section are the selective lists of sources organized under 250 topics based on Library of Congress subject headings. Entries provide complete bibliographic information with annotations. Supplemental notes provide historical information and additional sources. The two appendices are valuable aids to the researcher. The first lists additional guides, catalogs, indexes, and directories useful for obtaining government information. The second lists the bibliographies issued in the Subject Bibliographies series for sale by the GPO.

Archives and Manuscripts

The publication of catalogs and guides that describe collections and holdings of archival repositories has lagged behind the bibliographic apparatus that has enumerated and described printed holdings. Since 1960, catalogs of a number of major archival and manuscript collections have been published: *Guide to American Historical Manuscripts in the Huntington Library* (Huntington Library, 1979); *Catalog of Manuscripts of the Massachusetts Historical Society* (G. K. Hall, 1969); *Catalog of Manuscripts in the American Philosophical Society Library* (Greenwood, 1970); and the New York Public Library Manuscript Division's *Dictionary Catalog* (G. K Hall, 1967). Although manuscript cataloging in online databases began much later than cataloging for printed formats, there is now a growing body of archival cataloging in machine-readable form, making the location of manuscript holdings much easier to determine. The Research Libraries Group has an archival records database (entry 84), and the National Archives and Records Administration has begun machine-readable files for the presidential libraries and a number of other collections. The National Archives has maintained an internal machine-readable file of records for many years, but this file is not available for network access and is not distributed in any form by the National Archives.

The listings in this section do not reflect the collection and preservation of electronic information and data by archival repositories. Because so many records and data from the various departments and agencies of the federal government are maintained only in electronic form, the National Archives is becoming more and more an agency for the preservation of electronic data rather than of traditional paper archival materials. This growing universe of electronic information will be the research territory of the future.

The field of oral history is included in this section because original interview tapes and transcripts of interviews are housed in archival collections. Records for oral histories are included in the *National Union Catalog of Manuscript Collections* (entry 86). As the field has grown since its founding in the 1950s, reference tools have been published specifically in the area of oral history, although the majority of the publications have not been updated in recent years.

This section is divided into two subdivisions. The first division in on general manuscript and archival sources. The second is specifically devoted to oral history sources.

General Sources

82. Directory of Archives and Manuscript Repositories in the United States. 2nd ed. U.S. National Historical Publications and Records Commission. Phoenix: Oryx Press, 1988. 853p. ISBN 0-89774-475-6.

Intended as an aid for those writing to or visiting any of the 4,560 repositories listed, this directory was compiled through the use of questionnaires sent to the individual archival sites; thus, the completeness of the listings varies somewhat according to the responses from the institutions. Although directory information can become quickly outdated, the sheer number of repositories included in this directory make it a useful place to begin a search. The organization is geographical by state or territory, then by city and repository. The directory information includes address, telephone number, hours of opening, access policies, and user fees. In addition, there is a brief descriptive summary of the collections and holdings of each repository. There are two indexes, one alphabetical by name of repository, the other a subject index, with terms derived from the holdings descriptions. Although the information was gathered in the mid-1980s and some of the information has not been updated from the first edition in 1978, this is the most useful directory of its kind.

The *Directory of Archives and Manuscript Repositories* does not completely replace the *Guide to Archives and Manuscripts in the United States* edited by Philip M. Hamer (Yale University Press, 1961). The Hamer guide has been one of the foremost finding aids for manuscript collections for many years and is still useful for the fuller information it contains about the collections of the 1,300 repositories it covers.

83. A Guide to Manuscripts Relating to America in Great Britain and Ireland. Rev. ed. John W. Raimo. Westport, CT: Meckler Books for the British Association for American Studies, 1979. 467p. ISBN 0-930466-06-3.

The arrangement of this guide is geographical by county according to the new county structure established in Britain in 1974. The descriptions of the collections relating to the history and literature of the colonies and the directory information have been updated from the first edition by Crick and Alman. Over 100 new repositories were added in this 2nd edition, which is 65 percent longer than the first edition. Whereas the concentration in the original Crick and Alman guide was on political history, the definition of history was enlarged in the second edition to include immigration, economic, and social history. The second edition also includes information on private collections described under the National Register of Archives in London and Edinburgh, through which inquiries regarding those collections can be made. The indexing is detailed, with personal and geographical names, subjects, and archival repositories. Although it has not been updated in more than 10 years, this guide is still a useful one because of the large number of collections it locates for the researcher.

84.   **Guide to the National Archives of the United States.** Washington: National Archives and Records Administration, 1974. Repr, 1987. ISBN 0-911333-23-1.

The National Archives are the official repository of U.S. historical records from the First Continental Congress forward, including the records of all three branches of the U.S. government. There is no one main tool for identifying the vast collections of the U.S. National Archives, which has issued numerous finding aids and publications dealing with specific groups of collections. The *Guide to the National Archives of the United States* is an overall description of the collecting policies and collections of the National Archives. Originally published in 1974 (a much earlier guide was issued in 1948), it was reissued in 1987 with an introduction by Frank B. Evans. The 1987 publication does contain descriptions of some record groups added to the collections between 1970 and 1977, but it is not a revision of the 1974 edition. The arrangement is by government branch, then bureau or agency. The descriptions in the guide are very brief, and the index provides access not by collection or subject but according to the terms in the descriptions. Evans's essay is of some interest in the treatment of modern archival arrangement and descriptive techniques. A small catalog is usually issued annually by the National Archives, listing new publications and finding aids available for sale.

Collections in the National Archives are organized according to record groups, which are numbered according to accession order. A useful guide is the *List of Record Groups of the National Archives and Records Administration* (1985).

One of the more useful tools for research using National Archives materials is *National Archives Microfilm Resources for Research: A Comprehensive Catalog* (1986). The National Archives has an extensive microfilming program that has greatly facilitated access to the collections. This catalog lists the materials available for purchase and gives the "M" and "T" numbers by which microfilm is ordered. Arrangement is by government department or agency, with keyword and geographical indexes. Another series, entitled *Select Catalog of National Archives Microfilm Publications,* includes catalogs for individual collections such as black studies, American Indians, genealogy and biographical research, immigrant and passenger arrivals, military service records, and diplomatic records.

A recent special publication is the *Guide to the Holdings of the Still Picture Branch of the National Archives* (comp. Barbara Lewis Burger, 1990). There are over six million photographs and graphic images in the National Archives Still Picture Branch. The guide is arranged according to record group with descriptions of the photographs by topic, the name of the photographer, date range, and medium. There is a name and subject index.

One of the most recent and indispensable guides is not a publication of the National Archives and Records Service. *The Archives: A Guide to the National Archives Field Branches* (Salt Lake City: Ancestry Publishing, 1988) provides information on materials in the 11 field branches of the National Archives, which were created to house regional documents, including district court records. Records of a number of specific agencies (such as the Bureau of Indian Affairs and the surgeon general's office) and personnel and military records are located in field branches. In addition to storing original documents, the field branches contain duplicate microfilm collections of census records and other records pertinent to the region. The guide gives information on the holdings and services of each branch, both holdings shared by other branches and those unique to that branch. The guide also describes over 150 record groups, with information on published finding aids and the record groups availability of microfilm.

The Trust Fund Board of the National Archives and Records Administration publishes the journal *Prologue*. The purpose of the journal is to inform the public about the collections and resources of the National Archives. It contains articles about the collections of the various libraries and archival repositories under the administration of the National Archives and Records Service, with illustrations of some of the materials. The periodical also contains news on accessions, declassification of records, and other current information about the archives.

*85.   **National Inventory of Documentary Sources in the United States.** Alexandria, VA: Chadwyck-Healey, 1983– . Microform with CD-ROM indexes.

This ambitious commercial project began in 1983 and is ongoing. The purpose of the program is to film registers, catalogs, inventories, and all manner of finding aids for manuscript collections in the United States. A similar project for Great Britain is the *National Inventory of Documentary Sources in the United Kingdom.* Whereas other published guides and catalogs such as the *National Union Catalog of Manuscript Collections* (entry 86) give brief descriptions of collections and holdings, the *National Inventory* finding aids contain detailed listings of the contents of manuscript collections. The greatest number of the finding aids are unpublished inventories heretofore available only on-site. With the *National Inventory* microform reproduction of these finding aids, the researcher can determine contents without traveling to the repository. The U.S. project has four major divisions: (1) Federal records, including the National Archives, the presidential libraries, and the Smithsonian Institution Archives; (2) Library of Congress Manuscripts Division; (3) state archives, state libraries, and state historical societies; and (4) academic and research libraries and other repositories. Each section has updated indexes accompanying the microform text of the finding aids. By 1992 there were finding aides from approximately 170 repositories in part 3 and 118 in part 4. The *National Inventory of Documentary Sources in the United States* is complementary to the *National Union Catalog of Manuscript Collections* (entry 86) in that it provides the on-site finding aids for many of the collections listed in the *NUCMC*. The project is ongoing and must be checked periodically for additions of interest. Indexes to the finding aid are available in CD-ROM format.

86.   **National Union Catalog of Manuscript Collections 1959/61– .** Washington: Library of Congress, 1962– . Ann. ISSN 0090-0044.

The National Union Catalog of Manuscript Collections was established in 1959 as a cooperative cataloging program for libraries and archival repositories to report manuscript accessions. Each entry contains a brief description of the collection, including the number of items; scope and content; the holding institution; restrictions on access; finding aids; whether the holdings are original manuscripts or microform; the availability of microform copies; and so on. In 1970 the scope of the *NUCMC* was expanded to include listings of oral history tapes or transcripts and sound recordings. Indexes are issued separately and cumulated annually, then every five years. Names, places, subjects, and historical periods are indexed.

A 25-year cumulated *Index to Names in the National Union Catalog of Manuscript Collections, 1959–1984* was published by Chadwyck-Healey in 1988. Not only does this publication cumulate the name indexes, it also prints corrections and revisions to the original indexing contained in the six *NUCMC* indexes. Cross references are provided between variations of names and married and maiden names. Over 299,000 personal names are indexed.

A companion publication to the *Index to Names* is an *Index to Subjects and Corporate Names in the National Union Catalog of Manuscript Collections, 1959–1984.* Also published by Chadwyck-Healey (1993), this single, cumulated alphabetical index contains almost 300,000 subject and corporate names. Each entry for an organization, institution, association, or subject contains the *NUCMC* citation number. The two indexes by Chadwyck-Healey have greatly facilitated use of the *NUCMC*.

*87.   **Archives and Manuscripts Control (AMC).** Research Libraries Information Network (RLIN). Mountain View, CA: Research Libraries Group, 1983– . Online database.

In 1983 the Research Libraries Group began an automated system for the cataloging and retrieval of archival and manuscript records. The *AMC* is a machine-readable resource describing all types of archival materials. Since 1988, the current records for the *National Union Catalog of Manuscript Collections* (entry 86) have been incorporated into the database. As of late 1992 there were about 100 libraries and archival repositories contributing records to the *AMC* database. The number of archival records is over 370,000, including over 4,000 oral history records. The RLIN archival database is unique; researchers seeking archival or manuscript materials can learn of the existence and location of such materials through searching the database.

Oral History Sources

88.   **Directory of Oral History Collections.** Allen Smith. Phoenix: Oryx Press, 1988. 141p. ISBN 0-89774-322-9.

This directory of oral history collections in the United States was compiled from information returned by the 476 repositories listed. It provides the usual directory elements: address, telephone, hours of service, collection size, conditions of access, description of holdings (including special holdings), and catalogs or finding aids. The listings are objective and factual—that is, no attempt is made to describe, augment, or embellish the information provided in the questionnaire returns. As a directory, it is adequate and the most recently published source.

An older directory that is international in coverage is *Oral History Collections* by Alan M. Meckler and Ruth McMullin (Bowker, 1975). Although much of the directory information may be outdated, this compilation is still useful. It is divided into a name and subject section for collections and a directory section of 388 oral history centers. The directory is subdivided into a U.S. and a foreign section.

89.   **Oral History: A Reference Guide and Annotated Bibliography.** Patricia Pate Havlice. Jefferson, NC: McFarland, 1985. 140p. ISBN 0-89950-138-9.

Havlice's guide contains a brief history of the field of oral history and a bibliography of 773 entries of publications in oral history from the late 1950s to the early 1980s. The growth of the field can be seen in the increased numbers of items published in the 1970s. European and African oral history are covered, although the majority of the entries are on the United States and Canada. A section of basic reference sources is included, with abstracts, indexes, and societies and journals. There is a topical index to the bibliography. The Havlice work updates and replaces earlier bibliographies of oral history, such as those published by the Oral History Association in 1967, 1971, and 1975.

A manual for conducting oral history research is *Oral Historiography* by David Henige (New York: Longman, 1982). This title is satisfactory as a guide to the field and techniques of oral history, but the emphasis is on research in Third World countries. This aspect makes it of limited use for U.S. historians.

90. **The Oral History Collection of Columbia University.** Elizabeth Mason and Louis M. Starr, eds. New York: Oral History Research Office, 1978. 306p. ISBN 0-96024-920-6.

Columbia University has been credited as being the institution at which the field of oral history originated after World War II. The catalog of the founding oral history collection, first published in 1964, contains the early holdings. Interviews with political figures, publishers, authors, producers of plays, business leaders, and journalists are included, along with special projects of the Oral History Research Office. A later edition brought the holdings up through the middle 1970s. The additions since that time have been entered in the Research Libraries Group archives and manuscripts database (entry 87).

Another important early oral history collection is at the University of California at Berkeley. The *Catalogue of the Regional Oral History Office, 1954–1979* (Bancroft Library, 1980) was published to celebrate the twenty-fifth anniversary of the archive and contains a history of the project. Berkeley's Regional Oral History Office has a collection of over 1,000 interviews with people who have contributed significantly to the history of the western United States. There is descriptive information in the catalogue on 392 collections arranged alphabetically by title. An index of personal names and subjects is included.

91. **Oral History Sources.** Alexandria, VA: Chadwyck-Healey, 1988– . Microform.

The objective of this microfilming project is to construct a comprehensive source for finding what collections are in a particular repository and what projects and individual interviews are in a particular collection. The project reproduces on microfiche finding aids to oral history collections in universities, historical societies, state archives, and other repositories throughout North America. The printed index to the microfiche offers access by subject, geographical term, national origin, occupation, interviewer, interviewee, other personal name, corporate name, and project name. The publisher plans to offer a CD-ROM version and to merge the indexes for oral history with those of the *National Inventory of Documentary Sources in the United States* (entry 85). The project is ongoing and must be checked periodically for additions of interest.

Dissertations and Theses

History is by and large a research field. In order to analyze the past or to draft new historical interpretations, historians must conduct research. Original research leading to master's and doctoral degrees is integral to the field. The bibliographical apparatus for theses and dissertations has always been of primary importance. Even before the development of a comprehensive system of indexing for dissertations, the American Historical Association published a registry of *Doctoral Dissertations in History* (entry 94). The primary journals for specific fields include lists of doctoral dissertations; for example, dissertations in foreign affairs and military topics are listed in *Diplomatic Affairs* and *Military Affairs.* These specialized inventories tend to be less current than the general overall index, **Dissertation Abstracts International* (entry 92 below). The major indexing tools for dissertations and theses, both general and specialized historical works, are described in this section.

*92. **Dissertation Abstracts International.** Ann Arbor, MI: University Microfilms International, 1938–. **Humanities and Social Sciences.** Mo. **Worldwide.** Quart. ISSN 0307-6075. Available as an online database and in a CD-ROM format.

In 1938 a program was inaugurated to bring dissertations written in universities in the United States under bibliographic control. The publication program consisted of a bibliography of dissertations, with author-written abstracts and the microfilming of the manuscript of the dissertation. This program has been expanded to include more universities, and in 1976 the program began international coverage. It was not until 1988, however, that 50 universities in Great Britain became involved. More than 500 doctoral granting institutions now participate in the *Dissertation Abstracts* filming program. The index is divided into two subject sections for the U.S.—Humanities and Social Sciences in Section A, Sciences and Engineering in Section B—with Section C Worldwide, being international.

The bibliographic information in the printed index includes the author, title, degree-granting institution, date, and order number for copies of the dissertation produced from microfilm. The subject indexing in all UMI dissertation indexes is through key words from the title.

In 1973 a cumulated index to *DAI*, the *Comprehensive Dissertation Index, 1861–1972*, was published in 37 volumes. A further cumulative set for 1973–1982 in 38 volumes was published between 1983 and 1987. The *Comprehensive Index* is ongoing, with annual, five-year, and ten-year cumulations. The *Comprehensive Index* is useful for historical research in education or the development of research in particular areas, as well as for tracing the work of individuals.

The database includes all U.S. dissertations from 1861 to the present, British and European dissertations, and *Masters Abstracts International* (entry 95) beginning in 1988. The database can be searched online or using the CD-ROM format.

American Doctoral Dissertations is published annually on an academic-year basis by UMI. The purpose of this index compiled for the Association of Research Libraries is to provide information on doctoral programs rather than on individual dissertations. The citations are grouped by subject, and within each subject by institution. This organization allows the user to determine which dissertations have been written at particular universities. There is an author index so that individual dissertations may be found.

93. **Dissertations in History: An Index to Dissertations Completed in History Departments of United States and Canadian Universities.** Warren F. Kuehl. v.1, 1873–1960. Lexington: University Press of Kentucky, 1965. v.2, 1961–1970. Lexington: University Press of Kentucky, 1972. ISBN 0-8131-1264-8. v.3, 1970–June 1980 Santa Barbara, CA: ABC-Clio, 1985. ISBN 0-87436-356-X.

This title is the most current and comprehensive index devoted solely to doctoral dissertations written in history at U.S. and Canadian universities. It has the advantage of being a retrospective cumulated index. It uses the same subject headings as those used in *Recently Published Articles*. There are 7,000 dissertations indexed in volume 1; nearly 6,000 in volume 2; and 10,000 in volume 3, for a total of 23,000 dissertations in the 20-year period. Although it does not list dissertations solely in U.S. history, this is the quickest and most comprehensive source to consult for dissertations in history for the 20-year time span covered.

94. **Doctoral Dissertations in History.** Washington: American Historical Association, 1976– . Semiann. ISSN 0145-9929.

Doctoral Dissertations in History continues a former series published by the American Historical Association, *List of Doctoral Dissertations in History in Progress or Recently Completed in the United States* (1909–1970/73). In 1976, the AHA began publishing *Doctoral Dissertations in History* on a semiannual basis. This publication lists dissertations in progress as well as completed ones. The arrangement is both chronological and geographical by historical periods. U.S. history is subdivided by subject. A short abstract by the author is included with the bibliographical information. This publication has the advantage of listing only dissertations in the field of history, whereas the omnibus *DAI* includes dissertations in all fields.

95. **Masters Abstracts International.** Ann Arbor, MI: University Microfilms, 1962– . Quart. ISSN 0025-5106.

Hoping to duplicate its highly successful program for the indexing and filming of doctoral dissertations, UMI began a similar program for master's theses. A smaller number of institutions of higher education worldwide participates in the listing of the master's theses than in *DAI.* As is the case with the doctoral dissertations, the master's theses listed in *Master's Abstracts International* are microfilmed, and copies are available for purchase. *Research Abstracts* (University Microfilms), a quarterly that contains author-prepared summaries of postdoctoral and nondegree published research in subjects such as psychology and education, has been published as an addendum to *Masters Abstracts* since 1991. Master's theses are included in the online and CD-ROM *Dissertation Abstracts International* database (entry 92).

DICTIONARIES, ENCYCLOPEDIAS, CHRONOLOGIES, AND SOURCEBOOKS

The titles described in this section are works most likely to be utilized for answering many reference questions concerning U.S. history. A number of older standard works are included, as well as more recent publications. The majority of these reference works will be useful for students, librarians, researchers, and the general public.

Dictionaries and Encyclopedias

96. **Album of American History.** New York: Scribner's, 1960–1969. 6v. **Supp.** 1968– 1982. Scribner's, 1985. ISBN 0-684-17440-5.

The six-volume edition of this pictorial work is divided into historical periods. Within the chronological framework there are headings relating to major political occurrences, news events, or social and cultural trends of the period. The photographs are selected to best convey the emotional impact of events. All are reproduced in black and white with credits. The short descriptions or captions combine with the illustrations to give an excellent visual impression of the various periods in history. There is an index to facilitate searching for photographs on specific subjects or incidents. The supplement updates the coverage through 1982 and is organized into ten topical chapters. The presidency, Vietnam, social consciousness, business, ecological awareness, entertainment, and milestones are some of the subjects portrayed. The *Album of American History* is a perfect companion to assigned readings in both high school and undergraduate courses or for use by anyone seeking illustrations for historic events. It affords an overview of U.S. history through contemporary illustrations.

An older pictorial work is *Pageant of America: A Pictorial History of the United States* (New Haven: Yale University Press, 1925–29. 15v.). Although it has not been updated since its first publication, this standard multivolume work is a great source for older photographs. Unlike the *Album of American History*, the *Pageant of America* contains considerable text, both reference information and interpretation of the events depicted. An effort was made to secure contemporary photographs rather than later reproductions; the grainy early photographs evoke the era of the historical events. The set is organized in a chronological progression for the first nine volumes. The last six volumes each focus on a different theme or subject: religion, literature, art, architecture, the theater, and sports. Because of the different eras in which the *Album of American History* and the *Pageant of America* were compiled and the different editorial approaches they take, each is unique and valuable for historical study.

The *Pageant of America* is also available as a microfiche collection from University Microfilms.

97. **Dictionary of American History, 1878–1949.** James T. Adams. New York: Scribner's, 1976. 8v. ISBN 0-684-13856-5.

The original edition of James Truslow Adam's *Dictionary of American History* was published in 1940. It was thoroughly revised, expanded, and updated for the bicentennial edition. The arrangement consists of alphabetical signed entries, which vary in length according to the importance of the subject. The entries are both factual and interpretative. In the revised edition, science and technology, the arts and cultural activities, native Americans, and Afro-Americans were given greater emphasis. The index (v. 8) is a complete index to every item of information in the set including names. The original *Dictionary of American History* and the *Dictionary of American Biography* (entry 143) were published as a coordinated effort; thus, the former does not contain biographies. There is a great deal of information, however, to be gleaned from the name index in the U.S. history set. The index includes dates and parenthetical explanatory phrases. Place names are identified by territory, city, state, or country. This eight-volume encyclopedia is a standard reference work with a reputation for accuracy and thoroughness. It is suitable for use by student and scholar alike.

A one-volume abridged edition of the *Dictionary of American History* was published by Scribner's in 1983. More than 6,000 of the original entries were shortened and included in the abridged edition. The entries are not signed, and the use of the term "dictionary" is much more appropriate for the concise edition. However, the unabridged edition is to be preferred when available.

Another edition of this work with a different title was published by Scribner's in 1984. The *Scribner Desk Dictionary of American History* is based on the eight-volume bicentennial edition, but it is updated through the 1980 census. This edition was designed for personal home or office use and has very abbreviated entries. All editions of the Scribner *Dictionary of American History* include the text of the U.S. Constitution.

98. **Encyclopedia of American History.** 6th ed. Richard B. Morris, ed. New York: Harper & Row, 1982. 1,285p. ISBN 0-06-181605-1.

This ready reference work is more of a handy dictionary than an encyclopedia. The first section is a chronology of American history from the Asiatic origins of native Americans up through 1981. The next division is a topical section with separate chronologies under headings such as population and immigration, literature, science, and technology. A third section contains brief biographies of leading figures in U.S. history. The last section, on political history, gives the organization of the federal government and lists the presidents and their cabinets, Supreme Court justices, and others. The texts of the Declaration of Independence and the Constitution are included. The chronological organization makes it difficult to look up specific events or facts when the date of occurrence is not known, but there is an index. There are no references to sources, nor is there a separate bibliography. This one-volume reference is suitable for use by students and the general public.

99. **The Encyclopedia of Colonial and Revolutionary America.** John Mack Faragher. New York: Facts on File, 1990. 484p. ISBN 0-8160-1744-1.

The first-single volume work to cover both the colonial and revolutionary periods in U.S. history, this work provides information on individuals and topics in 1,500 short, alphabetical entries. The articles are written by a team of scholars, but most are not signed. The encyclopedia explains political, social, economic, and cultural terms, with many biographies of major and lesser-known figures. There are 26 topical guides for broad themes or subjects such as women, agriculture, colonial government, Spanish colonies, and so forth. These guides have a brief overview of the subject and lists of related terms, themes, references to biographies elsewhere in the volume, and a brief bibliography. Some of the articles give further bibliographic references. There are maps and illustrations. The encyclopedia is a good, quick reference tool for students, scholars, and the general public.

100. **Encyclopedia USA: The Encyclopedia of the United States of America Past & Present.** Gulf Breeze, FL: Academic International Press, 1983– . ISBN 0-87569-076-9.
    This reference work is projected to be a 50-volume set. As of 1991 there were 14 volumes published. The set is envisioned to encompass all major aspects of U.S. life. The arrangement consists of concise alphabetical entries for people, events, institutions, movements, and trends in U.S. history. The contributors are not all scholars. Only the longer or more significant entries are signed. Some entries include references to sources. The work is designed primarily for the general public and beginning researchers or as a general information source for specialists.

*101. **History of the U.S.** Parsippany, NJ: Bureau of Electronic Publishing, 1993– . CD-ROM.
    Over 107 books and 1,000 images are contained on the *History of the U.S.* disc. The product has been greatly expanded and updated from an earlier version titled *U.S. History on CD-ROM.* Texts included are historical documents such as the documents relating to the Constitution, biographies of historic figures, memoirs, and reports and commentary on great events. The works cover the geographic, political, social, military, economic, and scientific history of the United States, from discovery to the present. Hundreds of color and black-and-white maps, illustrations, photos, and tables accompany the texts. The multimedia features include famous speeches and eyewitness accounts, including Martin Luther King's "I Have a Dream" oratory. Animated maps show military, economic, and social trends; the technological evolution in U.S. history is also shown through animation. The topics can be searched for information on events, people, and subjects. Indexing is by title, theme, time period, and event. The database can be used as a reference resource and in conjunction with courses in the history of a broad range of subjects at the school and college level.

102. **The Reader's Companion to American History.** Eric Foner and John A. Garraty, eds. Boston: Houghton Mifflin, 1991. 1,226p. ISBN 0-395-51372-3.
    Sponsored by the Society of American Historians, this single volume is the most up-to-date and authoritative reference source for U.S. history. Three types of entries are combined into one alphabetical sequence: short factual entries, biographical entries, and thematic essays. The work was intended to truly be a "reader's companion," and the writing is concise, crisp, and interesting. The essays are historical overviews of pivotal events or sociological issues such as abortion, the family, and housework. The essay entries are written by scholars, are signed, and have a short bibliography. The text of the Declaration of Independence and the U.S. Constitution are included in the appendices. The organization and currency of this excellent reference source make it suitable for both reference work and research. Students and scholars will find it equally readable and informative.
    A previous work by John Garraty, one of the editors of *The Reader's Companion to American History*, is *1,001 Things Everyone Should Know About American History* (New York: Doubleday, 1989). This is an entertaining reference work divided into eight illustrated thematic sections. The entries are for songs, quotes, books, poems, people, slogans, battles, inventions, and more. Political and historical events are also included. There is an index.

Although it is a good place to find trivia, the work is also factual and informative and an excellent complement to more scholarly works.

Chronologies

103.   **The Almanac of American History.** Arthur M. Schlesinger, Jr. New York: Putnam, 1983. 623p. ISBN 0-399-12853-0.

Although basically a chronology, this reference work also has introductory essays by well-known historians. The work is divided into five time spans in U.S. history covering the years 986–1982. Each section contains an essay followed by a chronology of events. Major figures, events, and issues are given separate, fuller treatment in boxes. The essays offer a concise overview of the history of the United States. There are no bibliographies or references to further information sources and only a very brief index. This work is useful for those needing an approach to information by date or for students browsing for term paper topics.

104.   **The Encyclopedia of American Facts and Dates.** 8th ed. Gorton Carruth. New York: Harper & Row, 1987. 1,006p. ISBN 0-06-181143-2.

The arrangement of this reference work is at the same time advantageous and disadvantageous for the user. The organization is chronological by year. Within each year are four subject categories: governmental affairs; the arts and entertainment; business, science, philosophy, and religion; and sports, social issues, and crime. The four sections list chronological events by date and offer short accounts of significant inventions or issues that can be attributed to year but not a specific date. Thus, not every event in U.S. history has a dated entry. The emphasis is on a flow of history rather than on a daily recounting of unconnected events. The arts, entertainment, popular customs, and the like receive as much coverage as governmental and political events. This work is useful for scanning through time periods or specific years. It is not as suited as the *Almanac of American History* (entry 103) and other chronologies for a day-by-day approach. The attention given social and cultural issues makes this one-volume encyclopedia a good source for an overview of these aspects of U.S. history. The work is suitable for students and the general reader.

The Timetables of American History, edited by Laurence Urdang (Simon and Schuster, 1981), is also divided by subject. The emphasis in this work is on placing events in U.S. history in a time frame alongside significant happenings in world history. Sections are titled History and Politics, the Arts, Sciences and Technology, and Miscellaneous. Each section is further divided into subsections for the United States and "elsewhere." The introduction is by the noted historian Henry Steele Commager, and the coverage extends to 1980. There is an index by name and subject.

105.   **This Day in American History.** New York: Neal Schuman, 1990. 477p. ISBN 1-55570-046-2.

The most unique feature of this work is that it is organized by day rather than by year. Thus, one can find out what happened on a certain date in any year. Topics covered are as much popular as political and historical. Reviews of the book caution that there are factual errors, so the user is advised to validate the information obtained by using another reliable reference source.

Documentary Sourcebooks

106. **The Annals of America.** Chicago: Encyclopaedia Britannica, Inc., 1968–1974. 20v. ISBN 0-85229-140-X.

The most comprehensive set of primary source documents for U.S. history prior to 1968 is *The Annals of America.* Over 2,000 documents are reproduced in 18 text volumes arranged in chronological order from 1493 to 1968. A two-volume conspectus accompanies the text volumes. The conspectus is divided into 25 chapters, each containing an essay developing the theme of the chapter. Following the introduction, a reference section lists in chronological order the documents relevant to that chapter from the text volumes. There are cross references to other Encyclopedia Britannica reference works and recommended readings. Volume 21, covering the years 1977–1986, was published in 1987. This set of primary source documents is designed to be used with the two-volume interpretative conspectus by history students. It is useful for anyone seeking the text of significant documents in U.S. history along with recommended further readings.

107. **Documents of American History.** 10th ed. Henry Steele Commager, ed. Englewood Cliffs, NJ: Prentice-Hall, 1988. 2v. ISBN 0-13-217274-7(v.1); 0-13-217282-8(v.2).

The various editions of this standard reference work have been revised by retaining a core of documents, adding newer ones, and dropping a few older ones. There is no overall index that indicates which older edition a document may be found in if it is not in the latest edition. All editions have begun with the authorization for the voyage of Columbus and moved forward to modern documents. The tenth edition is divided into two volumes, the first covering the period up to 1898, the second from 1898 to the present. The last document in the tenth edition is the November 13, 1987, report of the congressional committee on the Iran-contra affair. Each document is accompanied by brief introductory notes and a short bibliography. The set is designed to be used by students seeking the text of important papers in U.S. history; it serves this purpose for all types of user.

108. **Historic Documents.** Washington: Congressional Quarterly, 1973– . Ann. **Historic Documents Index: 1972–1989.** Congressional Quarterly, 1991. ISBN 0-87187-566-7SB.

The majority of the primary source documents in this compilation are U.S. sources, although the series is not restricted to the United States. Between 50 and 100 significant documents from each year are arranged in chronological order, with an introduction placing them in historical perspective. The introductory text is presented in the form of an outline or overview. The types of documents included are presidential speeches, Supreme Court decisions, treaties, and government special studies and reports. Numerous cross-references to other volumes in the series enable a researcher to trace a particular issue through source documents over a number of years. A cumulated index also facilitates the tracing of issues over time. This series is a major reference source for primary documents of the last twenty years. It is useful for the general public, students, and researchers.

109. **New American World: A Documentary History of North America to 1612.** David B. Quinn, ed. New York: Arno Press and Hector Bye, Inc. 1979. 5v. ISBN 0-405-10759-5.

The focus of this collection is the discovery and settlement of North America up to 1612. The documents are drawn from printed sources and archives in Europe and North America. Foreign language documents are translated. In addition to administrative records, diplomatic correspondence, narratives, broadsides, and business records, there are 147 contemporary maps. Notes describe the text and provide references to original sources. A total of 851 documents are included, although not all in their entirety. The sources range from Aristotle up to the colonization of North America. The set is indexed, and there is a bibliography of all sources used. The references to foreign repositories and translations may be of use to the researcher as well as to students.

110. **Opposing Viewpoints American History Series.** San Diego, CA: Greenhaven, 1992– .

In this series, primary source materials are placed in a pro/con format in individual volumes, each devoted to a specific issue in U.S. history. The American Revolution, immigration, slavery, and the Cold War are the topics of the first volumes in the series. Chapter introductions place each issue in an historical context. Photographs and boxes give the volumes visual appeal. Bibliographies of sources for further research are provided. The sources are selected to aid in discussion and interpretation of issues. The series is suitable for students through the college undergraduate level.

STATISTICS AND DEMOGRAPHIC SOURCES

The U.S. government is the principal and largest collector of statistical data for the United States. In many instances, the federal government is mandated by law to collect data, such as the census, and is the only agency with the legal authority to do so. Although the data are produced by the government, many of the major access tools are maintained by private enterprise.

Current data are increasingly produced only in electronic formats. Beginning with the 1980 Census, much of the detailed data were never published but were available only in electronic form. For the 1990 Census, more information for detailed geographic areas was provided on CD-ROM disks than in printed summary reports. In addition to the print sources described below, there are many machine-readable datafiles available from government sources (entries 114, 115).

This section includes the most basic indexes and the long-running statistical publications that are most suitable for historical research. A fuller listing of statistical sources and datafiles produced by the federal government are included in the research guides and reference sources listed in the "Government Publications" section in chapter 2 of this reference guide. *Introduction to United States Government Information Sources* by Morehead and Fetzer (entry 69) describes government statistical sources. Both *Tapping the Government Grapevine* by Judith Schiek Robinson (entry 70) and *Using Government Information Sources* by Sears and Moody (entry 71) have explanatory sections on the use of government statistical sources, which are numerous and complex. These reference works may be used to identify additional sources to those described in this section of the reference guide.

Statistical Sources

*111. **American Statistics Index.** Washington: Congressional Information Service, 1974– . Mo., with quart., ann., and quad. cumulations. ISSN 0091-1658. Available online and as **Statistical Masterfile**, a CD-ROM product from the publisher.

The most comprehensive index to federal government statistics is the *American Statistics Index*. This title covers every type of statistical publication from hundreds of federal government agencies, including congressional committees, regulatory agencies, commissions and boards, judicial offices, statistical and research agencies, and special councils. Both depository and nondepository publications are indexed. The organization of the *ASI* is that of an abstracting tool. Data are indexed by subject, names, titles, categories or type of data breakdown (including demographic and geographic), and agency report number. These indexes refer to the abstract volumes that contain the bibliographic citation with SuDocs, ordering information, and an abstract which describes the organization, currency, and sources of the information. For statistical indexing prior to 1974, CIS has published a three-volume *Annual and Retrospective Edition,* which selectively indexes publications back to the early 1960s. Complete copies of the statistical sources are contained in the *ASI Microfiche Library* and available individually through an on-demand ordering service. The *ASI* is available online and in the CIS CD-ROM product *Statistical Masterfile.*

Statistical data published by state governments and the private sector are indexed in another CIS product. Since 1980 the *Statistical Reference Index* has been the counterpart to the federal *American Statistics Index.* Publications from associations and institutes, universities, research centers, state governments, and the commercial sector are indexed in the SRI. The organization is the same as that of the *ASI.* The *SRI* is contained in the *Statistical Masterfile* CD-ROM along with the *ASI.* Copies of data reports are also available in microfiche in the *SRI Microfiche Library.*

These indexes should be used by anyone seeking statistical data, either historical or current.

112. **Bureau of the Census Catalog of Publications, 1790–1972.** Washington: U.S. Department of Commerce, Bureau of the Census, 1974. Part 1, 1790–1945. 320p. Part 2, 1946–1972. 591p. Ann. eds., 1946–1984. Title changed to **Census Catalog and Guide,** 1985– .

A large proportion of the statistical data generated by the federal government is the responsibility of the Bureau of the Census. The most well-known of these responsibilities is the decennial population census, which is mandated by law to establish population shifts for the redistricting of Congress. The bureau also gathers, compiles, and publishes statistical data in the areas of agriculture, government, economics, and business. The business statistics are extensive, covering wholesale and retail trade, manufacturing and transportation, construction, mineral industries, and service enterprises. Most of these statistics are gathered every five years. The *Catalog of Publications, 1790–1972* consists of two parts. The first part is a reissue of the *Catalog of United States Census Publications, 1790–1945* by Henry J. Dubester (Government Printing Office, 1950), and the second part is the *General Catalog of Publications, 1946–1972,* which cumulates the annual Bureau of the Census catalogs for those years. Each section has its own index. This one-volume catalog forms a comprehensive historical bibliography of over 60,000 publications of the bureau. The *Catalog of Publications* will be of use to any student or researcher endeavoring to identify and locate publications of the Bureau of the Census. The historical volume is updated annually by the *Census Catalog and Guide.*

The Congressional Information Service has a number of microfiche collections that reproduce census publications. The collection of *Non-Decennial Census Publications* follows the two parts of the Bureau of the Census *Catalog of Publications, 1790–1972,* which have been reprinted by Greenwood Press to correspond to the microfiche collections. An index has been added to the second part that cross-references the catalog listings to the documents in microform. Separate collections for the 1970, 1980, and 1990 censuses are available in microfiche from CIS. These collections are drawn from the *American Statistics Index,* and the documents are accessible through the *ASI.*

The Bureau of the Census produces a number of CD-ROM databases of current demographic data by zip code and economic and agricultural data.

113. **Catalogs of the Bureau of the Census Library.** U.S. Bureau of the Census. Boston: G. K. Hall, 1976. 20v. ISBN 0-8161-0050-0. **Supp.** 1979. 5v. ISBN 0-8161-0296-1.

The Bureau of the Census Library was established in 1952. It contains a large collection of population surveys, census data, and government reports, both U.S. and foreign. The collecting emphases of the library are in economics, populations, state and local government finance, urban studies, statistical methodology, and data processing. The library also contains a strong retrospective collection of U.S. census publications from 1790 to the present, with materials covering census history, operations, and products. The catalogs are useful for identifying publications and statistical sources for historical research.

114. **Federal Statistical Databases: A Comprehensive Catalog of Current Machine-Readable and Online Files.** William R. Evinger, comp. Phoenix: Oryx Press, 1988. 670p. ISBN 0-89774-255-9

The federal government is the chief gatherer and source of statistical information in the United States. There are over 2,500 datafiles listed in this catalog, the majority being computer tapes, but diskettes, microfiche, and online databases are also included. The emphasis is on statistical information available from the federal government, arranged by department and agency. Many of the files are from the Bureau of the Census. Each entry includes the type of information, time period and geographic area covered, technical specifications for the file, contact persons and addresses, and price information. Related reference materials and reports are indicated. A subject index and an index by datafile title are provided, along with a National Technical Information Service (NTIS) order form. This catalog is a useful source for researchers making extensive use of statistical data who want to compile their own datafiles.

The U.S. Department of Commerce produces a *Directory of Computerized Data Files: A Guide to U.S. Government Information in Machine-Readable Format* (NTIS, 1988). There is a great deal of overlap between the NTIS directory and the Oryx Press publication.

115. **Guide to Resources and Services.** Inter-University Consortium for Political and Social Research. Ann Arbor, MI: Institute for Social Research, University of Michigan, 1977– . Ann. ISSN 0362-8736.

The foremost agency in the academic sector for the gathering and dissemination of statistical data is the Inter-University Consortium for Political and Social Research. The ICPSR was founded in 1962 at the Survey Research Center of the University of Michigan to advance the theory and research use of quantitative data in the social sciences. Approximately 360 institutions cooperatively participate in the consortium, which receives, processes, maintains, and distributes social science data. Information is received from other research centers and individual researchers, with ICPSR functioning as a central repository for maintenance and dissemination. The ICPSR database contains social, economic, political, historical, demographic, census survey international relations, and cross-national data from the U.S. and foreign sources. Figures for research on specific topics such as the aging process, leisure activities, and crime and criminal justice are gathered and maintained. In addition, the center provides training in the use of quantitative analysis and computer technology in the social sciences. Local access to ICPSR datafiles varies and can be obtained through a library, computer center, research center, or university academic department. The annual *Guide to Resources and Services* is a listing of available datafiles and studies indexed by researcher, subject, and ICPSR number.

116.   **Guide to U.S. Government Statistics, 1986.** Donna Andriot, Jay Andriot, and Laurie Andriot, eds. McLean, VA: Documents Index, 1986. 686p. ISSN 0434-9067.

Libraries that cannot afford the much more comprehensive (and much more expensive) *American Statistics Index* (entry 111) or have little need for it have an alternative source in the *Guide to U.S. Government Statistics.* This guide is a single-volume index to the statistical publications of federal government entities. The entries are arranged by SuDocs number and contain SuDocs class stem, title, depository item number, beginning and ending dates of the publication, frequency of publication, and earlier or later SuDocs numbers. The "Agency Class Chronology" feature is useful for tracing agency name and organization changes, as well as SuDocs author symbol changes. If a researcher wants to locate particular publications for a certain span of time or ascertain the publications of a certain agency, this guide can be useful. It can be used in conjunction with the *ASI* but does not substitute for the *ASI* when that index is also available.

117.   **Statistical Abstract of the United States.** U.S. Bureau of the Census. Washington: Government Printing Office, 1878– . Ann. ISSN 0081-4741.

If there is one indispensable statistical compilation, the *Statistical Abstract of the United States* would be that source. It presents summary tables of usually 10 to 20 years of social, political, and economic data drawn from federal statistical reports and publications. The coverage of topics is broad, ranging from information on business and economics, labor, vital statistics, education, energy, science, and transportation to social insurance and welfare services. Not only does the *Statistical Abstract* provide a wealth of recent statistical data, the tables are referenced as to the source of data, and there is a "Guide to Sources" bibliography at the end, as well as a guide to state statistical abstracts. The *Statistical Abstract* is also a major source for historical data, having begun publication in 1878.

Historical Statistics of the United States from Colonial Times to 1970 (2v., Government Printing Office, 1975; repr. Kraus International, 1989) is published as a supplement to the *Statistical Abstract.* Revised every few years, this compilation of over 1,000 pages contains data on the social, economic, political, and geographic development of the United States. A separate chapter contains colonial and pre-federal statistics. Notes at the beginning of the chapters explain the sources for and reliability of the data. Many of the tables are constructed in the same manner and categories as the *Statistical Abstract,* making the time series data compatible. There are indexes by time period and by subject. Researchers seeking historical data should first consult the two-volume *Historical Statistics* issued by the Bureau of the Census.

Another supplement to the *Statistical Abstract* is the *County and City Data Book* (Washington: U.S. Department of Commerce, Bureau of the Census, 1983). First issued in 1949, this compilation combined two earlier separate titles, one for county and one for city data. The compilation has usually been updated every five years from census data. Every county is the United States is covered, as are over 300 standard metropolitan areas, cities of over 25,000 population, and a few other regional categories. For the geographic areas covered, the statistical information in this publication is more detailed than the summary data in the main *Statistical Abstract.* The 1988 *County and City Data Book* is available in CD-ROM format.

Population and Demographic Information

118. **Federal Population Censuses, 1790–1890: A Catalog of Microfilm Copies of the Schedules.** Washington: U.S. National Archives and Records Service, 1979. 96p. ISBN 0-911333-63-9; **1900 Federal Population Census,** 1978. 84p. ISBN 0-911333-14-2; **1910 Federal Population Census,** 1982. 56p. ISBN 0-9911333-15-0; **1920 Federal Population Census,** 1991. 96p. ISBN 0-911333-86-X.

The U.S. National Archives and Records Service sells or rents positive microfilm copies of the original schedules of the first 14 federal population censuses. These pamphlets list the schedules in chronological order, with prices. Microfilm may be purchased through the Publications Services Branch.

Research Publications, Inc. also sells microfilm of decennial population census publications for the 1790–1970 censuses. The *Bibliography and Reel Index* (1975, 276p.) serves as a bibliography to the original publications and as a reel guide to the microfilm collection.

119. **Map Guide to U.S. Federal Censuses, 1790–1920.** William Thorndale and William Dollarhide. Baltimore: Genealogical, 1987. 420p. ISBN 0-8063-1188-6.

A publication that concentrates on the county governmental unit is valuable in historical population research because the U.S. decennial censuses have used the county as the base unit for gathering and reporting data. If county boundaries have changed, researching a location through several censuses can be difficult. This map guide uses the present county boundaries in each state and shows changes to the county boundaries by each census up through the 1920 census. Aside from the maps, there is a complete list of county names for each state that traces changes in names and spelling, including defunct counties. The availability of census information is also indicated. The introduction to the work gives historical information on the U.S. censuses and the records for each census. This guide is useful for state and local historians, genealogists, geographers, political scientists, and anyone else studying changes in demography.

A somewhat similar but more extensive and expensive project is a series entitled *Atlas of Historical County Boundaries* (Simon & Schuster). This project, edited by John N. Long, began in 1991 and will consist of 40 individual volumes by state. Each volume shows, by a consolidated chronology, the changes in territorial/state and county boundaries, with references to other sources. There are separate large-scale state maps and small-scale maps with county outlines for the census years. All volumes have a table of censuses for that state, maps, and text, making them useful to anyone needing historical geographical and census boundary information.

120. **Population History of Eastern U.S. Cities and Towns, 1790–1870.** Riley Moffat. Metuchen, NJ: Scarecrow, 1992. 242p. ISBN 0-8108-2553-8.

The U.S. Bureau of the Census reported population data only by county and incorporated townships until 1870. Constructing population histories for cities and towns that were unincorporated during this time period is very difficult. This work contains population figures for almost 7,000 cities and towns in the eastern portion of the United States from the Atlantic Ocean to Louisiana and Minnesota. The work is of use to historians, geographers, and genealogists.

Two more current reference works that contain historical data are *Township Atlas of the United States, Named Townships,* 2nd ed. (McLean, VA: Andriot Associates, 1979, Supp. McLean, VA: Documents Index, 1987) and the companion title, *Population Abstract of the United States* (Andriot Associates, 1983, 2v.). The atlas covers the 22 states that still have townships as civil divisions of the state. The maps are by individual state, with accompanying lists and indexes of incorporated and unincorporated places of 1,000 or more population. The *Population Abstract* gives population totals for states, counties, and cities with a population of 10,000 or more. Historical population statistics are included for the states, cities, and towns.

121. **Population in Nineteenth Century Census Volumes.** Suzanne Schulze. Phoenix: Oryx Press, 1983. 446p. ISBN 0-89774-122-6. **Population Information in Twentieth Century Census Volumes, 1900-1940.** Oryx Press, 1985. 274p. ISBN 0-89774-164-1. **Population Information in Twentieth Century Census Volumes, 1950-1980.** Oryx Press, 1988. 317p. ISBN 0-89774-400-4.

This three-volume set has been a boon to researchers trying to locate population information in census publications. The first volume covers the 11 censuses from 1790 to 1890. The first half of the twentieth century (up to World War II) is covered in the second volume. These two volumes use the Dubester number as the basic index number. (Henry Dubester's *Catalog of United States Census Publications: 1790–1945* [Government Printing Office, 1950] has been one of the reference works most often used for identifying census publications.) The years covered by the third volume are beyond the coverage of the Dubester catalog.

The Schulze volumes greatly simplify the process of identifying, locating, and retrieving printed population census information. One easy feature is the location of guides on inside covers, which serve as the first index to consult. The subjects are cross-referenced to the census year, volume, and part. The researcher proceeds to the citation for the appropriate census and volume for more detailed information. Complete bibliographic information for each part includes SuDocs number, Serial Set number, and availability in microform collections. Each decennial census is described in an essay providing history, scope, manner in which data were gathered, and unique features. Also included are lists of the subject inquiries of each census; congressional serial volumes containing census reports; and state censuses for the period. There is a section with definitions of terminology by census. This set forms the best and easiest-to-use index to census publications. It is the preferred reference tool for anyone seeking population information from the U.S. census.

122. **The Population of the United States: Historical Trends and Future Projections.** Donald J. Bogue. New York: Free Press/ Macmillan, 1985. 728p. ISBN 0-02-904700-5.

Social and economic trends as seen in population shifts from 1790 to 1980 are shown in this reference work. The 20 chapters are topically organized and include statistical tables, graphs, pie charts, and definitions of terms. The first chapter provides an overview of the U.S. population growth and distribution. A second section is devoted to population changes and includes figures on birth and death, marriages, divorces, and migration. Social and economic factors are covered in two separate chapters and include ethnicity, education levels, the labor force, income, and unemployment. The chapter on special topics contains information on Puerto Rico, religious affiliations, and political demography. There are many references to the source documents, and bibliographies and an index are included. This work emphasizes the years since 1960; an earlier work—*The Population of the United States* (Free Press, 1959)—emphasized the years preceding and following World War II. Although the data are drawn from Census Bureau publications, this work is interpretive and analytical.

An earlier publication that concentrates on the eighteenth and nineteenth centuries is *A Century of Population Growth: From the First Census of the United States to the Twelfth, 1790–1900* (Genealogical Publishing, repr. 1989, 303p.) This work was originally published by the Bureau of the Census in 1909 and has been reprinted several times. It reproduces much valuable data on the early population patterns of the United States. Besides data on age, race, sex, family characteristics, and social and economic factors, there are a number of statistics on slaves. Maps showing county boundary changes in the original 13 states plus Kentucky and Tennessee are given. Another interesting feature is a table of 4,000 surnames found in the 1790 census with spelling variations. There is much of historical value in this one volume that is useful for students and researchers.

123. **Researcher's Guide to United States Census Availability, 1790-1900.** Ann B. Hamilton. Bowie, MD: Heritage Books, 1987. 134p. ISBN 1-155613-066-X.
    This publication is a guide to U.S. census records on a county-by-county basis. The 1790-1900 U.S. censuses and indexes to those censuses are arranged by state and then by county. An introduction gives the type of data collected in each federal census. There is information on the existence of county histories and whether courthouse records were destroyed and have been reconstructed, plus a bibliography of publications issued by state and regional genealogical societies. This index can be used in conjunction with the *Map Guide to U.S. Federal Censuses, 1790-1920* (entry 119). It is intended for use by genealogists but is useful for anyone seeking local history information.

124. **A Retrospective Bibliography of American Demographic History from Colonial Times to 1983.** David R. Gerhan and Robert V. Well, comps. Westport, CT: Greenwood, 1989. 474p. (Bibliographies and Indexes in American History, no. 10). ISBN 0-313-23130-3.
    The emphasis in this reference work is on historical studies that concentrate on demographic changes over a period of time.
    There are over 3,800 citations to books and journal articles, including many from state and local history publications. The work is divided into six sections: general background; marriage and fertility; health and death; migration, pluralism, and local patterns; family and demographic history; and population, economics, and society. Within each section there are three chronological divisions for the early United States, the nineteenth century, and the modern United States. Indexes are by subject, author, and geographic names. This bibliography is most useful to students and scholars in the social sciences with some knowledge of demographic history.

ATLASES AND GEOGRAPHICAL SOURCES

The study of history often involves the need for reference works that present geographical or spatial information to assist in visualizing distances or terrain. Contemporary maps help the student and researcher enter the mind-set of people in the time period under study. Historical atlases present information that does not become obsolete. There has not been a scholarly atlas of U.S. history published in recent years; a number of classic sources are described in this section because they have not been superseded.
    U.S. libraries did not extensively collect maps until after World War II, according to Cobb in his introduction to *Guide to U.S. Map Resources* (entry 131). In the electronic age, static maps that the user must interpret are being replaced by geographic information systems (GIS), which are entered into computer databases and are capable of graphics manipulation. Geographic, census, and demographic data can be combined to create thematic maps to study growth patterns of a region, site businesses, and create new maps. Computer imaging techniques have been used to create three-dimensional battlefield maps (entries 381, 418).

The historian now has the power of enhanced visual imaging for the study of life and events from the past.

125. The American Heritage Pictorial Atlas of United States History. New York: American Heritage, 1966. 424p.

Like all American Heritage products, this atlas is very attractive, with all illustrations in color. It covers American history from "the ice age to the space age." Military history is emphasized, with battle maps of the Revolutionary and Civil wars and a section on the United States in World War I!. An unusual feature is the inclusion of maps of national parks. The accompanying text is not signed, but the expert contributors are listed in the volume. The atlas is intended for a general audience and is not as scholarly as the Scribner *Atlas of American History* (entry 126) or Paullin's *Atlas of the Historical Geography of the United States* (entry 128).

126. Atlas of American History. 2nd rev. ed. New York: Scribner's, 1984. 306p. ISBN 0-684-18411-7.

Although this atlas was first published in 1943, the latest revision was made after the 1980 census. New maps were added on such subjects as nuclear power plants, hazardous waste sites, and intercontinental ballistic missile bases. Information is presented solely through the maps and not in written text because the original publication was designed to accompany Scribner's *Dictionary of American History*. The lack of text with the design makes interpretation of some information difficult. The atlas is intended for students and a general audience.

127. Atlas of Ancient America. New York: Facts on File, 1986. 240p. ISBN 0-8160-1199-0.

This atlas offers an excellent overview of the culture, environment, and history of native Americans. The major Indian groups of North America, Mesoamerica, and South America are included. The volume spans prehistoric archaeology through the European discovery to the "Living Heritage," focused on present-day cultures. Illustrations are a mixture of black-and-white drawings, color maps, and photographs, with sidebars on cultural and behavioral aspects. There is reference value in the detailed gazetteer and subject index. The text is scholarly yet clearly written and suitable for students and the general public.

128. Atlas of the Historical Geography of the United States. Charles Oscar Paullin. Ed. John K. Wright. Washington and New York: Carnegie Institution of Washington and the American Geographical Society, 1932. Repr. Greenwood, 1975.

This atlas has been a standard for many years and has never been replaced as a basic historical atlas for U.S. history. The atlas is divided into two parts. The first contains the text, which refers to the plates contained in the second part. The first section of text covers geographical and geological features, plus temperature and climate. The next section, on cartography, reprints in very small format the early maps from 1492 up to Colton's map of 1867. There are sections on Indian tribes, the exploration of the West, population, political parties and opinion, religions, military history, and boundaries. The text contains a wealth of historical information. The reproductions are adequate. This atlas can still be consulted by any type of user when more recent publications do not contain the historical information sought.

129. **The Cartography of North America, 1500–1800.** Pierluigi Portinaro and Franco Knirsch. New York: Facts on File, 1987. 319p. ISBN 0-8160-1586-4.

The intent of this work is not to provide working copies of the maps but to trace the cartographic history of the New World. The 180 maps reproduced in this volume are by such well-recognized cartographers as Juan de la Cosa, Ortelius, Mercator, Champlain, the Blaeus, and others. There is an introductory essay on the history of cartography, mapmaking techniques of the past, and the exploration of North America. The maps are divided into the three centuries covered in the work. The maker, size, significance and, for some, locations of originals are given. Although the maps are necessarily reduced in size, some are reproduced in double-page spreads. Biographical information on cartographers and explorers is also included along with portraits. This work fulfills its intent; it is an excellent overview of the mapping of the New World. It can be used by anyone with an interest in the subject.

Another work that can be used in conjunction with *The Cartography of North America* is *Maps and Charts Published in America Before 1800: A Bibliography* (Yale, 1969). The maps are listed chronologically under regional headings, with scale, publisher, and other pertinent information given. This annotated bibliography will be of use to historians, historical geographers, and those interested in the extent of geographic knowledge and mapmaking skills in early North America.

130. **Guide to Cartographic Records in the National Archives.** U.S. National Archives and Records Service. Washington: Government Printing Office, 1971. 444p. ISBN 0-911333-19-3.

Since the founding of the nation, the U.S. federal government has extensively engaged in cartographic activities of a military, geographical, geological, and agricultural nature. The extent of the mapping activities can only be realized when the guide to 1.6 million maps and 9,000 aerial photographs in the collections of the National Archives Cartographic and Architectural Branch is perused. The introduction briefly traces the development of exploration, surveying, and mapping activities from 1777 to the present. The organization of the guide is by government branches and agencies. A brief historical account of each agency's responsibility and activities is given. The information includes record group title and number, with series subheadings showing inclusive dates and the number of items. Military maps for all wars are included, as well as peacetime aerial photography by the Department of Agriculture. The indexing in the guide was produced from a database and gives entry number, a list of major classifications by page numbers, and the inclusive dates of groups covered in the text.

Other extensive collections of maps in the federal sector are in the collections of the Library of Congress, which has published several catalogs and lists of these collections. *A List of Geographical Atlases in the Library of Congress with Bibliographical Notes* (1909–1974, 8v.) is the most comprehensive inventory. For U.S. history there is a separate *List of Maps of America in the Library* (1901; repr. B. Franklin, 1974), which describes many old state and county maps and city plans in the library's Map Division. Another is *United States Atlases: A List of National State, County, City and Regional Atlases in the Library of Congress* (1950–1953, 2v. Repr. Arno, 1971). The second volume of this title also lists atlases held by 180 other libraries with locations. The researcher will need to use all published lists and finding aids in endeavoring to make use of the vast cartographic resources of the National Archives and the Library of Congress.

131. **Guide to U.S. Map Resources.** 2nd ed. David A. Cobb, comp. Chicago: American Library Association, 1990. 495p. ISBN 0-8389-0547-0.

The ALA Map and Geography Round Table sponsors the compilation of this directory. The organization is alphabetical by state, city, and institution. Collections of 975 map libraries and their holdings are described, including chronological coverage, hours, and access policies. The first edition was criticized for the lack of subject indexing. This revised edition has greatly expanded indexing, adding a "Collection Strengths Index" with access points by area, name of special collection, and subject according to the Library of Congress map classification. There is a "Library Institution Index" that gives addresses and telephone numbers. The information was gathered by a questionnaire sent to academic, geoscience, private, public, and federal libraries. Because the maps in many collections do not appear individually cataloged in databases, ascertaining which institutions collect certain subjects may be the first step in finding maps for research.

There is another directory of map collections published by the Special Libraries Association, *Map Collections in the United States and Canada: A Directory* (4th ed., 1985). The two directories give much the same information; 805 collections are indexed in the Special Libraries directory edited by David K. Carrington and Richard W. Stephenson. Either directory can be used.

132. **Historical Atlas of the United States.** Washington: National Geographic Society, 1988. 289p. ISBN 0-87044-747-5.

Like all National Geographic products, this atlas is heavily illustrated with photographs, charts, paintings, graphs, and time lines in addition to the maps. The arrangement is in six broad areas, with additional chronological chapters by time period. The areas are the land, the people, boundaries, the economy, networks, and communities. There is a bibliography for the text and the sources of the illustrations. A subject index also covers text and illustrations. A portfolio of larger maps of the U.S. and regions accompanies the main volume. This is a recent historical atlas designed for general use.

133. **Historical Geography of the United States.** Ronald E. Grim. Detroit: Gale, 1982. 291p. (Geography and Travel Information Guide Series, v.5). ISBN 0-8103-1471-1.

The first two sections of this guide deal with cartographic and archival sources for the study and research of U.S. historical geography. The third section is a bibliography of primary sources published between 1965 and 1980. This bibliography updates an earlier work by Douglas R. McManis, *Historical Geography of the United States: A Bibliography* (Eastern Michigan University, 1965). The sources covered include historical atlases, urban and fire insurance maps, census records, and land records. The bibliography includes cultural geography, the physical environment, exploration and frontier settlement, and native Americans. There are indexes by author, title, and subject. The guide can be used by students learning the research process and by researchers in geography and history searching for specific types of source materials.

134. **Maps Contained in the Publications of the** *American Bibliography*, **1639–1819; An Index and Checklist.** Jim Walsh. Metuchen, NJ: Scarecrow, 1988. 367p. ISBN 0-8108-2193-1.

Both separate maps and maps within books are listed and indexed in this work, which is divided into three sections. The first section contains the maps in Evans's *American Bibliography* (entry 39), 1639–1800, arranged by Evans number. The next section covers the Shaw and Shoemaker *American Bibliography* (entry 42) for the years 1801–1819, arranged by Shaw/Shoemaker number. The last section is made up of six indexes by date of publication, place of publication, personal and corporate name, book title, map title, and geographic name. Anyone searching for maps of the Americas and the United States should use this time-saving tool.

*135.   **Omni Gazetteer of the United States of America.** Frank R. Abate. Detroit: Omnigraphics, 1991. 11v. ISBN 1-55888-336-3.

Available as a CD-ROM product from the publisher.

Approximately one and a half million place-names in the United States and territories are briefly described in this gazetteer, organized into nine regional volumes and by states within the regions. The regional volumes cover counties, cities, towns, islands, rivers, swamps, creeks, parks, churches, cemeteries, and historic buildings. Descriptions in the entries include the names and variants, zip code, county where located, map coordinates, and U.S. Geological Survey (USGS) topographic map in which the place-name can be found. Sources of information are given. An index to the set provides access by geographic names. The last volume, *U.S. Data Sourcebook*, contains seven appendices, including an index to USGS maps and list of U.S. airports, Indian reservations, and items on the National Register of Historic Places. There is a section titled "Acquiring and Using Maps and Other Topographic Resources." This is the most comprehensive U.S. gazetteer ever published and is of use to geographers, historians, and genealogists.

136.   **The Story of America: A National Geographic Picture Atlas.** Washington: National Geographic Society, 1984. 324p. ISBN 0-870-44-506-1.

Although this work is classed as a reference work for schools, it is suitable for students of any age. In spite of the use of the term "atlas" in the title, the work is really a pictorial history of the United States presented chronologically. The text contains a wealth of historical information, clearly written. The illustrations are photographs and reproductions of paintings, portraits, maps, artifacts, etchings, and engravings. Excerpts from diaries and letters bring history to life. There is an index to the volume that includes the illustrations as well as the text. A large poster accompanies the atlas volume depicting a time line in ten-year periods with categories such as population, government, the presidents, war, and way of life. The work is an excellent teaching aid and makes fascinating general reading.

BIOGRAPHICAL SOURCES

Biography is central to the study of history. Biographical sources for prominent persons have long existed, but the researcher making new history or the genealogist establishing family chronologies is searching for the not-so-famous, even the obscure. The hunt for biographical information has been made easier and faster in the past few decades with indexes that eliminate the need to consult a large number of biographical sources. A number of indexing tools are now also available in electronic formats. One current electronic database begun in 1980 is *The New York Times Biographical File*. This database contains biographical articles from the *New York Times* as well as obituaries. It will be a useful source for historical research as the database builds. Another current biographical database is found in the Marquis *Who's Who* publications.

This section describes comprehensive biographical indexes, indicating those available in electronic formats. Many older, classic biographical sources are also included. Although the new, comprehensive indexes eliminate the need to search the numerous older biographical sources for names, in many cases older reference works must still be used to obtain the actual biographical information.

Indexes

*137. **Biography and Genealogy Master Index.** 2nd ed. Barbara McNeil. Detroit: Gale, 1980. 8v. Ann. supp. with five-year cumulations, 1981–. ISSN 0730-1316. Available as an online database and in a CD-ROM format.

The first edition of this compilation in 1975 had the title *Biographical Dictionaries Master Index.* The second edition indexes the biographies in over 350 current and retrospective reference works. Prior to the publication of the first edition it was necessary to consult these works individually. The *Master Index* contains over 3 million entries from 675 biographical dictionaries, subject encyclopedias, indexes, and works of literary criticism. The emphasis is on U.S. individuals, but a number of foreign biographical tools are also included. Names are listed in one alphabetical sequence. For each name, abbreviated citations of biographical sources are listed. Variant forms of names have not been reconciled, so a person may be listed more than once. Some entries include birth and death dates. When this information is missing, it is difficult to distinguish between individuals with identical names. Entries indicate when a portrait is included with the biography. A less expensive version of the index is produced in microfiche under the title *Bio-Base.* The database for the master index is used to produce other biographical indexes by occupations and subject fields.

The *Biography and Genealogy Master Index* is available online and as a CD-ROM product. The database can be searched by name, birth or death years, source publication, and year of publication.

Prior to the second edition of the master index, which contains retrospective works, the *Historical Biographical Dictionaries Master Index* was published in 1980 (Gale). Thirty-four of the principal retrospective biographical reference works are indexed in this set. There are some living individuals in the historical index because of the sources included. A number of works are covered in both of the sources, such as the *Dictionary of American Biography* (entry 143). Others, such as *Appleton's Cyclopedia* (entry 141), are indexed only in the *Historical Biographical Dictionaries Master Index.* Not all retrospective reference works are in the historical index, so historical researchers must use both the *Historical Biographical Dictionaries Master Index* and the *Biography and Genealogy Master Index.*

*138. **Biography Index.** New York: H. W. Wilson. v.1– , 1946– . Quart. with ann. cumulations. ISSN 0006-3053. Available as an online database and in a CD-ROM format.

This work indexes biographical info.•nation from periodicals, collected biographical works, and biographical and nonbiograpical monographs. It is a general biographical source not limited to U.S. figures. The index is arranged alphabetically by the names of the subjects. A list by occupation or profession is also included. Basic bibliographic information on monographs indexed is given in a list of those works included in each issue. The number of years this index has been published makes it useful for historical research.

An index more restricted in scope is *People in History: An Index to U.S. and Canadian Biographies in History Journals and Dissertations* (ABC-Clio, 1988, 2v.). Edited by Susan Kinnell, this index was compiled from the *America: History and Life* database (entry 51). Each citation includes an abstract with brief biographical information and the subject, time period, and focus of the article or dissertation. A useful feature of *People in History* is a selective bibliography of references on the study of the writing of life histories, the craft of biography. There is a rotated subject index that provides access by occupation, ethnic group, religion, interests, national origin, and so on. There is also an index to the authors of the articles and dissertations.

139.   **Who Was Who in America with World Notables: Index, 1607-1993.** 12v. including index. Chicago: Marquis Who's Who, 1993. 272p. ISBN 0-8379-0218-5.

Marquis Who's Who has been a major publisher of current biographical sourceworks for nearly a century, producing *Who's Who in America* and a number of regional and specialized subject *Who's Who* volumes. The emphasis in the Marquis publications is on career achievement, and the entries contain brief factual information. *Who's Who in America* began publication in 1899 and can be used for historical research. The necessity of consulting many older volumes of *Who's Who in America* was eliminated when *Who Was Who in America* was published. The first volume, containing only deceased subjects, *Who Was Who in America: 1897–1942*, was published in 1943, with subsequent volumes pulling information from the current *Who's Who* sources as individuals died. A *Who Was Who in America: Historical Volume, 1607–1896* was published in 1963. It contains biographical information on individuals from the United States and other countries that played some role in U.S. history. All of the *Who's Who* titles, both current and historical, are grouped by the publisher under an umbrella title, *Who's Who in American History*. The index volume for all of the *Who Was Who* volumes and the historical volume is titled *Who Was Who in America with World Notables*. This latter set continues to update the *Who Was Who* series, with the addition of a cumulative index for volumes already published. The Marquis *Who's Who* publications are also indexed in the *Biography and Genealogy Master Index* (entry 137). The Marquis index to the *Who Was Who* series is a time saver for any student or researcher using those volumes.

The current *Who's Who in America* is supplemented by a number of regional biographical dictionaries begun in the 1940s. Separate publications focus on subject or professional specialties. The Marquis Who's Who current series are available for online searching and in a CD-ROM format.

Dictionaries and Collective Biography

140.   **The American Biographical Archive.** New York: K. G. Saur, 1986–1989. 1,842 microfiche. Printed **Index**, 19v. ISBN 0-86291-0 (set).

Biographical dictionaries and encyclopedias originally published between 1702 and 1920 in the United States, Canada, and England are reproduced in this microfiche collection. The 367 biographical works cover 300,000 individuals from the earliest period of North American history through the early twentieth century. All men and women of local, national, or international importance who resided in or were associated with the United States and Canada are included. The sources were reproduced, annotated, cross-referenced, and cumulated into one alphabetical sequence. The coverage of the collection is 15 times greater than the *Dictionary of American Biography* (entry 143). A printed index accompanies the microfiche collection. The index is a reference work in itself, giving birth and death dates, occupation, and a list of sources in which the individual appears, as well as the fiche number and frames where the full text of the entries is reproduced. It is likely the *American Biographical Archive* will only be found in large research libraries because it is an expensive acquisition. In those institutions in which it is available, it forms the most comprehensive biographical resource for U.S. history.

141.   **Appleton's Cyclopedia of American Biography.** James Grant Wilson and John Fiske, eds. New York: D. Appleton: 1881–1900. 7v. Repr. Gale, 1968.

One of the oldest established works in U.S. historical biography is Appleton's. Although it was largely superceded by the *Dictionary of American Biography* (entry 143), Appleton's is still consulted. The entries are constructed by family in chronological order rather than in a strictly alphabetical arrangement by individual names. Prominent persons have portraits with autographs. There are inaccuracies in the work and even fictious biographies. A study of these was published by Margaret Castle Schindler in the *American Historical Review* 42 (July 1937), 680–690. The original edition of Appleton's has an index of pen names, nicknames, and so on; a list of deaths; federal officials and unsuccessful candidates for office from 1789–1897; and an analytical index. A new, enlarged edition entitled *Cyclopedia of American Biography* (New York: Press Association Compilers, 1915, 6v.) was printed from the same plates as the original but omitted some articles and added new ones. There were six supplementary volumes published between 1918 and 1931. Appleton's is indexed in the *Biography and Genealogy Master Index* (entry 137).

142. **Current Biography.** New York: H. W. Wilson. 1940– . ISSN 0011-3344.

The number of years this title has been published make it useful for historical research despite its title. The biographies in this monthly periodical are taken mainly taken from news articles. A photograph is included with the majority of the sketches. Although the purpose of the periodical is to give current biographical information on newsworthy individuals, short obituaries are also included. The annual cumulation is titled *Current Biography Yearbook*. A cumulative index covers 1940–1985.

143. **Dictionary of American Biography.** New York: Scribner's, 1928–1937. 20v. Repr. 1943. 21v. 8 supp. with index, 1944–1989. ISBN 0-68416-794-8. **Comprehensive Index,** 1990. 1,001p. ISBN 0-684-19114-8.

This title is the best known of U.S. biographical reference tools, one reason being its similarity to the well-known British *Dictionary of National Biography* (*DNB*). The scholarly *DAB* was first published as a set with over 13,000 entries, sponsored by the American Council of Learned Societies. Supplements have brought the number of entries to over 18,000. The first set contained biographies with both career and personal information, but beginning with the fifth supplement the personal information has been excluded. Persons included are judged to have made significant contributions to U.S. history through politics or career achievements. Anyone who has resided in the U.S. or its territories may be included. The biographical articles feature a bibliography. The reprint edition has an errata section of corrections to the original first edition. The comprehensive index contains six separate listings: 1) names of biographees with authors; 2) contributors with the subjects of their articles; 3) birthplaces arranged by state or foreign country; 4) educational institutions attended by the biographees; 5) an occupations index; and 6) topical index. The *DAB* is also indexed in the *Biography and Genealogy Master Index* (entry 137).

An abridged version of the *Dictionary of American Biography* was first published by Scribner's in 1964. The most recent edition of the *Concise Dictionary of American Biography* is the fourth edition, published in 1990. This version contains condensed entries for all 18,000 individuals in the original set and eight supplements that provide coverage for those who passed away before 1971. All entries in the 4th edition of the *Concise DAB* are in one alphabetical sequence. This edition also contains an occupations index. The shortened articles in the concise edition may suffice for students and many researchers. Others may wish to consult the original volumes of the *DAB* for fuller information.

A work of great magnitude now in progress, with an expected publication date of 1995, is the *American National Biography,* edited by John Garraty for the American Council of Learned Societies. It will cover about 20,000 notables from every field of endeavor who died before 1991. It is anticipated as a 20-volume set, and contributors are scholars and specialists. Oxford University Press is the publisher.

144. **National Cyclopaedia of American Biography.** New York: James T. White, 1892–
1984. **Index**. 576p. ISBN 0-88371-040-4.

Although not as scholarly as the *Dictionary of American Biography* (entry 143), this
biographical compilation is useful for information on lesser-known figures in U.S. history.
The *National Cyclopaedia* is divided into two series. The first, or permanent, series contains
62 numbered volumes, which included only deceased persons. The second, or current, series,
published in lettered volumes (A-M), includes individuals still living at the time the volumes
were prepared. The last volume published is N-63, which is an update for both the permanent
series and the current series. The entries are lengthy, with some including portraits or
photographs and autographs. Information on family, education, career, and historical significance is indicated. Entries are not signed and do not have bibliographical references. A
cumulative index to all volumes in both series was published in 1984. It contains names and
topics in one alphabetical sequence. The *National Cyclopaedia of American Biography* is also
indexed in the *Biography and Genealogy Master Index* (entry 137).

*145. **Notable Americans From the National Portrait Gallery.** Washington: National
Portrait Gallery, Smithsonian Institution, 1990– . Ann. CD-ROM database available from Abt
Books, Inc.

Both color and black-and-white portraits are contained in this full-text graphics database.
Almost 4,000 high-resolution portraits of famous Americans from the National Portrait
Gallery, dating from 1615 to 1980, are included in the database. Enlargements of details from
200 of the art works make the database useful for art history as well as U.S. national history.

146. **Notable Americans: What They Did, from 1620 to the Present.** 4th ed. Linda S.
Hubbard, ed. Detroit: Gale, 1988. 733p. ISBN 0-8103-2534-9.

The first tabulated lists of distinguished Americans were issued in combination with the
indexes to the *National Cyclopaedia of American Biography* in 1906 (entry 144). The next
publication of the lists came under the title *White's Conspectus of American Biography* (James
T. White, 1937). The third edition was titled *Notable Names in American History* (James T.
White, 1973). With the fourth edition, Gale Research has taken up publication of the
compilation of lists. In the first three editions, biographies in the *DAB* (entry 143) were
referred to, but the compilation is now independent of any biographical source. *Notable
Americans* is a reference work, but it does not contain biographies. There are 19 subject
sections with chronological lists of over 42,000 individuals in cultural, philanthropic, religious, educational, government, business, labor, and professional organizations. Recipients
of awards and honors are also listed. A number of the sections are organized according to
periods in U.S. history; others are listings of corporate executives and leaders in other fields.
There are separate personal name and organization indexes. The indexes allow users to find
biographical information on an individual for membership or leadership roles. This work can
be consulted in conjuction with standard biographical sources giving fuller information.

147. **Research Guide to American Historical Biography.** Washington: Beacham, 1991.
4v. ISBN 0-933833-24-5.

This set contains biographies of 452 individuals prominent in U.S. history. Both historical personages and contemporary figures are included. The first three volumes of the set are
arranged alphabetically. The fourth volume contains a separate alphabetical sequence and a
cumulative index to the entire set. Women, native Americans, and minorities were emphasized
in the selection of biographees for the last volume. Most entries contain a chronology, a
section on activities of historical significance, an overview of biographical sources, and an
evaluation of the principal sources. Some sections contain a bibliography of additional

sources and, if pertinent, museums and historical landmarks connected with the biographee. The biographies are not signed, but a list of contributors, most of them historians, appears in each volume. This set is most useful to students or anyone just beginning research on an historical figure.

A similar biographical set is *Great Lives from History: American Series* (Salem Press, 1987, 5v.), edited by Frank N. Magill. The format for the set is signed biographical chapters giving dates, a section on early life, a career summary, and a bibliography of additional sources. There are no portraits or photographs. As with the above entry, this set is most suitable for students or those not familiar with the research process.

Bibliographic Sources

148. **American Diaries: An Annotated Bibliography of Published American Diaries and Journals.** Laura Arksey, et al. Detroit: Gale, 1983–1987. v.1, **Diaries Written from 1492–1864.** 1983. 311p. ISBN 0-8103-1800-8. v.2, **Diaries Written from 1845–1980.** 1987. 501p. ISBN 0-8103-1801-6.

The time span covered and the number of entries make this two volume set a major source for determining the existence of published diaries and journals. The first volume is a revision and expansion of *American Diaries, an Annotated Bibliography of American Diaries Written Prior to the Year 1861* by William Matthews (University of California Press, 1945). The first volume contains 2,780 entries, and the second volume has 3,263 items. The introduction explains the types of personal journals included and the sources used in compiling the bibliography. The definition of "American" is very broad, including material from all 50 states and Spanish-American sites. The arrangement is chronological by year in which the diary was begun, then alphabetical by author. The diaries cited are both separate publications and those published in periodicals or parts of larger works. The indexing is extensive, with subjects, geographical names, and names of primary authors as well as persons mentioned in the annotations. Many of the diaries are by individuals prominent in U.S. history, but others are not well known. This bibliography is of use to anyone seeking personal accounts for specific geographical regions, time periods, or specific individuals.

149. **American Autobiography, 1945–1980: A Bibliography.** Mary Louise Briscoe, ed. Madison: University of Wisconsin Press, 1983. 365p. ISBN 0-299-09090-6.

An earlier work by Louis Kaplan, *A Bibliography of American Autobiographies* (University of Wisconsin Press, 1961) included autobiographies published before 1945. The Briscoe bibliography begins with 1945 imprints but also includes earlier items not in Kaplan. Together these two bibliographies list over 11,000 autobiographies published in book form by private and trade presses. The definition of "autobiography" is very broad, encompassing all manner of personal accounts—diaries, journals, memoirs, and collections of letters. The arrangement is alphabetical by author in both bibliographies, with subject indexes by occupation, place, subject, and personal name. These bibliographies are useful for anyone seeking published first-person accounts by occupation, subject, locale, or specific individual.

150. **Biographical Books, 1876–1949.** New York: Bowker, 1983. 1,768p. ISBN 0-8352-1603-9. **1950–1980.** Bowker, 1980. 1,557p. ISBN 0-8352-1315-8.

The database for the retrospective and cumulative edition of *American Book Publishing Record Cumulative, 1876–1949* and later supplements is the source for the entries in the *Biographical Books* bibliographies. The term "biographical" is broadly defined to encompass all manner of works containing biographical material, including directories and juvenile literature. The entries give basic publication information on the books indexed. One feature of these compilations is the vocation index, which allows for research on occupations or areas of interest as well as individuals. There is a great deal of overlap between the Bowker bibliographies and those of Arksey (entry 148) and Briscoe (entry 149) above. All are useful depending upon their availability in local libraries.

Historiography

151. **Historians of the American Frontier: A Biobibliographical Sourcebook.** John R. Wunder. New York: Greenwood, 1988. 814p. ISBN 0-313-24899-0.

The 57 historians profiled in this work are treated in lengthy signed articles. In addition to biographical information, there are an analysis of the individual's work, a bibliography of the subject's writings, and secondary material about the person, plus a subject and title index. The work will be of interest for those researching the subjects or the U.S. frontier or those having an interest in historiography.

152. **Twentieth Century American Historians.** Clyde N. Wilson. Detroit: Gale, 1986. 427p. (Dictionary of Literary Biography v.17). ISBN 0-8103-1144-5.

There are three volumes devoted to U.S. historians in the Gale *Dictionary of Literary Biography* series. The other two titles are *American Historians, 1607–1865* (1984) and *American Historians, 1866–1912* (1983). In all three works, the individual biographies are written by different contributors and follow a set format. To be included, the historian had to be from the United States and write chiefly in U.S. history. The essays are interpretive and discuss the historian's contribution to the field. Included with each essay are bibliographies of the individual's writings and secondary sources, illustrations and photographs, and reproductions from documents. The biographies are authoritative and useful to anyone from student to researcher.

PART II

U.S. HISTORY—TOPICS AND ISSUES

Chapter 2

Politics and Government

Research in governmental and political topics has been heavily dependent upon government publications as primary source material. U.S. federal government publications and state documents have always been poorly cataloged and indexed by comparison with trade publications. In the past 20 years, the older bibliographic access tools for government publications have been almost entirely replaced by modern cumulative indexing, in many cases with the full text of documents reproduced in accompanying microform collections. Many of the indexes are now available in electronic formats allowing for sophisticated search and retrieval of bibliographic information.

Although researchers in the fields of political science, policy studies, and public administration do not use the same approach as those engaged in historical research, the reference tools employed in these fields are also of use to the historian. The main index in political science is *PAIS International*, published by the Public Affairs Information Service. This index includes many U.S. and foreign government documents, as well as articles from foreign journals and other publications. *PAIS* is available as an online database and as a CD-ROM product. Another general periodical index is *ABC POL SCI*, published by ABC-Clio. This is an indexing tool that lists tables of contents from 300 political science journals, broadly covering the field on an international basis. *ABC POL SCI* is available from the publisher in a CD-ROM format. Also available online is *United States Political Science Documents* (USPSD), compiled at the University of Pittsburgh. The database contains citations and abstracts from 150 scholarly U.S. journals dealing with political and social sciences including education, domestic and foreign policy, international relations, behavioral sciences, public administration, economics, law and contemporary problems, and world politics.

Since the advent of the computer age, disciplines in the social sciences have become increasingly data oriented. Political scientists make extensive use of election data, both current and historical. Because this is a guide to reference sources for historical research, a number of current awareness services and data sources produced mainly for the political science, communications, and sociology fields have not been included in this chapter. For the most part, reference tools have been omitted if they do not contain information dating at least as far back as 1970. A few exceptions are new tools that within a few years will contain a substantial amount of historical information. For a more complete array of current source materials for political and governmental topics, the researcher is referred to *Political Science: A Guide to Reference and Information Sources* by Henry E. York (Libraries Unlimited, 1990).

GENERAL

Reference works that broadly cover U.S. government and politics are included in this section. Those sources that concentrate on a single branch of the government are treated in the individual sections for the executive, legislative, and judicial branches. There are also separate sections for state and local government, political parties, and campaign materials.

153. **American Leaders, 1789–1991: A Biographical Summary.** Washington: Congressional Quarterly, 1991. 534p. ISBN 0-87187-594-2.

The key term in the title of this reference work is "summary," for the biographical information is very brief. The work is mainly an alphabetical listing of officeholders by categories: presidents and first ladies, vice presidents, cabinet members, Supreme Court justices, members of Congress, and state governors. The most serious limitation of the work is that the only index is of governors, making the most common approach of looking up a specific person very difficult. There are several useful lists: female and black members of Congress, length of term for governors, and congressional sessions since 1789. The most valuable features are the introductory essays to each section, which trace the development of a branch of government and describe the most significant historical events and trends. This work provides quick access to information, but users will need to consult other biographical sources to augment that information.

154. **The American Political Dictionary.** 8th ed. Jack C. Plano and Milton Greenberg. New York: Holt, Rinehart, and Winston, 1989. 608p. ISBN 0-03-002932-4.

This standard dictionary was first published in 1962 and has been updated periodically. It is classified by subject, with a comprehensive alphabetical index included to facilitate location of particular terms. One of the strengths of this dictionary is the coverage of important court cases and statutes. Each entry begins with a definition, followed by an explanation of the significance of the term or event. Chapters cover the U.S. Constitution, civil rights, the legislative and judicial processes, business and labor, health, education, foreign policy, and state and local government. This dictionary is of greater reference value and is more current than two other well-known similar works—Safire's *Political Dictionary* (Random House, 1978) and *The Dictionary of Concepts on American Politics* (Wiley, 1980).

155. **American Political Leaders from Colonial Times to the Present.** Steven G. O'Brien, et al. Santa Barbara, CA: ABC-Clio, 1991. 437p. ISBN 0-87436-570-8.

Although selective, rather than comprehensive, this is an excellent biographical work. It includes over 400 individuals, some of whom are lesser known but who had an important political role in U.S. history. The biographies not only give the pertinent facts about the individual, they also are well written and stress the significance of the individual to U.S. history. Brief bibliographies accompany the biographies, and some entries have portraits. Besides including all major party presidential candidates, the work also includes a selection of third-party candidates, all vice presidents, speakers of the house, chief justices of the Supreme Court, and secretaries of state. Not all of the persons included were officeholders. For those individuals profiled, *American Political Leaders* is a superior source to the standard biographical dictionaries.

156. **The HarperCollins Dictionary of American Government and Politics.** Jay M Shafritz. New York: HarperCollins, 1992. 656p. ISBN 0-06-270031-6.

The scope of this work is broader than the *American Political Dictionary* (entry 154). The *HarperCollins Dictionary* (former editions entitled the *Dorsey Dictionary*) has more than 4,000 entries covering U.S. politics and government at the federal, state, and local levels. Entries range from significant Supreme Court decisions to political slang. Brief biographies, major federal laws, journals and professional associations, and bibliographic references are included. The format is attractive, with illustrations, charts, and diagrams. Boxes treat specific events such as Great Society legislation, presidential vetoes and congressional overrides of vetoes between 1961 and 1985, and turnouts in presidential elections, 1920–1984. Five appendices include the text of the U.S. Constitution with annotations, a guide to federal government documents, information on online databases and statistical information, and an index that places all of the entries in the dictionary into concept lists by subject. The comprehensiveness and scholarly nature of this work make it one of the best single sources for reference information on U.S. politics and government.

157. **Encyclopedia of American Political History: Studies of the Principal Movements and Ideas.** Jack P. Greene, ed. New York: Scribner's, 1984. 3v. ISBN 0-684-17003-5.

Contained in this three-volume work are 90 essays, each written by a noted scholar in the field. The introductory essay is "Historiography of American Political History." It is important to note the subtitle of the work, as it emphasizes ideology, issues, movements, and trends. This is not a work one goes to for facts or short historical accounts. The articles average 10 pages in length and are arranged not in topical order but alphabetically by title from "Agricultural Policy" to "Women's Rights." There is an index, which includes subjects and personal names. Annotated bibliographies are included with each chapter, although these vary somewhat in length. For some, the major bibliographical sources receive in-depth treatment; in others the list of additional sources is short. Topics included range from articles on the seminal documents of U.S. history—the Declaration of Independence, the Constitution, the Bill of Rights—to more contemporary issues—women, ethnic minorities, and environmental concerns. This encyclopedia is an excellent source for background reading with interpretation of the trends and significance of the subjects. Scribner's has also published similar works for U.S. economic history (entry 904), foreign policy (entry 273), and social history (entry 422).

A visual record of U.S. politics is provided by *American Political Prints 1766–1876: A Catalog of the Collections in the Library of Congress* (G. K. Hall, 1991). Bernard F. Reilly, Jr., has selected prints from the Library of Congress collections to form a history and political commentary through editorial cartoons. U.S. presidents, other prominent politicians, businessmen, and minorities are lampooned and vilified but seldom praised. Political cartoons are usually biased and vitriolic. The work has notes and text to accompany the cartoons and is of interest to journalists, political scientists and historians.

158. **Political Facts of the United States Since 1789.** Erik W. Austin, with Jerome M. Clubb. New York: Columbia University Press, 1986. 518p. ISBN 0-231-06094-7.

The chief value of this work is that it collects data found in many different sources into one volume. The format consists of tables organized into topical chapters such as "Parties and Elections," "Wealth, Revenue, Taxation and Public Expenditure," and "Demographic Information." The work is mostly a collection of election statistics and lists of officeholders. The compiler consulted state and local sources and unpublished material as well as standard statistical sources. Examples of less common information are a list of assassination attempts on major political figures and a list of salaries of officeholders. The sources used to compile the tables are listed at the end. There is no index, but the tables are clearly listed in the table of contents. This work is most useful to consult when first searching for a fact or for a lead to other statistical sources.

A similar sourcebook is *Vital Statistics on American Politics* (Congressional Quarterly, 1988). This compilation is designed to initiate students to the use of statistics. The data are drawn from a number of standard reference works, such as the *Statistical Abstract of the United States* (entry 117) and other *Congressional Quarterly* publications. Among the best features of the work are the introductions to the chapters, which discuss the availability and use of statistics for that chapter topic. The coverage of current topics such as gun control, abortion, and the death penalty make this a handy reference work. Many of the tables do contain historical data.

159. **Public Administration in American Society: A Guide to Information Sources.** John Edward Rouse, Jr. Detroit: Gale, 1980. 553p. (American Government and History Information Guide Series, v.11; Gale Information Guide Library). ISBN 0-8103-1424-X.

The concentration in this bibliography is on the decade of the 1970s and the growth of the field of public administration and governmental bureaucracies. The bibliography of over 1,000 annotated entries also selectively covers the history of public administration since the end of the nineteenth century. The majority of the sources are articles in scholarly and professional journals from the fields of history, sociology, psychology, political science, business, management, and economics. Author, title, and subject indexes are included. Although the bibliography is not up to date, it serves as a historical overview of the development of the field of public administration and is a useful source for historians of government policy.

160. **United States Government Manual.** Washington: Government Printing Office, 1935– . Ann. ISSN 0887-8064.

Although it is designed to be a current information source, the manual began publication in 1935, and earlier editions are useful for historical information. The manual contains current information on the organization and personnel of the United States government and quasiofficial agencies. Also included are international organizations in which the United States participates. There is a brief description and history of each agency, including its role and functions within the federal government. Key personnel are listed with addresses and telephone numbers. Additional information can include publications, grants and contracts, and other appropriate information specific to a particular agency. Appendices contain abbreviations and acronyms, organization charts, lists of abolished agencies or transferred functions, and citations to agencies in the *Code of Federal Regulations*. There is an index by name, subject, and agency. This is one of the most useful and basic sources of information on the federal government. More detailed information on the organizational structure, regulatory documents of an agency, or presidential documents is published in the *Federal Register* (entry 173).

THE CONSTITUTION

A number of new reference works were issued in observance of the bicentennial of the U.S. Constitution in 1987. Many of these works are interpretative and analytical, with essays written by scholars. Several recent reference works focus on constitutional law in light of social issues since World War II. Only those sources that broadly cover the writing and historical development of the U.S. Constitution are described in this section. Reference sources for state constitutions are listed in the section headed "State, Local and Territorial Government."

161. **The American Constitution: An Annotated Bibliography.** Robert J. Janosik. Pasadena, CA: Salem Press, 1991. 254p. (Magill Bibliographies). ISBN 0-89356-665-9.

The compiler's intent with this bibliography is to provide source material for the study of the U.S. Constitution for students from the high school to university level and to present a diversity of viewpoints on the major issues in constitutional law. The bibliography contains citations to secondary source material written since 1970. The work is divided into four categories: reference works; the text of the Constitution; federal government institutions; and the individual and the Constitution. Like all products of Salem Press, this bibliography is an excellent basic reference tool that must be supplemented by more in-depth research for serious scholarship.

A complementary bibliography listing works published before 1978 is *U.S. Constitution: A Guide to Information Sources* by Earleen M. McCarrick (Gale, 1980). Both primary and secondary sources are included in this annotated bibliography. The first five chapters cover general sources and the history of the Constitution. The remaining chapters cover the three main branches of government and the amendments to the Constitution. There are three indexes by author, title, and subject. Although it is not comprehensive, this bibliography lists many generally available sources for the study of the U.S. Constitution and serves as a useful supplement to more current bibliographies.

162. **CQ's Guide to the U.S. Constitution: History, Text, Index, Glossary.** Ralph Mitchell. Washington: Congressional Quarterly, 1986. 108p. ISBN 0-87187-392-3.

A revised edition of *An Index to the Constitution of the United States with Glossary* (CQ, 1980), this guide gathers a number of elements into a single source. Both the text and a history of the Constitution are included. The history explains the importance of each of the major components of the Constitution and the historical currents and philosophy behind their incorporation into the document. The index in the guide gives references to the exact article or amendment, section, and paragraph. The glossary of terms is helpful in understanding the language of the Constitution. This guide is useful for teaching the Constitution and as a quick reference for students and researchers in all types of libraries.

An authoritative compilation, not as easy to use as the CQ guide, is the *Constitution of the United States of America, Analysis and Interpretation*, which is issued every 10 years by the Congressional Research Service of the Library of Congress, with biennial supplements between editions. The volume is known as the *Consititution Annotated* because every article and section is explicated, with citations to Supreme Court decisions. Tables are also included that list constitutional amendments with status (i.e., pending or ratified); acts of Congress and state and local laws that have been held unconstitutional by the Supreme Court; and Supreme Court decisions that were later overturned. There is an index.

163. **A Comprehensive Bibliography of American Constitutional and Legal History, 1896–1979.** Kermit Hall. Millwood, NJ: Kraus International, 1984. 5v. ISBN 0-527-37408-3. **Supp.** 1980–1987, 1991. 2v. ISBN 0-527-37414-9.

This bibliography of 18,000 entries ranging in date from 1896 to 1979 is indeed comprehensive. A two-volume supplement covering the years 1980–1987 updates the original five-volume work. Journal articles, books, documents, and dissertations are included. The bibliography is organized into seven chapters: general surveys and texts; institutions; constitutional doctrine; legal doctrine; and a chapter apiece for biographical, chronological, and geographical works. There are also subject and author indexes. Within the chapters the works cited are designated as primary or secondary sources according to their importance to the topic of the chapter. Works cited can be designated "primary" in more than one chapter. The chronological and geographical sections repeat the citations from the subject sections. This bibliography is a significant reference work in U.S. legal and constitutional history and should be of use to any serious researcher in those fields.

164. The Constitution of the United States: A Guide and Bibliography to Current Scholarly Research. Bernard D. Reams, Jr. and Stuart D. Yoak. Dobbs Ferry, NY: Oceana Publications, 1987. 545p. ISBN 0-379-20888-1.

The emphasis in this bibliography is on legal research, and the citations are to legal treatises, periodicals, and government documents published between 1970 and 1986. The organization is according to articles, amendments, and sections of the Constitution. The majority of works cited are focused on specific portions of the Constitution. There are an author index and a subject index by legal/constitutional heading. The emphasis on Supreme Court decisions and recent changes in the law make this bibliography less useful for historians than other works with a broader focus.

*165. The Constitution Papers. Orem, UT: Electronic Text Corporation, 1989– . Full-text database.

The complete texts of documents relating the history and development of the U.S. Constitution are included in this inexpensive database available from the producer, Electronic Text Corporation. The definition of the history of the U.S. Constitution is very broad, and documents included are wide ranging—the English Bill of Rights, the Mayflower Compact, the constitutions of the original 13 colonies, Hamilton's Plan of Union, Washington's first inaugural address—as well as the usual documents associated with the founding of the United States. The database is most useful for students studying the text of founding documents.

A similar database of texts is the *WESTLAW Bicentennial of the Constitution Database* (WESTLAW, file label BICENT). The complete texts of historical papers dealing with the origins of the United States are available in this online file.

166. The Constitutional Law Dictionary. Ralph C. Chandler, Richard A. Enslen, et al. Santa Barbara, CA: ABC-Clio, 1985–1987. 2v. ISBN 0874360315 (v.1); 087436440X (v.2). Supp. v.1, 1984–1986. 1987. ISBN 0-87436-484-1.

This reference work has been published in two volumes, with a supplement to volume 1 that updates it through the Supreme Court sessions of 1985–1986. Volume 1 is entitled "Individual Rights" and volume 2, "Governmental Powers." Chapters 1 and 8 of volume 1 have a dictionary arrangement and cover constitutionalism and legal words and phrases. The remainder of the volume, chapters 2–7, concerns amendments to the Constitution, with introductory essay material and significant court cases. Approximately 300 landmark Supreme Court cases are covered. Volume 2 covers over 200 cases affecting governmental powers. The emphasis is on recent decisions and the current thinking of the Court, but the definitions of concepts and the tracing of cases that shaped the law make the set useful for historical research. There is considerable overlap with the *Encyclopedia of the American Constitution* (entry 168), but both sources offer enough unique material to justify consulting each of them.

167. The Dynamic Constitution: A Historical Bibliography. Suzanne Robitaille Ontiveros, ed. Santa Barbara, CA: ABC-Clio, 1986. 343p. (ABC-Clio Research Guides, 19). ISBN 0-87436-470-1.

The area of constitutional history is broadly covered in this bibliography, which has 1,370 citations to 2,000 periodical articles, books, and dissertations from 1974 to 1985. The articles are annotated; books and dissertations are listed but not annotated. The first section is a general "Historiography, Bibliography, and Overview." The remaining four sections cover periods in the history and development of the Constitution up to 1985. A list of abbreviations is provided, along with an author index and a subject index. The text of the Constitution is reprinted. The bibliography is of value to historians and legal scholars.

*168. **Encyclopedia of the American Constitution.** Leonard W. Levy, editor-in-chief. New York: Macmillan, 1990, c1986. 4v. ISBN 0-02-918610-2. **Supp.** 1985–1991, 1992.

This encyclopedia contains 2,000 separate articles written by historians, political scientists, legal scholars, and practicing lawyers. Many of the contributors are well known, including Henry Steele Commager, Archibald Cox, and Eugene V. Rostow. There are three useful indexes, by name, case, and subject. The encyclopedia provides coverage of events and individuals significant in the history of the Constitution up through the Supreme Court term of 1984–1985. The articles range in length from brief definitions and short biographies to longer essays on historical periods, constitutional doctrines, and landmark court cases. Major concepts or issues such as freedom of speech, flag desecration, and euthanasia are treated. There is a glossary of legal terms, and a case index references over 21,000 cases. A detailed subject index is also included. The texts of the Constitution and related documents are reproduced in appendices. The history and development of the Constitution are traced in a chronology. A list of suggested readings is also provided. This is a comprehensive and excellent reference source on all aspects of the U.S. Constitution designed to be used by both general and specialist audiences. It is also available on CD-ROM.

169. **The Founder's Constitution.** Philip B. Kurland and Ralph Lerner, eds. Chicago: University of Chicago Press, 1987. 5v. ISBN 0-226-46387-7.

The purpose of this work is to reproduce documents that trace the writing of the Constitution and shed light on its philosophical underpinnings. Many of the documents are famous and well known, but there are also more obscure texts reprinted. Most of the *Federalist Papers* are included, as well as letters from Jefferson, Madison, Hamilton, Adams, and Washington. The first volume has a theme arrangement, with documents reproduced according to their relevance to a particular concept or theme in U.S. government. Essays on each theme place the documents in historical context. The remaining volumes follow the organization of the Constitution, with each document accompanying a particular article in the Constitution or the Bill of Rights. Some texts are reprinted more than once, and sometimes cross-references are given instead of text. The work succeeds in tracing the history of the Constitution through the documents involved in its preparation and ratification. It is not designed to be a quick reference work but rather one for the study of the historical development of the Constitution.

Words and phrases in the U.S. Constitution and the Bill of Rights are the focus of *The Language of the Constitution: A Sourcebook and Guide to the Ideas, Terms, and Vocabulary Used by the Framers of the United States Constitution* (Greenwood Press, 1991) by Thurston Greene. The two documents, plus other political writings and documents from the colonial period that may have influenced the framers of the Constitution, were scanned and made into a database, from which the passages containing 85 seminal words and phrases were extracted. Each extract is accompanied by a citation to the source. The purpose of the work is to set the words and phrases into the context of the time so that the contemporary meanings can be understood in the present. The work has a subject/source index. An 1872 "Concordance to the Constitution" by Charles W. Stearns is included as an appendix. The work is of use to students and scholars studying the formation of the Constitution.

BRANCHES OF THE
FEDERAL GOVERNMENT

The Executive

General

The executive branch and departments other than the presidency are described in this section. There are not a large number of reference works that deal with these offices and agencies. A number of very specialized works focused on one agency have not been included in this reference guide. Examples are biographical works such as *Principal Officers of the Department of State and United States Chief of Mission, 1778–1986* (U.S. Department of State, Office of the Historian, 1986) and *The Secretaries of the Department of the Interior, 1848–1969* (Washington: National Anthropological Archives, 1975). Only more general sources on the executive branch are included in this section.

170. **Biographical Directory of the United States Executive Branch, 1774–1989.** 3rd ed. Robert Sobel, ed. New York: Greenwood, 1990. 567p. ISBN 0-313-26593-3.

Although biographies of U.S. presidents and vice presidents can be located in many reference tools, this one-volume compilation also lists basic biographical information for all cabinet heads through 1989. The major accomplishments of each cabinet figure are provided, along with basic biographical information and political and religious affiliations. Many of the cabinet heads may be difficult to find except in the larger comprehensive biographical works. This publication is adequate as a ready reference source, but many users will probably seek fuller information.

171. **CIS Index to U.S. Executive Branch Documents, 1789–1909: Guide to Documents Listed in Checklist of U.S. Public Documents, 1789–1909, Not Printed in the U.S. Serial Set.** Bethesda, MD: Congressional Information Service, 1990. 5v. ISBN 0-88692-202-X.

The *CIS Index to U.S. Executive Branch Documents, 1789–1909* is the first part of a six-part set projected for completion in 1995. An accompanying microfiche collection contains the text of the documents in the index. The second part, published in 1992, extends coverage to 1925. The value of the set's being published by CIS is twofold: It serves as a subject index to the *1909 Checklist* (entry 77), and it lists documents not in that publication. The *1909 Checklist* was compiled from the shelflist of the Public Documents Library and is thus a record of the holdings of that institution. During the process of locating documents for filming, other documents not in the original *1909 Checklist* were located, indexed, and filmed. The printed resources are divided into index and reference bibliography volumes. There are indexes by subject/name, SuDocs number, title, and agency report number. The reference bibliography volumes give the dates of publication, pagination, frequency for serial publications, SuDocs number, report number, and subject descriptors and tell whether or not the title is indexed and whether or not the item is in the accompanying microfiche collection. Because CIS has an index and microfiche collection for the U.S. Serial Set (entry 196), those documents already filmed for that collection are not repeated in the executive branch collection. The SuDocs index provides the number for the documents in the Serial Set. *The CIS Index to U.S. Executive Branch Documents* and accompanying microfiche collection have greatly facilitated the identification and location of early executive branch records for research.

172. **The Executive Branch of the U.S. Government: A Bibliography.** Robert Goehlert and Hugh Reynolds, comps. New York: Greenwood, 1989. 380p. (Bibliographies and Indexes in Law and Political Science, no. 11). ISBN 0-313-26568-2.

The focus of this bibliography is toward the executive branch in general, particularly the departments other than the presidency and the White House. The bibliography contains 4,000 entries, including monographs, periodical articles, reports, and dissertations. The entries are not annotated. Because of the large number of entries, the bibliography will be useful for students and researchers seeking a fuller range of sources than those afforded by selective annotated bibliographies.

*173 **Federal Register.** Washington: Office of the Federal Register, 1936– . ISSN 0097-6326. Also available as an online database.

The *Federal Register* is the official publication of the U.S. government, in which all proposed and final text of rules and regulations, notices and orders issued by executive departments and agencies are published. Once a final notice is published it has the force of law. In 1984 CIS began publishing an index to the *Federal Register*. The index provides detailed and comprehensive access to the more than 35,000 items published annually in the *Federal Register*. The complete text from the beginning of the publication in 1936 is available on microfiche. There are also indexes prepared by the Office of the Federal Register. The earlier years of the *Federal Register* are useful for historical research concerning particular agencies or government regulations. The current issues are available as an online government database.

174. **A Guide to Pre-Federal Records in the National Archives.** Howard H. Webmann, comp. Rev. by Benjamin L. DeWhitt. Washington: National Archives and Records Administration, 1989. 375p. ISBN 0-911333-75-4.

The records in the National Archives created in or relating to the period before the Constitution went into effect on March 4, 1789, are described in this guide. These documents include those of the Continental and Confederation congresses, the Constitutional Convention, and the Continental Army and Navy. Records are included for the period of the Revolutionary War pertaining to commerce, Indian affairs, postal and customs operations, and land, pension, and other claims arising out of the military and civilian activities for the period. Diplomatic, fiscal, and judicial records for the Revolutionary War era are included. Information on each record group includes a brief history and describes the organization of the records, indicates availability in microform with reel numbers, and notes the existence of finding aids. There is a subject index that includes names, offices, places, and topics.

175. **Public Office Index. Volume 1: U.S. Presidents, Vice-Presidents, Cabinet Members, Supreme Court Justices.** Keith L. Justice, comp. Jefferson, NC: McFarland, 1985. 181p. ISBN 0-89940-137-0.

This volume is a good source for factual information on the government officials included. There are several useful lists of information not readily found, especially with respect to the members of the cabinet. An administrative index lists the presidents and the terms of office for each cabinet member. Another list conveys cabinet succession, giving the order in which individuals served. Dates given are more specific than in most reference tools, with the month and day included in addition to years of birth or terms in office. The dates of appointment, confirmation, and resignation are given for Supreme Court justices.

Another source for information on cabinet members is *The Vice Presidents and Cabinet Members: Biographies Arranged Chronologically by Administration* by Robert I. Vexler (Oceana Publications, 1975). This is a useful historical reference devoted to the major offices in the executive branch. The basic biographical facts are presented in articles from one to three pages in length. There are bibliographies for further research, one of the features that makes it still useful.

The President

The presidency and individual presidents have quite naturally been the subject of a voluminous amount of research. Consequently, the number of reference works in this subject area is also quite large. The works annotated in this section are recent publications pertaining to the office of the presidency in general. This guide does not list reference works on individual presidents. The works cited have been selected for their comprehensive coverage, currency, and usefulness in the research process. A large number of less scholarly reference works have been omitted. For works dealing with presidential campaigns see "Political Parties and Elections" in this chapter.

Library Resources

In addition to the documentary sources and manuscript guides described in this section, the researcher is referred to the "Manuscripts and Archival Resources" section in chapter 2 and specifically to entry 85, the *National Inventory of Documentary Sources,* which includes materials in seven presidential libraries and is a more detailed source of information than many printed collection guides.

176. **A Guide to Manuscripts in the Presidential Libraries.** Dennis A. Burton, et al, eds. College Park, MD: Research Materials Corporation, 1985. 451p. ISBN 0-934631-00-X.
Seven presidential libraries, from presidents Herbert Hoover to Gerald Ford, are included in this guide. Much of the information is drawn from the published guides to the individual libraries, but it is useful to have it all collected into one publication. The collections of each library are described, including manuscripts, microfilm, and oral history archives. Descriptions include the name, size, reference number, and *NUCMC* number, plus information about the contents of the collections and opening hours of the libraries. There is a subject and name index. This guide should be consulted by any researcher needing access to presidential papers.

177. **Modern First Ladies.** Nancy Kegan Smith and Mary C. Ryan, eds. Washington: National Archives and Records Administration, 1989. 184p. ISBN 0-911333-73-8.
Written for a popular audience, this work is designed to trace the evolution of the position of first lady throughout the twentieth century. As bureaucracy has grown, so has the "office" of the first lady, resulting in a large staff generating considerable documentation. This guide covers documentary materials available for research on 14 first ladies. They are treated in essays that survey their activities and place them in the historical context of their respective presidential administrations. Edith Roosevelt, Helen Taft, Ellen Wilson, and Edith Wilson are grouped in one essay because their papers are all in the Manuscript Division of the Library of Congress. The others, ranging from Lou Henry Hoover to Nancy Reagan, each receive a separate chapter. This basic guide is useful as a starting point for further research.

Bibliographical Sources

178.   **The American Presidency: A Bibliography.** Fenton S. Martin and Robert U. Goehlert. Washington: Congressional Quarterly, 1987. 506p. ISBN 0-87187-415-6.

Martin and Goehlert have compiled two enumerative bibliographies with very similar titles that were designed to be used in tandem. *The American Presidency* contains approximately 8,500 citations relating to the office of the presidency—"its history, development, powers, and relations with other branches of the federal government." The second work by the same authors is *American Presidents: A Bibliography* (CQ, 1987). This volume is devoted to the individual presidents and contains over 13,000 entries. There is no overlap between the two titles. One of the advantages of these bibliographies is that the publication period of the entries spans 1885–1986. These are research-oriented bibliographies, with references to scholarly monographs, journal articles, and dissertations. Government documents are excluded. Each contains an author and subject index. The entries are not annotated, so judging the relevance of sources may be a problem. Nevertheless, the comprehensiveness of these bibliographies makes them among the best sources for scholarly research.

179.   **The American Presidency: A Guide to Information Sources.** Kenneth E. Davison. Detroit: Gale, 1983. 467p. ISBN 0-8103-1261-1.

The approximately 4,000 citations in this bibliography are mainly from the 1960s and 1970s, with some dating back to 1945. There are two divisions to the bibliography: The first part is on the office of the presidency; the second part contains bibliographies of source materials on individual presidents from Washington to Reagan. Monographs, journal articles, and government documents are cited. There is an author, title, and subject index. This guide is suitable for students and beginning researchers.

The American Presidency: A Historical Bibliography (Santa Barbara, CA: ABC-Clio, 1984) can be used in conjunction with this information guide. This bibliography was drawn from the *America: History and Life* (entry 51) database. The 3,000-plus citations are for journal articles and essays published in the 1973–1982 time period, thus serving as a supplement to the Davison bibliography.

180.   **The Presidency: A Research Guide.** Robert U. Goehlert and Fenton S. Martin. Santa Barbara, CA: ABC-Clio, 1985. 341p. ISBN 0-87436-373-X.

The emphasis here is on primary source materials for the study of the presidency and individual presidents. The "Presidency as an Institution" section emphasizes presidential papers and other government documents, such as treaties and statutes. There are bibliographic citations to both primary and secondary sources for the "Oval Office" and "Running for Office." A fourth section is on constructing a research strategy. The addresses, holdings, hours, and access policies of the presidential libraries and other major repositories of research materials are given. An outline of the legislative process is also given, along with an explanation for tracing legislative history. The appendices contain election returns, sources of treaty information, and other helpful information. There is an author/title index. This guide is clearly written and organized for all levels of research and should be consulted at the beginning of the research process.

181.   **Religion and the U.S. Presidency: A Bibliography.** Albert J. Menendez. New York: Garland, 1986. 142p. ISBN 0-8240-8718-6.

For the most part, this is an uncritical, unannotated bibliography. There is an introductory section of general references on religion and the presidency, which are annotated. In the following section each president is treated separately in an alphabetical arrangement; the entries in this section are not annotated. The number of citations (696) is not large, and, quite naturally, the number of entries for each president varies according to how important or influential religion was deemed to be in his personal and political life. The material cited is from newspapers, monographs, journal articles, dissertations, and theses. The bibliography is fairly comprehensive for the topic, including obscure material that might be hard to locate. An author and a subject index are included. The bibliography is useful as a starting point for research on the topic.

Information Sources

182. **CIS Index to Presidential Executive Orders & Proclamations.** Bethesda, MD: Congressional Information Service, 1987. 20v. **Supp**. March 4, 1921–December 31, 1983; 1987, 2v. ISBN 0-88692-106-6.

This 22-volume index covers presidential documents issued between 1789 and 1983. It lists more than 75,000 documents and is organized chronologically into two parts. Part I covers the administrations of Washington through Wilson (1789–1921). Part II begins with Harding and ends in 1983, at which point the *CIS Federal Register Index* provides access to executive orders and proclamations. There is a two-volume supplement that includes another 5,300 documents located after the publication of part II. Each part of the index contains five separate approaches to the documents. There are indexes by subjects and organizations; by personal names; a chronological day-by-day list of all documents; a cross-reference of all executive orders that affect or are affected by other executive orders; and an index by site and document number. This tool may be used with the hard-copy publications or with the *CIS Presidential Executive Orders & Proclamations on Microfiche* collection. The microfiche collection contains the full texts of over 70,000 documents, plus over 3,000 maps and other descriptive attachments. The index and accompanying microfiche collection bring together and provide access for the first time to all numbered and unnumbered executive orders and proclamations. The set is useful to historians, political scientists, and legal researchers.

183. **Congressional Quarterly's Guide to the Presidency.** Michael Nelson, ed. Washington: Congressional Quarterly, 1989. 1,521p. ISBN 0-87187-500-4.

This volume is unique in the amount and variety of information it contains about the office of the presidency. The historical development of the office, the selection and removal of the president, the powers of the presidency, and the relationships within the executive branch and with other governmental agencies are all explored in an essay-chapter arrangement. The section on the "Daily Life of the President" includes information on the people who play an important role in his life. Much factual information is presented in the form of tables, charts, sidebars, and boxes with lists. These features, plus the numerous photographs and illustrations, make the work very attractive. There is a section for biographies of presidents, vice presidents, and first ladies. Other features are the reprinting of the text of selected documents relating to the presidency, approval ratings for presidents from Truman to Reagan, lists of cabinet members, and so on. Each chapter is referenced and includes an extensive bibliography. There is an index. The history of the presidency is contained in this one volume, which is the most comprehensive and useful work on the subject.

Another publication by *Congressional Quarterly* is *The Presidency A to Z: A Ready Reference Encyclopedia* (1992). The information in this work is arranged alphabetically in encyclopedic format rather than in chapters as in the *Guide to the Presidency*. There are 300 entries, both essay overviews and shorter, definitive items. Essays explain concepts and relationships such as constitutional powers and the budget process, whereas the shorter entries define terms, procedures, and the like. Biographies for all presidents, vice presidents, and other important figures are also included. The *A to Z* is designed to be easier and quicker to use than the *Guide to the Presidency*. Of the two, *A to Z* is more suitable for quick reference and as a starting point for research.

A new in-depth reference work is due for publication by Simon and Schuster at the end of 1993. Edited by Leonard W. Levy and Louis Fisher, *Encyclopedia of the American Presidency* will be a four volume work with more than 1,000 original articles covering every facet of the presidency. The source will be an authoritative tool for reference and research.

184. **Historic Documents of the Presidency: 1776–1989.** Michael Nelson, ed. Washington: Congressional Quarterly, 1989. 528p. ISBN 0-87187-518-7.

The full text of many seminal documents in U.S. history are reprinted here. Nearly 80 documents are reproduced, including the Articles of Confederation, the Monroe Doctrine, Roosevelt's "Four Freedoms" speech, Nixon's "Checkers" speech and the "smoking gun" transcript, and Carter's Camp David accords. This volume also contains more recent documents and other historical material that may not readily be found outside of government publications. Each document is prefaced by an introduction on its historical significance. This publication will be of use to anyone seeking a ready source for the text of historical documents.

A more limited source is *Speeches of American Presidents* (H. W. Wilson, 1988). Most of the orations in this volume are reproduced in full. Each president is the subject of a separate chapter, with the number of speeches varying from 4 to 10. Background information is given for each address. An introductory chapter gives an overview on the general subject of presidential speeches. This work contains a total of 189 speeches by 40 different presidents, making it a handy reference for students.

185. **Presidential Vetoes, 1789–1988.** U.S. Senate Library, comp. Washington: Government Printing Office, 1992. 595p.

A bill becomes law if the president does not veto it within 10 days after it has been presented to him. A cumulative listing of vetoes is compiled by the Senate Library. The arrangement is chronological by presidential administration and then by Congress within the administrative term. Each veto is numbered, and the index refers to the numbers. Information on the veto includes the date the legislation was returned to Congress; the reasons given for the veto; and the disposition of the matter by Congress (i.e., whether the veto was unchallenged, overridden, or sustained). There are a list of bills vetoed by each president and an index of names and subjects. This volume is useful in research pertaining to presidential administrations and in tracing the history of particular legislation.

186. **The Presidential-Congressional Political Dictionary.** Jeffrey M. Elliot and Sheikh R. Ali. Santa Barbara, CA: ABC-Clio, 1984. 365p. (Clio Dictionaries in Political Science, v.9). ISBN 0-87436-357-8.

Although designed as a current information tool, this reference work is also suitable for use in historical studies. Over 750 terms dealing with the relationship between the presidency and Congress are defined. The terms are arranged into topical chapters evenly divided between the presidency and allied executive agencies on one hand and Congress with its committees and staff on the other. Each term has a paragraph of definition or identification followed by a second paragraph on the significance of the term both currently and historically. A detailed index facilitates access to the entries. Appendices contain organization charts and tables of popular and electoral voting totals for president. The reference work can be used by students, the general public, and scholars seeking to learn more about the current and historical relationship between the president and Congress.

187. **Public Papers of the Presidents of the United States, Containing the Public Messages, Speeches and Statements of the President.** Washington: Office of the Federal Register, 1957– . Ann. ISSN 0079-7626.

In 1958 the Office of the Federal Register began publishing an annual compilation in chronological order of the public statements of the president. This series is the *Public Papers of the Presidents of the United States.* Subsequently, retrospective annual volumes were published, beginning with the Hoover administration in 1929. In 1965 the Federal Register also began publishing the *Weekly Compilation of Presidential Documents,* which contains the text of proclamations and executive orders, letters, messages, communications with Congress, news conferences, and so forth. Beginning in 1977 the annual *Public Papers* began cumulating all material from the *Weekly Compilation.* These publications provide a day-to-day account of history in the making and a comprehensive record of each presidential administration.

The *Cumulated Indexes to the Public Papers of the Presidents of the United States* (Kraus International) compiles the annual volumes of the *Public Papers* into a set for each presidential administration. In the compilations, "see" and "see also" references have been added. The cumulated set also has references to the page numbers in the original annual series. The cumulated indexes enable a researcher to locate material on one president much faster than by using each annual volume of the *Public Papers* series individually.

The forerunner to the *Public Papers* annual series is a 20-volume set, *A Compilation of the Messages and Papers of the Presidents...* (New York Bureau of National Literature, 1917). This title, originally published by the Government Printing Office from 1896 to 1899, covered the years 1789–1897, from George Washington to William McKinley. The compilation was updated to include administrations through the term of Calvin Coolidge in 1929, at which point the *Public Papers* series begins.

188. **Records of the Presidency: Presidential Papers and Libraries from Washington to Reagan.** Frank L. Schick, et al. Phoenix: Oryx Press, 1989. 309p. ISBN 0-89774-277-X.

Most reference works on the presidents are arranged in chronological order by presidential administration. This guide is arranged according to the type of institution in which presidential papers and records are to be found. The types are: 1) agencies responsible for the maintenance of presidential records, legislation relating to presidential libraries, guides to presidential records, and presidential book collections at historic sites; 2) presidential papers in the Manuscript Division of the Library of Congress; 3) presidential papers in historical societies and special libraries; and 4) the presidential libraries administered by the National Archives. Appendices provide statistical tables on the presidential libraries, directories of major presidential record collections and historic sites, and an explanation of the White House filing system. There are short biographies and bibliographies for each president and outlines of the collections. This guide is a useful overview of the organization and distribution of presidential papers and records. More detailed collection guides from the Library of Congress, the National Archives, and the individual presidential libraries will need to be consulted for specific research.

Separate indexes have been prepared to the microfilmed collections of presidential papers in the Manuscript Division of the Library of Congress. These indexes are not publications, but are collectively referred to as the *Presidential Papers Index Series* (Library of Congress, 1960–1976). An index has been prepared to the papers of 23 presidents— Washington, Jefferson, Madison, Monroe, Jackson, Van Buren, William Henry Harrison, Tyler, Polk, Taylor, Pierce, Lincoln, Andrew Johnson, Grant, Garfield, Arthur, Cleveland, Benjamin Harrison, McKinley, Theodore Roosevelt, Taft, Wilson, and Coolidge. The indexes are arranged by correspondent and by date with no subject aproach. These indexes are useful in searching for correspondence of particular individuals.

Biographical Sources

189. **Debrett's Presidents of the United States of America.** David Williamson. Topsfield, MA: Salem House, 1989. 208p. ISBN 0-88162-366-0.

This biographical reference focuses on personal and family history rather than taking the political focus of most presidential reference works. There is a genealogical chart of the president's family, and the photographs and portraits feature presidential wives and family members. Attention is given to the character of the man and his life before he became president. Although popular rather than scholarly, this source may contain information not found in other reference works on the presidency.

190. **Facts About the Presidents.** 6th ed. Joseph Nathan Kane. New York: Wilson, 1993. 432p. ISBN 0-8242-0845-5.

The longevity of this reference work attests to its usefulness. The sixth edition follows the established organizational pattern of the previous editions. The first part is arranged chronologically by president and concentrates on biographical facts, political career, and the significant policies and events of the administration. Suggestions for further reading are included. The second part contains lists and comparative data tables, in which the presidents are compared in such characteristics as age, college degrees, early occupation, and so forth. This reference work is suitable for use by students and the general public.

Another standard reference work is *The American Presidents* by David C. Whitney (7th ed., Prentice-Hall, 1990). This work is mainly biographical, although there are also tables with election results and other factual information about the presidents. The seventh edition is the same as the sixth edition, with the addition of information on President George Bush the only change.

Similar to the other two reference works is *The Complete Book of U.S. Presidents* by William A. DeGregorio (New York: Dembner Books, distr. W. W. Norton, 1989). Each president is the subject of a chapter, with a standardized format for biographical information divided into 38 subheadings. Both facts and commentary analysis are provided as well as references to the sources of the information. Comparative tables are not provided as in Kane's *Facts about the Presidents.*

191. **Political Profiles.** New York: Facts on File, 1976– .

This series, organized according to presidential terms, provides biographical information on individuals who played significant roles in the politics and government of the period covered. Five volumes have been published: *The Truman Years, The Eisenhower Years, The Kennedy Years, The Johnson Years,* and the *Nixon-Ford Years.* Biographees are not limited to officeholders but may include leaders in industry, labor, civil rights, and science and technology. The biographies are not only factual, they are also interpretative, placing the individual's contributions in a historical context. Articles are signed. Appendices include a chronology, a list of major officeholders, and a bibliography. These volumes give a sense of the presidential terms covered and concentrate factual and biographical information for each time period into one reference. They are written to be used by both students and researchers.

192. **The Presidents: A Reference History.** Henry F. Graff, ed. New York: Scribner's, 1984. 700p. ISBN 0-684-17607-6.

The concept of this work is similar to that of *Political Profiles* (entry 191). The biographical essays on 35 presidents from Washington through Jimmy Carter summarize the accomplishments of each administration. Each essay is written by a well-qualified historian or political scientist. The essays are analytical and attempt to assess the impact of key policies and events in the administration. The essays are not referenced, but each is accompanied by an annotated bibliography. This work is not a factual reference source, but an excellent overview source for students.

Another work similar in scope and objectives to the Graff volume is *The American Presidents: The Office and the Men*, edited by Frank N. Magill (Salem Press, 1986, 3v.). The essays are written by academics and focus on the impact made upon the presidency by each holder of the office. The work is illustrated, including official portraits. It is most useful to students as another source of information on the impact of individual presidents.

193. **The Presidents of the United States of America.** Frank Freidel. Washington: White House Historical Association, 1989. 91p. ISBN 0-912308-37-0.

The White House Historical Association and the National Geographic Society have joined to produce another edition of Freidel's popular work on the presidents. One feature of this reference work is a reproduction of the official White House portrait for each president and a listing of the artists. There is a short essay on each president's political career and administration. Other reference works contain more statistical and factual information, but for students and public libraries this book is a standard.

Also written in a popular vein for a general audience is *The Presidents, First Ladies, and Vice Presidents* (Congressional Quarterly, 1989). The biographies of the presidents include portraits. Biographies for vice presidents and first ladies are shorter. This work is in an attractive format similar to other CQ publications.

Unique in that it emphasizes the vice presidents and their wives is *Our Vice Presidents and Second Ladies* by Leslie Dunlap (Scarecrow, 1988). The arrangement is chronological according to administration. Each vice president and second lady are treated in an essay that begins with an outline of important events in their lives. A number of basic information sources are given at the end of each essay. There are no portraits or photographs. The treatment in this work is popular and personal. Much of the information is repeated from other sources, but this is a recent work concentrating on the vice presidency. It is useful for students but not the serious researcher.

*194. **U.S. Presidents.** St. Paul, MN: Quanta Press. CD-ROM.

Biographical and statistical information on 41 U.S. Presidents from George Washington to George Bush is included in this database. First ladies are also provided, as well as other historical information relating to the presidency. Portraits and photographic images are included in the full-text graphics database.

The Legislative

As the federal government bureaucracy has expanded in the twentieth century, there has been an ever-growing universe of publications to acquire and index. In the last 25 years, there have been great improvements in access and bibliographic control of congressional publications and documents. This section is organized into five segments. The first segment is devoted to the indexing and documentary services provided by the Congressional Information

Service. The other four segments cover standard archival, bibliographical, informational, and biographical resources.

A number of the printed sources annotated in this reference guide have been supplanted by the various CIS congressional indexes. The availability of individual reference works or the CIS indexes will vary according to a user's primary library collection; therefore, this reference guide cites a variety of useful works.

CIS Series

The CIS (Congressional Information Service) has a number of current and retrospective indexes, with full text of the indexed documents available in microfiche. These indexes are grouped together here under one entry to make clear the relationship between the various indexes. Although various GPO publications have indexed government documents, the indexing in many cases is not thorough, does not cover all years, and/or is contained in a number of different publications. One of the main advantages of the CIS indexes is that they have eliminated the necessity for using a number of different sources; in addition, they have supplied information not previously available.

The CIS congressional indexes are also available in CD-ROM format. The retrospective indexes are all contained in one integrated database, *Congressional Masterfile 1 (entry 198). CIS Index*, the current index that began in 1970, is produced as a separate database, *Congressional Masterfile 2 (entry 198).

The order of the section on CIS publications is not alphabetical or chronological, but rather from the more comprehensive indexes to the more specialized. The two broad indexes, *CIS Index* and the *CIS U.S. Serial Set Index, 1789–1969,* are described first. A number of more specific indexes follow them.

*195.   **CIS Index.** Bethesda, MD: Congressional Information Service, 1970– . ISSN 0007-8514.

The *CIS Index* is the current index to congressional documents. Since 1970 CIS has collected, analyzed, indexed, and microfilmed the publications generated by congressional committees, including hearings, reports, documents, and other miscellaneous publications. The indexes come out monthly, with annual cumulations accompanied by abstracts. The indexing is cumulated every five years, but the abstracts are not reprinted. This comprehensive index is useful to attorneys, historians, political scientists, students, and researchers in a variety of fields. Of even greater value for historical research are the retrospective indexes and accompanying microfiche collections listed and described below. The *CIS Index* is contained in the CD-ROM Masterfile 2 produced by CIS (entry 198).

*196.   **CIS U.S. Serial Set Index, 1789–1969.** Bethesda, MD: Congressional Information Service, 1986. Pts. 1–12, 3v. per pt. ISBN 0-812380-26-8.

Unique in the variety and comprehensiveness of the publications it includes, the Serial Set begins with the first session of Congress in 1789. Congressional publications such as committee reports, legislative journals, directories, manuals, and other publications have been included in the Serial Set. Also included are departmental and agency reports, serial publications, and nongovernmental publications such as reprints of newspaper, magazine, and journal articles. This wealth of information has historically been poorly indexed, and very few libraries own complete runs of the Serial Set. The printed index to the Serial Set published by CIS is in three volumes divided into 12 chronological parts. An alphabetical index contains some 2 million names and keyword subject terms derived from the titles of the publications indexed. There is a separate index for proper names that concern private legislation in the

"Private Relief and Related Actions Index of Names of Individuals and Organizations." The Serial Set reference number for all House and Senate reports and documents is given in the "Numerical List of Reports and Documents." There is a shelflist-order index for each Serial Set volume, which allows the review of the contents of each volume. Both the shelflist index and the numerical list give full information on the publication—Congress and session, publication type, volume, report or document number, and serial number. For those documents in the Serial Set, the *CIS U.S. Serial Set Index* for the most part replaces the early document indexes of Poore (entry 72), Ames (entry 73), the *Document Catalog* (entry 74) and the *Monthly Catalog* (entry 76). The Serial Set's coverage ends with the first session of Congress in 1969, coinciding with the beginning of the current index for congressional publications, the *CIS Index* (entry 195). The *CIS U.S. Serial Set Index* is the major retrospective index to government publications for historians and all other researchers. A number of more specific indexes for congressional documents are listed below.

*197.   **CIS U.S. Congressional Committee Hearings Index (1833-1969).** Bethesda, MD: Congressional Information Service, 1981. 8 pts. ISBN 0-88692-050-7.

More than 40,000 titles published between 1833 and 1969 are indexed in the *CIS Congressional Committee Hearings Index,* with the full text reproduced in the accompanying microfiche collection. The transcripts of testimony and supporting documentation of witnesses appearing before congressional committees are a gold mine of information on a wide variety of subjects. The index contains a reference bibliography that provides full information for locating printed hearings. Information on the hearing may include a description of the subject matter, bills considered, a list of witnesses and their affiliations, and the subject descriptors assigned to the hearing. There are indexes by title, subject, and organization; personal names; bill number; report and document number; and SuDocs number. As with the other retrospective indexes, the *Committee Hearing Index* has been continued since 1970 on a current basis by the *CIS Index* (entry 195).

Unpublished committee hearings are indexed in the *CIS Index to Unpublished U.S. Senate Committee Hearings (1823-1968)* and the *CIS Index to Unpublished US House of Representatives Committee Hearings (1833-1946).* The testimony and proceedings of many hearings were not made public for a variety of reasons, usually dealing with national security or the confidentiality of witnesses. A vast array of uncataloged and unindexed materials were filmed and indexed by CIS and made accessible to researchers for the first time. These two indexes, with the accompanying microfiche collections, contain the same access points as the index for published committee hearings.

Similar to the unpublished committee hearing reports are congressional committee prints. These are issued in limited numbers by the congressional committee and synthesize the research and issues germane to a given set of hearings. They are written as background papers for the members of Congress to be informed on important national and international issues, and they contain statistical, bibliographical, and other reference information. Committee prints for the years 1830-1969 have been gathered, filmed, and indexed in the *CIS U.S. Congressional Committee Prints Index.*

Senate executive documents and reports, like committee prints, have been distributed in very limited quantities, if not classified as secret. The *CIS Index to Senate Executive Documents and Reports (1817-1969)* makes these research materials available through both indexing and microfilming.

The user is reminded that the congressional indexes described here are also available in CD-ROM format, with six retrospective indexes contained in one integrated database, Congressional Masterfile 1 (entry 198).

*198. **Congressional Masterfile 1.** Bethesda, MD: Congressional Information Service, 1988. Available online and in CD-ROM format.

Congressional Masterfile 1 is a complete, integrated, multiple-index database. It contains six major CIS historical congressional indexes: *CIS U.S. Serial Set Index (1789–1969)* (entry 196); *CIS U.S. Congressional Committee Hearings Index (1833–1969)* (entry 197); *CIS Index to Unpublished U.S. Senate Committee Hearings (1823–1968)* (entry 197); *CIS Index to Unpublished U.S. House of Representatives Committee Hearings (1833–1946)* (entry 197); *CIS U.S. Congressional Committee Prints Index (1830–1969)* (entry 197); and *CIS Index to US Senate Executive Documents & Reports (1817–1969)* (entry 197). All of these indexes can be searched at once in the Congressional Masterfile 1 database. The current CIS indexes are contained in a separate CD-ROM database, Congressional Masterfile 2, which begins with 1970 and is updated quarterly. The CD-ROM products make research time more productive than it would be with the printed indexes, enabling researchers to retrieve citations from all of the indexes simultaneously.

Archival Resources

199. **Guide to Research Collections of Former United States Senators, 1789–1982.** Kathryn Allamong Jacob, ed. Washington: Historical Office, U.S. Senate, 1983. 352p. (U.S. Senate Bicentennial Publication no. 1). Repr. Gale, 1986. ISBN 0-8103-3334-2.

Parallel to the *Guide to Research Collections* for senators is *A Guide to Research Collections of Former Members of the United States House of Representatives, 1789–1987* (U.S. House of Representatives, Office of the Bicentennial, 1988), edited by Cynthia Pease Miller. Together these guides cover 3,000 house members and 1,800 senators. They are arranged alphabetically by names of congressmen and women. Collections of primary materials, including papers, oral histories, photographs, and other archival materials, are identified by repository. There are brief descriptions of the collections. Repositories are listed by state in the appendices. These guides are the only sources specifically devoted to location information on the papers of members of both houses of Congress. They serve as a starting point for a more thorough search for archival materials on specific individuals.

200. **Index, The Papers of the Continental Congress, 1774–1789.** John P. Butler, comp. Washington: National Archives and Records Service, 1978. 5v. ISBN 0-911333-56-8.

The National Archives produced this five-volume index as a bicentennial project. The documents indexed are available on microfilm from the National Archives and include the records of the two Continental Congresses, the Confederation Congress, and the Constitutional Convention, as well as the Declaration of Independence and the Articles of Confederation. The documents are organized not by congress but by type: Journals, committee reports, correspondence, and so forth are grouped together. There is a separately published index for the journals, *Index to the Journals of the Continental Congress, 1774–1769* (National Archives, 1976). Indexing for persons, places, and subjects is in one alphabetical sequence. Volume 5 is a chronological listing of all the documents, with originator and recipient of the document, number of pages, and location in the microfilm provided. These indexes are the only tools for working with the National Archives microfilm.

Since the publication of the two indexes by the National Archives in the late 1970s, a microfiche collection of *U.S. Congressional Journals* has been published by CIS. This collection is available in two components: one of all congressional journals from 1789 to 1978, and another that contains only those journals not in the *CIS U.S. Serial Set Index*. Researchers trying to locate congressional journals can inquire into the availability of the National Archives microfilm or the CIS microfiche publication.

201. **Members of Congress: A Checklist of Their Papers in the Manuscript Division, Library of Congress.** John J. McDonough, comp. Washington: Library of Congress, 1980. 217p. ISBN 0-8444-0272-9.

The papers of the members of Congress are not all deposited with the Library of Congress, but this is a useful source for quickly determining which collections are there. A total of 894 members of Congress are included, from the Continental Congress to the 95th Congress. Many of the collections listed have only a few items, but other collections are quite extensive. Each entry contains brief biographical information and a description of the holdings of the collection. A useful feature is a summary of microfilmed manuscripts from other repositories held by the Library of Congress, thus providing leads to collections with materials pertaining to the same individual. The entry notes if the collection appears in the *National Union Catalog of Manuscript Collections* (entry 86). There is also a listing of the members of Congress by state as well as by the Congress in which the member served. This checklist will be useful to the researcher seeking to locate personal papers of members of Congress.

Bibliographical Sources

202. **Legislative Reference Checklist: The Key to Legislative Histories from 1789–1903.** Eugene Nabors. Littleton, CO: F. B. Rothman, 1982. 440p. ISBN 0-8377-0908-3.

No references to statutory bill numbers are provided in the *U.S. Statutes at Large* from 1789–1903. This bibliography is arranged chronologically by Public Acts of Congress, with the chapter number, public law number, *Statutes at Large* volume number, beginning and end page citation, date of approval, and bill number for each law. Researchers are able to begin tracing the history of early legislation with this information. This bibliography is a valuable, time-saving aid to research.

203. **Sources of Compiled Legislative Histories: A Bibliography of Government Documents, Periodical Articles, and Books, 1st Congress–94th Congress.** Nancy P. Johnson, comp. Littleton, CO: F. B. Rothman for the American Association of Law Libraries, 1979– . Loose-leaf.

Another aid in tracing legislative histories, this bibliography lists published legislative histories to federal statutes. As such it is very valuable to the legal researcher, who will need to update the legislative history to the present but nevertheless will already have saved the time expended by a previous researcher. The bibliography will also be of use to the historian or political scientist who is not an expert at legal research but is researching subjects in which the interpretation of federal statutes is involved. The loose-leaf service has been kept up to date through the 1980s.

For more current research, the CIS CD-ROM Congressional Masterfile 2 (entry 198) provides a short CIS-prepared legislative history with abstracts of the congressional publications cited for any public law enacted since 1970.

204. **The Speakers of the U.S. House of Representatives: A Bibliography, 1789–1984.** Donald R. Kennon, ed. Baltimore: John Hopkins University Press, 1986. 323p. ISBN 0-8018-2786-8.

Both the individuals who have been Speaker of the House of Representatives and the office itself are thoroughly covered in this bibliography of over 4,000 articles, books, speeches, and dissertations. The first section concerns the office; the second part is devoted to individual speakers and is divided into four time periods. Each begins with a biographical section, followed by information on the location of manuscripts. The bibliography is divided into sections for writings or publications by the individual, and another section lists secondary materials. There are separate subject and author indexes. This volume is a comprehensive treatment of the office of Speaker of the House of Representatives and would be useful for students and researchers interested in the topic.

205.   **The United States Congress: A Bibliography.** Robert Goehlert and John R. Sayre. New York: Free Press, 1982. 376p. ISBN 0-02-011900-6.

Although this bibliography lists a large number of publications (over 5,000), it is admittedly not exhaustive, omitting biographies and many government publications. The focus is on the institution of Congress, its history, and legislative processes rather than on individuals or political and governmental issues. The sources cited include books, essays, journal articles, theses and dissertations, and selected government publications. The subject index is not adequate, and the entries are not annotated. The bibliography will serve as a basic guide for students and a base upon which researchers can build for further investigation.

Information Sources

206.   **Congress and Law-Making: Researching the Legislative Process.** 2nd ed. Robert U. Goehlert and Fenton S. Martin. Santa Barbara, CA: ABC-Clio, 1989. 306p. ISBN 0-87436-509-0.

Designed to serve as a basic introduction to the federal legislative process, this guide is a clearly written explication of the complex of publications, agencies, and procedures involved. A major part of the work is devoted to tracing the legislative process through both houses of Congress. The sections that follow deal with statutory and administrative law. Other sections concentrate on the congressional budget process, support agencies, foreign affairs and treaties, and elections. A large section is composed of a bibliography of secondary sources arranged by format and types of sources. A final section deals with library collections and the citing of government documents. This guide shows the relationship between the steps in the legislative process and the concomitant congressional publications. Those who discover it will carry it along as a companion in the research process.

Another research guide is that by Jerrold Zwirn, *Congressional Publications and Proceedings: Research on Legislation, Budgets, and Treaties* (2nd ed. Libraries Unlimited, 1988). This guide also focuses on tracing the legislative process but devotes separate chapters to the budget process and the ratification of treaties. Pertinent documents and publications are discussed as the processes are followed in essay chapters. Appendices include charts of standing committee jurisdiction and an annotated list by topics of legislative information sources. Indexes are by subject and documents.

207.   **Congressional Committees, 1789–1982: A Checklist.** Walter Stubbs, comp. Westport, CT: Greenwood, 1985. 210p. (Bibliographies and Indexes in Law and Political Science, no.6). ISBN 0-313-24539-8.

Although there are many reference works listing members of Congress and congressional delegations by state, information on committees is not so readily available. This checklist enables a researcher to use a subject approach, listing committees alphabetically according to a key word in the committee name. A subject index is also provided, with references to entry numbers. More than 1,500 standing, select, and special committees are listed. Besides the name of the committee, information given includes the legislation (with citation) creating the committee; the dates of establishment and termination; SuDocs number if the committee was assigned one; and serial set number and volume if a report was issued. A chronological list of committees by date of establishment provides another reference approach. There is a bibliography included. This checklist gathers information on congressional committees into one volume and is useful for those seeking citations to committee reports or information for committees dealing with particular topics.

A more recent work is *Committees in the U.S. Congress 1947–1992* (Congressional Quarterly, 1993). This two-volume work gives the membership of congressional committees, as well as the length of tenure and leadership positions held by each member. Volume 1 is organized by committee, and volume 2 is organized by individual members of Congress, giving the committee members' assignments throughout his or her career. The work is the most comprehensive reference for the years since World War II.

208. **Congressional Quarterly's Guide to Congress.** 4th ed. Washington: Congressional Quarterly, 1991. 1,188p. ISBN 0-87187-584-5.

The first edition of this guide was published in 1971. Each subsequent edition has emphasized the changes occurring in Congress since the previous edition. Each edition also has as its first section historical information on the origins and development of Congress. The second section reviews the powers of Congress; the third explains congressional procedures. A complete listing of members of Congress is included in each edition. Other sections vary according to the edition and the issues prominent in the time period covered. For example, the latest edition reviews effects of the Watergate scandal on Congress and the reforms that resulted. Taken as a series of editions, the *Guide to Congress* is both a current information tool and an historical reference work with an interpretative perspective. It is thoroughly indexed and includes hundreds of charts and tables. It is a reference that should be utilized by anyone studying the federal legislative process or researching any aspect of Congress.

Congress A to Z: A Ready Reference Encyclopedia (2nd ed. Congressional Quarterly, 1993) contains much the same information as the *Guide to Congress.* The format of the *A to Z* makes it much easier to use than the guide. The majority of the entries are brief historical or biographical sketches. Despite the encyclopedic approach, the emphasis is still on the role of Congress in the U.S. government and its historical development and influence. There are a number of longer essays on the committee system, the budget process, the legislative process, war powers, and Watergate. There are cross-references and an index of names and subjects. Besides photographs and charts there are appendices that list members of Congress by various categories. There are also lists dealing with congressional actions such as vetoes and overrides. There are maps and organization charts for Congress and the U.S. government. A bibliography is provided for further research. The arrangement and format of the *A to Z* make it ideal for ready reference, students, and the general public.

A new work is *Congressional Quarterly's American Congressional Dictionary* by Walter Kravitz (1993). Terms and phrases such as "balanced budget" are defined and explained in this comprehensive dictionary. Many of the explanations give the historical origins of the words. The work is an expansion of the glossaries in the back of several CQ publications. It will be a handy reference to use along with the two CQ guides to Congress.

A more specialized work also published by Congressional Quarterly is *Congressional Campaign Finances* (1992). Through a combination of chronology and narrative text, this work follows the issues in campaign finance reform from the Teapot Dome scandal to the present. Contributions and expenditures, political action committees (PACS), and political parties are included.

*209. **Congressional Record.** Washington: Government Printing Office, March 1, 1873– . Daily with bound editions for each Congress.

The *Congressional Record* provides a complete account of the debates on the floor of Congress. It also includes many items placed "on the record" by members of Congress, texts of bills, presidential messages, treaties, and other materials relevant to the legislative process. The *CR* is divided into four sections: the proceedings of the House (H) and Senate (S); the Extensions of Remarks (E); and the Daily Digest (D), which summarizes the day's proceedings. The bound edition is available from the GPO in printed and microfiche formats. The Congressional Information Service films the bound edition, which is considered to be the authoritative version for legal purposes. All volumes from 1873 to the present are available in the CIS microfiche collection. The predecessors of the *Congressional Record*—the *Annals of Congress* (1789–1824), the *Register of Debates* (1824–1837), and the *Congressional Globe* (1833–1873)—have also been microfilmed. Indexing for the *Congressional Record* has been provided by the GPO and also commercial firms. Current indexing for the *Congressional Record* is also available in a CD-ROM product from FD, Inc. (600 New Hampshire Ave. NW, Suite 355, Washington, DC 20037). Not just an index, this product is a complete full-text library of the *Congressional Record* that is updated monthly with cumulative indexing.

CIS also offers microfiche collections of *U.S. Congressional Journals* and *Congressional Bills, Resolutions, and Laws*. The collection of journals covers the years 1789–1978. The bills, resolutions, and laws are available from the 73rd Congress (1933–1934) forward.

210. The Historical Atlas of State Power in Congress, 1790–1990. Kenneth C. Martis. and Gregory A. Elmes. Washington: Congressional Quarterly, 1993. 190p. ISBN 0-87187-742-2.

This title is the third political atlas by Kenneth Martis and updates *The Historical Atlas of United States Congressional Districts, 1789–1983* (Free Press/Macmillan, 1982). Also by Martis is *The Historical Atlas of Political Parties in the United States Congress, 1789–1989* (Macmillan, 1989) (entry 249). The most recent atlas concentrates on the changes in Congress that have occurred after each census and how reapportionment affects the strategy of presidential campaigns. A historical introduction explains congressional reapportionment. The second part of the volume shows congressional reapportionment by decade. The third part treats major geographical trends showing when power shifts took place, how the balance of power swung from slave states to free states, how the West emerged as a separate region, and the growth of the Sunbelt. The atlas contains 33 color maps and 70 charts that analyze the changes in seat allocations and power shifts from 1790–1990. Overviews and case studies supplement the information in the graphic analyses and explicate the historical relationship between geography and public policy. This atlas is of interest to political historians, geographers, political scientists, journalists, and sociologists.

211. The United States Congressional Directories, 1789–1840. Perry M. Goldman and James S. Young. New York: Columbia University Press, 1973. 417p. ISBN 0-231-03365-6.

The material in this work was compiled from early congressional directories, copies of which are now scarce. The period covered is the first 50 years of the Congress, although directories could not be found for some years. One of the objectives in compiling the information was to provide material for the study of the role of "governing elites" in U.S. politics. When the 7th Congress began meeting in Washington, members of the House were listed according to boardinghouse groups rather than the states they represented. Information not included in the original directories has been added. This publication also lists committee memberships, which were added to the directories beginning in 1816. Persons omitted from the original lists and committee memberships before 1816 have been supplied. Biographical data is not supplied, and other reference works, such as the *Biographical Directory of the American Congress* (entry 213), must be consulted. *United States Congressional Directories* is a valuable resource for the research and study of early congressional membership and governing processes.

212.   **United States Congressional Districts, 1788–1841.** Stanley B. Parsons, William W. Beach, and Dan Hermann. Westport, CT: Greenwood, 1978. 416p. ISBN 0-8371-9828-3.

This is the first volume in a series projected to include demographic data by congressional district from 1788 through 1956. Two further volumes have been published with slightly different titles: *United States Congressional Districts and Data, 1843–1883* (Greenwood, 1986) and *United States Congressional Districts, 1883–1913* (Greenwood, 1990). The intent of the series is to enable researchers to analyze an individual legislator's behavior according to the socioeconomic and political makeup of the representative's district. In each of the volumes, data is organized into the decade breakdowns corresponding to the U.S. Census from which the data is derived. Although census data were not consistently collected for the same variables over the years, an effort has been made to make the data categories as similar as possible to allow comparison across decades. Data on variables is presented in tabular format by state and then county. There are state maps showing congressional district bounda-ries by congressional session, and there are political subdivision maps for cities or counties having more than one congressional district. These volumes can be used in conjunction with the Martis atlases (entry 210) and the concomitant congressional publications.

Biographical Sources

213.   **Biographical Directory of the American Congress, 1774–1971.** Washington: Gov-ernment Printing Office, 1971. 1972p. S/N 5271-0249.

Although this reference has not been revised in 20 years, it remains one of the major sources for biographical information on members of Congress. It spans the Continental Congress, September 8, 1774–October 21, 1788, and the 1st to the 91st Congresses, March 4, 1789–January 3, 1971. There are more than 10,800 biographies arranged alphabetically. In addition to congressmen, presidents who never served in Congress are included. There are lists of members arranged by Congress and then by state. There are also lists by administration of the officers of the executive branch. For information since 1971 the annual *Official Congressional Directory* (GPO) contains information on each congressional session, includ-ing biographies, statistical data, and lists of foreign representatives and consular offices, state delegations, and press representatives. This work is the primary source for biographical information on members of Congress.

Brief biographical sketches are also given in *Members of Congress Since 1789* (3rd ed., Congressional Quarterly, 1985). This publication is a directory listing alphabetically all members from the 1st to the 99th Congress. Information given includes birth and death dates, party affiliation, years of congressional service, and other political offices and appointments. There is a statistical section that includes lists of members by average age, religion, occupa-tion, race, and gender. There is also information on congressional leadership and party lineups. The *Biographical Directory* is more comprehensive, but the *CQ* publication is a good ready reference source.

The Judicial

Throughout history, the Supreme Court, in its role as the third branch of the U.S. government, has counterbalanced the other two branches. Many controversial issues dealing with state's rights, attacks on freedom of speech, desegregation, and abortion—insolvable through the legislative process—have come before the high court. Rulings on such volatile issues have kept the Court and its members before the public during periods of intense unrest in the history of the United States.

In 1974 the Supreme Court Historical Society was founded. It now has upward of 3,500 members, both individuals and institutions, engaged in historical research and the collection and preservation of artifacts dealing with the history of the Supreme Court. The society sponsors lectures, research projects, and the publication of historical studies, including an index to judicial opinions (entry 221). It publishes a newsletter and yearbook, as well as the *Annual Lecture Reprints* (111 2nd St. NE, Washington, DC, 20002, (202) 543-0400). The bicentennial of the Supreme Court was the impetus for the publication of a number of reference works. The majority of the works described in this section are recent publications.

Library Resources

214. **The Personal Papers of the Supreme Court Justices: A Descriptive Guide.** Alexandra K. Wigdor. New York: Garland, 1986. 226p. (Garland Reference Library of Social Science, v.327). ISBN 0-8240-8696-1.

All of the justices of the Supreme Court up to and including Chief Justice Warren Burger are listed in this reference work. Justices for whom no personal or judicial papers have been found are listed with that indication. Arrangement is alphabetical by justice. Information given on collections includes location, size, access restrictions, provenance, and a description of the collection as to correspondence and legal papers. The source of the information on the collections is also given. This work gathers much scattered information into one highly useful volume. It will be heavily used by those researching the Supreme Court, individual justices, and broad topics in constitutional history.

Bibliographical Sources

215. **How to Research the Supreme Court.** Fenton S. Martin and Robert U. Goehlert. Washington: Congressional Quarterly, 1992. 140p. ISBN 0-47187-497-3.

Both general research resources and advanced legal research tools are covered in this guide. It is useful for students and members of the general public with little knowledge of the research process and for advanced researchers in law, history, and political science. In addition to listing the resources according to format category, this guide describes the best use of the resources for the type of research being conducted. Bibliographies on the history of the Court and its relations with the other branches of government are included, as well as reference tables listing justices, appointments, and nominations. This guide is obligatory as a beginning point for research on the Supreme Court.

The authors of the research guide have also produced a bibliography emphasizing scholarly research sources. *The U.S. Supreme Court: A Bibliography* (Congressional Quarterly, 1990) can be used in conjunction with the research guide. It is an extensive, although not annotated bibliography that covers research monographs, journal articles, and dissertations. Government documents have been excluded. Subject sections include the history, work,and organization of the Court; civil liberties; equal rights; due process; regulation; and education. This bibliography is useful for anyone beginning research on the Supreme Court or sociopolitical topics.

216. **The Supreme Court and the American Republic: An Annotated Bibliography.** D. Grier Stephenson, Jr. New York: Garland, 1981. 281p. (Garland Reference Library of Social Science, v.85). ISBN 0-8240-9356-9.

Although there are more recent bibliographies on the Supreme Court, such as the Martin and Goehlert work, this bibliography of over 1,300 sources may not be entirely superceded. It offers a selective, annotated listing on a number of broad topics relating to the Supreme Court and constitutional history. Unlike the others, this volume includes citations to the *U.S. Supreme Court Reports.* It also features sections on the history and development of the Court; histories and studies of U.S. constitutional law; the judicial process; and the Court's role in constitutional interpretation, with court cases cited. References are included to the analysis and interpretation of Supreme Court decisions. Its broad coverage makes this bibliography useful for students and researchers. It should be used as a supplement to more recently published bibliographies.

Information Sources

217. **Congressional Quarterly's Guide to the U.S. Supreme Court.** 2nd ed. Elder Witt. Washington: Congressional Quarterly, 1990. 1,060p. ISBN 0-87187-502-0.

Between publication of the first edition of this guide in 1979 and the second in 1989, there were major changes in the outlook of the Supreme Court. In 1979, the Court was composed primarily of the appointments made during the liberal Kennedy, Johnson, and Carter administrations. By 1989 a more conservative orientation was manifest following appointments by presidents Reagan and Bush. The purpose of the guide is to show how the Court has been a major force in shaping law and government in the United States throughout its history. The second edition is a thorough revision. The organization remains the same, with every section updated to include significant rulings through the July 1989 term. The history of the Court and the development of its powers are traced from its inception to the present. A chapter titled "Pressures on the Court" looks at the societal and governmental issues involved in case decisions. Summary descriptions of more than 450 major decisions are arranged chronologically and include the date of the decision, the vote of the justices, case name, citation, and subject heading. Supreme Court nominees, a glossary of legal terms, and acts of Congress that were held as unconstitutional are included in appendices. There is a subject index and case name index. This is an excellent, comprehensive reference work for all inquirers. The guide is updated by *The Supreme Court Yearbook,* which *Congressional Quarterly* began publishing in 1991 with the 1989–1990 year.

Most recent is *The Supreme Court A to Z* (1993) published by *Congressional Quarterly* along with similar volumes on Congress and the presidency. This ready reference work covers the major cases, people, events, and procedures of two centuries of the Supreme Court. The work is alphabetically arranged and contains both short definitional passages and longer core essays on such topics as civil rights. Biographies of justices are included, along with many illustrations. Cases are indexed both by name and by subject. This work is useful for any level of user and most types of libraries. Another important guide is *The Oxford Companion to the Supreme Court of the United States,* edited by Kermit L. Hall (Oxford University Press, 1992). This work furnishes biographies and portraits of every justice who ever sat on the Supreme Court, as well as extensive essays on major issues the Court has faced.

218.   **Encyclopedia of the American Judicial System: Studies of the Principal Institutions and Processes of Law.** Robert J. Janosik, ed. New York: Scribner's, 1987. 3v. ISBN 0-684-17807-9.

This set is one of the encyclopedias in Scribner's American Civilization series, the others being on U.S. political history (entry 157), U.S. economic history (entry 904), U.S. foreign policy (entry 273), and U.S. social history (entry 422). The set furnishes a number of topical essays written by historians and legal scholars. For each article, a list of cited cases and a bibliographic essay are provided, with cross-references to relevant topics in other articles in the set. This encyclopedia is not a factual reference tool but more of an overview useful as reserve reading for a class in U.S. jurisprudence. It is written for an audience without legal training and serves both students and the general public.

219.   **The First One Hundred Justices: Statistical Studies on the Supreme Court of the United States.** Albert Blaustein and Roy M. Mersky. Hamden, CT: Archon Books, 1978. 210p. ISBN 0-208-01290-

Although much of the information in this publication can be found in other reference works such as the *Congressional Quarterly's Guide to the U.S. Supreme Court* (entry 217), there are some worthwhile features. One of these is a "rating" of the decisions of the justices. The ratings are compiled from the *U.S. Supreme Court Reports* and a 1970 opinion survey. The decisions for each justice are listed according to whether they authored, assented, or dissented. The work also contains biographical sketches and a bibliography. It is useful as a ready reference tool and for students and researchers specifically interested in an overview of the decisions of the Court and of individual justices.

220.   **The Supreme Court in American Life.** George J. Lankevich, ed. Millwood, NY: Associated Faculty Press. 1986–1987. 9v. ISBN 0-86733-060-0.

The volumes in this series are divided into nine historical periods: v.1, *The Federal Court, 1781–1801*; v.2, *The Marshall Court, 1801–1835*; v.3, *The Taney Court, 1836–1864*; v.4, *The Reconstruction Court, 1864–1888*; v.5, *The Fuller Court, 1888–1910*; v.6, *The Conservative Court, 1910–1930*; v.7, *The Court and the American Crises, 1930–1952*; v.8, *The Warren Court, 1953–1969*; v.9, *The Burger Court, 1968–1984*. Each volume follows the same format. There is a foreword by the author giving a historical overview of the period covered, focusing on significant events and issues of the period. The first part of the text proper is a chronology of major events, which provides a context for the issues and decisions of the Court. The second part, "Decisions and Documents," includes portions of the arguments in landmark decisions, dissenting opinions, constitutional amendments, and other documents pertinent to the founding and evolution of the Court. There is a biographical section with basic facts and portraits or photographs of the justices. The last section in each volume is a selective bibliography of scholarly articles and treatises pertaining to the era of the Court covered by the volume. The series and its division by historical period are intended to place the decisions of the Supreme Court into a historical context and to assess the impact of those decisions on the country. The volumes succeed in both presenting information and the prevailing philosophy of the Court in each period. The set is useful for students and the general public.

Another multivolume history of the Supreme Court is the Oliver Wendell Holmes Devise *History of the Supreme Court of the United States*, published by Macmillan. The first volume was issued in 1971, and the set is still ongoing. Designed for a varied audience from general readers to lawyers and scholars, the histories are based on personal papers and other original source documents. The volumes are being written by various legal and constitutional scholars, and the set is intended to become the definitive history of the Supreme Court.

221. **Supreme Court of the United States, 1789–1980: An Index to Opinions Arranged by Justice.** Linda A. Blandford and Patricia Russell Evans, eds. Millwood, NJ: Kraus International, 1983. 2v. ISBN 0-527-27952-8.

Certain types of reference works fulfill a distinct need and once published do not have to be revised. This index to opinions of Supreme Court justices is one such work. With its publication it became no longer necessary to search legal source materials repeatedly for the opinions. The editors have included an introduction and a handy "Note to Users." The introduction explains the seven categories into which the opinions have been classified. The complete case name and citation are provided for each opinion. The arrangement is alphabetical by justice and then within the seven categories. This index will be used by historians, political scientists, legal scholars, and students interested in issues placed before the Supreme Court. It forms a base for more current research, which can be conducted through database searching as well as printed sources.

Biographical Sources

222. **Biographical Dictionary of the Federal Judiciary.** Detroit: Gale, 1976. 381p. ISBN 0-8103-1125-9.

Only those judges who were appointed for lifetime tenure appear in this work; persons who served fixed appointments are not included. Coverage is from the administrations of George Washington through Lyndon Johnson, with a few justices from the Nixon era. A large number of the biographies are repeated from the Marquis *Who's Who* publications. The biographies are factual, typically listing place and date of birth, parent's names, spouses, degrees received, positions held, church membership, publications, political party, address, and date of death. An appendix lists judges alphabetically according to the appointing president. In addition to the biographical data there is an essay relating the judges' socioeconomic and political backgrounds. Contained within the essay are tables listing the religious and political affiliations and occupations of the judges. Although the biographical information for most of the judges listed can be found elsewhere, it is useful to have it gathered into one reference volume for study and research on the federal judiciary.

Another biographical work on the federal judiciary was compiled by the Bicentennial Committee of the Judicial Conference of the United States. *Judges of the United States* (2nd ed., The Committee, 1983, available from the Superintendent of Documents) includes all persons who served as a federal judge from the late eighteenth century through the Nixon administration. This directory also contains an appendix listing judges by appointing president.

223. **The Supreme Court Justices: Illustrated Biographies, 1789–1992.** Clare Cushman, ed. Washington: Congressional Quarterly, 1993. c440p. ISBN 0-87187-723-6SD.

This work, produced under the auspices of the Supreme Court Historical Society, is the first single-volume reference to provide in-depth biographies of each of the 105 men and one woman who have served on the Court. Besides presenting standard biographical information, the biographies describe the legal philosophy of each justice and the major issues on which each passed judgment. The volume is suitable for general audiences and students and will be used often for research on the justices of the Supreme Court.

A more thorough, though dated, analysis and interpretation of the first 97 justices may be obtained from *The Justices of the United States Supreme Court, 1789–1969* (Bowker, 1969, 4v.; v. 5, *1969–1978*, 1978), edited by Leon Friedman and Fred L. Israel. All five volumes were later reprinted by Chelsea House in 1980 as *Justices of the Supreme Court, 1789–1978.*

Another work with biographical information on Supreme Court justices is *The Supreme Court Compendium: Data, Decisions, and Developments* by Lee Epstein, et al. (Congressional Quarterly, 1993). For individual justices, such topics as political party affiliation, public support of opinions, backgrounds, nominations and confirmations can be researched. Other aspects of the Court, including its history and development as an institution, workload, cases, decision trends, and impact on society, can be researched. The volume has a detailed index and can be used by lay readers.

STATE, LOCAL, AND TERRITORIAL GOVERNMENT

This section is divided into sources for state and local government and resources for the study of urban politics. The study of state, local, and urban politics has not traditionally enjoyed as high a status for academic historians as the study of federal government policies and national issues and trends. Much state and local history has been carried out by genealogists and nonacademic historians.

The study of urban politics is a relatively new field in which research is carried out mainly by political scientists, sociologists, and public policy experts. The formation of the field can be seen in the beginning publication dates of the three main indexes, all of which began in the 1970s. The first of these is the *Index to Current Urban Documents* published by Greenwood Press. Documents for almost 300 metropolitan areas have been indexed in this publication since 1972. Two other indexes are *Sage Urban Studies Abstracts* (Sage, 1973–) and *Urban Affairs Abstracts* (National League of Cities, 1973–). There are not a large number of sources in urban studies specifically focused on historical research. Additional sources that focus on the sociological aspects of urban studies are listed in chapter 6 of this guide in the section on "Urban Studies."

State and Territorial Sources

224. **American Legislative Leaders 1850–1910.** Charles F. Ritter, et al. New York: Greenwood, 1989. 1,090p. ISBN 0-313-23943-6.

This biographical source profiles 1,390 persons who served as speakers of state legislatures. The biographical information consists of standard personal and professional facts of birth, family and career, religious and party affiliations, and death. The individual biographies do not highlight the accomplishments or influence of the legislators. There is an introductory essay that sets the state legislatures and their leaders into historical perspective. Statistical analyses on the lives and careers of the speakers are in tables in the eight appendices. A summary bibliography of sources is also included. The work is useful as a beginning source, but it is not comprehensive enough for serious historical research.

225. **American State Governors, 1776–1976.** Joseph E. Kallenbach and Jessamine S. Kallenbach. Dobbs Ferry, NY: Oceana Publications, 1977–1982. 3v. ISBN 0-379-00665-0.

The first volume of this three-volume set is the most useful. It contains information on each state derived from state bluebooks and other sources. The main purpose of volume 1 is to give an historical and factual background on each state and the electoral process in that state. The most useful information, gathered from a variety of sources, is that of the constitutional provisions for the election and succession of office of new governors. The second and third volumes in the set contain chronological listings of the governors by state, with brief biographical information. The biographical information can also be found in a number of other sources.

One such source is *American Governors and Gubernatorial Elections, 1775–1978* (1979), published by Meckler, with an updated volume for the years 1979–1987. In addition to containing brief biographical sketches, the book contains a section that provides election statistics, giving voting totals by party and by candidate. Bibliographies organized by state are provided both for states and individuals.

226. **Biographical Directory of American Colonial and Revolutionary Governors, 1607–1789.** John W. Raimo. Westport, CT: Meckler, 1980. 521p. ISBN 0-930466-07-1.

This title is one of a number of biographical directories of governors published by Meckler. Arrangement is geographical and then chronological by date of office. The standard biographical information is given, with fuller information when it is available. Many entries include a photograph. In the colonial volume, persons who held other positions of authority are included. This reference work includes individuals not found in the standard, more well-known biographical works such as the *Dictionary of American Biography* (entry 143). There are bibliographies for each state or colony and for individuals. A name index is provided. In 1984 another title, *Biographical Directory of American Territorial Governors* by Thomas A. McMullin and David A. Walker, was published by Meckler.

The governors biographical series published by Meckler is continued with a four-volume set, *Biographical Directory of the Governors of the United States, 1789–1978*, edited by Robert Sobel and John Raimo (1978). Two supplementary volumes have been published to this set: One, released in 1985, updates the work through 1983, and a second supplement, from 1989, covers men and women who were governors during the years 1983–1988 elections. Biographies in this set are brief.

Within the Meckler biographical sources, persons who served as governor in all states and territories of the United States from the colonial era to the 1980s are profiled. The history of the states and territories can be followed through the accomplishments and assessments of the terms in office of the governors. Although much of the information in these directories is gleaned from other sources, the accumulation of the information and its organization into one continuous set makes these directories a major reference tool.

Another reference source with biographical information is *The Governors of the American States, Commonwealths, and Territories, 1900–1980* (Council of State Governments, 1980). This volume contains much the same information as the Meckler directories in the same geographic organization, but the biographies are much briefer.

227. **The Book of the States.** Lexington, KY: Council of State Governments, 1935– . Bienn. ISSN 0968-0125.

The longevity of this publication makes it suitable for historical as well as current research. Much of the contents consists of contemporaneous directory information—members of the executive, legislative, judicial branches, and government services agencies, with addresses and telephone numbers. Historical and statistical data are provided for each state, with an emphasis on government affairs within the two years preceding the year of publication. The introductory essays and special feature articles are written by the staff of the Council of State Governments. These articles address issues in state government, such as consumer protection, education, and reapportionment. Thus, this reference work is valuable not only for directory and factual information but also for the comparative perspectives it provides for the handling of issues by state governments.

228. **The Constitutions of the States: A State by State Guide and Bibliography to Current Scholarly Research.** Bernard D. Reams, Jr. and Stuart D. Yoak. Dobbs Ferry, NY: Oceana Publications, 1988. 554p. ISBN 0-379-20970-5.

The arrangement of this bibliographic guide is by state. The articles cited are primarily from legal periodicals. The articles date from the 1970s, with the majority from the 1980s. The articles are arranged in order by section number of the state constitution. The full text of the constitutions is not included, but the date the constitution was ratified is given. Those constitutions in force during the preparation of the guide were the sources used. There are indexes by title, author, and case name. This reference work is most useful for legal and historical research. The authors also have a reference work on the *Constitution of the United States* (entry 164).

229. **Historical Dictionary of Reconstruction.** Hans L. Trefousse. Westport, CT: Greenwood, 1991. 284p. ISBN 0-313-25862-7.

The Reconstruction period in U.S. history covered in this dictionary is 1862–1896. Reconstruction was a program undertaken by the federal government to rule and then rehabilitate the Southern states that had been members of the Confederacy. The topics covered in this reference work by a distinguished historian of the period are politics, race relations, major figures, and the restoration of the states. All entries include bibliographic references, many to nineteenth-century sources. A chronology of the period is another feature of the dictionary. Because of the dictionary arrangement there are no indexes, but there are numerous cross-references. The viewpoint of the period expressed is that of current historical scholarship. This volume not only defines the terms and events of the Reconstruction period, it also provides a complete overview and interpretation of the period. It is useful for both students and researchers.

230. **The State and Local Government Political Dictionary.** Jeffrey M. Elliot and Sheikh R. Ali. Santa Barbara, CA: ABC-Clio, 1988. 325p. (Clio Dictionaries in Political Science, no.12). ISBN 0-87436-417-5.

Although the reference works in the ABC-Clio political science dictionary series are primarily focused on current politics, they do contain historical material. The format for each of the dictionaries uses a two-paragraph feature. Each term, event, concept, or person is defined or identified in the first paragraph. The second paragraph provides information on the significance of the item, be it contemporary or historical. The entries are not in a single alphabetical sequence but are grouped into topical chapters, some of which may be more useful historically than others. The work can be used in conjunction with other more historically oriented works by students, the general public, and scholars.

231. **State Constitutional Conventions from Independence to the Completion of the Present Union, 1776–1959: A Bibliography.** Cynthia E. Browne, comp. Westport, CT: Greenwood, 1973. 250p.

This title is the first in a series of bibliographies that accompany and index the microfiche collection *State Constitutional Conventions* begun by Greenwood and now published by Congressional Information Service. The bibliography and part 1 of the microform collection cover all 50 states. The official documents from the state conventions include the enabling legislation, journals, proceedings, resolutions and rules, the proposed draft of the constitution, and the final ratified constitution. Additional parts of the microfilm collection contain material produced by conventions and commissions between 1959–1988. An updated two-volume bibliography for the years 1959–1978 published by CIS accompanies parts 2–4 of the microform collection. Volume 1 provides full bibliographic information arranged by state and time period; volume 2 is arranged alphabetically by author and title within each state. There is also a separate annotated bibliography for the 1979–1988 time period accompanying part 5 of the microfiche collection. The bibliographies and microform collections are essential sources for those researching state constitutional conventions.

232. State Document Checklists: A Historical Bibliography. Susan L. Dow. Buffalo, NY: William S. Hein, 1990. 224p. ISBN 0-89941-739-6.

Bibliographic control of state documents has varied considerably among the states. Dow has compiled a bibliography by state that lists all the state checklists in chronological order according to publication date. The bibliography is evaluative as well as enumerative. Information is given on the scope and time span covered for each checklist. For the current checklists, ordering and full cataloging information are given. A title index is provided. In addition to the bibliography by state, there is an introductory essay on the history of the bibliographic control of state publications. Historians making extensive use of state documents will find this work helpful.

233. State Government Reference Publications: An Annotated Bibliography. 2nd ed. David W. Parish. Littleton, CO: Libraries Unlimited, 1981. 355p. ISBN 0-87287-253-X.

The overall arrangement of this annotated bibliography of 1,756 entries is by publication type, with listings by state within each of the nine sections. The major sections are for official state bibliography, bluebooks, legislative manuals, state government finances, statistical abstracts, directories, tourist guides, audiovisual guides, atlases and maps, and bibliographies and general reference. Indexes by author, title, and subject are included. This is the second edition of a well-known reference work useful for historical research.

234. State Legislatures: A Bibliography. Robert Goehlert and Frederick W. Musto. Santa Barbara, CA: ABC-Clio, 1985. 229p. ISBN 0-87436-422-1.

A compilation of scholarly writings concerning state legislatures, this bibliography includes dissertations, books, articles, and selected documents published between 1945 and 1984. The work contains 2,532 citations divided into two parts. The first part contains studies about state legislative processes, arrayed by subject, and the second part contains studies of individual state legislatures, arranged by state. There are separate subject and author indexes. The only bibliography of its kind, this reference work is indispensable for historical research on state legislatures.

Local Government Sources

235. Biographical Dictionary of American Mayors, 1820–1980: Big City Mayors. Melvin G. Holli and Peter d'Alroy Jones. Westport, CT: Greenwood, 1981. 451p. ISBN 0-313-21134-5.

Biographies of 647 mayors from 15 of the largest U.S. cities are included in this dictionary. The cities are Baltimore, Boston, Buffalo, Chicago, Cincinnati, Cleveland, Detroit, Los Angeles, Milwaukee, New Orleans, New York, Philadelphia, Pittsburgh, San Francisco, and St. Louis. The biographies are written by over 100 scholars who used local libraries and archives for their research. The arrangement is alphabetical by individual, but an appendix provides chronological listings by city. Other appendices list the mayors by place of birth, religious and party affiliations, and ethnic background. Each entry is signed and includes a list of sources. Standard biographical information is included as well as dates of terms in office. This work was thoroughly researched and provides information on individuals not found in previously published sources.

236. **Urban Politics: A Guide to Information Sources.** Thomas P. Murphy, ed. Detroit: Gale, 1978. 248p. ISBN 0-8103-1395-2.

Sources in this bibliography are from the 1970s. The work is useful for research in the history of urban government policies and structure as they evolved in the 1960s and 1970s. The bibliography is especially strong in the area of federal-state-urban relations. The annotated bibliography is divided into subject sections covering political parties and leaders, socioethnic relations, public policy, citizen participation, and governmental organization and structure. There are appendices, which are not annotated, listing further source materials. Indexes by author, title, and subject are provided. Anyone doing research in urban politics can use this as a base bibliography for publications prior to the mid-1970s.

A work with a narrower focus is *Citizen Groups in Local Politics: A Bibliographic Review* by John D. Hutcheson, Jr. and Jann Shevin (ABC-Clio, 1976). The bibliography is annotated, with unannotated lists of dissertations at the end of each chapter. The emphasis is on the organization and influence of citizen groups in the development of local government policy.

POLITICAL PARTIES AND ELECTIONS

As the capacity to analyze huge amounts of data has evolved, the study of political parties and campaigns has become focused more on socioeconomic factors than on political strategies. Traditionally, campaign elements such as slogans, songs, speeches, and newspaper coverage played a major role in campaign strategy. Since the 1960s, political campaigns have become ever more media-intensive, with predictive polls and sociopolitical strategies taking on increasing importance. Like the sections on politics and government, this section does not describe many contemporaneous publications for election statistics. Rather, the sources mainly concern historical campaign tools and tactics or the study of political parties in the United States.

Bibliographical Sources

237. **The People's Voice: An Annotated Bibliography of American Presidential Campaign Newspapers, 1828–1984.** William Miles, comp. New York: Greenwood, 1987. 210p. ISBN 0-313-23976-2.

Before the advent of radio and television, the primary campaign medium was the newspaper. The history and influence of the campaign press are discussed in the introduction to *The People's Voice*. The bibliography is chronological by election year and then subdivided by political party or candidate. Masthead title and slogan, beginning and ending dates, frequency, publisher, and place of publication are given for each newspaper. One of the most valuable features for researchers is the location and holdings information for the newspaper files. Anyone conducting research involving U.S. presidential campaigns will need to consult this work.

238. **American Political Parties: A Selective Guide to Parties and Movements of the 20th Century.** Lubomyr Roman Wynar, comp. Littleton, CO: Libraries Unlimited, 1969. 427p. ISBN 87287-011-1.

This annotated bibliography broadly covers the literature dealing with political parties in the United States. There are general sections on Congress, the executive branch, and the political and electoral processes, as well as sections devoted to particular political parties and movements. Sources cited are monographs, periodical articles, general reference sources, dissertations, and government documents. This bibliography is useful for the broad political scope and amount of material it includes. Further research will be necessary to update the bibliography.

239. **The Democratic and Republican Parties in America: A Historical Bibliography.** Santa Barbara, CA: ABC-Clio, 1984. 290p. ISBN 0-87436-364-0.

The origin of the two-party system in U.S. politics is traced in this bibliography, through chapters arranged by historical period. It includes source material on other parties influential in the political process. The bibliography is drawn from the database of *America: History and Life* (entry 51). The publication dates of the sources range from 1973 to 1981. Abstracts included with the citations often indicate the type of sources used in a particular work. Although it is not current, this bibliography is fairly comprehensive for the years 1973–1981.

240. **American Third Parties Since the Civil War: An Annotated Bibliography.** Stephen Rockwood, et al. New York: Garland, 1985. 177p. (Garland Reference Library of Social Science, v.227). ISBN 0-8240-8970-7.

Designed more for the student than the serious researcher, this selective bibliography emphasizes major monographic source material, although periodical articles are included. The organization is by political ideology, with parties of similar orientation grouped together. There are separate chapters for the Populist Party, Progressive Party, the Dixiecrats, and American Independent party. This bibliography serves as a useful complement to other bibliographies on similar topics in U.S. politics.

241. **The American Electorate: A Historical Bibliography.** Susan Kinnell, ed. Santa Barbara, CA: ABC-Clio, 1984. 388p. ISBN 0-87436-372-1.

Another bibliography drawn from the ABC-Clio *America: History and Life* database (entry 51), this work forms an excellent companion to reference works such as the *Congressional Quarterly*'s compilations of election statistics. The focus is on voter characteristics and behavior. The sources cited are from 1973–1982, and abstracts are included. There are subject and author indexes. This volume forms a base bibliography for research on U.S. elections and is useful for anyone seeking historical information on the electoral process.

242. **The Image Makers: A Bibliography of American Presidential Campaign Biographies.** William Miles. Metuchen, NJ: Scarecrow, 1979. 254p. ISBN 0-8108-1252-5.

Campaign biographies endeavor to portray the candidate in the best possible light. The comparison of campaign biographies to known biographical facts is an interesting exercise. This bibliography is not exhaustive, but it covers a broad range of sources and topics, including both favorable and unfavorable satirical material. All serious candidates for office, successful and unsuccessful, are included. As with most presidential campaign reference works, the organization is chronological by election year, beginning with 1824. The decline in the number of official campaign biographies in the latter half of the twentieth century is apparent from the number of entries. Campaign newspapers are not included in this bibliography (see entry 237). *The Image Makers*, a microfilm collection based on the Miles bibliography, has been published by University Microfilms. The bibliography is of interest to political scientists, media specialists, and historians.

243. **Songs, Odes, Glees, and Ballads: A Bibliography of American Presidential Campaign Songsters.** William Miles. Westport, CT: Greenwood, 1990. 200p. (Music Reference Collection, no.27). ISBN 0-313-27697-8.

Before the electronic media age, campaign songs were a prominent feature of election campaigns. This work contains an introductory overview of the place of the song in election campaigns, which makes for entertaining reading. The main part of the work is a bibliography of anthologies containing campaign songs from 1840 to 1964. Location of copies of the works cited is facilitated by the inclusion of the OCLC database accession number in the bibliographic information. Lists of secondary sources and discographies are in the appendices. There are indexes by name, title, and publisher. This bibliography will be of interest to historians, political scientists, and musicologists.

Information Sources

244. **The American Dictionary of Campaigns and Elections.** Michael L. Young. Lanham, MD: Hamilton Press, 1987. 246p. ISBN 0-8191-5446-6.

The terms in this dictionary are gleaned from scholarly and professional articles, but jargon is also included. Although the dictionary is designed to provide definitions for current terminology, many political terms have long been in use. The work is arranged into seven broad subdivisions, with titles such as "Electoral Strategies and Tactics" or "Money and Politics." There is an alphabetical index of the 725 terms included in the dictionary. This dictionary is of use to historians, political scientists, sociologists, and journalists.

245. **American National Election Studies Data Sourcebook, 1952–1986.** Warren E. Miller and Santa Traugott. Cambridge, MA: Harvard University Press, 1989. 375p. ISBN 0-674-02636-5.

This sourcebook is not a compilation of voting statistics but rather the results of surveys of voter opinion conducted biennially by the University of Michigan Center for Election Studies. The first publication contained data from 1952–1978. This edition updates the original through the 1986 national elections. Public opinion on issues such as abortion and school busing are analyzed over the time period the data have been collected. Voter demographics are also analyzed by party, race, income, and so forth. The last chapter synthesizes the information into a profile of issues that most influenced the voters on election day. Not only is the volume useful for the data it contains, it also serves as an index to portions of the raw data available from ICPSR (the Inter-University Consortium for Political and Social Research, entry 115) at the University of Michigan. This work is one of the best sources for tracing changes in public opinion on national issues since the 1950s.

Another source that discusses issues and the role of political parties in the United States is *The People Speak: American Elections in Focus* (Congressional Quarterly, 1990). This work covers elections since 1945, with the concentration on the 1980s.

246. **America Votes.** New York: Congressional Quarterly, 1956– . Bienn. ISSN 0065-678X

This biennial publication is the one of the best sources of twentieth-century election results for presidential, congressional, and gubernatorial elections. The organization is by state, and within each state by county, with separate tables for major cities. Population statistics are given along with the election results. Congressional district maps are included. The 1991 volume gave presidential election results on a state-by-state basis from 1920 to 1988 and the results of elections for governor and senator since World War II. Primaries and special elections are also included. This title does not attempt to analyze voting results in any way; it is strictly a reporting of election results.

Two compilations that cumulate presidential election statistics are *America at the Polls: A Handbook of American Presidential Election Statistics 1920–1964* (University of Pittsburgh Press, 1965) and *America at the Polls 2, 1968–1984* (CQ, 1988). In these two volumes, presidential election results are given by county from 1920 to 1984.

247. **Congressional Quarterly's Guide to U.S. Elections.** 2nd ed. Washington: Congressional Quarterly, 1985. 1,308p. ISBN 0-87187-339-7.

The purpose of this publication is to gather all statistics on U.S. presidential, congressional, and gubernatorial elections into one reference source. The data in the volume were obtained from the historical archive of the Inter-University Consortium for Political Research (entry 115) and a number of other sources. The presidential and senatorial data begin with the year 1789. Data for U.S. House of Representatives begin in 1824. Returns are given by state and not analyzed by further breakdowns. In addition to the data, topics such as the origins of the electoral college, nominating conventions, and southern primaries are addressed in narrative format, thus giving a look at the historical development of the election process. The appendices and indexes contain a variety of information, such as the number of U.S. immigrants by country of origin. Candidate indexes are for primaries and general elections and include major and minor parties. Maps, charts, and diagrams increase the ease of use. This title is the best source of historical election statistics and information on the electoral process for all types of users.

248. **Encyclopedia of Third Parties in the United States.** Earl R. Kruschke. Santa Barbara, CA: ABC-Clio, 1991. 223p. ISBN 0-87436-236-9.

This is a useful reference work both for identifying third parties in the United States and getting basic information about them. The historical information includes the founding of the party; the origin of the name; the party platform or agenda the party is identified with; personalities associated with the movement; and what became of the party. Candidates supported or elected are mentioned and pertinent election statistics provided. There is information on the type of material published or distributed. This work is more useful for students than the serious researcher.

249. **The Historical Atlas of Political Parties in the United States Congress 1789–1989.** Kenneth C. Martis. New York: Macmillan, 1989. 518p. ISBN 0-02-920170-5.

This reference is unique in that it illustrates congressional districts according to the party affiliation of the incumbent. National party maps for each session of Congress make up the majority of the work. A roster of the members of Congress and their districts and party affiliations accompany the maps. The introduction concentrates on the political party system in the United States and gives a good historical overview of the party system and voting patterns.

250. **Campaign Speeches of American Presidential Candidates, 1948–1984.** Gregory Bush, ed. New York: Ungar, 1985. 343p. ISBN 0-8044-1137-9.

This volume contains the text of selected campaign speeches. Included are nomination acceptance speeches and several other representative campaign speeches for the major-party presidential candidates. Third-party candidates are represented by one speech each. There is some essay commentary providing background information on the major campaign issues. An earlier volume, *Campaign Speeches of American Presidential Candidates, 1929–1972* (Ungar, 1976) provides the text of speeches for elections before 1948. The full text of speeches can be difficult to find. This publication is a useful source for students in history, political science, and communications.

Another work on elections produced by Congressional Quarterly is *Historic Documents on Presidential Elections 1787–1988* (1991). Editor Michael Nelson has selected 70 key speeches and documents that highlight developments in the presidential election process. The documents are preceded by a brief essay that sets the text in a historical context. Topics such as third parties, important party platforms, debates, and landmark speeches are included. The work is useful for students and teachers.

Presidential Election Campaign Documents, 1868–1900 is a microfilm collection that focuses on political issues in the period following the Civil War. The collection of 14 reels published by University Microfilms contains a wealth of political pamphlets and speeches and is another major resource for the study of presidential election campaigns.

251. **National Party Conventions, 1831–1988.** Washington: Congressional Quarterly, 1991. 289p. ISBN 0-87187-608-6SD.

This is one of the few reference works focusing entirely on the party conventions. Each convention receives a description that includes the major issues, platforms, and results of any votes taken. The candidates are profiled, with photographs and biographical information also presented. All parties that held conventions are included. The information is fuller for the twentieth-century meetings than for those held in earlier years. Historical information on the political parties is also provided. This publication is useful for students and researchers of the electoral process.

A more narrowly focused but complementary work is *National Party Platforms* (University of Illinois Press, 1978) and its supplement, *National Party Platforms for 1980* (University of Illinois Press, 1982), compiled by Donald Bruce Johnson. These volumes reprint the text of the platforms of the major and principal minor parties for presidential elections from 1840 to 1980. A brief history of the parties, a list of the candidates, and vote totals are also given. There are subject and name indexes.

252. **Political Parties and Civic Action Groups.** Edward L. Schapsmeier and Frederick H. Schapsmeier. Westport, CT: Greenwood, 1981. 554p. (Greenwood Encyclopedia of American Institutions, no.4). ISBN 0-313-21442-5.

Approximately 300 political organizations that had national influence at some point in U.S. history are included in this reference source. Many of the groups are familiar—the Women's Christian Temperance Union, Common Cause, the Grey Panthers. Some of the groups are still active, others defunct. In addition to descriptive and historical information on the origins, goals, and accomplishments of the organizations, citations for organizational publications and references to other sources of information are given. Appendices include a glossary of 200 terms; a subject listing of the organizations according to mission or function; and a chronology by founding dates. This reference source is useful to students and researchers in a broad range of disciplines in the social sciences.

253. **Political Parties & Elections in the United States: An Encyclopedia.** Sandy L. Maisel and Charles Bassett, eds. Hamden, CT, and New York: Garland, 1991. 2v. (Garland Reference Library of Social Science, v.498). ISBN 0-8240-7975-2.

Although this reference work contains much the same information as several others, it is a recently published, up-to-date source. It contains over 1,100 entries written by a group of 250 scholars. The scope is broad, covering political parties and elections from colonial times to the present. One strong point is that it gives more attention to some less prominent figures and terms than do other sources. The detailed index makes location of terms easy. This encyclopedia can be used in conjunction with other similar reference tools by inquirers at all levels.

254. **Presidential Also-rans and Running Mates, 1789–1980.** Leslie H. Southwick. Jefferson, NC: McFarland, 1984. 722p. ISBN 0-89950-109-5.

Although it is easy to find information on the winners of presidential elections, it is often not easy to even find the names of those who were not victorious in their quest for office. This source gives substantial biographical information on unsuccessful presidential candidates and their running mates. The arrangement is chronological by date of election, with brief historical information provided. The 1861 election for the Confederacy is also included, as well as an index and bibliography of sources.

255. **Presidential Elections Since 1789.** 4th ed. Washington: Congressional Quarterly, 1987. 235p. ISBN 0-87187-268-4.

There are a number of publications that focus on presidential elections. The first of these is *Presidential Elections Since 1789,* a work by Congressional Quarterly that repeats much of the information in the *Guide to U.S. Elections* (entry 247). Statistical information on the primaries, conventions, and electoral and popular votes by state are included. Biographical information on candidates and the text of election laws are also included.

Another compilation of presidential election results is *A Statistical History of the American Presidential Election Results* (Greenwood, 1981). This edition contains more than 100 tables of votes and percentages by state and by election from 1789–1980. The strength and usefulness of this work are in the information provided for each historical party.

The Pursuit of the White House by G. Scott Thomas (Greenwood, 1987) emphasizes statistics less than do either of the two publications above. The Thomas work contains both statistical election information organized by period, with biographical information on candidates. It repeats information found in a number of other sources.

Chapter 3

Diplomatic History and Foreign Affairs

GENERAL

The study of diplomatic history and foreign relations is one of the oldest categories of historical research. As in other areas of political history, government documents and archival materials are integral to research in the history of foreign policy. There are not a large number of reference works, however, in this area. Publication of a new index for U.S. foreign policy was begun in 1993 by Congressional Information Service. The *American Foreign Policy Index* is designed to be a comprehensive guide to the foreign relations of the U.S. government. This current information source will in the future form a thorough index for historical research. There is an accompanying microfiche collection that contains the text of documents listed in the *American Foreign Policy Index*.

There are many reference works on the government and politics of individual countries. ABC-Clio has in progress a World Bibliographical Series that will include more than 135 volumes, with an extensive bibliography of each country in the world. Scarecrow Press has a series of historical dictionaries on individual countries. Only a few reference works are available that are devoted to specific time periods or geographic areas. This section on foreign affairs is limited to reference works dealing directly with U.S. foreign policy and relations with other countries.

Documents, Treaties, and Papers

256. **American Foreign Policy Current Documents, 1950/55– .** Washington: U.S. Department of State, 1956– . Ann. ISSN 0501-9811.

The title and frequency of this publication can be misleading for users seeking current information. The Department of State began publishing this annual containing the text of important documents relating to foreign affairs in 1956, with the first volume containing documents from the five previous years. The annual publication takes up after the publication of *A Decade of American Foreign Policy: Basic Documents, 1941–1949* (Senate document 123, 81st Congress, 1st Sess.). The annual series has continued to publish documents on a retrospective basis, with approximately a five-year time lag. Since 1981, the printed text has been supplemented by accompanying microfiche with the full text of longer documents. The organization of the publication is topical/chronological. The principal foreign policy messages and congressional testimony by the executive branch make up the majority of the documents reproduced. The series is useful to researchers for topics in U.S. foreign relations since 1941.

A publication with a similar purpose and scope that also includes official statements and documents is *American Foreign Relations* (World Peace Foundation 1939–1952; Council on Foreign Relations, 1952–). This publication is more useful to those seeking a current awareness tool. For retrospective research, earlier years published under the title *Documents on American Foreign Relations* (1938/39–1973) are available in microform.

257.   **The Dynamics of World Power: A Documentary History of United States Foreign Policy, 1945–1972.** Arthur M. Schlesinger, comp. New York: Chelsea House, 1973. 5v. Repr. ISBN 0-8775-4259-7.

The texts of important documents in the history of U.S. foreign policy from the end of World War II to the end of the U.S. involvement in Vietnam in January 1973 are reproduced in this five-volume set. The set is divided geographically, with each volume edited by a different historian. Volume 1 is on Western Europe, edited by Robert Dallek; volume 2, on Eastern Europe and the Soviet Union, is edited by Walter LaFeber; volume 3, on Latin America, is edited by Robert Burr; volume 4, on the Far East, is edited by Russell D. Buhite; and volume 5, on the United Nations and sub-Saharan Africa, is edited by Richard C. Hottelet and Jean Herskovits. The documents are from official government sources, many from the *Department of State Bulletin*, but speeches of foreign leaders and nongovernment sources are also included. Through the documents in these five volumes, the interactions of the United States as a major world power with the nations of Europe, the communist world, the Third World, and the United Nations can be followed. Each volume attempts to place events within both the contemporary context and a larger historical perspective. The set is suitable for assigned reading in college courses and as a source for basic research in U.S. foreign policy.

258.   **Foreign Relations of the United States: Diplomatic Papers, 1861– .** Washington: U.S. Department of State, 1861– . Ann. ISSN 0780-9779.

As with *American Foreign Policy Current Documents* (entry 256), the years covered by this publication of the U.S. Department of State do not correspond to the publication year. For those researchers seeking diplomatic correspondence between the United States and foreign countries, this is the primary source. Also included are the text of treaties, the president's annual message to Congress, and special messages on foreign subjects. The years 1861–1956 are also available in microform. An index in two volumes was published covering the years 1861–1899 and 1900–1918 (Government Printing Office, 1902–1941). Kraus International has published *The Cumulated Index to the U.S. Department of State Papers Relating to the Foreign Relations of the United States, 1939–1945* (1980, 2v.). The Kraus index includes the regular annual volumes for the 1939–1945 period and the special volumes on China and the conferences attended by Presidents Roosevelt and Truman.

259.   **National Security Files, 1961–1969.** George C. Herring, gen. ed. Frederick, MD: University Publications of America, 1989–1991. Microform.

Over 150,000 pages of declassified archival materials from the Kennedy and Johnson presidential libraries have been microfilmed for the *National Security Files, 1961–1969.* The series is divided into separate collections for Latin America, Africa, Vietnam, Asia and the Pacific, the Middle East, Western Europe, the USSR and Eastern Europe, and the United States. International crises such as the Bay of Pigs, the Cuban Missile Crisis, Laos, Berlin, the Congo, the Six-Day War, and Vietnam took place in the 1961–1969 time period. The *National Security Files* contain primary source materials on national security, international relations, and the affairs of U.S. allies and adversaries worldwide. Each portion has a printed guide that contains document-by-document descriptions listing type of document, sender, recipient, brief description of subject matter, date of document, original classification, number of pages, and date declassified. There is also a comprehensive analytical subject index. The *National Security Files* microfilm collection makes an enormous volume of diverse documents available for research. The collection contains essential source materials for the study of U.S. foreign policy in the decade of the 1960s.

260. **A Reference Guide to United States Department of State Special Files.** Gerald K. Haines. Westport, CT: Greenwood, 1985. 393p. ISBN 0-313-22750-0.

The archival files described in this guide include materials in the National Archives and materials in the files within the Department of State. The bulk of the entries are for files from the 1940s and 1950s. The guide is arranged into 17 geographical and subject sections, mainly following the organization of the Department of State. For each entry there is a description of the file that includes the arrangement of the records, the existence of finding aids, the physical volume of the records in boxes or cubic feet, and information on the exact location of the records. For National Archives records the access number is given, along with any restrictions on access. In addition to conveying factual information, many of the descriptions give background on the file, including committees or individuals responsible for its generation. There are name, subject, and file number indexes. This reference guide is essential for those seeking information from Department of State files because the files are not all located in the National Archives.

261. **Treaties and Other International Agreements of the United States of America, 1776–1949.** Charles I. Bevans, comp. Washington: Government Printing Office, 1968–1976. 13v.

The compilation supervised by Bevans contains the text and an index for those agreements entered into by the United States in the 1776–1949 period. The Bevans set updates an earlier compilation by Mallow et al, which covered the 1776–1927 time period. Before 1950 when the U.S. Department of State began publishing *United States Treaties and Other International Agreements (UST)* the official texts of treaties and agreements were only found in the *United States Statutes at Large* or published in pamphlets in the Treaties and other International Acts, as of Dec. 27, 1945– series (Government Printing Office, 1946–) called *TIAS*. Thus, the Bevans set gathers together the text of treaties from a number of different sources. The first four volumes of the Bevans work contain multilateral treaties arranged chronologically. The next eight volumes contain bilateral treaties arranged alphabetically by country. The last volume is the general index. The Bevans volumes reproduce the treaties whether they are presently in force or not; thus the set is suitable for historical research. The work is useful for students and researchers seeking the text of treaties for the 1776–1949 time period.

262. **United States Treaty Index, 1776–1990 Consolidation.** Igor I. Kavass, ed. Buffalo, NY: W. S. Hein, 1992. 11v. ISBN 0-89941-770-1.

The *Consolidation* has replaced a number of treaty indexes published by W.S. Hein as it consolidates the information in the previous indexes. The set provides access to *TIAS* number, country or countries, and time frame. Unpublished acts from 1776–1950 and treaties and agreements from 1950–1990 not yet published are included. The first volume explains the five different treaty series and gives reference sources for U.S. and international treaties. Chronological lists of U.S. treaties from 1776 forward begin in volume 6. In volumes 8 and 9 treaties are listed chronologically by country, group of countries, or organization. Series citation and classification cross references are given. The last two volumes make up the subject index to the set including agreements by names of individuals and negotiating organizations. For historical research of U.S. treaties the *Consolidation* is now the starting point.

W. S. Hein produces a CD-ROM product, *Hein's United States Treaty Index on CD-ROM*. Access is provided to treaties and other international agreements from 1776 through January 1, 1990.

263. **Unperfected Treaties of the United States of America, 1776–1976.** Christian L. Wiktor. Dobbs Ferry, NY: Oceana, 1976–1984. 6v. ISBN 0-3790-0560-3.

The majority of reference aids for researching treaties and agreements are for those that were officially put in force. This unique reference work is an aid to those searching for information and the text of treaties that never went into force, the exclusions being Indian treaties and postal agreements. The text of the proposed agreements is accompanied by information on the parties involved, the place and date of signature, Senate actions, the location of the text of the treaty in the National Archives, and other historical details. The table of contents in each volume lists the treaties. There are a listing of works cited and an index. The last volume has a cumulative index for the set. This reference set will undoubtedly be of interest to diplomatic historians and other researchers concerned with U.S. foreign policy.

Bibliographical Sources

264. **American Foreign Relations: A Historiographical Review.** Gerald K. Haines and J. Samuel Walker, eds. Westport, CT: Greenwood, 1981. 369p. (Contributions in American History, v.90). ISBN 0-313-21061-6.

Scholars in the field survey the literature of U.S. foreign relations from the colonial era to the 1940s in this compilation of 16 review essays. The first 11 chapters proceed chronologically, whereas the next 4 essays focus on the regions of Asia, Africa, the Middle East, and Latin America. The final chapter concentrates on primary source materials for the study of U.S. foreign relations and the location and availability of the documents. Each essay provides a review and interpretation of the important literature and trends in research, with a discussion of further research topics. The cutoff point is the early years of the Cold War, which means that foreign relations since World War II are not treated to any extent. There is an author index. This collection of essays provides an overview of U.S. diplomatic history up through the period immediately following World War II. It is suitable for students and researchers seeking source materials in U.S. foreign relations.

265. **Arms Control and Disarmament: A Bibliography.** Richard Dean Burns. Santa Barbara, CA: ABC-Clio, 1977. 430p. (War/Peace Bibliography Series, no.6). ISBN 0-87436-245-8.

The subject of arms control has been especially prominent in the last half of the twentieth century. This bibliography lists over 8,000 citations to monographs and serials. Thirteen chapters are divided into two major sections: "Views, Overviews, and Theory" and "Accords, Proposals and Treaties." The first part includes works on the broad theories and issues of arms control and disarmament, surveys for specific periods and countries, as well as works on related topics. The second part lists works on specific proposals and treaties, the majority of which are twentieth-century negotiations, including the SALT initiatives. Although many of the sources cited are mainly in English, the second part contains considerably more foreign language sources. The bibliography broadly covers the subject of arms control and disarmament.

It can be used by students and researchers in history, political science, and international relations.

266. **The Department of State and American Diplomacy: A Bibliography.** Robert U. Goehlert and Elizabeth R. Hoffmeister. New York: Garland, 1986. 349p. (Garland Reference Library of Social Science, v.333). ISBN 0-8240-8591-4.

In the introduction to this bibliographical work, reference sources and research guides are listed, along with the publications of the Department of State and guides to U.S. government documents. The bibliography is divided both topically and geographically. The first chapter covers the functions of the Department of State and historical studies. The second chapter deals with the conduct of U.S. foreign policy, relations with the president and Congress, and so on. The third chapter is organized geographically and covers U.S. relations with other countries. The fourth chapter lists biographical source material on diplomats and members of the foreign service, with a separate section for the secretaries of state. The bibliography includes only English-language items published between 1945 and 1984. There are author and subject indexes. The work is useful for students at all levels and for researchers seeking information on any aspect of U.S. foreign policy.

267. **Foreign Affairs 50-Year Bibliography: New Evaluations of Significant Books on International Relations, 1920–1970.** Byron Dexter, et al. New York: Bowker, published for the Council on Foreign Relations, 1972. 936p. ISBN 0-8352-0490-1.

Each decade the journal *Foreign Affairs* publishes a bibliography. For the fiftieth anniversary bibliography, titles from the previous 10-year volumes were reexamined by 400 scholars in the field of international relations. The period from 1920–1970 is covered with a selection of 2,130 reviews, within which an additional 900 titles are cited. The arrangement is in three major sections, the same as the 10-year bibliographies: "General International Relations," "The World Since 1914," and "The World by Regions." The bibliographies are for scholars in the areas of international relations and foreign policy.

268. **Guide to American Foreign Relations Since 1700.** Richard Dean Burns, ed. Santa Barbara, CA: ABC-Clio, 1983. 1,311p. ISBN 0-87436-323-3.

This guide is a comprehensive bibliography to U.S. foreign relations, with evaluative annotations. The only comparable bibliography is a much earlier work by Samuel Bemis and G. G. Griffin published in 1935, *Guide to Diplomatic History of the United States, 1771–1921*. Not only does the new guide edited by Burns cover a longer time span, it also approaches U.S. foreign relations in a much broader context. The scope of the later work includes the impact of domestic politics on foreign affairs, public opinion, military and intelligence activities, and international economic and cultural relationships. The bibliography of over 9,000 items is arranged in 40 chapters, each by a different editor and each treating a major period or topic. After the first two chapters, which concern general sources and overviews of diplomatic themes and theories, each chapter contains an introductory essay, followed by listings of primary sources, biographical sources, and secondary sources. A detailed table of contents at the beginning of each chapter serves as a chronological subject index. Two appendices list presidents and key personnel in foreign relations, with a separate section of brief biographies of the secretaries of state. Separate indexes for author, subject, and persons complete the work. The Bemis and Griffin guide is still useful for the references to eighteenth- and nineteenth-century manuscript collections. The Burns guide is the standard source for the historical study of U.S. foreign relations and is designed to be used by students and researchers.

269. **U.S. Foreign Relations: A Guide to Information Sources.** Elmer Plischke. Detroit: Gale, 1980. 715p. (American Government and History Information Guide Series, v.6; Gale Information Guide Library). ISBN 0-8103-1204-2.

The Plischke book concentrates more narrowly on the foreign affairs process than does Burns (entry 268), which is broader in scope. This work is organized into four main sections: diplomacy and diplomats; conduct of U.S. foreign relations; official sources and resources; and memoirs and biographical material. Each major section is subdivided into chapters on more specific aspects of the general topic. Analytical, descriptive, and documentary sources from British and U.S. scholarship and some foreign language works are included. The annotated guide was prepared to assist serious students in doing research in U.S. foreign relations. It can be used in conjunction with the Burns guide, which covers a larger number of sources.

Another Gale bibliography of broader scope is *Economics and Foreign Policy* by Mark R. Amstutz (Gale, 1977). The focus of this work is the interrelationship between political and economic factors on the international level. Researchers concerned with these factors in connection with U.S. foreign relations may find sources cited that are not included in bibliographies devoted exclusively to the United States.

270. **Versailles and After: An Annotated Bibliography of American Foreign Relations, 1919–1933.** Linda Killen and Richard L. Lael. New York: Garland, 1983. 469p. (Garland Reference Library of Social Science, v.135; American Diplomatic History, v.2). ISBN 0-8240-9202-3.

Several exclusions make this bibliography only suitable as a basic source for undergraduate students. There are no materials dealing with Latin America because that area was to be covered by another work in the American Diplomatic History series. The bibliography also excludes articles from the major journals in the field, such as *Foreign Affairs, Current History*, and a number of others. The bibliography is a good basic guide for the sources it does include: English language monographic and journal literature, dissertations, and documentary and manuscript sources. The bibliography can be used as a beginning point for research by students.

Information Sources

271. **Chronological History of United States Foreign Relations 1776 to January 20, 1981.** Lester H. Brune. New York: Garland, 1985–1991. 3v. (Garland Reference Library of Social Science, v.196). ISBN 0-8240-9056-X (v.1–2); 0-8240-5690-6 (v.3).

The first two volumes of this work, from 1776 to the beginning of the Reagan presidency, form an overview of U.S. foreign relations, not just a chronological listing of events. Both historical and diplomatic significance are given in the descriptions, which vary in length according to the importance of the incident but can be as much as a page long. The author recommends a two-year approach when following specific events, the year preceding and the year following. The work is organized into four parts, each with an overview essay: "The Early Republic," "The Emergence of the United States in the Western Hemisphere," "Becoming a Global Power," and "The Nuclear Age." Political, economic, and national security issues are included. Over half of the chronology is made up of twentieth-century events. The closing event is the return of the hostages from Iran at the beginning of the Reagan administration. There are 24 outline maps and a 12-page bibliography. A third volume covering the Reagan years was published in 1991. This well-researched chronology is appropriate for general reference, students and researchers.

272.   **Dictionary of American Diplomatic History.** John E. Findling. Westport, CT: Green-wood, 1980. 622p. ISBN 0-313-22039-5.

Information in this dictionary is organized into one alphabetical arrangement of concise descriptive entries with bibliographies. The entries refer to concepts, events, treaties, organi-zations, persons, and popular slogans from the revolutionary era to 1978. The biographical information is complete, with dates, education, career information, posts and offices, publi-cations, family, and so forth. Asterisks are placed in the text to cross-reference terms that have separate articles. There is an index for individuals, terms, and topics not having separate entries. Appendices include a chronology and lists of diplomatic personnel by presidential administration and by of countries with which the United States has maintained diplomatic relations. Appendix E covers locations of manuscript and oral histories and is divided into two sections. The first section lists collections containing more than 100 pieces; the second lists oral histories pertaining to persons who are subjects of biographical entries in the volume. The extensive index lists persons and proper names, geographical units, and terms. Although much of the information in the dictionary can be obtained from other sources, the work is extremely useful for reference and research because of the amount of material contained in a single volume.

A new tool is the *Dictionary of American Foreign Affairs* by Stephen A. Flanders and Carl N. Flanders (Macmillan, 1993). It furnishes a comprehensive and authoritative coverage of events, ideas, personalities, and agreements relative to U.S. foreign policy involvement since the colonial period. A narrower work with a dictionary arrangement that focuses on foreign policy events subsequent to World War II is *A Concise Overview of Foreign Policy (1945–1985)* (Melbourne, FL: Krieger, 1986) by Kenneth L. Hill. The title briefly describes 174 events and can be used to supplement more extensive works such as the *Chronological History of United States Foreign Relations* (entry 271).

273.   **Encyclopedia of American Foreign Policy: Studies of Principal Movements and Ideas.** Alexander DeConde, ed. New York: Scribner's, 1978. 3v. ISBN 0-684-155036-6.

This encyclopedia contains 95 original articles on concepts and themes in U.S. foreign policy. The essays analyze the development of ideas, theories, and policies and explore the significance of major events in U.S. foreign policy such as "Isolationalism," "The Marshall Plan," and "Revisionism," among others. The encyclopedia does not function as a reference work for consultation on specific events, but volume 3 has a biographical section with information culled from standard biographical sources such as the *DAB* (entry 143). Each article has a bibliographical essay at the end. There is an extensive name and subject index. This work gives a scholarly overview of the field of U.S. foreign policy. It is suitable for supplemental reading at the college level, for beginning research on the topics covered, or for reading by interested laypersons.

A recent work with a narrower focus is *The Cold War: 1945–1991* (Gale, 1992–1993). Edited by Benjamin Frankel, a specialist on U.S. national security, foreign policy, and international relations, this three-volume encyclopedia is a definitive work on the Cold War period. The first two volumes are devoted to examining the careers and explaining the significance of individuals who played key roles in the Cold War including spies and scientists as well as political and governmental figures. The third volume discusses themes and events that had a major impact on the period. The set is amply illustrated with photographs, maps, and diagrams. It will be consulted by experts and general readers alike.

274.   **The Encyclopedia of American Intelligence and Espionage: From the Revolution-ary War to the Present.** G.J.A. O'Toole. New York: Facts on File, 1988. 539p. ISBN 0-8160-1011-0.

Material scattered over a number of sources has been brought together in this single volume on the subject of the U.S. intelligence community. The majority of the 700 alphabetical entries are biographical. Major figures in U.S. intelligence are covered, including many historical and current personages. The information was compiled from unclassified sources by O'Toole, a former CIA employee. There are essay-length entries on the role of intelligence in the major wars in U.S. history, and incidents such as the Bay of Pigs and the Cuban Missile Crisis. References are listed at the end of the entries. Some terms are also defined. The end of the book includes a listing of abbreviations, a 10-page unannotated bibliography, and an index. Similar, less current sources are *The Dictionary of Espionage* (St. Martin's, 1984) and the *Encyclopedia of Espionage* (Doubleday, 1972). This encyclopedia is the most comprehensive work devoted to the U.S. intelligence establishment and can be used by the general public and researchers alike.

A similar work that concentrates on the period since World War II is *United States Intelligence: An Encyclopedia* (Garland, 1990). Short entries are given for over 3,000 acronyms, terms, persons, agencies, and programs. Most entries have references to sources, and there is a complete bibliography to all sources at the end of the work. There is no index. A chronology of significant events in the U.S. intelligence sphere since 1941 is included. Significant documents affecting the intelligence community are reproduced in appendices. Together with O'Toole, which is more satisfactory from an historical perspective, this encyclopedia furnishes complete coverage of the modern intelligence operations of the United States.

AFRICA/MIDEAST

275. **The United States and Africa: Guide to U.S. Official Documents and Government-Sponsored Publications on Africa, 1785–1975.** Julian W. Witherell, comp. Washington: Library of Congress, 1978. 949p. S/N 030-000-00098-6.

Compiled by the chief of the African and Middle Eastern Division of the Library of Congress, this is a definitive bibliography of U.S. relations with the countries of Africa. Only Egypt is excluded. There are over 8,000 entries for publications issued or sponsored by the federal government. This definition includes treaties, contract studies, presidential and congressional documents, diplomatic papers, political and economic maps, space photography, and translations. The arrangement of the bibliography is in five chronological time periods: 1785–1819, 1820–1862, 1863–1920, 1921–1951, and 1952–1975. The bulk of the entries are concentrated in the last time period, reflecting the growing involvement of the United States in Africa. Each period is geographically divided, with subdivisions by subject for agriculture, education, economics, health, labor, and so on. The annotations indicate the scope and contents of the publication and include references to related publications, citations to the original for translations, and locations for materials not owned by the Library of Congress. There is an extensive index to authors, titles, and subjects. A partial update was published in 1984, *The United States and Sub-Saharan Africa; A Guide ... 1976–1980.* It includes an additional 5,000 publications. These bibliographies are extremely useful to historians, political scientists, economists, and any others with an interest in the growth and development of African nations and U.S. involvement in the governance of African affairs.

276. **United States Foreign Policy and the Middle East/North Africa: A Bibliography of Twentieth-Century Research.** Sanford R. Silverburg and Bernard Reich. New York: Garland, 1990. 407p. (Garland Reference Library of Social Science, v.570). ISBN 0-8240-4613-7.

The geographic areas included in this selective bibliography of over 3,000 entries are defined as all Arab nations plus the non-Arab nations of Iran, Israel, and Turkey. The introduction provides an overview of U.S. involvement in this area of the world, beginning in the late nineteenth century. The majority of the works cited are English language sources published after 1960. Monographs, journal articles, government publications, and doctoral dissertations are included. The arrangement is alphabetical by author, but there is a subject index. The bibliography is a current source of use mainly to those interested in developments in the Middle East since 1960. It is a good basic reference source for students and beginning researchers.

277.　**The United States in Africa: An Historical Dictionary.** David Shavit. Westport, CT: Greenwood, 1989. 298p. ISBN 0-313-25887-2.

Shavit has produced a number of dictionaries, each concentrating on a specific geographic region (entries 278, 283, 292) As with most of the dictionaries of this type, the majority of the entries are for individuals involved in establishing relationships between the U.S. and African countries. There are a considerable number of entries, however, devoted to institutions, organizations, and businesses. The entries are well written and contain references for further research. There are lists by occupation and profession, including authors, explorers, hunters, diplomats, and engineers. The dictionary functions as a basic information source and a reference for further study. It is the only single work concentrating on information in the historical relationship between the United States and African countries and is suitable for use by all types of library users.

278.　**The United States in the Middle East: A Historical Dictionary.** David Shavit. Westport, CT: Greenwood, 1988. 441p. ISBN 0-313-25341-2.

This work on the Middle East covers approximately 200 years of U.S. involvement in that region. The entries are mainly biographical, but institutions, events, and businesses, mainly oil companies, are included. The biographical information on individuals includes dates, education, role in the Middle East, length and places of service, and locations of archival materials. Each entry includes a list of further references. In addition to the alphabetical entries, there are a bibliographical essay on U.S.–Middle East relations; a list of modern place-names with historical equivalents; a chronology of events from 1787 to 1986; a list of U.S. chiefs of mission in the Middle East from 1831–1936; and lists of biographees by occupation or profession such as explorers, engineers, and so on. The dictionary for the Middle East is an excellent information source for general readers, students, and researchers.

The Middle East: A Political Dictionary by Lawrence Ziring (ABC-Clio, 1992) is similar to the Shavit work. The emphasis is more current, although this title also covers historical terms and events. The reference work is another in ABC-Clio's dictionaries in political science series, a feature of which is the two-part entry—one paragraph for definition, one for significance. The work is helpful for understanding the history of many of the tangled relationships between nations and factions in the Middle East.

279.　**United States/Middle East Diplomatic Relations, 1784–1978: An Annotated Bibliography.** Thomas A. Bryson. Metuchen, NJ: Scarecrow, 1979. 205p. ISBN 0-8108-1197-9.

Designed as a beginning reference work for students, this selective annotated bibliography has approximately 1,300 entries for English-language books, articles, and dissertations. The annotations are critical and note particular viewpoints. The bibliography is divided into 19 chronological sections, beginning with the "Barbary Pirates" and ending with the "Crucial Decade of the 1970s." Dissertations are listed separately in the last section and are not annotated. There is an author index but no subject index. The work is suitable as a basic information source, but it must be used in conjunction with other, more comprehensive bibliographies for scholarly research.

280. **U.S. Relations with South Africa: An Annotated Bibliography.** Y. G-M. Lulat. Boulder, CO: Westview Press, 1991. 2v. ISBN 0-8133-7138-4 (v.1); 0-8133-7747-1 (v.2).

The most comprehensive work on the subject to date, this bibliography of over 4,500 books, articles, government documents, reports of nongovernmental organizations, and dissertations includes English-language sources from the last 100 years. The organization of the bibliography is somewhat complex, with sources arranged by publication type and then by subject within those two groupings. Only about 40 percent of the entries are annotated, but those provide abstracts, tables of contents, and, for some important works, citations to book reviews. The main index lists authors, organizations, and subjects. There is a separate list of periodical titles. In addition, there is a "Guide to Sources of Current Information on U.S. Relations with South Africa." The recent publication date of this bibliography makes it useful to those seeking up-to-date information as well as those engaged in historical research.

ASIA

281. **The Allied Occupation of Japan, 1945–1952: An Annotated Bibliography of Western Language Materials.** Robert Edward Ward and Frank Joseph Shulman, et al. Chicago: American Library Association, 1974. 867p. ISBN 0-8389-0127-1.

The Joint Committee on Japanese Studies of the Social Science Research Council of the American Council for Learned Societies and the Center for Japanese Studies at the University of Michigan sponsored the compilation of this bibliography. The work lists over 3,100 items—books, periodical and newspaper articles, government documents, and archival materials, mainly in English. All aspects of the period of occupation are included, from the pre-occupation planning and staffing to the "direct consequences of the occupation and Japanese or foreign relations or reactions thereto." The arrangement is by topical sections. There is a list of "High Ranking Personnel," a list of periodical titles, and an author index. The bibliography is a definitive work on the subject, of use to scholars and students for research on the period of the occupation of Japan.

282. **Philippine-American Relations: A Guide to Manuscript Sources in the United States.** Shiro Saito. Westport, CT: Greenwood, 1982. ISBN 0-313-23632-1.

Primary resource materials for the study of U.S.-Philippine relations from the mid-nineteenth century to the present are described in this research guide. Materials located in the United States that contain contemporary descriptions of the relations between the two countries include manuscripts, official records, and other unpublished papers. Although there is material from the nineteenth century, items pertaining to internal affairs and the Spanish period of the Philippines (1521–1898) are not included—only material for U.S. involvement with the Philippines is examined. The first section of the book lists the collections alphabetically by person or institution. Descriptive information includes title and date of source material; size, scope, and contents of the collection, with evaluative comments; location of the material; and other sources of information about the material. The second section of the work is a geographical listing (by state) to manuscript sources. The last section includes a chronology, a general index, and an index by repository. This is a useful guide to primary source materials for a specialized area of research.

283. **The United States in Asia: An Historical Dictionary.** David Shavit. New York: Greenwood, 1990. 620p. ISBN 0-313-26788-X.

A basic information source on U.S.-Asian relations, this work follows the same organizational pattern as the other Shavit historical dictionaries (entries 277, 278, 292). The entries consist mostly of biographical sketches on individuals, with some entries for events and institutions. Although Shavit states in the preface of the work that military personnel who fought in World War II and the Korean and Vietnam conflicts are not included, there are a number of prominent military leaders profiled. As in the other Shavit works, sources to manuscript materials and other biographical sources are included with each biography. The entries range from the early trade and missionary contacts between the United States and Asia up to the present. The work provides a list of biographees by occupation and a list of the leaders of U.S. diplomatic missions in Asia from 1843–1989. It also includes a bibliographic essay on the development of U.S.-Asian relations. The dictionary is a useful reference work for all type of library users and a good basic information tool for students and researchers.

284. **The United States in East Asia: A Historical Bibliography.** Santa Barbara, CA: ABC-Clio, 1985. 298p. (ABC Research Guides, no.14). ISBN 0-87436-452-3.

This bibliography is another work drawn from the *America: History and Life* (entry 51) database, and it contains citations to 1,176 periodical articles, with abstracts, from the 1973–1984 time span. The bibliography is organized geographically by country, except for a beginning chapter with general articles on relations between the United States and two or more countries in East Asia. Separate chapters are devoted to China, Hong Kong, Japan, both Koreas, and Taiwan. There are separate computer-generated author and subject indexes. Because of the restricted time span from which the source materials are drawn, this bibliography is useful only as a supplement to other reference works. Researchers not having access to the electronic version of the database will welcome the bibliography, which eliminates the need to cull the articles from the printed indexes for the time period covered.

EUROPE

285. **The Anglo-American Relationship: An Annotated Bibliography of Scholarship, 1945–1985.** David Lincove and Gary R. Treadway, comps. Westport, CT: Greenwood, 1988. 415p. (Bibliographies and Indexes in World History, no.14). ISBN 0-313-25854-6.

Anglo-American relations from 1783 through World War II are covered in this scholarly bibliography. The entries are limited to materials in English, but both British and U.S. scholarship are surveyed. The bibliography is divided into two major sections, the first for nondiplomatic relations and the second for diplomatic relations. The first section is divided into topical categories: social and cultural relationships, immigration, education, political influences, trade, and financial cooperation. The diplomatic section is organized chronologically around specific events such as the War of 1812, the Trent Affair, and World War II. The bibliography lists scholarly books, articles, and British, Canadian, and U.S. dissertations. Primary source materials, archival materials, and documents are excluded. Appendices present two lists of ambassadors, one for each nation, and a selective list of reference sources consulted in compiling the bibliography. There are an author and subject index. The scholarly emphasis of this bibliography makes it an excellent source for research in Anglo-American relations.

286. **The Missile Crisis of October 1962: A Review of Issues and References.** Lester H. Brune. Claremont, CA: Regina Books, 1985. 147p. (Guides to Historical Issues, no.2). ISBN 0-941690-16-4.

The Cuban Missile Crisis is the incident in which the two superpowers, the United States and the USSR, came closest to nuclear war. In the beginning of this reference work there are several essay chapters giving the historical background and events leading up to the crisis and the sequence of events that took place during it. Brune analyzes the reactions of both Washington and Moscow and the maneuvers that defused the crisis. The second half of the book is a bibliographic essay referencing both contemporary accounts of the incident and later analyses of it. Both primary and secondary materials are cited, including news magazines and scholarly articles. The citations are annotated as to the significance of the source and the interpretations put forth in them. This is an excellent basic source for the historical background, understanding of the issues, and the later interpretations of the events. It is useful for all audiences with an interest in research on the subject of the Cuban Missile Crisis.

287. **NATO: A Bibliography and Research Guide.** Augustus Richard Norton, et al. New York: Garland, 1985 252p. (Garland Reference Library of Social Science, v.92). ISBN 0-8240-9331-3.

Despite its title, this work is really just an unannotated bibliography listing approximately 4,000 sources. There is very little in the way of research strategy or the explication of reference sources that constitute a proper research guide. As a bibliography, it is a good attempt to cover NATO (North American Treaty Organization), which began as the Atlantic Alliance in 1949 and eventually had 15 member nations. The bibliography lists primary and secondary English-language sources. The first section of the bibliography covers general subjects divided chronologically. The remaining sections are topical and cover such issues as disarmament; SALT; doctrines, strategies, and military issues; and alliance politics. There is an author index. The work is suitable for use by students and as a basic bibliography for research.

An earlier bibliography with a similar topic and scope is *The Atlantic Alliance: A Bibliography* by Colin Gordon (Nichols Publishing, 1978). This bibliography broadly covers the political and military development of the member nations of NATO. Some 3,000 books, articles, reports, and pamphlets drawn from U.S., European, and Soviet sources are listed in four chronological groupings beginning with 1945 and ending with 1977. The four sections are divided into five categories: legal, economic, national and regional, politico-military, and military-strategic. Most of the entries are not annotated, and there are no indexes provided. The work's main strength is that it gathers into one volume material otherwise scattered throughout a number of different indexing tools. It can be used in conjunction with more current reference sources.

288. **Origins, Evolution, and Nature of the Cold War: An Annotated Bibliographic Guide.** J. L. Black. Santa Barbara, CA: ABC-Clio, 1986. 173p. (War/Peace Bibliography Series, no.19). ISBN 0-87436-391-8.

The focus of this scholarly bibliography is the 1938–1950 time span, which covers the origins of the Cold War but not the extended period for which it lasted. The bibliography is divided into 13 topical sections, each with an introductory note. The approximately 1,300 entries include books, journal articles, dissertations, and government publications. Strengths of the work are chapters on the Soviet perspective and the historiography of the Cold War. There are author and subject indexes. Because of the focus on the origins of the Cold War, the work is most useful to historians and political scientists.

289. **The United States and Russia: The Beginning of Relations, 1765–1815.** Nina H. Bashkina, et al. Washington: Government Printing Office, 1980. 1,184p. S/N 022-002-00068-6.

A collection of 560 documents, this compilation was a joint effort by historians and archivists from the United States and the Soviet Union. The documents are not all political, covering commercial, scientific, and cultural as well as diplomatic issues. Many of the U.S. documents have been published previously, but an effort was made to find unpublished sources. The documents are reproduced in full in the writing style of the period except for some modernization in punctuation and correction of errors. Longer documents are sometimes summarized in part. The extent of the relations between the two countries can be surmised from the documents, which include dispatches and correspondence from the U.S. consul at St. Petersburg (1803–1815); the correspondence of Thomas Jefferson and Alexander I (1804–1808); business correspondence of John Jacob Astor; documents describing the U.S. reaction to the invasion of Russia by Napoleon; and dispatches from the Russian minister in London discussing the American Revolution. An introductory essay gives a brief historical overview of the period, and a chronology of events and a list of the documents are also present. The work is illustrated with a variety of portraits, maps, and facsimiles of the original documents. Appendices contain a list of diplomatic and consular appointments, a directory of archival and manuscript sources, lists of names and short titles, a bibliography, and an index. This excellent compilation is useful to students and historians of both countries.

LATIN AMERICA

Latin America as a region and the individual countries it encompasses have been subjects of intense study. There are many reference works and bibliographic guides for Latin American studies. The most comprehensive and well known is the annual *Handbook of Latin American Studies* compiled by the Hispanic Division of the Library of Congress and published by the University of Texas Press. The handbook is an annotated bibliography with introductory essays that evaluate the research and literature in specialized areas. It alternates each year between the humanities and the social sciences in the focus of the bibliography. It is a comprehensive resource for students and scholars of any aspect of Latin American studies.

This section contains only works directly related to the historical study of U.S. relations with Latin America. Works on individual countries not concerned directly with U.S. foreign relations are not listed.

290. **A Bibliography of United States–Latin American Relations Since 1810.** David F. Trask, Michael C. Meyer, and Roger R. Trask. Lincoln: University of Nebraska Press, 1968. 441p. **Supp.** University of Nebraska Press, 1979.

Published in 1968, this bibliography has long been a standard reference work on the subject of U.S.–Latin American relations. A supplement by Michael Meyer published in 1979 extends the coverage of the first edition. The combined bibliographies list over 14,500 sources on the history of U.S.–Latin American relations. Both follow the same organizational pattern. After a general sources chapter, the first section is arranged chronologically into distinct periods in the relationship between the two countries. The second large portion of the work is arranged alphabetically by country. Items are listed in only one section, but there are numerous cross-references and an author index. The supplement has additional chapters on current issues. Works listed are in several languages, and some are annotated. In spite of not being recently updated, this work remains the major bibliography for U.S.–Latin American relations for historians and students.

291. **The Controversy over a New Canal Treaty Between the United States and Panama: A Selectively Annotated Bibliography of United States, Panamanian, Colombian, French, and International Organization Sources.** Wayne D. Bray, comp. Washington: Library of Congress, 1976. 70p. ISBN 0-8444-0213-3.

An unusual feature is employed in this bibliography to indicate the relative importance of each source. A number is assigned ranging from a " 1" for essential material to a "3" for marginal sources. This feature will assist students and librarians less familiar with the topic in choosing which sources to use. The bibliography is an excellent resource for historical material but was published before the controversial U.S. decision to turn the Canal Zone over to the jurisdiction of Panama. It was extremely useful as a reference source during the negotiations. Researchers will have to update the bibliography for more recent scholarship and events in connection with the Panama Canal.

292. **The United States in Latin America: A Historical Dictionary.** David Shavit. New York: Greenwood, 1992. 471p. ISBN 0-313-27595-5.

The format of this dictionary is the same as for the other historical dictionaries David Shavit has authored (entries 277, 278, 283). The work is an alphabetical listing of definitions and biographies for people, terms, issues, and events in history of U.S. relations with the countries of Latin America. All countries south of the United States are covered, including the Caribbean islands and Mexico, with the exception of places that were annexed to the United States. The entries include biographical and bibliographical references. Appendices include a list of chiefs of U.S. diplomatic missions in Latin America, 1823–1990, and a list of biographees by profession and occupation. There is an index of names and subjects. This is a basic work suitable for all levels of library users and sound enough for use by scholars.

A work with a more current emphasis is *Latin America: A Political Dictionary* by Ernest E. Rossi and Jack C. Plano (ABC-Clio, 2nd ed., 1992). The current and historical significance are explained for the terms and events in this reference. It can be used in conjunction with the Shavit work for research on U.S.–Latin American relations.

Although not specifically focused on U.S. and Latin American relations, a recent work provides an excellent background in Latin American Studies. *Latin America and the Caribbean: A Critical Guide to Research Sources* (Greenwood, 1993) edited by Paula H. Covington. A section on electronic resources for Latin American research in the United States, Latin America, and Europe is particularly useful.

293. **Views Across the Border: The United States and Mexico.** Stanley R. Ross, ed. Albuquerque: University of New Mexico Press, 1978. 456p. ISBN 0-8263-0445-1.

This volume is a collection of papers, with responses, given at a conference sponsored by the Weatherhead Foundation in 1975. The format resembles that of the encyclopedias of commissioned essays that have been published in recent years. The papers reflect the different views of the participants from both sides of the border. Problems and issues in the border region are covered in the critical essays on culture, politics, economics, migrants, health, social psychology, and ecology. The nature and causes as well as solutions to the problems are explored in the volume. The extensive bibliography in the volume serves as a reference source. The work can be used to supplement course materials and as a beginning source for further research.

Chapter 4

Military History

The course of history has largely been determined by wars and military conquests. The Revolutionary War, the Civil War, and World War II stand out as the major conflicts in terms of military, diplomatic, and political history of the United States. These wars were the major focus of U.S. history until the recent redirection toward social history. The Vietnam conflict is now generally regarded as a turning point in the history of the United States. The Vietnam conflict, which was so divisive, has brought the political and social aspects of war to the forefront of research, pushing aside to some degree the study of troop movements, battle strategies, and military leaders. The effect of the increased interest in social issues is seen in the lack of development of tools for military research.

The equipment, weapons, vessels, and technology for waging war have been the object of much amateur and professional interest. However, works dealing specifically with military equipment have been excluded from this reference guide, with a few exceptions. Naval vessels have been treated. None of the excellent standard reference works in the Jane's series have been included. There are over 20 Jane's titles, all dealing with some aspect of military, naval, or aerospace equipment and are well known to buffs and scholars alike.

Publications concerning specific branches of the armed services have not been as numerous as those dealing with particular wars. There has not been a large number of new bibliographies and research guides produced in the last 20 years concentrating on the armed forces. The exception is U.S. naval history; it is being thoroughly covered by the Naval Institute Press, which has published a number of bibliographical and biographical reference works.

This chapter begins with a section of works on military history and the armed forces in general. The next section contains works focused on specific branches of the U.S. armed services. The wars or armed conflicts in which the United States has participated follow chronologically. Works on branches of the services concentrating on a particular war are in the section pertaining to that war.

GENERAL

Bibliographical Sources

294. **Air University Library Index to Military Periodicals.** Maxwell Air Force Base, AL: Air University Library, 1949– . ISSN 0002-2586.

The specialized subject focus of this periodical index is both an advantage and disadvantage. The scope is confined to military affairs, aeronautics, arms technology, and international relations. Sixty percent of the periodicals covered are not indexed anywhere else, and the other 40 percent are scattered over a wide variety of indexing tools. The emphasis is on the U.S.

armed forces and military affairs. The periodicals covered are English language military and aeronautical publications. The index is well produced, with an easy arrangement and plentiful cross-references. Even though many of the articles indexed are on narrow military topics, the thorough coverage of the field and the numerous citations make this index an excellent source for the serious researcher in defense policy and international relations. One disadvantage is that the periodicals indexed may not be carried in many libraries. The specialized nature of the index makes it the best—in some cases, the *only*—available source to consult for many of the topics covered.

Another source for military publications is *The Dougherty Collection of Military Newspapers* produced on microfilm by University Microfilms. Nearly 2,500 military newspapers are represented, most of them dating from World War II. Titles from all branches of the military are included, as well as some from the defense industries. A brief history of the collection and a printed guide written by Walter S. Dougherty accompany the 58 reels of microfilm. The collection complements those publications indexed in the *Air University Library Index to Military Periodicals* and will be of interest to researchers in military history, military science, and political science.

295. **America's Military Past: A Guide to Information Sources.** Jack C. Lane. Detroit: Gale, 1980. 280p. (American Government and History Information Guide Series, v.7; Gale Information Guide Library). ISBN 0-8103-1205-0.

The scope of this selective bibliography is limited to U.S. land and air forces. The naval forces are not included, and the user is referred to Myron Smith's *The American Navy* (entry 322). Nine other bibliographies are cited that the work does not overlap with. Books and periodical articles are included, but dissertations are not. The annotations are very brief, only a few lines. The compiler has attempted to be evaluative in the selection of items for inclusion. After a first introductory chapter on military historiography, civil-military relations, military philosophy, and general works, the arrangement is chronological by military epochs. The time span covered is from colonial times to the post-Vietnam era. This bibliography is still a relatively recent single source for information on U.S. military history and is useful for students and researchers alike.

296. **A Bibliography of Military Name Lists from Pre-1675 to 1900: A Guide to Genealogical Sources.** Lois Horowitz. Metuchen, NJ: Scarecrow, 1990. 1,080p. ISBN 0-8108-2166-4.

The arrangement of this bibliography is by time period and then locality. There are no indexes for branch of service, war, and so on. Both published and unpublished lists, including war records, rolls of servicemen, lists of veterans and pensioners, reports, journals, and histories are included in the bibliography. The work is most useful to genealogists, but it is also useful to other researchers tracing individuals who served in the military.

297. **Conscription: A Select and Annotated Bibliography.** Martin Anderson and Valerie Bloom. Stanford, CA: Hoover Institution Press, 1976. 453p. (Hoover Bibliographical Series, no.57). ISBN 0-8179-2571-6.

Although it has been almost 20 years since the publication of this bibliography, it is still the only separate work on the subject. Interest in conscription in the United States has waned since the peacetime draft was abolished in the 1970s. Thus, this bibliography forms a base that probably represents the bulk of the literature on the subject of conscription. The emphasis is on the history of conscription in the United States from colonial times to the 1970s. The experiences of Great Britain and other foreign countries are also touched upon. The bibliography includes books, articles, manuscripts, pamphlets, and government documents. The work is organized into 17 chapters by broad topics such as general history, selective service, universal military training, the National Guard and reserves, and conscientious objection. Legal, philosophical, and moral issues are dealt with. There are author and title indexes. This is a useful bibliography for the student or researcher's initial approach to the subject.

298. **Guide to the Sources of United States Military History.** Robin Higham. Hamden, CT: Archon Books, 1975. 559p. ISBN 0-208-01499-3. **Supps. I–III,** Robin Higham and Donald Mrozek, eds. **Supp. I.** 1981. ISBN 0-208-01750-X. **Supp. II.** 1986. ISBN 0-208-02072-1. **Supp. III.** 1992. ISBN 0-208-02214-7.

The bibliographical essay is the format for this guide and its supplements. The initial publication covers U.S. military history from colonial times to 1972. The first supplement updates the work to 1978, the second supplement to 1983, and the third supplement up through the Persian Gulf war. The third supplement updates all previous chapters from the original edition and the first two supplements, then offers three new chapters. The original publication contains 18 essay chapters written by scholars, most of them well-known military historians. Each chapter provides a broad survey of the literature of the subject, with an emphasis on primary materials. Social, political, and economic aspects are covered. Each essay includes suggestions for further research and about 300 selective bibliographic citations. The arrangement is chronological by historical period, with additional topical essays on military medicine, defense department policies, and museums as historical resources. The supplements, in addition to updating the bibliographies for the original topics, have new sections on nuclear war, military law, the Coast Guard, and the Corps of Engineers. There are no indexes. These bibliographies have long been regarded as a major resource for the study of military history. They are an important starting place for students and researchers.

A similar but more limited bibliography is *A Guide to the Study and Use of Military History* by John E. Jessup, Jr., and Robert W. Coakley (Center for Military History, U.S. Army, 1979). This bibliography is based on the extensive holdings of the U.S. Military Institute Library at Carlisle Barracks, Pennsylvania. The first section of the work is a general one on military history and sources. The major portion of the work is part II, which contains seven bibliographical essays on U.S. military history by period from 1607 to the early 1970s. The remaining two sections are devoted to the U.S. Army. The work is indexed.

299. **Intervention and Counterinsurgency: An Annotated Bibliography.** Benjamin R. Beede. New York: Garland, 1985. 312p. (Wars of the United States, v.5; Garland Reference Library of Social Science, v.251). ISBN 0-8240-8944-8.

The subject of this annotated bibliography is the small wars of the United States, the military interventions or occupations undertaken "under executive authority." The organization is by action, beginning with the Boxer Rebellion (1898–1901) and ending with Grenada in the 1980s. There are over 30 confrontations covered, including the *Pueblo* seizure and the *Mayaguez* incident. Excluded are political actions that did not involve the discharging of weapons. The more than 1,200 citations are to English-language books, periodical articles, dissertations, and documents, the majority of which are U.S. publications. An introduction defines the confrontations and provides general background; each section also has prefatory background material. There are author and subject indexes. This bibliography is the only source on the subjects covered. It is suitable for students and the general public, but the serious researcher will need to seek foreign source material in addition.

300. **Military History of the United States: An Annotated Bibliography.** Susan K. Kinnell, ed. Santa Barbara, CA: ABC-Clio, 1986. 333p. (Clio Bibliography Series, no.23). ISBN 0-87436-474-4.

Nearly 3,300 entries drawn from the *America: History and Life* (entry 51) database for the years 1973–1985 make up this bibliography, which can be updated by searching the index from 1985 to present. The bibliography with abstracts contains an initial chapter on historiography, followed by two main sections divided chronologically into 1860–1900 and 1901–1945. A final section covers the post–World War II era. The volume includes both an author index and an extensive subject index. The bibliography can be used in conjunction with other sources. It is fairly comprehensive for the time period of publications covered but is limited because the time span is so short.

301.   **Shield of the Republic, Sword of Empire: A Bibliography of United States Military Affairs, 1783–1846.** John C. Fredriksen, comp. New York: Greenwood, 1990. (Bibliographies and Indexes in American History, no.15). ISBN 0-313-25384-6.

Over 6,800 entries make up this specialized bibliography, including almost 2,000 citations to biographical materials. The majority of the sources cited are secondary sources, but the section on military campaigns lists a number of personal narratives. The bibliography includes books, articles from both scholarly and popular sources, dissertations, and state and local history publications. There are name and subject indexes as well as extensive cross-references. The bibliography is suitable for beginning research on the early development of the armed forces in the United States and U.S. military history from 1783–1846.

302.   **War Crimes, War Criminals, and War Crimes Trials: An Annotated Bibliography and Sourcebook.** Norman E. Tutorow and Karen Winnovich. New York: Greenwood, 1986. 548p. (Bibliographies and Indexes in World History, no.4). ISBN 0-313-24412-X.

Although the subject of war crimes is broadly covered, the preponderance of material in this bibliography consists of U.S. sources, including government documents. A large proportion of the material is related to World War II and the war crimes trials that followed. There are author and subject indexes.

Information Sources

303.   **American Badges and Insignia.** Evans E. Kerrigan. New York: Viking, 1967. 286p.

Although it has been over 25 years since its publication, this work is still useful historically. Together with another work by the same author, *American War Medals and Decorations* (Viking, 1963), it forms a comprehensive and detailed illustrated set on the military hierarchy and reward structure. Besides offering 1,100 illustrations, the volume provides details on the evolution of insignia and the developments and changes in uniforms and service organizations from 1776 to the 1960s. References and a bibliography are included. An older, similar work is by the National Geographic Society published in 1945, *Insignia and Decorations of the United States Armed Forces*. The illustrations in this work are regarded as superior to those by Kerrigan. Both are useful illustrated historical reference works.

Another illustrated and more general work is *Military Uniforms in America, Volume IV: The Modern Era—From 1868* by John R. Elting (San Rafael, CA: Presidio Press, 1988). This volume is the most recent in a set that depicts the history of military uniforms in the colonies and the United States from 1755 to the present. The three previously published volumes are *The Era of the American Revolution, 1755–1795; Years of Growth, 1796–1851;* and *Long Endure: The Civil War Period, 1852–1867.* The signed color drawings have been reproduced from a series of portfolios of unit histories published for collectors by the Company of Military Historians. There is no continuous narrative. Each color plate is accompanied by a facing page of text describing the uniform and its function as combat or dress attire. The text also includes a brief history of the unit, and other military equipment or weapons are shown. The text is interesting and gives references to sources. Authors and artists are listed for each entry. A glossary at the end of each volume defines terms used in the text. The set is useful for students, researchers, and others interested in the history of military uniforms.

304. **A Dictionary of Soldier Talk.** John R. Elting, et al. New York: Scribner's, 1984. 383p. ISBN 0-684-17862-1.

The definitions in this dictionary compiled by former U.S. Army personnel are linguistically valid. The work is entertaining and substantial. The main body of the dictionary presents Army slang and terminology, but there is also a section for Navy and Marine Corps terminology. The definitions cover the period from the beginnings of the U.S. military to the present. The dictionary is especially strong in post—World War II terminology. Both definitions and etymology are given, with references in appropriate contexts. The number of acronyms has been limited to avoid having the work become a dictionary of acronyms. The dictionary will be useful in all types of libraries for any user seeking definitions to military terms.

305. **Encyclopedia of Historic Forts: The Military, Pioneer, and Trading Posts of the United States.** Robert B. Roberts. New York: Macmillan, 1988. 894p. ISBN 0-02-926880-X.

More than 3,000 military posts and forts are listed alphabetically by state in this comprehensive work. Not limited to a particular time period, region, or conflict, the work gives the history of each fort, along with present visiting status and preservation efforts. Historical information includes major historical events; commanders; dates of construction, destruction, and reconstruction; architectural innovations; and name changes. The book concludes with a selective bibliography and listing of state archives and libraries for further research. There is an index of forts by name, but no chronological or geographical listings are given. There are maps and illustrations accompanying the text. Because of its comprehensiveness, this resource can be consulted before going to more specialized references on the subject.

306. **The Military History of the United States.** Christopher Chant. North Bellmore, NY: Marshall Cavendish, 1992. 16v. ISBN 1-85435-361-9.

The striking illustrations contribute to the effectiveness of this 16-volume work. The volumes are chronologically arranged and trace U.S. military history from the Revolutionary War to the Persian Gulf war in 1991. The text is authoritative in this set by Chant, who has produced several other works of military history. More than 1,500 illustrations from various media—photographs, engravings, contemporary paintings, maps, and drawings—adorn the set. Each volume has a bibliography and index. Volume 16 contains an index for the entire set and a glossary. The bibliographies from the individual volumes are repeated in volume 16. This attractive work is an up-to-date military history of the United States that will be of use to students, scholars, and the general reader.

307. **Reference Guide to United States Military History 1607–1815.** Charles Reginald Schrader, ed. New York: Facts on File, 1991. 277p. ISBN 0-8160-1836-7.

The series of which this is the first volume is intended to show that the history of the United States can be chronicled through the wars in which it has been engaged. Other volumes are planned on the period of the Mexican Civil War, the Spanish-American/World War I era, World War II, and Korea to the present. This volume covers the period from the Jamestown settlement to the War of 1812. There is a general introduction that discusses the history, development, and organization of the U.S. armed forces, with emphasis on the role of the military in a democratic society. The second section is made up of biographies, and the third section presents a detailed discussion of battles and events. There are numerous maps and illustrations of military leaders, battles, and other aspects of military life. A bibliography and an index are also included. This work is suitable for use by students or for background reading prior to beginning research.

Another work by the same author with a narrower focus is *U.S. Military Logistics, 1607–1991: A Research Guide* (Greenwood, 1992). It begins with an introductory chapter that defines the topic: the logistics of the supply and upkeep of the U.S. Army. Another chapter lists major holdings of manuscripts, government documents, and unit histories, repositories such as the National Archives. The other chapters are bibliographic citations in the theory and organization of logistics, specific periods, and units such as the Quartermaster Corps, Transportation Corps, and Subsistence Supply. Of particular use might be the appendices, which give Army expenditures and strength from 1775 to 1989. There is an index by author and subject. Another appendix contains key names in Army logistics.

308.   **The U.S. Defense and Military Fact Book.** C. W. Borklund. Santa Barbara, CA: ABC-Clio, 1991. 293p. ISBN 0-87436-593-7.

This work is an account of the growth of the U.S. Department of Defense and the military establishment since the end of World War II. There is a chronology of events influencing the department and an appendix of documents relating to its organization. There are also lists of personnel, with brief biographies. The section on the defense budget goes into detail on the makeup of military spending and the congressional appropriations process. The growth of expenditures since 1945 is traced in budgetary and statistical tables. Some sources are not given or not cited exactly, but references to the U.S. Code—the official publication of public laws in force that incorporates amendments and deletes repealed portions of the law—are complete. There is a selective bibliography. This reference work is appropriate for students, business people, and researchers.

309.   **The West Point Atlas of American Wars.** Vincent J. Esposito, ed. New York: Praeger, 1959. 2v.

Although it has not been updated or revised in over 30 years, the West Point atlas remains a standard reference source. It contains over 400 maps with supplemental text. The maps are three-color—black-and-white maps, with troop movements in red and blue. The two volumes are divided chronologically: v.1, 1689–1900; v.2, 1900–1953. The Civil War section of 137 maps has also been separately published (entry 386). Although primarily an atlas of land operations, the book also includes naval battles. Not all battles are covered for every war. The atlas ends with the Korean conflict. This atlas remains the best available U.S. military atlas.

Biographical Sources

310.   **Dictionary of American Military Biography.** Roger J. Spiller, ed. Westport, CT: Greenwood, 1984. 3v. ISBN 0-313-21433-6.

The biographies in this work are not limited to those individuals who served in the U.S. armed forces. Included among the nearly 400 subjects are political or civilian figures who had some influence upon or connection with military matters. The three-volume set begins with the French and Indian wars and ends with the Vietnam era. The biographical essays are written by over 200 specialists and include bibliographical references. The articles of approximately 1,500 words attempt to indicate the significance of the individual in U.S. military history and give specific accomplishments. A comprehensive index includes names of persons, places, units, battles and campaigns, and government agencies. Appendices include a chronology of the U.S. military and lists of rank designations, military organizations, birthplace of biographees, and names of contributors. This biographical work is well written and indexed. It is useful for any type of research on the U.S. military.

311. Fallen in Battle: American General Officer Combat Fatalities from 1775. Russell K. Brown. Westport, CT: Greenwood, 1988. 243p. ISBN 0-313-26242-X.

The criteria for inclusion in this biographical work make it very specialized. The 221 U.S. officers profiled held at death, previously held, or were posthumously awarded general or flag officer rank and died in combat or of wounds, were executed or died as prisoners of war, or became missing in action from the Revolutionary War through Vietnam. Officers of the Confederacy are included, along with an explanation of the criteria that determined officer ranks in the Confederacy. Almost three-fourths of the biographees died in the Civil War. Basic biographical facts about the officer are given, as well as a list of sources. Appendices include lists of officers killed, wounded, or captured according to the war, branch of service, and battles. One appendix lists officers who were noncombat fatalities during wartime. The author combed biographical works; service, unit and campaign accounts; and other reference works to compile the biographies. Almost two-thirds of the officers are not found in the *Dictionary of American Biography* (entry 143). This work is useful to genealogists, students, and military historians.

312. Webster's American Military Biographies. Robert McHenry. Springfield, MA: G. & C. Merriam, 1978. 548p. ISBN 0-87779-063-9.

The essays in the Webster's biographical dictionary are shorter than those in the *Dictionary of American Military Biography* (entry 310). Over 1,000 persons are included in this single-volume work. The definition of military is broad and includes civilians who played roles associated with the military, such as frontier scouts, nurses, Indian leaders, explorers, and shipbuilders. Biographies cover the person's whole life, not just the military affiliation. The appendices include lists of the secretaries of war, navy, and defense; tables of major commanders in the major wars; chronological listings of expeditions, wars, and battles; and lists of persons by career categories. All are referenced to pertinent biographies. This work is most useful as a quick reference for students and the general public.

BRANCHES OF THE
ARMED FORCES

There are many veterans, auxiliaries, and patriotic societies in the United States. In addition to the larger organizations such as the American Legion, the Veterans of Foreign Wars. AMVETS (World War II, Korea, and Vietnam), the Retired Officers Association, and the Retired Enlisted Association, each branch of the armed forces has its own associations, many for specific units. These societies are usually formed for the purpose of fostering patriotism, keeping memories alive, and sponsoring reunions. Many of the organizations sponsor scholarships, maintain memorial sites, issue newsletters, and sponsor occasional publications. Listings of such organizations can be found in the *Encyclopedia of Associations* under "Veterans, Hereditary, and Patriotic Organizations"; other historical societies can be found under "Cultural Organizations." A small number of such organizations are included in the introductory sections in this reference guide for the separate branches of the armed services.

Air Force

The Air Force is the youngest of the branches of the U.S. armed forces, having begun as a unit of the U.S. Army in 1907. It did not become a separate branch of the services until 1947. In 1954 the Air Force Historical Foundation was founded for the purpose of preserving the history of the U.S. Air Force and other units or subjects connected with U.S. air power. The foundation has 5,000 members and publishes the quarterly *Air Power History,* which covers all aspects of aerospace history. (Contact c/o Henry S. Bausum, Virginia Military Institute, Lexington, VA, 24450, (703) 464-7468.)

Since World War II a number of organizations have formed based on specific fighter units of the Air Force and Army Air Corps. The 17th Bomb Group, the 43rd Bomb Group, the 401st and 494th Bombardment Groups, the 381st Bomb Group, and the 304th and 369th Fighter Squadrons have associations for veterans. Many of these groups maintain memorials and biographical archives and promote research in the history of the unit and military history.

Many illustrated volumes on aircraft have been published, but such works are not listed in this reference guide. The subject of space exploration is also not covered. The Office of Air Force History in Washington has published a number of reference works for the study of Air Force history and two have been listed.

313. **An Aerospace Bibliography.** 2nd ed. Samuel Duncan Miller, comp. Washington: Office of Air Force History, 1979. 341p. S/N 008-070-000-427-5.

Although this work is identified as a second edition, it is not a revision exactly following the organization and format of *United States Air Force History: An Annotated Bibliography* by Mary Ann Cresswell and Carl Berger (Government Printing Office, 1971), which it claims to update. Some sections and citations from the first bibliography are not included in the second edition. Both treat the term "aerospace" broadly. The Air Force is the central topic, but anything related to aviation—equipment, missiles, space travel, UFOs—is included. The annotated entries, divided into 38 topical sections, are selective, but there is a more comprehensive listing of bibliographies in an appendix. Other appendices include lists of archives, libraries, and museum collections with materials of use to the aviation researcher. There are both author and subject indexes. Although this bibliography does not cover recent literature on the subject, it a good starting point for research.

314. **Historical Dictionary of the U.S. Air Force.** Charles D. Bright, ed. New York: Greenwood, 1992. 768p. ISBN 0-313-25928-3.

The comprehensiveness and inclusiveness of this one-volume reference work make it suitable for users at all levels. There are over 1,000 entries for persons, events, terms, and concepts, all relating to the U.S. Air Force. Included are acronyms, battles, campaigns, air bases, equipment, famous units, movies and TV shows, slang, and songs. Although many popular subjects are included, the work is authoritative. The time span ranges from the beginnings of aviation in 1907 to Operation Desert Storm. Entries range in length from short definitions to longer signed articles with references to other sources of information. There are numerous cross-references, including asterisks within articles marking terms that have a separate entry. This work is a current source for all inquirers seeking information about the U.S. Air Force.

315. **United States Air Force History: A Guide to Documentary Sources.** Lawrence J. Paszek, comp. Washington: Office of Air Force History, 1986. 245p. S/N 0870-00322.

Over 700 collections that have documents relating to the Air Force and historical material on aviation as far back as the use of balloons in the Civil War are described in this research guide. The organization is in five sections, divided according to type of repository. The first section lists Air Force official depositories. The second section describes the collections of the National Archives, presidential libraries, and federal records centers. Academic library collections occupy the third section. The Library of Congress, other federal and local government depositories, and historical societies are the subject of the fourth section. The last section describes other collections that have primary or secondary materials relating to the development of aviation in general. There is a general index and an index by name of depository. This guide is useful for historians and researchers interested in aviation history and the history of the U.S. Air Force.

The Army

The Army is the oldest branch of the U.S. armed services, dating back to June 14, 1775, when the Continental Congress created the Continental Army. A number of U.S. presidents served in the Army, including its first commander, George Washington, Ulysses S. Grant, and Dwight D. Eisenhower. The history of the U.S. Army is also one of technological evolution, from muskets to missiles with telegraph, radio, and satellite communications. The Army Historical Foundation plans to build a museum in Washington, D.C., but the group has been inactive for a number of years. There are numerous associations of Army infantry and other units. The majority of these are veterans organizations formed to honor those who fought with distinction in the world wars. A few of the associations do maintain museums or libraries.

Because of the Army's long history, there have been a number of reference works compiled on some aspect of it, although there have not been many new works in recent years. A few of the most useful reference works on the U.S. Army are listed in this section.

316. Histories, Personal Narratives: United States Army: A Checklist. Charles E. Dornbusch. Cornwallville, NY: Hope Farm Press, 1967. 399p.

Although it has not been revised in many years, this bibliography of unit histories is still a standard reference source. It updates an earlier, more restricted work published in 1956, *Histories of American Army Units, World Wars I and II and Korean Conflict.* Over 1,000 titles are listed in the expanded edition. One useful feature is that library locations are given for most entries. The checklist is a time saver for historians and genealogists searching for Army unit histories or personal accounts from particular Army units.

317. The Late 19th Century U.S. Army, 1865–1898: A Research Guide. Joseph G. Dawson, III. Westport, CT: Greenwood, 1990. 252p. (Research Guides in Military Studies, no.3). ISBN 0-313-26146-6.

The period covered in this research guide is that of the Old West and the Indian wars, a time span in which there were no major foreign conflicts. An excellent overview of the time period and the state of the Army introduces the guide. The first chapter describes manuscript collections, government documents, and the personal papers of such major military figures of the period as Ulysses S. Grant, William Tecumseh Sherman, and George Custer. The second chapter covers the reference literature. The ensuing chapters cover the phases of the Army and reconstruction, the Indian-fighting Army, and the Army in the late nineteenth century. Another chapter lists personal accounts of officers, wives, and others connected with Army life. Other chapters cover post life, coastal defense, and fictional depictions. Each chapter has an introductory bibliographical essay. The research guide is an excellent survey of the sources available for research on this period in the history of the U.S. Army. It is useful for students, researchers, and members of the general public interested in the Old West and U.S. Army history.

318. **List of Officers of the Army of the United States from 1779-1900...** William H. Powell. New York: L. R. Hamersly & Co., 1900. 883p. Repr. Gale, 1967.

Several separate lists of officers of all ranks make up this reference work. There is a list of officers arranged by years from 1779–1815. The Army list for 1815–1900, arranged alphabetically, also contains a brief biography for each name. Other lists focus on volunteer officers appointed by the president during the Civil War and brevets conferred during the Revolution and the War of 1812. There is a breakdown of names by grade, branch of the service, and regiment up through 1814. Appendices include a chronology of wars, conflicts, border disputes, and labor disturbances in which the Army was involved. This work has been used extensively by genealogists and historians since its first publication.

A similar work, equally well known, is that by Francis Heitman, *Historical Register and Dictionary of the United States Army from Its Organization ... to 1903*, a congressional document reprinted by the University of Illinois Press in 1965. The first volume of the two-volume set contains an alphabetized list giving the service records of all officers of the U.S. Army for the time period 1779–1903. The second volume includes lists of those killed, wounded in action, or taken prisoner. Information is also given on Army campaigns and losses, along with alphabetical and chronological lists of battles, actions, and so forth. Other information includes statistical tables, national cemeteries, and hospitals.

A somewhat specialized biographical source, the *Biographical Register of the Officers and Graduates of the U.S. Military Academy at West Point, N.Y. ...* was begun by George Washington Cullum. It was produced by various publishers from 1891 to 1950, with various other people editing different volumes. The work is organized into periods, starting with the first set for 1803–1890 (Boston: Houghton, Mifflin, 1891, v.1–3) and thereafter by decades to the last volume for 1940–1950. The work has been used through the years by genealogists and military historians.

319. **The Peacetime Army, 1900–1941: A Research Guide.** Marvin Fletcher. Westport, CT: Greenwood, 1988. 177p. (Research Guides in Military Studies, no.1). ISBN 0-313-25987-9.

The emphasis in this guide is on the development of the U.S. Army during the first part of the century preceding World War II. Because the focus is on peacetime changes, no references are included for the wars occurring during the time span covered, the Spanish-American War and World War I. The annotated references are to articles, books, and dissertations written since the end of World War II. The bibliography is divided into two time periods, before and after World War I. The chapters are topically subdivided into sections such as biography, management, technology, strategy, and political and social issues. There is an introductory essay and a chronology. Research ideas and an author/subject index are also provided. This work is an excellent introduction to sources and research in the history of the U.S. Army in the years before World War II.

The Marines

The U.S. Marine Corps grew out of two sharpshooter battalions in 1775 into the branch of the armed services that specializes in amphibious assault operations. The Marine Corps has an especially proud history, but an organization devoted to the Corps was not founded until relatively recently, in 1979. The Marine Corps Historical Foundation (PO Box 420,

Quantico, VA, 22134, (703) 640-6161) has a membership of 2,000 individuals and institutions. The foundation promotes the study and preservation of the history and traditions of the U.S. Marine Corps. It supports a museum; sponsors fellowships for thesis and dissertation work and a research grant fund; and underwrites publications and displays of manuscripts and artifacts focusing on the history of the Marine Corps.

Other organizations related to the Marine Corps for veterans and families are the 1st Marine Division Association; Loyal Escorts of the Green Garter; Marine Corps League Auxiliary; Military Order Devil Dog Fleas; Devil Pups; the Second Marine Division Association; and the Women Marines Association.

Although there are few reference works specifically focused on the Marine Corps, there is a recent bibliography.

320. **An Annotated Bibliography of U.S. Marine Corps History.** Paolo E. Coletta. Lanham, MD: University Press of America, 1986. 417p. ISBN 0-8191-5218-8.

The 4,000-plus entries in this bibliography make it a major source for materials on the history of the U.S. Marine Corps. The annotated entries include books, articles, documents, dissertations and theses, and films. Fictional works are included, as well as informational materials. The bibliography is divided by historical period and subdivided by format. In addition there is a subject section covering aviation, education, logistics, music, uniforms, women Marines, and division histories. There is a list of the personal papers of over 1,000 individuals that are deposited at the History and Museums Division at Marine Corps Headquarters in Washington. An unusual feature is the inclusion of classification numbers for the Marine Corps Historical Center Library. There is an author/subject index to the volume. This bibliography is of use to anyone beginning to search for information on the history of the U.S. Marine Corps.

An earlier, similar bibliography is *Creating a Legend: The Complete Record of the United States Marine Corps.* This bibliography compiled and self-published by a former Marine officer, John B. Moran (Moran/Andrews, 1973), lists all Marine Corps publications and a selection of articles from Marine Corps periodicals. The compiler endeavored to produce a comprehensive bibliography on the Marine Corps and included uncritically fiction, films, plays, and songs as well as standard book and periodical sources. The organization is by subject and title, with an author index. The bibliography may not be on hand in many libraries, but where available it can be used in conjunction with other bibliographies such as the entry above.

The Navy

Interest has always been high in the history of naval warfare. The Naval Historical Foundation was founded in 1926. It is open to members of the U.S. Navy, Marine Corps, and Coast Guard, and to civilians interested in U.S. naval history. The foundation (Bldg. 57, Washington Navy Yard, Washington, DC, 20374-0571, (202) 433-2005) has over 1,000 members. It maintains a library and has placed an extensive manuscript collection on deposit with the Library of Congress. It publishes *Pull Together*, a semiannual newsletter; the *Naval Historical Foundation Manuscript Collection Catalog*; and occasional monographs.

There are many other organizations focused on the history of the U.S. naval forces, including those for specific units or vessels. A few of the more general organizations are the United States Navy Memorial Foundation, the American Battleship Association, the Naval Order of the United States, the Tin Can Sailors, and the Waves National.

The literature of naval warfare and the history of naval vessels is extensive. Myron J. Smith has compiled five bibliographies on the U.S. naval forces alone (322, 324, 405). This reference guide does not attempt to cover the many popular and technical publications on naval vessels and aircraft. Only those reference works dealing with the history of the U.S. Navy are included.

The U.S. Navy is the only branch of the armed forces that has its own press, publishing high quality research and reference works. Trade publishers have also recently produced a number of reference works pertaining to the history of U.S. naval forces.

Library Resources

321. **U.S. Naval History Sources in the United States.** Dean C. Allard, et al. Washington: Naval History Division, Department of the Navy, 1979. 235p. S/N 008-046-00099-9.

Over 251 archival repositories throughout the United States are listed in this resource guide. Most collections described are of personal papers of officers, men, and civilians who had some connection with the Navy. Official Navy records, congressmen, and business firms that held naval contracts are also included in the sources listed. The arrangement is by state and then by repository. The information given on the collections includes the title, dates of coverage, and the volume of material. An index of names includes persons, institutions, and ships. This is an essential source for naval historians and others needing research materials on the U.S. Navy.

Bibliographical Sources

322. **The American Navy, 1789–1860: A Bibliography.** Myron J. Smith, Jr. Metuchen, NJ: Scarecrow, 1974. 489p. (American Naval Bibliography, v.2). ISBN 0-8108-8659-2.

Myron Smith has compiled a number of bibliographies in the American Naval Bibliography series. Two additional volumes with the same title covering the Navy for the years 1865–1918 and 1918–1941 have been published (Scarecrow, 1974). The first title cited above is composed of over 4,700 entries in a single alphabetical arrangement. The two subsequent bibliographies are divided chronologically by historical period. All three bibliographies contain citations to books, journal articles, dissertations, and theses, with no limitation on the time span of the publication dates of the sources cited. Government documents are treated in separate sections in all three works. Together, these bibliographies and the other Smith title listed in this section (entry 324) comprehensively treat the secondary literature on U.S. naval history. They can be used by students and researchers of any level to find source materials on naval history.

323. **A Selective and Annotated Bibliography of American Naval History.** Rev. ed. Paolo E. Coletta. Landham, MD: University Press of America, 1988. 523p. ISBN 0-8181-7111-5.

This is an update of a bibliography by the same author published by the Naval Institute Press in 1981. The first title, *A Bibliography of American Naval History*, listed over 4,800 sources, with very brief imprint information and short opinion phrases rather than full annotations. The revised edition updates the first bibliography up to 1987. The arrangement for both bibliographies is chronological by historical period beginning in 1689 and ending with the present. Sources include books, both fiction and nonfiction, articles, dissertations and theses, and government documents. A useful feature is that oral histories are also listed. The U.S. Marine Corps, Coast Guard, and other subjects as related to the U.S. Navy are also included. There are author and subject indexes; the latter includes biographies. These two bibliographies are adequate for students but not for serious research.

324.   **The United State Navy and Coast Guard, 1946–1983: A Bibliography of English-language Works and 16mm Films.** Myron J. Smith, Jr. Jefferson, NC: McFarland, 1984. 539p. ISBN 0-89950-122-2.

Smith's earlier bibliography series, the American Naval Bibliography set, was composed of five chronological volumes that ended with 1941 (entry 322). A further work, *World War II at Sea* (entry 405), covered those years. The work described here brings the bibliography of the U.S. Navy up to the 1980s. This volume alone contains over 10,000 entries, topically arranged. Materials listed are books, scholarly articles, dissertations and theses, and government documents. Some entries have very brief annotations when the content is not clear from the title. Films are listed separately. There are author and subject indexes. These are uncritical but comprehensive bibliographies suitable for students and researchers at any level.

Information Sources

325.   **American Naval History: An Illustrated Chronology of the U.S. Navy and Marine Corps, 1775–Present.** 2nd ed. Jack Sweetman. Naval Institute Press, 1991. 376p. ISBN 1-55750-785-6.

The entries in this illustrated chronology include battles, explorations, personnel, ships, technological developments, and events that influenced the development of the Navy in some way. The entries have very brief commentaries that explain the significance or consequences of events. This edition updates the 1984 work and includes the recent naval operations in the Persian Gulf war. Maps and a bibliography are included at the end. There is an index by vessel; a general index of persons, events, and subjects; and a calendar index for each day of the year. The illustrations make the work very attractive. This resource will be useful to any inquirer seeking an overview of naval history and specific facts about the U.S. Navy and Marine Corps.

326.   **Cruisers of the U.S. Navy 1922–1962.** Stefan Terzibaschitsch. Annapolis, MD: Naval Institute Press, 1988. 319p. ISBN 0-87021-974-X.

There have been a number of reference works on specific categories of naval vessels. This reference on cruisers is somewhat specialized. The work includes an overview of the development of this type of vessel, which was designed to provide fleet protection by virtue of speed and firepower. Numerous technological and strategical aspects of the cruiser are discussed. The major portion of the work deals with the different cruiser classes and then each ship individually. Changes in design and technology are covered for the cruiser classes. For each ship, a chronology of service life is given. Numerous photographs and line drawings illustrate the work. A brief bibliography and a series of technical tables are furnished. An even more specialized volume on naval cruisers also published by the Naval Institute Press is *U.S. Cruisers: An Illustrated Design History* by Norman Friedman (1984). The Terzibaschitsch work is suitable for the more general audience of naval enthusiasts, whereas the Friedman work is more technical.

327.   **Dictionary of American Naval Fighting Ships.** Washington: U.S. Department of the Navy. Naval Historical Center, 1959–1981. 8v. S/N 008-046-00101-4.

Naval vessels in both the Continental and the U.S. Navy are listed in this alphabetical reference work. Information on the ships includes service history, statistical description, and a discussion of the role and missions of the ship. The work is especially valuable because of the information on minor vessels, which is not to be found in most reference sources. Besides listing the ships in the eight volumes alphabetically, each volume contains appendices and statistical tables. Chronological listings by type of vessel begin in volume 1 and continue throughout the eight volumes. Volume 2 includes Confederate vessels. New ships and aircraft are in volume 5. There is a wealth of information on naval vessels in this comprehensive set, which will be useful for anyone seeking a description of a specific vessel or an historic overview of the naval fleet.

328. **List of Officers of the Navy of the United States and of the Marine Corps, from 1775 to 1900...** Edward William Callahan, comp. New York: Hamersly, 1901. 749p. Repr. Haskell House, 1969). ISBN 8383-0347-7.

The complete and lengthy title of this register compiled from official records of the Navy indicates that it includes all present and former officers of the U.S. Navy and Marine Corps commissioned, warranted, and appointed—regulars and volunteers—up to the time of publication. The volume also contains lists of all midshipmen cadet engineers and naval cadets who have entered the Naval Academy since its establishment. Alphabetical entries include date of entry into service, ranks held, and manner or reason for departing the service. Other information included in the volume is an appendix listing combat ships from 1797–1900 and a chronology of the Navy from 1775 to 1798. The work is useful to genealogists and naval historians.

Biographical Sources

329. **American Secretaries of the Navy.** Paolo E. Coletta, ed. Annapolis, MD: Naval Institute Press, 1980. 2v. ISBN 0-87021-073-4.

The chapters in this work are all written by naval historians and contain references to sources. The lives and influence of 60 secretaries of the navy are covered, beginning with the first-ever secretary of the Navy (appointed by President Adams) and continuing up to the term of President Nixon. Portraits are included along with biographical information. The sketches cover the abilities of each secretary, his influence upon the administration in which he served, and the impact his programs and policies had upon the navy. The biographies are arranged chronologically in the two volumes; the second volume begins with World War I. An introduction by Coletta describes the role of the office within the executive branch. This is a useful reference work for those seeking biographical information on secretaries of the navy or an historical overview of the office.

330. **Captains of the Old Steam Navy: Makers of the American Naval Tradition, 1840–1880.** Annapolis, MD: Naval Institute Press, 1986. 356p. ISBN 0-87021-013-0.

Only 13 naval officers are included in this biographical work focused on the time period in which the navy was in transition from sail- to steam-powered vessels. The biographies are interpretative essays showing the role of each man during the transition period. Each essay contains an annotated reading list, and there is a comprehensive bibliography at the end of the volume. The work is indexed and there are a few illustrations. It is useful for the study of U.S. naval history for the time period and the biographies of the specific individuals.

331. **The Chiefs of Naval Operations.** Robert William Love, Jr., ed. Annapolis, MD: Naval Institute Press, 1980. 448p. ISBN 0-87021-115-3.

The position of chief of naval operations was established in 1915 to counterbalance the civilian post of secretary of the navy. This work contains an introduction on U.S. naval administration and policy. Nineteen officers are profiled, each by a different naval historian. The biographies include photographs and a sketch of the life of the subject, with a concentration on the time spent in the position. Much can be learned about the growth of the Navy in the twentieth century and its role in U.S. foreign policy through the biographies. The work is of use to students and historians or anyone with an interest in U.S. naval history and foreign policy.

332. **Dictionary of Admirals of the Navy.** William B. Cogar. Annapolis, MD: Naval Institute Press, 1989. 217p. ISBN 0-87021-431-4.

Brief biographies of 211 officers are contained in this source, the first in a projected five-volume set. The first volume begins in 1862, when the rank of admiral was first used, and continues to 1900. The biographies provide a brief summary of the life of the subject, service record with ranks held, and the highlights of the officer's career, along with a photograph or portrait. Description and location of manuscripts and a bibliography of sources by and about the individual form part of each biographical sketch. Students and naval historians will find this biographical dictionary of Navy leadership useful.

333. **United States Naval Biographical Dictionary.** Karl Schuon. New York: Franklin Watts, 1964. 277p.

The specialized works issued in recent years by the Naval Institute Press have not entirely replaced this general biographical dictionary of naval personnel. Pioneers in naval science, oceanographers, engineers, and Medical and Chaplain Corps personnel are also included. This work with brief biographical sketches is still useful for biographies of individuals not listed in other biographical works.

Special Forces

334. **Special Operations and Elite Units, 1939–1988: A Research Guide.** Roger Beaumont. Westport, CT: Greenwood, 1988. 258p. ISBN 0-313-26001-X.

The preface to this work reveals the compiler's personal interest in the subject of special forces. A substantial introduction traces and describes the use of special forces and units in wars and intelligence operations since 1939. The annotated bibliography is divided into 10 topical sections arranged by author. The sources cited include popular and scholarly books and periodical articles as well as military field manuals and reports. Four appendices list current elite units, elite forces since 1939, counterterrorist operations since World War II, and principal airborne combat operations. There are separate indexes by author, title, and subject. This bibliography is unique among military reference works and will be of general interest as well as research use in military history and foreign affairs.

THE WARS

The only section in this reference guide organized chronologically is this section on the wars. Thus sources for a particular period in history, especially those that pertain to the Revolutionary period, are included in this section.

The number of reference works on each war varies, as would be expected, according to the magnitude of the conflict in the history of the United States. There have been a number of new reference tools published in recent years dealing with specific wars. Older, classic reference works are also included when they are still the most useful works for research.

The French and Indian War (1754–1763)

335. Struggle for Empire: A Bibliography of the French and Indian War. James G. Lydon. New York: Garland, 1986. 272p. (Wars of the United States, v.7; Garland Reference Library of Social Science, v.188). ISBN 0-8240-9069-1.

All aspects of the French and Indian War are covered in this annotated selective bibliography of over 1,500 entries. French, Spanish, Canadian, U.S., and British sources are included to represent the views of various factions involved in the war. Contemporary sources are cited, as is twentieth-century scholarship on the subject. The sources cited are books, articles, dissertations, and documents. A separate section lists audiovisual materials, film-strips, microformats, and cassettes. The bibliography is divided into two major sections; the first has 12 topical chapters and the second is subdivided geographically into New York state and the South.

Military, political, and social aspects of the war, including Indian relations, are covered in the first section. There are separate indexes by author and subject. The annotations are evaluative as well as factual. This bibliography is a thorough treatment of the subject and is suitable for use in research by all levels of inquirer.

Revolutionary War (1775–1783)

The Revolutionary War has quite naturally been the focus of much historical research. The Revolutionary period was the founding period of the country, when the American colonists fought to break away from England and, having been successful, formulated a new system of government. The major historical societies focused on the Revolutionary period are those for descendants of the original colonists or those who fought in the War of Independence. These include the Daughters of the American Revolution, the Sons of the American Revolution, the Society of Loyalist Descendants, the Society of the Descendants of Washington's Army, the Black Revolutionary War Patriots Foundation, and the Descendants of the Signers of the Declaration of Independence. Many of these organizations sponsor high school essay contests, scholarships and publications, raise funds for memorials and the preservation of historic sites, maintain historical/genealogical libraries, and sponsor activities to foster patriotism in U.S. society.

The bicentennial of the United States, celebrated in 1976, was the impetus for many historical publications and reference works. Interest in the Revolutionary period has tapered off somewhat since then, but new reference materials have been published in the years since the bicentennial. Those of most significance for historical research are described in this section.

Library Resources

336. A Bibliography of Loyalist Source Material in the United States, Canada, and Great Britain. Gregory Palmer, ed. Westport, CT: Meckler, 1982. ISBN 0-930466-26-8.

Three separate bibliographies prepared under the Program for Loyalist Studies have been gathered together and reprinted in this volume. The program was sponsored by four libraries: the American Antiquarian Society, the University of New Brunswick, the University of London, and the City University of New York. The objective was to locate Loyalist material in repositories in the United States, Canada, Great Britain, and Ireland. The organization of the bibliographies is geographical by repository, with collections briefly described. Reposi-tories are numbered, as are collections within the repository. Two appendices list Loyalist newspapers by state and imprints chronologically by date. There is an overall index covering all three bibliographies referenced by repository number. The researcher seeking loyalist materials is well served by this bibliography of library and archival collections.

337. **European Manuscript Sources of the American Revolution.** William J. Koenig and Sydney L. Mayer. New York: Bowker, 1974. 328p. ISBN 0-85939-001-0.

The only source that concentrates on archival sources in Europe for research on the period of the American Revolution, 1763–1785, this guide lists over 250 repositories. The organization is geographical by country, city, and repository. Museums, archives, and private collections from the British Isles, the Netherlands, France, Spain, Austria, Germany, Italy, the USSR, and Sweden are included. Diaries, diplomatic correspondence, journals, letters, newspapers, ships' logs, pamphlets, and other printed materials are included in the collections, which have brief summaries of contents. The entries also include references to other bibliographies and guides. There is a subject index, which is rather inadequate. Researchers making use of this bibliography will realize that there is a wealth of material on the American Revolution in European archives.

338. **Manuscript Sources in the Library of Congress for Research on the American Revolution.** Washington: Library of Congress, 1975. 372p. ISBN 0-8444-0122-6.

The American Revolution Bicentennial Office of the Library of Congress compiled this guide. It includes original manuscripts plus transcriptions, microfilms, and photoreproductions from collections in the Library of Congress that contain American Revolution materials. The guide is divided into two major sections: domestic collections and foreign reproductions. The domestic section is arranged into alphabetical lists of account books, journals, diaries, order books, and miscellaneous manuscripts. Brief information and biographical facts are provided for each collection. There are indexes of subjects and of repositories, domestic and foreign. Given the large amount of manuscript material in the Library of Congress, this guide is a necessary starting point for the researcher.

A much more specialized collection is located at Morristown National Historical Park in Morristown, New Jersey. *Hessian Documents of the American Revolution, 1776–1783: Transcripts and Translations from the Lidgerwood Collection* is a microfiche publication of over 20,000 pages of material, with a printed guide by author and subject (G. K. Hall, 1989). The Hessian soldiers were hired by King Frederick II of Prussia to fight in the American Revolutionary War. They recorded their daily experiences and official activities from 1775–1783. These documents, official journals, correspondence, and so on have been translated over a period of years beginning in 1906 and provide a firsthand view of life during the Revolutionary period. The collection will be of interest to students, scholars, and the general public.

339. **Revolutionary America, 1763–1789: A Bibliography.** Ronald M. Gephart. Washington: Library of Congress, 1984. 2v. ISBN 0-8444-0359-8 (v.1); 0-8444-0379-2 (v.2).

This bibliography forms a counterpart to the guide to manuscript sources in the Library of Congress described in entry 338 above. The work lists printed primary and secondary sources on the American Revolutionary period in the Library of Congress. Both monographs and periodical articles are included in the more than 20,000 titles given here, the majority of which have brief annotations. Collected works, *festschriften*, dissertations, and pamphlets are included. Given the completeness of the holdings of the Library of Congress, this is a definitive bibliography of the period for sources published before 1972. The first two chapters deal with reference works and regional and local histories. The next seven chapters proceed chronologically through the war up to the writing of the Constitution and the formation of the government. There are two chapters devoted to economic, cultural, social, and intellectual life. A biographical chapter lists works by and about 2,130 persons. An extensive bibliographic essay on the preservation and publication of documentary sources forms the last chapter. The index contains over 100,000 entries to people, places, and titles that appear in the citations, but it is not an adequate subject index. This is a major bibliography for the study of the American Revolutionary period. Researchers will need to update it for sources published after 1972.

Bibliographical Sources

340. **The American Controversy: A Bibliographical Study of the British Pamphlets About the American Disputes, 1764–1783.** Thomas R. Adams. Providence: Brown University Press; New York: Bibliographical Society of America, 1980. 2v. 0-87057-150-8.

The pamphlets printed in Great Britain expressing British views toward the American Revolution, or "American Controversy," have been bibliographically identified by Adams, who had previously published a bibliography of American pamphlets (entry 341). The bibliography lists 1,400 titles in 2,350 editions, including those first published in the colonies and reprinted in Great Britain. The pamphlets are listed chronologically and then alphabetically by author within each year. Later editions are listed in the year published and then cross-referenced back to the first edition. The bibliographical descriptions are a work of scholarship, with collations detailed to distinguish different printings, variant editions, and so on. Authorship of anonymous works, original price, and number of copies printed are included. Locations are given for libraries holding copies. There are two useful appendices. The "Pamphlet Exchange" traces the ongoing debate, tracking which pamphlets were responses to earlier ones. A publisher index lists pamphlets by publisher and gives places in England where the pamphlets were sold. There is a separate title index and a general index of names, places, and subjects. This bibliography is valuable for research in colonial and American Revolutionary history and for research in eighteenth-century printing.

341. **American Independence: The Growth of an Idea; A Bibliographical Study of the American Political Pamphlets Printed Between 1764 and 1776 Dealing with the Dispute Between Great Britain and Her Colonies.** Thomas R. Adams. Providence: Brown University Press, 1965. Repr. Austin, TX: Jenkins and Reese, 1980. 264p. (Contributions to Bibliography, 5).

The counterpart to the bibliography of British pamphlets (entry 340), this bibliography was previously published by the Colonial Society of Massachusetts. The 1980 reprint also contains a 1979 article, "The British Pamphlet Press and the American Controversy" by Adams, and a list of additions and corrections. There were fewer pamphlets published in the colonies than in Britain. The 231 pamphlets are listed chronologically, with bibliographical descriptions and locations of copies. A list of pamphlet exchanges is included. The bibliography shows the development of political thought in the colonies during the Revolutionary period and is a valuable research aid for historians of all aspects of the period.

342. **Navies in the American Revolution: A Bibliography.** Myron J. Smith, Jr. Metuchen, NJ: Scarecrow, 1973. 219p. (American Naval Bibliography, 1). ISBN 0-8108-0569-3.

The citations in this bibliography are to books, articles, poetry, dissertations, and documents, mostly in English and written between 1770 and 1972. Some of the approximately 1,500 citations have brief annotations. There are two appendices: One is an article by Smith, and the other is a list, "Vessels in the Public Service of the United States, 1775–1785." Smith has gathered information on publications concerning U.S. naval forces during the Revolutionary War into one volume useful to inquirers of any level.

343. **The War of the American Revolution: A Selected Annotated Bibliography of Published Sources.** Richard L. Blanco. New York: Garland, 1984. 654p. (Wars of the United States, v.1; Garland Reference Library of Social Science, v.154). ISBN 0-8240-9171-X.

All aspects of the era of the American Revolution, 1775–1983, are treated in this bibliography of over 3,700 items. The sources listed are mainly English-language secondary materials. The bibliography is aimed at a broad audience. The annotations are evaluative and in many cases indicate the appropriate level of readership. The bibliography is organized into 14 topical chapters. Social as well as martial aspects of the period receive attention. There are author and subject indexes. The work is a useful basic bibliography for students and readers of all levels.

A more highly selective bibliography also prepared for a broad audience is *Periodical Literature on the American Revolution: Historical Research and Changing Interpretations, 1895–1970* by Ronald M. Gephart (Library of Congress, 1971). Although somewhat dated, this bibliography of 1,122 entries arranged by subject is still suitable for students and general readers as a basic source to be used in conjunction with more recent bibliographies.

Information Sources

344. **Atlas of Early American History: The Revolutionary Era, 1760–1890.** Lester J. Cappon, et al. Princeton, NJ: Published for the Newberry Library and the Institute of Early American History and Culture by Princeton University Press, 1976. 157p. ISBN 0-691-04634-4.

Produced by a team of scholars in historical geography and colonial history, this atlas is a definitive achievement. The 286 maps, the majority in color, were produced for the volume and represent the best in cartography. They are divided into three periods: the colonial period up to 1776; the war; and the period of the Articles of Confederation. All aspects of life for the time period—social, political, and economic—are illustrated. The text is well written, giving an explanation and analysis of the maps, with numerous bibliographic references to primary and secondary sources. Maps include 15 cities important to the time period and also show Indian settlements, population density, water transportation and mail routes, political activities, and events of the war. The maps show comparative time studies of economic growth, exports, and agricultural products. The section on the Revolutionary War is organized into geographical areas, with the military activities shown in each area over time rather than in a battle-by-battle approach. The atlas is designed for use by all those with an interest in the study of the period of the American Revolution and is a significant research resource.

345. **Atlas of the American Revolution.** Kenneth Nebenzahl, ed. Chicago: Rand McNally, 1974. 218p. ISBN 528-83465-7.

Another atlas produced for the bicentennial, this volume is of more aesthetic and antiquarian interest than of reference use. There are 54 historical maps and battle plans originally engraved and published in the eighteenth century, some not having been reproduced before. The majority of the maps are by William Fiden, the principal mapmaker of the Revolution. Although they are interesting as contemporaneous accounts, the maps can be difficult to interpret for those seeking specific information. Commentary on the maps is provided by Kenneth Nebenzahl, a noted antiquarian map authority. The text is an essay by a scholar of the American Revolution, Don Higginbotham. The people of the time period are vividly described, along with military events and strategy. The maps and battle plans depict specific military and naval activities from Lexington and Concord to the British surrender at Yorktown. Street plans of the principal cities in North America are also included. There is an index of persons, places, and subjects. The atlas is of interest to cartographers and map collectors, military historians, and students of the Revolutionary period.

346. **A Battlefield Atlas of the American Revolution.** Craig L. Symonds. Baltimore: Nautical & Aviation Publishing, 1986. 110p. ISBN 0-933852-53-3.

If the researcher is seeking illustrations of troop movements, this atlas is the best reference to consult. The major battles of the American Revolution are analyzed, with symbols delineating the action. There are 41 black-and-white maps, with forces depicted in two shades of blue and movements shown by dotted lines. The maps are divided chronologically into four sections, each beginning with an overview: "Early Campaigns," "1777: The Turning Point," "A Global War," and "The War Moves South." Each map has explanatory text on a facing page. There is no index, but references for suggested reading are included with each map. The atlas clearly sets forth the military dimensions of the American Revolution. The maps are clearer and easier to interpret than those in the Rand McNally atlas (see entry 345), and the book contain specific battle information not included in the *Atlas of Early American History* (entry 344). It is useful for students and all but the most specialized researcher.

347. **The Bicentennial Guide to the American Revolution.** Sol Tember. New York: Saturday Review Press; distr. by Dutton, 1974. 3v. ISBN 0-84515-0311-7 (v.1); 0-8415-0313-3 (v.2); 0-8415-0316-8 (v.3).

The three volumes in this tour guide are *The War in the North*; *The Middle Colonies*; and *The War in the South*. Although the purpose of this set is to serve as a travel guide to battlefields, forts, and other historic sites of significance in the Revolutionary War, the set is well written and historically accurate, with contemporary accounts interspersed with the narrative. Each volume is divided by state into a geographical/chronological war narrative. There are detailed maps of each site with accompanying text that gives an account of the battle and the way it affected the outcome of the American Revolution. Routes, distances, hours of opening, and walking tours contribute to the usefulness of the set. The guide is of interest to students and the general public.

348. **The Blackwell Encyclopedia of the American Revolution.** Jack P. Greene and J. R. Pole, eds. Cambridge, MA: Basil Blackwell, 1991. 845p. ISBN 1-55786-244-3.

Ninety-six scholars from the United States. and Europe contributed to this authoritative encyclopedia reflecting recent scholarly thinking on the Revolutionary period. The major part of the work is 75 signed, thematic essays covering the military, political, social, economic, and religious underpinnings of the American Revolution. The first 9 essays examine such aspects of colonial history as the family, population, and cultural development; the next 17 follow events leading up to the war; the following 20 focus on events after 1776. The last 12 essays deal with concepts such as equality, sovereignty, suffrage, and nationalism. Following the essays is a section of signed biographical sketches of major participants and lesser-known figures, including a number of women. The last section is a chronology from 1688–1790. There is an index to the essay and biography sections that allows use of the volume for reference queries. The essay format of this encyclopedia presents a coherent view of the entire Revolutionary period. It is one of the best sources for high school and university students and has much to offer for researchers also.

A standard and well-known work with a similar title is the *Encyclopedia of the American Revolution* by Mark Boatner (MacKay, 1974). The previous edition was published in 1966, and the 1974 bicentennial edition was billed as "revised and expanded." The newer edition is almost an exact reprint of the 1966 volume except for a few recent bibliographical citations. The encyclopedia contains nearly 2,000 entries for people, places and events connected with the American Revolution. The Blackwell work is much superior as a source analyzing the broader social, economic, and intellectual components of the period. The Boatner work is useful as a source of definitions and factual information for all levels of investigators who are not seeking recent interpretative scholarship.

349. **Campaigns of the American Revolution: An Atlas of Manuscript Maps.** Douglas W. Marshall and Howard H. Peckham. Ann Arbor, MI: University of Michigan Press; Maplewood, NJ: Hammond, 1976. 138p. ISBN 0-472-23300-9 (University of Michigan); 0-8437-3125-7 (Hammond).

The authors' intent with this volume is to show the importance of maps in military campaigns. The majority of the 56 manuscript maps reproduced in the volume are from the collections of the William L. Clements Library at the University of Michigan. The maps are presented chronologically, from Lexington and Concord through the Revolution, ending with Pensacola in 1781. A narrative overview precedes each year, giving the events of that year. Each map has a few pages of text placing it in the context of the war and describing the map itself. The volume forms a military history of the Revolutionary period illustrated with contemporary maps that show the topography and the disposition of opposing forces for each campaign. There are bibliographical references for each map in a section of sources at the end of the volume. There is an index. The atlas is of most interest to historians of the American Revolution and those interested in military strategy and cartography. It is suitable for use by students.

350. **Historical Register of Officers of the Continental Army During the War of the Revolution, April 1775 to December 1783.** Repr. of the 1932 ed. Baltimore: Genealogical Publishing Co., 1982. 698p. ISBN 0-80630-176-7.

The original edition of the *Register* was published in 1893, with a revised reissue in 1914 and another reissue in 1932 that contained an addenda by W. H. Kelby. The source is an alphabetical list with service records of 14,000 officers of the Continental Army, including many state troops and militia who also served during the Revolution. The *Historical Register* is the most complete list available and has been used mainly by genealogists through the years. Another work reprinted by Genealogical Publishing is *Prisoners of the American Revolution* (1967) by Danske Dandridge, which lists over 8,000 prisoners. The U.S. naval forces during the Revolution were small and augmented by privateers. A list of *Mariners of the American Revolution, with an Appendix of American Ships Captured by the British During the Revolutionary War* was compiled by Marion J. Kaminkow and Jack Kaminkow (Magna Carta, 1967). The information in this publication, obtained mainly from British sources, lists almost 3,000 captives, including ship, origin, and date of capture if available. Besides these reference works there are a number of rosters by state. The names of those engaged in military actions during the American Revolution have been thoroughly researched and listed in various reference works for the benefit of students, historians, and genealogists.

351. **Index to Maps of the American Revolution in Books and Periodicals: Illustrating the Revolutionary War and Other Events of the Period, 1763–1789.** David Sanders Clark. Westport, CT: Greenwood, 1974. 301p. ISBN 0-8371-7582-8.

It is often not easy to find copies of original maps reproduced in sources commonly held in most academic and large public libraries. This index includes approximately 6,400 maps from more than 1,000 monographs and periodical articles. There are three parts to the index. The first part contains citations to the maps; the second part is a subject and name index; and the third part lists the sources indexed. The maps, arranged geographically, are chiefly military, but population, towns, roads, and boundaries are also shown. Although this work is nearly 20 years old and the references were written before 1965, it cites basic sources that will still be owned by most libraries. The work is therefore still useful for students seeking maps for the period.

352. **Sources and Documents Illustrating the American Revolution, 1764–1788.** 2nd ed. Samuel Eliot Morison. Repr. of the 1965 ed. New York: Oxford University Press, 1977. 308p. ISBN 0-19-500262-8).

Originally published in 1923, this sourcebook has been reprinted several times. An index was added in later reprints, the original not having one. The documents in the volume are not all reproduced in full; many are represented by excerpts. The focus is on the constitutional aspects of the revolution and not the military and diplomatic aspects. Included are important acts, royal instructions, state constitutions, and extracts from letters, pamphlets, debates, and other documents that influenced the resolve for independence. There is an introduction by Morison discussing the significance of many of the documents. The source-book is still a useful one for students seeking the text of formative documents of the Revolutionary period.

353. **Uniforms of the American Revolution, in Color.** John Mollo. New York: Macmillan, 1975. Reprint, New York: Sterling Publishing Co., 1991. 228p. ISBN 0-8069-8240-3.

Uniforms and equipment for the major armies—the American, French, and British—as well as other groups—Loyalists, Indians, and German troops—are depicted in this small volume. There are 334 numbered plates, followed by a section of text arranged primarily by campaigns describing the military action and the uniforms and equipment from the plates. There is an introduction for each of the major armies. Mollo engaged in considerable archival research to present a wider range of reconstructed uniforms than has any previous work on the subject. A bibliography of sources completes the volume. There is no index. This work is of interest to students, military historians, and others seeking information on military dress and equipment during the Revolutionary War.

354. **The War of the American Revolution: Narrative, Chronology, and Bibliography.** Robert W. Coakley and Stetson Conn. Washington: U.S. Army Center of Military History, 1975. 257p. S/N 008-029-00091-1.

Another bicentennial publication from the Center for Military History, this work is an excellent summary of the military history of the Revolutionary War from the first confrontation to the surrender at Yorktown. The history traces the development of the Continental Army and the diplomatic relations between the Americans, the British, and the French. A chronology covers events from 1763 to 1783. This selected bibliography of over 1,000 sources, although not up to date, is still a very useful resource for students.

Biographical Sources

355. **Biographical Sketches of Loyalists of the American Revolution.** Gregory Palmer. Westport, CT: Meckler, 1984. 959p. ISBN 0-930466-14-4.

Palmer has compiled a work that supplements one by the same title published by Lorenzo Sabine in 1864. The Sabine work contains about 9,000 names drawn from U.S. and Canadian sources. Palmer used the records of the Loyalist Claims Commission in the Public Records Office (PRO) in London to compile the supplemental information. Using the Sabine work as a base, the Palmer volume has one alphabetical sequence with names divided according to three categories: 1) those in the main section of Sabine; 2) those in the "Fragments" section, which contains little information; or 3) those not listed in Sabine. Over 70 percent of the entries in the supplement are names not included in Sabine. Although the Palmer entries refer to Sabine, there are no cross-references in Palmer to variant forms of names in the latter. Palmer's entries give the PRO record number for anyone needing that exact information. An introduction to the volume discusses Sabine's work and the use of the Loyalist Claims Commission records. This work is valuable for historians and genealogists.

356. **Fighters for Independence: A Guide to Sources of Biographical Information on Soldiers and Sailors of the American Revolution.** J. Todd White and Charles H. Lesser. Chicago: University of Chicago Press, 1977. 112p. (Clements Library Bicentennial Studies). ISBN 0-226-89498-3.

The information in this dictionary is gleaned from a variety of published sources and

Unlike the early biographical works, which concentrated on officers, this source prepared for the bicentennial focuses on Revolutionary soldiers and sailors. The first chapter is one of the most valuable features for researchers. It describes collections of manuscripts, microfilms, and printed material useful in finding biographical information on the soldiers and sailors, along with the guides available to those collections. The second chapter contains citations to lists of names and biographical sketches that other researchers have drawn from the sources described in the first chapter. The third chapter lists sources of biographical information other than those in chapter 1. The last chapter is an unannotated bibliography of primary sources— diaries, journals, autobiographies, and memoirs. There is a concise "major subjects" index. The work is useful to students, researchers, and genealogists for the sources of biographical information it identifies.

357. **Naval Officers of the American Revolution: A Concise Biographical Dictionary.** Charles E. Claghorn. Metuchen, NJ: Scarecrow, 1988. 363p. ISBN 0-8108-2096-X.

The information in this dictionary is gleaned from a variety of published sources and state and federal records. The names of 3,500 U.S. and French naval officers and privateers are listed. Other data are given when found, such as date and place of birth, commissioning, the ships served aboard, battles, and captures and rescues participated in. Date of death is not included unless death was military-related. This work brings information from a variety of sources together and indicates the sources along with the biographical data. It is useful for researchers, genealogists, and others pursuing such information.

358. **People and Events of the American Revolution.** Trevor N. Dupuy and Gay M. Hammerman, eds. New York: Bowker, 1974. 471p. ISBN 0-8352-0777-3.

The time span covered in this reference work (1733–1783) is longer than many works on the American Revolution. It is divided into two major sections: the first is a chronology of events and the second an alphabetical biographical section. The chronology gives dates, place, and a very brief description. "People of the American Revolution" lists patriots, loyalists, Indian leaders, and foreigners who had some role in the American Revolution. Other elements are a bibliography and a detailed index to the chronology. There is no analysis or interpretation; this is simply a factual information source suitable for students and the general public.

359. **Women Patriots of the American Revolution: A Biographical Dictionary.** Charles E. Claghorn. Metuchen, NJ: Scarecrow, 1991. 519p. ISBN 0-8108-2421-3.

The information contained in this dictionary is brief for most of the entries. There are short biographical sketches for 600 women and a separate section listing another 4,500, with references to the sources in which they are mentioned. The work seems to include all women not classified as Loyalists for which *any* information was found rather than those who were truly patriots. The main biographical sketches include the state in which the woman lived and the source of the information, indicated by a code to sources explained in a table at the front of the work. This work is useful for students and researchers for the number of names and the references to information sources it contains.

War of 1812 (1812–1814)

Although it is not regarded as a war of major proportions in the scheme of U.S. history, the War of 1812 has at least three patriotic societies that still perpetuate the memory of those who served in the conflict. The General Society of the War of 1812 is for male descendants of the veterans; the National Society, United States Daughters of 1812 is obviously for the women descendants of those who rendered service; a smaller organization is the Society of the War of 1812 in the Commonwealth of Pennsylvania. There have not been a large number of reference sources published for the War of 1812, but two sources published in the mid-1980s are described in this section.

360. **Free Trade and Sailor's Rights: A Bibliography of the War of 1812.** John C. Fredriksen, comp. Westport, CT: Greenwood, 1985. 399p. (Bibliographies and Indexes in American History, no.2). ISBN 0-313-24313-1.

The main value of this bibliography on the War of 1812 is in the chapter on manuscript collections, which describes over 100 groupings of personal papers in libraries in the United States and Canada. The bibliography of books and periodical articles is divided geographically by region and then by state. Within the states there are topical divisions. Other chapters in the bibliography are arranged by broad themes or topics. Appendices contain a chronology of the war, a list of military regiments that were active, and a list of wartime newspapers. There is a subject index but no author index. The bibliography is a good basic and reasonably current source for students and researchers and can be used in conjunction with the entry below.

361. **The War of 1812: An Annotated Bibliography.** Dwight L. Smith. New York: Garland, 1985. 340p. (Wars of the United States, no.3; Garland Reference Library of Social Science, v.250.). ISBN 0-8240-8945-6.

The Smith bibliography is more comprehensive and covers a wider range of sources material than the work by Fredriksen (entry 360). The Smith work includes 1,400 entries for published primary and secondary materials: books, articles, essays or chapters, diaries and memoirs, speeches, pamphlets, songs, literary works, sermons, and dissertations. Government documents, manuscripts, newspapers, and broadsides are excluded. Items cited are prior to 1981, in English, with very brief annotations. The arrangement is in nine broad categories with geographical and chronological classifications. The bibliography covers all aspects of the war and includes U.S., British, and Canadian viewpoints. A brief chronology of the war is included along with author and subject indexes. Used in conjunction with the work by Fredriksen, this bibliography provides excellent coverage of research materials for the study of the War of 1812. Both bibliographies will have to be updated for the decade of the 1980s and 1990s.

Mexican War (1846–1848)

362. **The Mexican-American War: An Annotated Bibliography.** Norman E. Tutorow, comp. Westport, CT: Greenwood, 1981. 427p. ISBN 0-3131-22181-2.

A total of 4,537 sources are listed in this annotated bibliography, which is arranged in eight sections according to format. There are sections for reference works, periodical articles, monographs, and miscellaneous works. The sections on primary source materials, manuscripts, government documents, and National Archives records are excellent. Appendices contain several maps, tables, lists of U.S. and Mexican naval vessels, and rosters of military personnel reprinted from other sources. This work is a thorough and comprehensive resource for researching the Mexican-American War. It is obligatory for any student or researcher seeking information on that period.

Civil War (1861–1865)

The war between the North and the South, the Union and the Confederacy, has been one of the most romanticized wars in history. It has been the subject of many publications, both of a popular and a scholarly nature. The character and personalities of the leading figures have been and continue to be the subject of biographical works. There are a number of societies and organizations focused on preserving battlefields and conducting research in Civil War history. One of the most well known is the Civil War Round Table Associates. This organization of 1,500 members was not founded until 1968, after the Civil War centennial in 1961. The Civil War Round Table has been active in the preservation of Civil War battlefields and historic sites. It holds an annual congress and operates the Confederate Historical Institute near a Civil War battlefield. The monthly *Civil War Round Table Digest* is a newsletter relating to the study and preservation of Civil War historic sites. (Contact at PO Box 7388, Little Rock, AK, 72217, (501) 225-3996.)

A similar group is the Civil War Society, a relatively young organization founded in 1975 that now has 3,500 members interested in the history of the U.S. Civil War. The society raises funds for the preservation of Civil War battlefields; sponsors lectures, workshops, and walking tours; conducts a high school essay contest; and bestows awards. It publishes *Civil War*, a bimonthly magazine. (Contact at 24 N. Buckmarsh St. PO Box 770, Berryville, VA, 22611, (800) 247-6253.)

Another organization that emphasizes the Civil War is the 2,000-member Confederate Memorial Association, founded in 1872. Composed of individuals interested in the literature and culture of the South and the Civil War, the association maintains the Confederate Memorial Hall museum and library in Washington. It operates a speakers' bureau and bestows awards in addition to sponsoring the Confederate Embassy Honor Guard and Confederate Calvary. (Contact at 1322 Vermont Ave., NW, Washington, DC, 20005, (202) 483-5700.)

Two specialized organizations are the Civil War Press Corps and the Confederate Memorial Literary Society. The Civil War Press Corps, founded in 1958, is composed of authors, artists, journalists, and others interested in the Civil War and concerned that the war receives "fair treatment" in the U.S. media. The Corps (7674 Heriot Drive, Fayetteville, NC, 26311, (919) 488-0598) sponsors a speakers' bureau, maintains a library and biographical archives, and publishes *Civil War Byline*. The Confederate Memorial Literary Society, founded in 1890, presents annual literary awards for historical research and writing on the Confederacy. It maintains a library that includes the Jefferson Davis collection. The society (1201 E. Clay St., Richmond, VA, 23219, (804) 649-1861) has 8,000 members, including authors, educators, students, and others interested in the study of Confederate history and culture. It maintains a museum of Confederate uniforms, weapons, flags, and espionage.

The Civil War also has a number of organizations for descendants of veterans: the Military Order of the Stars and Bars; United Daughters of the Confederacy; Sons of Confederate Veterans; Military Order of the Loyal Legion of the United States; Dames of the Loyal Legion of the United States of America; Daughters of Union Veterans of the Civil War; and Hood's Texas Brigade Association.

The centennial of the Civil War was observed from 1961–1965. At that time the Civil War was a prominent area of academic specialization, and several classic reference works in the field had already been published. During the 1960s the focus of historical studies began to shift away from the war's political and military aspects toward social, economic, and urban issues. Since the Civil War centennial there has not been a single landmark reference work published. Only in very recent years has the Civil War been the subject of new reference works. This section lists a few of the classic references on the Civil War along with significant newer works.

Library Resources

363. **Civil War Manuscripts: A Guide to Collections in the Manuscript Division of the Library of Congress.** John R. Sellers, comp. Washington: Library of Congress, 1986. 391p. ISBN 0-8444-0381-4.

The 1,064 collections of personal papers described in this guide are mainly from Northern sources. The individuals are both military and nonmilitary figures. The entries are alphabetical by name, with birth and death dates, occupation, and rank given for each individual if available. The number and type of items are given, along with a brief description of the scope and contents, for each collection. The size of the collections varies widely. Information is given on finding aids if they exist. There is an extensive name/subject index. This guide will be useful for researchers searching for primary materials dealing with the Civil War.

Chadwyck-Healey has published a microfilm collection, *A People at War*, of the papers of more than 350 Civil War era figures from the Library of Congress Manuscript Division. The collection contains papers of political and military figures from both sides. Included are noncombatants, women, freedmen, wives of soldiers, artists and photographers, and people from many other walks of life. The collection gives researchers access to a vast amount of original manuscript material without requiring them to visit the Library of Congress. The published index/guide to the collection has the same title.

364. **Civil War Maps: An Annotated List of Maps and Atlases in the Library of Congress.** 2nd ed. Richard W. Stephenson, comp. Washington: Geography and Map Division, Library of Congress, 1989. 410p. ISBN 0-8444-0598-1.

Originally issued for the Civil War centennial in 1961, this guide has been expanded in its second edition. The volume is an attractive one, with reproductions from maps in the collections. The 2,240 maps and 76 atlases are indexed by title, battle, cartographer, place, subject, printer, and engraver, among other things. One of the largest groups in the collection is the Hotchkiss Map Collection of 341 Confederate maps from the Army of Northern Virginia. Another collection, which belonged to General William T. Sherman, consists of 210 maps and 3 atlases showing fortifications and troop movements. The Library of Congress has an extensive collection of maps from the Civil War, and this list enables researchers to ascertain which maps are in the collection. It will be of interest to cartographers and Civil war historians, both amateur and professional.

365. **The Confederacy: A Guide to the Archives of the Government of the Confederate States of America.** Henry Putney Beers. Washington: National Archives and Records Administration, 1986. 536p. Repr. of the 1968 ed. ISBN 0-911333-18-5.

This guide is usually mentioned in tandem with the guide to Union records issued by the National Archives in 1962 (entry 369). The guide for the Confederacy includes collections in the Library of Congress and 29 other library and archival collections, plus additional information from guides and bibliographies to other sets of material. The 1968 edition has been reprinted with a new introduction by Frank G. Burke. The guide is arranged by governmental agency and lists records, finding aids, and other bibliographic references. Because the guide has not been updated in over 25 years, researchers may find more up-to-date information in *Confederate Research Sources: A Guide to Archive Collections* (Ancestry, 1986) by James C. Neagles. Used together, these two guides will provide the researcher with information on the major collections of Confederate government records.

366. **Confederate Imprints: A Check List Based Principally on the Collection of the Boston Athenaeum.** Marjorie Lyle Crandall. Boston: Boston Athenaeum, 1955. 2v. (Robert Charles Billings Fund publication no.11).

Crandall's two-volume bibliography was the first of a number of lists of Confederate imprints and has long been regarded as a classic in the field, not having been updated until 1987 (entry 374). The first volume lists official publications. The second volume lists unofficial publications and has a section of sheet music complied by Richard Harwell. Harwell also compiled *More Confederate Imprints* (Virginia State Library, 1957, 2v.), a supplement with 1,773 additional items arranged in the same categories as the first checklist. Another compilation by Harwell is *Confederate Imprints in the University of Georgia Library* (University of Georgia, 1964). A number of other libraries with extensive collections of Confederate imprints have published lists of holdings. Although these bibliographies have been largely superceded by the 1987 update to *Confederate Imprints,* they are still useful as guides to the holdings of particular libraries.

367. **The Era of the Civil War, 1824–1876.** Louise Arnold. Carlisle Barracks, PA: U.S. Army Military History Institute, 1982. 704p. (Special Bibliography, no.11). S/N 008-029-00123-3).

Although this is a bibliography only of the holdings of the U.S. Army Military History Institute library, the collections of Civil War materials owned by that agency are extensive. One useful feature of the bibliography is the extended time frame defined as the "era" of the Civil War—1820–1876. There are two introductory essays that concentrate on the manuscript collections and museum holdings of the institute. The bibliography is arranged topically into nearly 100 subjects, some of them biographies and specific campaigns, others broad topics such as minorities, prisons, and technology. There is no index. All serious researchers of the nineteenth-century United States should be aware of the collections of the U.S. Army Military History Institute. The bibliography is useful for identifying unique holdings in the institute collections and for identifying materials for site visits or interlibrary loan.

368. **Guide to Civil War Maps in the National Archives.** 2nd ed. Washington: National Archives and Records Administration, 1986. 139p. ISBN 0-911333-36-2.

The largest collection of cartographic records in the world pertaining to the Civil War is located in the Cartographic and Architectural Branch of the National Archives. This guide lists over 8,000 Civil War maps, charts, and plans held by the National Archives. The second edition includes maps from the War Department Collection of Confederate Records and is divided into two parts. The first part is a general guide organized by classification scheme with entry numbers. The map file number, which is necessary for ordering copies from the National Archives and Records Service, is supplied for each item. The second part describes 267 maps in greater detail. There is an index that includes geographical and personal names mentioned in the descriptions. The cartographic records described are useful in geographical, topographical, historical, and genealogical research.

369.   **The Union: A Guide to Federal Archives Relating to the Civil War.** Kenneth W. Munden and Henry Putney Beers. Washington: National Archives and Records Administration, 1986. 721p. ISBN 0-911333-46-0.

This resource lists and describes federal records from the Civil War period and records relating to the war created in subsequent years. It forms the counterpart to the *Guide to the Archives of the Government of the Confederate States* described above (entry 365). The majority of the records in the guide to the Union are in the National Archives, but those in federal records centers and other agencies are also included. The 11 chapters describe records of a major branch or agency of the federal government, with subdivisions for the various bureaus, offices, and other units. Each chapter begins with an historical analysis of the department's organization and wartime functions, with bibliographical references included. The guide then describes those records relating to the department as a whole and cites finding aids and items pertinent to the use of the records. Major collections of related records in the Library of Congress and historical societies are indicated. An appendix lists all groups of federals records relating to the Civil War, cross-referenced to the page in the guide where the records are described. There is also an index. Anyone conducting research on the Civil War will need to make use of the two guides to the records in the National Archives.

Bibliographical Sources

370.   **American Civil War Navies: A Bibliography.** Myron J. Smith, Jr. Metuchen, NJ: Scarecrow, 1972. (American Naval Bibliographies, v.3). ISBN 0-8108-1509-X.

Both Union and Confederate naval forces are included in the nearly 2,900 citations to English-language sources cited in this bibliography. The arrangement is alphabetical by author. Only a few of the items are annotated. The sources include monographs, periodical articles, and documents ranging in date from the 1850s to the 1970s. An appendix reprints the votes of thanks of the 37th and 38th Congresses to the Union naval officers. Another appendix reports on the demise of the federal freshwater Mississippi Squadron. There is a subject index. The bibliography thoroughly covers the literature on Civil War naval forces up to the 1970s. Naval historians, Civil War historians, and afficionados will all find the bibliography an aid to research.

371.   **Civil War Books: A Critical Bibliography.** Allan Nevins, et al. Baton Rouge, LA: Published for the U.S. Civil War Centennial Commission by LSU Press, 1967–1969. 2v.

Although this bibliography lists no scholarship on the Civil War published since the centennial, it remains in use as there has not been a comprehensive bibliography published to supercede it. The bibliography includes some 6,000 books selected and annotated by 15 historians. The entries are arranged in 15 subject sections. Volume 1 includes three sections on military aspects of the War. Volume 2 includes general works, biographies, memoirs, and collective works, with three sections each on the Union and the Confederacy. A cumulative author, title, and subject index covers both volumes. The bibliography is useful for monographic publications on the Civil War written prior to the 1960s, but anyone researching the period will need to search more recent compilations.

372. Civil War Eyewitnesses: An Annotated Bibliography of Books and Articles, 1955–1986. Garold L. Cole. Columbia, SC: University of South Carolina Press, 1988. 351p. ISBN 0-87249-545-0.

The main advantage of this bibliography is that it cites recent materials, the majority published after the 1961 Civil War centennial. The 1,395 items are divided into three subject categories: the North, the South, and anthologies. Sources include books, collected essays, memoirs, autobiographies, and periodical articles. An extensive index provides access to the entries by author, title, and subject. Although the focus of this bibliography is restricted to personal accounts, it is one of a few recent bibliographies on the Civil War. It is useful for researchers of all levels.

An earlier standard bibliography that has not been superseded is *Travels in the Confederate States: A Bibliography* by Merton E. Coulter (University of Oklahoma Press, 1948). This classic reference has been reprinted several times. The bibliography is a selective listing of 500 diaries, letters, regimental histories, and other personal accounts of life and conditions during the Civil War, written during the conflict and after by military figures and civilians, including foreign travelers. Researchers seeking personal accounts of the Civil War will need to use this bibliography and the Cole work cited above. The texts of works cited in *Travels in the Confederate States* have been published in a microform collection, with the same title available from Research Publications.

Another type of "eyewitness account" is found in newspapers. University Microfilms has a collection of *Civil War Newspapers,* an invaluable source for news of battle actions, casualty reports, troop movement notices, and reports on the economic disruptions and political decisions that affected the course of the conflict. *Frank Leslie's Illustrated Newspaper* published nearly 3,000 pictures of battles, sieges, and other war scenes sketched by Leslie's artists at the front. There is no bibliography for the Civil War newspaper microfilm collection. Inquiries can be made to University Microfilms for any newspaper titles falling within the scope of the collection. (Contact at 300 N. Zeeb Road, Ann Arbor, MI 48106-1346, 1-800-521-0600.)

373. The Civil War in the North: A Selective Annotated Bibliography. Eugene C. Murdock, New York: Garland, 1987. 764p. (Wars of the United States, v.9; Garland Reference Library of Social Science, v.254). ISBN 0-8240-8941-3.

The contents of this bibliography cover Abraham Lincoln and the Civil War in the North. The 5,600 entries to books and periodical articles are arranged under subject groupings such as government, the Army, minorities, soldier life, biographies, and personal accounts. The entries are annotated and the sources range from the nineteenth century to the present. There are author and subject indexes. This bibliography is one of the few recent ones on the Civil War, and, although limited to the North, it broadly covers the subject and should be consulted by researchers for any topic dealing with that period.

374. Confederate Imprints: A Bibliography of Southern Publications from Secession to Surrender. T. Michael Parrish and Robert H. Willingham, Jr. Austin, TX: Jenkins; Katonah, NY: Gary A Foster, n.d. 991p. ISBN 0-8363-0712-3.

There is no publication date on the piece, but this bibliography was published in 1987, 30 years after those by Crandall and Harwell (entry 366). There are 40 percent more Confederate imprints listed in this bibliography than were listed in Crandall and Harwell. The organization remains the same as the earlier volumes: official and unofficial publications. The official publications include the Confederate government departments and the states of the Confederacy. The 4,781 unofficial publications are divided into nine sections by format and subjects: military; politics; economics; and social issues; science and medicine; maps and prints; belles-lettres; music and entertainment; sheet music; education; and religion. Bibliographic information is complete, including page numbers and size. Holdings are recorded for over 400 libraries and private collections. Entry numbers are given for those items listed in Crandall and Harwell. An extensive index provides access by author, title, subject, name on broadside, place of publication, name of printer and publisher, and class of publication. There are illustrations of title pages and broadsides. This much-needed update to Crandall and Harwell replaces the two earlier bibliographies and smaller, separate publications for the most part. All researchers concerned with the Confederacy during the Civil War will have to make extensive use of the bibliography.

A microform collection of the texts, *Confederate Imprints, 1861–1865*, has been published by Research Publications. There is a reel index to the 144-reel set. The items have also been cataloged in the OCLC database. The bibliographies and the microfilm collection are central to any research on the Civil War period.

375. **Military Bibliography of the Civil War.** Charles Dornbusch. New York: New York Public Library, 1962–1972. 3v.

Particular attention is paid to military units, both Confederate and Union, in this bibliography of over 3,300 unannotated entries. Included are chronological listings by battle according to geographical region. Sources cited are books, periodical articles, official reports, and ephemera. The cutoff date for the items cited is 1962, although the bibliography was in progress for a number of years afterward. Entries include full bibliographic information and locations for library copies. There is an index of authors. The bibliography remains a standard source on the Civil War.

A microfiche collection based on Dornbusch's bibliography is being published by University Microfilms. *Regimental Histories of the American Civil War,* when completed, will contain 3,000 titles, including state adjutant generals' reports; rosters; published memoirs, letters, and diaries; prisoner of war accounts and other personal narratives; biographical sketches; and other documents. The organization of the microfiche collection follows the geographical groupings in Dornbusch and includes material from the U.S. Army Military History Institute at Carlisle Barracks, the Huntington Library, and the Newberry Library. Another microfiche collection published by UMI is *Pamphlets of the Civil War.* The emphasis in this collection of 1,758 titles is on the issues and attitudes that led to the conflict. The collection is accompanied by its own guide.

Information Sources

376. **A Battlefield Atlas of the Civil War.** Craig L. Symonds. Annapolis, MD: Nautical and Aviation Publishing Company of America, 1983. 106p. ISBN 0-933852-40-1.

This atlas was designed to answer the needs of students and members of the general public with an interest in the Civil War. Symonds is a professor at the U.S. Naval Academy; the cartographer for the atlas, William J. Clipson, is also at that institution. This same team has also produced an atlas for the American Revolution (entry 346). The *Battlefield Atlas of the Civil War* does not replace the older standard Civil War atlases—*The West Point Atlas of the Civil War* (entry 386) and *The Official Military Atlas of the Civil War* (entry 383), but it has many excellent features. This newer atlas is attractive, with portraits and photographs illustrating the text. Arrangement is in four chronological sections: "The Amateur Armies," "The Organized War," "Confederate High Tide," and "Total War." The maps are drawn to scale and use a simple scheme of symbols to show the placement, number, and kinds of troops. The 43 maps form a concise topographical survey of the major Civil War campaigns. Opposite each map is a brief essay that clearly explains the strategy and outcome of the event. The discussions of the battles are lively, with references to the numbered positions on the maps. A list of suggested readings is provided at the end. The atlas is suitable for use by anyone with an interest in Civil War battles.

377. **The Civil War Battlefield Guide.** Frances H. Kennedy. Boston: Houghton Mifflin, 1990. 317p. ISBN 0-395-52282-X.

The Conservation Fund is the sponsor of this chronological survey of 58 major Civil War battlefields. There is a summary account of each battle giving the events leading up to it, as well as the strategies and their significance to the outcomes. There is also a map for each battle showing the positions of the forces, the Union in blue and the Confederate in red. One purpose of this guide is to urge the preservation of battlefields that are not under public ownership. The maps show the boundaries for the portions that are publicly owned. Modern features that impact the sites, such as buildings and roads, are included in the maps. Symonds's battlefield atlas (entry 376) is much more suitable for the study of the battles, but *The Civil War Battlefield Guide* gives a broader perspective on the significance of the battles. It should be used in conjunction with other reference works on the Civil War.

An impressive and attractive set is *Battle Chronicles of the Civil War*, edited by James M. McPherson (Macmillan, 1989). This six-volume guide describes the course of every battle from 1861 to 1865, explaining strategies, tactics, and outcomes.

378. **The Civil War Dictionary.** Rev. ed. Mark Mayo Boatner. New York: McKay, 1988. 974p. ISBN 0-8129-1726-X.

The first edition of this title was published in 1959 in anticipation of the Civil War centennial. Although this edition is billed as revised, there are many indications that very little revision took place, the most telling being that the page numbers are identical and that bibliography, which is 30 years out of date, has not been updated. The volume contains 4,000 entries, with roughly half being short biographical sketches. The other half are terms, events, issues, statistics, and maps. The *Civil War Dictionary* remains useful as a quick reference source.

379. **Compendium of the Confederate Armies.** Stewart Sifakis. New York: Facts on File, 1991–1993.

Those who have studied the Confederate forces during the Civil War have longed for a reference comparable to that of Frederick Dyer's *Compendium of the War of the Rebellion* (entry 380), which presents statistics and historical material on each unit in the Union Army. At last there is a series on military units that fought in the Confederate Army. The series contains 10 volumes arranged by state and a last volume comprising tables of brigades and higher commands. Entries for each unit include organizational information, history, and final disposition; the name of the first colonel of the regiment, with an alphabetical listing of the field command; the higher assignments of the unit with dates; the service of the unit in the field; and a listing of available histories, memoirs, biographies, and diaries dealing with the unit. Each volume has an extensive bibliography and index. The Confederate compendium will be a much-used and essential reference source for all students, genealogists, and local and Civil War historians for many years to come.

380. **Compendium of the War of the Rebellion, Compiled and Arranged from Official Records of the Federal and Confederate Armies...** Frederick H. Dyer, comp. Dayton, OH: National Historical Society, in cooperation with the Press of Morningside Bookshop, 1979. 2v. Repr. of the 1908 ed. (Torch Press).

Dyer's *Compendium of the War of the Rebellion* has long been a unique reference for the study of the Union forces during the Civil War. Originally published in 1908 in one volume of 1,796 pages, it has been reprinted several times. An introduction by Civil War historian Bell Irvin Wiley was added in 1959 to the reprint by Thomas Yoseloff. The work is divided into three large sections. Part 1 is statistical, with numbers and organization; compositions and leaders of departments, armies, corps, division, and brigades; locations of national cemeteries; and sketches arranged numerically by state. In part 2 are lists taken from other sources of engagements and losses arranged by both state and chronology. Over 10,400 conflicts are also arranged by actions, battles, campaigns, and so on. The largest section is part 3, "Regimental Histories," consisting of a concise statement for each regiment and lesser unit telling where the units were organized and where they fought; service records and losses are included. In compiling the work, Dyer examined hundreds of original muster rolls, talked with thousands of veterans, and examined all available printed sources, including the 128 volumes of the *War of the Rebellion: Official Records of the Union and Confederate Armies* (U.S. War Department, 1880–1901). The Dyer work is an encyclopedia of federal units and actions. Archivists, researchers, and writers have consulted it constantly since 1908, and it remains the only source of its kind.

381. **Great Battles of the Civil War.** John Macdonald. New York: Macmillan, 1988. 200p. ISBN 0-02-577300-3.

The thesis put forth in this atlas is that terrain plays a large role in the operations of a military campaign. To illustrate this point, Macdonald selected 17 major Civil War campaigns and constructed three-dimensional landscape models via computer mapping of the geographical features of the battle sites. Troop movements are marked to show the effects of the terrain on the action. The maps are accompanied by text, graphs of troops and losses, and other illustrations. The interesting analysis using modern computer technology makes this a unique tool among Civil War reference works. It should be of interest to students, historians, and military history buffs.

There is another publication with exactly the same title, *Great Battles of the Civil War*, published by Beekman in 1989. This 96-page volume treats 36 of the most important Civil War battles through descriptive narratives illustrated with reproductions of chromolithographs from the late nineteenth century by Louis Kurz and Alexander Allison. In addition, there are diagrams, sidebars, and photographs that further illustrate the battles and facts about them. This attractive volume presents an overview of the Civil War through the narrative on the major battles.

382. **Historical Times Illustrated Encyclopedia of the Civil War.** Patricia L. Faust, ed. New York: Harper, 1986. 850p. ISBN 0-06-181261-7.

This work is the best single-volume reference for information on all aspects of the Civil War period. It contains 2,000 entries and 1,000 black-and-white illustrations. Although any work on the Civil War will of necessity be heavily weighted toward the military, in this work economic, social, cultural, political, diplomatic, and technological issues receive considerable space. The entries are signed and contain a wealth of detail. Most biographies have portraits, and sources are given for all photographs and illustrations. There is no index, but terms and names for which there are separate entries are set in upper case within the text of other entries, forming an effective cross-reference system. The encyclopedia is useful for students, researchers, and the general public.

An "encyclopedia" of the Civil War is the *USA–Civil War,* a CD-ROM database (Quanta Press, St. Paul, MN). The product is marketed by Wayzata Technology under the title *The*

Civil War. The database includes biographies, statistics, a chronology, information on battles, campaigns, and foreign involvement for the years 1860–1865.

A new reference work due to be published by Simon and Schuster in late 1993 is *Encyclopedia of the Confederacy*. The editor-in-chief of the projected 4 volume work is Richard N. Current. The encyclopedia will look at the confederation of states as a nation and not just as the adversary to the Union in the Civil War. The encyclopedia will contain approximately 1,500 articles including 860 biographies. The work will be heavily illustrated, cross-referenced and indexed. It will be an authoritative resource for the Confederacy and the Civil War period.

383. **The Official Military Atlas of the Civil War.** Calvin D. Cowles, comp. New York: Arno Press; New York: Crown Publishers, 1978. ISBN 0-405-11198-3 (Arno); 9-517-53407-X (Crown).

Originally published in 1891 by the U.S. War Department to accompany *The War of the Rebellion: Official Records of the Union and Confederate Armies* (1880–1901), this atlas has been reprinted several times. The military maps are contemporary from the war, many drawn on the spot and used in battles or to accompany action reports written by commanders. The originals have been reproduced with errors and mistakes uncorrected in order that the information be shown as it was available to the commanders at the time. A few general topographic maps drawn later were added to complete the information in the atlas. The maps are divided into four groupings in the atlas: military operations in the field; general topographic maps; military divisions and departments; and miscellaneous plates. In addition to the maps, there are engravings of fortifications, battle scenes, troops, and terrain. Uniforms, weapons, equipment, flags, and insignia are illustrated in 209 drawings. An introduction by noted historian Henry Steele Commager was added to the reprint edition in 1962. Further indexing was also provided to augment the original indexes. In contrast to modern maps drawn to explicate and illustrate battle strategies, the maps in the *Official Military Atlas* reproduce original source material. This volume will never be replaced as a definitive resource for research on Civil War military strategy.

384. **The Union Army 1861–1865: Organization and Operations. Volume I: The Eastern Theater. Volume II: The Western Theater.** Frank J. Welcher. Bloomington, IN: Indiana University Press, 1989. v.1: 1,065p. ISBN 0-253-36453-1. v.2: 1,088p. ISBN 0-253-36454-X.

The organizational history of the Union's 4 military divisions, 26 departments, 13 field armies and other subdivisions forms the core of this reference work. The set gives a complete account of all Union military divisions, departments, and subunits, including geographical boundaries and important dates. It makes it possible to track the activities of a specific unit. Information given includes the date of creation and the composition of each unit; changes in organization and commanders; and dates of the end of the unit. Details of personnel and maneuvers are also provided. Half of the first volume, on the Eastern Theater, deals with battles and campaigns, giving itineraries of all major units. Volume 2 includes extensive name and unit indexes for the set. This work contains much of the information in Dyer's *Compendium of the War of the Rebellion* (entry 380) but does not completely replace it. The modern work will be a core source for military historians and buffs of the Civil War.

385. **Warships of the Civil War Navies.** Paul H. Silverstone. Annapolis, MD: Naval Institute Press, 1989. 271p. ISBN 0-87021-783-6.

This is the first reference work that treats all of the vessels that participated in the naval forces during the Civil War. The work provides a comprehensive listing that includes detailed descriptions and brief war records. The vessels are divided into four categories: U.S. Navy warships, U.S. revenue cutter service, U.S. coast survey, and the Confederate States Navy. The Confederate section is divided geographically, and the federal sections are divided by size and mode of propulsion as well as type of duties. The descriptions include name, builder, construction date, dimensions, tonnage, machinery, armor, service record, later history, and other details. There is a list of shipbuilders and an index by ship name. The book is amply illustrated with photographs and drawings. Silverstone has brought a considerable amount of information together into this volume, which is a definitive reference on the naval vessels of the Civil War. It is useful for all researchers seeking information on ships of the period.

386. **The West Point Atlas of the Civil War.** Vincent J. Esposito, ed. New York: Praeger, 1962. 323p.

This work is accepted as the standard military atlas of the Civil War. The atlas was extracted from the larger *West Point Atlas of American Wars* (entry 308), developed for instructional use at the U.S. Military Academy. The Civil War atlas shows troop movements in great detail, even down to the hour of the day, through the use of symbols in color. Other details include troop strength, landmarks, topography, and fortifications. Although it is very detailed, the atlas is also clear and easy to understand. The accompanying text explains and evaluates the tactics and strategies of the opposing forces. There is an annotated bibliography, which is now quite out of date. The atlas is useful for students and all others interested in military strategy of the Civil War.

Biographical Sources

387. **Biographical Dictionary of the Confederacy.** Jon L. Wakelyn. Westport, CT: Greenwood, 1977. 601p. ISBN 0-8371-6124-X.

Approximately 650 individuals who played prominent roles—political, military, economic, and social—in the Confederacy are profiled in this biographical work. The information is drawn from other published biographical sources, although these are not indicated. In addition to the biographical sketches there is a computer analysis of 72 variables from information in the biographies. Wakelyn analyzes the quantitative information in four chapters at the beginning of the work. There is a bibliography and an index. Five appendices show 1) general mobility before and after the Civil War; 2) principal occupations; 3) religious affiliation; 4) education; and 5) pre- and postwar political party affiliations. The biographical information on Confederate commanders does not supercede that of other works, including *Generals in Grey* by Ezra Warner (entry 390n). This dictionary is a good one-volume reference work on prominent individuals in the Confederacy. It is suitable for use by students, researchers, and the general public.

388. **Biographical Register of the Confederate Congress.** Ezra J. Warner and W. Buck Yearns. Baton Rouge, LA: LSU Press, 1975. 319p. ISBN 0-8071-0092-7.

The Confederate Congress is not heard of often because it was only in existence during the war years and did not play a large role in the military conduct of the war. Nonetheless, the biographies of its 267 members collected into one volume do expand the amount of established reference information on the Confederacy. Many of the men who served in the Confederate Congress had been U.S. Congressmen prior to the war. The biographies contain all the information the authors were able to find through extensive research, but some of the figures remain relatively obscure in spite of the effort. The work contains four appendices that furnish information on the sessions of the Confederate Congress, standing committees, membership, and maps of the Occupied Confederate Territory, 1861–1864. A bibliography of sources used to compile the biographical information completes the volume. This biographical work is rather specialized and will probably only be used by researchers seeking information on the Confederate Congress or individuals who served in that body.

389. **The Confederate Governors.** W. Buck Yearns, ed. Athens, GA: University of Georgia Press, 1985. 291p. ISBN 0-8203-0719-X.

The role of the governors of the 13 Confederate states during the war is approached through biographical essays. All but 2 of the 15 men who served in office during the war were born in the South; most were young lawyers with political experience. Most of those elected early in the war years were Democrats, but as the war wore on Whigs and Unionists were elected to office in some states. The immense problems faced by the state governments are apparent: feeding the civilian population and supplying troops; overcoming serious financial difficulties; dealing with the Confederate government; maintaining home defense; and numerous others. This book brings together discussions of the kinds of problems faced by the Southern states during the war and the responses to those problems. The editor concludes that the governors effectively aided the war effort. The volume forms an excellent political history of the states of the Confederacy traced through the men who led during that difficult time. A bibliography comes at the end and an index. The work can be used both as a biographical reference work and as a scholarly treatment of the subject by students and researchers.

390. **Generals in Blue: Lives of the Union Commanders.** Ezra J. Warner. Baton Rouge, LA: LSU Press, 1964. 679p.

This work and its earlier companion volume, *Generals in Grey* (LSU, 1959) by the same author, have been well known as standards on the Civil War since their publication. Warner spent years researching the two biographical works, contacting descendants and searching family records and newspapers files, to establish facts about the lives of 425 Confederate and 583 Union generals. The biographies contain sound opinions and analysis as well as biographical facts. The two works have not been surpassed or replaced by any subsequent reference publications and are still the most useful for serious research.

A recent work that complements the two titles by Warner is *Civil War Generals: Categorical Listings and a Biographical Directory* (Greenwood, 1986). This volume features a conspectus arrangement of listings by rank, date of birth and death, college, and vocation before and after the war. There is also a listing by battle of those killed, with dates. Following the listings are four-line biographical sketches. This work does not contain as much information as do the Warner titles. The presentation of the information makes it more of a quick reference source, but the Warner titles are to be preferred for serious research.

391. **Who Was Who in the Civil War.** Stewart Sifakis. New York: Facts on File, 1988. 766p. ISBN 0-8160-1055-2.

Biographies of approximately 2,500 individuals, both military and civilian, are contained in this *Who Was Who*. The essay biographies concentrate on the individual's wartime activities and accomplishments but also follow through during the postwar period. The biographies are lively and interesting, often quoting humorous comments made by or about the individual. Some entries give references to other sources for more information. Illustrations from the period are interspersed throughout the volume. There is a selective critical bibliography, a list of illustrations (with sources indicated by codes), and a glossary of place names. One appendix contains a chronology of Civil War battles and events, and the other gives a list of Union officers thanked by the U.S. Congress. There is an index that includes occupational titles, lists each side's participants by rank, and cites references to places and events. The biographical information is fuller than that given in Boatner's *Civil War Dictionary* (entry 378). Both works are useful as reference tools for students, researchers, and the general public, but *Who Was Who* is the preferred biographical work.

Facts on File has published two volumes extracted from *Who Was Who in the Civil War;* the titles are *Who Was Who in the Confederacy* (1988) and *Who Was Who in the Union* (1988). The duplication makes it unnecessary for libraries to own the individual volumes, but inquirers can use either the one-volume or the two-volume formats, as both contain the same information.

Spanish-American War (1898)

392.   **The Spanish-American War: An Annotated Bibliography.** Anne Cipriano Venzon. New York: Garland, 1990. 255p. (Wars of the United States, v.11; Garland Reference Library of the Humanities, v.1,120). ISBN 0-8240-7974-4.

The entire time period of the Spanish-American War, extending to 1902 through the U.S.-Phillipine conflict, is covered in this selective bibliography of over 1,000 items. It contains English-language source materials written between 1898 and 1986, including: scholarly monographs, periodical articles, dissertations, personal accounts, War and Navy Department reports, and other government documents. Fiction, poetry, and music are included but not annotated. Only printed source materials are cited in the bibliography, but there is a section on special collections for further research. The entries are organized into topical chapters. Several chapters are devoted to public opinion on the issues raised by the war, such as expansionism and anti-imperialism. The bibliography is useful for students, scholars, and general readers.

World War I (1914–1918)

There are many associations and societies that encompass both world wars, probably because the two conflicts were waged within one generation of each other and were fought on some of the same terrain, with the German adversary in common. Groups specifically focused on the first World War are the Veterans of World War I of USA, Widows of World War I, World War I Overseas Flyers, and Allied Airborne Association.

The first World War has been eclipsed in history by the magnitude of the second World War. There have been but a few reference works published in recent years that focus on World War I.

393.   **America and World War I: A Selected Annotated Bibliography of English-Language Sources.** David R. Woodward and Robert Franklin Maddox. New York: Garland, 1985. 368p. (Wars of the United States, v.6; Garland Reference Library of Social Science, v.259). ISBN 0-8240-8939-1.

The topical organization of this bibliography of over 2,000 items provides an overview of the impact of the war upon the United States. The main bibliographic chapters proceed chronologically from the origins and outbreak of the war, touching upon the home front, the war's military aspects, its social and intellectual impact, diplomacy, and the peace settlement. The entries are varied and include books, periodical articles, dissertations, review essays, and films. Two reference chapters cover printed works and collections for archival research, including oral history collections. A chronology of events from August 1914 through June 1919 is provided. There are author and subject indexes. The sources were published before 1983, making this bibliography still reasonably current. It is useful for all students and researchers of the World War I period and the impact of the war.

A more limited work is by A.G.S. Enser, *A Subject Bibliography of the First World War: Books in English, 1914–1987* (Brookfield, VT: Gower, 1990). This bibliography of monographic works includes personal memoirs. It has a topical arrangement, but there are author and anonymous title indexes. A list of subject headings eases access to the volume's contents.

394.   **The American Field Services Archives of World War I, 1914–1917.** L. D. Geller, comp. Westport, CT: Greenwood, 1989. 87p. (Bibliographies and Indexes in World History, no.16). ISBN 0-313-26794-4.
   This slim volume describes the collections of the archives of the American Field Service, a voluntary medical organization that operated in France from 1914–1917, at which time it became part of the U.S. Army. The volume contains an essay on the American Field Service and the sources in the archives, followed by descriptions of over 50 archival collections. An appendix contains box and folder lists. There is a name and subject index. The small volume is attractively illustrated with over 50 photographs from the AFS archives. A grant from the National Historical Publications and Records Commission contributed to the completion of the bibliography. Students and scholars of World War I will want to explore the research materials contributing to perspectives on the conduct of the war in France, Franco-American relations, and the contributions of the leaders and volunteers of the American Field Service to the war effort.

395.   **Army Uniforms of World War I: European and United States Armies and Aviation Services.** Andrew Mollo. Poole, England: Blandford Press, 1977; distr. by Sterling Publishing, 1986 printing. 219p. ISBN 0-7137-1928-1.
   The illustrations in this work are drawings based on actual uniforms or photographs, resulting in consistency and accuracy in the details depicted. The only pieces not illustrated are the various insignia, which are only described in the text. The uniforms included are from the U.S. and European forces and are arranged by country. The accompanying text covers detailed aspects of the uniforms and traces the changes in type and design throughout the war. The work is of interest to all military enthusiasts as well as historians.

396.   **Chronicle of the First World War.** Randal Gray and Christopher Argyle. New York: Facts on File, 1990–1991 2v. ISBN 0-8160-2139-2 (v.1); 0-8160-2595-9 (v.2).
   Every aspect of World War I, military, political, and international, is tracked in this two-volume chronology. Volume 1 spans the period from before the assassination of Archduke Ferdinand in 1914 to 1916. Volume 2 continues through 1917 to the end of the war in 1918 and the finalization of the peace process in 1921. The volumes present a day-by-day record of the war accompanied by critical analyses of events. Each volume is illustrated with maps and contains a foreword, glossary, tables, statistics, bibliography, and index. Volume 2 contains a biographical section of over 100 key figures in the war. The source is scholarly and can be used for quick reference or read vertically as an overview of the war.

397.   **Great Battles of World War I.** Anthony O. Livesey. New York: Macmillan, 1989. 200p. ISBN 0-02-583131-3.
   Macmillan has published computer-produced atlases for the Civil War (entry 381) and World War II (entry 406), as well as a general volume, *Great Battles of the World*. In the World War I work, 18 major battles are presented in three-dimensional maps constructed through computer graphics. The book is a comprehensive history of World War I with photographs, paintings, and drawings in addition to the maps. The text is accompanied by sidebars focusing on weaponry, uniforms, ships, planes, and notable persons. The work illustrates the horrors of the trench warfare and the tactics that resulted in the high casualty

rate (over 8 million killed). The work can serve as a reference source or as supplemental reading for students.

Another Macmillan publication, the *First World War Atlas* (1971), contains 159 clearly drawn maps. The atlas is one of a series by Martin Gilbert; the World War I work has an introduction by Viscount Montgomery of Alamein. Chronologically arranged, the maps visually cover the political, economic, military, and diplomatic aspects of the war. Statistics accompany the maps. A short bibliography and index complete the work. Although not a definitive military source, the atlas can be used by students and the general public and in conjunction with the *West Point Atlas of American Wars* (entry 308).

398. **Subject Catalog of the World War I Collection.** New York Public Library. Boston: G. K. Hall, 1961. 4v.

One of the largest collections of materials relating to World War I is in the New York Public Library. The catalog, published by G. K. Hall, is an alphabetical subject listing of books, pamphlets, and analytics for periodical articles. The collection contains European materials in many languages as well as English-language materials. Although the catalog does not contain recent scholarly literature, it is a comprehensive source for contemporary publications produced during the war and in the years immediately afterward. It is useful not just as a record of the holdings of the New York Public Library but also as a reference for scholarly research on the World War I period.

399. **World War I Aviation Books in English: An Annotated Bibliography.** James Philip Noffsinger. Metuchen, NJ: Scarecrow, 1987. 305p. ISBN 0-8108-1951-1.

This bibliography of over 1,600 items is arranged in one alphabetical sequence by author. Not all entries are annotated, but the bibliography is fairly comprehensive for monographic works on World War I aviation, including rare editions. The subject matter of the titles cited ranges from technical aspects of the aircraft to personal memoirs and biographies of the famous pilots and other personalities of the period. The work is attractively illustrated, and there is a subject index. The bibliography partially updates that of Myron J. Smith, *World War I in the Air* (Scarecrow, 1977), but does not replace it, because the Smith work covers a wider variety of source materials. It has an aviation chronology for the war years and a list of Aces by country, ranked by number of "kills." Both bibliographies will be of interest to World War I historians, aviation historians, and enthusiasts.

World War II (1941–1945)

In the second World War fighting began on much the same terrain as in World War I, but the technology of weapons, airplanes, and sea craft was much advanced. Because many people in Europe and the United States still had memories of the earlier war, the second war was entered very reluctantly. Once the United States was committed, however, the war became global. The last major officially declared war, it was fought on all continents except Australia. The Cold War that followed lasted for four decades. The fiftieth anniversary of the United States' entrance into World War II was observed in 1991.

The American Committee on the History of the Second World War is a small organization (300-plus members) composed of academic and government historians and others interested in promoting historical research on all aspects of World War II. The organization meets annually in conjunction with the American Historical Association and publishes a semiannual *Newsletter* that includes books reviews and emphasizes archival and bibliographical resources (c/o Clayton James. Virginia Military Institute, Department of History and Politics, Lexington, VA, 24450, (703) 464-7243).

The global scope of World War II has occasioned the formation of many societies and organizations, some by type of military unit, some by geographical region. There are approximately seven pages of associations with a World War II focus in the *Encyclopedia of Associations*. There are still many veterans of the second World War living, and the history of that conflict will be preserved through video records, which had just reached a level of sophistication sufficient to capture the reality of war.

Many popular works on aircraft, ships, tanks, artillery, and the like have been published. Only a few such recently published works are described in this section. The majority of the reference works in this section are for scholarly research.

Library Resources

400. Subject Catalog of the World War II Collection. New York Public Library. Boston: G. K. Hall, 1977. 3v. ISBN 0-8161-0074-8.

Material in more than 200 subjects under the heading "World War II," plus material from many other related subject headings, is brought together in this catalog from the New York Public Library research collections. Although the information gained from the catalog will have to be updated for more current references, the breadth of the New York Public Library collections makes the catalog a major reference tool for researchers of World War II.

Another major resource for World War II research is the National Archives. *Federal Records of World War II* is a descriptive listing of the records in the National Archives. First published in a two-volume set by the National Archives in 1950–1951, the title was reprinted by Gale in 1982. Although it has not been updated, the volumes reflect the records deposited with the National Archives after the war. Volume 1 lists records of civilian agencies and volume 2 lists records of military agencies. The set has a name, acronym, and analytical index contained in volume 2. The set is useful for helping researchers determine World War II holdings in the National Archives.

Bibliographical Sources

401. Investigations of the Attack on Pearl Harbor: Index to Government Hearings. Stanley H. Smith, comp. New York: Greenwood, 1990. 251p. (Bibliographies and Indexes in Military Studies, no.3). ISBN 0-313-26884-3.

The surprise attack on Pearl Harbor by the Japanese has been the subject of eight official inquiries by branches of the armed services and Congress. The reports of the hearings were published as the *Hearings before the Joint Committee on the Investigation of the Pearl Harbor Attack* (40 parts, Government Printing Office, 1946). In addition to the testimony, the volumes contain exhibits, charts, and illustrations prepared for the hearings. Although two indexes to congressional proceedings that include the Pearl Harbor hearings have been published—*Witness Index to the United States Congressional Hearings: 25th–89th Congress, 1839–1966* (Greenwood, 1974, microfiche) and *CIS U.S. Congressional Committee Hearings Index, Part V: 79th–82nd Congress, 1943–1952* (CIS, 1981)—there did not exist a separate satisfactory index to the Pearl Harbor investigations until the Smith work was published. The index references people, places, aircraft, ships, and events mentioned in the reports. A preface includes background information on the hearings and reports. The index makes the hearings and accompanying documents accessible to anyone seeking information on the events in the Pacific theater in World War II.

402. **The Second World War: A Select Bibliography of Books in English Since 1975.**
Arthur L. Funk. Claremont, CA: Regina Books, 1985. 219p. ISBN 0-941690-15-6.

The expiration of the 30-year rule for archival materials dealing with World War II opened up new avenues for research, resulting in numerous studies dealing with the war. There are two bibliographies that have focused on monographs published since 1975: the work by Funk and *A Subject Bibliography of the Second World War, and Aftermath; Books in English, 1975–1987* by A.G.S. Enser (Gower, 1990). Enser also has a similar bibliography on the First World War (entry 393n). Of the two World War II bibliographies, Funk's work is more suitable for serious research. It is divided into five sections. The first contains bibliographies, research aids, and collections of documents; section two has works dealing with the international situation during the war; the third section contains titles on military tactics and strategy, political and diplomatic issues, economics, and technology; the fourth section lists monographs devoted to the consequences of the war. A last section lists titles on the individual nations involved in the war. The Enser work is organized alphabetically by subject with author and subject indexes and is less complicated to use. Both are suitable for use by students and the general public, but the Funk work is more suitable for advanced research.

403. **The War Against Japan, 1941–1945: An Annotated Bibliography.** John J. Sbrega. New York: Garland, 1989. 1,050p. (Wars of the United States, v.10; Garland Reference Library of Social Science, v.258). ISBN 0-8240-8940-5.

The scope of this bibliography, its currency, its broad coverage, and its excellent annotations make it the best resource on the war in the Pacific. There are over 5,200 citations to works published through 1987. Sources included are reference works, histories, biographies, articles, fictional works, official reports, and other government documents. The volume is organized into six chapters that follow the LC classification. Military matters make up a goodly portion of the work, but political, social, economic, and religious aspects of the Pacific war are well covered. The appendices include a list of periodicals consulted; a directory of Japanese-American relocation centers; a chronology; and author and subject indexes. This bibliography should be used by students and all researchers seeking resources on the war in the Pacific.

404. **World War II: The European and Mediterranean Theaters: An Annotated Bibliography.** Myron J. Smith, Jr. New York: Garland, 1984. 450p. (Wars of the United States, v.2; Garland Reference Library of Social Science, v.217). ISBN 0-8240-9013-6.

Although he is best known for the American Naval Bibliography series, Myron J. Smith has expanded coverage of World War II to include the air and land conflicts. The 3,000-plus sources cited in this selective bibliography are all in English. Publication dates are from 1940 to 1983. Sources include books, periodical articles, theses, and dissertations. A documentary film guide is a special section. There is a list of periodicals consulted. The bibliography is divided into reference works, special studies, "The War in the Air," "The War on Land," and "The War at Sea." The bibliography is suitable for all levels of research.

405. **World War II at Sea: Bibliography of Sources in English.** Myron J. Smith, Jr. Metuchen, NJ: Scarecrow, 1976. 3v. ISBN 0-8108-0884-6 (v.1); 0-8108-0969-9 (v.2); 0-8108-0970-2 (v.3).

This three-volume bibliography of over 10,000 items published between 1939 and 1973 has been supplemented by *World War II at Sea: A Bibliography of Sources in English, 1974–1990* (Scarecrow, 1990). Together these two works form a comprehensive bibliography for the study of the maritime aspects of World War II. The first two volumes are divided into the European (v.1) and Pacific (v.2) theaters. The third volume covers general works, aircraft, ordnance, ships, and the Allied and Axis home fronts. Volume 3 also includes the "All Hands Chronology" of the war years and comprehensive indexes for the three volumes. The supplemental volume follows much the same organization. Items listed include books, periodical articles, theses, and dissertations, but not literary works. The sources reflect popular, academic, and military periodicals. Complete bibliographic information is given, but the majority of the entries are not annotated, and those that are have only a line or two. These bibliographies are both up to date and comprehensive. They will be used by all students and researchers seeking information on naval actions during World War II.

Information Sources

406. **Battles and Battlescenes of World War II.** New York: Macmillan, 1989. 160p. ISBN 0-02-897175-2.
      The essential facts and a concise summary of 52 of the most important battles of World War II are given in this popular reference work. Air, land, and sea battles in Europe, Asia, and North Africa are included. Each entry contains factual information on date, location, object, opposing sides, casualties, and results. Each section contains a narrative about the battle and a list of suggested readings. Maps and photographs are provided for each battle. There is a chronological table at the end that gives data, location, opposing sides, and the nature of the battle. There is an index. This informative work should appeal to students and the general public.

407. **Destroyers of World War II: An International Encyclopedia.** M. J. Whitley. Annapolis, MD: Naval Institute Press, 1988. 320p. ISBN 0-87021-326-1.
      All destroyer-class ships in existence during the time period 1939–1945 for all nations, including completed and constructed vessels, are recorded in this encyclopedia. The arrangement is alphabetical by country and then by class of destroyer. Technical data are given for the class, displacement, length, beam, draught, machinery, and so on. The class is then described in three categories—design, modifications, and service. There is a short introduction and history for each country's vessels. An historical essay on torpedo boats/destroyers is at the beginning of the volume. Numerous photographs and drawings of individual ships illustrate the text. There is an alphabetical index of ship names. The encyclopedia is suitable for serious research by military historians and naval historians or others with a keen interest in World War II and naval battles.

408. **Historical Encyclopedia of World War II.** Marcel Braudot. New York: Facts on File, 1989. 574p. ISBN 0-8160-2109-0.
      A single-volume encyclopedia can only cover the essentials on a subject such as World War II. This encyclopedia is suitable as a recent source for use by students and the general public or as a quick reference source. It is illustrated with over 100 black-and-white maps and figures. There is a bibliography but no index.

409. **U.S. Army Ships and Watercraft of World War II.** David H. Grover. Annapolis, MD: Naval Institute Press, 1987. 280p. ISBN 0-87021-766-6.
      Although the subject of this work would seem somewhat specialized, it certainly is not small. The U.S. Army had over 127,000 naval vessels of various types in operation during World War II, nearly twice as many as did the Navy. This was not a fleet of battleships but rather a miscellany of ships needed for various chores—tugboats, hospital ships, tankers, transports, and communication ships. Each chapter in the work is devoted to a particular class

of ship with data and facts such as dimension, tonnage, build, engines, and builder. The postwar fate is also given. A glossary, bibliography, and index to the volume are presented. The work is attractively illustrated with photographs. The little-known subject makes this work valuable to those interested in naval history and World War II, students and researchers alike.

410. **War Maps: World War II, from September 1939 to August 1945, Air, Sea and Land, Battle by Battle.** Simon Goodenough. New York: St. Martin's Press, 1982. ISBN 0-312-85584-2.

The 200 maps, battle plans, and theater charts in this work make it an ideal companion to keep close by when reading historical works on World War II. The larger portion of the work, the first 140 pages, covers the European theater. The last 45 pages are devoted to the Pacific theater. There is an index to the maps at the end. In addition to the maps, there are explanatory text and photographs. The maps vary in scale, but the quality is high. This work will appeal to students, teachers, and librarians seeking a visual reference work to supplement other works on World War II.

411. **World War II: America at War, 1941–1945.** Norman Polmar and Thomas B. Allen. New York: Random, 1991. 940p. ISBN 0-394-58530-5.

The U.S. point of view is emphasized in this encyclopedia on World War II. The work covers political, military, and social issues of the war. The first part of the book is a chronology from 1941 to 1945 with short descriptions. There is a "War Guide, A–Z" with 2,400 entries, their length depending upon the significance of the person, event, or subject. The "War Guide" is illustrated throughout with maps, photographs, tables, and drawings. Appendices include military ranks, battle streamers, and stars for each of the armed forces. A subject bibliography of additional sources is provided. Two indexes, a "Personality Index," and a "Code and Project Names Index," conclude the book. This encyclopedia is an up-to-date and useful general reference work on World War II. It compares favorably to similar works such as the *Dictionary of the Second World War* by Elizabeth-Anne Wheal (Bedrick, 1990). It is of use to students and the general public and for quick reference by researchers.

Korean War (1950–1953)

The last "wars" after World War II were not officially declared wars but limited conflicts in which the United States endeavored to help one half of a divided country in its struggle against the other half, which maintained a totalitarian form of government. The patriotism of World War II began to wane during the Korean conflict. The long years of the Vietnam conflict involved a new generation not inured to the casualties that had been deemed necessary to preserve democracy in previous wars. The Korean War is remembered by the Korean War Veterans Association, the Chosin Few, and Korean Veterans International.

There are not many reference works published that focus strictly on the Korean conflict. The Vietnam War has only in recent years begun to attain sufficient historical distance to become a subject for objective research. The reference works on these two recent wars are described in the last two sections of this chapter.

412. **Historical Dictionary of the Korean War.** James I. Matray, ed. Westport, CT: Greenwood, 1991. 626p. ISBN 0-313-25924-0.

The purpose of this work is to contribute to an understanding of the issues surrounding U.S. involvement in the Korean War. The approximately 500 signed entries cover prewar events, battles, strategies, documents, diplomacy, and truce talks. There are biographical sketches of government and military leaders from the United States, China, North and South Korea, and the USSR. Journalists and diplomats from other countries are also included. Cross-references and bibliographical references are given in the entries. There are 20 detailed maps of major battles and offensives placed in the front of the book. Statistical information on casualties, prisoners of war, lists of commanders, and so on are given in appendices. There is a chronology and a selective topical bibliography. The work is scholarly and has a detailed index. It can serve as a factual reference work or as a resource volume for serious study of the Korean War.

A full-text graphics database, *USA Wars—Korea*, is available from Quanta Press, Inc. (St. Paul, MN) and also through Wayzata Technology under the title *The Korean War*. The database includes biographies, a chronology, and information on U.S. and U.N. forces and campaigns.

413. The Korean War: An Annotated Bibliography. Keith D. McFarland. Garland, 1986. 463p. (Wars of the United States, v.8; Garland Reference Library of Social Science, v.189). ISBN 0-8240-9068-3.

This selective annotated bibliography lists over 2,300 English-language items dealing with the Korean conflict. Sources included are monographs, journal articles, government publications, personal accounts, and theses and dissertations. The work is divided into 23 topical chapters preceded by a chronology of the war. Topics covered include the background of the war and the U.S. decision to intervene, the home front, the U.S. Army in Korea, the United Nations and the war, the Truman-MacArthur controversy, and a last chapter on analyses and consequences. A map of Korea is provided, and there are author and subject indexes. Although not an exhaustive bibliography, the work forms an overview of the subject. It is the first bibliography since that by Carroll Blanchard in 1964, *Korean War Bibliography and Maps of Korea* (Korean Conflict Research Foundation). The work will be useful to all levels of readers with an interest in the Korean War.

414. Korean War Almanac. Harry G. Summers, Jr. Facts on File, 1990. 330p. ISBN 0-8160-1737-9.

The *Korean War Almanac* focuses more on the United States and its military involvement in the Korean War than does the *Historical Dictionary of the Korean War* (entry 412). The work is divided into three parts. The first part, "The Setting," discusses the two Koreas. The second part is a chronology from June 25, 1950 to September 6, 1953. The largest portion of the work is the third section, "The Korean War A-Z," which contains 375 entries covering people, weapons and equipment, campaigns and battles, military terms, and political factors, issues, and events. Some entries provide references for further reading. The articles on weapons are very detailed. Biographical sketches cover the person's life, with an emphasis on the individual's role in the Korean War. There are 10 maps and numerous black-and-white photographs, as well as a selective bibliography and an index. The coverage in this work is not as balanced and objective as that of the *Historical Dictionary of the Korean War*. The almanac is useful for general readers and students, but researchers will want to use other reference works in addition to this one.

Vietnam War (1957–1975)

The Vietnam conflict was the first war in history to be covered on daily television news broadcasts. It is generally acknowledged that the immediacy of the news coverage had a large influence on the population back home. Modern technology also brings graphic images to a CD-ROM database, *USA Wars—Vietnam, available from Quanta Press (St. Paul, MN) and also through Wayzata Technology under the title *Vietnam Remembered. The full-text graphics database covers U.S. involvement in Vietnam from the late 1950s to 1975. Information and images include unit histories, order of military rank, order of battle, medals and awards, and all names listed on the Vietnam War Memorial in Washington, D.C. The addition of images makes this database an attractive source for historical information on the Vietnam conflict. It can be utilized by students and the general public in conjunction with the printed reference sources listed below.

The Vietnam Veteran's Memorial has become one of the most frequently visited sites in Washington, D.C. The families and friends of those listed on the monument are organized into Friends of the Vietnam Veterans Memorial (2030 Clarendon Blvd., Ste. 412, Arlington, VA, 22201, (202) 628-0726). The organization seeks to insure that the legacy of Vietnam is not forgotten and sponsors the Remember Them Project, which gathers biographical data and oral histories relating to persons listed on the wall.

The Veterans of the Vietnam War, with 30,000 members, maintains a veterans locator service, POW/MIA listings, and collections of literature on Agent Orange and post-traumatic stress syndrome (760 Jumper Rd., Wilkes-Barre, PA, 18702-8033, (717) 825-7215).

Although U.S. involvement in Vietnam began before the term of President Kennedy in 1960, it did not end until 1975. The Vietnam period is only just beginning to recede into the historical past. A number of reference works have been published for the purpose of assisting in historical research on the Vietnam conflict and its aftereffects.

415. **America and the Indochina Wars, 1945–1990: A Bibliographic Guide.** Claremont, CA: Regina Books, 1992. 286p. (New War/Peace Bibliographical Series, no.1). ISBN 0-941690-43-1.

The Center for the Study of Armament and Disarmament of California State University, Los Angeles is responsible for the New War/Peace Bibliographical Series. The United States was involved in three wars in Vietnam, Cambodia, and Laos. This bibliography concentrates on sources published since 1980, including books, periodical articles, and dissertations. The work reviews the history and background of the areas, the military conflicts, and the effect of the wars on life and politics in the United States during and after the wars. A reference chapter includes guides to library and archival collections and other useful reference works. The entries are not annotated except for an occasional one-line description. There are author and subject indexes and tables for war casualties and expenditures. The value of the bibliography lies in its coverage of literature published after the Vietnam War ended.

416. **Dictionary of the Vietnam War.** James S. Olson, ed. New York: Greenwood, 1988. 585p. ISBN 0-313-24943-1.

The 30 years between 1945 and 1975 are the focus of this work. Brief entries with a few longer essays cover the people, legislation, military operations, and controversies of the U.S. involvement in Vietnam. Each entry includes references for further research. Asterisks within the entries cross-reference related topics. Two appendices describe the population and minority groups of South Vietnam. Another appendix is a glossary of war acronyms and slang expressions. A selective bibliography, chronology, and maps of the Republic of Vietnam are also included. There is a name and title index, which includes names of aircraft, naval vessels, and weaponry. The dictionary is designed as a reference source for students and scholars.

Another reference source is *Vietnam War Almanac* by Harry G. Summers, Jr. (Facts on File, 1985), which is similar to the *Korean War Almanac* (entry 414) by the same author. After an introductory essay about the war, there is a chronology. The main part of the book is an "A to Z" of persons, events, weapons, battles, and so forth. Every aspect of the war's history—military, political, social, diplomatic, and strategic—is covered. The volume is illustrated with 21 maps and more than 120 photographs. It is suitable for readers at any level as a general reference source.

417.   The United States in the Vietnam War, 1954–1975: A Selected, Annotated Bibliography. Louis A Peake, New York: Garland, 1986. 406p. (Wars of the United States, v.4; Garland Reference Library of Social Science, v.256). ISBN 0-8240-8946-4.

The compiler of this bibliography is a Vietnam-era Army veteran, not a librarian or bibliographer. The annotated bibliography of 1,667 citations includes a number of useful features. One of these is a listing of accounts of the war by North Vietnamese. Another is the inclusion of films, art, and recordings. The bibliography is strong in references on the controversial issues and aftermath of the war. The organization is by topical chapters—"The Media War" and "The Domestic Impact of the Vietnam War," for example. A chronology and glossary are furnished. There are subject and author indexes, although they are somewhat inadequate. The limitation to English-language sources makes this work most suitable for the general public and students.

A work with a narrower focus is *Air War in Southeast Asia 1961–1973: An Annotated Bibliography and 16mm Film Guide* by Myron J. Smith, Jr. (Scarecrow, 1979). Military strategy in the Vietnam War made heavy use of air strikes and other aerial technology, such as the spraying of herbicides. Although this bibliography is no longer current, it still pulls together into one volume sources on all aerial aspects of the Vietnam War. There are over 3,000 English-language sources covering the administrative and operational aspects of the air war for the 1961–1973 period. The majority of items are periodical articles. Studies from the Air War College and the Air Command Staff College are cited, as are popular sources. The films are primarily those produced by the military. There is a subject index that includes persons, aircraft, organizations, missions, and places. The variety of source material and the simple organization make this bibliography suitable for use by students and researchers.

418.   Vietnam: The Decisive Battles. John Pimlott. New York: Macmillan, 1990. 200p. ISBN 0-02-580171-6.

Another in the Macmillan military atlas series, this volume also features computer-generated three-dimensional maps. Seventeen key battles ranging from the French defeat at Dien Bien Phu in 1954 to the fall of Saigon in 1975 are depicted in two-page color spreads. In addition to the computer-generated maps, there are numerous diagrams, photographs, and drawings that further illustrate and relate to the battles. The volume contains a foreword written by Shelby L. Stanton. Military, political, and historical aspects of the war are covered in the notes accompanying the illustrations, and there is a military analysis of each battle. This work contributes to an understanding of the military conduct of the war and is a useful reference work for students and all others with an interest in the topic.

David B. Sigler has compiled a more detailed and comprehensive account of military engagements, *Vietnam Battle Chronology: U.S. Army and Marine Corps Combat Operations, 1965–1973* (McFarland, 1992). This work traces more than 600 Army and Marine ground combat operations for the time period 1965–1973. The information given includes the dates, code names for the operation, geographical location, all military units involved, the objectives of the operation or targets, and casualties. In addition, there is a chronological list of operations according to command unit and an alphabetical listing by Army or Marine combat operation. One of the most useful features is a bibliography for each command unit that gives the National Archives record numbers for the Operational Reports. Name, subject, and military unit indexes conclude the volume.

419. **Vietnam War Bibliography.** Christopher L. Sugnet, John T. Hickey, et al. Lexington, MA: Lexington Books/D. C. Heath, 1983. 572p. (The Lexington Books Special Series in Libraries and Librarianship). ISBN 0-669-06680-X.

Although this is a bibliography of the John M. Echols Collection at Cornell University, the number and depth of resources in the collection make the work a comprehensive bibliography for the Vietnam War. The sources span the mid-1940s to 1975, with the majority of sources concentrated during the period of heaviest military involvement. Over 4,000 of the more than 7,000 items in the Echols Collection are listed in the bibliography. Sources include books, pamphlets, manuscripts, documents, maps, serial titles, and archival and audiovisual materials. The sources are in English and foreign languages, including French and Vietnamese. The bibliography is computer produced and divided into three sections: a register, an index, and an appendix. The register is an alphabetical listing by title with basic bibliographical information such as date range, alternative titles, and call number/location within the Cornell libraries. The index is by authors, personal and organizational names, topics, and alternative titles. The appendix is a listing of acronyms and cross-references. The John M. Echols Collection is one of the largest and richest of primary and secondary source materials on the period of the Vietnam War. The bibliography will be useful to anyone engaged in scholarly research on the war in Southeast Asia.

University Microfilms has made available several microformat collections on the Vietnam War. The first of these is *The Echols Collection: Selections on the Vietnam War.* The collection covers prewar and wartime history as well as the aftereffects of the war worldwide. It contains a variety of social and political commentaries, including views of anti- and pro-war factions, religious groups, and governments in the United States, Vietnam, and other countries. Another collection offered by UMI is *The History of the Vietnam War,* which spans 25 years and includes 365,000 pages of material. Included are unclassified and declassified U.S. government documents; captured documents; prisoner of war interrogation reports; newspaper and periodical clippings from U.S., Vietnamese and other foreign newspapers; transcripts of speeches and press conferences; and propaganda leaflets and manuscripts by Vietnamese writers. These microform collections contain essential materials for research on the period of the Vietnam War.

420. **Writing About Vietnam: A Bibliography of the Literature of the Vietnam Conflict.** Sandra M. Wittman. Boston: G. K. Hall, 1989. 385p. (Reference Publication in Literature). ISBN 0-8161-9083-6.

English-language works relating to the Vietnam experience by U.S. and foreign authors are listed in this bibliography of 1,734 citations. The bibliography is divided into 13 sections by literary format arranged alphabetically by author. Dissertations and nonfiction narrative works are included. There are author and title indexes.

A similar work by John Newman, *Vietnam War Literature* (Scarecrow, 1988), concentrates on literary works. The Wittman bibliography covers a broad range of sources, and the time span is from the French period up to recent writings about the Vietnam experience. This specialized bibliography of first-person narrative works is of use to general readers or researchers probing the psychological and sociological ramifications of the Vietnam War.

Chapter 5

Social, Cultural, and Intellectual History

Of the historical divisions utilized in this guide, sociocultural and intellectual history furnishes the largest concentration of tools and resources. These studies have undergone a great deal of review and examination in light of the heightened activity of the past few decades. Implications for scholars, students, librarians, and interested laymen are obvious in the numerous materials published on different topics and issues.

This chapter opens with a section on ideological trends and identifies reference tools dealing with the broad spectrum of sociopolitical thought from extreme right to radical left. Genealogy, the somewhat controversial auxiliary science, has been given equal footing with more established subfields and shares a section with immigration. This is followed by a look at works dealing with ethnic, gender, and racial influences, each of which is treated separately. This reference guide is the first to deal with the gay movement and to bring up-to-date coverage of works on the various ethnic minorities that contribute to our nation. The diverse segments of our cultural and social existence are represented—church, school, the law, entertainment, and so on. Purposely excluded are the visual arts, both popular and serious, and literature. The reader is advised to consult the appropriate specialized guides for those subject areas.

A useful tool of a general nature is *Sage Family Studies Abstracts,* which treat books, articles, documents, and other literature on a variety of topics relevant to family studies, marriage, gender issues, and employment among them. The emphasis is on current affairs, but historical writings are covered as well. Also of interest to the modern social historian is *Family Resources,* a database published by the National Council on Family Relations. It is available through DIALOG and furnishes coverage of the psychosocial literature relating to family studies.

GENERAL

421. **American History and Culture: Research Studies by the National Park Service, 1935–1984.** Alexandria, VA: Chadwyck-Healey, 1986. Microfiche.
Another of the monumental efforts by Chadwyck-Healey, this microfiche source collection of more than 5,500 reports issued by the National Park Service over a 50-year period is valuable to scholars and serious students. Scope is extensive and covers three major areas: history, including oral history; archaeology and ethnology; and architecture and landscape, including interiors and artifacts related to the more than 300 national parks. Arrangement is geographical, with the country being divided into nine different regions. Reports vary in content and in depth of research; among them are identifications, descriptions, evaluations,

and field studies of sites, furnishings, objects, and so on. Maps, photographs, drawings, and documents are given.

Purchase of the complete set above ($24,500) includes *The Cultural Resources Management Bibliography* (*CRBIB*) on microfiche. *CRBIB* is an automated inventory of the reports issued by the National Park Service; the publisher's fiche edition furnishes access by location, subject, author, title, date, and category of study. This work is updated annually with the addition of current reports.

422. Encyclopedia of American Social History. Mary Kupiec Cayton, et al., eds. New York: Scribner's, 1992. 3v. ISBN 0-684-19246-2.

Rather than emphasize isolated events and political phenomena, this work describes the processes by which people have defined their existence. Beginning researchers should find that the 180 essays furnish adequate depth and insight into the nature and composition of U.S. life from the precolonial period to the present. Essays vary from 8 to 16 pages and are organized into 14 topical segments covering such factors as social change, methodology, social identity, ethnic and racial subcultures, family history, and social problems. Included are maps, charts, and bibliographies. Each essay is written by an academician who has special interest or expertise in the topic. There is a comprehensive index to provide access.

A forthcoming biographical dictionary is *American Social Leaders: From Colonial Times to the Present* by James McPherson and Gary Gerstle (ABC-Clio). Expected in 1993, the work covers 350 individuals who provided meaningful contributions to social development in the United States.

423. Index to America: Life and Customs—Twentieth Century to 1986. Norma Olin Ireland. Metuchen, NJ: Scarecrow, 1989. 361p. (Useful Reference Series, no.107). ISBN 0-8108-2170-2.

Best described as a popular bibliography of popular culture, this index has placed emphasis on titles that are common to most libraries. Included are articles from such publications as *People* magazine and various almanacs and handbooks, as well as recently published historical surveys and turn-of-the-century-writings. These focus on U.S. life and custom in all facets. Historical events are deemphasized in favor of descriptions of family life, personalities, and social and political trends. The work has been criticized both for erratic coverage, with entries not always representing the most recent information within the framework of the stated time coverage, and for certain notable omissions. The author's three earlier volumes in this series covered the seventeenth, eighteenth, and nineteenth centuries. Arrangement is by subject, and the entire series should be considered more useful to the beginning student than to the serious inquirer.

424. Social History of the United States: A Guide to Information Sources. Donald Fred Tingley. Detroit: Gale, 1979. 260p. (American Government and History Information Guide Series, v.3; Gale Information Guide Library). ISBN 0-8103-1366-9.

Compiled by a professor of history, this bibliography of about 1,000 items, most of them books, represents a selective rather than an enumerative work. It has been susceptible to criticism regarding notable omissions within its 26 chapters. Organization is similar to other works in this series, with introductory chapters on general works and reference materials followed by topical coverage. Such topics as "Religion," "Ethnic Groups," "Popular Culture," and the "Nature and Practice of Social History" are provided. Entries are annotated briefly in a nonjudgmental manner and serve to inform the inquirer regarding the scope of each work. Because of the volume's rather unique breadth of coverage and its expansive scope (early to recent history), users at all levels will want to examine its contents. It is indexed by author, title, and subject, assuring easy access to contents.

425. **This Remarkable Continent: An Atlas of United States and Canadian Society and Culture.** College Station, TX: Published for the Society for the North American Cultural Survey by Texas A & M University Press, 1982. 316p. ISBN 0-89096-111-5.

The information used to construct the maps in this atlas is based on "detailed field surveys and interviews." The distribution of elements of culture and folklife, past and present, is depicted in 390 black-and-white maps. Topics covered include architecture, ethnicity, religion, language, food, politics, urban design, and leisure activities, presented with intro-ductory material. The volume is more suitable for browsing than for a search for specific information, but it can be used as a supplementary source for data on ethnic groups, a study of regional patterns, and the geographic differences in attitudes of U.S. citizens. The first stage in the development of a comprehensive atlas by the society, it represents a unique source for scholars, students, and the general public. There is a bibliography of sources and an index.

426. **U.S. Cultural History: A Guide to Information Sources.** Philip I. Mitterling. Detroit: Gale, 1980. 521p. (American Government and History Information Guide Series, v.5). ISBN 0-8103-1369-3.

This annotated bibliography lists over 2,500 entries, mostly books with some periodical articles, in the relatively broad field of cultural history. Emphasis is on titles published since 1950, but more important earlier sources are included. Eleven periods, beginning with the colonial era, are covered, with fairly equal treatment given to such topics as architecture, biography, literature, popular culture, science and medicine, and education. Annotations are brief and include, in many cases, judgments of value and importance. The author is a professor of history and social science who seems to have succeeded in furnishing a representative body of literature in a convenient format, which should prove useful to a wide range of users. Like other volumes in this series, separate indexes cover author, title, and subject.

IDEOLOGICAL TRENDS AND MOVEMENTS

This country was created with a sense of pluralism and found strength in its diversity. In this section, one can find sources of information regarding philosophical orientations, sociopolitical movements and organizations, and trendy eras that have earmarked our past. For sources on the New Deal, see chapter 8, "Depression and Recession."

The Center for Socialist History was founded in 1981 in Berkeley, California to aid in the study of the U.S. left. The institution has published its *Interbulletin* on an irregular basis since 1982. The Historians of American Communism, an organization of 120 members headquartered in Washington Depot, Connecticut, offers a quarterly newsletter. For study of the U.S. right, the Intercollegiate Studies Institute was founded in 1953 and has 35,000 members. Operating out of Bryn Mawr, Pennsylvania, it has published the semiannual *Continuity: A Journal of History* since 1980 and the *Intercollegiate Review* since 1965.

Library Resources

427. **The American Left, 1955–1970: A National Union Catalog of Pamphlets Published in the United States and Canada.** Ned Kehde, comp. Westport, CT: Greenwood, 1976. 515p. ISBN 0-8371-8282-4.

Defining "left" as those publications issued by Awareness for Democratic Action or by persons or groups to the left of the ADA, Kehde has furnished a listing of about 4,000 titles derived from the *National Union Catalog* and the card catalogs of the New York Public Library and the State Historical Society of Wisconsin. In addition to listing pamphlets, the work includes important leaflets, brochures, instructional manuals, and religious tracts. No annotations are provided, and there are no suggestions for how to obtain the material. The period of coverage dates from the initial year of the *Village Voice* and the beginning of the civil rights movement and ends with the year 1970, after which the New Left became relatively inactive. Titles are arranged alphabetically by author and include date (if available) as well as imprint, physical description, and holding library. This represents a valuable bibliographic control device for what is often difficult-to-find literature.

428. **Peace Archives: A Guide to Library Collections of the Papers of American Peace Organizations and of Leaders in the Public Effort for Peace.** Marguerite Green, comp. and ed. Berkeley, CA: World Without War Council, 1986. 66p.

This brief guide was created as a result of a historical program initiated in 1980 by the World Without War Council, the purpose being to analyze the peace movement in this country since 1930. This particular effort identifies documents and manuscripts held by approximately 30 major archive collections in this country. Included in each entry are the name of the curator, specific collections on the topic, types of services available, and services offered to donors and contributors. Although the guide has been termed of limited value by reviewers because of minimal information provided about the quality of each collection covered, it facilitates the search for such material and merits consideration by any researchers. Included in the appendix is a listing of 70 additional collections; there is a bibliography of search guides and manuals.

Bibliographical Sources

Of interest to social historians is the *Alternative Periodicals Index,* operating since 1969 and issued on a quarterly basis. It is the leading index of leftist or radical literature and furnishes coverage of the pertinent articles from over 200 periodicals. It includes listings of monographs, reviews, and essays; coverage embraces the environment, women's issues, anarchy, and the gay/lesbian movement, among other things. It is published by the Alternative Press Centre in College Park, Maryland. Similar coverage is given in *The Left Index: A Quarterly Index to Periodicals of the Left*, published since 1985 by The Left Index of Santa Clara, California. This work indexes some 75 left-wing periodicals, both U.S. and European, on a variety of subjects, issues, and topics. Book reviews are listed separately.

429. **American Communes 1860–1960: A Bibliography.** Timothy Miller. New York: Garland, 1990. 583p. (Sects and Cults in America Bibliographic Guides, v.13; Garland Reference Library of Social Science, v.402). ISBN 0-8240-8470-5.

One of the publisher's two titles on communes issued during 1990, this work covers a period of 100 years normally considered a hiatus in communal development. Miller has shown that this is not true and furnishes excellent coverage in his identification of over 3,000 books, chapters, articles, theses, and dissertations. Entries are arranged alphabetically by community name and follow two general sections of bibliographies and reference works. Communities are both religious and secular in nature; each is given a brief description and historical treatment. Sections are subdivided by type of source material. Both primary and secondary source material is given. A comprehensive name index furnishes access.

The other Garland effort of the same year is Philip N. Dare's *American Communes to 1860: Bibliography,* which identifies over 1,900 works covering the early period of communal development to the onset of the Civil War. Structure and arrangement is similar to that of its counterpart above, although this volume has received more criticism for omissions in coverage and failure to explain its selectivity.

430. **American Students: A Selected Bibliography on Student Activism and Related Topics.** Philip G. Altbach and David H. Kelly. Lexington, MA: Lexington Books, 1973. 537p. ISBN 0-699-85100-0.

This book represents an expansion and enlargement of a 1968 publication by Altbach, which also lists books, periodical articles, and doctoral dissertations on the subject of student activism. Three major classifications are presented: "Students and Student Activism"; "Minority Students in American Higher Education"; and "Students and Student Life in America." These classes are subdivided by topics. There are no annotations except for those given for items in the bibliographic essay on "Student Activism and Academic Research." There is a detailed table of contents that is important in providing access, because there is no index to the work. This is an unfortunate oversight—convenience is an important consideration for a work of this kind. A good tradeoff, however, is the employment of asterisks as symbols for those items of most importance.

431. **Anti-Intervention: A Bibliographical Introduction to Isolationism and Pacifism from World War I to the Early Cold War.** New York: Garland, 1987. 421p. ISBN 0-8240-8482-9.

This extensive compilation of references gives annotations to about 1,600 monographs, periodical articles, essays, and dissertations; government documents are not covered, however. Beginning with the opposition to participation in World War I, the historical development of such resistance is traced to the late 1950s and the defeat of isolationism as a viable policy. The work is divided into five chapters: general works; World War I; the period from World War I to the 1950s; opinion-making elements; and ideological groups and leaders. Although the organization of this tool is excellent, the annotations are not consistent in length and utility. Some are too truncated to be viable, others nonexistent. Because material on these subjects is elusive, however, the work should be examined by all levels of inquirers.

432. **Communism and Anti-Communism in the United States: An Annotated Guide to Historical Writings.** John Earl Haynes. New York: Garland, 1987. 321p. ISBN 0-8240-8520-5.

As the editor of the "Newsletter of Historians of American Communism," Haynes is well qualified to prepare this bibliography of over 2,000 items on the topic. The bibliography is divided into 37 major categories, such as "Schismatic Communist Movements" and "Right-Wing Anti-Communism and McCarthyism"; in many cases, these are subdivided into smaller categories. The detailed table of contents identifies these categories and subcategories, encompassing a variety of subjects. Included are books, periodical articles, and even some dissertations. The period covered is primarily from the beginning of U.S. Communism in 1917 to the decline of the American Communist Party in the mid-1950s and should provide both scholars and students with useful materials. There is an author index, but no subject index is provided. The introduction is most useful in describing the periods of writing and providing perspective.

433. **From Radical Left to Extreme Right: A Bibliography of Current Periodicals of Protest, Controversy, Advocacy, or Dissent.** 2nd ed., rev. and enl. Robert H. Muller, et al. Ann Arbor: Campus Publishers, 1970–1976. 3v. ISBN 0-8108-1967-8.

The first edition of this work was compiled in 1967 by Muller, at which time he mentioned the need for subsequent editions of a bibliography devoted to current periodicals of protest because of their ephemeral nature. The second edition was compiled by Muller along with Theodore and Janet Spahn in an expanded three-volume version issued between 1970 and 1976. This version identified 1,324 periodicals, as compared with 163 in the earlier edition. Only 280 periodicals are given full treatment, which includes name of editor, frequency, price, date of inception, circulation, and format. Brief narratives or summaries for each title describe content and offer quotations. Entries are alphabetically arranged under 21 chapter headings—e.g., "Civil and Human Rights," "Peace," and "Libertarian." There are three indexes providing access to titles, names, and opinions found in the narratives. Of importance is the cessation list for titles included in the second edition.

434. **The Ku Klux Klan: A Bibliography.** Lenwood Davis and Janet L. Sims-Wood, comps. Westport, CT: Greenwood, 1984. 643p. ISBN 0-313-22949-X.

This is the second major book-length bibliography on the Klan and serves to complement the coverage by William Harvey Fisher (see below). Davis and Sims-Wood have produced a rather selective but generous listing of nearly 9,800 entries organized by sections covering major works, books, and pamphlets; dissertations and theses; KKK material; and government documents. Included are references to speeches of Klansmen and articles from *Kourier Magazine*, the *New York Times*, and regional newspapers. Although the work has been criticized for omitting materials from Jewish and other ethnic presses, it represents an important source for both students and researchers. There is a directory of archival repositories in the appendix. An author index furnishes access.

William Harvey Fisher's *The Invisible Empire: A Bibliography of the Ku Klux Klan* (Scarecrow Press, 1980) was the initial bibliography of large proportions, furnishing several thousand entries arranged under nineteenth- and twentieth-century divisions. No newspapers are treated, but coverage is given to subdivisions by form—dissertations, manuscripts/archives, government documents, monographs, and periodical articles. Annotations are brief. There are author and subject indexes.

435. **Margaret Sanger and the Birth Control Movement: A Bibliography, 1911–1984.** Gloria Moore and Ronald Moore. Metuchen, NJ: Scarecrow, 1986. 211p. ISBN 0-8108-1903-1.

Normally, in a literature guide of this type, there is a purposeful attempt to avoid including materials on a single individual. In this case, however, the birth control movement is inextricably linked to Ms. Sanger's life, as is apparent in the organization of this extensive bibliography. More than 1,300 items, most of them annotated, are arranged chronologically by year from 1911 to 1966, the year of Ms. Sanger's death. The following sections contain materials written between 1967 and 1984. Sanger's own writings precede those of others in the 1911–1966 segment. Materials are varied and include monographs, periodical articles, newspaper articles, pamphlets, dissertations, even novels. Annotations tend to be brief but useful. Additional coverage includes listings of special collections of relevant material, legislative bills, and hearings. The work represents an earnest attempt to include all materials available through academic or college libraries.

436. **Peace and War: A Guide to Bibliographies.** Berenice A. Carroll, et al. Santa Barbara, CA: ABC-Clio, 1983. 580p. (War/Peace Bibliography Series, no.16). ISBN 0-87436-322-5.

This bibliography of bibliographies identifies all types of listings: full-length bibliographies, sections of books and periodical articles, pamphlets, and unpublished materials on the subject of war and peace. There are almost 1,400 entries arranged into 34 sections that fall under one of three broad parts: "Peace and War," "Peace," and "War." Sections emphasize topical elements such as "War and Children," rather than individual wars with the exception of the two World Wars. Entries are listed in chronological order within the section. Annotations are relatively detailed in providing a number of items, including time period covered, and original language. Emphasis has been placed on U.S., then European, perspectives, although coverage is global. Backed by a grant from the National Endowment for the Humanities, the compilers were able to actually examine most materials. There are both author and subject indexes to facilitate access. A recent selective bibliography that is complementary to the above is *The American Peace Movement: References and Resources* by Charles F. Howlett (G. K. Hall, 1991). It furnishes approximately 1,600 annotated entries of books, articles, dissertations, reports, and documents organized under 12 subjects such as the U.S. peace movement, arbitration, and religious pacifism.

437. **Progressive Reform: A Guide to Information Sources.** John D. Buenker and Nicholas C. Burckel. Detroit: Gale, 1980. 366p. (American Government and History Information Guide Series, v.8). ISBN 0-8103-1485-1.

This is a useful and convenient selective bibliography of the important writings on the topic. There are more than 1,600 entries, with annotations ranging from very brief to more than 100 words. The Progressive period embraces the time following the 1893 depression to the end of World War I, and the entries are well chosen for scholarly inquiry. Included here are research monographs, journal articles, biographical works, and dissertations. Government documents are omitted, however. Arrangement is topical under 13 subject headings such as "Urban Reform," "Progressive Thought," "Social Welfare Issues," and "Decline, Persistence and Legacy." Coverage of topics is considered to be excellent, and the work is valuable to both students and researchers. Detailed indexes to authors and subjects assure access.

438. **Progressivism and Muckraking.** Louis Filler. New York: Bowker, 1976. 200p. (Bibliographic Guides for Contemporary Collections). ISBN 0-8352-0875-3.

This work presents four sets of bibliographic essays comprising 46 sections that identify secondary sources describing the origins and developments and evaluating the successes and failures of these reform movements from the turn of the century to the Watergate era. The first grouping is entitled "A Man for Modern Times" and contains 9 sections, followed by "Progression" with 24 segments, "Progression: Second Phase" with 10, and "Search for Values," with only 3 sections, all focusing on the aftermath of the Reform era. All told, there are about 1,000 references, accessible by both an author index and a subject/title index. There is a feature intended for scholars, "Work that Needs to be Done," as well as coverage of audiovisual materials useful to classroom teaching found at the end of each chapter.

439. **Protest, Direct Action, Repression: Dissent in American Society from Colonial Times to the Present: A Bibliography.** Dirk Hoerder, comp. and ed. Munchen: Verlag Dokumentation, 1977. 434p. ISBN 3-79407-009-7.

This German work is keyed loosely to the holdings of the John F. Kennedy Institute of American Studies at the Free University of Berlin, but it surpasses that institution's collections in the total number of titles. It represents an attempt to codify dissent under three major segments: "General Literature," "Protest and Repression in Mainstream American History," and "Minorities in the United States." In each section, general readings precede listings subdivided by specific topics. Beginning researchers would find the listing helpful, although such bibliography when developed with a European perspective is vulnerable to the criticisms of omission (no references to underground/terrorist groups) and inequity (few references to women's liberation). More serious are the oversimplifications found in the historical introductions provided the various sections. Most successful is the coverage accorded racial issues.

440. **Radical Periodicals in America, 1890–1950: A Bibliography with Brief Notes.** Walter Goldwater. New Haven: Yale University Press, 1964. 51p.

After nearly 30 years, this brief effort retains its stature as a good source of information on the nature and character of radical left-wing periodicals published during a trying period marked by fear and repression in U.S. society. Considered a work of exacting scholarship in its attention to bibliographic detail, it is praised also for the pithy commentary furnished by Goldwater, the proprietor of a bookstore near Columbia University. This was a difficult work to produce, because there was much reluctance on the part of many editors to concede an association with the journals for which they were responsible, a poignant reminder of the period of McCarthyism. Arrangement of entries is alphabetical. The brief descriptions often employ subjective interpretation of the liberal/radical involvement of the journal named and may properly be challenged by others with a different viewpoint. This volume's greatest impact was the inspiration given to Greenwood Press to engage Goldwater to edit the massive reprint series *Radical Periodicals in the United States: 1890–1960* (entry 444n).

441. **Right Minds: A Sourcebook of American Conservative Thought.** Gregory Wolfe. Chicago: Regnery Books, 1987. 245p. ISBN 0-89526-583-4.

In response to the surge of conservative thinking that has emerged over the recent decades comes this bibliographic guide prepared under the auspices of the *National Review* through Regnery Books. There is a foreword by William F. Buckley, Jr. who provides tribute to the conservative cause and praises the volume for its success in representing the essence of conservatism. The first part of the tool furnishes a bibliography of such writing organized under 22 subject headings such as "Education" and "The Welfare State." Part 2 renders a biographical dictionary of 75 leading conservatives from the beginning of the republic to 1985. The author serves as the editor of a conservative periodical, and in certain cases the application of the label "conservative" to some of the individuals named is questionable. Nevertheless, the volume serves the needs of both scholars and students, who profit from the final section, which identifies publishers, special collections, journals, and so on.

442. **Social Reform and Reaction in America: An Annotated Bibliography.** Santa Barbara, CA: ABC-Clio, 1984. 375p. (Clio Bibliography Series, no.13). ISBN 0-87436-048-X.

This bibliography of nearly 3,000 items is derived from the publisher's monumental database *America: History and Life* (entry 51) and serves as a convenient access tool to abstracted journal articles and book chapters on the subject of social reform. It deals with both the U.S. and the Canadian experience and can serve as an aid to comparison studies of these trends in northern North America. Publications included in this volume were issued between 1973 and 1982 and draw not only from journals of history but also those of the entire social science realm and certain segments of the humanities. Arranged in six chronological sections, the entries appear alphabetically by author under topical subject divisions: e.g., "Education," "Religion," "Civil Liberties." Detailed author and subject indexes facilitate access and make this a useful source for both scholars and students.

Available online from the American Studies Program of George Washington University in Washington, D.C. is *Rose Bibliography,* which cites periodicals, books, and pamphlets on all aspects of reform activity and social change in the country during the late nineteenth and early twentieth centuries. There are 4,000 entries with dates of publication ranging from 1865 to 1917.

443. **Unity in Diversity: An Index to the Publications of Conservative and Libertarian Institutions.** Carol L. Birch, ed. Metuchen, NJ: Scarecrow, 1983. 263p. ISBN 0-8108-1599-0.

Prepared under the auspices of the New American Foundation, a conservative research firm, this work provides indexing to the periodical and monographic literature issued by the organization and 14 others of similar mind (among them the American Enterprise Institute for Public Policy, Cato Institute, and Hudson Institute). Publications date from between 1970 and 1981, thus providing a fairly intensive survey of conservative thought over this limited time period. The value of the work lies in its uniqueness, for most of these items have not been indexed by other services. Entries are arranged alphabetically by author under subject headings taken primarily from *Public Affairs Information Services* (PAIS). The work has been criticized for inconsistency or inadequacy of cross-referencing and for limitations of the selective subject index. The author index is detailed and includes editors, compilers, and contributors.

Information Sources

444. **The American Radical Press, 1880–1960.** Joseph R. Conlin, ed. Westport, CT: Greenwood, 1974. 2v. ISBN 0-8371-6625-X.

In hiring Walter Goldwater to edit and prepare the ambitious reprint program described below, Greenwood Press commissioned the writing of introductory essays for each of the journal titles that was reprinted. These essays were well-developed and maintained a high standard for accuracy and detail—so much so that it was decided to issue a collection of these essays as a separate work, with Conlin as editor. Through these writings, one is able to gain perspective on the nature of radicalism as well as specific information regarding the parties, movements, and developments. Many of these periodicals are obscure, and this work provides a real boost to scholarly inquiry on the nature of the radical press and its impact on the U.S. milieu. Conlin furnishes a general introduction as well as brief introductions to each of the chronological sections.

Radical Periodicals in the United States: 1890–1960, edited by Walter Goldwater (Greenwood, 1970), was a successful 410-volume endeavor to reprint the entire volume runs of 109 different radical periodicals over a 70-year period. Scholars were engaged to write introductory essays (reprinted in the above work). In view of the fact that the cost of the multivolume set was over $17,000 at the time, distribution and sales were quite successful, and scholars have an excellent sourcebook to the U.S. left. Goldwater was offered the editorship because of his effort in producing *Radical Periodicals in America, 1890–1950* (entry 440).

445. **Dictionary of American Communal and Utopian History.** Robert S. Fogarty. Westport, CT: Greenwood, 1980. 271p. ISBN 0-313-21347-X.

As editor of the *Antioch Review* with a background in the research of communal history, Fogarty was especially well prepared to develop this work. It has been limited to communal existence from 1787–1919 and provides both biographical and historical descriptions of the notable and noteworthy. The biography section contains about 150 sketches of individuals prominent in the founding and development of communes, or utopias, as they were called. Each sketch concludes with a bibliography of the individual's writings and a list of additional source materials. The other major segment furnishes historical passages describing nearly 60 communal societies, along with lists of sources. Criteria for selection are described in the preface to the work, and the introduction furnishes an overview of communal existence. A useful feature in the appendix is a listing of 270 communes. Access is provided by a name index.

446. **Dictionary of American Conservatism.** Louis Filler. New York: Philosophical Library, 1987. 380p. ISBN 0-8022-2506-3.

This one-volume dictionary of conservative thought is an interesting and even "lively" information piece, the intent being to provide a definition of concepts both past and present. Included are the "visible personalities," "symbolic slogans and ideas," and representative figures rather than a comprehensive or in-depth examination. As a result, the tool has been reviewed as lacking a balanced viewpoint. Filler, a prolific historian-writer of conservative orientation, seems to enjoy the process of creating reference books to espouse his philosophy: Gun control is defined as a "cause generally identified with liberals"; within the entry on abortion, one learns that "freedom of choice" is a euphemism for "legalization of abortion." Arrangement of entries is alphabetical, and length varies from a brief paragraph to more than a full page for certain individuals, such as Ronald Reagan, and broad topics.

A companion work is the author's *A Dictionary of American Social Change* (Krieger, 1982), which is an update of a 1963 publication with a slightly different title. Topics range from "abolitionism" to "Zoar Society." Most are treated concisely; like Filler's other works, it leaves no doubt of the author's sociopolitical stance.

447. **Encyclopedia of the American Left.** Mari Jo Buhle, et al., eds. New York: Garland, 1990. 928p. (Garland Reference Library of Social Science, v.502). ISBN 0-8240-4781-8.

This recent effort represents one of the few comprehensive works on the subject of the left in U.S. society. Over 300 contributors have provided 600 articles that describe major events, important personalities, institutions, and sources of information. Defining the left as that segment of society pursuing fundamental change in economic, political, and sociocultural systems, the work provides the student and inquirer with an informative introduction to ideological study. The period covered begins with the latter part of the nineteenth century and extends to the present day. Entries are full and detailed for the most part and provide insight into the topic; a bibliography is given at the conclusion. A special feature is a glossary of terms and acronyms, and access is furnished by both name and subject indexes.

448. **Historical Dictionary of the 1920s: From World War I to the New Deal, 1919–1933.** James Stuart Olson. New York: Greenwood, 1988. 420p. ISBN 0-313-25683-7.

Professor Olson, a prolific author, has produced a well-regarded series of reference dictionaries for Greenwood. In the present work, one is able to examine the flapper era through a collection of 700 entries, moderate in size (about a half-page long) but informative. They are arranged alphabetically for easy access and furnish information on people, events, legislative acts, legal cases, and the issues of the day, such as Prohibition. Also treated are organizations, fads, radio shows, and ideas. This well-chosen and well-developed selection of components is designed to inform the student or researcher of the importance of the topic and its impact on U.S. life. All entries furnish listings of additional readings and are connected by cross-references. There is a useful chronology of events for the years 1919–1933 and a fairly extensive bibliography keyed to various topics. An index provides access primarily to names covered within the entries.

449. **Historical Dictionary of the Progressive Era, 1890–1920.** John D. Buenker and Edward R. Kantowicz, eds. New York: Greenwood, 1988. 599p. ISBN 0-313-24309-3.

Although there is no attempt on the part of the publisher to formalize a series title, this work fits in with the historical coverage of other Greenwood products (see entry above). Like the others, it represents a useful and comprehensive examination of the period in question. Progressivism is seen as a response by the citizenry to the emergence of the United States as a great power. There are over 800 signed entries prepared by expert contributors who have provided factual description and interpretation. Entries cover personalities, organizations, social topics and issues, laws, court cases, and movements, among other things. Like others in the Greenwood line of historical dictionaries, this book has well-written and carefully developed entries. There is a 12-page chronology designed to place the period in perspective. Access is provided through name, title, and subject indexes.

The Gay Nineties in America: A Cultural Dictionary of the 1890s by Robert L. Gale (Greenwood, 1992) furnishes 500 entries describing events, personalities, and published works representing that extraordinary period. There is a detailed bibliography as well as an index by occupation to aid access.

450. **The Ku Klux Klan: An Encyclopedia.** Michael Newton and Judy Ann Newton. Hamden, CT: Garland, 1991. 639p. (Garland Reference Library of Social Science, v.499). ISBN 0-8240-2038-3.

This short-entry encyclopedia furnishes informative factual descriptions of several sentences in length, rather than broad-based interpretive analysis. It is a convenient tool, with alphabetical arrangement of entries designed to enlighten students to the nature and activity of what has been described as the "world's oldest terrorist organization." There are references within each entry to sources used by the authors, sources that have themselves been compiled as a bibliography at the back of the volume. These for the most part represent secondary sources of a popular rather than scholarly nature, such as wire service articles from newspapers (with an emphasis on the *New York Times*), magazines, and books of general interest. There is a brief, interesting history of the organization provided in the preface; listings of groups, individuals, and geographical entries are given at the beginning in place of an index.

Biographical Sources

451. **American Peace Writers, Editors, and Periodicals: A Dictionary.** Nancy L. Roberts. New York: Greenwood, 1991. 362p. ISBN 0-313-26842-8.

A useful biographical dictionary that targets individuals associated with peace movements dating from the colonial era to modern times, this tool provides sketches of 400 writers and editors who attempted to enlighten their leadership to the issues of war and peace. The individuals selected for inclusion represent a wide range of interests, from well-known writers employed by mainstream publications to relatively obscure writers known only by readers of alternative periodicals published by church bodies and peace organizations. The entries are well done and informative and furnish personal information, description of peace activities and of publications. Additional biographical sources are listed. In a work of this type, reviewers will question inclusions and omissions, but generally it should prove to be of substantial use to all inquirers. There is a chronology along with useful bibliographies of both peace publications and serious studies.

452. **American Reformers: A Biographical Dictionary.** Alden Whitman, ed. New York: H. W. Wilson, 1985. 930p. (H. W. Wilson Biographical Dictionary). ISBN 0-8242-0705-X.

Containing just over 500 biographical essays of U.S. figures involved with reform movements dating from the seventeenth century to modern times, this work furnishes the researcher and the student of history a convenient package of useful information. Both well-known and the obscure individuals appear, the common thread being that all contributed to the character of the reform movement. Entries range from 600 to 3,000 words and furnish dates, areas of reform, family background, education, and so forth, along with a summary of accomplishments. Photos and bibliographies are included. Prepared by a former obituary editor for the *New York Times* with the aid of an impressive panel of historians, the work touches on all aspects of reform: abolition, civil rights, health, labor, temperance, and women's rights, among others. There is a list of reformers at the beginning; at the end is a list of reformers by category, which employs some 60 topical headings.

A recent effort by Louis Filler, a prolific author of Conservative persuasion, is *Distinguished Shades: Americans Whose Lives Live On* (Belfry, 1992). Fifty-six men and women of the mid-eighteenth to mid-twentieth century, largely of liberal and progressive belief (reformers, politicians, feminists), are revealed through detailed three- to five-page biographical sketches. Coverage appears to be fair-minded and enlightening.

453. **Biographical Dictionary of the American Left.** Bernard K. Johnpoll and Harvey Klehr, eds. Westport, CT: Greenwood, 1986. 493p. ISBN 0-313-24200-3.

A well-conceived and well-developed tool consisting of nearly 400 biographical essays, the work succeeds in providing a cross-section of leading personalities treated within the ideological context of their time, place, and milieu. About 50 contributors, mostly young scholars, have been utilized, provoking some justifiable criticism of certain inequities, imbalances, and omissions. Regardless, the essays are informative and well-researched for the most part, and they furnish an excellent perspective on the U.S. left through all its practitioners (e.g., socialists, communists, anarchists). The essays range in length from less than one page to nearly eight pages, reflecting the relative stature of the individual. Dates, personal and professional background, political affiliations, and activities are covered; sources for further study are listed. The work concludes with appendices that attempt to qualify or categorize some of the data reported and a useful index.

Covering the other side is *Biographical Dictionary of the Extreme Right Since 1890* by Philip Ross (Simon & Schuster, 1991). This is a well-written compilation of biographical sketches covering the influential conservatives of the 20th century.

454. **Dictionary of American Temperance Biography: From Temperance Reform to Alcohol Research, the 1600s to the 1980s.** Mark Edward Lender. Westport, CT: Greenwood, 1984. 572p. ISBN 0-313-22335-1.

This is a useful biographical dictionary consisting of about 375 entries of men and women considered to be activists in the temperance movements since the colonial period. The entries are written in three segments, beginning with brief summaries of life and achievements, followed by essays of one to two pages on the subject's involvement with temperance, and concluding with bibliographies of up to six works by the biographees and up to six works about them. Selection of the individuals is somewhat arbitrary, with no criteria for inclusion listed, but those included appear to merit consideration because of their activism or their intellectual productivity. Most of them are of historical importance, with relatively little representation of contemporary individuals responsible for the recent resurgence of the issue. Access is provided by an index of subjects, names, and organizations.

GENEALOGY AND IMMIGRATION

In the past, genealogy as an auxiliary study has been held suspect by historians as a relatively undisciplined "popular" exercise in self-fulfillment. More recently, however, following the success of Alex Haley's *Roots,* with its systematic methodology, and the broadened focus on social history, there has been greater acceptance in many (but not all) quarters of the potential utility and historical value of genealogical inquiry.

Prior to beginning the task, the investigator needs to become acquainted with the study through use of the genealogy handbooks listed here. A useful source is an article by L. D. Bookstruck, "Four Centuries of Genealogy: A Historical Overview" appearing in the Winter 1983 issue of *Reference Quarterly (RQ)*, pp. 162–170.

It is also important to consider the services and products offered by the Genealogical Department of the Church of Jesus Christ of Latter-Day Saints in Salt Lake City, Utah, as well as the various commercial distributors of genealogical products. The church, through sale of its Family Search product line, offers CD-ROM access to various files, the most important being *The Family History Library Catalog*, which lists and describes the vast holdings in Salt Lake City. Many local church branches have the equipment to conduct searches for patrons. The Genealogical Publishing Company has been the leading publishing house. The American Genealogical Lending Library in Bountiful, Utah, is an important supplier offering several useful publications through its subsidiary, Historic Resources, Inc., also in Bountiful. Its *AGLL Fiche Catalog* is an ongoing semiannual listing that continues to provide awareness of available items.

As the representative sources included here illustrate, the study of British origins is relatively well supported by documentation. A useful guide to such materials is Ann Wuehler's "Genealogical Sources for England and Wales," which appeared in *Reference Services Review* in the Spring 1989 issue, pp. 65–70, 80. Recently there has been an increased interest in family lines of various ethnic groups. In this section we have included materials of ethnicity and gender. Additional materials pertinent to the study of both genealogy and immigration may be found in this chapter in those sections dealing with the various ethnic, racial, and gender influences.

The National Genealogical Society of Arlington, Virginia, has 9,500 members and was founded in 1903. It has published the *National Genealogical Society Quarterly* since 1912.

The Immigration History Society of Chicago, Illinois, was founded in 1965 by scholars interested in the study of human migration, especially immigration to the United States and Canada. Membership (830) is made up of historians, economists, sociologists, and others interested in research in the field of immigration history. The society bestows the Theodore Saloutos Memorial Book Award in Immigration History.

The Immigration History Society publishes *Journal of American Ethnic History*, a semiannual journal, and *Immigration History Newsletter.*

Library Resources

455. Dictionary Catalog of the Local History and Genealogy Division. New York Public Library, Local History and Genealogy Division. Boston: G. K. Hall, 1974. 20v. ISBN 0-81610-784-X. **Ann. Supp.** 1977– .

This is one of the major resource tools for both local history and genealogy based on the extensive holdings of the New York Public Library. G. K. Hall, publisher of important library catalogs, produced this multivolume access tool in the mid-1970s to cover the material cataloged by the library through the end of 1971. Since that time, the materials have been listed in the Library's *Dictionary Catalog of the Research Libraries*. Since 1976, these materials have been supplemented on an annual basis in the Library's *Bibliographic Guide to North American History* (entry 45). The 20-volume work (which itself includes a two-volume supplement of local history) bears the unmistakable design of the G. K. Hall company and is simply a reproduction of the catalog cards of items in this collection. About 100,000 titles were identified in the original 20 volumes.

456. **The Ellis Island Sourcebook.** August C. Bolino. Washington: Kensington Historical Press, 1985. 306p.

This is considered to be the most extensive and comprehensive survey of materials relating to Ellis Island. It was undertaken as part of the Ellis Island restoration effort; the author was a member of that commission and spent several years researching the materials. It was necessary to visit major cities affected by ethnic immigration (Pittsburgh, Chicago, Cleveland, and others) in order to gain perspective on existing material. The resulting work provides locations of much existing material on Ellis Island immigration activity and includes government agencies at various levels, church records, ethnic presses, and various fraternal groups and social clubs, among others. Oral history is covered, as are audiovisual materials. The bibliography presented is over 100 pages long and identifies books, articles, and dissertations. Unfortunately, there is no index.

457. **Genealogies in the Library of Congress: A Bibliography.** Marion J. Kaminkow, ed. Baltimore: Magna Carta Book Company, 1972. 2v. ISBN 0-91094-615-9. **Supp. 1972–1976**, 1977. 285p. ISBN 0-91094-619-1; **Second Supp. 1976–1986**, 1987. 861p. ISBN 0-91094-630-2.

Still considered a monumental work, this 1972 title superseded earlier efforts from 1910 and 1919 in identifying U.S. and English family histories in the Library of Congress. The more than 20,000 entries included all listings in the Family Name Index of the library's Local History and Genealogy Room and furnished the most comprehensive bibliography of its kind. Both published and unpublished genealogies, arranged by family surname and representing various countries of origin, are listed through mid-1971. Microfilm as well as print editions are identified. Five years later, Kaminkow produced a one-volume supplement covering 23,000 more items added to the collection to mid-1976. In 1987, a second supplement was issued by the author covering genealogies added between 1976–1986. Numerous cross-references facilitate use of these Kaminkow volumes. *Genealogies Cataloged by the Library of Congress Since 1986: With a List of Established Forms of Family Names and a List of Genealogies Converted to Microform Since 1983* (Library of Congress, 1991) continues the coverage through mid-1991 with over 10,000 family-name entries and more than 22,600 cross-references.

Kaminkow's *A Complement to Genealogies in the Library of Congress: A Bibliography* (Magna Carta Book Company, 1981) identifies genealogies found in an additional 45 libraries, excluding the Library of Congress. Also treated are supplements, corrections, and new editions. About 20,000 entries are furnished.

458. **Guide to Genealogical Research in the National Archives.** National Archives Trust Fund Board. Washington: National Archives Trust Fund Board, National Archives and Records Administration, 1985. 304p. ISBN 0-911333-00-2.

Divided into four major sections, this work is a revised and expanded version of a 1969 publication; it describes groupings of records in the National Archives in terms of their content and access. The first section, "Population and Immigration Records," describes census holdings, passenger lists, and naturalization records. The second segment, "Military," covers service records of the various military branches, with additional information on volunteers and pension files, among other things. The third part, "Records Relating to Particular Groups," includes collections relating to wartime activities of the civilian population, such as blacks, American Indians, and merchant seamen. Finally, a miscellaneous category, "Other Records," includes those relating to land claims, court proceedings, and cartography. There is a five-page introductory segment on the value and limitations of government records for genealogy. This includes an overview of the general organization of records, the various special programs at the archives, and the use of finding aids. Appendices provide various listings, and access is furnished through a detailed index.

459. **Immigrants from Great Britain and Ireland: A Guide to Archival and Manuscript Sources in North America.** Jack W. Weaver and DeeGee Lester, comps. Westport, CT: Greenwood, 1986. 129p. ISBN 0-313-24342-5.

This is the first volume of another Greenwood series and offers a listing of archival resources in various repositories on this continent as they relate to the Anglo-Irish experience. English, Welsh, Scottish, and Irish immigration manuscripts, unpublished and relatively obscure in most cases, are identified through institutional responses to questionnaires on their holdings. The centers listed represent just about every state in the United States and every province in Canada. Some repositories are uncertain about how much they own of the Anglo-Irish culture. Entries furnish name of source, address, phone number, hours and accessibility, and availability of photoreproduction. Brief descriptions are included, and arrangement is alphabetical under state or province, then city, then repository. Much effort has gone into this work, and although there are notable omissions, its value is evident.

460. **The Immigration History Research Center: A Guide to Collections.** Suzanna Moody and Joel Wurl, comps. and eds. New York: Greenwood, 1991. 446p. ISBN 0-313-26832-0.

Another of the Greenwood products in this area, this guide enumerates the holdings of the Immigration History Research Center (IHRC) created at the University of Minnesota to remedy the short-sightedness apparent in U.S. libraries' failure to collect such materials. There is a strong emphasis on Central and East European culture, although southern Europe is also represented. In all, there are 24 different national groups ranging, alphabetically, from Albania to Ukraine, with Jewish immigration also being treated. There is a separate chapter for each group for which the holdings of IHRC are described. Included in these collections are manuscripts, newspapers, monographs, and serials. Emphasis is given to the period just prior and subsequent to the turn of the century, a period for which the causes of immigration are examined and experiences are recorded. Full information is given regarding the operation and accessibility of IHRC.

461. **The Library: A Guide to the LDS Family History Library.** Johni Cerny and Wendy Elliott, eds. Salt Lake City: Ancestry, 1988. 763p. ISBN 0-916489-21-3.

In approaching any study of family history, the Mormon influence on collecting such information is a primary consideration. This work serves as a guide to the collections and services offered through the Church of Jesus Christ of Latter-day Saints (LDS), its monumental library in Salt Lake City, and the numerous branch libraries located throughout the world. The United States is divided into 10 regions, for which information is given concerning historical background, migration, and settlement. Various records are described that are relevant to all phases and stages of life (census, court, church, cemetery, etc.). Charts and checklists are furnished with the data for each region to highlight the types of records held for any jurisdiction. The remainder of the world is covered through a series of 14 different essays in which Europe is treated most thoroughly. Africa and South America are both represented, making the guide a valuable starting point for the more difficult searches. The researcher should check the catalogs of both the church and other publishers for relevant tools.

462.   **The Library of Congress: A Guide to Genealogical and Historical Research.** James C. Neagles and Mark C. Neagles. Salt Lake City: Ancestry, 1990. 381p. ISBN 0-916489-48-5.

This recent publication does a superb job in guiding the user through the array of materials related to genealogy. Not limited to those materials in the Local History and Genealogy Reading Room, it points out the value of various divisions and catalogs of the LC in conducting such research. Arranged under three major sections, the first of which serves as an introduction to the entire library, the guide was compiled by several librarians who cooperated in providing this useful access tool. Part II identifies the categories of research and publication; part III represents the bulk of the text in describing nearly 3,000 source publications by state and by region. An index is included at the end.

A tool that complements the above work is P. William Filby's *Directory of American Libraries with Genealogy or Local History Collections* (Genealogical, 1988), which identifies and describes library collections and services throughout the U.S. and Canada. Arrangement is alphabetical by state or province; also, there is an index of libraries with collections of relative importance for out-of-state searches.

Bibliographical Sources

463.   **American Family History: A Historical Bibliography.** Santa Barbara, CA: ABC-Clio, 1984. 282p. (ABC-Clio Research Guides, no.12). ISBN 0-87436-380-2.

Another of the publisher's spin-off guides based on the database that produces *America: History and Life* (entry 51), this annotated bibliography furnishes over 1,150 entries relevant to both Canadian and U.S. family history. Limited to the publication years 1973–1982, the work furnishes a useful survey of contemporary thought. Coverage is provided in four major chapters: "The Family Historical," "The Family and Other Social Institutions," "Familial Roles and Relationships," and "Individual Family Histories." Over 2,000 journals in history and the social sciences have been searched for relevant contributions. Included in each entry are the usual bibliographic elements, along with significant abstracts. The arrangement of entries is alphabetical by author within the different chapters, and both subject and author indexes provide access to the material.

464.   **American Genealogical-Biographical Index to American Genealogical, Biographical and Local History Materials.** Fremont Rider, ed. Middletown, CT: Godfrey Memorial Library, 1952–1992. v.1–168. (In progress).

This effort originally began as a card file of names from genealogies held by several cooperating libraries back in the mid-1930s. Since that time it has been published in book format as the *American Genealogical Index* over a 10-year period from 1942 to 1952 (48v.), when it was superseded by the present title. Through it all, Fremont Rider, the eclectic, enterprising, and somewhat eccentric librarian at Wesleyan University guided its fortunes. Although Rider died in 1962, his work goes on with volume 168, published in 1992. The intent is to furnish a comprehensive index to names in published family genealogies that are not themselves indexed. There appears to be merit in the claim that the index will prove to be a time saver owing to the large number of names drawn from thousands of sources.

The fifth edition of the *Index to American Genealogies and to Genealogical Material Contained in All Works Such as Town Histories* (Munsell, 1900; Supp. 1908; Repr. Gale,

1966), although old, represents comprehensive indexing of family names found in scattered sources (e.g., biographies, local histories, proceedings). It treats about 16,000 names with 60,000 references.

465. Genealogical and Local History Books in Print. 4th ed. Nettie Schreiner-Yantis, comp. Springfield, VA: Genealogical Books in Print, 1985–1990. 4v. ISSN 0146-616X.

This work began in 1975 as *Genealogical Books in Print* and has continued as a useful tool, providing awareness of available materials for purposes of inquiry, a marketing device for authors and publishers, and an ordering tool for librarians, researchers, and collectors. Entries are arranged by subject and furnish bibliographic information and, in some cases, annotations. The present edition greatly expands the coverage of the previous effort, and reflects the growing interest in the field. The first three volumes were published in 1985, with volumes 1 and 2 furnishing coverage under subject areas subdivided by states. Volume 3 lists family genealogies; there is an index of family names. Volume 4 was issued in 1990 as a supplement to the fourth edition and includes listings and ordering information for materials published since 1985. Listings are based on submissions by publishers; therefore, coverage is not comprehensive.

466. Immigrant Women in the United States: A Selectively Annotated Multidisciplinary Bibliography. Donna R. Gabaccia, comp. New York: Greenwood, 1989. 325p. (Bibliographies and Indexes in Women's Studies, no.9). ISBN 0-313-26452-X.

This recent bibliography updates the Cordasco volume treated in the paragraph below. A more comprehensive effort, this one identifies more than 2,000 items (books, journal articles, dissertations) of a scholarly nature dealing with the subject of immigrant women and their daughters born in this country. Chapters focus either on format/type, such as "Bibliography" or "General Works," or on topical elements ("Migration," "Family," "Work," etc.). There is a useful introduction in each chapter, and many of the entries are annotated. Arrangement is alphabetical by author within the chapters. The entries are accessible through no less than four indexes, which cover authors, persons, groups, and subjects.

The earlier bibliography, by Francesco Cordasco, *The Immigrant Woman of North America: An Associated Bibliography of Selected References* (Scarecrow, 1985), furnishes 1,190 entries, some annotated, drawn from a variety of books and journals. These examine the female experience in immigration history. There are six broad categorical headings, both form/format ("Bibliography" and "General References") and topical ("The Workplace" and "Political Encounters"). The material is accessed by both subject and author indexes.

467. Immigrants and Their Children in the United States: A Bibliography of Doctoral Dissertations, 1885–1982. William A. Hoglund. New York: Garland, 1986. 491p. (Garland Reference Library of Social Science, v.303). ISBN 0-8240-8748-8.

This represents a comprehensive and briefly annotated bibliography of doctoral dissertations on immigrants to the continental United States since 1789. These dissertations were accepted between the years of 1885 and 1982. Over 3,500 dissertations are represented here and arranged alphabetically by author. Entries include name, title of dissertation, degree-granting institution, major field, and year of completion. Also furnished is the reference number employed by *Dissertation Abstracts International* (entry 92), which serves as the major source for the entries. Excluded from consideration here are works on Eskimos, native Americans, Puerto Ricans, blacks as slaves (involuntary immigrants) and Spanish-speaking people in the American southwest during the seventeenth and eighteenth centuries. As a special feature, there is a listing of 82 dissertations on ethnic groups arriving in the United

States before 1789. There is an index for ethnic and national groupings that is essential because of the author arrangement.

The Immigrant Experience: An Annotated Bibliography by Paul D. Mageli (Salem, 1991) furnishes a selective listing of books and articles, largely of a popular nature, that should prove useful to the student or interested layperson. Annotations are detailed, and coverage is given to various ethnic groups and time periods beginning with the mid-nineteenth century.

468. Jewish Immigrants of the Nazi Period in the U.S.A. Herbert A. Strauss, ed. New York: K. G. Saur, 1978–1986. v.1–3,5. (Projected 6v.). ISBN 0-89664-026-4.

This set represents a large-scale, ambitious project designed to provide access to documents and secondary sources that trace the immigration and resettlement in this country of German Jews fleeing the Nazi menace. Sponsored by the Research Foundation for Jewish Immigration and planned as a six-volume work, it is only partially complete. It comprises: volume 1, *Archival Resources* (1978), compiled by Steven W. Siegel; volume 2, *Classified and Annotated Bibliography of Books and Articles on the Immigration and Acculturation of Jews from Central Europe to the USA since 1933* (1981), compiled by Henry Friedlander, et. al.; volume 3, part 1 , *Guide to the Oral History Collection of the Research Foundation for Jewish Immigration* (1982), compiled by Joan C. Lessing; volume 3, part 2, *Classified List of Articles Concerning Emigration in Germany* (1982), compiled by Daniel R. Schwartz; and volume 5, *The Individual and Collective Experience of German-Jewish Immigrants, 1933–1984* (1986), compiled by David Rohrbaugh. Volume 4 is to be similar to volume 5, with documents and primary source material. Volume 6 will provide a social and communal history of Jewish immigrants. Judging by what has been accomplished thus far, the work provides full and detailed scholarship and is a must for this type of inquiry.

469. Passenger and Immigration Lists Bibliography, 1538–1900: Being a Guide to Published Lists of Arrivals in the United States and Canada. 2nd ed. P. William Filby and Dorothy M. Lower, eds. Detroit: Gale, 1988. 324p. ISBN 0-8103-240-6.

This is the most recent edition of a work first issued in 1981 and supplemented in 1984. It supersedes these efforts by including all the lists in the two earlier volumes and adding 750 others. This bibliography is a real asset to those undertaking the challenge of genealogical investigation or immigration history. All told, there are over 3,300 published sources here. Arrangement is alphabetical by author; entries include full bibliographic description as well as informative annotations describing the content and value of the work in question. There is a detailed index that provides access to topics (e.g., "Illinois—Arrivals") and is subdivided by such elements as nation of origin.

Filby's *Passenger and Immigration Lists Index: A Guide to Published Arrival Records of 500,000 Passengers Who Came to the United States and Canada in the Seventeenth, Eighteenth, and Nineteenth Centuries* (Gale, 1981; Ann. Supp. 1982–) provides an enormously useful index of names taken from passenger lists. Arrangement is alphabetical and includes age, date and place of arrival, source list, symbol/page number, and names and relationship of accompanying passengers. The 11 supplements (1982–1992) have increased the total number of names to over 2 million.

Genealogy Handbooks

470. **Ancestry's Red Book: American State, County & Town Sources.** Alice Eicholz, ed. Salt Lake City: Ancestry, 1989. 758p. ISBN 0-916489-47-7.

Designed as a guide to family research in each of the 50 states and Washington D.C., this useful manual provides state-by-state descriptions of records of all kinds (census, land, probation and court, tax, cemetery, church, military). Local history is covered, and collections are identified and located in libraries and historical societies. Useful charts are provided, along with location of county and town records and earliest date of extant primary sources. Records of immigration are enumerated, including those important to native American inquiry. Beginning with an easy-to-understand explanation of its use and ending with an excellent detailed index, this book is one of the best sources to the breadth of material available throughout the country.

471. **Black Genesis.** James Rose and Alice Eichholz. Detroit: Gale, 1978. 326p. (Gale Genealogy and Local History Series, v.1). ISBN 0-81031-400-2.

In the study of the black experience, many problems are encountered in tracing ancestry. This annotated bibliography creates an interest in black ancestry and helps researchers reclaim or retrace that part of history. There are two major sections. Part I contains seven chapters, including "Oral History" and "War Records." Part II presents a survey of the United States, the West Indies, and Canada, in which state, regional, and local records are identified. These include records of federal origin and cemetery, church, military, personal, and slave records. There is a list of projects that need to be done. Annotations are brief but informative.

Black Genealogy by Charles L. Blockson and Ron Fry (Prentice-Hall, 1977) furnishes the inquirer with a handbook providing awareness of the sources necessary to trace African ancestry. Although it is not as comprehensive as the Rose and Eicholz volume, there are many useful features. Especially noteworthy is the listing of important newspapers and the directory of research resources identifying information centers both in the United States and elsewhere. There is helpful information on how to search in the introductory chapters.

472. **The Encyclopedia of Jewish Genealogy. Volume I: Sources in the United States and Canada.** Arthur Kurzweil and Miriam Weiner, eds. Northvale, NJ: Jason Aronson, 1991. 226p. ISBN 0-87668-835-0.

With the growing interest in family origins, the more specialized manuals that deal with problems specific to an ethnic or racial group have become increasingly important. To the Jewish people, family study has always been a major interest, and location of records has been an important task. This recent entry is the first of what is projected to be a three-volume work. In this volume, there are three major chapters: immigration and naturalization; U.S. institutional resources arranged by city; and Canadian resources arranged by city. The second chapter is the most important: In directory fashion, first by state, then by city, it identifies and describes the collections and resources of a variety of institutions (libraries, cemeteries, synagogues, funeral homes). Canada is treated in similar fashion by province, then city. Chapter 1 describes immigration and naturalization records and identifies passenger and steamship listings. Volume 2 will cover sources throughout the rest of the world, and volume 3 will provide a topical approach.

473. **The Researcher's Guide to American Genealogy.** 2nd ed. Val D. Greenwood. Baltimore: Genealogical Publishing Co., 1990. ISBN 0-8063-1267-X.

This work was established as the premiere text on U.S. genealogy with its first edition in 1973. It was considered to be thorough, understandable, and exceptionally informative in explaining the location and utilization of existing records. The new edition continues that legacy with its excellent treatment of various records and their analysis. New sources and new techniques are carefully and clearly described. Search strategies are enumerated; new technology, such as the home computer, is embraced and endorsed in the development of worksheets and charts. There is a new chapter on family historians as well. Classes of records are described in detail, as in the earlier version. Bibliographies have been updated, and the book is still the best source of initial inquiry for both the beginner and the specialist.

Genealogical Research and Resources: A Guide for Library Use by Lois C. Gilmer (American Library Association, 1988) is intended to furnish assistance to reference librarians with limited collections in genealogy. Brief but informative treatment is given to genealogical research, its practice, and its source materials. It represents a useful tool for the beginning researcher.

474. **The Source: A Guidebook of American Genealogy.** Arlene Eakle and Johni Cerny, eds. Salt Lake City: Ancestry, 1984. 786p. ISBN 0-916489-00-0.

More of a resource guide than a manual of genealogy practice, this work is divided into three major sections. The first one covers sources of records (family, home, cemetery, marriage, divorce, business, prison, military). Part 2 treats the published sources (directories, newspapers, genealogical tools), and part 3 enumerates special resources related to ethnic influences (immigrant origins, Spanish and Mexican records, as well as those of blacks, Asian-Americans, Jewish-Americans, etc.). In all, there are 23 chapters divided along these and similar lines. This would appear to fulfill its purpose of providing a "solid introduction to the major U.S. record types from their beginnings to 1910." Also useful are the frequent illustrations of documents and sources.

Ethnic Genealogy: A Research Guide by Jesse Carney Smith (Greenwood, 1983) was an early entrant in multicultural genealogy and facilitates the search for information pertaining to the family life of American Indians, Asian-Americans, black Americans, and Hispanics. This serves as a manual for conducting such searches and provides helpful listings of the various resources and records.

Other Information Sources

475. **The Abridged Compendium of American Genealogy: First Families of America. Genealogical Encyclopedia of the United States.** Frederick A. Virkus and Albert Nelson Marquis, eds. Baltimore: Genealogical Publishing Co., 1987. 7v. ISBN 0-8063-1171-1.

This work was begun in 1916 in response to the need for evidence to prove citizenship lineage for those applying for jobs in war-related or war-sensitive organizations, agencies, and firms. The final volume appeared in 1942, at a time when it was again necessary for some to obtain this sort of proof. Bearing a 1970 copyright date, the work has recently been reprinted with a new foreword by noted genealogy writer P. W. Filby. The work represents an extensive listing of first families (earlier rather than most prominent), with information having been gathered mostly from people born in the second half of the nineteenth century, describing their earlier lineage. This is not a "vanity" publication: Much was discarded by the editors, and an attempt was made to verify the dates. Entries appear as biographical narrative and identify the degree of descent from particular ancestors. There is a name index to provide access.

476. **Bonded Passengers to America.** Peter Wilson Coldham. Baltimore: Genealogical Publishing Co., 1983. 9v. in 3. ISBN 0-8063-1003-0.

This is a comprehensive listing of names of individuals who were forcibly sent by judicial action from England to this country from the early seventeenth century to 1775. Crimes range from petty theft and indebtedness to more serious felonies. Following an introductory essay in the first volume on the history of transportation from 1615 to 1775, coverage in each of the following volumes is based on the conviction list of the various British judicial districts or circuits—for example, volume 3, "London, 1656–1775," and volume 8, "Northern Circuit, 1665–1775." The 50,000 names are arranged alphabetically in each volume and stand as the largest listing of immigrants to the U.S. colonies prior to the Revolutionary War. Entries include the date of sentencing, the name of the ship, and in some cases indication of the nature of the crime and/or place of arrival.

An earlier work, not so extensive, is Marion J. Kaminkow's *Original Lists of Emigrants in Bondage from London to the American Colonies, 1719–1744* (Magna Carta, 1967), which identifies nearly 7,300 people who were sent to this country for assorted crimes and misdemeanors.

477. **The Complete Book of Emigrants, 1607–1660.** Peter Wilson Coldham. Baltimore, MD: Genealogical Publishing Co., 1988. 600p. ISBN 0-8063-1192-4.

This work targets British emigration to the Americas during a limited time segment of the seventeenth century and furnishes a listing of 15,000 available names. There is duplication of certain information previously published by Hotten (entry 480) and in other public records. Coldham has examined over 30 archival sources such as those issued by the British Public Record Office in producing this listing. The names are limited to English only and do not include Irish or even Scottish or Welsh families. When available, information concerning age, family relationships, status and ship are included for each entry. Because much of the emigration record has been lost through the years, Coldham's energetic effort represents a great asset to those who conduct such studies. Arrangement of entries is chronological, with access provided by a name index.

Supplementary works by Coldham are *The Complete Book of Emigrants, 1661–1699* (1990) and *The Complete Book of Emigrants, 1700–1750* (1992). With these two volumes, an additional 60,000 names are furnished in the same manner as the initial work. The fourth and final volume, covering the period from 1751 to 1776, is planned for early 1993.

478. **The Dictionary of American Immigration History.** Francesco Cordasco, ed. Metuchen, NJ: Scarecrow, 1990. 784p. ISBN 0-8108-2241-5.

The editor has been a prolific bibliographer in a variety of fields but most frequently in ethnic studies. In this dictionary, various ethnic groups are described, along with personalities, organizations, societies, topical themes (such as pluralism), legislation, and unions. It is a product of large proportions, with over 90 contributors from this country, Canada, and the United Kingdom. There are more than 2,500 entries, arranged alphabetically and varying in length from a single paragraph to several pages depending upon the importance of the subject. Brief bibliographies are furnished at the end of the entries. American Indians as a group have been excluded from coverage because of extensive treatment given in numerous other publications. Certain omissions occur (such as gypsies). There is a brief but useful introduction that describes immigration policies in this country for a period of 100 years beginning with the 1880s. There is no index.

479.   **Germans to America: Lists of Passengers Arriving at U.S. Ports, 1850.** Ira A. Glazier and P. William Filby, eds. Wilmington, DE: Scholarly Resources, 1988– . v.1–20 (in progress). ISBN 0-8420-2279-1.

In recent years, there has been much more interest in the publication of tools to aid the investigation of German immigration. Glazier and Filby have produced a large-scale effort that reached its twentieth volume in 1991. Complete passenger lists are furnished beginning with the year 1850 and continuing through the late 1960s. Entries furnish age, gender, trade or occupation, place of origin, and destination for every passenger from Germany who arrived in any of the major ports in this country. A name index furnishes access to the proper list.

A complementary effort, also recent, is *German Immigrants: Lists of Passengers Bound from Bremen to New York 1842–1867 with Places of Origin*, compiled by Gary J. Zimmerman and Marion Wolfert (Genealogical Publishing Co., 1985–1988) in three volumes. About 100,000 names are given of those who arrived through the well-traveled route of Bremen to New York. The work is of value because of its focus on an elusive time period.

480.   **The Original Lists of Persons of Quality; Emigrants; Religious Exiles; Political Rebels; Serving Men Sold for a Term of Years; Apprentices...** John C. Hotten, ed. Repr. Baltimore: Genealogical Publishing Co., 1986. 580p. ISBN 0-8063-0605-X.

This offering has been a major aid for investigation since its publication in 1874 and is one of the best-known sources. Hotten employed the public records of the Chancery and the Exchequer to create a listing of names representing a wide range of individuals who emigrated to American plantations from Great Britain during the years 1600–1700. As stated in the extensive subtitle, in addition to "persons of quality" there were emigrants, religious exiles, political rebels, indentured servants, apprentices, "children stolen" and "maidens pressed." Entries include ages, localities of origin, and names of the ships whenever possible.

Over 100 years later, the work was supplemented by James C. Brandow, who edited *Omitted Chapters from Hotten's Original Lists ... Census Returns, Parish Registers and Militia Rolls for the Barbados Census of 1679/80* (Genealogical Publishing Co., 1982). Hotten's rather surprising omission of Barbados records was brought to light and corrected by Brandow, who scoured the registers, rolls, and landholder lists to produce the names of an additional 6,500 persons. This is quite important, because many of those who arrived in Barbados later relocated in this country.

ETHNIC, RACIAL, AND GENDER INFLUENCES

Since the 1960s, there has been a real interest in ethnicity and national origins, which has inspired the production of an array of trade and reference publications on the topic. Authors, editors, and publishers have both followed and encouraged the public interest in the awakening of pride within ethnic, racial, and gender segments of U.S. society during the past 30 years. This focus is in keeping with the emphasis on such societal factors in modern historiography. Following a slight lapse of enthusiasm for the subject during the late 1970s, there has been a renewed interest in the 1980s and 1990s with the country's growing commitment to the promotion of multicultural studies and appreciation of its cultural diversity.

The American Society for Ethnohistory in Chicago was founded in 1953 and has 1,200 members. Since 1954, it has published the quarterly journal *Ethnohistory*, which treats past cultures all over the world. Also relevant is the Immigration History Society and its publications (p. 177).

General

This subsection treats the more generic or comprehensive sources, such as those on racism in general or those covering more than one ethnic group. Works having a more specific focus, be it ethnic, racial, or gender-based, are treated in listings for each of the particular groups. Included in the general subsection are materials that may be pertinent to the study of immigration, addressed in the previous unit of this chapter, and also to economic history, the topic of chapter 7.

Library Resources

481. **Ethnic Collections in Libraries.** E. J. Josey and Marva L. DeLoach, eds. New York: Neal-Schuman, 1983. 361p. ISBN 0-918212-63-4.

Referring to the lack of a "communications link" to material on the four non-European ethnic groups—native Americans, African-Americans, Asian Americans, and Hispanic Americans—the editors have produced a collection of 18 original essays by different writers on existing collections of these materials. The work is divided into three major sections or parts: "Diversity of Ethnic Collections," "Major Collections on Ethnic Minorities," and "Archives, Programming, Federal Policy, and Linkages." Chapters describe historical development, future projections for the collections of each group, and problems in acquisitions. Holdings are given for both academic and public libraries in this country. Emphasis is placed on separate essays on technical considerations of access and criteria, whereas the advocacy of balanced ethnic collections represents a common theme to the various writers.

Bibliographical Sources

A current abstracting service of interest is *Sage Race Relations Abstracts* (Sage, 1975–) which is issued quarterly and abstracts books, periodicals, essays, and pamphlets relating to both U.S. and European happenings. Occasionally, historical topics are treated.

482. **A Comprehensive Bibliography for the Study of American Minorities.** Wayne C. Miller, et al. New York: New York University, 1976. 2v. ISBN 0-8147-5373-6.

As its title indicates, this volume represents an expansive bibliography in terms of its coverage, and although it is aging it should continue to prove fruitful for those seeking information on multicultural elements within the U.S. milieu. Containing over 29,000 entries bearing concise but informative annotations, the work is not limited to the black and native American experience but includes treatment of the various European influences as well as those of the Middle East and Asia. Coverage is broad and includes history, sociology, religion, education, and language. There is a historical-bibliographical introductory essay for each ethnic group treated, followed by the extensive bibliographic listing. Each of the nearly 40 distinct groups is treated in this way in a separate chapter. Both author and title indexes provide access in this extremely useful work. The introductory essays have been reprinted in another work by Miller published at the same time.

483. **The Economics of Minorities: A Guide to Information Sources.** Kenneth L. Gagala. Detroit: Gale, 1976. 212p. (Economics Information Guide Series, v.2). ISBN 0-8103-1294-8.

As an economist who has special expertise on the topic of economic conditions of nonwhite peoples, Gagala was well-prepared to assume the responsibility of producing a useful bibliography. The work consists of annotated listings of books and articles from a wide range of studies (political science, sociology, psychology, education, etc.). Nonwhites have been defined as black Americans, American Indians, Mexican-Americans, and Puerto Ricans. Materials were published between 1965 and 1974 and reflect the impact of the race riots of the mid-1960s in terms of an increased number of relevant publications. Entries are arranged alphabetically by author within 12 categorical or topical chapters. With few exceptions, the citations are complete. There is a subject index that contains cross-references and an author index and title index as well.

484. **Ethnicity and Nationality: A Bibliographic Guide.** G. Carter Bentley. Seattle: University of Washington, 1981. 381p. ISBN 0-295-95853-7.

There are over 3,300 published items covered in this useful bibliographic guide to ethnicity and nationality sponsored by the School of International Studies at the University of Washington in a project begun in 1975. English-language articles published between 1961 and 1979 are treated in one of two major sections. The first section provides a straight alphabetical listing of the 308 annotated entries the author has judged to be most significant. Annotations are longer and well developed and should prove helpful for subsequent use. The second section, "Unannotated Entries," contains the remaining listings arranged alphabetically by author. All entries are coded by content, geographical area covered, and group. This work received mixed reviews when it appeared, but in general it should serve the needs of students and general inquirers.

485. **Minority Studies: A Selective Annotated Bibliography.** Priscilla Oaks. Boston: G. K. Hall, 1975. 303p. ISBN 0-8161-1092-1.

This is a useful annotated bibliography of 1,800 books on selected groups of U.S. minorities (native Americans, Mexican-Americans, Puerto Ricans, Afro-Americans and Asian-Americans). As is the case with many of the efforts of the mid-1970s, there was a purposeful omission of white ethnic minorities in recognition of the need to target people of color. This effort begins with a general section that includes periodical titles, followed by separate sections on each of the groups covered. Subsections are divided by format and, in some cases, by topic. Annotations are brief but informative; there is an author/title index.

Minorities and Women: A Guide to the Reference Literature in the Social Services by Gail Ann Schlachter and Donna Belli (Reference Service Press, 1977) furnishes reference to more than 800 English-language entries. Arrangement is by format division, such as information sources (e.g., fact books, biographies) or bibliographic sources (bibliographies, indexes, etc). These are subdivided by the minority groups; American Indians, Asian-Americans, black Americans, Spanish-Americans, and women. There are separate author, title, and subject indexes.

486. **Race and Ethnic Relations: An Annotated Bibliography.** Graham C. Kinloch. New York: Garland, 1984. 250p. (Garland Bibliographies in Sociology, v.3; Garland Reference Library of Social Science, v.226). ISBN 0-8240-8971-5.

A fairly recent and thereby useful effort in the area of race relations is this annotated bibliography of nearly 1,100 books and articles published between 1960 and 1979. One may benefit from an excellent overview, encompassing 20 years of writing, of the changes and changed pace of ethnic relations. Approximately 120 social science journals were searched to turn up the relevant texts. The work is divided into four sections beginning with "General Bibliography and Research Trends," which bears 18 entries, followed by "Theory and Methodology" with 154. "Race and Ethnic Relations in the United States" is the major category, with 696 entries; other societies are covered in the final segment, with 198 entries.

Both author and subject indexes provide access to this effort, which should benefit both scholars and students.

487. **Racism in the United States: A Comprehensive Classified Bibliography.** Meyer Weinberg, comp. New York: Greenwood, 1990. 682p. ISBN 0-313-27390-1.

The compiler has served as a history instructor in the community college system in Chicago and projects a real interest in the nature and effects of racism. This annotated bibliography furnishes about 10,000 items alphabetically arranged under 87 different subject headings. Materials include books, articles, monographs, hearings, and dissertations. Each topical area concludes with a listing of bibliographies on that subject. With such an extensive listing of titles, the work is considered a useful product for serious inquiry, although it has been criticized for incompleteness and inconsistency in the citations themselves. There is an index of authors but not of subjects.

Jahid A. Momeni's *Demography of Racial and Ethnic Minorities in the United States: An Annotated Bibliography with a Review Essay* (Greenwood, 1984) updates his 1983 effort on the black population but places emphasis on sources of social statistics pertinent to Asians, Hispanics, Jews, and native Americans. Such topics as fertility patterns, health and mortality, and migration are covered with nearly 700 books, articles, and dissertations, accompanied by lengthy annotations. A detailed bibliographic essay serves to introduce the text. This is a useful product for serious inquirers on non-white and Jewish people. There are both author and minority subject indexes.

A more recent effort is *Discrimination and Prejudice: An Annotated Bibliography* compiled by Halford H. Fairchild and others (Westerfield Enterprises, 1991), which identifies books, articles, and dissertations in five separate bibliographic segments: Afro-Americans, American Indians, Asian-Americans, Hispanic-Americans, and a multiethnic listing.

Information Sources

488. **Dictionary of Race and Ethnic Relations.** 2nd ed. Ernest E. Cashmore with Michael Benton, et al. London: Routledge, 1988. 325p. ISBN 0-415-02511-7.

The first edition of this useful work was issued in 1984 and was recognized for its coverage of both British and U.S. racial relations. The more recent edition is similar to the first in providing in-depth articles (essay-length in most cases) on major figures and socio-logical elements related to the study of ethnic influences. Treatment is given to theories and concepts, for which much of the material has been rewritten or updated since the 1984 work. Many topics have been added, including such elements as "ethnic monitoring" and "racial choice theory." Although this book is useful to the student of U.S. history, there is feeling on the part of at least one reviewer that this basically British publication could have provided more coverage of U.S. issues than it now does. Certain omissions (such as communism and socialism) have been noted. An index is provided.

489. **Encyclopedic Directory of Ethnic Newspapers and Periodicals in the United States.** 2nd ed. Lubomyr R. Wynar and Anna T. Wynar. Littleton, CO: Libraries Unlimited, 1976. 248p. ISBN 0-87287-154-1.

This volume updates a 1972 work and needs to be revised itself at this point in time. The effort is still useful for its breadth, still greater than the more recent effort by Sally M. Miller (entry 491). The Wynar effort was enlarged to cover 63 ethnic groups, as compared to 43 in the first edition, and it gives background information on nearly 1,000 different serial titles. Information was obtained by Wynar, who served as Director of the Center for the Study of Ethnic Publications at Kent State University. Arrangement is alphabetical within the 51 sections, and entries are separated by languages employed (English or native/bilingual). Entries give dates, frequency, circulation, subscription rate, and scope of each publication, plus addresses and phone numbers of editors. Statistical information is found in the appendix, and an introductory essay explores the nature of the ethnic press.

490. **Ethnic Information Sources of the United States: A Guide to Organizations, Agencies, Foundations, Institutions, Media, Commercial and Trade Bodies, Government Programs...** 2nd ed. Paul Wasserman and Alice E. Kennington, eds. Detroit: Gale, 1983. 2v. ISBN 0-8103-0367-1.

This useful broad-based directory attempts to identify and describe "as many sources of information about ethnic groups which are available in the United States as it was possible to accumulate." Because of the presence of numerous tools dealing with racial minorities, this work excludes blacks, American Indians, and Eskimos. It instead provides a focus on the sources relevant to the study of over 100 European and Asian ethnic groups. The groups are arranged alphabetically in the first section from Afghan to Yugoslav; sources are then listed under 26 headings—"Embassy and Consulates," "Information Offices," "Fraternal Organizations," and so on. Information was secured in a variety of ways, including correspondence and questionnaires, library research, and interviews with experts. Although the book has been criticized for attempting too broad a coverage in terms of the 26 types of sources identified in the subtitle, its utility for the inquirer is evident.

491. **The Ethnic Press in the United States: A Historical Analysis and Handbook.** Sally M. Miller, ed. New York: Greenwood, 1987. 437p. ISBN 0-313-23879-0.

Although not as comprehensive as the earlier work by Wynar (entry 489), which covers 63 ethnic groups, this more recent effort furnishes in-depth historical analysis. Scholarly, essay-length articles contributed by ethnic studies specialists describe the newspapers of 27 different ethnic groups. Included are both the better-known and the more obscure newspapers. The editor from the staff of the *Pacific Historian* regards the ethnic press as the "best primary source for an understanding of the world of non-English speaking groups in the United States." Prior to World War I, there were as many as 1,300 foreign-language newspapers in this country; the decline was brought about by immigration restrictions. Essays treat the background of each ethnic group and the cultural-political atmosphere contributing to the origin and development of its publications. Bibliographies are provided; there is an index of subjects, titles, and names.

492. **Harvard Encyclopedia of American Ethnic Groups.** Stephan Thernstrom, et al., eds. Cambridge: Harvard University Press, 1980. 1,076p. ISBN 0-674-37512-2.

Nearly 300 expert contributors and consultants were commissioned to generate this comprehensive one-volume encyclopedia covering 100 U.S. ethnic groups. Articles are essay-length and range from 3,000 to 40,000 words, describing not only each of the individual groups but also an additional 29 themes and topics (American identity, folklore, politics, etc.). The articles are well-written and readable and include select bibliographic narratives. They furnish information on historical background, migration, settlement, culture and language, organization, and group maintenance. Although somewhat uneven in coverage of the different groups (owing to the participation of the various experts), this is a pioneering effort contributing to the information store available on ethnic peoples. "Ethnic" is interpreted broadly and includes some U.S. Caucasians, such as Mormons and inhabitants of the Appalachians, as well as American Indians and blacks.

493. **Multiculturalism in the United States: A Comparative Guide to Acculturation and Ethnicity.** John D. Buenker and Lorman A. Ratner. New York: Greenwood, 1992. 280p. ISBN 0-313-25374-9.

With the recent interest in multiculturalism, Buenker and Ratner have been quick to respond to what is to become a driving issue. This new history of the various groups in our country is a comprehensive source, treating both the traditional immigrant cultures from various parts of Europe and the more recent Latin American immigration. Nor does it neglect native Americans. The various chapters succeed in providing informative profiles of individual cultures written by scholars in their own areas of expertise. As is the case with most multiauthor works, there is a certain inconsistency both in style and treatment among the different chapters. Both students and researchers should profit from the description of major institutions for each tradition. Each chapter has a full bibliography for further examination.

494. **Peoples of the World: North Americans: The Culture, Geographical Setting, and Historical Background of 37 North American Peoples.** Joyce Moss and George Wilson. Detroit: Gale, 1991. 441p. ISBN 0-8103-7768-3.

Designed more for the layman and high school or undergraduate student rather than the practicing historian, this recent work provides an excellent overview of the people who have inhabited the North American continent. As such, it will be in great demand for a variety of needs associated with the new emphasis on multicultural elements within our society. Beginning with the early inhabitants who came prior to the European settlements, the book enumerates a mix of native cultures, including three lost cultures as well as 34 current groups. Entries profile these peoples and emphasize the human dimension in terms of their cultural achievements. In so doing, they provide an excellent awareness of the continent as a melting pot of diverse cultural composition. Maps and illustrations accompany the text and help to illustrate the cultural movements.

495. **Refugees in the United States: A Reference Handbook.** David W. Haines, ed. Westport, CT: Greenwood, 1985. 243p. ISBN: 0-313-24068-X.

This is a broad-based reference tool designed to cast light on the refugee problem in this country as it has unfolded over the past 25 years. The recency of its coverage makes this an unusual and desirable resource for social historians interested in tracing contemporary influences. The editor was formerly associated with the Federal Refugee Resettlement Program and has brought expertise to the subject. The work comprises two major parts. Part 1 examines the resettlement of refugees in this country, identifies programs, and describes obstacles and adjustments within the process of migration. Part 2 offers chapters on the major refugee groups (Chinese, Cubans, Haitians, Hmong, Khmer, Lao, Salvadorans, Guatemalans, Soviet Jews, and Vietnamese). Chapters are written by specialists and furnish background history of the homeland, the migrations, and the adjustments. There is a detailed index as well as a selective bibliography.

496. **We the People: An Atlas of America's Ethnic Diversity.** James P. Allen and Eugene J. Turner. New York: Macmillan, 1988. 315p. ISBN 0-02-901420-4.

As a work seven years in the making, this cultural atlas is the product of a happy union of the two geographers, Allen as a specialist in immigration and Turner as an expert in computer mapping. The data are arranged by ethnic group and are taken from the 1980 census. Presentation is excellent thanks to the use of 115 maps, most of which are in color. Nearly 70 racial and ethnic groups are treated, their movements and distributions charted from 1920 to 1980. Subsections are given to the coverage of special groups, such as Catholic and Protestant Irish, Sephardic Jews, and Chinese from Vietnam. Accompanying text of about three pages for each group describes settlement patterns and reasons for locating in certain geographic locales. Indexes of ethnic population and place provide access to the content.

The Asian Experience

Compared to the other ethnic influences on this country, the Asian-American experience has suffered from neglect and lack of documentation. This neglect has persisted longer than it did in the case of European ethnic minorities, who did benefit from a surge of interest in ethnicity during the 1970s. With the relatively recent focus on multi-culturalism, reference tools on Asian-Americans have begun to appear. It should be pointed out that one of our only reference tools targeted to a juvenile audience is included here (entry 500) because of the void in such coverage at more sophisticated levels.

The Chinese Historical Society of America was founded in 1963 in San Francisco and has 500 members. It has published *Chinese America: History and Perspectives* on an annual basis since 1980.

497. Asian-American Periodicals and Newspapers: A Union List of Holdings in the Library of the State Historical Society of Wisconsin and the Libraries of the University of Wisconsin–Madison. Maureen E. Hady and James P. Danky, comps. Madison, WI: State Historical Society of Wisconsin, 1979. 54p. ISBN 0-87020-191-3.

The State Historical Society of Wisconsin has one of the more important collections of materials relating to social history. As a result, there are numerous access tools based on its holdings. This listing of over 100 titles spanning 30 years prior to the book's publication in 1979 is useful in its union of the society's library holdings with those of various libraries of the University of Wisconsin. Titles are arranged alphabetically and are treated with bibliographic information, editorial information, indication of subject, and microfilm availability. The collection is reported to be strongest in its holdings of publications issued through university presses. Four indexes provide excellent access to expedite research through geographical, chronological, name, and subject approaches.

498. Asian-American Studies: An Annotated Bibliography and Research Guide. Hyung-Chan Kim, ed. Westport, CT: Greenwood, 1989. 504p. ISBN 0-313-26026-5.

This is a fine bibliography of nearly 3,400 items drawn from a variety of sources such as newspapers, periodicals, books, and dissertations dealing with Asian-Americans. Many of the entries furnish informative annotations. An introductory essay on research precedes the listings. There are 13 chapters covering historical perspectives and 14 chapters dealing with contemporary existence. This bibliography serves the needs of historical inquiry with respect to a variety of topics. Historical chapters cover such issues as community, justice, and religion. There is good coverage of the Japanese internment. These chapters are subdivided by format and medium (books, periodicals, theses). Creative writing is purposely excluded because it is covered in another recent source. There is a detailed subject index. This is the second of three projected works by the editor, the first of which is *Dictionary of Asian American History* (entry 502).

499. A Buried Past: An Annotated Bibliography of the Japanese American Research Project Collection. Yuji Ichioka, et al., comps. Berkeley: University of California, 1974. 227p.

This is a catalog of the collection held by the UCLA Research Library regarding Japanese government primary source materials relating to Japanese immigration and resettlement in the United States. It consists of 1,500 documents and records of various types organized under 18 different subjects. These categories include "history," "education," and "poetry," as well as "religion," "economics," and "society." Also included is a useful segment on "wartime internment." Each category opens with an introductory historical summary providing an overview of the listings on the issue. The work was undertaken as a special project of the Asian American Studies Center at the university, which succeeded in producing a valuable access tool. There is a 10-page general introduction examining the current status of publications on the topic. The work is carefully done and designed to facilitate access.

500. **The Chinese-American Heritage.** David M. Brownstone. New York: Facts on File, 1988. 132p. ISBN 0-8160-1627-5.

This offering is considered one of the best in this series intended for young adults. It provides a well-written, heavily illustrated treatment of Chinese-American history. The Asian-Americans are slow to have assimilated into the mainstream United States. Coverage is given to the historical and cultural background of the early Cantonese immigrants, followed by a description of living conditions in China. The early experiences in the United States begin with the period of the Gold Rush, when discrimination and prejudice were highest, and ends on a positive note with easing of immigration laws and lessening of racial tensions. Of course, publication of this history preceded the very recent outbreak of physical assaults upon Orientals in a U.S. society driven by anger and fear of a declining economy. There is a bibliography and an index.

501. **Chinese Newspapers Published in North America, 1854–1975.** Karl Lo and H. M. Lai, comps. Washington: Center for Chinese Research Materials, Association of Research Libraries, 1977. 138p.

A comprehensive union listing of Chinese-American newspapers, this directory took 10 years to compile. It covers a span of 122 years and is a valuable source of information for both researchers and students. The newspapers were published either by or for Chinese people in the United States or Canada, and most were written in Chinese or Chinese and English, although English-language items are also included. There is a concise but useful history of Chinese journalism in the United States and Canada. "Newspapers" are defined rather broadly in terms of being serial publications that report news; entries are arranged in chronological sequence under names of cities. Included in each are dates, names and titles (romanized through the Wade-Giles System), and holdings symbols for 40 libraries of various types (special, public, archives, etc.). There is an index of titles.

502. **Dictionary of Asian American History.** Hyung-Chan Kim, ed. New York: Greenwood, 1986. 627p. ISBN 0-313-23760-3.

The first of three works projected by the editor for Greenwood Press (entry 498), the dictionary is an important source of brief information found through nearly 800 entries, dealing with all aspects of Asian-American history. Entries describe major events, personalities, places, and ideas "that have left indelible marks," and they run from a few lines to two pages; many have lists of additional readings and cross-references. Both individual, and collective experiences of the major groups are treated. In addition, there are 15 thematic essays of from 4 to 15 pages in length. The first seven essays cover histories of particular groups in the United States (Chinese, Japanese, and Southeast Asians). The other essays are topical (immigration law, justice, politics, economics, education, mental health, literature, and popular culture). There is a chronology, a selective bibliography, and a useful detailed index.

503. **The Koreans in America, 1882–1974: A Chronology and Fact Book.** Hyung-Chan Kim and Wayne Patterson, comps. and eds. Dobbs Ferry, NY: Oceana, 1974. 147p. (Ethnic Chronology Series, no.16). ISBN 0-379-00513-1.

This brief chronology and handbook is a unique contribution to the history of Korean-Americans. There is no attempt to be exhaustive, merely a desire to furnish an additional aid to the few that exist. The work consists of three major sections, beginning with the chronology that identifies in sequence the events and activities involving Koreans in the Hawaiian Islands and the continental United States over a period of 90 years. The second segment, treating documents, creates a little confusion because it is not limited to source documents but includes reprints of journal articles and an unpublished paper by Professor Kim. The third section furnishes a selective bibliography on the topic. Although criticized for omissions in the chronology and typographical errors, the work is useful to students and beginning researchers. There is a name index to provide access.

504. **Literature of the Filipino-American in the United States: A Selective and Annotated Bibliography.** Irene P. Norell. San Francisco: R and E Research Associates, 1976. 84p. ISBN 0-88247-388-3.

Another of the reference tools on ethnic studies produced in the mid-1970s, this bibliography of books and journal articles on Filipino-Americans adds to the small store of material on the topic. At the time of publication, Filipino-Americans represented the second-largest group of immigrants entering the country and numbered over 500,000 residents. They are among the least understood of cultures, not only by Caucasians but by other Oriental groups as well. There had been very little bibliographic work done prior to its publication and, unhappily, little has been done thereafter. The entries, mostly historical and demographic in nature, are organized under seven major categories dealing with different social issues such as immigration and exclusion, race and racism, and socioeconomic factors. California and Hawaii receive special attention because of their prominent Filipino populations.

The Black Experience

Only a few reference tools were recognized as standard sources on blacks and Afro-Americans until the 1960s and 1970s, when such publications were encouraged by the increased interest in social responsibility and racial pride. Mainstream authors and publishers found ready markets in libraries and bookstores. Small black publishing houses emerged during this period, but they encountered difficulty in producing their materials in supplies adequate to market them effectively. There has been some decline in interest since then among trade publishers, who have given higher priority to the female experience. Reference book publishing remains steady, however, and both bibliographic and information sources are purchased readily. Especially noteworthy is the recent activity of Carlson Publishing Company.

Included in this section are books on various topics and issues treated elsewhere in this guide. Our rationale gave primacy to the racial consideration as the primary criterion. Therefore, here one will find books on the following aspects as they relate to African-American history: the female experience, education, religion, urban studies, demography, ideological trends, business, and labor. Exceptions are tools on black genealogy, which are found in "Genealogy and Immigration" section of this chapter, and those on blacks in film, which are found in the section on "Entertainment and Recreation: Popular Culture," also in this chapter. For books on the Ku Klux Klan, see "Ideological Trends" in this chapter. For works on desegregation, see "Education" in this chapter.

One of the oldest organizations in the field of black studies is the Association for the Study of Afro-American Life and History, headquartered in Washington, D.C. Founded in 1915, it has 2,200 members and has issued the quarterly *Journal of Negro History* since 1916.

Library Resources

505. Afro-Americana: A Research Guide to Collections at the University of California at Berkeley. Phyllis Bischof. Berkeley: General Library and the Department of Afro-American Studies, University of California, 1984. 76p.

A convenient and informative guide to the resources of the University related to the black experience, this work surveys the various branches and departments, including the Bancroft Library. It provides useful information regarding the locations and essential character of the resources. Operations and procedures are described in order to expedite access. Also covered is the online catalog, MELVYL, with suggestions and recommendations for its use, and descriptions of relevant periodical indexes. Subject headings from the card catalog are enumerated, and a list of dissertations that utilized the collection is given. There is a list of reference materials, followed by an author-title index.

The Amistad Research Center's *Author and Added Entry Catalog of the American Missionary Association Archives, with Reference to Schools and Mission Stations* (Greenwood, 1970) is a standard listing of primary source materials in this area. Now located at Tulane University, the center offers a wide variety of documents in its catalog of over 100,000 items, most of which relate to correspondence. Because of its traditional concern over "the Negro problem," the Amistad Center has amassed a fine collection of items of historical importance on such aspects as the Underground Railroad.

506. Black History: A Guide to Civilian Records in the National Archives. Debra L. Newman, comp. Washington: National Archives Trust Fund Board, 1984. 379p. ISBN 0-911333-21-5.

This guide, which has been described as a "roadmap" to the National Archives' holdings on what has been called "civilian" records, represents a time saver to researchers in the field. The materials are summarized and described and include textual, photographic, and audiovisual resources of over 140 federal agencies (Bureau of the Census, Customs, Department of Commerce, Coast Guard, etc.). A history of each agency is given, and its relevance to the black experience is examined. The records are identified by record group number. Descriptions of holdings are by necessity brief, but access is measurably aided by the inclusion of a detailed index that specifies names, sites, ships, and so on and sharpens the focus on events and occurrences. The researcher should not hesitate to use this tool to find information on either an individual or a broad topic.

507. Dictionary Catalog of the Schomburg Collection of Negro Literature and History. New York Public Library. Boston: G. K. Hall, 1962. 9v. **1st supp.** 1967. 2v. **2nd supp.** 1972. 4v. **3rd supp.** 1976. 2v. **Ann. supp.** 1976– .

G. K. Hall produced another of its valuable catalogs of notable library collections with its coverage of the famous Schomburg Collection of the New York Public Library. The initial issue provides copy of catalog cards arranged alphabetically by author, title, and subject of some 36,000 bound volumes of materials of international scope on the black experience both historical and contemporary. The three supplements furnish additional materials cataloged subsequent to publication of the basic edition. The *Bibliographic Guide to Black Studies* (Schomburg Center for Research and Black Culture, G. K. Hall, 1976–) is an annual update of the Schomburg catalog beginning with the year 1975, thus continuing the earlier works. Arrangement of entries is similar to those publications.

The *Dictionary Catalog of the Jesse E. Moorland Collection of Negro Life and History* (Moorland-Spingarn Research Center, Howard University, G. K. Hall, 1970; supp., 1976, 3v.) is a basic catalog of this famous collection. It consists of references to over 100,000 books, pamphlets, periodical titles, theses, compositions, clippings, and pictures on the black experience, with special emphasis on the slave trade and abolition. A three-volume supplement was issued in 1976 and listed additions to the book collection but not manuscripts, music, or photography.

508. **The Kaiser Index to Black Resources, 1948–1986.** Brooklyn: Carlson, 1992. 5v. ISBN 0-926019-60-0.

Another of the valuable access tools based on the magnificent collection at the Schomburg Center is this comprehensive five-volume guide to selected periodical holdings spanning a period of nearly 40 years. Over 150 periodicals covering the black experience in all its facets are treated, thus furnishing scholars, students, and interested laypersons with a wealth of information. The effort was supported by a grant from the National Endowment for the Humanities and the Aaron Diamond Foundation and represents the enormous effort expended in converting the great card file to publication format. The file was started as a reference tool of answered questions, with full indication of the periodical source material that provided the answers. Over the 40-year period, the file grew to the 174,000 items in this work, having been codified, edited, and organized during the mid-1980s. Arrangement is alphabetical by Library of Congress subject headings. A CD-ROM edition is planned for the future.

The *Index to the Schomburg Clipping File* (Chadwyck-Healey, 1986-1988) also was made possible by an NEH grant and furnishes access to this extraordinary resource, which now is available on microfiche. Here one is able to locate through a topical approach the facts, personalities, and events preserved by librarians of the past over a period of 50 years, from 1924 to 1974. Arrangement of the index is alphabetical by topic. Source material is preserved in over 9,500 microfiche and is available from the publisher as *Schomburg Clipping File, Part I, 1924–1974* ($20,000). *Part II, 1975–1988* ($17,000) contains 4,500 microfiche, for which an index is in preparation.

509. **Slavery in the Courtroom: An Annotated Bibliography of American Cases.** Paul Finkelman. Washington: Library of Congress, 1985. 312p. ISBN 0-8444-0431-4.

This is a valuable guide to the holdings of the Library of Congress related to the question of slavery and the law. While serving as the Jameson Fellow at the Library, Finkelman was moved by the discovery of numerous uncataloged pamphlets on fugitive slave cases stored in the Law Library. This discovery led to extensive research on approximately 30,000 cards on the library's Trial Collection. Because there is no subject access to this collection, Finkelman has performed an important service for students and researchers of both legal and social history with respect to this topic. Organized into seven major chapters (e.g., the "Slave in a Free Jurisdiction" and "Abolitionists in the South"), materials date from 1772 to the beginning of the Civil War. The guide covers most important considerations. Also included are a "Table of Cases," lists of pamphlets and illustrations, a select bibliography, and an index.

Bibliographical Sources

510. African-American Community Studies from North America: A Classified, Annotated Bibliography. Fred J. Hay. Hamden, CT: Garland, 1991. 234p. (Applied Social Science Bibliographies, v.5; Garland Reference Library of Social Science, v.420). ISBN 0-8240-6643-X.

This classified bibliography of community studies performed on the black community from the 1890s through the 1980s is of value to social historians and serious students. The methodology of the "community study" invokes ethnographic and sociological premises in documenting the nature and social conditions relevant to race and culture. This work includes both sociological studies and those less systematic inquiries more representative of "folklorist" traditions. A variety of source materials (some relatively obscure) is presented: books, theses, dissertations, bulletins, and reports. Entries are organized by decade beginning with the 1890s and should be useful for historical inquiry. Annotations are detailed and describe population, education, economics, and religion, among other things. There are cross-references to related subjects; the specialized classified scheme is described in a separate chapter.

511. Afro-American Demography and Urban Issues: A Bibliography. R. A. Obudho and Jeannine B. Scott. Westport, CT: Greenwood, 1985. 433p. ISBN 0-313-24656-4.

Containing nearly 5,300 citations on the subject of urban affairs and demography, this volume ranks as the most comprehensive bibliography of materials relevant to the black experience. There are seven general chapters representing key topical elements such as "Housing and Residential Patterns" and "Ghettoization." These follow a chapter devoted to listings of nearly 1,200 bibliographies. Entries are alphabetical by author, are numbered, and furnish complete bibliographic information for all titles (books, journal articles, conference papers, theses, dissertations, government documents, and unpublished items). Dates of publication between 1960 and 1980 are emphasized, although the range is from the eighteenth century through 1984. There is a guide to 35 major collections on the topic, as well as a lengthy list of periodicals consulted. A useful tool for both researchers and students, it is accessed by an author index.

512. Afro-American Education, 1907–1932: A Bibliographic Index. Richard Newman. New York: Lambeth, 1984. 178p. ISBN 0-931186-05-6.

With the publication of *Education Index* beginning in 1932, the H. W. Wilson Company relieved the government of the responsibility for maintaining bibliographic control over education literature. The 1907–1932 period spans that era of governmental responsibility. In this work, entries are in alphabetical order and were taken from an earlier 12-volume effort that brought all the government-indexed materials into one publication. The present work furnishes 461 entries related to the black educational experience in the United States, the Caribbean, and Africa. Annotations are furnished by the editor and are arranged alphabetically by author. There is a listing of journals indexed, and a detailed general index locates entries by various topics.

Frederick Chambers's *Black Higher Education in the United States: A Selected Bibliography on Negro Higher Education and Historically Black Colleges and Universities* (Greenwood, 1978) furnishes listings under several major divisions covering doctoral dissertations, institutional histories, periodical literature, master's theses, books, and miscellaneous materials. Coverage extends from the antebellum period to the 1970s.

513. **Afro-American History: A Bibliography.** Dwight L. Smith, ed. Santa Barbara, CA: ABC-Clio, 1974–1981. 2v. (Clio Bibliography Series, nos.2, 8). ISBN 0-87436-123-0 (v.1); 0-87436-314-4 (v.2).

This bibliography of article abstracts related to Afro-American history drawn from the quarterly abstracting service *America: History and Life* (entry 51) is particularly useful because of the convenience of its packaging. Volume 1 covers international periodical literature over a wide range of history and the social sciences dating from 1954 to 1972; volume 2 furnishes articles issued from 1964 to 1978. Abstracts are organized in a classified arrangement by topic and furnish complete bibliographic information. They tend to be brief, ranging from one sentence to a concise paragraph, but are informative of the content. The volumes are organized into six chapters covering cultural traditions, colonial America, slavery, Reconstruction, twentieth-century society, and the contemporary scene (subsequent to 1945). There is an author index and the publisher's SPIndex (Subject Profile Index), as used in the parent work.

514. **Afro-American Literature and Culture Since World War II: A Guide to Information Sources.** Charles D. Peavy. Detroit: Gale, 1979. 302p. ISBN 0-8103-1254-9.

Covering much more than literature in a literary sense, this annotated bibliography of books and articles treats 26 subjects and topical issues of interest to social historians, among them black studies, economics, Jews, religion, civil rights movement, movies, politics, roots, television, theatre, and women. Both famous and obscure writings and writers are treated, the major criterion being that they describe the black experience subsequent to World War II. As is true of any work of this type, there are some notable omissions, but generally this title is valued by both researchers and students. There are three well-designed indexes to facilitate access by author, title, and subject. The subject index is quite detailed and useful. Both scholars and students would do well to consult this work before starting a new project on the topic.

515. **Afro-American Nationalism: An Annotated Bibliography of Militant Separatist and Nationalist Literature.** Agustina Herod and Charles C. Herod. New York: Garland, 1986. 272p. (Canadian Review of Studies in Nationalism, v.6; Garland Reference Library of Social Science, v.336). ISBN 0-8240-9813-7.

This annotated bibliography furnishes more than 600 books and articles published subsequent to 1945 on the little-understood theme of black nationalism. The work is useful to both students and researchers because of its comprehensive nature and substantial annotations. Beginning with the legacy of the Free Negro prior to the Civil War, the work provides historical coverage to the present time through a sequence of 10 sections representing different chronological periods. There are also sections on religious black nationalism (where one will find references to works on Malcolm X, among others) and "Garveyism." There is an author index, but the work would have profited from better subject access.

On Malcolm X specifically, there are two important bibliographies dating from the mid-1980s: *Malcolm X: A Selected Bibliography* (Greenwood, 1984), compiled by Lenwood Davis, the prolific bibliographer of African-Americana, and Timothy V. Johnson's *Malcolm X: A Comprehensive Annotated Bibliography* (1986), a Garland endeavor. The first work identifies over 1,150 books and articles on Malcolm X, along with brief annotations. The Johnson compilation, as its title implies, is more thorough, yet both titles suffer from lack of currency. It is likely that these bibliographies will soon be updated, supplemented, or superceded—particularly in view of new interest in the subject elicited by Spike Lee's explosive 1992 motion picture *Malcolm X.*

516. **Afro-American Reference: An Annotated Bibliography of Selected Resources.**
Nathaniel Davis, comp. and ed. Westport, CT: Greenwood, 1985. 288p. (Bibliographies and
Indexes in Afro-American and African Studies, no.9). ISBN 0-313-24930-X.

Designed to supersede the guide published 10 years earlier by Guy Westmoreland, this
effort is a worthy successor. It is divided into 17 major subject and format divisions, for which
the entries represent the reference literature (bibliographies, indexes, directories, selected
anthologies, and dictionaries). Some periodical articles are included also. Nearly 650 titles
are identified and described in lengthy and well-developed manner (some reach 200 words
in length). Certain of the subject classes are of special interest to social historians, such as
genealogy, mass media, family and related studies, and medicine and health care. The work
has achieved its purpose as "a point of departure for research on most aspects of
Afro-American history and culture." Access to the content is facilitated by the presence of
three indexes: author, title, and subject.

517. **Afro-American Religious Studies: A Comprehensive Bibliography with Locations
in American Libraries.** Ethel Williams and Clifton F. Brown. Metuchen, NJ: Scarecrow,
1972. 454p. ISBN 0-810-80439-5.

This work has become a standard source of bibliographic information on the black
experience since its publication two decades ago. At the time there was a real need for a work
that would examine in a thorough manner the religion of U.S. blacks from its origins through
different historical periods. About 6,000 entries are furnished under five classes: "African
Heritage," "Christianity and Slavery in the New World," "The American Negro and the
American Religious Life," "The Civil Rights Movement," and "The Contemporary
Religious Scene." Subdivisions are given by county and by denomination, if appropriate.
The entries consist of books, articles, speeches, and reports. Some are easily located in
libraries; others are more obscure. Appendices contain lists of serials, manuscript collections,
and sources consulted. An author index provides access.

518. **Black Access: A Bibliography of Afro-American Bibliographies.** Richard Newman,
comp. Westport, CT: Greenwood, 1984. 249p. ISBN 0-313-23282-2.

Over 3,000 bibliographies and discographies related to the Afro-American experience
are cited in this valuable guide, which begins with an excellent introduction examining 50
years of collecting. The work excludes the Caribbean, Latin America, and Africa; blacks in
Canada are covered, however. This extensive listing has utilized most of the standard sources,
both general and specific to Afro-American life. The idea was to find all relevant bibliographies that exist independently as books, pamphlets, guides, articles, and book chapters.
Although the Civil War has been excluded, the Reconstruction period and the slavery issue
are well covered. Entries are arranged alphabetically by main entry and are accessible through
both subject and chronological indexes.

Nineteen bibliographies are reprinted in Betty K. Gubert's *Early Black Bibliographies,
1863–1918* (Garland, 1982). Such historically important efforts as those by W.E.B. DuBois
(1900, 1905, 1910), Arthur Schomburg (1918), and Samuel May (1863) address social,
cultural, creative, and political interests through books, articles, and so on. At the beginning
of each bibliography the compiler provides a brief historical description. There is a comprehensive name index to provide access.

519. **Black Business and Economics: A Selected Bibliography.** George H. Hill. New York: Garland, 1985. 351p. (Garland Reference Library of Social Science, no.267). ISBN 0-8240-8787-9.

Only recently has attention been paid to the economic base from which black Americans operate. This bibliography of over 2,650 books, dissertations, theses, government documents, and articles for journals, newspapers, and magazines offers a wide range of source material related to black capitalism and ownership, employment, and economic mobility in the corporate world. The purpose is to provide researchers and students with both published and unpublished materials written over the past 100 years. Most of the material was issued during the 1960–1980 period. There are 16 chapters that represent different topics, such as banking, capitalism, income, insurance, organization, and clubs. The first chapter offers entries of 100 books (the only annotated segment of the work), and chapter 2 lists government documents. Although criticized for certain omissions, it represents a unique and needed source.

520. **The Black Family in the United States: A Revised, Updated, Selectively Annotated Bibliography.** Lenwood G. Davis, comp. New York: Greenwood, 1986. 234p. ISBN 0-313-25237-8.

Professor Davis has been compiling bibliographies on the black experience for many years, and with this effort he has furnished a revision of a 1978 publication for research and study in social history. This bibliography gives 725 annotated entries of books, articles, and dissertations written over the 25 years prior to its publication. Entries are classified by format in four divisions (major books, books, articles, and dissertations), then by topical subdivisions covering such elements as slavery, children, adoption, abortion, poverty, sickle-cell diseases, and stress. Some of these have been added since the original effort. Annotations are detailed and run about a paragraph for each. An author-subject index furnishes access.

A more comprehensive title (although not fully annotated) is *Black American Families, 1965–84: A Classified Selectively Annotated Bibliography,* edited by Walter R. Allen et al. (Greenwood, 1986). It appears as number 16 in the series "Bibliographies and Indexes in Afro-American and African Studies" and contains over 1,100 entries (about one-fourth annotated) of books, journals, and dissertations published during the vital 20-year period. Indexing is excellent, with a keyword index of titles, classified subject index, and co-author index.

521. **Black Index: Afro-Americana in Selected Periodicals, 1907–1949.** Richard Newman. New York: Garland, 1981. 266p. ISBN 0-8240-9513-8.

For an extremely useful cumulative listing, one should consult this index to more than 10,000 articles and book reviews taken from more than 350 periodicals from the United States, Canada, and Great Britain over a span of 43 years. Drawn from the Faxon Company's *Annual Magazine Subject Index 1907–1979,* it goes further and identifies articles in periodicals not covered in the Faxon work. Most of the listed items have not been indexed before; access is provided by author (includes book reviewer) and by subject, for which listings have been expanded. The fact that it targets little-known publications makes it a unique source of bibliographic information.

The *Index to Periodicals by and About Blacks* (G. K. Hall, 1973–1983) was an annual publication begun in 1950 as *Index to Periodicals by and About Negroes* and was compiled by the staff of the Hallie Q. Brown Memorial Library at Central State University in Wilberforce, Ohio. It indexed several thousand articles and features for nearly 25 Afro-American periodicals each year. Its major weakness was lack of promptness; historically, it remains an important source.

522. **Black Labor in America, 1865–1983: A Selected Annotated Bibliography.** Joseph Wilson and Thomas Weissinger, comps. and eds. New York: Greenwood, 1986. 118p. (Bibliographies and Indexes in Afro-American and African Studies, no.11). ISBN 0-313-25267-X.

Another of the Greenwood publications, this work identifies nearly 600 books, pamphlets, government documents, private studies, and collections of papers. The more significant entries receive full annotations; in other cases, annotations are brief or nonexistent. They are arranged alphabetically by main entry. One can only conjecture about the omission of journal articles, but one suspects that the purpose was to provide a focused perspective regarding the monographic literature. Also excluded are sources that do not have the black worker as the central theme and certain occupational categories, such as athletics and the military. Although the production is shoddy in some respects (titles arranged alphabetically by first words, *including* the article adjectives; omissions; inconsistencies; and typographical errors), there is an obvious need for the content. Indexing is provided by a title index and a subject index.

523. **Black Slavery in the Americas: An Interdisciplinary Bibliography, 1865–1980.** John D. Smith, comp. Westport, CT: Greenwood, 1982. 2v. ISBN 0-313-23118-4.

This is a comprehensive classified bibliography of nearly 16,000 English-language books, articles, theses, dissertations, and essay reviews covering all facets of slavery except for the political. It is extremely valuable because of its exhaustive nature; both scholars and students will need to use it for their inquiries. The two-volume work is organized into 25 chapters with broad headings such as "Slave Culture," "African Background," "The Slave Trade," and "Geography." In this case, breadth has been sacrificed for depth, and there are no annotations provided. Arrangement is alphabetical by main entry, and access is furnished through both subject and author indexes.

Slave Life in America: A Historiography and Selected Bibliography by James S. Olson (University Press of America, 1983) is not as extensive as the Smith work but is targeted to the needs of the undergraduate student. Two brief essay chapters cover the historical treatment of the topic and precede well-selected listings of books and articles. No annotations are given.

524. **Blacks in the American Armed Forces, 1776–1983: A Bibliography.** Lenwood G. Davis and George Hill, comps. Westport, CT: Greenwood, 1985. 198p. (Bibliographies and Indexes in Afro-American and African Studies, no.3). ISBN 0-313-24092-2.

Another of the Davis bibliographies is this thorough and well-designed treatment of the black experience with respect to military service. This has been an elusive topic in the past, and the relatively recent effort is welcomed by both students and researchers. The major coverage of the book is in the first of two segments, which contains 10 chronological sections with each one covering a war or campaign. Entries are arranged alphabetically within these sections; no annotations are given, although they would have been useful. The range of coverage is from the American Revolution to the small wars following Vietnam. The second segment is auxiliary in nature and furnishes four appendices: "Black American Generals and Flag Officers," "Ships Named for Black Americans," "Black Soldiers in Films" and, finally, one containing documents from World War I.

525. **Education of the Black Adult in the United States: An Annotated Bibliography.** Leo McGee and Harvey G. Neufeldt, comps. Westport, CT: Greenwood, 1985. 108p. ISBN 0-313-23473-6.

An interesting and unique coverage of nearly 370 books, articles, and dissertations proves useful to beginning researchers and students in helping to trace the history of black adult education from the precolonial days to the present. There are five major sections to the work, under which the annotated entries are alphabetically arranged. The first part, "Pre-Civil War (1619–1860)," covers education on the plantation and the influence of the Quakers; the next deals with "Civil War and Reconstruction," in which government responsibility and illiteracy are treated; the third segment, "Separate but Equal, 1880–1930," covers the withdrawal of federal protection and the beginnings of segregated education; and the fourth section examines "The Modern Era, 1930– ," which has witnessed the renewal of federal intervention. Part 5 includes items not fitting into the classified arrangement of the others. There are subject and author indexes.

526. **Health of Black Americans from Post Reconstruction to Integration, 1871–1960: An Annotated Bibliography of Contemporary Sources.** Mitchell F. Rice and Woodrow Jones, Jr., comps. Westport, CT: Greenwood, 1990. 206p. (Bibliographies and Indexes in Afro-American and African Studies, no.26). ISBN 0-313-26314-0.

This annotated bibliography is meant to complement an earlier effort by the compilers that covered the more recent literature (1970s and 1980s) on the health of U.S. blacks. The historical effort furnishes nearly 600 entries, most of which are references to journal and periodical literature written over a span of 90 years. Entries are organized under three major chronological periods, beginning with post-Reconstruction to the early twentieth century (1871–1919), followed by the 1920–1950 period (which provides the bulk of the cited entries), and concluding with the 1950–1960 period. Entries are arranged alphabetically and numbered sequentially within each division. Annotations are well developed and detailed; they vary from a paragraph to nearly a full page. There is a fine introductory essay on health and working conditions of blacks from the time of slavery; both author and subject indexes furnish access.

527. **Index to Afro-American Reference Resources.** Rosemary M. Stevenson, comp. New York: Greenwood, 1988. 315p. (Bibliographies and Indexes in Afro-American and African Studies, no.20). ISBN 0-313-24580-0.

This recent addition to the Greenwood series furnishes a useful subject index to material found in nearly 190 reference sources of various types (dictionaries, encyclopedias, abstracts, catalogs, indexes, and bibliographies). Also included are social commentaries and historical texts that treat blacks in America, including substantial coverage of Canada, the Caribbean, and South America. The work is well developed as a source of additional information and is divided into five parts, beginning with an introduction that furnishes a bibliographical essay on recent publications. This is followed by a section on cited works, which lists the tools indexed. The third section is the heart of the text and provides subject access to the material. Also included are author and title indexes, which furnish references to the listings in the subject index.

528. **The Progress of Afro-American Women: A Selected Bibliography and Resource Guide.** Janet L. Sims-Wood, comp. Westport, CT: Greenwood, 1980. 378p. ISBN 0-313-22083-2.

Although not a definitive work by any means, this bibliography is comprehensive enough to provide both researchers and students with a useful source of information. This effort follows several other titles produced in the 1970s on black women and is a more extensive source. More than 4,000 titles of books, articles from journals or newspapers, and dissertations are enumerated under 34 useful subject categories. Each of these is subdivided for greater specificity (the arts, family life, medicine, politics, sex). Certain segments, such as the one on science, provide access to information that is relatively obscure. Biographies are also treated in one of these categories. A comprehensive index expedites access to needed information.

Information Sources

529. **Black Journals of the United States.** Walter C. Daniel. Westport, CT: Greenwood, 1982. 432p. (Historical Guides to the World's Periodicals and Newspapers, no.1). ISBN 0-313-20704-6.

This work is of value to historical inquiry in providing full descriptions of more than 100 popular and scholarly magazines of Afro-American character dating from 1827 to the 1980s. These profiles are arranged alphabetically by title, the average entry being several pages long. There is an overview of the purpose and format of the periodical, and the background surrounding the periodical's origin is described. Also included are sources, notes, publication history, current circulation figure, and imprint, along with indication of indexing tools, location sources, title changes, and editor. The appendices contain a chronology of events in black history relating to the establishment of journals. There is a name/subject index.

The Afro-American Periodical Press, 1838–1909 by Penelope L. Bullock (Louisiana State University, 1981) is a similar work that covers 97 general and special-interest magazines, beginning with *Mirror of Liberty* (1838) and finishing with *Negro Business League Herald* (1909) and NAACP's *The Crisis* (1910). These titles are profiled with historical description as well as editorial biography. Appendices identify holding libraries and geographical and chronological data. A general index provides access.

530. **Chronology of African-American History: Significant Events and People from 1619 to the Present.** Alton Hornsby, Jr. Detroit: Gale, 1991. 526p. ISBN 0-8103-7093-X.

This recent chronology from Gale is of use to inquirers at all levels. It is introduced by a historical description, beginning with African origins and ending with contemporary conditions. Of interest here is an analysis of the effects that each U.S. president has had on black society in the United States. The chronology spans a period of more than 370 years, from the arrival of the first slave ship in Virginia in 1619 to the appointment of a black president of a college in Georgia in 1990. Entries are annotated briefly but effectively; they are organized under 11 different chapter headings representing different periods of history. Appendices furnish excerpts from various documents, speeches, and laws, which have been enumerated in the chronology, as well as statistical tables and lists. The work concludes with a lengthy bibliography and index.

531. **Dictionary of Afro-American Slavery.** Randall M. Miller and John D. Smith, eds. New York: Greenwood, 1988. 866p. ISBN 0-313-23814-6.

Two leading authorities have collaborated in producing this valuable reference tool for the nonspecialist and general reader. Researchers will also find it useful for the full treatment given the nearly 300 topics contributed by over 200 specialists, beginning with the first English settlement and closing with Reconstruction after the Civil War. Entries emphasize the social, institutional, intellectual, and political aspects of slavery and include bibliography and cross-references. The listings provide a real service in summarizing the scholarly perspective found in more recent multidisciplinary historical inquiry; they treat of broad subjects, such as the slave trade and abolition, as well as topics of specific interest, such as conditions in a particular city or state. Although there are the usual omissions to a work of this kind, this is a highly important source. A detailed subject index provides good access.

532. **Encyclopedia of African-American Civil Rights: From Emancipation to the Present.** Charles D. Lowery and John F. Marszalek, eds. New York: Greenwood, 1992. 658p. ISBN 0-313-25011-1.

From Greenwood Press comes this new dictionary of the fight for civil rights, the product of the effort of two historians from Mississippi State University. There are over 800 articles, each averaging just under a page in length, covering all important elements and considerations of the 100-year-long struggle. Entries describe personalities, events, court cases, organizations, and important legislation. Arrangement is alphabetical and furnishes easy access to the specific topic treated. There are cross-references to related articles and useful bibliographic references for additional reading. Enhancing the text are numerous illustrations, both photographs and drawings, designed to further the reader's comprehension. The work opens with a foreword by David J. Garrow, winner of the 1987 Pulitzer Prize for his work on Martin Luther King, Jr., who describes this encyclopedia as a rich and valuable source even for senior scholars.

533. **Encyclopedia of Black America.** Augustus Low, ed. New York: McGraw-Hill, 1981. 921p. ISBN 0-07-038834-2.

This is a good overview of the black experience and has been called "the first comprehensive encyclopedia of Afro-American history" in its coverage, which extends from the slave trade to the present day. The purpose was to produce a reliable yet comprehensive and expansive work providing both factual narrative and interpretation concerning both the past and the present. It is primarily a biographical dictionary, with 1,400 of its 1,700 articles devoted to various personalities. Also covered is black involvement in the professions such as politics, theatre, education, banking, and medicine. Articles vary in size but tend to be brief, a page or less, although some are of essay length. More than 100 specialists have contributed to the production of this title. Arrangement of entries is alphabetical, and access is assured by the provision of a comprehensive detailed index.

534. **The Harlem Renaissance: A Historical Dictionary for the Era.** Bruce Kellner, ed. Westport, CT: Greenwood, 1984. 476p. ISBN 0-313-23232-6. Repr. New York: Methuen, 1987. ISBN 0-416-01671-5.

This excellent information tool describes an era of excitement, self-awareness, and creative expression as it developed around the black population of Harlem from 1917 to 1935, when the first riot occurred. Kellner and seven other contributors, mostly university professors, have furnished over 800 signed entries that range from a few lines to two pages in length. Coverage is given to personalities, books, periodicals, newspapers, groups, associations, musical comedies, and significant places associated with those dynamic years. As one would expect, the period embraced various types of people (politicians, educators, and clergy, as well as poets, artists, and especially musicians and entertainers). Separate chronologies of events, books, and plays are presented in the appendices, along with a listing of serial publications and even a glossary of Harlem slang. The work concludes with a substantial bibliography and good analytical index.

535. **Historic Landmarks of Black America.** George Cantor. Detroit: Gale, 1991. 372p. ISBN 0-8103-7809-4.

Of interest to both students and scholars, this much-needed travel book covers historical landmarks and monuments important to the black experience in this country. These sites are listed in the publisher's *Negro Almanac* (entry 537), but Cantor furnishes descriptive commentary for each landmark varying in length from one paragraph to one page. The author is a journalist who brings excellent form and style and combines a subtle sense of humor with good, informative summaries. Included are details regarding the site's importance, plus information on location and access. The 300 entries are arranged in directory fashion, first by region, beginning with the Midwest; then alphabetically by state; then by city. All types of sites are represented: birthplaces, battlefields, cemeteries, and so on. There is a chronology and a lengthy bibliography, as well as an index of proper names.

536. **The Historical and Cultural Atlas of African Americans.** Molefi K. Asante and Mark T. Mattson. New York: Macmillan, 1991. 198p. ISBN 0-02-897021-7.

Of special interest to students, this attractive atlas covers the black experience in the United States from the period of the slave trade to the present day. Arranged in chronological sequence, the work gives encyclopedic treatment to developments through easy-to-understand textual narrative. Most important are the 65 maps emphasizing historical trends and contemporary demographics. These are accompanied by photographs, diagrams, and charts. The two editors, although qualified through experience in African-American matters and cartography, respectively, are criticized by at least one reviewer for a Eurocentric emphasis representing the perspective of Caucasians to the exclusion of the music, culture, art and belief systems derived from an African tradition. Although certain factual errors are noted, the work should be of value because of the uniqueness of its content.

537. **The Negro Almanac: A Reference Work on the Afro-American.** 5th ed. Harry A. Ploski and James Williams, comps. and eds. Detroit: Gale, 1989. 1,622p. ISBN 0-8103-7706-3.

Ploski was part of the editorial team for the initial edition of of this work in 1967 and has consistently revised and upgraded it ever since. Like its predecessors, the fifth edition has great scope, and it has been completely revised and updated since the fourth edition in 1983. More than 30 chapters provide exposition and description of the black experience. Although emphasis is placed on the current role of blacks in politics, law, business, education, and the arts, ample treatment is given to historical interpretation, beginning with the continent of Africa and progressing through African-American development. There are listings of black achievements, personalities, and historical landmarks. The general index has been improved and now is more detailed. The subject bibliography is limited to publications appearing subsequent to the fourth edition.

538. **The Social and Economic Status of the Black Population in the United States, 1790-1978: An Historical View.** U.S. Bureau of the Census. Washington: U.S. Department of Commerce, Bureau of the Census, 1979. 271p. (Current Population Reports, Special Studies Series P-23, no.80). SuDoc No. C3.186:P23/80.

Derived from government census reports, this useful source of historical statistics covers a period of nearly 200 years. Black population changes and characteristics are shown clearly with the use of graphs, charts, and tables, accompanied by historical overviews for each area covered. The major segment, the first of a two-part arrangement, presents historical trends from 1790 to 1975. The second part illustrates recent trends from 1975 to 1978. This source is valuable for all historical inquiries because it summarizes the societal changes that have marked the black population since the adoption of the Constitution: income levels, employment characteristics, housing, voting, and so on. The appendices furnish definitions, explanations, and sources. There is a detailed table of contents but no index; therefore the researcher must study the organization of the tool to expedite its use.

Biographical Sources

539. **Black Americans in Autobiography: An Annotated Bibliography of Autobiographies and Autobiographical Books Written Since the Civil War.** Rev. and exp. ed. Russell C. Brignano. Durham, NC: Duke University, 1984. 193p. ISBN 0-8223-0559-3.

This is a revision and expansion of a 1974 bibliographic effort by Brignano that targets autobiography with a historical perspective. Of use to students and researchers at all levels, the work is divided into two major sections. The first part, "Autobiographies," lists volumes that cover significant amounts of the authors' lives, whereas the second part, "Autobiographical Books," contains listings of diaries in journals, collections of essays, eyewitness accounts, personal experiences, and so forth. Annotations are well written but brief, and bibliographical information is accurate for each entry. In the old tradition of bibliographies intended to aid scholarship, library locations are given by symbol for up to 10 libraries. Several useful indexes are furnished that provide access through various points: occupation, organization, institution, geographical location, chronological sequence by first date of publication, and title.

540. **Black Biography, 1790–1950: A Cumulative Index.** Randall K. Burkett, et al., eds. Alexandria, VA: Chadwyck-Healey, 1990. 3v. ISBN 0-89887-085-2.

As the access tool of a large-scale microfiche project described below, this extensive index to nearly 300 biographical dictionaries and collective biographies covers more than 30,000 names. Because of its high price ($900), the index and its parent sourcebook (see below) will be purchased only by those agencies serving the needs of serious inquirers. Many of the titles indexed are of historical importance, as publication dates range from 1790 to 1950. Entries are organized alphabetically and provide name, gender, birth date, birthplace, death date, occupation, religion, biographical source, and location of illustrations. Volume 3 serves as both a bibliography and summary index volume that classifies the entries by birthplace, religion, occupation, and gender.

Black Biographical Dictionaries, 1790–1950 (Chadwyck-Healey, 1987) is the major microfiche source providing copy of all 300 biographical works. It represents an enormous project, with a correspondingly high price of about $5,500 at time of publication. A product of some 20 years in the making, it furnishes a highly valuable aid to scholarship and education.

541. **Black Leaders of the Nineteenth Century.** Leon Litwack and August Meier, eds. Urbana: University of Illinois, 1988. 344p. (Blacks in the New World Series). ISBN 0-252-01506-1.

Composed of 16 chapters, each by a different scholar (one of the chapters is coauthored), this is a valuable title for both students and researchers. Most of the chapters cover a single individual of large stature, such as Harriet Tubman (examined by Benjamin Quarles), Frederick Douglass (by Waldo E. Martin, Jr.), and Nat Turner (by Peter H. Wood). Collective biography is represented by two chapters on Reconstruction leaders. The essays are well written and full and include pictures.

Part of the same series is the earlier work by Litwack and Meier, *Black Leaders of the Twentieth Century* (University of Illinois, 1982). Fifteen major leaders are treated individually in scholarly essays written by different historians. Covered are such illustrious and at times controversial figures as Booker T. Washington, Malcolm X, Marcus Garvey, Mary McLeod Bethune, and, of course, Martin Luther King, Jr.

542. **Black Photographers, 1840–1940: An Illustrated Bio-bibliography.** Deborah Willis-Thomas. New York: Garland, 1985. 141p. (Garland Reference Library of the Humanities, v.401). ISBN 0-8240-9147-7.

One of the more interesting and revealing aspects of the historical record of the black experience is the body of images preserved in the camera work of black photographers. This element of historical inquiry has received little attention in the past; its study is benefited greatly by this work. Willis-Thomas has produced a bio-bibliography that, although not comprehensive, provides valuable insight for both students and scholars. Coverage is furnished for 65 U.S.-born black photographers who plied their trade for the first hundred years after introduction of the daguerreotype. Entries provide brief biographies, descriptive commentary on their works, and bibliographies. These are organized under four time periods: 1840–1859, 1860–1899, 1900–1919, and 1920–1940. The most impressive part is the selection of photographs taken by nearly half the individuals covered. These show a valuable slice of life from urban to rural regions.

543. **Blacks in the Humanities, 1750–1984: A Selected Annotated Bibliography.** Donald F. Joyce, comp. New York: Greenwood, 1986. 209p. (Bibliographies and Indexes in Afro-American and African Studies, no.13). ISBN 0-313-24643-2.

The compiler has been an active contributor to African-American history and has produced a unique source in terms of its scope. It covers leading black personalities and their contributions over a wide range of the humanities and creative arts spanning a period of over 200 years. The humanities are defined broadly to include art, music, drama, literary criticism, linguistics, philosophy, science, history, and even library science. Coverage is provided for over 600 monographs, journal articles, and dissertations, offering both students and researchers well-selected and carefully developed listings. Annotations range from brief to very full; entries have been taken from numerous sources (bibliographies, indexes, union lists, encyclopedias, biographical dictionaries, catalogs, textbooks, etc.). Access is provided by both subject and author/title indexes of comprehensive nature.

544. **Dictionary of American Negro Biography.** Rayford W. Logan and Michael R. Winston, eds. New York: Norton, 1982. 680p. ISBN 0-393-01513-0.

Serving as a complement to the *Dictionary of American Biography* (entry 143), this distinguished, comprehensive, and scholarly biographical tool is limited to U.S. blacks who died before 1970. There are over 700 signed entries, ranging in length from two paragraphs to several pages and covering individuals who were considered to be major influences either nationally or regionally. Historical significance, rather than fame, fortune, or visibility, was the major criterion for inclusion. Many of the names are relatively obscure today, but all of these individuals played meaningful roles as black participants in U.S. society, serving in such capacities as cowboys, explorers, and ship captains. This large project took ten years to complete and involved the contributions of over 250 scholars and specialists. Although there are omissions of important people, the work is of great importance to serious students and researchers.

A more specialized source of note is Eric Foner's most recent effort, *Freedom's Lawmakers: A Directory of Black Officeholders During Reconstruction* (Oxford University Press, 1993), which furnishes brief biographical coverage of 1,500 officials in both the North and South during the period following the Civil War. Offices range from constables to congressmen.

545. **A Guide to Research on Martin Luther King, Jr., and the Modern Black Freedom Struggle.** Comp. by staff of the Martin Luther King, Jr., Papers Project. Stanford, CA: Stanford University Libraries, 1989. 185p. (Occasional Publications in Bibliography Series, no.1). ISBN 0-911221-09-3.

This is the first of what is anticipated to be a multivolume effort of the Martin Luther King Papers Project. It began as an access tool to materials housed at the Center for Non-Violent Social Change in Atlanta, which itself is part of a larger database maintained at Stanford University. Included are listings of books and articles, most scholarly but some popular, as well as dissertations, theses, government documents, reference works, and audiovisual materials. Microform materials and manuscripts are included as well. Brief annotations are provided. All works by King are included when readily accessible, along with representation of other materials on the movement as well. Access to the database at Stanford University is now possible through Internet.

Marcus Garvey: An Annotated Bibliography (Greenwood, 1980) is yet another relevant annotated bibliography provided by Professor Lenwood G. Davis, who has spent most of his professional career documenting the Afro-American heritage. There are more than 550 books, articles, newspapers, journals, theses, dissertations, and documents on the founder of the "Back to Africa Movement" who inspired much emotion in the 1920s. A special feature is the full text of the "Constitution of the Universal Negro Improvement Association," an organization he founded.

546. **In Black and White: A Guide to Magazine Articles, Newspaper Articles, and Books Concerning More than 15,000 Black Individuals and Groups.** 3rd ed. Mary M. Spradling, ed. Detroit: Gale, 1980. 2v. ISBN 0-8103-0438-4. **Supp.** 1985. 628p. ISBN 0-8103-0439-2.

Originally published in 1971 as a relatively small compilation, this work has grown fivefold and has increased its scope beyond its previous focus on African-Americans to the present international perspective. The two-volume third edition indexes approximately 15,000 individuals and groups who were given biographical coverage in monographs, serials, pamphlets, newspapers, and calendars. Although the emphasis is on the current scene, there is ample coverage given to historical figures, and both the famous and the obscure are identified. It has been noted that most of the references are to the journal literature; entries briefly identify the individual with an occupational category, which forms the basis for a special index by occupation of biographees. The 1985 supplement furnishes an additional 6,700 entries from the same types of sources.

547. **Index to Black American Writers in Collective Biographies.** Dorothy W. Campbell. Littleton, CO: Libraries Unlimited, 1983. 162p. ISBN 0-87287-349-8.

This index furnishes access to biographical information concerning nearly 1,900 African-American writers, ranging from creative writers of fiction and literature to journalists, historians, bibliographers, social critics, and even illustrators. About 270 works on collective biography and reference are used, with publication dates spanning a 145-year period between 1837 and 1982. Included are entries on certain foreign nationals who spent some time and did some publishing in this country. Entries are arranged alphabetically and furnish references to exact pages in the indexed works where the biographical coverage can be found. They give dates, fields of interest or activity, and variant names employed by the different biographical tools indexed. Inquirers at all levels should profit from this tool in gaining access to what has been elusive material in the past.

548. **Notable Black American Women.** Jessie C. Smith, ed. Detroit: Gale, 1992. 1,334p. ISBN 0-8103-4749-0.

This is an interesting and useful source of information on the lives of 500 black females born between 1730 and 1958 who achieved stature. They represent all areas of endeavor and include businesswomen, artists, political activists, educators, scholars, and professionals, with decidedly less emphasis given to sports figures. They range from those of monumental historical significance (Sojourner Truth, Harriet Tubman, Mary McLeod Bethune) to the notables of today (Whoopi Goldberg, Maya Angelou, Rosa Parks). Also included are the more obscure but equally worthy individuals in every historical period. With the resources of Fisk University at her disposal, librarian Smith and her advisory board were able to select an interesting and wide-ranging group of people. Pictures are included for a number of the personalities, who are alphabetically arranged.

Another recent publication of this type is a valuable 2-volume effort, *Black Women in America: An Historical Encyclopedia* (Carlson Publishing, 1992). The new work is edited by Darlene C. Hine, who previously edited several multivolume efforts for the same publisher. This title furnishes biographical sketches of more than 800 black women by over 400 contributors. These women achieved in all fields of endeavor from the time of slavery to the present. The work contains 400 photographs, a detailed chronology, and a large comprehensive index.

The most recent effort is *African American Women: A Biographical Dictionary* by Dorothy C. Salem (Garland, 1993), which covers 270 individuals from all walks of life. Coverage ranges from the colonial era to the present, and biographees are arranged alphabetically.

549. **Who's Who Among Black Americans.** 4th ed. William C. Matney, ed. Lake Forest, IL: Educational Communications, 1985. 1,043p. ISBN 0-915130-96-3.

An important ongoing publication, this biographical dictionary of black U.S. figures has been issued periodically since its initial edition in 1976. Criteria for inclusion in the latest edition have not changed and emphasize the attainment of elective and appointive office or distinctive achievements in "meritorious" careers. Biographical sketches are derived from the biographees themselves through questionnaires. It is an important source inasmuch as African-American achievers have not been documented very well up to the present time. Very few of the biographees are covered in *Who's Who in America* (entry 139n). There are both geographic and occupational indexes.

A much earlier, now historical, publication is *Who's Who in Colored America: A Biographical Dictionary of Notable Living Persons of Negro Descent in America* (Burckell, eds. 1–7, 1927–1950). Even earlier coverage is provided by *Who's Who of the Colored Race: A General Biographical Dictionary of Men and Women of African Descent*, first published in 1915 and later reprinted by Gale in 1976. These are similar to the newer work in terms of coverage of contemporary professionals and the type of access to the entries.

The European Experience

In terms of documentation through the reference literature, European-Americans benefited from the resurgence of interest in ethnic studies brought on by the expansive spirit of the 1960s and 1970s. The 1970s and 1980s witnessed a steady output of reference tools (many of which were singular in nature) furnishing bibliographic and/or historical coverage of minority Americans of various European persuasions. Commonly, the author or editor was of ethnic extraction, served as a librarian or professor, and produced a work on his or her tradition. The following segment is organized by geographic regions of Europe. It is clear that certain traditions ,such as those of Germany and of Italy, receive disproportionate coverage. It is hoped that with the recent, more vigorous pursuit of multicultural studies, much of the aging material dating from the 1970s on the European-American groups will be updated.

General

550. **American Ethnic Groups. The European Heritage: A Bibliography of Doctoral Dissertations Completed at American Universities.** Francesco Cordasco and David N. Alloway. Metuchen, NJ: Scarecrow, 1981. 366p. ISBN 0-8108-1405-6.

This is an extremely useful source to scholars and serious inquirers who wish to utilize the work of doctoral students or determine the state of the literature with respect to dissertations. There are more than 1,400 dissertations identified that have attempted topical treatment of the European heritage in this country, interpreted broadly to include any element of the U.S. ethnic experience. Entries are annotated and arranged in chapters under two major headings: "Western and Northern Europe" and "Central, Southern, and Eastern Europe." Nations or regions are treated, as are subsections on multigroup studies, emigration/immigration, and history, among others. Jewish people are considered under "European Jewry" as a special category defying geographic classification. There are some limitations in the omission of certain titles and needed cross-references. Author and subject indexes furnish access.

Central/Eastern Europe

The Finnish-American Historical Society of the West was founded in 1962 and has 400 members. Headquartered in Portland, Oregon, it offers a periodic historical monograph series as well as quarterly newsletter.

551. **Guide to the American Ethnic Press: Slavic and East European Newspapers and Periodicals.** Lubomyr R. Wynar. Kent, OH: Center for the Study of Ethnic Publications and School of Library Science, Kent State University, 1986. 280p.

This is a unique effort in terms of its content and its focus on the Slavic and East European press. The author is a bibliographic specialist in the area of ethnic studies and has compiled what amounts to the first annotated encyclopedic directory of currently operating newspapers and journals representing the interests and viewpoints of Americans of Slavic or East European descent. The value of this enterprise to social historians is unmistakable: Much of the record regarding the customs, traditions, and socioeconomic status of these groups has been furnished by the ethnic press. There is an introductory essay that covers the nature of the Slavic and Eastern European presses; the entries are well developed and furnish information on sponsorship, editors, language, frequency, circulation, and price. The work concludes with an appendix of useful statistics, followed by a geographical and title index.

552. **Polish American History and Culture: A Classified Bibliography.** Joseph W. Zurawski. Chicago: Polish Museum of America, 1975. 218p.

Riding the wave of ethnic consciousness developing in the early 1970s came this 1975 bibliography of over 1,600 English-language entries related to Polish-Americans, the single largest Slavic community in this country. There have not been a great many attempts at controlling the literature on the impact of Eastern or Central European cultures, and this tool was definitely needed for study. It was not intended to be a definitive work but rather was meant to cover a wide range of topics, for which a representative group of titles is provided (some annotated). Even so, it is of use to both students and scholars beginning their study. Topics of interest to the social historian are Polish-American history, as well as the segments on political, cultural, social, and economic life; separate chapters are given to creative expression, such as one titled "Polish-American Poetry." An author index furnishes access.

553. **The Romanians in America and Canada: A Guide to Information Sources.**
Vladimir Wertsman. Detroit: Gale, 1980. 164p. ISBN 0-8103-1417-7.

Another reported "first" is this annotated guide to informational materials concerning Romanian-Americans. This resource joins with the author's chronology and fact book, published in 1975, and supplies needed material on the Romanian influence. The guide covers titles of general reference, humanities, and social sciences. There are several directory-type listings of organizations, periodical titles, churches, and research centers representing Romanian-American culture and history. There are over 900 annotated entries of relevant books and periodical articles from both English- and Romanian-language presses. Annotations vary in size from very brief to ample. This tool will suit the needs not only of undergraduates and beginning researchers but also of the general public. Access is provided through three indexes: title, name, and subject.

554. **Slavic Ethnic Libraries, Museums, and Archives in the United States: A Guide and Directory.** Lubomyr R. Wynar and Pat Kleeberger. Chicago: Association of College and Research Libraries, American Library Association; and Kent, OH: Center for the Study of Ethnic Publications and School of Library Science, Kent State University, 1980. 164p.

Another of the principal author's directories of ethnic studies is this 1980 publication, which revised and expanded the Slavic sections of his more general work completed two years earlier. Fully 14 Slavic-American groups are given separate treatment by chapters: Bulgarian, Byelorussian, Carpatho-Ruthenian, Cossack, Croatian, Czech, Macedonian, Polish, Russian, Serbian, Slovak, Slovenian, Sorbian-Lusatian, and Ukrainian. There is also a general treatment of Slavic-Americans. The work identifies nearly 200 different libraries, museums, and archives representing nonprofit cultural institutions established and supported by individuals or organizations within the communities. These agencies are listed alphabetically within the appropriate chapters; each entry furnishes name and type of institution, address, founding date, staff numbers, chief officers, policies, costs, scope and size of collection, publications, and general commentary. Each chapter opens with a brief introductory description of the important institutions.

555. **Ukrainians in Canada and the United States: A Guide to Information Sources.**
Aleksander Sokolyszyn and Vladimir Wertsman. Detroit: Gale, 1981. 236p. ISBN 0-8103-1494-0.

This is a useful directory to various types of information sources pertaining to Ukrainians, who number an estimated 2,000,000-plus in the United States and more than 600,000 in Canada. This publication, as is true of others covering Eastern or Central European groups, is unique in dealing with a national influence that had largely been ignored. The guide has over 1,000 annotated entries representing both the historical and contemporary perspectives. It is divided into several major segments broadly covering general reference works, immigration and settlement, culture and heritage preservation, education, and social structure. There is a directory of organizations, churches, and other institutions. Included in the bibliography are books, articles, dissertations, and pamphlets. The content is indexed by author, title, and subject.

556. **Ukrainians in North America: A Biographical Directory of Noteworthy Men and Women of Ukrainian Origin in the United States and Canada.** Dmytro M. Shtohryn, ed. Champaign, IL: Association for the Advancement of Ukrainian Studies, 1975. 424p. ISBN 0-916332-01-2.

This unique work provides biographical treatment to a group of people who had not received much coverage in the literature. Entries furnish personal and professional data on a wide range of individuals, from movie stars to nuclear scientists. It is, indeed, the first of its kind for Ukrainians—a biographical dictionary of 1,800 notable people. Inclusion was decided on the basis of individuals' position of responsibility; scientific, scholarly or professional work; cultural, social or political involvements; and past achievements. The author was serving as head of Slavic cataloging at the library of the University of Illinois and had access to a large array of source material. Because this is a current dictionary limited to living people, it will be most useful to students of contemporary history. There is a segment with several entries covering individuals who died during the preparation of the work (1973–1975).

Northern/Western Europe

The Swedish-American Historical Society is located in Chicago and has a membership of 1,200. Founded in 1948, it has published the *Swedish American Historical Quarterly* since 1950. The Swiss-American History Society, also in Chicago, was begun in 1927 and has 375 members. Since 1965, it has published its *Review*, which now appears three times a year. The American Irish Historical Society of New York City was founded in 1897 and has issued *The Recorder* since 1901. Since 1985, it has appeared twice a year.

557. The Cultural Heritage of the Swedish Immigrant: Selected References. O. Fritiof Ander. Rock Island, IL: Augustana College Library, 1956. Repr. New York: Arno, 1979. 191p. ISBN 0-405-11629-2.

This is a standard work on the rich heritage and traditions of the Swedish-American people. It was published under the auspices of Augustana College Library in 1956 and later reprinted by Arno Press, where it became part of Arno's "Scandinavians in America" series. The work represents a comprehensive bibliography developed to provide broad coverage of the history and traditions of the Swedish-American people. The work is divided into 10 major segments, beginning with a bibliography of bibliographies and continuing through Swedish emigration, U.S. books, emigrant guides, Swedish acculturation in U.S. life, church, religion, literature, performing arts, and periodic publications. Unfortunately, there are no indexes.

E. Walfred Erickson's *Swedish-American Periodicals: A Selective and Descriptive Bibliography* (Arno, 1979) is another useful source from the same series. Erickson furnishes a bibliography of over 100 Swedish-American serials published between 1850 and 1930, mostly in the metropolitan centers that received larger numbers of Swedish immigrants. Entries contain the usual information: title, dates, publishers, editors, frequencies, formats, price, content notes, descriptions, and locations. There is no subject or title index, but an appendix offers an index of names.

558. Dutch Americans: A Guide to Information Sources. Linda P. Doezema. Detroit: Gale, 1979. 314p. (Gale Information Guide Library; Ethnic Studies Information Guide Series, v.3). ISBN 0-8103-1407-X.

This offering comes from Gale Press and from the solid effort of the author, a librarian of Dutch descent who extended her master's thesis into the development of an excellent bibliographic guide. The work furnishes 800 annotated entries for both students and researchers. It represents a unique source, the first of its kind on Dutch-Americans who, like other groups in this country, were finally documented in some fashion during the 1970s. The period covered spans nearly 300 years from the growth of commerce in the 1660s to the migrations of the twentieth century following World War II. There are four major chapters, the first two listing reference works and general works. The other two divide into historical periods and are subdivided by topics such as religion, sociology, politics, and language. Annotations are brief. The work contains author, title, and subject indexes.

559. **German-American History and Life: A Guide to Information Sources.** Michael Keresztesi and Gary R. Cocozzoli. Detroit: Gale, 1980. 372p. (Ethnic Studies Information Guide Series, v.4). ISBN 0-8103-1459-2.

This is a comprehensive guide designed to expedite the study of German-American history. There are nearly 1,300 annotated entries organized in 22 chapters that deal with topics such as immigration, regional and state history, special groups, utopian communities, sociopolitical factors, economic concerns, and culture. The authors' intent was to compile the best available source information in the various areas for differing levels of sophistication; therefore, both the student and the more seasoned scholar should find it of value. Of use to historical research is the chapter on archival and library resources, as well as a listing of the contents of leading periodicals. Features include a glossary of terms, happenings, and ideas relevant to the study. Annotations are brief, especially with respect to the serial literature. There are author, title, and subject indexes.

560. **German-Americana: A Bibliography.** Don H. Tolzmann, comp. Metuchen, NJ: Scarecrow, 1975. 384p. ISBN 0-8108-0784-X.

This bibliography is one of the more expansive, containing over 5,300 entries of books, pamphlets, records, photography albums, dissertations, government documents, newspapers, and periodical articles judged to be of value to the study of German-American history, literature, and culture. Entries are not annotated for the most part, and descriptive comments are brief when they appear. They are arranged in 10 chapters covering various aspects of German-American culture and life, such as history, language, book trade, religion, education, and business. There is a segment on biography and one on genealogical works. Of real value are the directory segments of the tool; listings are furnished for several types of agencies; German national organizations in this country, periodicals, books, homes, schools, societies, and research centers. The work is indexed by author only.

561. **German-American Relations and German Culture in America: A Subject Bibliography, 1941–1980.** Arthur R. Schultz. Millwood, NY: Kraus International, 1984. 2v. ISBN 0-527-71572-7.

This is the most respected and most comprehensive effort at bibliographic control that has appeared since Henry A. Pochman's standard 1953 work (see below). Schultz's volume has nearly 21,000 entries, many annotated, of books, articles, dissertations, manuscripts, collections, and unpublished works; it continues the Pochmann coverage. Drawn particularly from the annual bibliographies appearing in *The American German Review* and *German Quarterly* between 1942 and 1971, the book covers writings on every aspect of German influence in this country and Canada. The work is divided into 12 segments covering philosophy, sociology, culture, history, and so on. Indexing amounts to over 100 pages and identifies authors, editors, reviewers, places, and other topics.

Pochmann's *Bibliography of German Culture in America to 1940* (Kraus International, 1982), was recently corrected and revised by Schultz, who now has furnished us with an indispensable guide. The revised edition contains nearly 5,000 addenda and hundreds of corrections. The two publications now serve as companion volumes.

562. **The German Language Press of the Americas, 1732–1968: History and Bibliography.** 3rd rev. ed. Karl J.R. Arndt and May E. Olson. München: Verlag Dokumentation, 1976–1980. 3v. ISBN 3-794-03422-8.

This book represents an update and expansion of what amounts to a historical and bibliographic directory of large proportions and of great importance to historical inquiry. Volume 1, *History and Bibliography, 1732–1968* (1976), originally appeared in 1961 and in

1965 as *German-American Newspapers and Periodicals, 1732–1955.* Volume 2, *History and Bibliography, 1732–1968: Argentina...* and 16 other countries, was issued in 1973. These comprehensive volumes furnish bibliographic listings with essential data on every German-language newspaper or periodical ever published in the Americas. The first volume for the United States lists the presses by state, then city or town; volume 2 organizes the countries of Central and South America alphabetically from Argentina to Venezuela. Both volumes have title indexes, and provide access by holding libraries; they furnish historical narrative regarding the various presses and their publications. Volume 3, *German-American Press Research from the American Revolution to the Bicentennial* (1980), contains 23 essays written in German on the history of German journalism in the Americas.

563.   **Guide to Swedish-American Archival and Manuscript Sources in the United States.** Chicago: Swedish-American Historical Society, 1983. 600p. ISBN 0-914819-00-3.
        Sponsored by the Swedish-American Historical Society, this bibliographic guide developed from a survey funded by the National Endowment for the Humanities is concerned with the materials on Swedish immigration and acculturation in this country. Nearly 130 U.S. libraries and archives are listed, first by state, then by city; file holdings (both personal and organizational), histories, and photographic materials are described. A total of 30 states is represented, although the major bulk of the material (over 1,200 of the approximately 3,100 items) comes from Augustana College (see entry 557) or from the closely linked Swenson Swedish Immigration Research Center. Entries furnish brief, informative narratives; cross-references are supplied. This work has found broad acceptance among wide varieties of researchers and interested inquirers. Access is provided by an index of proper names.

564.   **Guide to the Archival Materials of the German-Speaking Emigration to the United States After 1933.** John M. Spalek. Charlottesville, VA: University Press of Virginia, 1978. 1,133p. ISBN 0-81390-749-7.
        This guide is the result of a four-year project aimed at locating the existence of papers and manuscripts of about 700 prominent German-speaking intellectuals who arrived in this country after 1933. That year marked the beginning of a general exodus from Germany of creative people who were beginning to feel stifled and constrained by the political climate (Arendt, Brecht, Einstein, Mann, and Schönberg, for example). The author has provided a real service in making accessible a wealth of material by such important contributors to U.S. society. Arrangement of entries is alphabetical by name. Holdings of 200 libraries and many more private collections are reported and described briefly in terms of status and conditions. Materials are listed and classified by symbols. There are appendices of names for which little or no information has been found and of material that has changed location.

565.   **Immigrants from the German-Speaking Countries of Europe: A Selective Bibliography of Reference Works.** 2nd ed. Margrit B. Krewson. Washington: Library of Congress, European Division, 1991. 76p. ISBN 0-8444-0715-1.
        The author is a specialist with the European Division of the Library of Congress and has produced bibliographic works of interest to both area and social history. At the same time, they serve as finding lists for the Library of Congress collection. This effort is a revision and expansion of *Germanic People in the United States,* a 1983 publication, and is the most recent title to deal with the German tradition in this country. There are separate sections for Austria, Germany, and Switzerland, all of which have been subject to a variety of influences affecting their German "character." Although less provincial in terms of origin, an interesting culture such as that of the Pennsylvania Dutch has been categorized only under "Germany." There

is an introduction covering patterns of migration, which has been criticized for omitting ethnic Germans from Eastern Europe.

566. The Irish-American Experience: A Guide to the Literature. Seamus P. Metress. Washington: University Press of America, 1981. 220p. ISBN 0-8191-1694-7.

As the first book-length bibliographic guide on the topic, this work seeks to provide access to a wide range of material embraced in the Irish experience. Government documents are omitted, as are archival materials. Instead, entries cite books, articles, theses, dissertations, and chapters of books on a host of topics, chiefly from the social sciences (anthropology, economics, geography, history, political science, psychology, sociology); the arts and literature are excluded. Entries are organized under 15 chapter headings, each dealing with a specific topic (e.g., "Migration to the United States," "Irish Nationalism," "Irish Americans in Politics"). There are no indexes.

A recent effort from Greenwood's Material Culture Directory Series is Susan K. Eleuterio-Comer's *Irish-American Culture: A Directory of Collections, Sites and Festivals in the United States and Canada* (Greenwood, 1988). It describes the holdings of nearly 100 museums, libraries, historical societies, and archives responding to a questionnaire. It locates over 40 historical sites and festivals relevant to Irish-American traditions. The introduction provides a brief history. The most recent effort is Patrick J. Blessing's *The Irish in America: A Guide to the Literature and the Manuscript Collections* (Catholic University of America, 1992). This useful tool serves both as a bibliography of print material of all types and as a dictionary of manuscript collections arranged by state.

Southern Europe

The American Italian Historical Association, headquartered at the University of Rhode Island in Providence, was founded in 1966 and has 450 members. It has published *Italian Americana*, a semiannual journal, since 1974.

567. Basque Americans: A Guide to Information Sources. William A. Douglass and Richard W. Etulain. Detroit: Gale, 1981. 169p. (Ethnic Studies Information Guide Series, v.6). ISBN 0-8103-1469-X.

Another product of the recent increased interest in ethnic studies is this bibliographic guide to materials on Basque Americans. The authors (both experts on Basque culture) were assisted in their effort by the work of seven contributors who produced the 413 entries. The sources are drawn primarily from the holdings of the Basque Collection at the University of Nevada in Reno. Basques have been misunderstood and ignored in the literature for reasons relating to their almost total agrarian/shepherd existence, largely in the U.S. West, their avoidance of metropolitan centers, and their lack of literary productivity. As a result, the present work represents a unique and valuable tool. Divided among 16 sections—some topical, such as "History in U.S.," a few by form, such as "Bibliographies and Reference Works"—the entries are annotated in an evaluative manner. There is a subject index, although it is somewhat lacking in detail.

568. A Bibliographic Guide to Materials on Greeks in the United States, 1890-1968. Michael N. Cutsumbis. Staten Island, NY: Center for Migration Studies, 1970. 100p.

This brief work received little attention at the time it appeared, at the onset of the revival of ethnic interest in this country. Very little has been done on Greek-American culture; this bibliography was sponsored by the Center for Migration Studies. The tool is well planned and well executed, with entries organized under 12 chapter headings, most of which are related to form and format: "Books by Greeks in the United States," "Articles," "Publications Dealing with the Greek Orthodox Church," "Unpublished Works," "Serials Currently Published," "Fraternal Publications," "Manuscript Collections," and so on. No annotations are given, but location symbols are provided for many of the entries. Although quite selective in the titles chosen, this resource provides a good perspective of representative publications of every type.

569. **Italian-Americans: A Guide to Information Sources.** Francesco Cordasco. Detroit: Gale, 1978. 222p. (Gale Information Guide Library; Ethnic Studies Information Guide Series, v.2). ISBN 0-8103-1397-9.

Cordasco is a prolific bibliographer who is especially active with respect to the literature on Italian-Americans. This title complements an earlier publication that is less comprehensive yet more detailed (see below). It is divided into seven chapters ("General Reference Works," "Social Services," "History and Regional Studies"). A concise introduction states the purpose of producing a bibliographic resource that covers all really important materials. In its attempt at comprehensiveness, this volume lists almost 2,000 books, articles, theses, and papers of both historical and current interest, written in both English and Italian, many accompanied by annotations. All were published between 1842 and 1977. Author, title, and subject indexes are furnished.

Cordasco's *The Italian-American Experience: An Annotated and Classified Bibliographical Guide, with Selected Publications of the Casa Italiana Educational Bureau* (Burt Franklin, 1974) is more selective, with fewer than 350 entries, but furnishes lengthy annotations, some reaching essay proportions. Arrangement is by subject. The impact of Cordasco's continuing efforts on behalf of Italian-Americans is noteworthy.

570. **Italian-Americans and Religion: An Annotated Bibliography.** Silvano M. Tomasi and Edward C. Stibili. New York: Center for Migration Studies, 1978. 222p. ISBN 0-913256-25-0.

This annotated bibliography of the religious experience of Italian-Americans is divided into two major sections. Of use to historians is the first segment, "Primary Materials," which enumerates locations and describes the content of a number of depositories and archival agencies holding various types of documents. The second part, "Secondary Sources," covers bibliographies, serials, dissertations, histories of various parishes, and books and articles. Nearly 1,200 entries are given, and annotations are provided, some of which, however, are too brief to be of real use. The importance of this work cannot be overlooked: The immigrant tradition has not been examined in the major religious bibliographic works of the past, so both scholars and students will need to consult this one in beginning their studies. The index furnishes entry numbers of listed materials.

571. **Italians in the United States: An Annotated Bibliography of Doctoral Dissertations Completed at American Universities, with a Handlist of Selected Published Bibliographies, Related Reference Materials, and Guide Books for Italian Emigrants.** Francesco Cordasco and Michael V. Cordasco. Fairview, NJ: Junius, 1981. 229p. ISBN 0-940198-00-2.

Another of the Cordasco bibliographic efforts on Italian-Americans is this guide to over 500 doctoral dissertations and masters theses. The work is composed of six chapters: "Italians and the American Experience," "Inter-ethnic and Related Studies," "Emigration/Immigration: History, Politics, Economics and Policy," "Miscellany," "Selected Published Bibliographies and Related Reference Works," and "Guide Books for Italian Emigrants." Annotations are furnished based on information provided primarily by *Dissertation Abstracts*

International (entry 92). This work serves as a partial update of Cordasco's 1972 publication, *Italians in the United States: A Bibliography of Reports, Texts, Critical Studies and Related Materials* (Oriole Editions, 1972). This was not limited to dissertations and theses but also furnished journal articles, books, critical studies, and reports—a total of 1,400 entries in all. The focus on doctoral work in the present effort makes it a useful tool for scholars, researchers, and serious students, the idea being that the conduct of research confirms the legitimacy of ethnic historiography. A report on affirmative action is found in the appendix; name and subject indexes are provided.

572. **The Portuguese-Americans.** Leo Pap. Boston: Twayne, 1981. 300p. (The Immigrant Heritage of America). ISBN 0-8057-8417-9.

This is another important title by Pap (see entry 573), furnishing a unique comprehensive survey-history of a little-understood and relatively undocumented minority in the U.S. milieu. Beginning with the initial contacts of the Portuguese in the days of exploration, Pap describes their immigration and settlement from the periods of colonization to modern times. Emphasis has been placed on the earlier movements as compared to the post-1965 period. Immigrant life and conditions are revealed in an interesting and enlightened manner; economic factors, religious influences, newspapers, organizations, and civic groups are explained. The work has been criticized for not being vigorous enough in its interpretation of some of the dynamics involved in the more recent treatment of immigration history—e.g., social mobility, assimilation—although these aspects are described. The description of immigrant communities is especially revealing. An excellent bibliography accompanies the text.

573. **The Portuguese in the United States: A Bibliography.** Leo Pap. Staten Island, NY: Center for Migration Studies, 1976. 80p. (Bibliographies and Documents Series). ISBN 0-913256-21-8.

As a scholar with a longtime interest in speech patterns of Portuguese-Americans, Pap has more recently become involved with the documentation of their history and development (entry 572). This brief bibliography was the first of its kind and furnishes about 800 unannotated entries treating books, articles, doctoral dissertations, and masters theses. As an access tool, it has been well received by both students and researchers, and subsequent to its publication, supplements have appeared in an annual, *Essays in Portuguese Studies* published under the auspices of the University of New Hampshire's International Conference Group on Portugal. Pap has divided his work into two segments, the first of which covers Portuguese in the United States and the second, Portuguese in Portugal. It covers a time span from the period of exploration to the present day. There is no author index.

The Female Experience

The past 20 years have seen many changes in the role and position of women in U.S. society. The struggle over the Equal Rights Amendment crystallized much of the dualism surrounding women's employment, rights, and status as a whole; as well as the the latent fears of both males and females when such issues were "pushed." Since then, the agenda has been well publicized regarding spouse abuse, parity in the sexual act, and health issues through the efforts of such forces as the National Organization of Women. The rise of social consciousness in the 1960s and 1970s led to an increased production of books concerning women's issues. Since the 1970s, publishers from the mainstream have increased their activity regarding the social conditions and social conditioning relevant to the U.S. woman. At the same time, small female publishing houses have come into operation. Reference book publishers have been quick to respond with production of a variety of sources.

Reference tools included here embrace many areas covered elsewhere in this work, the rationale being that, other than race, gender is the criterion of primary importance. Therefore, one will find books in this section on the following topics as they relate to the female experience in U.S. history: politics, ideological trends, education, labor, science, entertainment and sports, religion, and the military.

The National Women's History Project of Windsor, Canada was founded in 1977 and has a staff of eight to promote women's history. It publishes *Women's History Network Directory* semiannually and *Women's History Resource Catalog* on an annual basis.

Library Resources

574. **Women in the First and Second World Wars: A Checklist of the Holdings of the Hoover Institution on War, Revolution, and Peace.** Helena Wedborn, comp. Stanford, CA: Hoover Institution, Stanford University, 1988. 73p. (Hoover Press Bibliography Series, v.72). ISBN 0-8179-2722-0.

From the Hoover Institution on War, Revolution, and Peace comes this brief catalog of its holdings as of 1987 on women's history as it relates to the two World Wars. There are nearly 400 entries for each war representing both printed and archival holdings, although no correspondence is included. Because the organization has a noteworthy collection on various issues relevant to social change, it is important to the historian that access tools are being developed. Two catalog listings are provided, the first one covering the period 1914–1918, the second listing materials between 1939 and 1945. Entries are organized in classified manner using Library of Congress subject headings. The format presents a slight problem with no table of contents. The lack of specificity in some of the Library of Congress terms is disconcerting, but the search results are worthwhile.

575. **Women's History Sources: A Guide to Archives and Manuscript Collections in the United States.** Andrea Hinding, et al., eds. New York: Bowker, 1979. 2v. ISBN 0-8352-1103-7.

This two-volume set is considered to be one of the most important contributions to research and scholarship on the history of U.S. women in the last 20 years. It represents an immense undertaking and is the product of several years effort. Funded by a large grant from the National Endowment for the Humanities, a survey was conducted of nearly 7,000 archives and manuscript repositories regarding their holdings of primary source materials related to women's history. From the survey and subsequent fieldwork, nearly 1,600 repositories were selected offering more than 18,000 collections in their charge. These collections are composed of personal papers, correspondence, diaries, photographs, organizational records, and oral history tapes, most of which had never been documented. Volume 1 is the main volume and lists the entries arranged alphabetically by state and city. The collection is described in terms of document type, size, date, access, and content. Volume 2 is an index volume providing both subject and geographic access in detailed fashion.

A useful supplementary source is the more recent *Women in the West: A Guide to Manuscript Sources* by Susan Armitage and others (Garland, 1991). This directory identifies the holdings of numerous collections and archives of varied size that document the history of women in the U.S. West over a period of 300 years beginning in 1610.

576.   **Women's Periodicals and Newspapers from the 18th Century to 1981: A Union List of the Holdings of Madison, Wisconsin Libraries.** James P. Danky, ed. and Maureen E. Hady, et al., comps., in association with the State Historical Society of Wisconsin. Boston: G. K. Hall, 1982. 376p. ISBN 0-8161-8107-1.

Another of the union lists of Madison, Wisconsin, libraries produced by the librarian of the State Historical Society of Wisconsin, this work identifies and locates over 1,450 women's periodicals and newspapers published between 1759 and 1981. It gives information regarding the periodicals in the Herstrong Collection of the Women's History Research Center in Berkeley, California, and indicates libraries with microfilm holdings of that collection. Varied aspects of female existence and a wide array of periodicals—literary, political, historical, general, feature—are included. An attempt is made to exclude certain titles targeted to professions such as nursing or home economics because of their narrow focus. Entries are informative and furnish most recent title, date, frequency, subscription and editorial information, address, indexing, availability, library locations, and so forth. Multiple indexes (geographic, subject, language) furnish excellent access.

577.   **Women Religious History Sources: A Guide to Repositories in the United States.** Evangeline Thomas, et al., eds. New York: Bowker, 1983. 329p. ISBN 0-8352-1681-0.

This is a useful guide and directory to the collections and archival repositories of nearly 575 women's religious communities in this country. Arrangement of entries is by state, then by city. Entries furnish location and holdings information obtained through a survey funded by the National Endowment for the Humanities, which took four years to complete. Of real value is the brief but informative historical description of each religious community. Coverage is given to those female devotees identified as sisters or nuns in the Catholic, Orthodox, and Episcopal churches and to the deaconesses in the Lutheran, Methodist, and Mennonite churches. There is a useful glossary as well as a 16-page bibliography. Appendices furnish a chronological listing of founders, with references to appropriate entry. There is a main-entry name index.

Bibliographical Sources

Women's Studies Abstracts is a quarterly abstracting service of periodical articles and books relevant to women's studies. There is a history section that includes various sources, most often those pertinent to the United States. It is published by Rush Publishing and has operated since 1972.

578.   **The American Woman in Colonial and Revolutionary Times, 1565–1800: A Syllabus with Bibliography.** Eugenie A. Leonard, et al. Philadelphia: University of Pennsylvania, 1962. Repr. Greenwood, 1975. 169p. ISBN 0-8371-7883-5.

One of the earliest reference works in response to the need for women's materials, this syllabus with bibliographic references is organized through various topical subject headings, such as marriage, religion, and political rights, as well as European backgrounds of immigrants. Subsections cover geographic locales. These headings and subheadings are introduced briefly but effectively, with useful summary information. All aspects of the life and achievements of colonial women are covered by the 1,500 listed entries, which represent books, journals, memoirs, and diaries. Following the syllabus is a list of more than 100 outstanding women chosen as representatives of different backgrounds, religions, and professions. Their contributions to solutions of social problems are described. Finally, there is a useful bibliography of nearly 1,100 books and articles for additional reading.

579. **American Women and the Labor Movement, 1825–1974: An Annotated Bibliography.** Martha J. Soltow and Mary K. Wery. Metuchen, NJ: Scarecrow, 1976. 247p. ISBN 0-8108-0986-9.

The first edition of this useful annotated bibliography appeared four years earlier with a slightly different title and covered the 1825–1935 period. By way of comparison, the present effort expands the coverage nearly 40 years and adds nearly 270 more entries; it furnishes 726 as compared to 458 numbered items. The work is divided into eight sections, which serve as chapter headings: "Employment," "Trade Unions," "Working Conditions," "Strikes," "Legislation," "Worker Education," "Labor Leaders," and an interlibrary segment on "Supportive Efforts," which covers the workings of the National Women's Trade Union League. Under each chapter, the entries are alphabetically arranged by title. The appendix contains a listing of personal and organizational names, with references to useful archival collections. There are author and subject indexes, as well as a cross-reference index that lists chapter headings along with related entries.

580. **American Women's Magazines: An Annotated Historical Guide.** Nancy K. Humphreys. New York: Garland, 1989. 303p. (Garland Reference Library of the Humanities, v.789). ISBN 0-8240-7543-9.

Designed to expedite research and inquiry, this recent annotated bibliography is viewed by its author as an introductory compilation of writings about women's magazines. Nearly 900 entries are presented here, drawn from nearly 30 indexes and abstracting services. Entries are arranged alphabetically in one of the two major divisions: alternative and mainstream publications. Articles for mainstream newspapers were purposely excluded; only periodicals in the English language are covered. The time span ranges from the later nineteenth century to the late 1980s. Alternative publications are subdivided into sections on earlier magazines for women's rights and on feminist periodicals from the 1960s on. Mainstream publications are classed as nineteenth-century ladies' magazines, twentieth-century women's magazines, women's pages in newspapers, and romance/confession magazines. Annotations are brief but informative; there is a subject index.

581. **Bibliography in the History of Women in the Progressive Era.** Judith Papachristou. Bronxville, NY: Sarah Lawrence College, 1985. 70p. (Sarah Lawrence College Women's Studies Publication).

From Sarah Lawrence College comes this brief bibliography of the role of the U.S. woman in what has been called the Progressive Era. Roughly, the period covers the 40 years from 1890 to 1930 and embraces various ideological and social developments such as the flapper era, Prohibition, wartime activities, and new professionalism, The 650 citations refer to books, book chapters, and journal articles; excluded are dissertations, bibliographies, and writings on artists and most writers. The entries are classed under nine subject categories: "Women and Work," "Gender and the Family," "Education," "Religion," "Community Activities and Social Change," "World War I," "Feminism and Suffrage," "Minority Women," and "Biography and Autobiography." Topical subheadings cover a variety of issues. This should be of use primarily to students but also to researchers as an initial step in their search. There is a subject index.

582. **The Female Experience in Eighteenth- and Nineteenth-Century America: A Guide to the History of American Women.** Jill K. Conway, et al. New York: Garland, 1982. 290p. (Garland Reference Library of Social Science, v.35). ISBN 0-8240-9936-2. Repr. Princeton: Princeton University Press, 1985. ISBN 0-6910-0599-0.

This is a fine selective bibliography of real value to beginning researchers and serious students in its coverage of both private and public lives of U.S. women over a span of two centuries. Much of the strength of the work lies in its organization of books, articles, and dissertations (both primary and secondary sources) into broad subject categories; each of these is furnished with an excellent introductory essay describing and interpreting important events and developments. These categories are "U.S. Culture and Society," "Industrialization," "Women's Work and the Transformation of the Household," "The Cultural Roles of Middle-Class Women," "Women's Religious Life and the Reference Tradition," and "Biology and Domestic Life." These chapters are subdivided by topic (family life, legal status, social work) or format (diaries, travel accounts, etc.). There is an author index.

Another selective bibliography is *Victorian American Women 1840–1880: An Annotated Bibliography* by Karen R. Mehaffy (Garland, 1992), issued as volume 1181 of the Garland Reference Library of the Humanities series. The middle-class woman of the period is the subject of the work, and coverage includes books, articles, and other publications dealing with social and family life. Unfortunately, there is no index, and access is dependent upon the table of contents.

583. **The History of American Women's Voluntary Organizations, 1810–1960: A Guide to Sources.** Karen J. Blair. Boston: G. K. Hall, 1989. 363p. (G. K. Hall Women's Studies Publications). ISBN 0-8161-8648-0.

This is a well-constructed, annotated bibliography of books and articles culled from a number of standard indexing sources. It is useful for historical studies in its sharp focus on women's voluntary organizations recognized by the author-historian as being vital to both personal and political change. Arrangement of the nearly 700 entries is alphabetical by author; there is a symbol for each entry indicating its coverage of one of 13 classes representing either charitable or socially active organizations involved in patriotism, temperance, peace, suffrage, racial awareness, religious causes, and so on. Trade unions have been excluded (see entry 579). The annotations are thorough and provide both information and critical interpretation. There is a brief bibliography of sources used. A detailed index provides access by subject and name of association.

584. **Index to American Women Speakers, 1828–1978. Beverley Manning.** Metuchen, NJ: Scarecrow, 1980. 672p. ISBN 0-8108-1282-7.

This unique bibliographic product provides a real boost to women's studies and documentation of the female experience in the United States. The author, an academic librarian, has examined a variety of sources—anthologies, documentaries, histories, published conference proceedings, government documents, and periodicals—in an attempt to identify and locate speeches given by U.S. women. More than 3,000 speeches are listed from 225 sources. Virtually none of these were listed either in *Speech Index* or *Vital Speeches* which, as indexing tools, have not been prone to include women's contributions. The expansive coverage of this 150-year period makes this tool an important asset for social historians and serious students. The speechmakers range from the very famous (Susan B. Anthony and Bella Abzug) to the now obscure. Author, subject, and title indexes are furnished.

585. **Women in America: A Guide to Books, 1963–1975; with an Appendix on Books Published 1976–1979.** Barbara Haber. Urbana: University of Illinois Press, 1981. 262p. ISBN 0-252-00826-X.

Considered to be an excellent and reliable bibliographic tool, this paperback offering updates Haber's 1978 guide, which furnished annotated listings of 400 nonfiction books relevant to studies of the U.S. woman. The present version repeats that listing, which covers books published between 1963 and 1975 and includes a bibliographic essay in the appendix covering 200 additional titles published between 1976 and 1979. Designed as both a reading guide and a selection tool, the text is arranged under 18 topical chapters (e.g., "Abortion," "Education," "History"). Each chapter opens with a brief description followed by major entries with lengthy, critical annotations. Additional titles receive less detailed coverage. There is an author and title index.

Although criticized for its "haphazard inclusions and exclusions" as well as the preponderance of misspellings, Virginia R. Terris's *Woman in America: A Guide to Information Sources* (Yale, 1980), furnishes beginning researchers and students with a classic annotated bibliography of nearly 2,500 numbered entries of books, periodical articles, government documents, and pamphlets organized under 10 chapter headings. There are 10 appendices listing centers, collections, agencies, and the like. Author, title, and subject indexes are furnished.

586. Women and Feminism in American History: A Guide to Information Sources.
Elizabeth Tingley and Donald F. Tingley. Detroit: Gale, 1981. 289p. (Gale Information Guide Library; American Government and History Information Guide Series, v.12). ISBN 0-8103-1477-0.

With coverage given to works on suffragism, equality, and activity promulgating action necessary for women to obtain their rightful status, this annotated bibliography aims to provide access to sources of information relevant in a historical or contemporary context. Entries to books and collections are arranged in 22 chapters under three major divisions. The first part covers general resources such as manuscript collections, biographical directories, and periodical titles, whereas the second segment furnishes chapters on historical periods through the 1920s. The third section contains topical chapters regarding the status of women as well as their societal role and impact. The tool will be helpful to the student and nonspecialist with its ample listings of book titles. Annotations are brief. Author, title, and subject indexes furnish access.

587. Women and Sexuality in America: A Bibliography. Nancy A. Sahli. Boston: G. K.
Hall, 1984. 404p. (G. K. Hall Women's Studies Publications). ISBN 0-8161-8099-7.

This annotated bibliography contains nearly 1,700 entries under 15 topical chapters covering such issues as "Children and Adolescents," "Sexual Dysfunction," "Lesbians," "Psycho-Analytic Views," and "Adolescent Sexuality," The purpose is to document the changing perspective of female sexuality as expressed in the professional literature of this country during the nineteenth and twentieth centuries. Each chapter opens with a brief historical description, which is then followed by the annotated entries. Entries identify books drawn primarily from the social and behavioral sciences (history, sociology, psychiatry, and medicine). Then follow listings of periodical titles representing the same disciplines. This work is useful for both students and beginning researchers who wish to study trends from a historical perspective. Both an author/title index and a subject index assure access.

588. Women and the American Left: A Guide to Sources. Mari J. Buhle. Boston: G. K.
Hall, 1983. 281p. (G. K. Hall Women's Studies Publications). ISBN 0-8161-8195-0.

This annotated bibliography on the role of women and the U.S. left identifies nearly 600 entries concerning the "woman question" written over a period of 110 years from 1871 to 1981. Entries represent books, articles, and pamphlets and include biographies, autobiographies, fiction, plays, and poetry. The question as to what role women could play in furthering the cause of the working class while pushing their agenda for liberation is addressed in a variety of ways through these materials. Entries are organized under four time periods relevant to the U.S. left—1871–1900, 1901–1919, 1920–1964, and 1965–1981—then subdivided by form and format. Annotations are full and detailed, describing the scope and content of the documents chosen; they range from one paragraph to a full page. Full bibliographic data is given. There is a dictionary-style index combining authors, titles, and subjects for easy access.

589. **Women, Education, and Employment: A Bibliography of Periodical Citations, Pamphlets, Newspapers, and Government Documents, 1970–1980.** Renee Feinberg. Hamden, CT: Library Professional Publications, 1982. 274p. ISBN 0-208-01967-7.

Of more interest to the undergraduate student than the researcher of recent history, this bibliography lists various types of ephemeral material and government documents from the decade of the 1970s. Over 2,500 entries are organized into two major divisions: "Women, Education and Training" and "Women: Employment." They are drawn from the databases of 15 important indexing and abstracting services and were chosen on the basis of accessibility as well as value to women's studies. They appear to cover opposing viewpoints. The categories are subdivided by topics and subtopics, under which entries are alphabetically arranged. Excluded are books, dissertations, superficial short articles, and, unfortunately, the products of alternative and limited-circulation women's journals. No annotations are given. Both subject and author indexes facilitate access.

590. **Women in American History: A Bibliography.** Cynthia E. Harrison, ed. Santa Barbara, CA: ABC-Clio, 1979. 374p. (Clio Bibliography Series, no.5). ISBN 0-87436-260-1.

Drawing from the first 14 volumes (as well as a number of selections from later volumes) of *America: History and Life* (entry 51), Ms. Harrison has produced a comprehensive collection comprising nearly 3,400 abstracted entries of scholarly periodical articles. These represent all types of activity and areas of inquiry—sociology, anthropology, literature, religion, economics—as they touch on the female experience in this country's past. About 550 journals and 5 anthologies are represented, covering a span of some 13 years from 1963 to 1976. The abstracts are substantive, which is characteristic of the parent source. There are detailed subject and author indexes. The work is continued with volume 2, *Women in American History: An Annotated Bibliography* (ABC-Clio, 1985), issued as number 20 in the Clio series. This work furnishes 3,700 abstracted articles from 600 periodicals, newsletters, review media, and anthologies issued between 1976 and 1983.

A more recent effort is *Journal of Women's History Guide to Periodical Literature,* compiled by Gayle V. Fisher (Indiana University Press, 1992). It furnishes a listing of over 5,500 articles relevant to women's history culled from 750 journals. About 75 percent of the entries concern women in this country. *Women in U.S. History: An Annotated Bibliography* (The Common Women Collective, 1976) is an earlier and far more selective listing designed to facilitate research and study by both laypeople and academicians. Availability of materials, representation of the feminist perspective, and coverage of obscure groups are several of the criteria for inclusion. Annotations are descriptive and useful, and the illustrations are noteworthy.

591. **Women of Color in the United States: A Guide to the Literature.** Bernice Redfern. New York: Garland, 1989. 156p. (Garland Reference Library of Social Science, v.469). ISBN 0-8240-5849-6.

One of the products of the recently awakened interest in people of color is this listing of over 630 entries on the experience of the non-Caucasian female. The work contains four major divisions covering Afro-American women, Asian-American women, Hispanic-American women, and native American women. Included are books, articles, chapters, and dissertations published since the mid-1970s. Each of the four chapters begins with a summary of the available literature, which should prove useful to serious inquirers. These are followed by subdivisions based on form and format (e.g., bibliographies, life histories, etc.). There are topical segments as well (history and politics, literature and the arts). Emphasis is placed on scholarly contributions, and only those popular works deemed significant are included. Both author and subject indexes are furnished, the latter providing good access to the various topics.

592. **Women's Education in the United States: A Guide to Information Sources.** Kay S. Wilkins. Detroit: Gale, 1979. 217p. (Gale Information Guide Library; Education Information Guide Series, v.4). ISBN 0-8103-1410-X.

One of the bibliographic tools to focus on women's education in this country, this title updates earlier efforts and has been prominent in women's studies since its appearance. There are about 1,100 annotated entries citing books, documents, and articles arranged into 19 topical sections, including: historical accounts, women's colleges, physical education, and so on. Although most of the entries were published between 1969 and 1978, there is representation of earlier "classic" writings on the question of educating women and on the history of women's education. Annotations are brief but useful in describing content. Various academic school subjects from different educational levels are treated. The work should be considered a good starting point for more serious inquiry as well as a useful aid for understanding the various issues. There are author, title, and subject indexes providing good access.

593. **The Women's Rights Movement in the United States, 1848–1970: A Bibliography and Sourcebook.** Albert Krichmar, et al. Metuchen, NJ: Scarecrow, 1972. 436p. ISBN 0-8108-0528-6.

Of importance to both students and scholars, this comprehensive listing of nearly 5,200 entries covers the various issues related to women's rights over a period of nearly 126 years. Subject matter includes the status of women with respect to politics, economics, religion, education, and the professions. Entries include books, articles, dissertations, pamphlets, and both state and federal government publications. Separate sections furnish coverage of over 400 manuscript collections and of women's liberation serial publications. Some annotations are furnished. Four separate indexes provide excellent access.

A strong focus on recent history is provided in Krichmar's *The Women's Movement in the Seventies: An International English Language Bibliography* (Scarecrow, 1977). Although coverage is provided of nearly 100 countries, about two-thirds of the 8,600 English-language publications, books, dissertations, articles, and government documents relate to the United States. The brief period of publication (1970–1975) indicates the vast interest of publishers on this topic during that time. There are author and subject indexes.

594. **Women's Work in Britain and America from the Nineties to World War I: An Annotated Bibliography.** Mary D. McFeely. Boston: G. K. Hall, 1982. 140p. ISBN 0-8161-8504-2.

Intending to provide a stimulus to both students and scholars for research on the topic, the author has furnished an annotated listing of more than 500 books (including fiction), pamphlets, essays, and periodical articles published between 1890 and 1980. Covered here are writings on the subject of women's work in both England and the United States during a brief historical period preceding World War I. The bibliography is divided into two major sections, one for each country, providing excellent resource material for comparative study. Major considerations are treated such as work in shops, factories, social organizations, and agencies. The attempt is not to duplicate material in Soltow and Wery's *American Women and the Labor Movement, 1825–1974* (entry 579) but rather to complement its coverage. Author, title, and subject indexes are provided.

Information Sources

595. Almanac of American Women in the 20th Century. Judith F. Clark. New York: Prentice-Hall, 1987. 274p. ISBN 0-13-022658-0.

This chronology and handbook on U.S. women of this century is a handy ready reference tool for all types of users. Coverage begins with January 1900 and extends to the time of publication in 1987. Narratives and expositions that range from a half-page to a full page in length are interspersed with the normal dated listings. Most of these essays are biographical in nature, but some also deal with social issues such as child care. The work is divided into nine chapters, each of which deals with pertinent events that happened during a single decade. Emphasis is given to women who have contributed to societal change rather than those active in the arts or the professions. The entries are classified by categories such as popular culture, science, and ideas/beliefs. There is a name index but, unfortunately, not one for subjects.

596. American Women in Sport, 1887–1987: A 100-Year Chronology. Ruth M. Sparhawk, et al., comps. Metuchen, NJ: Scarecrow, 1989. 149p. ISBN 0-8108-2205-9.

Providing a quick overview of the achievements of U.S. female athletes since the Victorian period, this first-of-its-kind chronology is divided into four periods. These periods are determined by the social perspective toward women engaged in sports: the preorganizational era, 1887–1916; the organizational years, 1917–1956; the competitive period, 1957–1971; and, finally, the Title IX period, 1972–1987. Entries are arranged chronologically within each time period for which names and accomplishments are enumerated. The gradual changes from individual to group or team competition can be studied in terms of their social acceptability. Included are large numbers of individuals and their feats; they range from very famous figures such as Babe Didrikson Zaharias and Billie Jean King to obscure and all-but-forgotten heroines for a day. Included is a bibliography for further reference and inquiry. There are indexes by name and by sport.

597. Atlas of American Women. Barbara G. Shortridge. New York: Macmillan, 1987. 164p. ISBN 0-02-929120-8.

A most welcome source is this recent atlas designed to illustrate important data concerning demographics, employment, education, social roles and relationships, health, and crime. Based on the 1980 census data and other sources, the work clearly indicates the contrasting conditions that prevail in different parts of the country. There are nearly 130 maps, which in many cases are accompanied by charts and diagrams. Textual narrative is detailed and well-developed in terms of comparative analysis. An interesting point of coverage is the section on women's sports. This work was one of several that appeared at the same time, all bearing feminist orientation. Both students and scholars of recent social history will find it of value in studying the various distributions presented. There is a bibliography and an index.

598. Handbook of American Women's History. Angela H. Zophy, ed. New York: Garland, 1990. 763p. (Garland Reference Library of the Humanities, v.696). ISBN 0-8240-8744-5.

This one-volume handbook was designed to provide quick and easy-to-gather information on women's history for students and beginning researchers. Although reviewers have noted a number of inconsistencies in style and organization of entries, it appears to succeed in furnishing basic information in easily digestible manner. Entries are alphabetically arranged, and although there are omissions, a variety of events, people, issues, organizations, books, jobs, ideas, and laws are represented. For each entry there is a brief bibliography for additional reading. Coverage is at times unconventional, producing narratives of such cultural phenomena as soap operas along with more weighty issues of concern. The entries are well developed for the most part, although there is some unevenness in the treatment of various topics. There is a detailed index.

599.   **Women Remembered: A Guide to Landmarks of Women's History in the United States.** Marion Tinling. New York: Greenwood, 1986. 796p. ISBN 0-313-23984-3.

This is an interesting and useful directory of more than 2,000 sites—monuments, parks, memorials, homes, workplaces—of historically important contributors to women's history in this country. Women chosen for inclusion made an impact on society through either their performance of heroic deeds or their participation in historic events. Bystanders (wives, daughters) are excluded, as are living individuals. Of real value are the brief but well-developed biographical essays for each entry. Locations are given and accessibility is described, along with hours of opening. There are indicators of the subject's inclusion in *Notable American Women* (entry 604). Entries are organized under five regional divisions, then by state, city, and personal name. Only those sites open to the public are treated. There are listings classified by occupations, a chronology of dates, a brief bibliographic narrative, and a personal name index.

Biographical Sources

600.   **American Political Women: Contemporary and Historical Profiles.** Esther Stineman. Littleton, CO: Libraries Unlimited, 1980. 228p. ISBN 0-87287-238-6.

Although the emphasis of this biographical dictionary is on the current scene in U.S. politics at the time of publication, there is an attempt to provide a historical perspective. Inclusions are Jeannette Rankin, Dianne Feinstein, Pat Schroeder, Bella Abzug. It is selective to be sure, only furnishing 60 biographical sketches of women who operated at various levels of government, from city mayors to congresswomen and presidential advisers. Both students and researchers of recent history will appreciate the lengthy treatment given to women, most of whom served during the 1970s. The sketches are generally two to three pages long. Selected speeches are also included, as are bibliographies for additional reading on each subject. There is a general bibliography, and several useful appendices provide listings of women in various key positions.

601.   **American Women Managers and Administrators: A Selective Biographical Dictionary of Twentieth-Century Leaders in Business, Education, and Government.** Judith A. Leavitt. Westport, CT: Greenwood, 1985. 317p. ISBN 0-313-23748-4.

Included in this biographical dictionary are sketches of over 225 women who held prominent positions in business, education, or government. In addition to giving credit to women who were "first" to serve in their capacities, the book lauds those who have been recognized for major accomplishments in their fields of management or who founded businesses and educational institutions. The sketches are brief but informative and include bibliographies of materials both by and about the subject. Arrangement of entries is alphabetical; there appears to be a good balance of early leaders such as Jeannette Rankin and contemporary figures such as Elizabeth Dole. Sketches of current personalities may well include quotations on their style of management taken from the returned questionnaires. A list of "firsts" appears in the appendix; both a bibliography and an index are furnished.

602. Biographies of American Women: An Annotated Bibliography. Patricia E. Sweeney. Santa Barbara, CA: ABC-Clio, 1990. 290p. ISBN 0-87436-070-6.

Especially useful to the student or beginning researcher is this recent annotated bibliography of nearly 1,400 biographies of 700 U.S. women from various fields. Entries are arranged alphabetically by personal name. Obviously, there will be some inequity in number of titles listed for the various subjects; Eleanor Roosevelt has nearly 20 items, whereas others are limited to only one. The number of listings a woman has, of course, represents her importance as perceived by writers rather than a bias on the part of the author of this work. Publications vary widely and include many of the offerings of the popular literature as well as those from university presses and even doctoral dissertations. To have been included, the biography must have been at least 50 pages long; annotations are brief but evaluative. There is an appendix of biographies by profession and an author/title index.

Portraits of American Women: From Settlement to the Present by G. J. Barker-Benfield and Catherine Clinton (St. Martin's, 1991) is a highly selective and detailed collective biography of only 25 women from different historical periods and representing different ethnic groups. Arrangement is under historical period, and a portrait accompanies each sketch. There is no index.

603. Funny Women: American Comediennes, 1860–1985. Mary Unterbrink. Jefferson, NC: McFarland, 1987. 267p. ISBN 0-89950-226-1.

About 80 female performers, mostly from the twentieth century, are given generally good biographical coverage. Entries vary from less than a full page to seven pages in length. Comedy routines had their origins in the days of stage and vaudeville; such performers are well represented here, including Fanny Brice, Mae West, and Sophie Tucker. Those who made their impact on radio, television, and film are not neglected, and there is ample coverage of the familiar funny ladies of today, such as Goldie Hawn and Lily Tomlin. The work is divided into eight chapters, beginning with the early days of radio and finishing with a segment on rising stars. Several of these rising stars have since "made it"—for example, Whoopi Goldberg and Elayne Boosler. There is an index of personal names, titles, and awards.

604. Notable American Women, 1607–1950: A Biographical Dictionary. Edward T. James, et al., eds. Cambridge, MA: Belknap Press of Harvard University, 1971. 3v. ISBN 0-674-62731-8.

This is the major work of its type. It appeared as a three-volume retrospective biographical dictionary in response to a need to address the achievements of women, who largely had been ignored by the *Dictionary of American Biography* (entry 143). Covering a period of nearly 350 years, this set presents biographical sketches of nearly 1,400 women of notable stature who died prior to 1951. To be included here, a woman had to have earned distinction in her own right; only the wives of presidents were included as a result of their husbands' achievements. Entries are well developed and represent women from all fields of endeavor, from politics to the entertainment media and lively arts. They vary in length but are generally two or more pages long. Bibliographies are furnished for each entry.

Notable American Women, The Modern Period: A Biographical Dictionary, edited by Barbara Sicherman and Carol H. Green (Belknap Press of Harvard University, 1980), supplements the above title by furnishing over 440 additional biographies of women who died between 1951 and 1975. Both the format and the high quality of the earlier effort has been retained.

605. **Through a Woman's I: An Annotated Bibliography of American Women's Autobiographical Writings, 1946–1976.** Patricia K. Addis. Metuchen, NJ: Scarecrow, 1983. 607p. ISBN 0-8108-1588-5.

Nearly 2,225 autobiographical publications of U.S. women are identified in annotated listings arranged alphabetically by the author. All materials cited are at least 25 pages long and were issued during a 30-year period. This work serves to supplement Louis Kaplan's *Bibliography of American Autobiographies* (entry 149n), which covers autobiographies of both males and females published through 1945. Entries in the present work appear to be readily available in U.S. libraries and represent various literary forms—autobiographies, journals, letters, diaries, travel narratives, and memoirs. Annotations are brief but informative as to content, and cross-references are used to identify name variations and synonyms. Given in each entry are the writer's birth and death dates, when known, as well as complete bibliographic information. An author index categorizes the writers by occupation, whereas subject and title indexes furnish easy access.

606. **Women in Particular: An Index to American Women.** Kali Herman. Phoenix: Oryx, 1984. 740p. ISBN 0-89774-088-2.

This is a useful index to sketches of U.S. women. The sketches appear in more than 50 biographical dictionaries, ranging from *Notable American Women* (entry 604) to the *Slavonic Encyclopedia*. More than 15,000 women are treated, and access is aided by a noteworthy array of classification approaches. First, there is a field and career index, which is divided into areas of endeavor, such as education or fashion and etiquette. This segment represents the bulk of the volume. Second, there is an index by religious affiliation, followed by a third index by racial and ethnic background and a fourth by geographic location. Names are listed in all applicable indexes in chronological fashion. Entries furnish name, date, career information, religion, workplace, and residence, as well as references to biographical dictionaries. There is a final alphabetical index, which is comprehensive to the work.

607. **Women in the Scientific Search: An American Bio-Bibliography, 1724–1979.** Patricia J. Siegel and Kay T. Finley. Metuchen, NJ: Scarecrow, 1985. 399p. ISBN 0-8108-1755-1.

This title attempts to furnish information on an array of U.S. female scientists spanning a period of 250 years. It should be noted that only a few of the more than 150 women covered date back to the eighteenth century. Arrangement of entries is chronological under scientific discipline (anthropology, archaeology, biochemistry, zoology). Brief biographical sketches are furnished that appear to be accurate and well developed. There are a number of omissions, which is to be expected of a work of this type. Included with all entries is a bibliography of works about the subjects (not by them), making this more of a tool for the undergraduate than the scholar. An annotated section of general biographical works introduces the listings.

608. **Women in the United States Congress, 1917–1972: Their Accomplishments, with Bibliographies.** Rudolf Engelbarts. Littleton, CO: Libraries Unlimited, 1974. 184p. ISBN 0-87287-083-9.

This dictionary was produced in the mid-1970s following a period of rising awareness of the role of women in seeking political redress of grievances. It covers 81 women who served in Congress over a span of 55 years during the twentieth century. Although the author at times displays his political inclinations in chiding a self-indulgent, reactionary Congress, treatment given to the subjects appears to be useful and easily digested. Each entry is furnished with a bibliography of books and articles the undergraduate student would find useful in researching the topic. The entries vary in length with what seems to be their subjects' tenure in office, with the longtime politicians receiving more detailed analysis. Some errors have been detected by reviewers with reference to committee memberships. There is an index to facilitate access.

609. **Women's Diaries, Journals, and Letters: An Annotated Bibliography.** Cheryl Cline. New York: Garland, 1989. 716p. (Garland Reference Library of the Humanities, v.780). ISBN 0-8240-6637-5.

This recent annotated listing of nearly 3,000 primary source writings by women (mainly Americans, but also heavily representative of French and British thought) is of importance to both scholars and students. Other parts of the world receive far less treatment; for example, Africa has a total of seven entries. Entries describe private writings, mainly letters, diaries, journals, and travel accounts, mostly in the English language. There is a wealth of historical background on an array of topics such as divorce, religion, slavery, and the arts, enabling a slice of female life to be placed in historical perspective. There is an introductory segment describing the use of letters and diaries and problems in editing. Entries are then arranged under form and type divisions (e.g., critical works, anthologies, letters). It is indexed by authors, subjects, locations, and titles.

The Hispanic Experience

Like other ethnic groups, Hispanic-Americans have received increased documentation in the trade literature since the 1970s. Reference sources and bibliographic tools have not kept pace, however, and the culture fares badly when compared to reference sources produced on blacks, women, and American Indians. Mexican-Americans have received the most coverage here, largely through the efforts of Matt S. Meier. One of the tools (entry 618) defines Hispanics in terms of a pure Spanish origin. In this section, Mexican-Americans are treated separately; Puerto Rican and Cuban-American material is merged with the more general sources in the "other" category. For related material on Puerto Rico and its people, see chapter 6, "Regional History," under "Territories and Possessions."

Since 1978, *Hispanic American Periodicals Index* (*HAPI*) has been issued through the UCLA Latin American Center on an annual basis. Occasionally historical topics are treated in the 250 journals indexed but the emphasis is on current conditions in Latin America. The important journals treating Hispanics in the United States are included as well.

The Hispanic Society of America addresses both history and culture and was founded in 1904 in New York City. There are 400 members today.

Mexican-Americans

610. **Bibliografia Chicana: A Guide to Information Sources.** Arnulfo D. Trejo. Detroit: Gale, 1975. 193p. (Gale Information Guide Library; Ethnic Studies Information Guide Series, v.1). ISBN 0-8103-1311-1.

Part of the surge of interest in ethnic traditions in the 1970s, this literature guide on Mexican-Americans was prepared by a library science professor using the Winchell (now Sheehy/Balay, entry 23) alphanumeric system of classification. Arrangement of entries is alphabetical within subject divisions. Presented here are about 350 monographic works, each of which is annotated in critical fashion. Annotations in many cases include excerpts or quotations from the works themselves. The guide begins with a section on general reference works; this is followed by sections given to the humanities, social sciences, history, and applied sciences. Although beginning to show its age, this tool should be helpful to both scholars and students in beginning their inquiries; the monographs covered date back to the mid-nineteenth century. Special features include a list of serials, directory of publishing firms, and a glossary.

611. **Bibliography of Mexican American History.** Matt S. Meier, comp. Westport, CT: Greenwood, 1984. 500p. ISBN 0-313-23776-X.

Covering materials written between 1842 and 1982, this must be considered the most comprehensive of all bibliographies of English-language publications on Mexican-Americans. As such, it has value for historians and beginning researchers, furnishing 4,500 entries representing both primary and secondary sources. Students at the secondary school level will also find it beneficial. It begins with a chapter on general works; then follow five chapters on chronological periods, beginning with the colonial era and ending with the 1980s. Finally, three topical chapters cover labor, civil rights, and culture. Within these chapters, there are subdivisions based on formats (books, dissertations, articles, etc.). Annotations are given for more than two-thirds of the entries; these are brief and average one or two sentences in length. Both author and subject indexes are furnished.

612. **Dictionary of Mexican American History.** Matt S. Meier and Feliciano Rivera. Westport, CT: Greenwood, 1981. 498p. ISBN 0-313-21203-1.

Through a combination of the efforts of the two authors, both academicians, as well as 30 contributors, this work furnishes quick access to information on people, places, events, and organizations that have influenced Mexican-American history. Although coverage begins with the sixteenth century, emphasis is given to mid-to-latter nineteenth-century and twentieth-century developments. About 1,000 entries are furnished that vary in length from a few lines to several pages, depending on the perceived importance of the topic. The intention is to furnish a useful source for students at all levels. There are a few compromises on the inclusion of popular figures such as Trini Lopez. Articles are not signed, although contributors are listed in the preface. Also included are a bibliography, chronology, glossary, list of journals, statistical tables, and maps. An index is furnished to aid access.

613. **The Education of the Mexican American: A Selected Bibliography.** Mario A. Benìtez and Lupita G. Villarreal. Austin, TX: Dissemination and Assessment Center for Bilingual Education, 1979. 270p. ISBN 0-89417-353-7.

Of great use to the study of Mexican-Americans is this bibliography of historical importance regarding their education. The work lists materials of all types: books, monographs, journals, theses, dissertations, ERIC documents, federal laws, court decisions and documents issued by both state and federal government. Publication and issue dates range from 1896 to 1976. Nearly 3,250 entries are arranged in chronological fashion under nine different topical divisions following an initial segment on bibliographies. After opening with a generic category, the volume gives coverage to Mexican-American students; school; curriculum; migrant education, bilingual education; higher education, adult education; and community. Emphasis is given to studies and reports of research; there are no curriculum guides, textbooks, or other instructional aids. The work is categorized by both an author index and a chronological index.

614. **The Mexican American: A Critical Guide to Research Aids.** Barbara J. Robinson and Joy C. Robinson. Greenwich, CT: JAI, 1980. 287p. (Foundations in Library and Information Science, v.1). ISBN 0-89232-006-0.

This represents a major effort in furnishing sources of information on the Mexican-American tradition, an effort for which the authors are well prepared by virtue of their positions as a Latin-American bibliographer and a professor of history. The bibliography furnishes nearly 670 titles of books, book chapters, articles, pamphlets, dissertations, and documents that are placed within 17 chapters divided into two major divisions, "General Works" and "Subject Bibliographies." General works include chapters on bibliographies, guides, and biographies, whereas subjects include history, education, and labor. Annotations are of the critical nature and are useful in evaluating significance. Emphasis is given to twentieth-century writings, especially the 20 years prior to 1978, the cutoff date.

Mexican Americans: An Annotated Bibliography of Bibliographies by Julio A. Martinez and Ada Burns (R&E Publishers, 1984) is a compact volume considered to be supplementary to the above. Selection of bibliographies is concentrated in the period following the coverage of the earlier work beginning with 1978 for the most part. Annotations provide both descriptive and evaluative information.

615. **Mexican American Biographies: A Historical Dictionary, 1836–1987.** Matt S. Meier. New York: Greenwood, 1988. 270p. ISBN 0-313-24521-5.

The author, a historian and frequent contributor to the literature of the Mexican-American, has provided biographical coverage of 270 *prominentes* ranging from sports figures to politicians. Coverage spans 150 years from the mid-1830s, the Texas revolutionary period, to the 1980s. Emphasis is on the current scene, with about 75 percent of the personalities being contemporary figures. The historical biographees are those who generally have been treated in published surveys of Mexican-American history, whereas the current ones achieved prominence through professional or civic endeavors. Entries are arranged alphabetically and give biographical descriptions of varying length (dependent to some degree on the amount of available information). Emphasis is placed upon accomplishments, preparation, and training rather than family or marital details. Appendices list individuals by state and by field of endeavor. There is no index.

616. **Reference Materials on Mexican Americans: An Annotated Bibliography.** Richard D. Woods. Metuchen, NJ: Scarecrow, 1976. 190p. ISBN 0-8108-0963-X.

Although dated, this literature guide to materials on Mexican-Americans is still useful to inquirers at all levels who need to make determinations regarding sources of information. Nearly 400 reference works are enumerated, most of which have been published in the United States. Those published in Mexico contain material pertinent to Mexicans in this country. The guides listed represent sources of information to a variety of materials, both print and nonprint, much of which are useful in teaching situations. The monographic literature included in this work is oriented toward scholarship and serious inquiry and should prove a fruitful place to begin research. Included also are bibliographies, checklists, indexes, guides, and directories. Brief annotations of up to 100 words describe content adequately. There are three indexes to assure access to author, title, and subject.

Other Hispanics

617. **Cubans in the United States: A Bibliography for Research in the Social and Behavioral Sciences, 1960–1983.** Lyn MacCorkle, comp. Westport, CT: Greenwood, 1984. 227p. (Bibliographies and Indexes in Sociology, no.1). ISBN 0-313-24509-6.

MacCorkle's research bibliography on Cuban-Americans covers a 24-year period and is a real asset to scholars and serious students. It represents the initial effort of another of the Greenwood bibliographic series. Selection is limited to research studies as reported in journals, dissertations, government reports, conference papers, and miscellaneous other unpublished materials. The author has furnished about 1,600 entries, which are listed under several major categories: "Economics," "Education," "Public Administration," "Psychology," "Health," "Politics," "Sociology," and "Demography." These categories are well developed for use by researchers; the restrictions on content will discourage those with a desire for less rigorous literature. Although additional bibliographic work is needed to control the abundant popular literature, the present effort is a valuable contribution for historians at all levels. There is an author index to furnish access.

618. **The Hispanic Presence in North America from 1492 to Today.** Carlos M. Fernandez-Shaw. New York: Facts on File, 1991. 375p. ISBN 0-8160-2133-3.

Originally written in Spanish by the former Spanish consul-general in Miami and published as *Presencia Española en los Estados Unidos* (Cooperación liberoamerica [Spain], 1987), this English-language translation has been both abridged and updated. Comprehensive in scope, the work furnishes both students and scholars with a one-volume history of Spanish influence in the United States. Each state is treated within its region. The effort represents another area of inquiry in U.S. history assumed by Facts on File in its design to provide coverage of the cultural heritage of the various U.S. ethnic groups. In this work, the term "Hispanic" is applied to *influences* emanating from Spain, rather than Spanish-speaking *peoples*; Spain's role in U.S. history is described in an introductory essay to the regional segment. Useful listings of officers, missions, historical societies, and so on are given in the appendices.

619. **Latinas of the Americas: A Source Book.** K. Lynn Stoner. New York: Garland, 1989. 692p. (Garland Reference Library of Social Science, v.363). ISBN 0-8240-8336-1.

Ms. Stoner has made a real contribution to both study and research of the female experience within the Americas with this excellent resource. More than 3,000 studies, both published and unpublished, are organized under 15 different chapter headings. All but two of them are topical in nature. Such subjects as history, health, demography, household and family studies, religion, and urban/rural development are treated. Two segments deal with anthologies and bibliographies exclusively. Each chapter is prepared by a different specialist or scholar, and each opens with a bibliographical essay providing an overview of the subject and the works cited; these are followed by listings of entries without annotations. Coverage is given to studies on Hispanic women in this country as well as those in the various parts of Latin America. The work is indexed by author, country or region, and subject.

620. **Puerto Ricans and Other Minority Groups in the Continental United States: An Annotated Bibliography.** Diane Herrera, ed. Detroit: Blaine Ethridge Books, 1979. 397p. ISBN 0-87917-067-0.

This is mostly a reprint of a 1973 effort by Ms. Herrera that focused solely on the Puerto Rican tradition and cited more than 2,150 books and articles published through the year 1972, primarily on the education of Puerto Rican children. For the present work, Francesco Cordasco, a prolific bibliographer of ethnic traditions, has added an introductory essay and some 300 titles on bilingual and bicultural education, only a few of which bear more recent imprint dates. The work retains its initial emphasis on the educational experiences of Puerto Ricans in this country. There is a peripheral and slight coverage given to Mexican-Americans, blacks, Cuban-Americans, American Indians, and Jews, but not enough to warrant a researcher's interest. A few of the sources furnish information on social and historical topics. There is an author index, but it does not include the supplementary Cordasco listings.

621. **Sourcebook of Hispanic Culture in the United States.** David W. Foster, ed. Chicago: American Library Association, 1982. 352p. ISBN 0-8389-0354-1.

Giving broad coverage to the influences of Hispanic-Americans, this excellent bibliographic source treats the three major cultural traditions of Cuba, Puerto Rico, and Mexico. Both students and scholars will benefit from the excellent organization and commentary provided by the individual scholars and specialists who prepared each of the chapters. The Cuban segment has only one chapter on sociology; the Puerto Rican section furnishes four chapters on history, anthropology, sociology, and art; the Mexican segment has those and a fifth chapter on literature. Both Cuban and Puerto Rican literature are covered in a fourth, general section, along with generous treatment of literature, education, and music. In addition to the opening essay, there is an annotated bibliography in each chapter. Each of the 17 scholars seems to have done a thorough job. An author-title index furnishes access.

The Native American Experience

The plight of the native North American has received a great deal of news coverage since the 1960s. This coverage, in turn, has inspired a great deal of publishing by trade-book publishers, both mainstream and small press. Reference publishers have followed suit with bibliographic sources to control the increasing volume of literature, as well as information sources to furnish data and interpretation in convenient packages. Coverage spans the entire realm of American Indian life and addresses social ills, health problems, political involvement, and customs and traditions. History can be approached through study of individual tribes, cult of personality, or more generally through the development and progress of ideas and social response.

This section includes works on a variety of topics, some of which are addressed in more generic fashion elsewhere in this guide. As in the case of blacks, the racial/ethnic factor is considered dominant. Those issues examined here as part of the American Indian experience include those relating to education, law, the female experience, and medicine (science). For works relating to the treatment of American Indians in film, see "Entertainment and Recreation: Popular Culture—Cinema" in this chapter.

The American Indian Heritage Foundation of Falls Church, Virginia, was founded in 1963 and has an extraordinarily large membership numbering 260,000. Contemporary concerns are foremost, but historical aspects are also treated in the quarterly newsletter. The Cherokee National Historical Society of Tahlequah, Oklahoma, has 900 members and has operated since 1963. It also issues a quarterly newsletter.

Library Resources

622. **American Indian and Alaska Native Newspapers and Periodicals, 1826–1924.** Daniel F. Littlefield and James W. Parins. Westport, CT: Greenwood, 1984. 482p. (Historical Guides to the World's Periodicals and Newspapers). ISBN 0-313-23426-4.

This is the first of three volumes issued by the authors over a period of two years and furnishes listings and holdings information for nearly 225 periodicals published by American Indians or Alaskan natives. It covers a span of nearly 100 years, from 1826 to 1924, and examines titles in depth, with entries running several pages in length. Entries are alphabetically arranged and contain general descriptions, information on indexing, library holdings, publication history, and editorship. There is a useful segment on titles known but not located. Appendices furnish listings of titles arranged chronologically by publication date, state, and tribe. A general index of subjects includes persons, places, and topics.

The second volume was issued in 1986 and continues the coverage with an additional 500 newspapers and periodicals published between 1925 and 1970, and the third volume (also 1986) completes the coverage, adding another 1,000 titles published between 1971 and 1985. These efforts were aided by the contributions of more than 30 specialists for each volume.

623. **American Indian Archival Material: A Guide to Holdings in the Southeast.** Ronald Chepesiuk and Arnold M. Shankman, comps. Westport, CT: Greenwood, 1982. 325p. ISBN 0-313-23731-X.

This directory of resources was compiled through responses to a mail questionnaire sent to institutions throughout the southeastern United States. From a total of 2,300 repositories in 11 states, there were just over 500 responses, the majority of them indicating that they held no archival or manuscript materials pertinent to the study of North American Indians. In addition to receiving 168 positive answers, the compilers were able to develop entries from secondary sources for six nonresponding agencies, producing a total of 174 archival centers. Although by no means complete, the listing is more comprehensive on the topic of native American materials than any previous effort. Entries are organized in directory fashion by state, then city, and furnish the expected information regarding the collections. Appendices list both nonresponding agencies and those reporting no holdings. There is a general index of names, places, and subjects.

624. **American Indian Legal Materials: A Union List.** Laura N. Gasaway, et al., comps. Stanfordville, NY: E. M. Coleman, 1980. (American Indians at Law Series). 152p. ISBN 0-930576-31-4.

In an attempt to control the elusive material on legal matters relevant to the native American, the compilers have prepared a listing of over 4,500 entries held by libraries of 28 law schools, law firms, and governmental agencies. No annotations are given for the entries; arrangement is alphabetical by main entry, with each given a sequential entry number. Included are a variety of materials: monographic works on tribal codes, resolutions, constitutions, and so on. Quality of informational materials for the research of legal history varies widely, with many inclusions of novels as well as titles on education and on ethnology. Even so, the uniqueness of the content makes this an important resource for both scholars and students. There are three indexes to assure access by tribe, geography, or subject.

625. **Dictionary Catalog of the American Indian Collection, Huntington Free Library and Reading Room, New York.** Boston: G. K. Hall, 1977. 4v.

This is another of the G. K. Hall efforts furnishing photoreproduced copies of the catalogs of important and significant libraries. This four-volume edition covers more than 35,000 items on the anthropology, art, archaeology, history, and contemporary conditions of Indians in the Western Hemisphere. Included are books, periodicals, periodical articles, and newspapers. The library of the Museum of the American Indian (Heye Foundation), located at the Huntington Free Library, houses the largest collection of materials on American Indians in the country; there are strong collections of anthropological papers issued by universities, journals from historical societies, and field materials from specialists. Because much of the indexing and cataloging was completed over a long time span, quality and even legibility of the entries vary considerably. Both the scholar and the serious student will find many obscure and unknown resources that may be of value to their inquiries.

626. **Guide to Records in the National Archives of the United States Relating to American Indians.** Edward E. Hill, comp. Washington: National Archives Trust Fund Board, 1981. 467p. S/N 022-002-00098-8.

Of real value to scholars and serious students is this guide, which facilitates the use of the magnificent holdings of the National Archives with respect to the American Indian. As such, it is a specialized effort supplementary to the more generic guide to the archives (entry 84) and is organized in similar fashion. Beginning with prefederal records, it examines Indian treaties from 1789 to 1871, then covers the Bureau of Indian Affairs. From that point, there is a rather complex chronological coverage of U.S.-Indian affairs by different agencies. Entries describe these agencies in terms of their impact and their collections of records. Records vary and range from print narratives to photographs and maps. The work is indexed by subject, as well as by both personal and tribal names.

An additional research aid is *The American Indian*, published by the Archives in 1972, which furnishes a listing of important records available on microfilm. It is part of the Select Catalog Series (entry 84n).

627. Images of the Other: A Guide to Microform Manuscripts on Indian-White Relations. Polly S. Grimshaw. Champaign-Urbana, IL: University of Illinois Press, 1991. 174p. ISBN 0-252-01759-5.

This recent bibliographic guide enumerates the holdings of 65 repositories for which collections have been reproduced and made available for purchase in microformat. They represent European perspectives on the American Indian and, as such, have value for both serious students and scholars of intellectual and social history. It has been noted that length of time of commercial availability varies considerably for the entries, and work is required in tracking down the present holders of some of the sets. Each entry is described at length, beginning with a history of the collection and its significance. Then follows enumeration of content, editorial strategies, and listings of guides and help aids. Even the legibility of the documents is covered. Sets are organized into several categories, such as reports, letters, treaties, and organizations, and coverage ranges from 1631 to the late 1970s. There are author and subject indexes.

628. Native American Periodicals and Newspapers, 1828–1982: Bibliography, Publishing Record, and Holdings. James P. Danky, ed. and Maureen E. Handy, comp. Westport, CT: Greenwood, 1984. 532p. ISBN 0-313-23773-5.

Issued during the same year as the first volume of Littlefield's and Parins's *American Indian and Alaska Native Newspapers and Periodicals, 1826–1924* (entry 622), this work drew favorable reviews for its more comprehensive nature in covering over 1,160 titles published over a 155-year period. Even with completion of the other (now three-volume) effort, this still remains a useful source of information that also should be used by inquirers at various levels. Entries tend to be brief but accurate and informative and furnish dates, frequency, editor, publisher, title variations, holding libraries, and availability in microform. The work is indexed extensively by subject, author, editor, publisher, geography, and chronology. Much of the material is held by the editor's library at the State Historical Society of Wisconsin, thus furnishing excellent resource material to develop this useful tool.

Bibliographical Sources

629. The American Indian in Graduate Studies: A Bibliography of Theses and Dissertations. Frederick J. Dockstader and Alice W. Dockstader, comps. New York: Museum of the American Indian, Heye Foundation, 1973–1974. 2 pts.

This is a two-part bibliography issued by the Museum of the American Indian, Heye Foundation, covering theses and dissertations produced on the native American experience since 1890. Frederick Dockstader was the director of the museum and a well-known authority on anthropology; he developed part 1, which covers the years from 1890 to 1955 and was originally issued in 1957. This part consists of nearly 3,700 titles of theses and dissertations on all aspects of Indian life in the Americas. Part 2 treats nearly 3,800 additional titles completed between 1955 and 1970. For the present edition, a small added section was relocated from part 1 to part 2, and the original index was deleted. Numbering of items is sequential in both parts and furnishes an excellent listing of academic research over an 80-year period, documenting various attempts at exposition, interpretation, and suggested resolution. There is an excellent comprehensive index to both parts at the end of part 2.

630. **American Indian Women: A Guide to Research.** Gretchen M. Bataille and Kathleen M. Sands. Hamden, CT: Garland, 1991. 423p. (Garland Reference Library of Social Science, v.515; Women's History and Culture, v.4). ISBN 0-8240-4799-0.

This recent effort is considered to be the most comprehensive bibliography of scholarly and literary work by and about native North American women. It furnishes nearly 1,575 items, both print and nonprint. Excluded are dissertations, pamphlets, children's literature, and any materials not in the English language. Annotations are brief and descriptive of content; many offer interesting and revealing facts related to the topic or the document. The entries are organized under eight different topical and form divisions, beginning with "Bibliographies and Reference Works." Following are "Ethnography, Cultural History, and Social Roles," "Policies and Law," "Health, Education and Employment," "Visual and Performing Arts," "Literature and Criticism," "Autobiography, Biography and Interviews," and "Film and Video." The work is indexed by time period, tribe, name, and subject and should serve the needs of both students and scholars.

631. **An Annotated Bibliography of Northern Plains Ethnohistory.** Katherine M. Weist and Susan R. Sharrock. Missoula, MT: Department of Anthropology, University of Montana, 1985. 299p. (Contributions to Anthropology, no.8).

This volume represents a real asset to serious inquiry on the Northern Plains Indians. It furnishes almost 700 annotated entries of primary sources (books, articles, and reports) on the pre-reservation period from 1690 to 1880. Because the amount of material covering the topic is massive in volume, inclusion was limited to titles written by authors present at that time and reporting their observations, regardless of publication date (some items date to the mid-1970s). Arrangement of entries is alphabetical by author; tribes covered include the Blackfoot, Gros Ventre, Assiniboine, Cree, Ojibwa, Crow, Cheyenne, and Arapaho. Full bibliographic data is given for each entry; annotations are ample and range from 100 to 150 words each. Included are lists of relevant secondary sources and of bibliographies on the subject. There is an index of names, tribes, and subjects.

632. **Annotated Bibliography of the Literature on American Indians Published in State Historical Society Publications, New England and Middle Atlantic States.** Arlene B. Hirschfelder. Millwood, NY: Kraus International, 1982. 356p. ISBN 0-527-40889-1.

This annotated bibliography furnishes a total of 1,182 articles derived from the issues of 37 journals and newsletters published by state historical societies from 11 New England and Middle Atlantic states. Materials both by and about American Indians are listed. Each journal is covered from its first issue to its final one or, if still operating, through its last full volume published during 1979. Although there is emphasis on tribes that lived in the area covered by Connecticut, Delaware, Maine, Maryland, Massachusetts, New Hampshire, New York, New Jersey, Pennsylvania, Rhode Island, and Vermont, other area tribes treated infrequently in those journals are included as well. Entries are arranged alphabetically and are accompanied by an ample annotation of descriptive nature. There are three indexes: by subject; by person, place, and title; and by Indian nation.

633.   **A Bibliographical Guide to the History of Indian-White Relations in the United States.** Francis P. Prucha. Chicago: University of Chicago, 1977. 454p. ISBN 0-226-68476-8.

Prucha, a noted bibliographer-historian and expert on the history of native Americans, made this excellent contribution to research and study. More than 9,700 entries are furnished; these touch on every aspect of Indian-white relations, including those covering the British colonial period. Neither Canadian nor Spanish materials are given. Materials collected represent books, journals, periodical articles, pamphlets, and dissertations published through the year 1975. There are two major divisions. Part I offers a guide to source materials such as archives and government documents; part II represents the bulk of the text and furnishes a classified listing of materials in such categories as "Treaties and Councils," "Trade and Traders," and "Legal Relations."

The above title is supplemented by Prucha's *Indian-White Relations in the United States: A Bibliography of Works Published, 1975–1980* (University of Nebraska, 1982). Here, another 3,400 entries are furnished in the same style and organization of the earlier publication. Both volumes contain author and subject indexes.

634.   **Bibliographical Series.** Newberry Library. D'Arcy McNickle Center for the History of the American Indian. Bloomington, IN: Indiana University Press, 1976– . (In progress). ISSN 4200-4912.

This useful series began in the year of the bicentennial in response to a need for better documentation of the life and culture of the American Indian. Beginning with an effort on historical demography, the series steadily produced a variety of titles completed by different scholars ranging from tribal-specific works on the Cherokees, the Delawares, and the Ojibwas, to volumes on more generic topics, such as sociology. The authority for the series changed several times but most commonly was regarded as the Newberry Library Center for the History of the American Indian, with publication being handled by Indiana University. The pattern for the series is an opening bibliographical essay followed by an alphabetical listing of all works cited in the essay. Two sets of recommended titles (for beginners and for basic library collections) complete the package, which generally runs about 100 pages or less. After the 29th issue, covering the native American female experience, in 1983, the series was thought to have ended and was identified as a ceased publication by OCLC. For a complete listing of these titles, see Sheehy (entry 23). Happily, the series seems to have been resurrected with subsequent publication of *Scholars and the Indian Experience: Critical Reviews of Recent Writing in the Social Sciences* by W.R. Swagerty in 1984 and *The Seminole and Miccosukee Tribes: A Critical Bibliography* by Harry A. Kersey, Jr. in 1987. The authority for the series is now known as the D'Arcy McNickle Center for the History of the American Indian.

635.   **A Bookman's Guide to the Indians of the Americas: A Compilation of Over 10,000 Catalogue Entries with Prices and Annotations, Both Bibliographical and Descriptive.** Richard A. Hand. Metuchen, NJ: Scarecrow, 1989. 750p. ISBN 0-8108-2182-6.

A recent effort that serves as both a bibliography and relative price guide to materials on native Americans, this is a useful source of information for scholars and librarians as well as dealers and collectors. There are nearly 6,750 titles; additional copies of these titles are given also, which brings the total number of entries to 10,000. These items sell for at least $10 and were found through examination of 200 catalogs issued by 21 book dealers. Prices are quoted from the catalogs themselves, which furnish an accurate picture for only a limited time. The work is most valued as a bibliography and brings together books and monographs of interest and value to the study. Dates of imprints range from 1821 to 1985. There is a subject index to provide access.

636. **Ethnographic Bibliography of North America.** George P. Murdock and Timothy J. O'Leary. 4th ed. New Haven, CT: Human Relations Area Files, 1975. 5v. ISBN 0-87536-205-2. **Supp. 1973–1987.** 1990. 3v. ISBN 0-87536-254-0.

The fourth edition, a five-volume effort, represents a computer-produced revision of a monumental and classic tool first issued in 1941. Considerable expansion of coverage in the areas of history, psychology, biology, and current native American affairs, combined with an explosion of written material on Indians following publication of the third edition in 1960, contributed to the increased size. Listed are 40,000 entries, arranged geographically, with each volume covering a different geographic region. Entries represent books and articles; the introduction furnishes description of other types of sources, such as government publications, ERIC documents, dissertations, and maps. Nearly 270 different native American cultures are treated, ranging from those in northern Mexico to the Eskimo in Alaska.

Finally, there is a three-volume supplement, *Ethnographic Bibliography of North America, 4th Edition Supplement, 1973–1987*, by M. Marlene Martin and Timothy J. O'Leary (Human Relations Area Files, 1990), furnishing 25,000 more books and articles published during the indicated period. Citations represent all western languages; 21 more groups have been added. There is access by author and subject indexes; the work is also available on floppy disk.

637. **Guide to American Indian Documents in the Congressional Serial Set, 1817–1899: A Project of the Institute for the Development of Indian Law.** Steven L. Johnson. New York: Clearwater, 1977. 503p. ISBN 0-88354-107-6.

For the scholar and serious inquirer, this chronological listing identifies about 10,650 documents related to native Americans in volumes of the Serial Set (entry 196), issued between 1817 and 1899. This subject index is the result of an extraordinary project carried out by a team of bibliographers headed by Johnson, who examined each document from the first session of the 15th Congress (December 1, 1817) through the 55th Congress second session (March 3, 1899). Up to the time that Johnson issued his work, access was possible only through titles, by using the standard guides in the field. In addition to the subject index, there is a chronological section listing the documents by date and furnishing a brief enumeration of the contents. Appendices identify documents in both Poore's catalog (entry 72) and Ames (entry 73) which are not in the Serial Set. The work is indexed by subject, tribe, and region.

638. **Guide to Research on North American Indians.** Arlene B. Hirschfelder, et al. Chicago: American Library Association, 1983. 330p. ISBN 0-8389-0353-3.

Another excellent guide by Hirschfelder, this highly selective classified bibliography of 1,100 books, articles, and documents represents useful English-language writings of Indians of this country. Several items on Canadian and South American Indians are also included. Lengthy annotations of 200 to 400 words describe background and content. Entries are organized into 27 different subject chapters, each of which opens with an important informative essay describing the topic and placing it into perspective; problems of writing and research are addressed here. Topical chapters address such subjects as archaeology, Indian relations, war, economic influences, and the law. Entries in this volume are cited in the series for the Newberry Library Center (entry 634), but this title provides a handy single-volume survey for all levels of users, from interested laypersons to scholars. There are author-title and subject indexes.

639. Health and Disease of American Indians North of Mexico: A Bibliography, 1800-1969. Mark V. Barrow et al., comps. Gainesville, FL: University of Florida, 1972. 147p. ISBN 0-8130-0331-8.

The health and hygiene of America's disadvantaged ethnic, racial and gender minorities has become a much more important issue since the 1970s and generally receives treatment as one section or chapter of a more comprehensive work. The present effort, although aging, is a specialized book-length bibliography on the health and diseases of American Indians as treated historically in the literature over a period of 170 years. All types of materials are included with the exception of travel narratives; entries are organized into 22 categories representing diseases and physiological problems. The purpose of the work is to furnish a listing of materials relevant to the clinical treatment of diseases suffered by American Indians. Three indexes are provided: by author, by tribe, and by disease subject.

640. Index to Literature on the American Indian, 1970-1973. San Francisco: Indian Historian Press, 1972-1975. 4v. Ann. ISSN 0091-7346.

This was a short-lived but valiant attempt to furnish an annual index of books and periodical articles on American Indians. Sponsored by the American Indian Historical Society, it attempted to fill a void created by the cessation of the *American Indian Index* (see below), which suffered from numerous problems, both financial and technical, during its 16-year history. The more recent effort began with coverage of the year 1970, which was published in 1972. It ended with coverage of 1973, published in 1975. The work furnished an index, by author and subject, of monographs and articles selected from over 250 periodicals. No annotations were provided; entries represented a wide range of subjects, from agriculture to the U.S. government. Listings of native American publications are given, along with acquisitions information.

The *American Indian Index* (R.L. Knor, 1953-1968) was issued eight times per year and covered a wide spectrum of materials. It was recognized as a useful source but apparently suffered from lack of interest. Both titles now serve historical interests in terms of their retrospective coverage.

641. Indian Land Tenure: Bibliographical Essays and a Guide to the Literature. Imre Sutton. New York: Clearwater, 1975. 290p. (The Library of American Indian Affairs Series). ISBN 0-88354-104-1.

Because of the importance of the topic with regard to events of the past two decades, this bibliography relating to land occupancy and use by American Indians is helpful to both researchers and students. The work is divided into two major sections, the first of which furnishes seven bibliographic essays on topics important to research: "Aboriginal Occupancy and Territoriality," "Land Cessions and the Establishment of Reservations," "Land Administration and Land Utilization," "Aboriginal Title and Land Claims," "Title Clarification and Change," "Tenure and Jurisdiction," and "Land Tenure and Culture Change." These essays cover the socio-legal-political literature on the topic. The second part contains a bibliography of over 1,000 entries, alphabetically arranged. Three indexes furnish access to the materials: a subject index, which includes cross-references; a tribal index to authors; and a geographical index to authors.

642. **Indians of North America: Methods and Sources for Library Research.** Marilyn L. Haas. Hamden, CT: Library Professional Publications, 1983. 163p. ISBN 0-208-01980-4.

Prepared as a bibliographic aid for the beginning researcher and student, this book makes for an excellent starting point for research and inquiry. The guide opens with a segment on library methodology, furnishing information on use of the public catalog, classification systems, and various types of reference tools, including databases. The evaluation of these tools is useful in helping the inquirer make reasonable choices. The second part consists of an annotated bibliography of books arranged by topics such as agriculture, art, and games. Each topic is accompanied by a list of relevant subject headings and a list of journals. The final segment provides an unannotated bibliography of books arranged by specific tribes. Most entries in this work are written in English and were issued during the two decades prior to its publication. The materials are accessed by a useful detailed index.

The above work represents an expansion of the author's "A Basic Guide to Reference Sources for the Study of the North American Indian," which appeared as a special feature in the July/September 1979 issue of *Reference Services Review (RSR)*.

643. **Indians of the United States and Canada: A Bibliography.** Dwight L. Smith, ed. Santa Barbara, CA: ABC-Clio, 1974–1983. 2v. (Clio Bibliography Series, v.3, 9). ISBN 0-87436-124-9 (v.1); ISBN 0-87436-149-4 (v.2).

This is another of the publisher's specialized bibliographies derived from the massive database of *America: History and Life* (entry 51). The first volume was published in 1974 and consists of the abstracts of 1,600 articles published between 1954 and 1972. The second volume was issued in 1983 and covers an additional 3,200 entries similarly drawn from hundreds of journals in history and the social sciences. Coverage is extended to 1978 in terms of publication dates. Arrangement is similar in both volumes and parallels the parent work's three broad chronological divisions: pre-Columbian history; tribal history, 1492–1900; and the twentieth century. Subdivisions are furnished for tribes and cultural areas. Each volume is indexed separately, with volume 2 having incorporated the publisher's Subject Profile Index, a useful scheme employed in *America: History and Life* (entry 51).

644. **Native American Bibliography Series.** Metuchen, NJ: Scarecrow, 1980–1992. v.1– 16. (Projected 20v). ISSN 1040-9629.

This series began in 1980 with *Bibliography of the Sioux* by Jack W. Marken and Herbert T. Hoover and was projected as a 20-volume effort covering an array of topics and tribes. Since then progress has been steady, and the series has gained an excellent reputation for scholarly products. Comprehensiveness and depth compare favorably to the *Bibliographical Series* (entry 634) and other efforts that attempted similar coverage of specific tribes. Those volumes that are topical rather than tribal-specific are generally of the same high quality. Most volumes in the series list from one thousand to several thousand books, articles, government publications, newspaper items, and pamphlets, with the dates ranging from precolonial times to the present. The series volumes, enumerated in sequence, are: volume 2, *A Biobibliography of Native American Writers, 1772–1924* by Daniel F. Littlefield, Jr. and James W. Parins (1981); volume 3, *Bibliography of the Languages of Native California, Including Closely Related Languages of the Adjacent Areas* by William Bright (1982); volume 4, *A Guide to Cherokee Documents in Four Archives* by William L. Anderson and James A. Lewis (1983); volume 5, *A Biobibliography of Native American Writers, 1772– 1924: Supplement* by Littlefield and Parins (1985); volume 6, *Bibliography of the Osage* by Terry P. Wilson (1985); volume 7, *A Guide to Cherokee Documents in the Northeastern United States* by Paul Kutsche (1986); volume 8, *In Pursuit of the Past: An Anthropological and Bibliographic Guide to Maryland and Delaware* by Frank W. Porter III (1986); volume

9, *The Indians of Texas: An Annotated Research Bibliography* by Michael L. Tate (1986); volume 10, *Bibliography of the Catawba* by Thomas J. Blumet (1987); volume 11, *Bibliography of the Chickasaw* by Anne Kelley Hoyt (1987); volume 12, *Kinsmen Through Time: An Annotated Bibliography of Potawatomi History* by R. David Edmonds (1987); volume 13, *Bibliography of the Blackfoot* by Hugh A. Dempsey and Lindsay Moir (1989); volume 14, *The Upstream People: An Annotated Research Bibliography of the Omaha Tribe* by Michael L. Tate (1991); volume 15, *Languages of the Aboriginal Southeast: An Annotated Bibliography* by Karen M. Booker (1991); and volume 16, *Yakima, Palouse, Cayuse, Umatilla, Walla Walla, and Wanapum Indians: An Historical Bibliography* by Clifford E. Trafzer (1992).

645. Native Americans: An Annotated Bibliography. Frederick E. Hoxie and Harvey Markowitz. Pasadena, CA: Salem, 1991. 325p. (Magill Bibliographies). ISBN 0-89356-670-5.

With the emphasis in the past few decades on eliminating stereotypes and the caricature-type formula from writings on American Indians, this product represents a useful and timely effort. It is an annotated bibliography of books and articles determined to be more genuine and truthful than most writings in their representation of events and conditions. In many cases, these works were aided in having native American authors, collaborators, and contributors. Restricted to English-language material, most of which has been published since 1970, entries are organized into topical sections following the initial unit on general and reference works. There is a short segment on history, followed by sections on the various culture areas. Material tends to be scholarly rather than popular in nature. Annotations are descriptive of content. There is a personal name/author index.

Information Sources

646. Atlas of American Indian Affairs. Francis P. Prucha. Lincoln; University of Nebraska Press, 1990. 191p. ISBN 0-8032-3689-1.

The author, a well-known historian, has been a prolific writer on the native American experience. This atlas opens with a brief preface, then delivers nearly 110 large-scale black-and-white maps on a variety of themes. Maps are arranged by topics such as population, land cessions, reservations, the army, the Indian frontier, and agencies and other institutions. There is a segment of 10 maps by Rafael Palacios, reprinted from an earlier publication, covering the frontier and various army campaigns against American Indians. Narrative is slight and is offered in the introduction and in the historical notes, which are separated from the maps. Statistical data is furnished in tables. When appropriate, maps are targeted to regions rather than to the entire country. It is complementary to Waldman's *Atlas of the North American Indian* (entry 647).

647. Atlas of the North American Indian. Carl Waldman. New York: Facts on File, 1985. 276p. ISBN 0-87196-850-9.

Broader in scope and furnishing more textual narrative than does Prucha's *Atlas of American Indian Affairs* (entry 646), this volume furnishes a comprehensive atlas and history of native Americans. Organization is topical and the work is composed of seven broad divisions, beginning with a perspective on "Ancient Indians." Following are "Ancient Civilizations," "Indian Lifeways," "Indians and Explorers," "Indian Wars," "Indian Land Cessions," and "Contemporary Indians." Narrative is extensive on these topics, which are illustrated by over 100 two-tone maps and line drawings. The movements and migrations are well developed; early chapters cover the spread of native American cultures into North America. Interpretation is sound and clear. Appendices contain a general chronology and a listing of place names and societies. Following a brief bibliography of two pages, the work concludes with a general index.

648. A Concise Dictionary of Indian Tribes of North America. Barbara A. Leitch. Algonac, MI: Reference Publications, 1979. 646p. ISBN 0-917256-09-3.

This work begins with an introduction by well-known native American author Vine Deloria. Considering that all of the articles in this useful handbook on individual tribes was the work of a single person, it represents an impressive effort. There are over 280 articles on tribes, alphabetically arranged for easy access. The entries for the most part furnish extensive detailed narrative on the history, culture, language, and tradition of each group. The narratives are followed by brief bibliographies; there are illustrations that include both photographs and drawings from early books. Of use to students and beginning researchers are the several maps created by different contributors on language groups, culture groups, Indian communities, and regions. Scholarship and careful planning are evident. There is a very brief glossary of 20-odd citations, and an index is furnished to aid access. A second edition has been slated to come out since 1991, and should be issued in 1993.

649. Encyclopedia of Native American Tribes. Carl Waldman. New York: Facts on File, 1988. 293p. ISBN 0-8160-1421-3.

This one-volume encyclopedia will be appreciated by a variety of students from junior high school to undergraduate levels. It furnishes easily digested, descriptive information on the culture, tradition, and history of over 150 different tribes of the United States, Canada, and Mexico. The author has served as an archivist for the New York State Historical Association and has produced a highly regarded atlas on the American Indian (entry 647). In this encyclopedia, entries for tribes are alphabetically arranged, and narratives vary in length from less than a page to several pages according to the size and historical impact of each group. Selection for inclusion of tribes was based on their historical significance and culture. Along with single tribes, certain classes of tribes, such as cliff dwellers, and language families have their own entries. There are over 300 color illustrations, a glossary, a bibliography, and an index.

Targeted to the same audience and providing similar coverage is the *Encyclopedia of Native American Religions* by Arlene B. Hirschfelder (Facts on File, 1991). Entries of varying length examine ceremonies, rituals, and personalities associated with the observance of religion among Native American peoples. Also included are sites involved in public disputes and litigation, but not the location of undisturbed sacred grounds. There is a bibliography and an index.

650. A Guide to the Indian Tribes of the Pacific Northwest. Robert H. Ruby and John A. Brown. Norman, OK: University of Oklahoma, 1986. 289p. ISBN 0-8061-1967-5.

This is a general guide and encyclopedic work to more than 150 Indian tribes that either did reside or still reside in the Pacific Northwest region. It serves as a companion volume to a 1981 history by the same authors. The present effort furnishes an alphabetical approach, with entries varying in length according to the size or significance of the group. Illustrations are numerous and include both historical and recent photographic efforts. Cross-references are helpful in showing the relationship between tribes, and each entry ends with a list of suggested readings. Of interest to both students and beginning researchers, the tool furnishes information on historical traditions, customs, treaties, and population figures, among other things. There is a detailed index.

The companion work by the same authors, volume 158 in the Civilization of the American Indian series, is *Indians of the Pacific Northwest: A History* (University of

Oklahoma, 1981). It presents an excellent, well-constructed narrative, with emphasis on Indian-white relations over a period of 150 years, from 1750 to 1900. Included are maps and illustrations to aid comprehension.

651. **Handbook of American Indians North of Mexico.** Frederick W. Hodge. Washington: U.S. Government Printing Office, 1907–1910. 2v. (U.S. Bureau of American Ethnology, Bulletin No. 30). Reiss. Smithsonian Institution, 1912. Repr. New York: Pageant Books, 1959.

This two-volume reference work was originally issued as a two-part bulletin, then reissued by the Smithsonian Institution (see also entry 652 below) during the early years of this century. It remains the standard and classic volume on the subject of the American Indian. Since its first issue, it has been considered a beginning point for all serious research. It should not be neglected today, even though more recent material is available. All tribes north of Mexico are treated, including the Eskimo; inclusions are made for certain tribal affiliates that reside south of the border as well. Entries furnish brief descriptions of every linguistic stock, confederacy, tribe, subtribe, tribal division, and settlement known to have existed, as well as the origin of every name. Cross-references are liberally applied. Information is given regarding ethnic relations, history, migratory influences, culture, art, customs, and social institutions. Biographies of important leaders are included. References to additional sources create an invaluable aid to research.

652. **Handbook of North American Indians.** William C. Sturtevant, gen. ed. Washington: Smithsonian Institution, 1978–1990. Dist. U.S. Government Printing Office. v.4–11, 15. (Projected 20v.).

Projected as a 20-volume set, this fine reference source represents a cooperative effort on the part of scholars and specialists to produce a work of permanent value. The series began in 1978 with the publication of three volumes. Progress has been slow and steady, with the completion of nine volumes to date, the last one being issued in 1990. Each volume has an editor and multiple contributors of lengthy essays on the topics covered. Those sections covering tribal groups have segments on synonymies, identifying variant names by which the groups have been known. Each of the 700- to 800-page volumes concludes with a bibliography and index. All are profusely illustrated. The plan for the set has the 20 volumes divided into three groupings. Volumes 1–4 are to furnish an overview of social-historical conditions. Of this group, only volume 4, *History of Indian-White Relations*, edited by Wilcomb E. Washburn (1988), is available. The second group is made up of volumes 5–15 and furnishes coverage of major cultural areas. Available are volume 5, *Arctic*, edited by David Damas (1984); volume 6, *Subarctic*, edited by June Helm (1978); volume 7, *Northwest Coast*, edited by Wayne Suttles (1990); volume 8, *California*, edited by Robert F. Heizer (1978); volumes 9–10, *Southwest*, edited by Alfonso Ortiz (1979, 1984); volume 11, *Great Basin*, edited by Warren L. D'Azevado (1986); and volume 15, *Northeast*, edited by Bruce B. Trigger (1978). None of the volumes in the third group, which is to cover technology, linguistics, and biography, are completed. Volume 20 will be the index volume.

653. **Handbook of the American Frontier: Four Centuries of Indian-White Relationships.** J. Norman Heard. Metuchen, NJ: Scarecrow, 1987–1990. v.1–2. (Projected 5v.). (Native American Resources Series, no.1). ISBN 0-8108-1931-7 (v.1). ISBN 0-8108-2324-1 (v.2)

As a first issue of a new series from the publisher, this projected five-volume work by a librarian and writer on native Americans is being developed to cover all aspects and considerations of Indian-white relations. The plan is for each of the volumes to treat a different region. Presently volume 1 examines the Southeastern Woodlands and volume 2 handles the Northeastern Woodlands. volume 3 will be given to the Plains, volume 4 to the Southwest and Pacific Coast. The final volume will furnish a comprehensive index to the set, a chronology, and a bibliography. Judging by the first two volumes, the work is well constructed and should prove useful to students and beginning researchers. Entries are alphabetically arranged and provide a surprising amount of detail on the tribes, leaders, explorers, traders, missionaries, battles, and events. They vary in length from a few sentences to a full page.

654. **The Indian Tribes of North America.** John R. Swanton. Washington: Smithsonian Institution, 1952. 726p. (U.S. Bureau of American Ethnology, Bulletin No. 145). Repr. Brighton, MI: Native American Book Publishers, 1990. ISBN 1-8785-9218-1.

Another of the excellent government publications regarded as an important tool in the field, this handbook of information on Indian tribes still provides useful information for present-day students and inquirers. Of course, it should be augmented by more recent material, especially because its intent was to furnish all levels of inquirers with a "gazetteer of present knowledge." It was originally published in 1952, and coverage extended through the year 1944. Arranged in directory fashion, first by state, then by other countries on this continent, entries for each tribe give information on location, history, population, noteworthy circumstances, names and their meanings, villages, and so forth. The work is comprehensive in terms of its inclusion of Indian tribes; the bibliography is extensive and carefully developed. A special feature is the inclusion of four fold-out maps of tribal territories. A detailed index completes the work.

655. **Nations Within a Nation: Historical Statistics of American Indians.** Paul Stuart. New York: Greenwood, 1987. 251p. ISBN 0-313-23813-8.

This recent compendium of historical statistics on American Indians is of use to both researchers and students. The information was drawn from an array of works published over the last 100 years, federal and state documents, books and monographs, articles, and reports. The author is a university professor in social work who has had an extensive professional interest in native Americans and has prepared this volume as a statistical overview and starting point for scholarly research of the eight general areas into which the work is divided. These general topics are land holdings and climate, population, relocation (including urbanization), vital statistics (including health), government activities, health care, employment, and economic development. There are numerous tables and charts, primarily furnishing information from years subsequent to 1870. These are footnoted with additional references. There is an extensive bibliography of primary sources, and an index is also furnished.

656. **Native American Testimony: A Chronicle of Indian-White Relations from Prophecy to the Present, 1492–1992.** Peter Nabokov, ed. New York: Viking, 1991. 386p. ISBN 0-670-83704-0.

This recent sourcebook by a well-known social historian containing native American commentary on the events of the past 400 years is of immense value to study and research. It opens with a foreword by native American researcher and writer Vine Deloria, Jr., and constitutes an anthology of various types of primary source material found in autobiographies, government documents, and personal narratives. Uniquely, it presents a response from the perspective of the native Americans to their life and times as shaped by their relationship with whites. It begins with the period of Columbus's exploration and progresses through the difficult years of war, retaliation, humiliation, and relocation, up to the present day and the attempts to redress earlier wrongs. The tales are poignant and effectively told through a good selection of documents, and commentary by the author is enlightening.

*657. **North American Indian & Eskimo Culture.** South Dennis, MA: Quevillon Editions. CD-ROM.

Available in CD-ROM format is the complete text of the Smithsonian Institution's four-volume set of Bureau of American Ethnology publications of 1879–1960. The sourcebook contains the text of 150 titles producing 8,500 plates, along with exposition and descriptive narrative on the culture of Eskimos and North American Indians. Anthropological discoveries are described; coverage is well developed and furnishes excellent in-depth information on nineteenth- and twentieth-century conditions and development. Insight is given into the lifestyles, legends, religious rites, art, and culture of these peoples. Included are relevant publications of the U.S. Geological Survey.

A similar CD-ROM product is *North American Indians*, available from Quanta Press of St. Paul, Minnesota. This title furnishes historical descriptions of native Americans, including their tribal heritage, religion, family life, and customs. Material is derived from the U.S. Bureau of Ethnology.

Biographical Sources

658. **Biographical Dictionary of Indians of the Americas.** 2nd ed. Newport Beach, CA: American Indian Publishers, 1991. 2v. ISBN 0-937862-29-0.

As a small publishing house, American Indian Publishers of Newport Beach, California, has produced several multivolume sets that are considered to have value for the scholar and student. As with the output of other small publishers, its efforts are not always picked up by the general reviewing media. One of the recent titles is a two-volume biographical dictionary of native Americans, both living and dead, who have had some impact on their tribe or nation. In many cases, these are notables and celebrities, such as the Tallchief sisters, Maria and Marjorie, who achieved international acclaim as prima ballerinas. Others have been obscured by time, such as Tarhe, the Wyandot chieftain who opposed Tecumseh. More than 2,000 individuals are covered in concise biographical sketches. Brief bibliographies are included whenever possible; there are over 900 pictures and a listing of variant names.

659. **The Commissioners of Indian Affairs, 1824–1977.** Robert M. Kvasnicka and Herman J. Viola, eds. Lincoln: University of Nebraska Press, 1979. 384p. ISBN 0-8032-2700-0.

To those researching government involvement in the field of Indian affairs, this biographical dictionary will be of great value. Covering a period of 150 years, it presents informative, well-developed biographical sketches of all men who served as commissioner of Indian affairs. These individuals generally were not well known during their terms and historically have passed into obscurity. Many of them have had a real impact on government policy, however, and have been key figures in bringing about changes and establishing directions. This volume, published over a decade ago, is unique in its choice of subject matter. More than 30 specialists and experts contributed the articles on the 43 commissioners. Also included are a description of sources and a list of Commissioners' Annual Reports.

660. **Great North American Indians: Profiles in Life and Leadership.** Frederick J. Dockstader. New York: Van Nostrand Reinhold, 1977. 386p. ISBN 0-422-02148-8.

Another of the standard works in the field is this biographical dictionary of 300 American Indians, all of whom are deceased. The author has covered both men and women judged to be of importance from the standpoint of Indians; he has sought to raise the consciousness of a literate public. The entries are clear in composition, concise yet informative. There are many photographs and illustrations that add to the value of the work. There is some inequity of coverage, but selection is broad and representative; included are individuals with as little as one-eighth Indian blood. Coverage spans a 400-year period from the sixteenth century to the 1970s. Useful appendices include an enumeration of tribal divisions along with their biographees and a chronology of these personalities beginning with Hiawatha. There is a name index and cross-references to variant names.

661. **History of the Indian Tribes of North America, with Biographical Sketches and Anecdotes of the Principal Chiefs, Embellished with Eighty Portraits from the Indian Gallery in the War Department at Washington.** Thomas L. McKenney. Philadelphia: J. T. Bowen, 1848–1850. 2v. Repr. Kent, OH: Volair, 1978. ISBN 0-93148-012-4 (v.1).

   This monumental project completed between the years 1836 and 1844 is one of the real classics of the literature on American Indians. McKenney, as head of the Bureau of Indian Affairs from 1824 to 1830, was able to enlist aid and support in producing this work, which is described in the full title. It was published in two volumes, 1848–1850, after much trial and tribulation. McKenney begged, borrowed, and enticed both writers and graphic artists to participate, including his coeditor, James Hall. In the end, the effort met with little remuneration; the historical narrative and biographical sketches were all but forgotten in what was referred to as the "Great Portfolio" or "Indian Portrait Gallery." Those prints are especially valuable, the original volumes selling for thousands of dollars today. The work has been reprinted at various times and is available on microfilm. The 1978 reprint by Volair contains 120 portraits "from the Indian Gallery"—i.e., 40 more portraits than in the original printing.

662. **Who Was Who in Native American History: Indians and Non-Indians from Early Contacts Through 1900.** Carl Waldman. New York: Facts on File, 1990. 410p. ISBN 0-8160-1797-2.

   Waldman's third effort (see also entries 647 and 649) is produced for the popular interest rather than scholarly inquiry and offers biographies of more than 1,000 individuals who had some impact on Indian-white relations. There are almost as many non-Indians as native Americans: Coverage given to people such as George Washington and Andrew Jackson identifies dates and occupations and describes their relationships to Indians. Entries range from a paragraph to two pages; native Americans are identified in terms of tribal connections, contributions, and family ties. These entries furnish alternative spellings and translations for names. Generally, there is a chronological coverage of the persons' lives; also included are cross-references to others who participated in certain events. Unfortunate omissions include a bibliography of additional readings and/or source materials and an index.

The Gay Experience

The most recent struggle for fair treatment and equality is being waged by homosexual men and women, who previously had been hidden, concealed, fearful of detection. Beginning with a riot against the police in a Greenwich Village bar, the Stonewall Inn, in 1969, the past two decades have witnessed increasingly overt behavior among homosexuals, with demonstrations of pride and strength. These demonstrations not surprisingly have met with hostility and support from different quarters. All gay people do not agree, of course, on their social obligations or ethical roles, and some have felt victimized by an increasingly strident movement that has exposed ("outed") them despite their wishes to remain closeted. Through it all, Americans have become more aware of the various issues that represent the focus or core of the struggle for fair treatment and acceptance. Matters of health, employment, parenthood, and military service have been well publicized in the recent past.

The trade literature has been growing in volume and has changed direction with respect to its more recent focus on homosexuality as an acceptable lifestyle. Liz McMillen's "From Margin to Mainstream: Books in Gay Studies" in *The Chronicle of Higher Education*, July 22, 1992, pp. A8–A13, is the most recent exposition of publishing developments and the receptivity of mainstream publishers, especially university presses, to what has proved to be an extremely marketable topic. Series are being instituted by Oxford University, Duke University, New York University, and the University of Chicago.

An excellent review appears in *Choice*, July/August 1991, pp. 1743–1751, as "Bibliographic Essay: A Gay and Lesbian Core Collection," by Elizabeth M. Wavle. This scholarly piece traces publishing developments in areas such as psychology, history, and moral and religious aspects as they concern homosexuality. Leading works are described, and a bibliography is furnished. Reference materials are emphasized in the June 1, 1988, *Reference Books Bulletin*'s practical annotated bibliography, "Reference Materials for or About Gays and Lesbians," pp. 1647–1652. Both scholarly and alternative publishers are represented.

663. **About Time: Exploring the Gay Past.** Rev. and exp. ed. Martin B. Duberman. New York: Meridian, 1991. 480p. ISBN 0-452-01081-0.

The author is a well-known advocate, reporter, and historian of the gay experience who has put together an informative collection of both source materials and reflective essays furnishing a homosexual perspective. These pieces originally appeared in a 1986 publication, but here the set has been revised and in several ways augmented. The work is divided into three major segments, with the first part containing the original source material, which includes letters, excerpts from journals, and documents. The second section comprises reprinted material from Duberman's column from the *New York Native*, a periodical that since 1980 has been representing the gay viewpoint and advocating gay liberation. Finally, there is an extensive and useful bibliography of books and periodical articles covering a wide range of relevant topics in both the humanities and social sciences.

Another recent compilation, edited by Duberman and others, is *Hidden from History: Reclaiming the Gay and Lesbian Past* (New American Library, 1989). About 30 contributors have furnished scholarly essays on the homosexual experience from ancient to modern times in various parts of the world. Insight is given into the pattern of development that has led to the emerging awareness on the part of gay people in modern U.S. society.

664. **An Annotated Bibliography of Homosexuality.** Vern L. Bullough, et al. New York: Garland, 1976. 2v. (Garland Reference Library of Social Science, v.22). ISBN 0-8240-9959-1.

This is the most extensive of the bibliographic efforts on the topic and furnishes nearly 12,800 books and articles representing coverage from various languages and subjects. Arrangement is by broad topical and format categories. Annotations tend to be brief and describe the content of most of the works included. Although the tool has been criticized for lack of expressed selection criteria, its breadth of coverage will assure its use by scholars and serious inquirers. Not only factual materials but also creative literary efforts and biographical works are enumerated. The strength of the work lies in its comprehensive nature and its employment of an interdisciplinary concept. The work is international in scope but gives ample coverage to U.S. issues and developments.

665. **The Construction of Homosexuality.** David F. Greenberg. Chicago: University of Chicago Press, 1988. 635p. ISBN 0-226-30627-5.

This is a cross-cultural comparative history of the nature of homosexuality and its impact on various societies and cultures. The author, a professor of sociology, begins his study with an examination of primitive tribes and clans, then traces developments through ancient and medieval periods and into modern times. He examines the character and structure of each time period and furnishes exposition of the nature of homosexual activity and the types of responses generated by each society. His examination is designed to explore why certain forms of homosexual practice emerged in the various cultures and to explain the types of attitudes that prevailed. Homosexuality, therefore, is treated to a unique type of scrutiny, providing opportunity for new interpretations within existing theories. It provides good background information to the scholar and researcher interested in U.S. studies.

666. **Gay American History: Lesbians and Gay Men in the U.S.A., A Documentary History.** Rev. ed. Jonathan N. Katz. New York: Meridian, 1992. 702p. ISBN 0-45201-092-6.

The work was originally issued in 1976, after which it was reprinted on several occasions. It has served as a documentary history of the gay presence in North America from the sixteenth century to the 1970s. Included here are complete and excerpted documents of various types: letters, journals, diaries, newspaper pieces, magazine and journal articles, reports, books, and interviews. The documents are arranged chronologically within six broad thematic sections: "Trouble" (early opposition/condemnation); "Treatment" (attempts at "curing" homosexuality); "Passing Women" (women who passed for men); "Native Americans/Gay Americans"; "Resistance"; and "Love." A feature of the new edition is an up-to-date 21-page bibliography of major texts for the study of lesbian and gay history in this country. The work remains one of the major sources of historical study.

The Rise of a Gay and Lesbian Movement by Barry D. Adam (Twayne, 1987) is a more comprehensive narrative history describing the social, economic, and political conditions associated with the rise of the movement on a global scale, from its seeds of origin in the French Revolution to its development in Germany in 1897, then its various phases in both Europe and the United States throughout the twentieth century. There are both lists of references and an annotated bibliography; the work places the U.S. gay movement within the perspective of a worldwide phenomenon.

667. **The Homosexual and Society: An Annotated Bibliography.** Robert B.M. Ridinger, comp. Westport, CT: Greenwood, 1990. 444p. (Bibliographies and Indexes in Sociology, no.18). ISBN 0-313-25357-9.

This is a well-constructed, highly useful bibliography of articles and selected monographs published through 1987. Arrangement is under seven major realms "where homophobia has been expressed in coherent form: adoption and foster care, child custody, the military establishment, employment discrimination, censorship, religion, and police attitudes and actions." Nearly 860 entries are arranged chronologically under these issues, affording a convenient historical perspective. Entries date from the aftermath of the Stonewall Riots of 1969, generally considered to be the overt beginning of the gay liberation movement in this country. Articles are drawn primarily from three of the major journals of the gay community—*The Advocate*, *The Ladder*, and *The Mattachine Review*—as well as mainstream newsweeklies. Annotations are full and descriptive in content. There is an index of names and broad topics. Ridinger is a librarian and author of *An Index to the Advocate: The National Gay Newsmagazine, 1967–1982* (Liberation Publications, 1987).

668. **Homosexuality: A Research Guide.** Wayne R. Dynes. New York: Garland, 1987. 853p. (Garland Reference Library of Social Science, v.313). ISBN 0-8240-8692-9.

Containing more than 4,850 entries, this well-constructed annotated bibliography furnishes coverage of studies on various topics. Emphasis is given to history, psychology, sociology, and law, but also covered are an additional 20 categories such as language, politics, and anthropology. These categories are generally subdivided by more specific subtopics and furnish excellent access to needed material. There is a predominance of U.S. publications but also prominent German, Dutch, French, and Italian studies. Annotations are full and objectively describe content. The coverage is noteworthy for its balanced inclusion of studies relating to both past and current issues as well as U.S. and international influences. Also noteworthy are its interdisciplinary nature and its representation of all points of view. There is a name index and a subject index.

More recently, Dynes has served as principal editor for the two-volume *Encyclopedia of Homosexuality* (Garland, 1990), which gives a thorough look at issues, personages, and movements, with good historical emphasis.

669. Homosexuality: A Selective Bibliography of Over 3,000 Items. William Parker. Metuchen, NJ: Scarecrow, 1971. 323p. ISBN 0-8108-0425-5. **1st Supp. 1970–1975.** 1977. 337p. ISBN 0-8108-1050-6. **2nd Supp. 1976–1982.** 1985. 395p. ISBN 0-8108-1753-5.

Parker's initial effort in 1971 is recognized as an important standard in the field in terms of its bibliographic coverage of the topic. Homosexuality had not been documented well up to that time. This comprehensive work furnishes over 3,000 entries, with emphasis on books, research articles of scholarly nature, and pamphlets. Also included are dissertations and newspaper and magazine articles. Arrangement is by format, with access through author and broad subject indexes. Furnished are significant works from ancient times through 1969 that have appeared in English.

Homosexuality Bibliography: Supplement, 1970–1975 is Parker's first updating, covering 3,000 items published during the six-year period following the original edition. It marks the growing interest on the topic and represents a change in its emphasis on works that treat homosexuality as an acceptable lifestyle rather than a disorder. *Homosexuality Bibliography: Second Supplement, 1976–1982* lists over 3,500 items published during the seven-year period. The three volumes represent an important tool for scholarship.

670. Sexual Politics, Sexual Communities: The Making of a Homosexual Minority in the United States, 1940–1970. John D'Emilio. Chicago: University of Chicago Press, 1983. 257p. ISBN 0-226-14265-5.

The Chronicle of Higher Education review cited in our introductory narrative to this section describes D'Emilio's efforts to publish this work, which is considered to be the first published monograph on the history of gay life in the United States, and his gratefulness that the University of Chicago accepted it. Since then the market has exploded, and D'Emilio, an academic, has the services of an agent. This work examines the 30-year period prior to the Stonewall Riots in New York (1969) describing and interpreting the conditions that led to the emergence of gay liberation. The study began as part of the author's doctoral dissertation and is now recognized as a superb contribution, employing such records as personal letters, oral histories, and newspaper accounts. It examines both individual contributions and group efforts in order to place the movement within the context of other social developments. D'Emilio has a new compilation entitled *Making Trouble: Essays on Gay History, Politics, and the University* (Routledge, 1992).

Eric Marcus's book *Making History: The Struggle for Gay and Lesbian Equal Rights, 1945–1990: An Oral History* (HarperCollins, 1992) narrates the fight for homosexual rights up through very recent times through personal eyewitness accounts. *Before Stonewall: The Making of a Gay and Lesbian Community* by Andrea Weiss and Greta Schiller (Naiad, 1988) is a concise and well developed popular history written by two principals involved in the making of an important documentary film of the same name. The formation of the gay subculture is described and its emergence explained.

SOCIAL WELFARE AND PHILANTHROPY

The question of philanthropy is associated with a variety of personal motivations on the part of the donor. These range from the self-serving to the altruistic. It is as important to study the motivations of the donors as they relate to the values and ideas of a group, class, or time period as it is to study the impact of the gifts on societal existence. Revisionist historians continue to probe these areas and furnish provocative theories about the giving of gifts and endowments on the part of both the private and public sectors. Regardless of the reasons for giving, such gifts benefit social welfare agencies and institutions. Closely related to the study of such social issues is the history of public works in this country.

Reference tools on these topics are not as abundant as one might have hoped. Additional sources relevant to this topic may be found in chapter 8, "Economic History," especially in the section on "Depression and Recession," which identifies sources on the Roosevelt era and New Deal measures.

Sociological Abstracts (1953– ; five times/year) is a product of Sociological Abstracts, Inc. and abstracts the periodical literature of sociology and related fields. Historical writings appear regularly. It is available online through DIALOG and in CD-ROM format as *SOCIOFILE.*

The Public Works Historical Society (Chicago, IL) was founded in 1975 and has 1,900 members. It publishes an *Essay Series* along with its *Oral History* on an annual basis. The Social Welfare History Group was founded in 1956 and has 250 members. It operates out of the Michigan State University School of Social Work and meets in conjunction with the Council on Social Work Education. The SWHG offers an annual bibliography as well as a newsletter.

671. **American Philanthropy, 1731–1860: Printed Works in the Collections of the American Philosophical Society, the Historical Society of Pennsylvania, the Library Company of Philadelphia.** Cornelia S. King, comp. New York: Garland, 1984. 529 col. (Garland Reference Library of Social Science, v.183; Americana to 1860, v.1). ISBN 0-8240-9080-2.

Supported by a grant from the Mellon Foundation, officials of three Philadelphia libraries with major historical collections agreed on the development of a union catalog of historical materials on U.S. philanthropy, education (entry 676), natural history (entry 738), and agriculture (entry 920) covering a period of 130 years, from the colonial period to the onset of the Civil War. The work is of value to the scholar and serious student of history and other social science areas. This published catalog on philanthropy and the succeeding efforts in the other fields serve as excellent bibliographies. The effort on philanthropy furnishes over 3,700 entries of monographs, agency reports, and serial titles. Arrangement is alphabetical by authors of monographs and titles of serials, covering a wide range of social problems and remedial measures. Appendices furnish a listing of institutions and a chronology of publications.

672. **Biographical Dictionary of Social Welfare in America.** Walter I. Trattner, ed. New York: Greenwood, 1986. 897p. ISBN 0-313-23001-3.

This biographical dictionary of 330 deceased men and women active in the social welfare field from the colonial period to the present day should be of interest to students and beginning researchers. Entries are written by 200 specialists with expertise on the subject and are arranged alphabetically. Excluded here are the theoreticians, philosophers, donors, philanthropists in favor of the participants and practitioners. Similarly, labor leaders, feminists, and abolitionists are omitted. The field is defined loosely, with Cotton Mather and Benjamin Franklin included alongside Jane Addams. Entries are signed and furnish essay-length descriptions and analyses of the career and impact of each individual covered. There are selective bibliographies accompanying all entries. Appendices contain a chronology and listings of subjects by place and year of birth. . A subject index furnishes access.

673. **Corporate Philanthropy: An Annotated Bibliography.** David R. Farber and Susan M. Levy, comps. and eds. Chicago: Donors Forum of Chicago, 1982. 58p.

This unique work focuses on corporate philanthropy; it should prove useful to scholars and researchers at various levels. It is an annotated bibliography of more than 350 items divided into 10 sections, beginning with an overview, then describing status, promotional efforts, types, and advice given, along with directories and general information on corporations. An academic with the University of Chicago's Project on the History of Philanthropy and Public Policy, Farber has produced an enlightening array of citations from a variety of sources—newspapers, journals, books, newsletters, research reports, magazines, and annual reports—issued between 1972 and 1981. Items listed explain how corporate philanthropy works, what has been said about it, and how to improve and promote it. There is a separate segment on philanthropy in Chicago and a listing of the Foundation Center's extensive collections.

674. **Public Works History of the United States: A Guide to the Literature, by the Public Works Historical Society.** Suellen M. Hoy and Michael C. Robinson, comps. and eds. Nashville: American Association for State and Local History, 1982. 477p. ISBN 0-910050-63-5.

The history of public works in this country is closely tied to social welfare, which is covered in some detail along with political and management considerations in this annotated bibliography. As one might expect, the emphasis is placed on the engineering and construction of public projects. Included here are books, dissertations, and journal articles dealing with the history of public works projects. Entries bear publication dates ranging from the nineteenth century to the 1920s and are organized into 14 segments on an array of topics and subtopics. Covered are roads, streets, highways, railroads, highway traffic controls, mass transportation, airways, community water supply, flood control, irrigation, electric power, sewage, solid wastes, educational facilities, public housing, recreation, and aerospace. Within these segments, some of the great dams, parks, and structures are treated. The major criterion was that the entry was written as a history.

675. **Social Welfare in America: An Annotated Bibliography.** Walter I. Trattner and W. Andrew Achenbaum, eds. Westport, CT: Greenwood, 1983. 324p. ISBN 0-313-23002-1.

This is an excellent bibliography of more than 1,400 entries of all types of important materials of interest to scholars and serious students. Several major chapters divide the works; three were prepared by contributing specialists. An introduction provides perspective on the process and progress of social welfare. Chapter topics represent problems in the stages of human life: the care of infant and child, problems of youth, relief of domestic crises of adulthood, economic problems of adults, and coping with old age. The final chapter examines the need for a research agenda for the future. Each of the chapters is divided into a standardized sequence of syntheses, period pieces, and so forth. The subject index is especially useful in bringing entries together, because entries are duplicated in the sections when appropriate.

EDUCATION

From its beginnings, this country has looked to its educational institutions as the means by which citizens better themselves to achieve the American Dream. Operating upon democratic principles designed to make allowances for delayed maturation, educators have shown no inclination to place students on different "tracks" at an early age in line with performance on examinations. Rather, the tendency has been to extend public education through the university levels in a nondiscriminatory manner. Following the dissent, protest, and riot period of the 1960s, the college campus has become relatively quiet, but the student voice in governance is a given in contemporary campus life and has become more of a factor in secondary and even elementary schools.

The majority of tools in this section are bibliographic in nature, most of them being on higher education, where scholars and observers tend to conduct their investigations. Specific issues such as school prayer and desegregation of schools are treated, along with less volatile historical development.

The History of Education Society of Eugene, Oregon, has operated since 1960 and has 450 members. It has published *History of Education Quarterly* since 1961.

Library Resources

676. American Education, 1622–1860: Printed Works in the Collections of the American Philosophical Society, the Historical Society of Pennsylvania, the Library Company of Philadelphia. Cornelia S. King, comp. New York: Garland, 1984. 354p. (Americana to 1860, v.3). ISBN 0-8240-8966-9.

Supported by a Mellon grant, this is the third of the four union catalogs of specific subject holdings of three major historical collections in the city of Philadelphia. The first covers philanthropy and was also compiled by Ms. King (entry 671). The other two were handled by another individual and covered agriculture (entry 920) and natural history (entry 738). The present effort, like others in the series, is an extremely useful bibliographic source of early printed materials in this country. There are nearly 4,900 entries representing pedagogical treatises, official publications of organizations, societies, institutions, and school systems issued over a period of nearly 140 years prior to the Civil War. Serial publications are included as well. Arrangement of entries is alphabetical, primarily by author. Appendices provide valuable listings of institutions and organizations of various kinds. Neither textbooks nor dissertations or library catalogs are included.

A major project underway since 1987 is the *History of Education* microfiche collection (Research Publications), based on the extensive holdings of the Milbank Library, Teachers College at Columbia University (see Bibliographical Sources section below). Expected to eventually comprise some 12,000 titles, the *History of Education* set reproduces the full text of monographs in the history and philosophy of education, classical educational treatises, general works in education, and obscure pamphlets and lectures published from the fifteenth through the nineteenth centuries, with significant coverage of U.S education. Examples include late nineteenth-century texts on "Special Kinesiology of Educational Gymnastics" and a "History of Tufts University." A printed *Guide to the Microfiche Collection* provides a detailed listing by fiche number but is of very little help for author/title/subject searches. Broad educational subjects are grouped together in "units" (e.g., psychology/philosophy of education, health education and gymnastics, U.S. universities). A subject index is anticipated.

Bibliographical Sources

The most important current index of English-language materials is the *Education Index* published by the H. W. Wilson Company, one of the major index producers in this country. It has been issued since 1929 and now appears quarterly. Major emphasis is on the periodical literature, with over 300 titles covered, however, monographs, yearbooks, and reports are indexed as well. Historical topics are covered in some of the journals indexed. The tool is available on both CD-ROM (WILSON-DISC) and online (WILSONLINE).

Also useful are the two main government-sponsored abstracting services, *Resources in Education* (*RIE*) and *Current Index to Journals in Education* (*CIJE*), which began in 1966 and 1969, respectively. *RIE* identifies documents, and *CIJE* indexes periodical literature. *RIE* is issued through the U.S. Department of Education's Educational Resources Information Center (ERIC) and is available in print format on a monthly basis; it is also merged with *CIJE* for online access through DIALOG Information Services as File 1, the *ERIC* database. *CIJE* originally was published on a monthly basis by Macmillan, but since 1979 it has been issued in print format by Oryx. The combined *ERIC* database is available in CD-ROM through various distributors.

The *Bibliographic Guide to Education* (G. K. Hall, 1978–) is the annual supplement to the *Dictionary Catalog of the Teachers College Library, Columbia University* (G. K. Hall, 1970; 36v.) and its three supplements (1971–1977). Besides listing publications cataloged by the Teachers College at Columbia, the *Bibliographic Guide* also gives selected publications in the field of education cataloged by the Research Libraries of the New York Public Library (see entry 36).

677. The American College President, 1636–1989: A Critical Review and Bibliography. Ann H.L. Sontz. Westport, CT: Greenwood, 1991. 176p. (Bibliographies and Indexes in Education, no.10). ISBN 0-313-27325-1.

This recent effort is of value to both scholars and serious inquirers; it is the first bibliographic source on the subject in many years. Studies on college presidents have been numerous, and it is thought that the quality of such studies has improved in the past few decades. The work opens with a foreword by an academic, then introduces the selection criteria. A bibliographic narrative is furnished, as are tables of statistics on the literature and on the presidents. The author hopes that the current emphasis on evolutionary historical process rather than personal contribution can be reassessed and balanced more equitably. Also, the administration of less familiar institutions should be studied in terms of their sociointellectual theories. Included are sections on background material, presidential biographies, and presidential works, which account for the bulk of the text.

678. American Educational History: A Guide to Information Sources. Michael W. Sedlak and Timothy Walch. Detroit: Gale, 1981. 265p. (Gale Information Guide Library; American Government and History Information Guide Series, v.10). ISBN 0-8103-1478-9.

Of use to the student and beginning researcher is this annotated bibliography of books, articles, and a few dissertations on the history of U.S. education from the colonial period to the present. The purpose was to reveal sources that had not previously been covered in bibliographies, the emphasis being on titles published after 1965. The volume is organized into nine chapters revealing socioprofessional concerns, beginning with an overview of educational development from 1632 to 1975. This is followed by seven topical chapters on pedagogy, higher education, outsiders, race, delinquency, cities, and the workplace. The final chapter covers guides to research and enumerates general histories, historiographies, and reference bibliographies. All chapters contain a brief introductory narrative. Annotations are brief for each entry. There are both author and subject indexes.

679. **A Bibliographic Guide to American Colleges and Universities: From Colonial Times to the Present.** Mark Beach. Westport, CT: Greenwood, 1975. 314p. ISBN 0-8371-7690-5.

In 1975 this represented an exceptional comprehensive bibliography designed to bring together important books, articles, and dissertations relevant to the history of both individual colleges and universities and of higher education in various states. Arrangement of the guide is in directory fashion, first by state, then alphabetically by name of institution. Those entries furnishing more generic coverage of history within the states are listed prior to the division by institutions. More than 2,800 entries appear, representing a considerable yield to those scholars and students attempting to find material, especially on individual colleges and universities. This is one of the earlier Greenwood efforts in which the company took special interest in providing distinctive topical coverage within various professional studies. There is a good subject index to aid the user's search.

For more recent coverage in a similar vein, see the work by Arthur Young (entry 682). It serves as a companion title to Beach's *A Subject Bibliography of the History of American Higher Education* (entry 688).

680. **Dissertations in the History of Education, 1970–1980.** Edward R. Beauchamp. Metuchen, NJ: Scarecrow, 1985. 259p. ISBN 0-8108-1742-X.

Intending to facilitate the search by scholars and serious students for doctoral dissertations on the history of education, the author manually searched *Dissertation Abstracts International* (entry 92) and was able to generate nearly 2,450 entries produced between 1970 and 1980. The entries are organized into eight chapters representing geographic regions of the world. The chapter on the United States represents about 1,800 dissertations, or about 75 percent of the total. The U.S. chapter is subdivided by various topics, such as medical, business, and military education. Entries furnish bibliographic identification, author, degree, title, institution, number of pages, and reference to the abstract in *DAI.* Order numbers for microfilm are also furnished. There is a subject index to this desirable convenience tool.

681. **Education Literature, 1907–1932.** Malcolm Hamilton, ed. New York: Garland, 1979. 25v. in 12. ISBN 0-8240-3700-6 (v.1). (Each volume has individual ISBN).

Another useful tool for scholars and serious students is this large-scale facsimile reprint of the serial bibliographies from the U.S. Bureau of Education. The *Bibliography of Education* was published between 1907 and 1911, and the *Monthly Record of Current Education Publications* spanned a 20-year period of publication between 1912 and 1932. Included in these sources were books, proceedings, pamphlets, and periodical literature on education and related aspects at all levels. Over 700 periodical titles were covered during different periods; 44,000 entries are revealed. In some cases annotations were provided. Important here is the work done in unifying these serials; a separate volume now furnishes a comprehensive name and subject index to the entire work. This source affords a great advantage over the use of the original annual indexes, which were difficult and inconsistent and changed categories frequently from one volume to the next.

682. **Higher Education in American Life, 1636–1986: A Bibliography of Dissertations and Theses.** Arthur P. Young, comp. New York: Greenwood, 1988. 431p. (Bibliographies and Indexes in Education, no.5). ISBN 0-313-25352-8.

Another of the Greenwood publications that focuses on research literature in education is this excellent comprehensive listing of both doctoral dissertations and master's theses on higher education in the U.S. social milieu. This broad-based theme involves numerous elements touched by university life, such as institutions, curriculum, athletics, and personalities. Nearly 4,600 entries are furnished, about 3,300 doctoral efforts and 1,300 master's theses. The work is divided into two parts, the first segment offering directory-style coverage of 1,000 individual institutions. (This is similar to another Greenwood effort completed 13 years earlier—see entry 679.) The second part furnishes topical coverage, with studies organized under various headings. Entries provide the usual bibliographic information for works of this type and include order numbers for microform copy from University Microfilms. There are both author and subject indexes.

683. **The History of American Education: A Guide to Information Sources.** Francesco Cordasco, et al. Detroit: Gale Research, 1979. 313p. (Gale Information Guide Library; Education Information Guide Series, v.7). ISBN 0-8103-1382-0.

The principal author, a prolific bibliographer of the U.S. ethnic experience, collaborated with two others to furnish a literature guide of nearly 2,500 books, articles, and source collections dealing with a broad range of content relevant to the history of U.S. education. Categories are fluid and, when appropriate, represent historical periods, subjects, topics, and formats. Although omissions are pointed out by reviewers, the breadth of coverage should prove useful to students and nonspecialists. Entries furnish the usual bibliographic information; some are accompanied by brief annotations discussing the content. There are author, title, and subject indexes.

Cordasco's earlier effort, *A Bibliography of American Educational History: An Annotated and Classified Guide* (AMS, 1975) was a joint effort with William W. Brickman. It identifies general bibliographies, encyclopedic works, source collections, and histories, with individual sections on various states, the federal government, the education of women, biographical works, and other topics. Various specialists have prepared the different segments.

684. **Private School Education in the U.S.: An Annotated Bibliography, 1950–1980.** Alice H. Songe. Jefferson, NC: McFarland, 1982. 89p. ISBN 0-89950-045-5.

Of interest to inquirers at all levels is this selective annotated bibliography of the rarely documented private school. There are nearly 425 publications, arranged alphabetically under format divisions: books, monographs, and serials; government publications of both federal and state origin; journal articles; and doctoral dissertations. Publication dates cover a critical 30-year period, embracing the Supreme Court desegregation decision—Brown v. Board of Education—that gave visibility to the role of the private school in a pluralistic society. Annotations are brief but informative for most entries; they are excluded in the case of doctoral dissertations because *Dissertation Abstracts International* (entry 92) fills that need. Quality education and the differences in a private school environment compared to a public school environment have been important topics of argument and debate; these writings provide an excellent record of that controversy. Included is a list of associations concerned with private education; there are both author and subject indexes.

685. **From Brown to Boston: Desegregation in Education, 1954–1974.** Leon Jones. Metuchen, NJ: Scarecrow, 1979. 2v. ISBN 0-8108-1147-2.

Of importance to both students and scholars, this two-volume annotated bibliography of critical studies on the topics of integration and segregation begins with the 1954 case of *Brown v. Board of Education of Topeka*, the landmark decision that outlawed school segregation in

1954. The work concludes with the 1974 *Miliken v. Bradley* case and the traumatic conditions in Boston at the time. The author, an education professor, and in volume 1 lists nearly 2,850 articles and about 440 books, each in separate sections by date of publication. In this manner the 20-year period is covered, with excellent perspective given on the quantity of publication with passing of time. Volume 2 lists over 1,750 legal decisions. Entries in both volumes are annotated in depth. Indexes provide access by author-title, case-legal issue, and by subject.

686.   **Research in Higher Education: A Guide to Source Bibliographies.** 2nd ed. Richard H. Quay. Phoenix, AZ: Oryx Press, 1985. 133p. ISBN 0-89774-194-3.

This bibliography of nearly 1,000 bibliographies has great value for both the student and researcher of the educational scene. It is a revision and expansion of an earlier effort (1976) that furnished close to 600 entries published between 1960 and 1975. Scope has been increased in this version, with publication dates ranging from 1960 to 1985. The period of recent coverage is of great importance, for it was during these years that the idea of accountability began to take hold in U.S. schools. Entries are arranged into 15 chapters, where they are listed alphabetically by author. Brief annotations are furnished when needed to clarify the content. Included are a brief bibliography and a directory of research centers. The work is indexed by author and by subject.

687.   **School Prayer and Other Religious Issues in American Public Education: A Bibliography.** Albert J. Menendez. New York: Garland, 1985. 168p. (Garland Reference Library of Social Science, v.291). ISBN 0-8240-8775-5.

In 1992, a conservative Supreme Court followed the lead of previous, more liberal courts in its interpretation of the inviolable nature of the separation of church and state as it concerns school prayer. This bibliography of more than 1,600 books, periodical articles, law journal reviews, dissertations, theses, and newspaper articles represents a timely source for study and research of a powerful issue. Of the 21 chapters, 5 deal with the history, legal basis, and politics of school prayer, as well as arguments for and against. Others treat the Bible, celebration of Christmas, and moral education, among other subjects. Publications span 120 years, from the 1850s to the 1970s. The recent action on the part of the Court is a good indication of the multifaceted nature of the issue. There is an author index and a cursory subject index that focuses on geographic locales.

688.   **A Subject Bibliography of the History of American Higher Education.** Mark Beach, comp. Westport, CT: Greenwood, 1984. 165p. ISBN 0-313-23276-8.

In Beach's 1975 work (entry 679) he furnished a bibliography of books, articles, and dissertations that was unique in its focus on individual institutions. This more recent effort was designed as a companion volume rather than a supplement and provides a broad-based topical bibliography on the history of higher education. Again, he lists books, articles, and dissertations of consequence; arrangement of entries is alphabetical within classes or topics, which themselves are arranged alphabetically from "academic costume" to "zoology." None of these classes relate to specific colleges and universities; little duplication with the earlier effort is evident. Both scholars and students should benefit from this tool for its breadth and comprehensive nature with respect to the field as well as its selective inclusion of "major" writings. Both author and subject indexes furnish access.

689.   **U.S. Higher Education: A Guide to Information Sources.** Franklin Parker and Betty J. Parker. Detroit: Gale, 1980. 675p. (Gale Information Guide Library; Education Information Guide Series, v.9). ISBN 0-8103-1476-2.

This is another useful bibliography by the same team that produced a bibliographic series of U.S. dissertations covering foreign education. The present effort is an annotated bibliography of books and reports relating to higher education in *this* country. Included are writings on history, philosophy, finance, administration, and student life. Nearly 3,200 entries are listed alphabetically by author, representing what might be considered a comprehensive coverage of twentieth-century and selective coverage of nineteenth-century material. Entries furnish the usual bibliographic identification, author, title, imprint, and number of pages. Brief descriptive annotations then follow. Most useful is the coverage given to new techniques and technologies, as well as the needs of minorities and of university personnel and clienteles. Indexes are furnished by subject, title, and even author, which is superfluous in view of the arrangement of entries.

Information Sources

690. **American Universities and Colleges.** 13th ed. Produced in collaboration with the American Council on Education. Hawthorne, NY: Walter de Gruyter, 1987. 2,024p. ISBN 0-89925-179-X.

This is considered to be the most useful directory of higher education with respect to its listing of institutions and is of real value to students, researchers, specialists, and librarians. Important to historians is the information given in each entry regarding each institution's origin and developmental history. Nearly 2,000 colleges and universities receive good, informative descriptions. In addition, information is furnished regarding the school's calendar, organization, admission policy, degree requirements, fees, graduate work, financial aid, student life, sports, dormitories, library collections, and so on. Of value also are the survey articles on educational topics at the beginning of the work and the numerous tables, charts, and listings in the appendices. Although the work has appeared every four years since 1928, the 1987 edition remains the latest issue at this time.

691. **The Encyclopedia of Education.** Lee C. Deighton, ed. in chief. New York: Macmillan, 1971. 10v.

This 10-volume work represents a comprehensive and detailed picture of the workings, personalities, projects, and events surrounding education. The emphasis is on U.S. education, for which a good proportion of the total of 1,100 signed articles cover historical material. Theory, research, and philosophy are examined under broad subject headings in detailed narratives averaging several pages in length, with more than 30 entries containing coverage of over 25 pages (a throwback to the earlier days of encyclopedia construction). Hundreds of scholars and specialists contributed to the work in response to a felt need for a modern tool of this type. There are few biographies, but bibliographies are included in most entries. The final volume is devoted to the index.

A work of importance historically is the five-volume *A Cyclopedia of Education*, edited by Paul Monroe (Macmillan, 1911–1913. Repr. Gale, 1968), which served as a partial model for the title above. Like its successor, its emphasis was education in this country. Both historical and biographical articles are included. An analytical index furnishes access to the signed articles. For a more theoretical coverage of education, see the *Encyclopedia of Educational Research*, 5th edition, edited by Harold E. Mitzel (4v., Free Press, 1982), which contains 256 thoroughly researched, signed articles covering topics ranging from academic freedom to high school driver education programs. Historians will be interested in the early editions of this work, which was first issued in 1941.

Biographical Sources

692. **Biographical Dictionary of American Educators.** John F. Ohles, ed. Westport, CT: Greenwood, 1978. 3v. ISBN 0-8371-9893-3.

More than 1,650 entries furnish biographical sketches averaging about a page in length for individuals who had reached the age of 60, retired, or died by the year 1975. These people had been prominent at either the national or state level in their roles as teachers, reformers, theorists, or administrators. There is purposeful inclusion of both genders as well as ethnic minorities in keeping with the agenda of book production in the 1970s. Entries provide information regarding the biographee's education, professional accomplishments, contribution or impact, and participation in professional associations and activities. Useful appendices give listings by birthplace, state, and field of activity. Included also is a chronology of birthdates. A general index in volume 3 furnishes adequate access. The work should benefit both scholars and students.

693. **Who's Who in American Education: An Illustrated Biographical Dictionary of Eminent Living Educators of the United States and Canada.** Ed. 1–23. Nashville: Who's Who in American Education, 1928–1968. Bienn.

This work represents an effort, now of historical importance, that ceased publication with its 23rd edition in 1968. It had been published since 1928, mostly on a biennial basis, and later incorporated a slight change in subtitle. The early editions cover many now-obscure figures who during their time played an active role in the educational process at all levels. There are many administrators of both primary and secondary schools and systems, college and university faculty, and a variety of people in related fields, including public librarians and public relations executives.

For those professing an interest in current history, there is a recent product of the same name (without subtitle), edited by Jeffrey Franz and Pamela R. Jones, that was intended as an annual publication. The 1988–1989 inaugural edition (National Reference Institute, 1988) furnished 10,000 biographical sketches of personalities of reference interest. A second volume followed in 1990; none has appeared since. It is now published by Marquis Who's Who (4th ed. 1993).

RELIGION

This country has always professed to be a nation under God; much of its real strength is thought to lie in its pluralistic outlook, which permits religious beliefs to be observed in a personal manner. Great care has been taken to preserve the right to free religious expression and to assure separation of church and state. The Supreme Court has ruled in consistent fashion on this issue, most recently in a surprising manner, considering the conservative orientation of the justices in 1992.

The literature of religion is abundant, and reference books examine both generic topics and specific issues, some of which remain controversial and deep-rooted. This section is divided along the lines of the religious traditions that dominate Western society. The general subsection contains materials that are comprehensive in their treatment of both Christian and non-Christian denominations. Many of these titles cover cults, sects, and alternative faiths. The other subsections show the relative abundance of materials covering Protestant, as compared to Catholic, traditions in this country. Only now have slamic-American history materials begun to appear. The Jewish faith alone is covered in what constitutes the non-Christian subsection.

The American Society for the Study of Religion operates out of Toronto, Ontario, and has 85 members. It was created in 1960 and is affiliated with the International Association for the History of Religion. It publishes a newsletter.

General: Christian and Non-Christian

Bibliographical Sources

The major current index of a general nature in religion is *Religion Index One*, which was issued from 1953 to 1977 as *Index to Religious Periodical Literature*. Periodical articles and book reviews are covered in this semiannual publication issued by the American Theological Library Association. Emphasis is on English-language publications and on Protestant faiths, although other languages and religions are not excluded. The companion work is *Religion Index Two*, which has been issued since 1978 on an annual basis and indexes collective works by more than one author taken from anthologies, compilations, and so on. Material of interest to the history of religion in the United States routinely appears in both titles; both are available online through DIALOG as *Religion Index*.

694. **American Religion and Philosophy: A Guide to Information Sources.** Ernest R. Sandeen and Frederick Hale. Detroit: Gale, 1978. 377p. (Gale Information Guide Library; American Studies Information Guide Series, v.5). ISBN 0-8103-1262-X.

Considered to be a supplementary effort to the important bibliography by Burr (entry 697), this work emphasizes books and articles published since 1961, although earlier materials are included. Nearly 1,650 entries are grouped into 21 different chapters representing chronological periods. Opening the work is a chapter on general and reference works; next, there is one on the religion of native North Americans. Subsequent coverage is given to the Great Awakening, origins of denominations, and the Revolutionary era. Succeeding chapters deal with the nineteenth and twentieth centuries up through contemporary religious movements. Philosophy receives little attention, with only three chapters, one of which covers Judaism. Both scholars and students will find the work to be useful. Author and title indexes are also supplied.

695. **Bibliography of Religion in the South.** Charles H. Lippy. Macon, GA: Mercer University, 1985. 498p. ISBN 0-86554-161-2.

From the press of a small college with denominational origins comes this useful comprehensive bibliographic source on the religions of the South. The author is a professor of history at Clemson University and is well qualified to approach the task. He does so with vigor and has furnished a listing of 5,000 books, articles, monographs, essays, dissertations, theses, and recordings. Entries are placed into 22 chapters, each of which opens with a detailed bibliographic essay by the author. These are impressive in terms of scholarship and in their evaluation of the literature. Bibliographic listings follow the essays and are arranged topically. The focus is primarily on Christianity and Judaism, with a number of the chapters covering denominational traditions. Related cultural elements such as art, music, and literature are treated. No index is provided.

696. **Church and State in America: A Bibliographical Guide.** John F. Wilson, ed. New York: Greenwood, 1986–1987. 2v. ISBN 0-313-25236-X (v.1); 0-313-25914-3 (v.2).

Volume 1 covers the period of colonial existence through the early national period; volume 2 examines the Civil War period to the present. Each of the volumes of this important work furnishes 11 bibliographic essays prepared by young scholars (doctoral candidates and recent graduates) on the controversial issues of church and state. Essays are lengthy and examine various topics and philosophical interpretations. Chapters mainly cover historical periods, geographic divisions, or topical elements such as the Puritans in New England (volume 1) or Women and Religion from 1870 to 1920 (volume 2). Each of the essays is followed by an excellent listing of about 250 monographs, articles, and book-length bibliographies. Some of these listings are classified by topic; others are divided into primary source/secondary source groups. The work is of substantial value to scholars and serious students.

The subject of religious conflict is examined in *Religious Conflict in America: A Bibliography* by Albert J. Menendez (Garland Reference Library of Social Science, v.262, 1985). The author, having completed an earlier bibliography on church-state relations, then furnished this unannotated bibliography of religious conflict covering a period of history from the colonial era to the present. Various issues such as politics, cults, and the radical right are treated. All types of materials are included.

697. **A Critical Bibliography of Religion in America.** Nelson R. Burr, et al. Princeton, NJ: Princeton University Press, 1961. 2v. (Princeton Studies in American Civilization, no.5).

Although getting on in years, this work remains important in the field because it provides an excellent bibliographic commentary on the history of religion in the United States. Published as volume 4 (in two volumes) of *Religion in American Life* by James Ward Smith and A. Leland Jamison, the bibliography is often listed separately and remains the most important contribution of the set. It is comprehensive and provides the best coverage of the topic to date, with the inclusion of both primary and secondary sources. It begins with a general introductory section on bibliographic guides, followed by sections covering the evolutionary development of U.S. religion, religion and society, religion in the arts and literature, and intellectual history and theology. Christianity receives the most emphasis, reflecting its prominent position in this country, but other religions are not overlooked.

Burr furnished an updated but abridged edition entitled *Religion in American Life* as part of the Goldentree Bibliographies in American History series (Appleton-Century-Crofts, 1971). This version is intended for graduate and undergraduate students. Books, articles, and dissertations are listed in 22 main divisions, all of which are subdivided. An author index is given.

698. **New Religious Movements in the United States and Canada: A Critical Assessment and Annotated Bibliography.** Diane Choquette, comp. Westport, CT: Greenwood, 1985. 235p. (Bibliographies and Indexes in Religious Studies, no.5). ISBN 0-313-23772-7.

This annotated bibliography furnishes comprehensive coverage of more than 700 writings from the 1960s and 1970s on a variety of alternative faiths: Eastern religions, New Age and spiritualist sects, and the occult, as well as Christian variants (Jesus People, and the People's Temple). This is another in the Greenwood series designed to cover various faiths and is of use to scholars, students, and serious laypeople in its focus on both scholarly and popular literature. Entries represent books, periodical articles, dissertations, conference papers, unpublished works, and some audiovisual materials. Annotations are descriptive and sometimes critical. Arrangement of entries is by category or type—e.g., reference works, types of scholarly studies, popular titles. Many of these sections are subdivided by subject.

Entries are alphabetically arranged within these categories. There is a general index of authors, titles, and subjects that furnishes good access to content.

699. **Religion and American Life: Resources.** Anne T. Fraker, ed. Urbana, IL: University of Illinois Press, 1989. 236p. ISBN 0-252-01588-6.

This recent effort, an annotated bibliography, is very selective in its inclusion of 116 books and 121 articles on the relationship of religion to U.S. tradition and culture. The work grew out of a two-year series of symposia conducted under the joint sponsorship of Indiana and Purdue universities and is intended as a guide to undergraduate students. The product is useful for all levels of inquirers, however, including scholars and researchers, in its excellent choice of material. Its lengthy descriptive/critical annotations average about 350-400 words for each book and about 250 words per article. Selection of entries and writing of annotations was completed by a group of 40 specialists participating in the symposium. Selections represent civil religion as well as fundamentalism and include coverage of minority groups.

Religion and Society in North America: An Annotated Bibliography, edited by Robert de V. Brunkow (ABC-Clio, 1983), is an extensive listing of about 4,300 periodical articles published between 1973 and 1980 on the history of religion in the United States and Canada. It is another of the convenience packages derived from *America: History and Life* (entry 51), the monumental abstract database. It is designed to facilitate information searches for those with scholarly interests and furnishes a subject index to locate the materials on a wide range of topics and denominations.

700. **Religious Books, 1876–1982.** New York: Bowker, 1983. 4v. ISBN 0-8352-1602-0.

This massive bibliography of 130,000 entries provides a listing of more than 100 years of religious titles published and distributed in this country. Organized by LC subject headings, this tool draws on the database of the *American Book Publishing Record*, which contains all U.S. monographs from the *National Union Catalog* (entry 38) and MARC tapes in addition to those cataloged by Bowker. Aside from the core religious subjects (Bible, church history, denominations), it includes peripheral topics such as astrology, magic, and psychology. The first three volumes employ a subject approach through LC subject headings, and volume 4 provides author and title access. The work has been criticized for errors in certain subject headings, inclusion of questionable peripheral subject areas, and the listing of only first authors in the author index.

For currently available titles, there is Bowker's biennial publication, *Religious & Inspirational Books & Serials in Print*, which began in 1978–1979 under a slightly different title. The information is drawn from the records of *Books in Print* and *Forthcoming Books*. Over 50,000 entries from nearly 2,500 publishing houses are arranged under topical headings.

701. **Religious Seminaries in America: A Selected Bibliography.** Thomas C. Hunt and James C. Carper. New York: Garland, 1989. 231p. (Garland Reference Library of Social Science, no.539). ISBN 0-8240-7732-6.

This represents the completion of a trilogy, the first two volumes of which covered religious schools and religious universities, respectively. Sixteen specialists from the world of academe furnished these chapters, which vary in quality and consistency and cover a wide range of seminaries. Books, articles, dissertations and masters theses, even mimeographed reports and photocopied materials are included among the total of nearly 1,150 items. Following an introductory chapter on seminaries and civil government, coverage is given to Baptist, Catholic, Christian Church, Church of the Brethren, Episcopal, Hellenic, Independent, Jewish, Lutheran, Nazarene, Presbyterian, Reformed, Seventh-Day Adventist, United Church of Christ, and United Methodist denominations. The chapter on independent seminaries covers several denominations but omits others, such as the Quakers. Annotations vary in length but generally are brief. The work is indexed by author and subject.

Information Sources

702. **The Encyclopedia of American Religions.** 3rd ed. J. Gordon Melton. Detroit: Gale, 1989. 1,102p. ISBN 0-8103-2841-0. **Supp.** 1992. ISBN 0-8103-6903-6.

This title has achieved a prominent position with inquirers at all levels. The new edition covers nearly 1,600 religious bodies in a manner similar to that of its predecessors. The increase of 250 entries over the second edition (1987) reflects more comprehensive inclusion of Canadian groups. Similar here is the categorical arrangement of religious families into 22 segments, each furnishing a concise essay that places groups into historical context and supplies references. Traditional denominations such as Lutheran, Reformed, Presbyterian, and Pietist-Methodist, are treated, along with more modern affiliations such as Communal, Metaphysical, Psychic, and New Age. Directory-type entries follow, providing information on the various religious bodies (history, development, organizational aspects, and periodicals published) as well as a bibliography and bibliographic notes. Additional coverage is given to unclassified churches. No fewer than six indexes furnish access by institution, periodical, geographic location, name, subject, and group. The new supplement adds another 100 entries and updates information appearing in the third edition.

Another recent effort is *An Encyclopedia of Religions in the United States: One Hundred Religious Groups Speak for Themselves,* edited by William B. Williamson (Crossroad, 1992). This work furnishes general information on founders, major leaders, doctrines, worship, and contributions to U.S. culture of various Judeo-Christian groups having at least 100,000 members. Additional bodies are treated in the appendices.

703. **Encyclopedia of Religion in the South.** Samuel S. Hill, ed. Macon, GA: Mercer University, 1984. 878p. ISBN 0-86554-117-5.

Students and beginning researchers of both religion and area history will find this treatment of religion in the South a useful starting point. The editor is a religion professor and has pooled the contributions of over 200 specialists in an encyclopedic one-volume work. There are more than 500 signed articles; nearly half of them furnish biographical sketches. Average length is a half-page, although there are 16 lengthy essays covering individual state histories originally written for a work published a year earlier by the editor. Bibliographies accompany most entries. Coverage is wide-ranging, from the history and ideology of over 50 denominations to the description of various organizations, movements, events, and activities. Most biographees are deceased and represent various stations of life, including politics and literature. An index is provided.

704. **Encyclopedia of the American Religious Experience: Studies of Traditions and Movements.** Charles H. Lippy and Peter W. Williams, eds. New York: Scribner's, 1988. 3v. ISBN 0-684-18062-6 (set).

This three-volume encyclopedia is a throwback to an earlier period, when encyclopedias featured monograph-type essays of substance and depth. There are 100 essays averaging about 17 to 18 pages each; these are produced by young scholars writing in a clear and readable style. Each essay concludes with a summary paragraph and a bibliography of books and articles. Considered to be a product of excellent scholarship in terms of both breadth and depth of coverage, it explores both historical and contemporary conditions. Entries are organized into nine major segments dealing with approaches to religion, religious groups, religious movements, the arts, politics, and education, among other subjects. The work is exhaustive and includes coverage of most pertinent topics. It will serve as both a reference tool for students and scholars and an agreeable reading experience for those interested. There is an excellent detailed index.

705. Encyclopedic Handbook of Cults in America. Rev. ed. J. Gordon Melton. Hampden, CT: Garland, 1992. 407p. (Garland Reference Library of Social Science, v.797.) ISBN 0-8153-1140-0.

This informative handbook of alternative religions has been revised and expanded since the second edition in 1986. Melton, long an authority on religion in U.S. life and founder of the Institute for the Study of American Religion, has continued to produce an objective compendium of information. Especially useful are the introductory essays defining cults and their opponents in the United States. Coverage is given to 33 different groups ranging from the more established Rosicrucians to the more recent and publicized movements such as Unity School, Unification Church, and Krishna units. Each group is described in terms of leading figures, belief systems, organizational structure, and controversies. Bibliographies are provided. A name index and a detailed table of contents facilitate access.

706. Profiles in Belief: The Religious Bodies of the United States and Canada. Arthur C. Piepkorn. San Francisco: Harper & Row, 1977–1979. 4v. in 3. ISBN 0-06-066582-3 (v.2); 0-06-066581-5 (v.3–4).

When Piepkorn, a Lutheran scholar, died in 1973, he had prepared the copy for the first four volumes of what was to be a seven-volume work. These four volumes were published posthumously under his name. The first two volumes, on Catholicism and Protestantism, still are considered outstanding by scholars and students for their exposition of history, beliefs, statistics, liturgy, and practice. Volume 3, (*Holiness and Pentecostal*) and volume 4 (*Evangelical, ·Fundamentalist, and Other Christian Bodies*) were issued in one binding, with volume 3 approaching the level of quality associated with the earlier volumes. Although volume 4 displays less familiarity with the subject matter, when taken as a set the work represents an indispensable tool for scholarly inquiry.

For more up-to-date and less detailed information on the denominations one may consult the Melton encyclopedia (entry 702) and the old standard *Handbook of Denominations in the United States* by Frank Spencer Mead. It is revised about every fifth year by Samuel S. Hill and is now in its ninth edition (Abingdon, 1990). There are brief descriptions of the history, doctrine, organization, and status of nearly 300 religious bodies; coverage is even and considered to be objective. *Religious Bodies in the United States: A Directory*, also by J. Gordon Melton (Garland, 1992), identifies and describes all religious groups operating in this country as of 1991. There are listings of periodicals for each of the bodies.

707. Historical Atlas of Religion in America. Rev. ed. Edwin S. Gaustad. New York: Harper & Row, 1976. 189p. ISBN 0-06-063089-2.

Originally published in 1962, this more recent edition substitutes maps of countries for those of states. (State maps were considered by the publisher to be inconsequential.) This atlas attempts to show the expansion and development of religion in the United States from colonial times in the mid-seventeenth century to 1970. The emphasis is on Christianity, but other faiths are examined as well. The maps are integrated with descriptive narrative and charts and tables to provide insight into the type of development that took place within church groups and denominations. One is able to follow the development of religious influence in terms of numerical distributions. There are separate indexes for authors and titles, places, and religious bodies, as well as for names and subjects.

Two useful atlases by Peter L. Halvorson and William M. Newman furnish graphic presentation of the changes in size and locale of denominations in this country. The *Atlas of Religious Change in America, 1952–1971* (Glenmary Research Center, 1978) contains information on nearly 40 denominations ranging in size from several thousand to multiple millions as in the case of Roman Catholics. Information is based on data developed by the publisher. The *Atlas of Religious Change in America 1971–1980* (Glenmary Research Center, 1987) continues the coverage.

708. **The Religious Heritage of America.** Albert M. Shulman. San Diego: A. S. Barnes, 1981. 527p. ISBN 0-498-02162-9.

Intended as a handbook of religious groups for the student, beginning researcher, or information seeker, this one-volume work takes an encyclopedic approach to the six major U.S. religious groupings. These are treated in individual chapters following the introductory essays covering religious life in the United States. Over 100 religions are examined, the intent being to furnish salient facts about religions, cults, and sects in an easy-to-understand, comprehensive manner. Pattern of coverage generally begins with a chronological profile in which major events and dates are sequentially listed. Concise but informative narratives describe the group's origins, divisions, name, structure, and polity as well as doctrines and beliefs. Researchers would be more inclined to favor Piepkorn (entry 706) for depth, but nonspecialists may appreciate the brevity in this effort. There is a selective bibliography and three indexes.

Biographical Sources

709. **Biographical Dictionary of American Cult and Sect Leaders.** J. Gordon Melton. New York: Garland, 1986. 354p. (Garland Reference Library of Social Science, v.212). ISBN 0-8240-9037-3.

This useful biographical tool was developed in response to a clear need for material on leaders of divergent, nonmainstream groups. Both scholars and students should profit from the focus on what have come to be called alternative religions. Melton has provided comprehensive coverage of 213 founders and major leaders of U.S. cults and sects. Coverage is limited to deceased figures. A sect is considered to be a group in protest of the mainstream church, and a cult is defined as a more radical new spiritual option. Some of the groups have become mainstream, such as the Mormon Church. The biographies are well written and informative, numbering from 300 to 500 words in length and including bibliographies by and about the individual. Appendices provide classification by tradition, birthplace, and religious influences. A good general index is given.

710. **Dictionary of American Religious Biography.** Henry W. Bowden and Edwin S. Gaustad, eds. Westport, CT: Greenwood, 1977. 572p. ISBN 0-8371-8906-3.

Useful to both scholars and students, this retrospective biographical dictionary covers notable figures from all time periods in this country. Included are religious leaders, philosophers, reformers, and controversial figures. Here one will find the Mathers, Cardinal Cushing, Martin Luther King, and Malcolm X, an interesting and well-designed mix of diverse personalities. The editors were able to present the information in an unbiased manner and furnish a perspective respectful of the nation's pluralistic tradition. Each entry begins with a brief career overview and personal and educational data. Following this is a detailed narrative sketch giving both expository and evaluative commentary. A special attempt has been made to include women and minorities as well as dissidents from mainstream activity. Bibliographies that provide references by and about the biographee are tacked on to each entry. There is a name and subject index.

A more specialized effort is *The Conversion Experience in America: A Sourcebook on Religious Conversion Autobiography* by James C. Holte (Greenwood, 1992). Holte furnishes in-depth treatment of religious conversions described by 30 Americans over a period of 350 years. Most are Protestant, but also represented are Roman Catholics, Black Muslims, and Shakers. Seven of these converts are female, and nine are from minority groups. The autobiographies are analyzed through descriptive narrative as well as critique and assessment.

711. Religious Leaders of America: A Biographical Guide to Founders and Leaders of Religious Bodies, Churches, and Spiritual Groups in North America. J. Gordon Melton. Detroit: Gale, 1991. 604p. ISBN 0-8103-4921-3. ISSN 1057-2961.

This recent effort by the prolific author represents a biographical dictionary of nearly 1,050 personalities, all of whom made their contribution subsequent to the Civil War. Coverage extends over a wide range of figures from both the traditional Judeo-Christian heritage and the alternative or fringe areas. Minority figures, females, blacks, and native Americans are listed in a purposeful attempt to be inclusive. Although most of the entries are for deceased individuals, there is a good representation of living people: Pat Robertson, Jesse Jackson, Billy Graham, and Madalyn Murray O'Hair. Entries furnish birth and death dates, birthplaces, and religious affiliations, together with a well-developed biography. There is an appendix of religious affiliation classifying the subjects into various groups. A comprehensive index identifies individuals, organizations, and publications.

712. Twentieth-Century Shapers of American Popular Religion. Charles H. Lippy, ed. New York: Greenwood, 1989. 494p. ISBN 0-313-25356-0.

This is a most unusual and welcome tool for both scholars and students because of its detailed biographical essays on these leading figures, both living and dead, who represent some form of "popular" religion. Religions of this type are considered to be outside the mainstream, focused on a charismatic leader and utilizing (or exploiting) the media. Television evangelists of today along with the capable spokesmen of the past are represented. Coverage is highly selective, limited to just over 60 men and women representing this unique U.S. experience. Included here are leaders such as Mordecai Kaplan, Harvey Cox, Marcus Garvey, Amy Semple McPherson, Malcolm X, and Pat Robertson. Others have been included for their influence, such as Sinclair Lewis for his Elmer Gantry. Entries include an evaluation, critical summary, and bibliography. A detailed index is given.

Christian

Catholic

The *Catholic Periodical and Literature Index* is the leading current index of books and articles pertinent to Catholicism. Routinely it cites writings useful to the study of the history of Catholicism in this country. It is published bimonthly and indexes more than 150 periodicals. Book reviews are included as well. Initially two separate publications, it has been issued since 1930 by the Catholic Library Association in Haverford, Pennsylvania; the present title was adopted in 1968.

The American Catholic Historical Association was founded in 1919 and is headquartered at Catholic University of America in Washington, D.C. It has 1,100 members and issues the *Catholic Historical Review* on a quarterly basis. The U.S. Catholic Historical Society first appeared in 1884 and has 1,200 members. It operates out of East Brunswick, New Jersey, and has issued a quarterly journal, *U.S. Catholic Historian,* since 1980.

713. **The Catholic Church in America: An Historical Bibliography.** 2nd ed. Edward R. Vollmar. New York: Scarecrow, 1963. 399p.

This bibliography of books, articles, dissertations, and theses has proven useful to both students and researchers over the past three decades. The author, a Jesuit priest, had chosen to include only those theses and dissertations that were completed at Catholic colleges and thereby may have eliminated much useful research produced by students at other institutions. Even so, the work is unique in targeting the history of the Catholic Church in this country. The paucity of such efforts, especially in regard to the development of an up-to-date comprehensive history, is noted by the author in his useful overview. Entries are arranged alphabetically by author. The period of coverage of these writings is 1850–1961. Many entries are annotated in a descriptive manner. There is a detailed index to provide access.

714. **Dictionary of American Catholic Biography.** John J. Delaney. Garden City, NY: Doubleday, 1984. 621p. ISBN 0-385-17878-6.

A useful tool for quick answers to questions from all types of inquirers, this biographical dictionary lists 1,500 deceased personalities who have made a noteworthy contribution to the Catholic Church and/or to this country. Coverage represents a long time span, from the period of exploration to the present or recent past. Both men and women are treated in entries that are concise but well developed and carefully researched. As one might expect, the majority of the entries represent church people at various levels, but a good proportion of laypersons are included as well. Such people as Bing Crosby, Arturo Toscanini, Babe Ruth, and John F. Kennedy demonstrate the scope and breadth of coverage. No bibliographies are furnished with the entries, an omission that does limit its value to scholarship.

715. **Documents of American Catholic History.** John T. Ellis, ed. Wilmington, DE: Glazier, 1967-1987. 3v. ISBN 0-894-53611-7 (v.1).

The author has been one of the most respected historians of the Catholic Church in the United States for the past 35 years, having produced a concise historical survey the same year the original edition of this work came out in 1956. In the revised two-volume edition published in 1967 by H. Regnery, the first volume contained source material dating from 1493 to 1865 and volume 2 continued the coverage to 1966. What was offered was interesting documentary material showing the full flavor of Catholic existence. Included are laws, charters, papal documents, and so on, as well as John Adams's perception of a mass he attended, comments of Mr. Dooley on various issues, and poetry by Joyce Kilmer. The most recent edition offers a reprint version of the earlier two-volume effort, along with a new third volume covering the years 1966–1986.

716. **A Guide to American Catholic History.** 2nd ed., rev. and enl. John T. Ellis and Robert Trisco. Santa Barbara, CA: ABC-Clio, 1982. 265p. ISBN 0-87436-318-7.

The principal author has been one of the more prolific recorders of the U.S. Catholic experience for the past three decades (see entry 715 above) and revised the initial edition of this work some 23 years after its issue in 1959. The more recent effort furnishes an annotated bibliography of more than 1,250 entries, of which nearly 500 are newly added. The majority of the 800 original entries have been retained, with little revision evident. Both monographic and journal literature are treated along with dissertations; issue and publication dates run to 1979. Arrangement of entries is by classes covered in various chapters, some of which are very pertinent to the needs of social historians. The segment on manuscript depositories, once considered useful to the needs of scholarship, has been eliminated. There is a comprehensive index to subjects, authors, and titles.

Protestant

Many of the Protestant denominations have a historical society or association promoting research and publication. For example, the Historical Commission of the Southern Baptist Convention of Nashville, Tennessee, was founded in 1951 and has issued a quarterly journal, *Baptist History and Heritage*, since 1965. The American Baptist Historical Society (1853) is located at Linfield College in McMinnville, Oregon, and has 270 members. It has published the *American Baptist Quarterly* since 1958. The Unitarian Universalist Historical Society of Boston (1978) has 600 members and publishes newsletters and proceedings. The Historical Society of the United Methodist Church was founded in 1988 and has 1,100 members. Its quarterly journal, *Methodist History*, was started by the church in 1962. The Evangelical and Reformed Historical Society and Archives of the United Church of Christ was founded in 1863 and operates out of Lancaster, Pennsylvania. It has 1,600 members and publishes a newsletter as well as archival bibliographies.

Library Resources

717. Guide to the Manuscript Collections of the Presbyterian Church U.S. Robert Benedetto and Betty K. Walker. Westport, CT: Greenwood, 1990. 570p. (Bibliographies and Indexes in Religious Studies, no.17). ISBN 0-313-27654-4.

An excellent resource for scholarly study is this guide to the various manuscript collections available on the Presbyterian Church, U.S., the denomination founded in the South as the Presbyterian Church in the Confederate States of America in 1861. The principal author furnishes a brief, informative history and description of the nature and character of the unit until its 1983 merger with the northern factions into the present Presbyterian Church. Nearly 1,400 different collections are identified, most of which are located at the Department of History of the Presbyterian Church, U.S., in Montreat, North Carolina. Others are found in a variety of institutions, such as Davidson College. Arrangement of materials is by name of the person who developed the collection or created the materials. All types of source materials are cited, including diaries, correspondence, and photographs. A subject index is provided.

718. Methodist Union Catalog, Pre-1976 Imprints. Kenneth E. Rowe, ed. Metuchen, NJ: Scarecrow, 1975–1985. v.1–6. (Projected 20v.). ISBN 0-8108-0880-3 (v.1).

This union catalog of the holdings of over 200 Methodist libraries in the United States and Europe has progressed steadily if not rapidly since its initial volumes in 1975. The editor has served as the Methodist librarian at Drew University and has compiled what should become the standard bibliography of books, pamphlets, and theses on Methodism, as well as the writings of Methodists (even if not related to religious inquiry). Each volume furnishes between 6,000 and 7,000 entries, and arrangement is alphabetical by author. Publication dates start with the beginning of the movement in 1729 and continue up to the present day. There are six completed volumes thus far, and all bear a reputation for excellence in terms of comprehensiveness and adherence to high bibliographic standards. The sixth volume (1985) brings the alphabetical coverage through the letter "I." Symbols for locations of participating libraries accompany each entry. Index volumes are to be included to the entire set. Volume 7 is expected in 1993.

719.   **A Mormon Bibliography, 1830–1930: Books, Pamphlets, Periodicals, and Broadsides Relating to the First Century of Mormonism.** Chad J. Flake, ed. Salt Lake City, UT: University of Utah, 1978. 825p. ISBN 0-87480-016-1. **Supp.** 1989. 413p. ISBN 0-87480-338-1.

This work serves a dual role as both an important scholarly bibliography and a union catalog of various printed materials relating to the Mormon faith during its first hundred years. Included here are the formats enumerated in the title; excluded are specific articles, manuscripts, maps, and prints. There are over 10,000 entries representing the holdings of nearly 200 libraries. Arrangement is alphabetical by author in the manner of the *National Union Catalog* (entry 38). Entries provide bibliographic identification as well as symbols indicating library locations. The lack of a subject index is one drawback to its use as a convenient tool by scholars and serious students.

The supplement compiled by Flake and Larry W. Draper, *A Mormon Bibliography, 1830–1930: Ten Year Supplement* (University of Utah, 1989) is organized in the same manner and furnishes listings of additional citations covering the same time period. Rare materials available in over 40 libraries are identified.

720.   **A Presbyterian Bibliography: The Published Writings of Ministers Who Served in the Presbyterian Church in the United States During Its First Hundred Years, 1861–1961, and Their Locations in Eight Significant Theological Collections in the U.S.A.** Harold B. Prince, comp. and ed. Metuchen, NJ: American Theological Library Association and Scarecrow, 1983. 452p. (ATLA Bibliography Series, no.8). ISBN 0-8108-1639-3.

An extremely useful source for scholars and serious students, this union list cites nearly 4,200 published works by ministers of the Presbyterian Church of the Confederate States of America and its successor, the Presbyterian Church in the United States. Historically, it represents an extremely important time following the disunion of the nation into warring camps and the division of the Presbyterian Church along those same lines. The holdings of eight theological libraries are treated here with references to relevant items in their collections. Arrangement of entries is alphabetical by author and furnishes a unique perspective on church development as seen by its majority. There is a subject index to provide access.

The *Bibliography of Published Articles on American Presbyterianism, 1901–1980* by Harold M. Parker (Greenwood, 1985) is the fourth entry of the Bibliographies and Indexes in Religious Studies series. It is another useful reference with which to identify nearly 3,000 articles in 17 library locations. Included here is material from natural and regional secular reviews; house organs of churches are excluded. A valuable topical index furnishes access.

Bibliographical Sources

721.   **American Evangelicalism: An Annotated Bibliography.** Norris A. Magnuson and William G. Travis. West Cornwall, CT: Locust Hill, 1990. 495p. ISBN 0-933951-27-2.

This bibliography and the Blumhofer and Carpenter entry below appeared at the same time and cover much of the same ground. This one is the more extensive, however, with twice the number of books and articles. Even so, there is a surprising lack of duplication in areas touched by both works, such as "The Bible." One is able to detect a greater emphasis on monographic literature than on periodical literature in this title. Also, there is a greater focus on the literature of evangelicalism rather than literature on the topic of evangelicalism. Although this work is primarily focused on the twentieth century, the nineteenth century is surveyed as well. Annotations are brief, and there is an author index.

Twentieth Century Evangelicalism: A Guide to the Sources by Edith L. Blumhofer and Joel A. Carpenter (Garland, 1990) is another offering of the Garland Reference Library of Social Science (volume 521). More selective than the above effort, it serves as a useful complementary vehicle, with a helpful introductory segment and a good subject index. Annotations are slightly longer than those of Magnuson and Travis. Another useful tool, *Holy Ground: A Study of the American Camp Meeting* by Kenneth O. Brown (Garland, 1992), furnishes good bibliographical coverage of the literature as well as an informative history of the camp meeting, which originated in the South during the late eighteenth and early nineteenth centuries.

722. **American Puritan Studies: An Annotated Bibliography of Dissertations, 1882–1981.** Michael S. Montgomery, comp. Westport, CT: Greenwood, 1984. 419p. (Bibliographies and Indexes in American History, no.1). ISBN 0-313-2437-2.

This convenient listing of doctoral dissertations on the Puritan movement in this country is primarily intended for the scholar and researcher. Since its publication it has been regarded as a solid and useful effort, supplying the serious inquirer with good information. It is the initial offering in another of Greenwood's bibliographic series. Nearly 1,000 entries are presented from universities located not only in this country but in the United Kingdom, Canada, and Germany as well. Arrangement is chronological, covering 100 years of dissertations, then alphabetical by author. Annotations are brief and descriptive, based on the titles or abstracts reported in other access tools. There are helpful features, such as the indication of availability of unpublished dissertations. Four indexes yield access by author, institution, short title, and subject.

723. **A Guide to the Study of the Pentecostal Movement.** Charles E. Jones. Metuchen, NJ: American Theological Library Association and Scarecrow, 1983. 2v. (ATLA Bibliography Series, no.6). ISBN 0-8108-1583-4.

This is another of the interesting and important bibliographies produced through the increased desire to cover the writings on various denominations. The Pentecostal movement developed out of an emotional conviction that at times discouraged scholarly inquiry. This two-volume effort, authored by a religious scholar and librarian, presents a unique listing of more than 6,000 books and articles from a variety of sources and representing various languages. Many denominations are treated within a broad-based definition of Pentecostalism. Historical narrative is included with respect to churches, schools, associations, and missionary agencies. The emphasis is on U.S. Pentecostalism, but foreign movements are covered as well. This work is important to inquirers at various levels, ranging from student to scholar. A helpful directory is included as a special feature. Several indexes furnish adequate access.

724. **Jehovah's Witnesses and Kindred Groups: A Historical Compendium and Bibliography.** Jerry Bergman. New York: Garland, 1984. 370p. (Garland Reference Library of Social Science, v.180; Sects and Cults in America, Bibliographical Guides, v.4). ISBN 0-8240-9109-4.

Another excellent resource for the scholar and serious student is this comprehensive bibliography and history issued during the centennial year of Jehovah's Witnesses. The author is a psychology professor who has produced a well-organized and thorough tool; there is a fine introductory essay describing the history and development of the church, which should be read by people with a scholarly interest. Entries are arranged under five major divisions providing logical access: official publications of the organization; the Russell movement; works about the movement; U.S. offshoots; and non-U.S. related groups. Format subdivisions generally follow. Coverage of Jehovah's Witnesses has been sparse in the past, making this an especially valuable tool. There is a directory of related groups in the appendix. Access is furnished through a detailed index of personal and corporate authors.

725. **Mennonite Bibliography, 1631–1961.** Nelson P. Springer and A. J. Klassen, comps. Scottdale, PA: Herald, 1977. 2v. ISBN 0-8381-1208-3.

This is a useful bibliography of writings of all types on the Mennonites. It represents a comprehensive listing of more than 28,000 books, periodicals, pamphlets, dissertations, *festschrift*, symposia, and conferences, and even includes individual articles from encyclopedias and periodicals. Book reviews are also identified. U.S. Mennonites can trace their beginning to both the Swiss and Dutch wings of Anabaptism, which developed in Switzerland in the sixteenth century. It embraced parts of Germany and spread to the United States through various groups such as the Amish and the Hutterites. Volume 1 of this work covers the international aspects of the Mennonite faith, with volume 2 targeting its presence in North America. Entries are arranged under various topics as they fall under geographical divisions. There are indexes to author, subject, and book review.

726. **Shaker Literature: A Bibliography.** Mary L.H. Richmond, comp. Hancock, MA: Shaker Community; distr. Hanover, NH: University Press of New England, 1977. 2v. ISBN 0-87451-117-8.

Mother Ann Lee arrived in this country in 1774; subsequently, 18 Shaker communities were founded at different times. The Shakers as a religious group have most certainly attracted attention of both scholars and popular writers to a degree disproportionate to their relatively small number in U.S. religious history. This title provides an excellent bibliography with introductory essays. About 4,000 entries are divided into two volumes. The first volume furnishes over 1,700 entries and covers material by Shakers. Volume 2 covers material *about* Shakers. Included in the two volumes are references for books, parts of books, pamphlets, periodical articles, broadsides, almanacs, catalogs, advertisements, leaflets, and notices. Library locations are furnished. Of great interest is the segment on court decisions in volume 1, and the anti-Shaker tracts listed in volume 2. The annotations are useful in describing content. There is an index of titles and joint authors.

Information and Biographical Sources

*727. **Encyclopedia of Mormonism: The History, Scripture, Doctrine, and Procedure of the Church of Jesus Christ of the Latter Day Saints.** Daniel H. Ludlow, ed. New York: Macmillan, 1992. 4v. ISBN 0-02-879605-5.

This is a detailed and comprehensive compendium of the Mormon Church edited by a prominent professor of religion. Entries are well written and organized under five major topics: history of the Church; scriptures of the Church; doctrines of Mormonism; organization of the Church; and practices of Church members in society. Controversial topics such as feminism, abortion, and racism are treated in a frank and forthright manner, although doctrinal concepts may be difficult to grasp. There is an optional fifth volume that contains the sacred scriptures of Mormonism. Contributors to the encyclopedia are religious scholars of various affiliations. The CD-ROM version is available through Infobases of Orem, Utah; it does not contain the sample Mormon hymns.

The Presidents of the Church: Biographical Essays, edited by Leonard Arrington (Deseret Books, 1986), is a biographical dictionary primarily useful for students who are interested in pictures and biographical descriptions of the life and times of the 13 men who have served as head of the Church of Jesus Christ of Latter-Day Saints, the major arm of the Mormon faith. Beginning with Joseph Smith and ending with Ezra Taft Benson, who served as the secretary of agriculture under Dwight Eisenhower, biographies furnish highlights of each man's career and provide a human focus on their accomplishments. The tool's importance to scholarship is somewhat limited because of its failure to supply footnotes to source material. This work replaces the 13th edition of the same title completed in 1974.

Jewish

The Jewish influence on the course of events in this country has been strong since the Revolutionary War. As they have done in other countries in which they settled and to which they migrated, the Jewish people have added immensely to the cultural, educational, business, scientific, and recreational achievement of the United States. This section lists sources that treat both the Jewish religion and the Jewish social tradition.

The *Index to Jewish Periodicals*, published by The Index in Cleveland Heights, Ohio, has been issued since 1963 and is the leading current index of Jewish periodical literature. It covers about 50 periodicals in the English language and includes book reviews. Material of interest to U.S. Jewish history appears on a routine basis. Beginning with volume 26 (1988), it changed from a semiannual to an annual publication.

The American Jewish Historical Society of Waltham, Massachusetts, was founded in 1892 and has 3,300 members. Its quarterly journal, *American Jewish History*, has been published since 1893. One of the society's most ambitious publishing projects to date is the just-completed five-volume history, collectively entitled *The Jewish People in America* (1992), for which Henry L. Feingold served as general editor. Coverage of volume 1 begins with the first immigration of 23 Jews to New Amsterdam in 1654; succeeding immigrations are treated through volume 5, which covers the period subsequent to World War II. Jewish life in the United States is examined in depth from immigration through assimilation.

728. An American Jewish Bibliography: Being a List of Books and Pamphlets by Jews, or Relating to Them, Printed in the United States from the Establishment of the Press in the Colonies Until 1850. Abraham S.W. Rosenbach. Baltimore: American Jewish Historical Society, 1926. 486p. (Publications of the American Jewish Historical Society, no.30). Repr. Millwood, NY: Kraus, 1977.

The Rosenbach work has long been recognized as a standard bibliography relating to the study of U.S. Jewish history. It was issued in 1926 and remains a valuable source for research and scholarly inquiry. Originally a publication of the American Jewish Historical Society, it has since been reprinted. About 700 books and pamphlets are listed in chronological order and represent publications either by or about Jews from colonial times to 1850.

Two years after Rosenbach's death, there appeared a supplement: *Jewish Americana: A Catalogue of Books and Articles by Jews or Relating to Them Printed in the United States from the Earliest Days to 1850 and Found in the Library of the Hebrew Union College— Jewish Institute of Religion in Cincinnati* (American Jewish Archives, Monograph No. 1, 1954). Subsequently coverage was continued through Allan F. Levine's *An American Jewish Bibliography: A List of Books and Pamphlets by Jews or Relating to Them, Printed in the United States from 1851–1875, Which Are in the Possession of the Hebrew Union College— Jewish Institute of Religion Library in Cincinnati* (American Jewish Archives, Monograph No. 11, 1959).

729. **American Jewish History: A Bibliographical Guide.** Jeffrey S. Gurock. New York: Anti-Defamation League of B'nai B'rith, 1983. 195p. ISBN 0-88464-037-X.

This relatively compact work was hailed as the first critical inventory of U.S. Jewish history in 30 years; it was the first full-scale bibliography since the Brickman effort described below. The work is intended for all levels of users, from scholars to the general public, and features a guide to the titles considered most useful for examination of the major issues relevant to Jewish history in this country. It contains a series of brief but informative bibliographic essays that treat the basic introductory and reference titles concerning the topic from the colonial period to the present day. Special topics such as the Holocaust and Zionism are included. Author and title indexes are furnished.

William W. Brickman's *The Jewish Community in America: An Annotated and Classified Bibliographical Guide* (Franklin, 1977; Franklin Ethnic Bibliographical Guides, No. 2) presents an annotated critical bibliography of more than 800 histories, autobiographies, documents, and memoirs in various languages on the Jewish experience in this country. Coverage extends from the colonial period to the present day, with emphasis on adjustment to life in the United States. Arrangement of entries is by both format and topic, then alphabetical by author. Scholars and laymen alike derive benefit. The book is indexed by author and title.

730. **American Synagogue History: A Bibliography and State-of-the-Field Survey.** Alexandra S. Korros and Jonathan D. Sarna. New York: M. Wiener, 1988. 247p. ISBN 0-910129-90-8.

Developed as a resource for both scholarly and popular inquiry, this bibliography of nearly 1,200 synagogue and community histories is arranged alphabetically by state. Synagogue histories are of different varieties and include separate publications, parts of larger community histories, periodical articles, chronicles, and even souvenir publications and pamphlets. The work opens with an introduction by a noted historian, Jonathan D. Sarna, and follows with a useful survey article by Daniel J. Elazar, raising important considerations pertaining to the development of the synagogue in the United States. Entries are subdivided by congregational and community history and furnish the usual bibliographic identification. Brief annotations accompany some but not all citations. Special features include a separate bibliography on synagogue architecture as well as a selected listing of secondary sources. The work is of value because of the uniqueness of its content. An author index is provided.

731. **A Biographical Dictionary of Early American Jews: Colonial Times Through 1800.** Joseph R. Rosenbloom. Lexington: University of Kentucky Press, 1960. 175p.

This unique biographical tool is of real value to students and researchers of Jewish genealogy and colonial history and represents an extraordinary effort in its utilization of many sources. About 4,000 men and women who lived in the U.S. between the mid-seventeenth century through 1800 are listed alphabetically. Entries vary in depth according to what was revealed by the source material. Information provided includes name, residence, dates of birth, marriage, and death, and citation to source. Additional information is furnished when available, including names of parents, outstanding facts, marriage partners, and so on. As one would expect, most of the biographees are from the older Jewish communities, such as New York and Philadelphia. One is also able to appreciate the effort and careful scrutiny of publications by the American Jewish Historical Society.

732. **Conservative Judaism in America: A Biographical Dictionary and Sourcebook.** Pamela S. Nadell. Westport, CT: Greenwood, 1988. 409p. (Jewish Denominations in America). ISBN 0-313-24205-4.

Conservative Judaism emerged in the nineteenth-century United States as a compromise between the almost total accommodation to modern U.S. life of the new Reform movement and the unwavering observance of Hebrew tradition of the Orthodox school. This biographical dictionary is first of a series from Greenwood Press and opens with three brief, informative essays on the history, ideology, and organization of Conservative Judaism. Institutions such as the Jewish Theological Seminary are identified and explained. The bulk of the work consists of biographical sketches of roughly 130 individuals considered to be leading figures of Conservative Judaism, most of them rabbis active in the movement. Entries furnish biographical information, evaluation of achievements, bibliography of the subject's writings, and references about them. Also included are a glossary of Hebrew terms, a bibliography, and appendices listing names and dates. There is a detailed subject index.

733. **The Jewish Experience: A Guide to Manuscript Sources in the Library of Congress.** Gary J. Kohn, comp. Cincinnati, OH: American Jewish Archives; distr. Hoboken, NJ: KTAV, 1986. 166p. (Monographs of the American Jewish Archives, no.11). ISBN 0-87820-014-2.

Another guide to the massive holdings of the Library of Congress pertinent to a specific topic, this title has proved of value to research and scholarly study. One may lament its failure to furnish critical analysis or even descriptive annotations, but in this case the identification and enumeration of such primary source material is justification enough for its issue and use. Arrangement of the tool is in three sections, beginning with a listing of over 130 collections in the library that contain some material on the topic. Second, there is a listing of about 300 individual collections containing papers of prominent Jews or corporate bodies. Finally, there is a topical listing that identifies papers on such subjects as the Holocaust. Entries furnish collection name, subjects, and location file number.

734. **Jewish Heritage in America: An Annotated Bibliography.** Sharad Karkhanis. New York: Garland, 1988. 434p. (Garland Reference Library of Social Science, v.467). ISBN 0-8240-7538-2.

This relatively recent bibliography of nearly 325 books and 800 articles represents a good selection of both popular and scholarly literature. The author is the librarian of a community college in New York City and has culled his entries from nearly 90 journals spanning a period of over 60 years from 1925 through 1987. Selection was based on the significance of a topic and its treatment, with recognition of the need to present a balanced listing. Excluded are autobiographies, biographies, poetry, and fiction. Availability was a factor, with some emphasis on access through medium-sized libraries. Arrangement of entries is under seven broad categories, such as historical perspective and anti-Semitism, all of which are further divided by subcategories; books and articles are listed under topic. Descriptive annotations are lengthy. Author, title, and subject indexes are furnished.

The Jewish Experience in America: A Historical Bibliography (ABC-Clio, 1983) is another of the publisher's convenience packages drawn from the enormous database that generates *America: History and Life* (entry 51). This particular title furnishes over 800 entries treating the historical, political, and cultural (rather than religious) aspects of Jewish-American life published between 1973 and 1979 in a variety of journals ranging from the well-known to the obscure. Abstracts vary considerably in length. For more coverage of religious aspects, see *Religion and Society in North America* (entry 699n).

735. **Jewish-American History and Culture: An Encyclopedia.** Jack Fischel and Sanford Pinsker, eds. Hamden, CT: Garland, 1992. 710p. (Garland Reference Library of the Social Sciences, v.429). ISBN 0-8240-6622-7.

Reviewers consider this a ground-breaking work because it presents a well-designed, clearly written, comprehensive, one-volume source of information revealing the richness and depth of contribution of the Jewish people in the United States. Entries are alphabetically arranged and describe all aspects of life, including the arts, economics, history, the humanities, the military, science, social institutions, organizations, and popular culture. Personalities are covered in liberal fashion. Entries range from brief sketches to detailed surveys and furnish not only description but also, in many cases, critical evaluation. Useful bibliographies accompany most entries, enabling the reader to research the topic further. Contributors to the work are specialists in the field of Jewish studies and provide an enlightening and fair-minded exposition. Useful listings include Jewish Nobel Prize winners and libraries with extensive collections on the subject.

736. **Manuscript Catalog of the American Jewish Archives, Cincinnati.** Boston: G. K. Hall, 1971. 4v. ISBN 0-816-10899-4. **Supp.** 1978. 909p. ISBN 0-816-10934-6.

The American Jewish Archives was founded in 1947 at Hebrew Union College in Cincinnati as a documentation center for the history of U.S. Jewry. Today it houses several million items relating to the history and sociology of the Jewish tradition in the Western Hemisphere. The catalog was issued in 1971 as a four-volume effort; a supplementary volume was published in 1978. Together the five volumes represent an important access tool for the scholar and serious student, one in which the library catalog cards have been reproduced. In 1991 the publisher reprinted this work as a microfilm edition in four reels.

The *Guide to the Holdings of the American Jewish Archives* by James W. Clasper and M. Carolyn Dellenback (American Jewish Archives, 1979) was issued as number 11 in the Publications of the American Jewish Archives series. It is relatively handy and describes the scope and variety of materials in the various collections. Divided into four major parts or types of collections (manuscripts, microfilm from other repositories, theses and dissertations, and special files), it is accessible by a name and subject index. The *Index to the American Jewish Archives*, volumes I–XXIV by Paul F. White (American Jewish Archives, 1979) furnishes a 24-year index of the semiannual historical journal, covering the 1948–1972 period.

SCIENCE, TECHNOLOGY, AND MEDICINE

In U.S. universities the history of science, as a cultural, philosophical, and intellectual pursuit, was formalized during the second decade of this century with the active involvement of George Sarton. Today, the field remains a steady if not quite popular course of study for both graduate and undergraduate students. A quarterly publication, *Isis* (1913–) (see entry 746), is produced by the History of Science Society (HSS) of Worcester, Massachusetts. Founded in 1924, the society has an international membership of around 3,000. It publishes book-length studies in its review journal, *Osiris* (1936–1968; 2nd ser., 1985– , ann./irreg.), and produces a quarterly newsletter. Every two or three years, the society issues the *Guide to the History of Science*, which describes the organization and activities of the HSS; lists similar societies and organizations, periodicals and newsletters, and graduate programs and centers of research in the discipline; and serves as the society's membership directory. Much has been written about every phase of the study of science in its historical perspective, with numerous monographic histories and bibliographies on different branches, individuals, pursuits, and geographical regions.

This segment contains those reference tools that are linked specifically to the history of progress, development, and products in the United States. International coverage can be gained by examination of works such as S. A. Jayawardene's *Reference Books for the Historian of Science: A Handlist* (Science Museum [London], 1982).

The Society for the History of Technology (SHOT) at the Department of Social Sciences, Michigan Technological University, Houghton, Michigan, was founded in 1958 and has 2,600 members. It publishes *Technology and Culture* on a quarterly basis. The American Association for the History of Medicine (AAHM), formed in 1925 and based at the Boston University School of Medicine, boasts some 1,300 members and produces the quarterly *Bulletin of the History of Medicine*. The American Academy of the History of Dentistry, based in Chicago, has been publishing the *Bulletin of the History of Dentistry* on a semiannual basis since 1952.

Ralph S. Bates's *Scientific Societies in the United States*, 3rd edition (MIT Press, 1965), though dated, serves as a useful guide covering scientific societies in the United States from a historical perspective.

Library Resources

737. Catalog of Books in the American Philosophical Society Library. American Philosophical Society. Westport, CT: Greenwood, 1970. 28v. ISBN 0-8371-3266-5.

As part of its program to publish catalogs of some of the great libraries in this country, Greenwood Press produced this 28-volume work of the holdings of the American Philosophical Society of Philadelphia. This catalog is of real significance to historical study because of its broad, comprehensive coverage of the publications of scientific academies. Material relating to Benjamin Franklin and to the study of evolution are especially important, as are the holdings relevant to American Indian linguistics. The catalog, like others of its type, reproduces catalog cards for each of the entries. Access is available primarily through author or subject. Journal articles in certain specialized areas are also included.

During the same year, Greenwood published a *Catalog of Manuscripts in the American Philosophical Society Library, Including the Archival Checklist* in 10 volumes. Again, catalog cards are reproduced, identifying a wealth of primary source material on early U.S. history. History of science materials date from about 1700. The most up-to-date guide to the Library's manuscript and archival collection is *A New Guide to the Collections in the Library of the American Philosophical Society. Memoirs of the American Philosophical Society*, v.66 by J. Stephen Catlett (APS, 1987). Information on these collections is also available through RLIN (p. xxi).

738. Natural History in America (1609–1860): Printed Works in the Collections of the American Philosophical Society, the Historical Society of Pennsylvania, the Library Company of Philadelphia. Andrea J. Tucher, comp. New York: Garland, 1985. 287p. (Americana to 1860: Four Bibliographies of Printed Works in the Collections of Three Philadelphia Libraries, v.4; Garland Reference Library of Social Science, v.232). ISBN 0-8240-8965-0.

This is the fourth volume in the series designed to provide commercial access to a union catalog of holdings in four subject areas of three great historical libraries in Philadelphia. It targets natural history, excluding anthropology. Included here are a wide variety of papers and publications of historic value, such as scientific reports, museum and society publications, travel logs, and broadsides. Organization of the work follows the pattern of previous volumes dealing with philanthropy (entry 671), agriculture (entry 920), and education (entry 676). The Mellon Foundation, by providing an endowment for the original project, has furnished a real benefit to scholars and serious students, although it has been suggested that, for this particular subject, the holdings of the Academy of Natural Sciences should have been included. Arrangement of entries is by author; there are subject indexes.

Bibliographical Sources

The *General Science Index* is a current monthly index of periodical articles. It has been produced by the H. W. Wilson Company since 1978 in print and since 1984 on CD-ROM. It is also available online through WILSONLINE. Publications treating the history of science are included. Historical coverage is also given in the bimonthly publication *Science Citation Index*, available since 1961 from the Institute for Scientific Information. This massive ongoing index is also available on both CD-ROM and online through DIALOG Information Service, where it comprises four different files.

739. **America in Space: An Annotated Bibliography.** Russell R. Tobias. Pasadena, CA: Salem, 1991. 327p. (Magill Bibliographies). ISBN 0-89356-669-1.

Like the other Salem Press Magill bibliographies, this work is intended for the less sophisticated inquirer and should serve both undergraduate and high school students needing material for term papers and reports. The strength of this work lies in its being recent and up to date in covering over 30 years of both technical and popular-interest publications of various types, including government documents. Annotations are well developed and furnish enough detail to describe and afford understanding of the work. Entries are arranged under several broad topical categories such as "Propulsion," "Manned Spacecraft," and "Earthbound Support." Some limitations noted by reviews suggest a rather weak index in terms of providing access for less knowledgeable patrons. Even so, the bibliography should benefit those individuals.

740. **American Medical Imprints, 1820–1910: A Checklist of Publications Illustrating the History and Progress of Medical Science, Medical Education, and the Healing Arts in the United States: A Preliminary Contribution.** Francesco Cordasco. Totowa, NJ: Rowman & Littlefield, 1985. 2v. ISBN 0-8476-7338-3.

There are nearly 36,000 titles of monographs, addresses, and off-prints furnished in this comprehensive bibliography of early medical imprints from the United States. The author is a well-known bibliographer and has arranged this work into nine divisions by decade of publication. Arrangement of entries is alphabetical by author within these groupings. The work started as an interest piece for Cordasco, who is a hobbyist-collector of eighteenth-century medical books and has patterned his work as a continuation of Robert B. Austin's *Early American Medical Imprints, 1668–1820* (U.S. Department of Health, Education and Welfare, 1961). The decade ending in 1910 was chosen because of its pivotal nature as a benchmark in the transition toward modern medical practice. Although most entries are not annotated, descriptive comments do appear. Because of the unique coverage of this effort, it retains an important position in the minds of scholars and serious students.

741. **Bibliography of the History of Medicine.** Bethesda, MD: National Library of Medicine, 1965– . No.1– . Ann.

The leading U.S. serial bibliography on the history of medicine, this title began in 1965 when the *Bulletin of the History of Medicine* (described in the paragraph below) ceased publication. Its specific nature makes it a real asset to serious inquiry in the field and brings together journal articles and monographs from all over the world in a variety of languages.

Most articles are drawn from *Index Medicus*, produced by the MEDLARS/MEDLINE database. Also included are symposia, congresses, and conference proceedings, as well as specific sections or parts of general monographs. There is an attempt to avoid duplication with the bibliographic portion of *Isis* (entry 746). The history of U.S. medicine receives a greater proportion of the total coverage than it receives in its British counterpart, *Current Works in the History of Medicine* (Wellcome Historical Medical Library), which has been issued as a quarterly since 1954.

The *Bibliography of the History of Medicine of the United States and Canada, 1939–1960* by Genevieve Miller (Arco Press, 1964; repr. 1979) is a compilation and consolidation of the bibliographies published annually from 1940 to 1960 in the *Bulletin of the History of Medicine*. The basic classified arrangement under 16 major headings was established originally by the noted scholar Henry Sigerist. After 1964, the bulletin ceased its publication of the bibliography; since then the bibliography has been continued as an annual, with quinquennial cumulations by the U.S. Public Health Service of Bethesda, MD.

742. **Early American Scientific and Technical Literature: An Annotated Bibliography of Books, Pamphlets, and Broadsides.** Margaret W. Batschelet. Metuchen, NJ: Scarecrow, 1990. 136p. ISBN 0-8108-2318-7.

Considered one of the best historical bibliographies for its year of publication by a committee of the American Library Association's Reference and Adult Services Division, this selective, recent work supplies over 800 entries relevant to U.S. science and engineering published between 1665 and 1799. The natural and physical sciences are covered, as are medicine and technology. Entries represent primary source material of use to scholars and serious inquirers and are arranged chronologically in three major sections covering medical titles, technical science titles, and physical science titles. Annotations are furnished in most entries, which are brief but informative. Most titles are included in the *Early American Imprint Series* (entry 49n), for which identification numbers are furnished. The work is accessed by both author and subject indexes, the latter of which has been criticized as being minimal in depth. A more intensive effort is the one by Harkanyi (entry 747).

743. **A Guide to the Culture of Science, Technology and Medicine.** [Updated ed.]. Paul T. Durbin, gen. ed. New York: Free Press, 1984. 735p. ISBN 0-0290-7890-3 **(paperback).**

One of the few titles in this section not linked specifically to U.S. science is this outstanding guide underwritten by both the National Science Foundation and the National Endowment for the Humanities. It is an update of a 1980 effort. It consists of a series of nine essays, each accompanied by a set of bibliographic listings. The sections range from nearly 40 to nearly 70 pages in length, each written by a scholar in the field. Emphasis is given to the history of disciplines, with analyses of their methods, technologies, and relationships to other studies. Social and cultural values are examined, and the current conditions of the historical and philosophical disciplines are described with respect to their study of science, technology, and medicine. Meaning and relationship of values to science and technology are described extensively in the introductory section. More than 3,200 titles are furnished in the bibliography; scholars and serious students profit from the effort.

744. **The History of Science and Technology in the United States: A Critical and Selective Bibliography.** Marc Rothenberg. New York: Garland, 1982. 242p. (Garland Reference Library of the Humanities, v.308; Bibliographies of the History of Science and Technology, v.2). ISBN 0-8240-9278-3.

The author, a historian of science who previously edited the Joseph Henry papers at the Smithsonian Institution, is especially well qualified by experience and expertise to develop a survey bibliography of this type. He has done an excellent job in selecting the list of over 830 secondary sources from an initial pool of twice that number. This volume provides a modern perception of the discipline—most references date from between 1940 and 1980. Medicine is excluded as a topic. Entries represent books, articles, and dissertations and are arranged in several chapters covering bibliographies, special themes, physical sciences, biological sciences, social sciences, and technology. Entries furnish annotations, many of which are evaluative in nature, and will benefit inquirers at all levels. Both author and subject indexes provide access.

American Science and Technology: A Bicentennial Bibliography by George W. Black, Jr. (Southern Illinois University, 1979) identifies 1,065 articles derived from a base of some 1,500 journals cited in five of the Wilson Company indexes. The major limitation, historically, is that the articles are all published in 1976, a constraint that limits its value for serious inquiry. Coverage is broad, and most science/technology areas are included, resulting in a useful work for the interested layperson and possibly the beginning researcher.

745. **The History of Surgery in the United States, 1775–1900.** Ira M. Rutkow. San Francisco: Norman, 1988. v.1– . (In progress). (Norman Bibliography Series, no.2; Norman Surgery Series, no.2). ISBN 0-930405-02-1.

This is the first volume of a projected four-volume annotated bibliography of various publications written by U.S. surgeons. It thus serves as an access tool to primary source material relevant to the development of surgery in this country. Included here are surgical monographs, textbooks, studies, and treatises published during a period of 125 years beginning with the Revolutionary era. More than 550 books are cited in eight chapters covering different types of surgery (general surgery, ophthalmology, otorhinolaryngology, orthopedic surgery, gynecology, urology, colon/rectal surgery, and neurosurgery). Arrangement of entries is chronological within the chapters. Annotations vary in length and may include not only content description but also biographical information on authors and illustrators, as well as printing history. There are 130 reproductions taken from some of the listed works and a selective bibliography of study material. Access is provided through a name/subject index.

746. **Isis: An International Review Devoted to the History of Science and Its Cultural Influences. Current Bibliography.** Philadelphia: History of Science Society, 1913– . Ann. ISSN 0021-1753.

The major journal of international proportions began in 1913 with the efforts of George Sarton and today continues as the official journal of the History of Science Society. The *Current Bibliography* (known until 1988 as the *Critical Bibliography*) is issued at the close of each year and furnishes a comprehensive listing of secondary publications in the field (books, essays, journal articles, and reviews). The pattern generally has been to cover reference and general interest publications in the initial segment, followed by the various branches and periods of study. U.S. science is treated, along with that of other nations. There is an index of names.

Retrospective bibliography is well served with *Isis Cumulative Bibliography: A Bibliography of the History of Science Formed from Isis Critical Bibliographies 1–90, 1913–1965*, edited by Magda Whitrow (Mansell, 1971–1989, 6v.). This work is supplemented by *Isis Cumulative Bibliography, 1966–1975: A Bibliography of the History of Science Formed from Isis Critical Bibliographies 91–100, Indexing Literature Published from 1965 Through 1974*, edited by John Neu (Mansell, 1980-1985. 2v.) and finally by *Isis Cumulative Bibliography, 1976–1985*, also by Neu (Mansell, 1989. 2v.). Of real benefit to research is the publication of the first *Isis Cumulative Index, 1953–1982* in 1985, which facilitates a search for specific issues and topics.

747. **The Natural Sciences and American Scientists in the Revolutionary Era: A Bibliography.** Katalin Harkanyi, comp. Westport, CT: Greenwood, 1990. 510p. (Bibliographies and Indexes in American History, no.17). ISBN 0-313-26547-X.

This is a comprehensive bibliography of about 5,100 entries on science and scientists in this country during its formative period. Publications were issued between 1760 and 1789 and represent a fertile yield for the scholar and serious student. Writers and authors were American colonists and U.S. citizens. Natural science as a branch of study was broadly interpreted to include such disciplines as mathematics and geology, as well as architecture and travel literature. Although the work is comprehensive in nature, certain categories or types of people were excluded: Canadians, émigrés, and immigrants who arrived after the middle of the century. There are several appendices, including a chronology of accomplishments and listings of scientists by discipline. Brief annotations are given in some of the entries. For a more selective work, see the one by Margaret Batschelet (entry 742).

748. **Technology and Values in American Civilization: A Guide to Information Sources.** Stephen H. Cutcliffe et al. Detroit: Gale, 1980. 704p. (Gale Information Guide Library; American Studies Information Guide Series, v.9). ISBN 0-8103-1475-4.

Of value to scholars and serious students, this unique guide to technology in U.S. life identifies a variety of materials and therefore can facilitate the beginning of research. Nearly 2,150 items are listed that include monographs, articles, bibliographies, symposia, government documents, newsletters, and indexing and abstracting services. Entries are organized under 20-odd broad subject divisions, with general overview sections followed by specific study areas such as "Labor and the Work Process," "Transportation," and "Art." Arrangement of entries is alphabetical by author or title within these segments, and annotations are descriptive of content. The value of this work lies in its focus on technology and its effects on civilization; history of science is excluded. Access is enhanced by a detailed table of contents as well as author, title, and subject indexes.

Information Sources

Science in America: A Documentary History, 1900–1939, edited by Nathan Reingold and Ida H. Reingold (University of Chicago, 1981), provides useful and immediate access to source documents, such as correspondence, as well as descriptive narrative regarding issues, institutions, and individuals involved in U.S. science in the early twentieth century.

749. **Great American Bridges and Dams.** Donald C. Jackson. Washington, DC: Preservation Press, 1988. 357p. (Great American Places Series). ISBN 0-89133-129-8.

This attractive, well-illustrated work was developed by the National Trust for Historic Preservation as a guidebook to the most important extant bridges and dams from the nineteenth and twentieth centuries. The author, a technology historian, provides exposition of each site with respect to its place within the framework of technological development in this country. The book places emphasis on older structures but includes a full array of types and sizes. Three introductory essays describe the history of bridges and dams and offer a plea for increased attempts at preservation. Entries for individual sites are divided into six geographical regions, which are subdivided by state, then city in directory fashion. Brief narratives are furnished, with key details of construction highlighted in the margins. An index concludes the work, which should appeal to all levels of inquirers.

750. **The Historic American Engineering Record.** Alexandria, VA: Chadwyck-Healey. (n.d.). 870 microfiche.

The Historic American Engineering Record (HAER) was created in 1969 as a joint undertaking of the Library of Congress, the American Society of Civil Engineers, and the National Park Service. Catalogs and other publications have generally been published under the auspices of the National Park Service. Recently, Chadwyck-Healey, in one of its large microfiche projects, has made available certain selected reports, along with illustrations documenting sites and structures throughout the United States. Included are over 20,000 pages of text and 24,000 photographs describing over 1,800 canneries, mines, railways, arsenals, breweries, dams, gristmills, bridges, and windmills; even a rocket launcher is treated. The entries were selected for their capacity to provide enlightenment in the development of U.S. technology and to furnish both historical descriptions and technical analyses. Arrangement of entries is alphabetical by place name under state, then county. Each state begins on a separate set of microfiche.

751. **Medicine and Society in America: 1660–1860.** Richard H. Shryock. New York: New York University Press, 1960. 182p. (Anson G. Phelps Lectureship on Early American History).

Before his death in 1973 at the age of 81, Professor Shryock established an enviable reputation as a medical historian. This work contains the four talks he delivered while serving as the Anson Phelps Lecturer on early U.S. history at New York University in 1959. Coverage is given to "Origins of a Medical Profession," "Medical Thought and Practice, 1660–1820," "Health and Disease, 1660–1820," and "Medicine in Society and Transition, 1820–1860." Because the content's origin lies within the realm of oral communication, documentation is lightly treated, but the insights and wealth of information make this a useful work for all levels of inquirers. The author is especially adept at tracing the development of his specialties within the fabric or context of both social and political history. It is still considered a rewarding and enlightening vehicle (although not a reference tool).

752. **Two Centuries of American Medicine, 1776–1976.** James Bordley and A. McGehee Harvey. Philadelphia: Saunders, 1976. 844p. ISBN 0-7216-1873-1.

Considered the standard history of U.S. medicine, this work was developed as a historical survey to benefit both physicians and the educated public. Only about 100 pages, or one-eighth of the total, is given to the first of the three historical segments (1776–1876) into which the work is divided. Progress in U.S. medicine was linked to discoveries in England and on the European continent during this time. The period 1876–1945 is covered thoroughly, with improved treatments and diagnoses being described along with the developing awareness of the role of microorganisms, hormones, and diets. The final period, 1946–1976, occupies more than half the total narrative and delineates the great advances in this brief span. In each segment, coverage is given to education, public health, preventive medicine, hospitals, and research.

A new publication is *Disease and Medical Care in the United States: A Medical Atlas of the 20th Century* by Gary W. Shannon and Gerald F. Pyle (Macmillan, 1993). This work enumerates the patterns of disease and medical care through regional, state, and metropolitan area maps. A glossary is provided.

Biographical Sources

753. **American Engineers of the Nineteenth Century: A Biographical Index.** Christine Roysdon and Linda A. Khatri. New York: Garland, 1978. 247p. (Garland Reference Library of Social Science, v.53). ISBN 0-8240-9827-7.

Because biographical information on technologists and engineers is relatively difficult to find, this unique biographical index of some 2,000 individuals who were active during the middle and later stages of the nineteenth century is especially useful. All individuals were deceased by the end of the year 1900 and were associated with engineering projects involving railroads, canals, or innovative applications of iron and steel processes. Entries cite coverage in over 30 technical periodicals. References are also furnished to biographical information in the *New York Times* and the *Dictionary of American Biography* (entry 143). Entries furnish birth and death dates, field of interest and activity, and indication of portraits. The work is a convenient tool for scholars, students, and members of the general public who have an interest in the topic.

754. **American Men & Women of Science, 1992–1993: A Biographical Directory of Today's Leaders in Physical, Biological and Related Sciences.** 18th ed. New York: Bowker, 1992. 8v. ISBN 0-8352-3074-0 (complete set).

This is one of the respected biographical dictionaries and represents coverage of some 150,000 living scientists from every field from mathematics to public health and computer sciences. Historically, the publication has been important since its debut in 1906; "& women" was added to the title after the 11th edition (1968). Early editions furnish useful biographical information of past achievers, many of whom are obscure today. The work enjoys an excellent reputation for maintaining a high standard with respect to invited entries; quality research or a significant and influential position is a required for inclusion. Information is supplied to the editorial staff through questionnaires returned by the biographees, producing entries on achievements and career developments. Publication has been irregular throughout its existence; the 18th edition (1992) was issued only two years after the 17th in 1990. A cumulative index to the first 14 editions was published in 1983.

755. **American Nursing: A Biographical Dictionary.** Vern L. Bullough, et al., eds. New York: Garland, 1988–1992. 2v. (Garland Reference Library of Social Science, v.368, 684). ISBN 0-8240-8540-X (v.1); 0-8240-7201-4 (v.2).

Volume 1 of this biographical dictionary furnishes coverage of 177 U.S. nurses (175 female, 2 male) who are considered to have made an important contribution to the profession and were either deceased by 1988 or born prior to the year 1890. Volume 2 extends the coverage to those born between 1891 and 1915 or deceased between 1988 and 1991. Numerous contributors furnish lengthy biographical essays describing the biographees' career accomplishments and personal information and listing books and articles written by them. Also included is a bibliography. Indexes furnish access by decade of birth (before and beyond 1840), nursing school attended, special interest, or activities. This should prove useful to both researchers and students.

Similar coverage is given by Martin Kaufman in the *Dictionary of American Nursing Biography* (Greenwood, 1988), which treats 196 nurses who were historically important and died prior to January 31, 1987. Entries furnish basic biographical coverage such as education, contributions, and writings, with references supplied. There appears to be more emphasis on contemporary nurses here than in the Bullough effort, although 109 of the nurses are covered in both titles. Appendices furnish listings by birthplace and specialty. Indexing is detailed.

756. **Biographical Index to American Science: The Seventeenth Century to 1920.** Clark A. Elliott. Westport, CT: Greenwood, 1990. 300p. (Bibliographies and Indexes in American History, no.16). ISBN 0-3132-6566-6.

This is a comprehensive biographical index prepared as a companion volume to the *Biographical Dictionary of American Science* (described below). It is extensive in its coverage and furnishes brief biographical entries for about 2,850 individuals representing a real cross-section of scientists from all disciplines over a period of 250 years. Entries are arranged alphabetically and furnish information regarding dates, field of activity, and occupation. References to various sources for further and more extensive biographical coverage are included as well. Sources used are biographical dictionaries, scientific journals, proceedings of associations, and collective biography. There is an index of scientists by subject field.

The *Biographical Dictionary of American Science: The Seventeenth Through the Nineteenth Centuries*, also compiled by Elliott (Greenwood, 1979), is a useful biographical dictionary of nearly 600 individuals who were not included in the *American Men & Women of Science* (entry 754), as well as 300 who were. Entries run between 300 and 400 words. Appendices furnish listings by birth date, birthplace, and education. An index is provided. The two Elliott titles are complementary to each other and are useful to inquirers at all levels.

757. **Dictionary of American Medical Biography.** Martin Kaufman, et al., eds. Westport, CT: Greenwood, 1984. 2v. ISBN 0-313-21378-X.

Considered a real contribution to the study of U.S. medicine, this work assumes the same title as the Kelly publication described below. The recent effort furnishes biographical coverage of more than 1,000 persons perceived to have made contributions to medicine or public health between the seventeenth and the twentieth centuries. Biographees were all deceased by the end of 1976. There is a conscious inclusion of blacks and women and a variety of occupations other than physicians; covered are nurses, administrators, educators, biochemists, even health faddists and patent medicine manufacturers. Entries are arranged alphabetically and furnish dates, geographical information, career information, family circumstances, education, and writings. Several appendices offer various listings; the work is indexed.

The *Dictionary of American Medical Biography: Lives of Eminent Physicians of the United States and Canada from the Earliest Times* by Howard A. Kelly and Walter L. Burrage (Appleton, 1928) was originally issued in 1912, then again in 1920 under a different title. Biographies of more than 2,000 deceased physicians and surgeons from the colonial period to 1927 are provided. It has been reprinted on several occasions, most recently in 1978 by Longwood Press of West Newfield, Maine.

758. **Who Was Who in American History—Science and Technology: A Component of Who's Who in American History.** Chicago: Marquis Who's Who, 1976. 688p. ISBN 0-8379-3601-2.

Part of the Marquis *Who's Who* series, this work furnishes about 10,000 biographical sketches of deceased Americans prominent in science and technology from the colonial period to the mid-1970s. Entries are brief and describe inventors, scientists, and engineers in the customary familiar format of the publisher. Selections were drawn from the first six volumes of *Who Was Who in America* (entry 139), with coverage up to 1973. Given are birth and death dates, parentage, education, marriage, positions, accomplishments, publications, honors, and awards. Another plus is the inclusion of pronunciation symbols for a number of names perceived to be difficult. The Marquis publications are respected for their high quality and maintenance of standards in terms of selection. In the cases of unverified entries, these are so noted; the work should be useful for inquirers at all levels.

THE LAW AND CRIME

U.S. jurisprudence has long been the subject of scrutiny in terms of its fairness, application, and administration. Crime and its subsequent punishment has been examined in similar manner and recently has become a topic of increasingly volatile debate, especially as it concerns the death penalty. Included in this segment are those tools, primarily bibliographic, that may prove useful to the social historian interested in such issues.

Related materials may be found in other segments of this guide; Constitutional history with its legal interpretations is found in chapter 3, "Politics and Government." Slavery as a legal question is treated elsewhere in the present chapter, in the section on "Ethnic, Racial and Gender Influences" in the coverage given to "The Black Experience."

The American Society for Legal History was founded in 1956 and has 1,100 members. It operates out of the Department of History at the University of Mississippi and has published a semiannual journal, *Law and History Review,* since 1983.

Bibliographical Sources

The varied types of publications in the field of law include law reviews, scholarly journals, legal newspapers, and bar association publications. The online services *WESTLAW* (West Publishing) and *LEXIS* (Mead Data Central) furnish both bibliographic and full-text information to federal and state case law for lawyers and legal researchers. For legal historians, the monthly index from the H. W. Wilson Company, *Index to Legal Periodicals,* should also prove beneficial. Dating back to 1908, it indexes several hundred periodicals from English-speaking countries. Now an annual cumulation, it furnishes access to author, subjects, cases, and book reviews. It is available online through WILSONLINE. A complementary work is *Index to Periodical Articles Related to Law,* a quarterly publication from Glanville Publishers that has been issued since 1958. It identifies in selective fashion important articles from journals not covered by the Wilson index. *Criminology & Penology Abstracts* (Kluger Publications, 1980–) began as *Excerpta Criminologica* (1961–1968) and from 1969 to 1979 was known as *Abstracts on Criminology and Penology* before finally assuming its present name in 1980. It is the premier international abstracting service for criminological studies. For more applied research on crime and the criminal, one should consult both *Criminal Justice Abstracts* (National Council on Crime and Delinquency, 1977–), available on microfiche, and *Criminal Justice Periodical Index* (University Microfilms). The latter indexes over 100 journals, newsletters, and law reporters on all types of crime. It is available through DIALOG and is updated monthly.

759. **American Judicial Proceedings First Printed Before 1801: An Analytical Bibliography.** Wilfred J. Ritz, comp. Westport, CT: Greenwood, 1984. 364p. ISBN 0-313-24057-4.
This comprehensive bibliography furnishes listings of all judicial proceedings on record as having occurred prior to 1801. Included are law reports, trials, rules of court, and separate events for which something other than newspaper accounts was printed. Both primary and secondary source materials are included. The value of the effort lies primarily in the uniqueness of its coverage of the earliest years of U.S. jurisprudence prior to the adoption of the Constitution. Included also are English judicial proceedings relating to the colonies and U.S. reprints of European proceedings. There is an introduction, followed by an analytical section identifying references in over 65 bibliographic sources such as Evans (entry 39) and locations in over 100 libraries. Many of the materials are available in microform through the *Early American Imprints Project* (entry 49n).

760. **Capital Punishment in America: An Annotated Bibliography.** Michael L. Radelet and Margaret Vandiver. New York: Garland, 1988. 243p. (Garland Reference Library of Social Science, v.466). ISBN 0-8240-1623-8.

This is a listing of more than 1,000 publications in the English language reflecting the growing interest and debate on the topic. Emphasis is on the post-1972 period, and events of the 1970s to 1980s are covered well, complementing the Triche work described below. Accessibility of material is one criterion for inclusion, and the books and articles are considered readily available in public and academic libraries. Annotations are brief and informative. Arrangement of entries is alphabetical by author as organized under three major format divisions: books and articles, congressional publications, and Supreme Court decisions. Newspaper articles have been purposely omitted because of what was perceived as a lack of accessibility. A subject index is furnished.

Charles W. Triche's *The Capital Punishment Dilemma, 1950–1977: A Subject Bibliography* (Whitston, 1979) furnishes an extensive listing of books, essays, pamphlets, and government documents written over a span of more than 25 years prior to its publication. Unlike the more recent effort above, Triche's volume includes newspaper writings. An author index provides access.

761. **Crime in America: Historical Patterns and Contemporary Realities.** Francesco Cordasco and David N. Alloway. New York: Garland, 1985. 345p. (Garland Reference Library of Social Science, v.264). ISBN 0-8240-8901-4.

Like most of Cordasco's other bibliographies, this one furnishes an extensive listing and thus serves researchers and students as a useful tool, providing access to literature dating from the mid-1960s. Entries are organized into 17 chapters that treat broad topics. Recent phenomena such as computer crimes and victimology are conspicuous by their presence and should increase the volume's appeal to the general public. Coverage includes listings of major reference works, periodical titles, and organizations in the field. There is an author index to provide access.

Crime and Punishment in America: A Historical Bibliography (ABC-Clio, 1984) is another spin-off from the great database that produces *America: History and Life* (entry 51). This tool focuses much more intensively on the periodical literature than does the Cordasco effort. Nearly 1,400 entries (with abstracts) identify articles published between 1973 and 1982; they cover criminal justice in this country from the colonial period to the present. Both author and subject indexes are given.

762. **Criminal Activity in the Deep South, 1700–1930: An Annotated Bibliography.** A. J. Wright, comp. New York: Greenwood, 1989. 261p. (Research and Bibliographical Guides in Criminal Justice, no.1). ISBN 0-313-23798-0.

Initiating a new series for Greenwood Press is this bibliography focused on regional crime over a period of 140 years. The South has presented the world with a great enigma, being the most hospitable of regions yet capable of perpetrating violent inhuman acts to protect its way of life. Wright separates a good part of the South from this work, excluding crimes associated with slave revolts, Klan activities, Indian-white encounters, and military and labor violence. What is left is the general antisocial behavior found in any region or state (murder, robbery, etc.), here limited again to acts associated with economic gain. More than 1,250 entries are arranged alphabetically by author, then organized by state and format (monographs, dissertations, theses, journal and newspaper articles). There are indexes by author, subject, and personal name.

763. Criminal Justice in America, 1959-1984: An Annotated Bibliography. John D. Hewitt, et al. New York: Garland, 1985. 347p. (Applied Social Science Bibliographies, v.2; Garland Reference Library of Social Science, v.271). ISBN 0-8240-8813-1.

Focusing on the recent past, this annotated bibliography identifies over 800 books, articles, dissertations, and government documents in the field of criminal justice over a 25-year period. The work is organized under three major areas of inquiry—law enforcement, courts, and corrections—each of which is covered in four chapters devoted to history, organization, process, and issues. Entries are placed within the proper segments and are given lengthy annotations describing their content. All users will profit from this work, including students, scholars, practitioners, and the general public. Coverage varies with each segment depending upon the availability of literature on the topics. The authors, academicians in sociology and criminal justice, were able to make good judgments in their selection of the "essential literature." There are indexes of personal names and of subjects.

764. Criminological Bibliographies: Uniform Citations to Bibliographies, Indexes, and Review Articles of the Literature of Crime Study in the United States. Bruce L. Davis, comp. Westport, CT: Greenwood, 1978. 182p. ISBN 0-313-20545-0.

Of real interest to historians is this bibliography of bibliographies on criminology. Each of the works cited either was published in the United States or has substantial segments of the text devoted to U.S. efforts. There are upwards of 1,400 bibliographies published over a period of more than 100 years from the third quarter of the nineteenth century to 1977. The focus is on materials of value to social science study, so both scholars and students benefit from the use. Bibliographic works include separately published bibliographies, indexes, review articles, current serials, and catalogs on the topic. Legal literature is excluded. Arrangement of entries is chronological within seven broad divisions, each of which furnishes a detailed subject index. There is a general table of agency sources and a comprehensive index to compilers at the end. In many cases, library locations are given for the bibliographies.

765. Criminology Index: Research and Theory in Criminology in the United States, 1945-1972. Marvin E. Wolfgang, et al. New York: Elsevier, 1975. 2v. ISBN 0-444-99002-X.

Resulting from a National Science Foundation grant to determine the availability of and need for literature on criminology, this work lists over 3,000 articles and 550 books and reports representing both theoretical and empirical inquiry. Because of the piece's focus on research, scholars and serious students benefit most from the coverage given the various topics in what turns out to be a combination bibliography and citation index to the publications of a period of 27 years. The work is divided into three major segments, the first of which is a bibliography of two parts covering articles, books, dissertations, and reports. This section has complete citations; both the subject index and the citation index give brief references to the source index. The citation index lists all references (footnotes) used in the entries in the source index and therefore occupies the bulk of the two volumes.

766. Law Books, 1876-1981: Books and Serials on Law and Its Related Subjects. New York: Bowker, 1981. 4v. ISBN 0-8352-1397-8.

Another of the spin-off bibliographies, this one is drawn primarily from the Bowker database that produces *American Book Publishing Record* in combination with the *National Union Catalog* (entry 38) and MARC tapes from the Library of Congress. Truly comprehensive in nature, it contains about 130,000 entries of books on law and law-related topics classified under 39,000 subject headings employed by the Library of Congress. Entries are arranged alphabetically by author within those subjects and furnish complete title, author statement, imprint, collation, and series statement. Also given are content note, LC classification number, Dewey Decimal classification number, LC card number, and tracings. In this manner, the entries are duplicated several times under different subjects. The fourth volume provides author and title indexes to all entries as well as listings of publishers, distributors, database suppliers, and vendors.

767. **Watergate: An Annotated Bibliography of Sources in English, 1972–1982.** Myron Smith. Metuchen, NJ: Scarecrow, 1983. 329p. ISBN 0-8108-1623-7.

Because of Watergate's importance in the shaping of history, social historians at all levels will continue to study the episode and its implications for many years. As a result, it is the only specific event given coverage among the works in this section. More than 2,500 English-language publications representing both primary and secondary source material are identified and listed alphabetically. These were published over a span of 10 years tracing the revelations through newspaper accounts, books, articles, scholarly papers, government documents, dissertations, theses, and personal memoirs. There is a listing of video and sound recordings at the end. Entries are given annotations of varying length ranging from a sentence to a full paragraph. There is a chronology of events from 1972 to 1975, and a House Judiciary Committee report on the Nixon impeachment investigation.

Information Sources

768. **The Encyclopedia of American Crime.** Carl Sifakis. New York: Facts on File, 1982. 802p. ISBN 0-87196-620-4.

This is an interesting and useful reference book furnishing more than 1,700 entries on the topic of crime in the United States. Sifakis is a crime reporter who carefully researched the records and provides clear descriptions of people, events, reports, and organizations. Included are explanations of various crimes, historical treatment of different agencies, exposition of trials, and definitions of slang. Coverage varies in length and extends from the precolonial period to the present day. Individual biographies present a diverse group of criminals, detectives, lawyers, reporters, criminologists, and judges, beginning with some of the early Vikings and ending with John Hinckley. There are numerous black-and-white photographs, charts, and drawings. Cross-references are furnished between entries, and the index provides access through subject and geographic headings.

Criminal Justice History (Meckler, 1980–) is an international annual devoted to the history of crime and criminal justice, particularly in their broader social, legal, and institutional contexts. It publishes research and historiographical articles, comparative and interpretive essays, conference assessments, book reviews, and reviews of the discipline and of current historical issues. Significant attention is given to the history and analysis of crime and criminal justice in the United States.

769. **The Guide to American Law: Everyone's Legal Encyclopedia.** St. Paul, MN: West, 1983–1985. 12v. ISBN 0-314-73221-1. **Ann. Supp.** 1990– . ISSN 1052-8253.

Because of its comprehensiveness and thorough coverage of the field, this work has been included here when others have been omitted. Considered the only guide of this size designed to explain legal concepts to laymen and nonjurists, it succeeds admirably in furnishing exposition of over 5,000 topics. Students of history profit from its inclusion of material pertinent to landmark documents, constitutional rights, and the famous trials of the past. There were numerous contributors to these volumes, and most of the articles are signed. Arrangement of entries (and volumes) is alphabetical, with each volume containing a detailed subject index. Heightening the interest and utility of this work for all its users is the inclusion of old prints, cartoons, and photographs. Since 1990, the title has received an annual supplement.

Historic U.S. Court Cases, 1690–1990: An Encyclopedia, edited by John W. Johnson (Garland, 1992), is a handy compilation of essays on important court cases tried over a 300-year period. There are more than 170 essays written by 80 specialists that identify major themes in U.S. history and law and probe the decisions. The work is useful to students of history, specialists, and even laypersons.

JOURNALISM

The free press is one of the necessary ingredients to a free society. It is through the notable efforts of journalists that some of history's great scandals and governmental excesses have been brought to light and recorded. Journalism is broadly interpreted here to reflect the various media by which information is disseminated. The history of U.S. journalism, both print and nonprint, offers a rich and varied study reflecting the diversity of the individual and of society.

The reference tools in this section represent that diversity, focusing on the personalities as covered in biographical sources. It is largely through the study of the lives of the more colorful, memorable, and often prominent and influential writers and reporters that the United States has come to appreciate its fourth estate.

The American Photographic Historical Society was founded in 1969 in New York City. It has 500 members and has issued a quarterly journal, *Photographica*, since 1969. Both photojournalists and hobbyists subscribe.

Library Resources

770. **Guide to Sources in American Journalism History.** Lucy S. Caswell, ed. and comp. New York: Greenwood, 1989. 319p. (Bibliographies and Indexes in Mass Media and Communications, no.2). ISBN 0-313-26178-4.

Issued as the second offering in the recent Greenwood series, this title serves as a guide to resources relating to the study of the history of U.S. journalism. The work is prepared under the auspices of the American Journalism Historians Association and opens with several essays on historiography; bibliographic works, including indexes, abstracts, and bibliographies; computerized databases; and oral history. The major segment of the tool furnishes a directory of the major repositories of archival and manuscript materials found in about 40 states, primarily in universities or historical agencies. Beneficial to scholars and serious students, it arranges entries alphabetically by state and furnishes brief descriptions and identifications. Included are names, addresses, phone numbers, hours, and holdings, with an indication of size of collections in linear feet and a brief exposition of subjects.

Bibliographical Sources

Today, a number of indexes, both print and online, are available with which to search the content of newspapers. See the subsection on newspapers under "Bibliographies and Catalogs" in chapter 1.

771. **ABC News Index.** Woodbridge, CT: Research Publications, 1986– . Quart. with ann. cum. ISSN 0891-8775.

A specialized index of importance to students and researchers of recent history in the field of journalism, this work identifies transcripts on microfiche available through *ABC News Transcripts* (Research Publications, 1986–), which gives complete transcripts of the important ABC news programs. *ABC News Closeup, Nightline, 20/20, World News Tonight,* and others are furnished on a quarterly basis from 1970 to the present. The Index furnishes quick access to content of transcripts also on a quarterly basis, with the fourth number issued as a hardbound annual cumulation. A 1970–1985 cumulated index was issued in two volumes in 1990. Arrangement is topical by Library of Congress subject headings, alphabetically arranged. Brief abstracts are given, along with dates, program, and fiche number. It furnishes access by name, subject, and program.

A similar publication is the *CBS News Index* (University Microfilms International, 1975–), a quarterly index with annual cumulations enumerating CBS news transcripts on microfilm. The monthly *Television News Index and Abstracts* (Vanderbilt Television News Archive, 1968–) identifies Vanderbilt University's massive videotape holdings (some 27,000 hours of broadcast time to date) of network evening news programs.

For some time, Journal Graphics, Inc. has provided transcripts and/or videotape copies of over 160 news magazines and talk shows (such as CNN's *Crossfire,* ABC News' *20/20* and *Nightline,* and *Larry King Live*) as well as PBS, cable, and network documentaries (such as *Frontline* and *CBS News Special Reports*), some going back to 1968 and thus of great historical value. A very useful source providing access to Journal Graphics' vast and growing news/documentary archives is the *Journal Graphics Video and Transcript Index Guide* (Journal Graphics, Inc., 2v., ann., with monthly updates), also available online through the *CARL library consortium database, *LEXIS/NEXIS, and *Dow Jones News Retrieval. Broadcasts are indexed under over 250 topic headings, such as "abortion" or "capital punishment"; abstracts of each program are also provided. There is a "topic alert service" that keeps customers informed of any new broadcasts covering a given subject. There are also specialty indexes covering newsworthy topics such as the environment, political/social issues, and banking and finance. Those wishing to order transcripts and/or video tapes or who wish further information on the service may call toll-free 1 (800) 825-5746 or write Journal Graphics, 1535 Grant St., Denver, CO, 80203.

772. **American Journalism History: An Annotated Bibliography.** William D. Sloan, comp. New York: Greenwood, 1989. 344p. (Bibliographies and Indexes in Mass Media and Communications, no.1). ISBN 0-313-26350-7.

This useful and convenient annotated bibliography furnishes scholars and serious students with a listing of more than 2,650 books and articles relevant to the history of both print and nonprint journalism. Selection was limited to those items perceived to be the most useful and includes biographies, histories, expositions, and other types of materials. Entries are organized chronologically under categories ranging from "The Colonial Press, 1690–1765" to "Contemporary Media, 1945–Present." Annotations vary in size from very brief to 150–200 words long. There is a miscellaneous segment at the beginning that treats general history from the colonial period to the present. Access is furnished by a general index of names, subjects, and titles.

The Journalist's Bookshelf: An Annotated and Selected Bibliography of United States Print Journalism by Roland Wolsey (R. J. Berg, 1986), now in its eighth edition, excludes broadcast journalism and furnishes listings suitable to the general public. Entries are arranged under topical divisions.

773. **Newspapers: A Reference Guide.** Richard A. Schwarzlose. New York: Greenwood, 1987. 417p. (American Popular Culture). ISSN 0193-6859.

From Greenwood Press comes this unique bibliography on U.S. newspapers that should prove useful to both students and scholars interested in the history and development of the newspaper press. About 1,700 books and articles are identified through bibliographic essays organized into nine chapters covering reference sources, newspaper histories, newspaper work, production, social role, legal issues, technology, and so forth. Text focuses on the research value of the books and articles enumerated; essays are followed by listings of the publications in each chapter. All materials are in English and considered to be readily available in university libraries. The essays are well written and offer historical perspective on the role of the newspaper in U.S. society. There is a chronology, a listing of research collections, and an index of authors, titles, and subjects.

774. **The Nineteenth Century Photographic Press: A Study Guide.** Robert S. Sennett. New York: Garland, 1987. 97p. (Garland Reference Library of the Humanities, v.694). ISBN 0-8240-8544-2.

Historically, the photographic press has played an important role in the documentation of U.S. history, especially since the period of the Civil War and the work of Matthew Brady. This concise guide is an important vehicle for research and study, providing focus on those early years and the coverage given to photography's emergence during that period. The journal literature of the years 1840–1899 is identified here, the intent being to include listings from every U.S. and European journal relevant to the study of photography. Coverage is selective rather than comprehensive. Although there are the usual number of omissions and technical flaws characteristic of a work of this type, it should be used by those with a serious interest. Entries are arranged chronologically under journal titles, which are organized alphabetically.

Information Sources

775. **Special Edition: A Guide to Network Television Documentary Series and Special News Reports, 1955–1979.** Daniel Einstein. Metuchen, NJ: Scarecrow, 1987. 1,051p. ISBN 0-8108-1898-1.

This useful handbook furnishes a great deal of information to both researchers and students of recent history interested in the coverage and composition of network television documentaries and special reports over a period of 25 years. It is organized into three major divisions, the first of which covers network documentary series. This is a major segment and constitutes nearly 3/4 of the total. Smaller, separate segments are given to the programs of David Wolper, recognized as the major pioneering figure in the medium, and to network specials and special reports. Arrangement of entries is chronological within the groupings. Given for each entry are dates, titles, writers, directors, producers, and narrators, as well as brief descriptions of content. Over 7,000 individual programs and 120 series are enumerated. There are indexes of personalities and personnel, but the work suffers for lack of subject access.

For more recent coverage of documentaries, see the *Journal Graphics Video and Transcript Index Guide* (entry 771n).

Biographical Sources

776.   **American Magazine Journalists, 1741–1850.** Sam G. Riley, ed. Detroit: Gale, 1988. 430p. (Dictionary of Literary Biography, v.73). ISBN 0-8103-4551-X.

This is the first volume of a selective three-part work covering journalists who were productive over the 220-year period from 1741 to 1960. This first volume covers 1741–1850 and furnishes biographical essays of 48 individuals, most of whom have been treated in other volumes of this series and also in the *Dictionary of American Biography* (entry 143). The focus in the present work is on their magazine contributions; the biographical sketches are newly written by scholars and specialists. The essays are of considerable length, and extensive bibliographies are furnished.

American Magazine Journalists, 1850–1900, also edited by Riley (Gale; *DLB* v.79, 1989), is the second issue of this set and furnishes 50 biographical sketches of writers. Entries follow the same format as that used in the previous effort and give lengthy coverage along with bibliographies. There is an informative expository essay on publishing trends relative to political, social, and economic developments of this time period. Photographs are included. *American Magazine Journalists, 1900–1960, First Series* (Gale; *DLB* v.91, 1990) is the first of two volumes on this time period. Again, Riley serves as editor. Biographies and photographs of 37 editors and publishers of the twentieth century are furnished here in the manner of previous volumes.

777.   **American Newspaper Journalists, 1690–1872.** Perry J. Ashley, ed. Detroit: Gale, 1985. 527p. (Dictionary of Literary Biography, v.43). ISBN 0-8103-1721-4.

Similar to the coverage given magazine journalists in the previous entry is the treatment accorded newspaper journalists by Ashley for this *Dictionary of Literary Biography (DLB)* work. This is the first volume in terms of scope and coverage but the last one published. Like others in the series, it provides lengthy biographical sketches with critical interpretation rendered by scholars and specialists. Inclusion is highly selective, and bibliographies are furnished. Included here are 66 biographies of prominent contributors to newspaper journalism over a period of 180 years. Illustrations are provided.

American Newspaper Journalists, 1873–1900 (Gale; *DLB* v.23, 1983) furnishes biographical essays of 42 individuals prominent during the fourth quarter of the nineteenth century. Included are such noteworthies as Samuel Clemens, Ambrose Bierce, and Joel Chandler-Harris. *American Newspaper Journalists, 1901–1925* (Gale; *DLB* v.25, 1984) covers this burgeoning period of newspaper development with critical biographical essays of 47 personalities. Ring Lardner and William Randolph Hearst are among the group covered. *American Newspaper Journalists, 1926–1950* (Gale; *DLB* v.29, 1984), the final volume on U.S. journalists, continues the pattern that has worked so well for the entire series, furnishing biographical and critical essays of the careers of 54 prominent journalists such as Heywood Broun, H. L. Mencken, and Ernie Pyle, who were dominant forces during the second quarter of the twentieth century. A new title by Ashley is American Newpaper Publishers, 1950–1990 (Gale, 1993). It is offered as volume 127 of the *DLB* series and provides similar coverage of notable publishers.

778.   **Biographical Dictionary of American Journalism.** Joseph P. McKerns, ed. New York: Greenwood, 1989. 820p. ISBN 0-313-23818-9.

This handy biographical dictionary furnishes brief sketches varying from one to two pages in length of 500 men and women who were prominent in either broadcast or print journalism over a period of nearly 300 years, from 1690 to the present. Several of these individuals are still alive although at the tail end of their careers. The format emulates that of the *Dictionary of American Biography* (entry 143) and furnishes dates, summary of achievements, a biographical essay, and a bibliography of writings by and about the subject. Contributions are signed by the 130-odd academicians who furnished them. As with other works of this type, one will find fault with some of the "popular" inclusions, but more likely the exclusions and omissions will generate interest or concern. Nevertheless, this resource is useful for inquirers at all levels.

779. **Encyclopedia of Twentieth-Century Journalists.** William H. Taft. New York: Garland, 1986. 408p. (Garland Reference Library of the Humanities, v.493). ISBN 0-8240-8961-8.

A useful one-volume biographical dictionary, this work examines the lives of some 750 men and women who have achieved prominence in a variety of activities within the field of journalism during the twentieth century. Written in a popular style, the volume is eminently readable and should interest inquirers at all levels of interest and expertise. "Journalist" is here defined in a broad manner and includes such figures as cartoonists, photographers, broadcasters, and media managers as well as editors, reporters, and publishers. Just as diverse is the list of personalities, which includes George Will, Bob Woodward, Paul Harvey, Edward R. Murrow, Roger Ebert, Katherine Graham, and Hedda Hopper. Biographies vary in length from a few lines to several paragraphs.

780. **Journalists of the United States: Biographical Sketches of Print and Broadcast News Shapers from the Late 17th Century to the Present.** Robert B. Downs and Jane B. Downs. Jefferson, NC: McFarland, 1991. 391p. ISBN 0-89950-549-X.

Written by an eminent former librarian and library school dean, now deceased, this recently published biographical dictionary provides slightly more comprehensive coverage than does the related work, the *Biographical Dictionary of American Journalism* (entry 778), with treatment of about 100 more personalities from both print and broadcast journalism. It contains 600 biographical sketches ranging from a few lines to two pages. Greater emphasis is given to the eighteenth and nineteenth century figures than to contemporary personalities. It is the inclusion of seventeenth- and eighteenth-century figures that is most useful to both scholars and students of history. The electronic media of today are covered in equitable fashion. There is an index of names, periodicals and newspapers, organizations, and subjects.

URBAN STUDIES

The city has been the setting for a number of U.S. novels and motion pictures, and it has been both damned and praised for its role in fostering the energies that shaped the lives of the heroes and heroines. It has been either credited with harboring the forces that lead to progress or blamed for encouraging the processes of decline and decay. Cities have served as "melting pots" of ethnic acculturation and were frequently the predetermined destinations of past generations of immigrants. Political party affiliations formed along the lines of labor, as opposed to farm or entrepreneurial interests, and the Democratic Party gained a strong foothold in the early decades of this century. Several histories have been written on the subject, but relatively few reference books are available, as shown by the paucity of selections in this segment.

Sage Urban Studies Abstracts is a current quarterly service that has been issued since 1973 by Sage Publications. It abstracts a wealth of materials (books, articles, dissertations, speeches) on a variety of topics, including urban history. Also issued since 1973 is *Index to Current Urban Documents*, a quarterly guide from Greenwood Press that identifies documents and report literature produced by 300 of the municipal governments of the larger metropolitan areas in the United States and Canada.

781. **Cities and Towns in American History: A Bibliography of Doctoral Dissertations.** Arthur P. Young, comp. New York: Greenwood, 1989. 438p. (Bibliographies and Indexes in American History, no.13). ISBN 0-313-26588-7.

For scholars and serious students, this is of real value in listing the research products of doctoral students through the year 1987. More than 4,300 dissertations are cited, their content relevant to urban U.S. development dating from the colonial period to modern times. As a convenience tool, the work is successful and spares the researcher the need to examine the various volumes of *Dissertation Abstracts International* (entry 92). There are two major sections, the larger of which is the first part, providing over 3,800 entries arranged alphabetically under state and territory, then subdivided by city or town. Cities with more than 25 entries are further subdivided by subjects. The second section classifies around 500 entries by topic. Entries furnish the usual bibliographic identification and include order numbers for University Microfilms International.

782. **City Directories of the United States, 1860–1901: Guide to the Microfilm Collection.** Woodbridge, CT: Research Publications, 1984. 487p. ISBN 0-89235-081-4.

In the past, Research Publications has prepared microfilm copies of thousands of city directories and with this work now offers a guide to its massive collections. This directory and resource guide describe the three segments of the massive microform project. It is organized chronologically under city; entries enumerate the directories' time period and give bibliographic data. There is an index by state, region, and city. Scholars, students, and genealogists profit from the tool.

The microform project itself is entitled *City Directories of the United States.* Segment 1, which furnishes complete copies of city, state, and regional directories published prior to 1860, was issued in nearly 6,300 microfiche. Segment 2 places the directories published between 1861 and 1881 on about 365 reels of microfilm. Segment 3 provides coverage from 1882 through 1901 on roughly 750 microfilm reels. Segment 4, which is not covered in the guide, offers additional coverage from 1902 through 1935.

783. **Fire Insurance Maps in the Library of Congress: Plans of North American Cities and Towns Produced by the Sanborn Map Company.** Library of Congress. Geography and Map Division. Reference and Bibliography Section. Washington: U.S. Government Printing Office, 1981. 773p. ISBN 0-8444-0337-7.

This resource represents a real benefit for scholars and serious students. Insurance maps generally serve as excellent indicators of the physical condition, construction, and composition of dwellings and commercial buildings of the various geographic regions. The work is a checklist or guide to thousands of maps and sheets on nearly 10,000 cities and towns prepared by the Sanborn Map Company, one of the leading cartographers of U.S. cities and towns. Maps date from 1867 to the present day and furnish information on details of construction and locations of such features as exits, windows, and water mains. Valuable detail is given regarding boundaries, block numbers, and construction features, as these were prepared to help determine the degree of risk and hazard for insurance purposes. Arrangement of entries is by state, with indexes of counties and cities.

The *Union List of Sanborn Fire Insurance Maps Held by Institutions in the United States and Canada* (Western Association of Map Librarians, 1976–1977) is a two-volume source complementary to the above entry that furnishes listings of maps held by over 160 U.S. and Canadian libraries.

784. **Periodical Literature on United States Cities: A Bibliography and Subject Guide.**
Barbara S. Shearer and Benjamin F. Shearer, comps. Westport, CT: Greenwood, 1983. 574p.
ISBN 0-313-23511-2.

More than 4,900 entries are furnished in this bibliography of periodical literature dealing
with U.S. cities. The authors are librarians, and they have provided a useful guide for social
scientists and social historians emphasizing relatively recent literature. Publication dates
range from 1970 to 1981 and cover cities of 100,000 or more residents. Entries are arranged
alphabetically by city and subdivided into eight categories. Included are articles on architecture, education, the environment, government, housing, economic conditions, and transportation, which follow the introductory subsection on general works. Selection is based on
availability and informational quality. No annotations are provided, an omission that, along
with the exclusion of local documents, limits somewhat the volume's contribution to scholarly
inquiry. There are both author and subject indexes to furnish access.

785. **Urban America: A Historical Bibliography.** Neil L. Shumsky and Timothy Crim-
mins, eds. Santa Barbara, CA: ABC-Clio, 1983. 422p. (Clio Bibliography Series, no.11).
ISBN 0-87436-638-2.

This is another of the spin-off specialized bibliographies drawn from the database of
periodical articles that form the basis of *America: History and Life* (entry 51). More than
4,000 entries are furnished, all of which are considered relevant to the history of U.S. cities.
These entries include international efforts, although the great majority are U.S. publications.
The editors are academicians who have selected their material from volumes 11 to 17 of
America: History and Life, published between 1974 and 1980. The abstracts vary in length
depending on the perceived importance as determined by the parent source. The work is
divided into five segments, covering U.S. and Canadian cities from 1607 to modern times,
plus American Indian settlements, historiography, and methodology. The work represents a
useful convenience tool for all inquirers and is accessible by author and subject indexes.

786. **Urban History: A Guide to Information Sources.** John D. Buenker, et al. Detroit:
Gale, 1981. 448p. (Gale Information Guide Library; American Government and History
Information Guide series, v.9). ISBN 0-8103-1479-7.

Although this guide is beginning to show its age, it is still recognized as a useful starting
point for both scholarly inquiry and student investigation. Compiled by several academics,
the work furnishes over 1,900 entries to books, articles, and dissertations relevant to urban
studies of every historical period and for every geographic region. Emphasis has been placed
on literature published since 1960, although earlier efforts of significant impact are included
as well. Availability was also a consideration for inclusion. Arrangement of entries is
alphabetical under chapter divisions representing both topical and format categories, the first
of which (general studies) contains material useful to the teaching of urban history. Access
to materials is assured by the inclusion of three indexes by author, subject, and title.

ENTERTAINMENT AND RECREATION: POPULAR CULTURE

The many facets of popular culture and the entertainment arts have always represented an important consideration for civilized society. Modern cultural historians examine the impact and representative expression of these elements rather than the quality of the product. More recently, especially in this country, remuneration for sports personalities and entertainment figures has hit all-time highs and has somewhat distanced these heroes from the mainstream. The history of U.S. involvement with the various media has presented a fertile field for investigation, with the theatre and the cinema being the chief interests of numerous scholars and popular writers.

This section opens with a segment on general sources that cover more than one medium or recreational art. Following are separate sections on radio and television; cinema; theater and stage; and, finally, sports and games. We have excluded from our coverage art, music, and literature; investigators are referred to the various literature guides, which consider these areas in more depth than would be permitted here.

The Popular Culture Association at Bowling Green (Ohio) State University was founded in 1964 and has 2,500 members. It has published the *Journal of Popular Culture* since 1967 and the *Journal of American Culture* since 1978, both on a quarterly basis.

General

Library Resources

787. Motion Pictures, Television, and Radio: A Union Catalogue of Manuscript and Special Collections in the Western United States. Linda H. Mehr, comp. and ed. Sponsored by the Film and Television Study Center, Inc. Boston: G. K. Hall, 1977. 201p. (A Reference Publication in Film). ISBN 0-8161-8089-X.

Another of the G. K. Hall efforts in reproducing the catalogs of important libraries, this union catalog covers the holdings of 73 libraries out west where exist some of the better collections on the entertainment arts. The purpose is to furnish scholars and serious inquirers with the knowledge or awareness of what exists and where it is located. Nearly 75 libraries, museums, and historical societies are identified in 11 states with California being the major provider. Entries furnish names, addresses, hours, and accessibility along with descriptions of the content of collections. The directory was funded by grants from the National Endowment for the Arts and others, and represents a useful tool for initiating research. The index is useful since it furnishes both a general index, and one by occupation of people who are covered in the collections.

A more recent effort is *Popular Entertainment Research: How to Do It and How to Use It* by Barbara J. Pruett (Scarecrow, 1992) which identifies and describes resource centers, library collections, journals, and databases of importance to the researcher and student. Along with descriptions, suggestions are provided for gaining access to and utilizing resources and for conducting research.

Bibliographical Sources

788. American Popular Culture: A Guide to Information Sources. Larry N. Landrum. Detroit: Gale, 1982. 435p. (Gale Information Guide Library; American Studies Information Guide Series, v.12). ISBN 0-8103-1260-3.

Nearly 2,200 books with a sprinkling of periodical articles have been identified and annotated under form categories such as "Bibliographies, Indexes, and Abstracts" and "Anthologies and Collections." Many of these categories are subdivided by specific topics, and there are chapters on sports, games, music, dance, theatre, etc. Interpretation of popular culture is broad and the entries represent a wide range of subject material. The compiler, a professor of literature and popular culture, is "selective and unabashedly eclectic," which probably accounts for the presence of such interesting and disparate items as an encyclopedia of the occult and a history of the Olympic games. Annotations vary in length from brief or non-existent (subtitle only) to what may be considered a full paragraph. A name index includes not only authors and editors but subjects as well. The subject index includes all titles of books, motion pictures, and television programs that have been treated as subjects by the works listed.

789. American Popular Culture: A Historical Bibliography. Arthur F. Wertheim, ed. Santa Barbara, CA: ABC-Clio, 1984. 246p. (Clio Bibliography Series, no.14). ISBN 0-87436-049-8.

This is another of the specialized bibliographies spun off from the database of *America: History and Life* (entry 51). Like others in the series, this guide contains only periodical articles, along with the abstracts developed for them in the parent work. More than 2,700 entries are furnished for works published between 1973 and 1980. Popular culture here encompasses seven broad subject headings under which the entries are arranged: the historical perspective, popular arts, mass media, folk culture, customs, science and religion, and theory and research. These categories generally are subdivided under topical units. Although scholars and researchers will make use of this convenience tool, it is important that the parent tool be searched for a more fully developed investigation not limited to periodical literature. Access is provided by the publisher's SPIndex (Subject Profile Index) of subjects and an author index.

Information Sources

790. Blacks in American Films and Television: An Encyclopedia. Donald Bogle. New York: Garland, 1988. 510p. (Garland Reference Library of the Humanities, v.604). ISBN 0-8240-8715-1.

The author is regarded as a reputable historian of blacks in the entertainment industry, and with this volume he offers a critical interpretation on the manner in which black characters have been developed in some 260 films and more than 100 television series, motion pictures, and specials. More than 100 black performers and directors are profiled, their careers examined and contributions evaluated. Arrangement of entries is alphabetical, thus precluding the establishment of a historical perspective such as might have been provided in a chronological arrangement. As part of the Garland humanities series, the work provides useful information and provocative commentary for students, scholars, and the interested public. There is a bibliography of additional readings and numerous illustrations, as well as a comprehensive index to furnish access.

791.   **Handbook of American Popular Culture.** 2nd ed., rev. M. Thomas Inge, ed. New York: Greenwood, 1989. 3v. ISBN 0-313-25406-0 (set).

This three-volume handbook updates the first edition, which was issued between 1978 and 1981 and has been a regular choice of students and researchers of popular culture. The new work revises and expands the earlier effort, adding new subjects and updating those retained. All are now covered in an A-to-Z alphabetical arrangement. Coverage is handled through 48 essays on topics ranging from advertising to women. Literature has been excluded because it is covered in depth in a separate publication by the same author. Entries are well written and furnish historical perspective, followed by bibliographic narratives describing major reference works, description of research collections, and critical materials. There is a bibliography of books and articles as well. The tone and intent are scholarly; the essays have been authored by young academicians. Indexes of names and subjects furnish access in what must be considered an important effort.

792.   **Image as Artifact: The Historical Analysis of Film and Television.** John E. O'Connor, ed. Malabar, FL: Krieger, 1990. 344p. ISBN 0-89464-312-6.

The author is a film historian and professor who has developed a useful manual for scholars and serious students on methodology for the utilization of moving images (films and television programs) as historical documents and artifacts. These elements of popular culture furnish a rich source of documentation and are capable of supporting a body of critical scholarship that can enhance the understanding of social history. The work is divided into five chapters, the first two of which lead with an introduction and describe data collection on the contents, production, and reception of a moving-image document. Chapter 3 consists of four frameworks for perceiving the moving image, each of which is examined in essays by three contributing historians. These different types of inquiries are discussed in terms of methodological concerns in working with evidence. The final chapters offer a case study and an introduction to visual language. Both a bibliography and an index are supplied.

793.   **Mass Media: A Chronological Encyclopedia of Television, Radio, Motion Pictures, Magazines, Newspapers, and Books in the United States.** Robert V. Hudson. New York: Garland, 1987. 435p. (Garland Reference Library of Social Science, v.310). ISBN 0-8240-8695-3.

This chronology is beneficial to both students and scholars of the mass media because it divides the coverage between the media's dual roles: entertainment and information. Organization of the work is by divisions of 16 chronological periods, beginning with 1638–1764 and concluding with 1973–1985. Within the periods the entries are arranged chronologically by medium (books, broadsides, pamphlets, radio, and television). Entries vary in length from a few lines to a few paragraphs and enumerate various events, along with their key figures and sites. Exposition is furnished on the importance of the happenings, which include the founding of publications, the release of movies, court cases, and technical advances. The work begins with an informative history of mass media and a listing of "firsts," along with references to where they are treated in the chronology. There is a detailed index.

794.   **Sourcebook for the Performing Arts: A Directory of Collections, Resources, Scholars, and Critics in Theatre, Film, and Television.** Anthony Slide, et al., comps. New York: Greenwood, 1988. 227p. ISBN 0-313-24872-9.

This is a comprehensive directory in terms of its coverage of a wide spectrum of the performing arts (television, radio, theatre, and film), yet it is selective in its inclusion of entries. The work is divided into three major sections, the first two making up the bulk of the total text. The first section lists institutions and their collections. These entries are arranged alphabetically by state and indicate the usual directory information (name, address, telephone number, and description of collection). The second section furnishes brief biographical coverage of various personalities associated with the study (historians, librarians, etc.). The final section gives a brief listing of addresses of various participating units, agencies, and organizations, such as journals, book publishers, bookshops, studios, and production companies. There is an index to entries covered in the first two sections.

Biographical Sources

795. **Performing Arts Biography Master Index: A Consolidated Index to Over 270,000 Biographical Sketches of Persons Living and Dead, as They Appear in Over 100 of the Principal Biographical Dictionaries Devoted to the Performing Arts.** 2nd ed. Barbara McNeil and Miranda C. Herbert, eds. Detroit: Gale, 1982. 701p. (Gale Biographical Index Series, no.5). ISBN 0-8103-1097-X.

This is a convenience tool derived from the massive coverage of *Biography and Genealogy Master Index* (entry 137). Beginning as *Theatre, Film, and Television Biographies Master Index* (Gale, 1979), the new title expanded and increased coverage, more than doubling the number of entries. The number of biographical dictionaries indexed was increased in similar fashion, from about 40 to over 100 sources. Entries are alphabetically arranged and provide coverage of personalities representing a wide spectrum of the performing arts (theatre, film, television, classical and popular music, dance, puppetry, magic). Entries furnish dates of birth and death and references to the biographical dictionaries (including page numbers). The biographical sources are considered readily available in library collections, making this a practical reference tool for both students and researchers in need of background information on significant and obscure entertainers.

A work of wider scope but less comprehensive is *American Cultural Leaders: From Colonial Times to the Present* by Richard Ludwig and others, to be published by ABC-Clio in 1993. The work covers not only performing artists but also painters, architects, writers, and so on. Over 350 individuals are treated in narratives ranging from 500 to 1,500 words.

796. **Variety Obituaries: Including a Comprehensive Index.** Chuck Bartelt and Barbara Bergeron, proj. eds. New York: Garland, 1988–1992. v.1–13. (In progress). ISBN 0-8240-0835-9 (v.1).

From Garland Press comes this multivolume compilation of obituaries and related articles of entertainment figures as they appeared in *Variety* over a time span of more than 80 years. The work is of real value to researchers and serious students. Arrangement and format are similar to that of *Variety Film Reviews,* and entries appear in chronological sequence: volume 1 contains obituaries published between 1905 and 1928. Much of the material originated as news stories and editorials rather than as obituary listings. Personalities from all aspects of entertainment are represented, ranging from performers to business employees in fields from the circus to television. No photographs are included. Volume 11 is an index to the first 10 volumes and completes a set covering the years 1905–1986. The work continues with separately indexed volumes on a biennial basis: volume 12 covers the period 1987–1988, and volume 13 treats 1989–1990.

Jeb H. Perry has authored *Variety Obits: An Index to Obituaries in Variety, 1905–1978* (Scarecrow, 1980) for those who have *Variety* on microfilm and need only an index to the material.

Radio and Television

Reviews of television shows of historical interest may be found in a recent publication, *Variety Television Reviews, 1923–1988: The First Fifteen Volumes of the Series Including a Comprehensive Index*, edited by Howard H. Prouty (Garland, 1989–1991, 15v). This set consists of reviews as they appeared in *Daily Variety* out of Hollywood, California, from 1946–1960 (v.1–2) and *Variety* out of New York from 1923–1988 (v.3-14). Volume 15 is an index. The series continues on a biennial basis, with volume 16 (1992 publication) covering the reviews of 1989–1990.

For related works on news broadcasting, see the "Journalism" section in this chapter.

797. **Encyclopedia of Television: Series, Pilots, and Specials.** Vincent Terrace. New York: Zoetrope, 1985–1986. 3v. ISBN 0-918432-69-3 (v.1).

For over 15 years, Vincent Terrace has been producing compilations of various programs and actors in both radio and television (entries 798 and 801). This three-volume effort furnishes a comprehensive listing of more than 7,000 television series, pilots, experimental programs, and specials over a period of nearly 50 years. The guide provides plot summaries, cast information, number of episodes aired, networks, running times, syndication, and cable information. Also included are songs, vocalists, and musicians associated with production. Volume 1 covers the period 1937–1973; volume 2 examines the period 1974–1984; and volume 3 is the index giving access by names of individuals.

An earlier work by the author that helped establish his reputation in the field is *The Complete Encyclopedia of Television Programs, 1947–1979* (Barnes, 1979, 2v), which itself was a revision and second edition of an earlier work covering the period 1947–1976. The more recent effort gives comprehensive coverage of information regarding television programs for a period of more than 30 years. A name index furnishes access.

A more recent work of greater scope is *Les Brown's Encyclopedia of Television* (Gale, 1992), now in its third edition. Brown has furnished 800 entries treating performers, programs, and events in alphabetical order. The publication originated in 1977 as the *New York Times Encyclopedia of Television* and subsequently has been revised and expanded.

798. **Fifty Years of Television: A Guide to Series and Pilots, 1937–1988.** Vincent Terrace. Cranbury, NJ: Cornwall Books; distr. Associate University Presses, 1991. 864p. ISBN 0-8543-4811-6.

The most recent of Terrace's efforts (see also entries 797 and 801) is a comprehensive directory of more than 4,850 television series and pilots that ran between 1937 and 1988. Included here are entertainment series, experimental programs, and pilots (even those that were not aired). Excluded are mini-series, television movies, daytime serials, specials, and sports and news programs. Entries are arranged alphabetically and include the information normally associated with the author's handbooks: one- or two-sentence plot descriptions, type of program (e.g., comedy, western), cast lists, producers, dates, running times, networks, syndication, and cable information. Much of the information was gathered through viewings of the programs rather than release information furnished in press releases or *TV Guide*. The work should prove useful to inquirers at all levels because of its breadth and comprehensiveness. There is a selective index of performers.

Screen Gems: A History of Columbia Pictures Television from Cohn to Coke, 1948–1983 by Jeb H. Perry (Scarecrow, 1991) is a more specialized source that begins with a brief corporate history. The work then furnishes listings of series with descriptions, pilots, and specials produced by Columbia Pictures. Cast listings are provided, along with a chronology of premieres and cancellation dates.

799. **Radio: A Reference Guide.** Thomas A. Greenfield. Westport, CT: Greenwood, 1989. 172p. (American Popular Culture). ISBN 0-313-22276-2.

Another of the Greenwood issues in the American Popular Culture series, this bibliographic guide should prove useful to students and researchers at all levels. Over 500 books, articles, dissertations, and monographs are treated in bibliographic essays divided among chapters relating to the history of radio (in which both stations and networks are examined), more specifically of music, drama, comedy, news, sports, and advertising. Important personalities are also treated within the various topical segments as leaders of their genre. The guide is well organized and carefully developed to meet the needs of both undergraduates and more serious investigators. The essays are readable and informative; the concluding bibliographers for each chapter were carefully selected. Also included are listings of organizations, serial publications, indexing services, and important collections. There is a corporate index of names, titles, and subjects.

800. **Radio and Television: A Selected, Annotated Bibliography.** William E. McCavitt. Metuchen, NJ: Scarecrow, 1978. 229p. ISBN 0-8108-1113-8. **Supplement One: 1977–1981.** 1982. 155p. ISBN 0-8108-1556-7. **Supplement Two: 1982–1986.** 1989. 237p. ISBN 0-8108-2158-3.

The initial bibliography furnishes 1,100 items, mostly books, written over a time span of 50 years, from 1926 to 1976. Comprehensive coverage is given to all areas of broadcasting activity, with entries arranged under broad subject categories such as history, society, regulations, and audience, along with format categories such as annuals, periodicals, and bibliographies. The organization tends to be a weakness, as certain subjects seem to be scattered throughout rather than integrated as a unit. This problem is lessened somewhat by the inclusion of cross-references. Annotations vary in length and quality, with many entries not given any description at all. There is an author index.

The first supplement was completed by McCavitt in 1982 and furnished an additional 500 entries organized under 27 categories representing the literature from 1977 to 1981. *Supplement Two: 1982–1986* was compiled by Peter K. Pringle and Helen H. Clinton and identifies an additional 1,000 publications listed under six major categories.

801. **Radio's Golden Years: The Encyclopedia of Radio Programs, 1930–1960.** Vincent Terrace. San Diego: A. S. Barnes, 1981. 308p. ISBN 0-9603574-2-4.

When Terrace completed this work in 1981, it was seen as complementary to his 1979 title, *Complete Encyclopedia of Television Programs* (entry 797n). Since that time his efforts have been primarily directed toward furnishing revisions and expansions of the television reference works in response to the ever-changing television scene. Radio programming, of course, no longer has national perspective; except in the case of certain talk shows. Therefore this illustrated treatment of the golden years from 1930 to 1960 remains a standard tool. About 1,500 nationally broadcast programs are listed alphabetically and described in the familiar Terrace manner: plot, cast lists, announcer, music, sponsor, network information, and length and date of broadcasts. Of special interest is the coverage given to program openings, which include familiar quotations. Because of its comprehensive nature, this effort is useful for purposes of identification. A name index provides access.

802. **The Stars of Stand-up Comedy: A Biographical Encyclopedia.** Ronald L. Smith. New York: Garland, 1986. 227p. (Garland Reference Library of the Humanities, v.564). ISBN 0-8240-8803-2.

Comedy and humor retain an important position within the realm of popular culture, and the study of such performance receives continual attention among scholars and students. This biographical coverage of stand-up comedians furnishes useful information for all inquirers. More than 100 individuals and comedy teams are covered. Arrangement of entries is alphabetical and performers vary considerably. Included here are Groucho Marx, Lily Tomlin, and Bob Hope, as well as Lenny Bruce, Tom Lehrer, and Eddie Murphy. Most of the performers did earn their reputations at least in part through appearances on radio or television. Entries provide illustrations, dates, recordings, television appearances, films, biographies, and books written by subject. Essays are informative and cover background, philosophy, and brand of humor in well written two- to three-page formats.

803. **Television, A Guide to the Literature.** Mary B. Cassata and Thomas Skill. Phoenix, AZ: Oryx Press, 1985. 148p. ISBN 0-89774-140-4.

This is a bibliographic essay divided into three segments, each of which was initially published in *Choice* (January, February, and April 1982). More than 450 publications are identified and described in the three sections. The introductory "Test Patterns" furnishes historical perspective, general efforts on communication, and reference tools; "The Environment" treats the research concerned with various processes and influences of television, news, politics, and service to youth; and "Directions" furnishes coverage of the industry, its criticism and collected works. Because the work unfolded in separate segments, these sections retain separate identities rather than standing as a synthesized examination of the field as a whole. Nevertheless, both students and scholars find it useful in helping to define segments of the field in which they are interested. The work is indexed by author, title, and subject.

804. **Tube of Plenty: The Evolution of American Television.** 2nd rev. ed. Erik Barnouw. New York: Oxford University, 1990. 607p. ISBN 0-19-506483-6.

This work was originally issued in 1975, reprinted with additions in 1977, and first revised in 1982. Written by one of the leading scholars and historians of the industry, it continues to offer one of the most useful survey histories of the communications revolution. The author has diligently and capably recorded the changes within the social fabric and related them to developments within the broadcasting industry. In more recent years we have seen the decline of the major networks and the expansion of cable and pay-TV, with emphasis on specialized audiences such as those for MTV.

Much of the intellectual foundation of this work was derived from the author's scholarly three-volume *History of Broadcasting in the United States* (Oxford University, 1966–1970, 3v). This massive work is a merger of three separate publications that combine to form an in-depth retrospective. Coverage begins with volume 1, *A Tower of Babel*, which treats the beginnings of the industry up to Roosevelt's first inauguration in 1933. *The Golden Web* is the title of the second volume, which examines the next two decades, and volume 3, *The Image Empire*, covers the period from 1953 through the Eisenhower years to the moon landing.

Cinema

Motion picture reviews published in the *New York Times* are provided in *New York Times Film Reviews, 1913–1968* (New York Times, 1970, 6v). Since then it has been updated on a biennial basis, with the most recent issue published in 1992 and covering the years 1989–1990. *Variety* reviews are found in *Variety Film Reviews, 1907–1980* (Garland, 1983. 16v). Publication continues on a biennial basis through R. R. Bowker. Additionally, there is a comprehensive two-volume index by Patricia K. Hanson and Stephen L. Hanson entitled *Film Review Index* (Oryx, 1986–1987) that identifies substantial reviews from a variety of sources on films considered important to film researchers. Coverage extends from 1882 to 1985.

Magill's Survey of Cinema (Salem Press, 1980–) is an annual review of motion pictures furnishing lengthy and detailed treatments. It is available online through DIALOG, where it is updated twice a month. The complete file has about 35,000 reviews.

Bibliographical Sources

805.   **Film: A Reference Guide.** Robert A. Armour. Westport, CT: Greenwood, 1980. 251p. (American Popular Culture). ISBN 0-313-22241-X.

This bibliographic essay written by a professor furnishes a well-organized systematic examination of popular U.S. films from the nineteenth century to the present. Nearly 1,500 English-language books are identified and arranged under 11 chapter headings; coverage includes film history, criticism, and production techniques, as well as genres, major actors, and individual films. As part of the Greenwood American Popular Culture series, the volume places emphasis on popular U.S. fare, with description accorded to individual titles through a bibliographic narrative. Bibliographic listings follow in each chapter. The quality of the selections is without question of high caliber, and the work is useful to students and researchers at all levels. Of value is the comprehensive coverage in terms of time periods and topics treated. There are indexes by author and subject to provide access.

806.   **The Film Index: A Bibliography.** Comp. by the Workers of the Writers' Program of the Work Projects Administration in the City of New York, 1935–1940, with the Museum of Modern Art, New York. New York: The Museum of Modern Art Film Library and H. W. Wilson, 1941 (v.1). Kraus, 1985 (v.2–3). Repr. Kraus, 1988 (v.1). ISBN 0-527-29329-6 (v.1). ISBN 0-527-29334-2 (v.2). ISBN 0-527-29335-0 (v.3).

Because of cutbacks at the WPA in 1939, only the first volume, *The Film as Art*, appeared on time in 1941. It was produced jointly by the Wilson Company and the Museum of Modern Art and furnishes an extensive annotated bibliography of books and articles on the history, technique, and types of motion pictures. The work is based primarily on the collections of the Museum of Modern Art and the New York Public Library. The cards for the two remaining volumes were held in the archives of the museum; Kraus finally arranged for their publication. Volume 2, *The Film as Industry*, covers English-language materials excluding newspapers based on the holdings of the New York Public Library, with additional listings derived from periodical indexes. Entries are classified under major subject headings in alphabetical order. Volume 3, *The Film in Society*, identifies books and articles under such topics as education, censorship, and moral and religious aspects. All annotations are original from their period of preparation, and the complete set is an important contribution to film research.

Information Sources

807.   **The American Film Industry: A Historical Dictionary.** Anthony Slide. Westport, CT: Greenwood, 1986. 431p. ISBN 0-313-24693-9.

Slide and his team of eight research associates have put together a rather unique and detailed dictionary of the historical development of the film industry in this country. Coverage is given to about 600 entries, alphabetically arranged; the writing is smooth and the descriptions well developed, and cross-references are furnished. The work treats many facets of the industry, with special attention given to business organizations, industrial techniques, and technology. Also covered are producing and releasing companies, film series, genres, organizations, and specific terms peculiar to the field. Entries vary in length from only a few lines to several pages, depending upon the importance of the subject, and may include addresses, bibliographies, and archival resources. The work concludes with a general bibliography for additional reading on film history, plus a name index of persons, subjects, and organizations.

808. **The American Indian in Film.** Michael Hilger. Metuchen, NJ: Scarecrow, 1986. 196p. ISBN 0-8108-1905-8.

Films with American Indians as characters have always been popular with the U.S. public. More recently there has been much criticism of the adverse treatment given these characters and the less-than-accurate portrayals accorded them. Hilger has furnished a filmography of motion pictures that included either native American characterization or plot development of substantial proportion. Arrangement of entries is chronological, with the intent being to facilitate scrutiny of the changes occurring over time. There are four major chronological divisions, beginning with silent films and ending with the 1970s-1980s period. Entries provide title, distribution company, date, director, and plot summary, as well as quoted commentary of film reviewers regarding Indian characters. There are black-and-white illustrations. Access is furnished through indexes by actor name and by topic.

The Hispanic Image on the Silver Screen: An Interpretive Filmography from Silents into Sound, 1898–1935 by Alfred C. Richard, Jr. (Greenwood, 1992) examines the negative and demeaning portrayal of Hispanics over a period of 40 years. Coverage is given to 1,800 films listed chronologically and described in depth. The work is well indexed and serves as the first volume of a projected series.

809. **American Political Movies: An Annotated Filmography of Feature Films.** James E. Combs. New York: Garland, 1990. 173p. (Garland Filmographies, v.1; Garland Reference Library of the Humanities, v.970). ISBN 0-8240-7847-0.

This is a useful tool for scholars and researchers who are interested in the thematic material examined or interpreted in motion pictures about politics. Such films, as well as those with purposeful political orientation, are treated, as are those that reflect on the political climate. Films are treated in nine chapters, eight of which generally follow a chronological sequence of coverage. The first chapter is most impressive, providing an overview and philosophical interpretation of film as a maker of popular opinion and political direction. The remaining chapters describe the involvement of politics in Hollywood fare from the early days to the 1980s. Interpretation is given to the various political orientations, with films being used as examples. The work concludes with a bibliography of books and articles and a filmography of some 350 "political" films. There is a subject index.

Picture This! A Guide to Over 300 Environmentally, Socially, and Politically Relevant Films and Videos by Sky Hiatt (Noble, 1992) examines films as propaganda and as instruments of social impact. Included are many titles that have been banned, blacklisted, and criticized for a variety of reasons. Such themes as morality, intolerance, and revolution are examined in this useful analysis.

810. **American Film Studios: An Historical Encyclopedia.** Gene Fernett. Jefferson, NC: McFarland, 1988. 295p. ISBN 0-89950-250-4.

This is an informative historical treatment of the origins and development of U.S. film studios of varied nature and importance. Coverage is given not only to the major studios but to the more obscure as well. More than 60 studios are covered, with informative, well-developed narratives furnishing clear and revealing insight and perspective regarding the various organizations treated. Emphasis in this work is on the early years, with many modern studios being omitted. Entries cover major personalities of all types (actors, producers, directors, and owners), promotional literature, and photographs. They vary from one page to several pages in length and furnish a surprising amount of detail of the nature and composition of the studios. Both scholars and students benefit from the treatment. There is a detailed name index to assure access.

811. **Doing Their Bit: Wartime American Animated Short Films, 1939–1945.** Michael S. Shull and David E. Wilt. Jefferson, NC: McFarland, 1987. 198p. ISBN 0-89950-218-0.

Unique and useful coverage is provided both the film historian and the military historian on the production of animated cartoons related to World War II. In addition, this offering adds to the growing body of literature on animation, which has become a more popular study in recent years. The filmography of 271 entries gives title, distribution, company, date, producer, director, writer, animation personnel, and music director, as well as a plot synopsis. Cartoons are treated in serious manner: There is an informative and well-developed exposition of nearly 70 pages on the importance of this medium as an indicator of popular sentiment and a gauge of wartime attitudes. Several appendices provide various listings, such as an index of featured characters and selected topics. An index to the filmography is furnished.

812. **Encyclopedia of American Film Comedy.** Larry Langman. New York: Garland, 1987. 639p. (Garland Reference Library of the Humanities, v.744). ISBN 0-8240-8496-9.

Film historian Langman (see also entry 813) has produced what purports to be the first one-volume encyclopedia of cinematic comedy. As one might expect, coverage is comprehensive but relatively brief. Included here are numerous performers, both individuals and teams, male and female, dating from the one-reelers of the second decade of this century to the films of the mid-1980s. Coverage is given not only to actors but also to directors and screenwriters, all of whom vary widely from one to another in terms of their success or impact. Also included are more than 150 comedy films representative of various styles and even entries for series, such as the Andy Hardy films. Entries vary from a few sentences to three pages in length and generally supply a brief filmography for each actor. There is a brief general bibliography; cross-references within entries furnish access in lieu of an index.

A more recent effort is *Quinlan's Illustrated Directory of Film Comedy Actors* by David Quinlan (Holt, 1992), which provides brief treatment of 300 film comedians, mainly U.S. and British. Entry length ranges from half a column (John Belushi) to three pages (Chaplin, Keaton); filmographies accompany each entry. Stage and television contributions are described whenever applicable.

813. **Encyclopedia of American War Films.** Larry Langman and Ed Borg. New York: Garland, 1989. 696p. (Garland Reference Library of the Humanities, v.873). ISBN 0-8240-7540-4.

Another of Langman's interesting and useful contributions is this comprehensive listing of some 2,000 U.S. films depicting wars in which this country was engaged. Entries are listed alphabetically by title and vary somewhat with the importance of the motion picture. Most entries furnish a brief plot summary or short review with some critical interpretation. The strength of this work lies in its breadth of coverage, and it appears to succeed in its purpose to treat every U.S. film of this genre, major and minor, made over a period of 90 years, from 1898 through 1988. All wars are represented, as seen in one of the appendices, which links the wars to their related films. Also listed here are Oscar-winning films and a subject-arranged bibliography of film biographies.

A unique approach is taken by Mark Walker in *Vietnam Veteran Films* (Scarecrow, 1991), which covers motion pictures that include a Vietnam veteran among the characters. Plot summaries are given for 215 films, and genre classification is furnished (biker, vigilante, police, war, horror).

814. **Handbook of American Film Genres.** Wes D. Gehring, ed. New York: Greenwood, 1988. 405p. ISBN 0-313-24715-3.

This offering covers the genres of U.S. film in more comprehensive fashion than does any previous publication. It identifies 18 different forms, organized under five broad divisions: action-adventure, comedy, fantastic, songs and soaps, and nontraditional. Within these divisions are chapters devoted to specific genres: adventure films, westerns, gangster films, film noir, social-problem films, screwball comedies, parodies, black humor, and so forth. Film scholars contribute informative essays giving definitions and historical perspective and identifying books and articles on the topic. Coverage of each genre tends to be well developed and insightful and concludes with a brief filmography of important productions of each type. There is an index of names, films, and titles drawn from the essays, filmographies, and publications. Although quality of coverage varies with the contributor, the work is useful to both students and scholars.

815. **History of the American Cinema.** Charles Harpole, gen. ed. New York: Scribner's, 1990– . v.1–3. (Projected 10v.). ISBN 0-684-18413-3 (v.1). ISBN 0-684-18414-1 (v.2). ISBN 0-684-18415-X (v.3). ISBN 0-684-16740-9 (v.5).

This projected 10-volume history, edited by an academic, will cover the story of the cinema from 1895 to 1980 when completed. It represents a massive effort, with individual volumes commissioned to different scholars and historians in the field. The first three volumes, all published in 1990, show depth and critical perspective in analyzing the personalities and developments within their time periods. Volumes are detailed and include numerous illustrations of productions, advertisements, cartoons, and so on; they conclude with an index. Volume 1, *The Emergence of Cinema: The American Screen to 1907* by Charles Musset of Columbia University, examines the beginning years and the development of the art form. Volume 2, *The Transformation of Cinema, 1907–1915* by Eileen Bowser, curator of film at the Museum of Modern Art, and volume 3, *An Evening's Entertainment: The Age of the Silent Feature Picture, 1915–1928* by Richard Koszarski, curator of film at the American Museum of the Moving Image, continue the coverage. The remaining volumes are scheduled for completion by 1994. Volume 5, *Grand Design: Hollywood as a Modern Business Enterprise, 1930–1939* describes the beginnings of the studio system and such innovations as color and the big musicals. The remaining volumes are scheduled for completion by 1994.

816. **Hollywood and American History: A Filmography of Over 250 Motion Pictures Depicting U.S. History.** Michael R. Pitts, comp. Jefferson, NC: McFarland, 1984. 332p. (United States in Motion Pictures). ISBN 0-89950-132-X.

This is a most interesting filmography in terms of content, because included in the definition of history is a wide range of influences representing various aspects of U.S. social and political development. The 250 entries are arranged alphabetically by title and enumerate the production company, date, running time, and color/b&w. Production credits are given for producers, directors, and screenwriters, followed by cast listings, then brief essays summarizing the films' historical context and plot, and, finally, critical interpretation. In many cases the commentaries extend to other, related films. Films represent a variety of themes, from wars to gangsters; in many cases the portrayals represent Hollywood versions rather than historically accurate ones. A conservative political leaning is evident in both inclusions and exclusions, as well as in the commentary. A general index of names, subjects, and titles furnishes access.

817. **The New York Times Encyclopedia of Film.** Gene Brown and Harry M. Geduld, eds. New York: Times Books, 1984. 13v. ISBN 0-8129-1059-1 (set).

Similar to the *New York Times Film Reviews* in format, this monumental collection of articles from the nationally read newspaper is arranged chronologically from 1896 to 1979. Included are all types of writings pertaining to motion pictures: news items, features, interviews, reports, and promotional pieces. As one might expect, reviews are studiously avoided so the other publication can retain its uniqueness in that area. Many illustrations are included, although the work has been criticized for the poor quality of the reproductions. Many subjects are covered, with a good proportion of the articles about personalities (producers, commentators, critics, news correspondents, and performers). There is an alphabetically arranged index volume providing access to the desired subject through identification of the month, day, and year the articles were published.

Theater and Stage

Reviews of theatrical productions published in the *New York Times* can be located through *The New York Times Theatre Reviews, 1920–1970* (New York Times, 1971. 10v), with coverage continuing on a biennial basis ever since. Earlier retrospective coverage has been provided through a five-volume set published in 1976 covering the years 1870–1919. *The New York Theatre Critics Review* (Theatre Critics Review, 1940–) has furnished copy of reviews as they appeared in a variety of New York newspapers and periodicals and even on television. Frequency has varied through the years from weekly to monthly, and cumulative indexes were issued for 1961–1972 and 1973–1986. In 1992, the publisher offered *Opening Night on Broadway*, a loose-leaf service furnishing reprints of playbills.

The Theatre Historical Society of America was founded in 1968–1969 and immediately began offering *The Marquee* as a quarterly journal. It operates out of Springfield, Pennsylvania, and has 1,000 members. The Burlesque Historical Society of Helendale, California, was founded in 1963 and has 500 members. It offers several publications on Jennie Lee, the "Bazoom" girl.

Library Resources

818. American Theatrical Arts: A Guide to Manuscripts and Special Collections in the United States and Canada. William C. Young. Chicago: American Library Association, 1971. 166p. ISBN 0-838-90104-2.

This is a highly useful directory of 138 institutions that have collections of primary source material on the theatrical arts (legitimate theater, vaudeville, burlesque, motion pictures, television, dance, opera, and circus). Included in these collections are manuscripts, playbills, theater history, promptbooks, posters, letters, diaries, logbooks, brochures, scrapbooks, photographs, recordings, contracts, and the like. Much of the material has not been cataloged and is not entered in any national listings, making the tool an extremely valuable aid to inquiry and research. The materials are linked to various types of theatrical personalities, including actors, directors, authors, designers, choreographers, composers, critics, and dancers. Entries are arranged alphabetically by state, then by institution, and they indicate quantity of items and furnish brief descriptions. Access is by name and subject indexes.

Louis A. Rachow's *Theatre and Performing Arts Collections* (Haworth, 1981) surveys half a dozen of the important special collections in articles written by the curators or heads of the collections. Included are the Billy Rose Theatre Collection at the New York Public Library and the Library of Congress.

819. **Catalog of the Theatre and Drama Collections.** New York Public Library, Research Libraries. Boston: G. K. Hall, 1967–76. 51v. **Supp.** 1973. 3v. **Ann. Supp.** 1976– . ISSN 0360-2788.

Another of the important G. K. Hall efforts is this massive reproduction of the card catalog of the New York Public Library's outstanding collection of theater and drama materials established in 1931. This catalog has been published in several parts related to different components of the collection. Parts I and II were published in 1967. Part I, *Drama Collection: Author Listing* (6v.) and *Listing by Cultural Origin* (6v.), consists of 120,000 entries for plays published separately or in anthologies or even in periodicals. Part II, *Theatre Collection: Books on the Theatre*, has over 120,000 entries from over 23,500 volumes relating to all aspects of the theater (history, biography, acting, etc.). A 548-page supplement to part I and a two-volume supplement to part II were published in 1973. Part III, *Non-Book Collection*, was published in 30 volumes in 1975 and represents over 740,000 cards on such items as programs, photographs, portraits, and press clippings.

Coverage for parts I and II has been continued by an annual supplement, *Bibliographic Guide to Theatre Arts*, since 1976. This work lists materials newly cataloged by the New York Public Library, with additional entries furnished from the Library of Congress MARC tapes.

820. **The Federal Theatre Project: A Catalog-Calendar of Productions.** Fenwick Library, George Mason University. New York: Greenwood, 1986. 349p. (Bibliographies and Indexes in the Performing Arts, no.3). ISBN 0-313-22314-9.

The Federal Theatre Project was a product of the New Deal carried out through the WPA. It was the only federally funded theatre in this country and operated between 1935 and 1939, employing many professionals and helping young people to shape their careers. Hopes for a permanent national theatre, unfortunately, were shattered by mounting criticism regarding the FTP's moral and political character. The materials from the project were housed in the archives of George Mason University's Fenwick Library on indefinite loan from the Library of Congress and remained in the archives section for 10 years between 1974 and 1984. This catalog calendar identifies nearly 2,800 individual productions, arranged alphabetically by title and including date and location of performance, theater, and name of director or choreographer. Materials in the collection are identified and indexed and include costume and set designs, playscripts, music, photographs, and programs, among other things.

Bibliographical Sources

821. **A Guide To Reference and Bibliography for Theatre Research.** 2nd ed., rev. and exp. Claudia J. Bailey. Columbus, OH: Ohio State University Library Publications Committee, 1983. 149p. ISBN 0-88215-049-9.

Originally issued in 1971, the present work is designed to furnish both students and scholars with a basic list of reference and resource material. The effort is divided into two major sections, the first of which covers general reference and bibliography. Included here are sources covering national bibliographies, library catalogs, periodical and newspaper indexes, dissertation listings, and so on. The second section targets more specialized materials within the realm of theatre and drama, with emphasis on U.S. and British productions. More than 650 entries published to mid-1979 are identified. Arrangement is by author, geographical location, or chronological sequence. Entries are annotated briefly with respect to content and furnish the usual bibliographic information—author, title, and imprint. There is an author-title index to give access.

A more specialized guide is *The Political Left in the American Theatre of the 1930s: A Bibliographical Sourcebook* by Susan Duffy (Scarecrow, 1992), which identifies various sources: books, chapters, newspaper and periodical articles, playscripts, and anthologies. Most of the items were published in the 1930s, but they range from the 1920s to the 1940s. There are useful suggestions for doing long-distance research.

822. **Topical Bibliographies of the American Theatre.** Barbara N. Cohen-Stratyner, ed. New York: Theatre Library Association, 1987. 195p. (Performing Arts Resources, v.12). ISBN 0-932610-09-0.

From its inception in 1974–1975, the yearbook series of the Theatre Library Association has set an excellent standard for high quality bibliographic and critical products useful to scholars and serious inquirers. The first volume surveyed several of the leading research collections in this country. Subsequently there has been coverage of a variety of resources, with greater interest on foreign contributions and more obscure elements. Volume 12 continues the high quality of previous efforts with a useful treatment of topical bibliographies of the U.S. theater. This work comprises five essays, each written by different experts and authorities. Included here are a checklist and bibliographies of early printed children's plays, nineteenth-century sources on women in nineteenth-century theatre, Civil War drama, female impersonation, and labor plays of the 1930s. The selections are well chosen and should prove beneficial to those who consult them.

Information Sources

823. **American Theatre Companies, 1749–1887.** Weldon B. Durham. New York: Greenwood, 1986. 598p. ISBN 0-313-20886-7.

The first of a three-volume set on resident acting companies in the United States, this work covers a most interesting and creative period, 1749–1887. Included are P. T. Barnum's American Museum Stock Company and the Thalia Theatre company, a prominent and successful German-language troupe in New York City. Coverage begins with the first important English-speaking company in the colonies and continues through the creation of the last company organized and managed in the style of the English playhouse. A total of 81 theater groups are treated. Entries provide dates and locations of operation, managers, description of artistic and business practices, performers, designers, technicians, and other information. An analytical description of the group's repertory and a bibliography of published and archival resources for further study are included. The excellent factual analysis makes this an important tool.

American Theatre Companies, 1888–1930, also edited by Durham (1987), is the second volume of the series and continues the first-rate coverage, with treatment of 105 more companies ranging over a span of 40-plus years. *American Theatre Companies, 1931–1986* (1989) completes Durham's effort on behalf of Greenwood Press, extending coverage an additional 55 years.

824. **Annals of the New York Stage.** George C.D. Odell. New York: Columbia University, 1927–1949. 15v.

This massive set chronicles the period from 1699 to 1894 and remains the legacy of a single individual who persevered in the effort for more than 20 years. Unfortunately, Odell was to fall short of his goal of reaching the year 1900, but his scholarship, care, and attention to detail have enabled thousands of scholars, researchers, students, and critics to draw upon a wealth of well-organized information. Each volume proceeds in chronological sequence, covering a period of years (volume 1, to 1789; volume 2, to 1821). Included in the record are the actors, plays, theaters, critical commentary, and historical background of the period. Plays are identified along with cast listings and comments from contemporary critics and reviewers.

Many portraits of now-obscure performers are included, for which access has been facilitated through the publication of the *Index to the Portraits in Odell's Annals of the New York Stage* (American Society for Theatre Research, 1963).

The *Encyclopedia of the New York Stage, 1920–1930*, edited by Samuel Leiter (Greenwood, 1985) in two volumes, is the first of a series designed to describe legitimate plays of every type produced either on or off-Broadway. The pattern of coverage identifies type, author, lyricist, director, opening date, and so on, along with plot description and critical commentary. Each title covers a decade. Subsequently, Leiter has furnished an additional two volumes: *The Encyclopedia of the New York Stage, 1930–1940* (issued in 1989) and *The Encyclopedia of the New York Stage, 1940–1950* (1992).

825. **Best Plays of 1894/1899–1989 and Yearbook of the Drama in America.** New York: Dodd, Mead, 1920–1989. Ann. ISSN 0276-2625.

This annual review of play production has been an excellent vehicle for keeping abreast of developments in the world of theater. Although the title has varied in the past, as did the frequency in the early years, it is now simply referred to as the Best Plays series, or "Burns Mantle" after its initial editor. Mantle provided retrospective coverage of the early years with two volumes: *1899/1909* (1944) and *1909/1919* (1933). These volumes identify plays and furnish lists of plays produced with date, theater, and cast. The annual began in 1920 under Mantle and, after his death in 1948, continued under others, who also completed the final retrospective volume, *1894/1989*, in 1955. The annuals furnished digests and descriptions of selected plays, including author, number of performances, theater, and cast. Various listings of actors, productions, awards, and statistics were offered. There are indexes of authors, plays, casts, and producers. Since 1990, the work has been renamed *The Burns Mantle Theater Yearbook* (Applause Theater Book Publishers), edited by Otis L. Guernsey and Jeffrey Sweet. Guernsey's *Directory of the American Theater, 1894–1971* (Dodd, Mead, 1971) is a convenient index to the series by author, title, and composer for a period of over 75 years.

826. **The Encyclopedia of the American Theatre, 1900–1975.** Edwin Bronner. San Diego: A. S. Barnes, 1980. 659p. ISBN 0-498-01219-0.

A useful handbook for basic research, rather than an encyclopedia in the true sense, this volume furnishes information on nonmusical plays by U.S. or Anglo-American playwrights performed either on or off-Broadway during the first 75 years of this century. Arrangement is alphabetical by title, and coverage includes date of opening, theater, number of performances, and capsule reviews. Authors are sometimes listed within the body of comments, with quotations from contemporary reviews as well as critical comments from Bronner. Cast members, producers, directors, and revivals are also noted, as are some set and costume designers. There are six appendices: notable premieres of the century, debut roles, debut plays, 100 longest-running productions, statistical records by season, and listings of major awards. A name index provides access.

A specialized tool is *A History of Hispanic Theatre in the United States: Origins to 1940* by Nicolas Kanellos (University of Texas Press, 1990). The work describes the development of playhouses and theatrical groups in the United States, Spain, Mexico, and Puerto Rico from the nineteenth century through the first decades of the twentieth century.

827. **Famous American Playhouses.** William C. Young. Chicago: American Library Association, 1973. 2v. (Documents of American Theater History, v.1–2). ISBN 0-838-90136-0 (v.1); 0-838-90137-9 (v.2).

The author is linked to the field of theater through his acting, writing, and teaching, and he planned this work as part of a series documenting the history of U.S. theater. He described famous playhouses in this two-volume segment, with volume 1 covering the period 1716–1899 and volume 2 covering the years 1900–1971. A variety of interesting materials have been collected, most of which are primary sources. Excerpts are provided from newspapers, periodicals, letters, diaries, journals, autobiographies, reviews, magazines, playbills, publicity materials, and architectural descriptions. Some 200 buildings of historical, architectural, or sociocultural prominence are included. Sections on New York theaters, regional theaters, and so on are arranged within chronological periods. Three indexes provide access by name, geographical location, and personal name.

828. **The Oxford Companion to American Theatre.** Gerald M. Bordman. New York: Oxford, 1984. 734p. ISBN 0-19-503443-0.

This is the first edition of a specialized version of the Oxford Companion series, and it provides a comprehensive source of information on the U.S. theater. Especially strong is the biographical coverage of performers, playwrights, composers, librettists, choreographers, producers, managers, directors, and designers, as well as orchestrators, photographers, publicists, critics, scholars, and even architects. Represented in addition to the legitimate stage are various forms of live theater, such as minstrel shows and vaudeville. Unlike *The Oxford Companion to the Theatre* (Oxford, 1983), this volume covers individual plays, musicals, and revues. Entries include production date, plot, summary, and commentary. Organizations, companies, unions, clubs, societies, periodicals, and newspapers are included, making this an extremely welcome resource for the specialist and layperson alike.

An abridged version was issued three years later by Bordman as *The Concise Oxford Companion to American Theatre* (1987). It eliminated about 280 pages by deleting minor plays and personalities, retaining only the material of greater interest. It serves well the popular good.

829. **The Tony Award: A Complete Listing, with a History of the American Theatre Wing.** Isabelle Stevenson, ed. New York: Crown, 1989. 212p.

Of interest to the historian are these essays describing the origin and development of both the Tony Awards and the American Theatre Wing, which founded the Tonys. These brief but informative expositions cover the major points in readable fashion. The major focus of the tool is a complete listing of recipients of the Antoinette Perry (Tony) Awards over a period of 40 years, from 1947 to the present. Listings include nominees, except for the period 1947–1955, when only the winners are enumerated. Arrangement of entries is chronological by year. All major categories of the awards are included in both the performance and technical operations. There are additional listings of regulations and theaters eligible for competition. There are indexes of winners of both regular and special category awards. First issued in 1980, the work has been updated at intervals ranging from two to four years.

830. **Variety Entertainment and Outdoor Amusements: A Reference Guide.** Don B. Wilmeth. Westport, CT: Greenwood, 1982. 242p. (American Popular Culture). ISBN 0-313-21455-7.

This one-volume history covers a wide range of popular entertainments in its 12 chapters, which cover such topics as outdoor amusements, the circus, Wild West shows, dime museums, early musical theater, stage music, tent theaters, and floating palaces. In this convenient source of information on a variety of U.S. pastimes, each chapter opens with a brief historical description of the topic. This perspective is followed by a bibliographic essay identifying additional information centers, as well as useful books and periodicals and a detailed bibliography of the more important sources. The author is a prolific writer in the area of popular U.S. culture and with this work has produced an interesting and informative overview of those amusements that were "presented by professional showmen for profit." There is a selective index to aid access.

Biographical Sources

831. **American Actors and Actresses: A Guide to Information Sources.** Stephen M. Archer. Detroit: Gale, 1983. 710p. (Performing Arts Information Guide Series, v.8; Gale Information Guide Library). ISBN 0-8103-1495-9.

Archer has furnished an extensive annotated bibliography of publications covering the lives and careers of about 225 important U.S. actors and actresses of the professional legitimate theater. More than 3,200 entries are identified, an average of about 15 items for each individual. Most of the personalities are deceased, and all are of historical significance in terms of their achievements. Inclusion is limited to those who were established through performance in U.S. productions; few are foreign-born. Certain important directors and instructors have been treated because of their influence on the U.S. theater. The work is useful to both scholars and students. There are author, title, and subject indexes.

American Actors, 1861–1910: An Annotated Bibliography of Books Published in the United States in English from 1861 Through 1976 (Whitson, 1979), edited by Ronald L. Moyer, provides comprehensive coverage with the purpose of furnishing a complete listing of books containing substantial information on U.S. actors over a period of 50 years beginning with the Civil War period. About 360 English-language books are listed and annotated at some length regarding content. An index furnishes access.

832. **Notable Names in the American Theatre.** New and rev. ed. Clifton, NJ: J. T. White, 1976. 1,250p. ISBN 0-883-71018-8.

As the second edition of Walter Rigdon's *Biographical Encyclopedia and Who's Who of the American Theatre* (Heinemann, 1966), this work is useful although aging. Its nine major sections provide comprehensive coverage. Included are segments listing New York productions, 1900–1974, U.S. premiers, and U.S. plays abroad, listing title, author, date, and run. Also furnished are theater group bibliographies, New York theater buildings, and listings of awards. Important coverage is given to biographical bibliography, through references to books about theater personalities, and to necrology, through a comprehensive listing of deceased individuals from the colonial period to the present. The major segment is, of course, that on notable names, providing detailed biographical descriptions of then-living individuals (many of whom are now deceased). Actors, designers, producers, and writers of all levels of achievement are included.

William C. Young's *Famous Actors and Actresses on the American Stage* (Bowker, 1975) is a companion work to Young's volumes on theaters (entry 827) and furnishes biocritical information, employing excerpts from reviews, memoirs, and so forth. Portraits are included, as are references to the sources of the critiques for 225 actors and actresses.

Sports and Games

Because of the U.S. fascination for spectator sports, there are many almanacs, guides, statistical handbooks, and other information sources of a popular nature, many of which are issued periodically. Included here are representative sources that serve the needs of both popular and scholarly interests. *Sport Bibliography* (Human Kinetics Publishers, 1986–) is an annual listing of monographs, articles, and theses from all over the world. Of course, U.S. sport receives a good proportion of the coverage, and historical treatment is frequent. The bibliography is available online through DIALOG in a file of over 250,000 records. A similar effort on CD-ROM is *Sport Discus that identifies articles, monographs, dissertations, report, and proceedings on an international basis. Beginning in 1981, it draws from over 2,000 periodicals and furnishes abstracts for most entries.

The North American Society for Sport History was founded in 1972 at Pennsylvania State University in University Park. It has some 900 members and publishes the *Journal of Sport History* three times per year.

833. The Ballplayers: Baseball's Ultimate Biographical Reference. Mike Shatzkin, et al., eds. New York: Arbor House/William Morrow, 1990. 1,230p. ISBN 0-87795-984-6.

The most comprehensive of the biographical works on baseball, this well-illustrated tool covers more than 6,000 players and managers and another 1,000 umpires, broadcasters, front office types, scouts, and so on. Also included are players from the Japanese, Mexican, and Negro leagues. There is excellent coverage given to historical figures—about 1,000 of the listed personalities date back to the nineteenth century. Entries are arranged alphabetically and offer biographical sketches varying in length from a few sentences to several pages. Sketches identify position, team, nickname, years of service, career statistics, and achievements. Awards, all-star selections, World Series performances, and other information of interest to baseball enthusiasts and researchers. The various contributors have signed their entries and are listed separately at the end.

834. Biographical Dictionary of American Sports: Basketball and Other Indoor Sports. David L. Porter, ed. New York: Greenwood, 1989. 801p. ISBN 0-313-26261-6.

This is one of a series of biographical dictionaries by the author, all of which employ a similar format and treat important figures from the major spectator sports. This volume on basketball does include a number of other indoor sports, some of minor significance to the U.S. viewing and cheering public. Of the nearly 560 personalities, more than half are basketball players, officials, and other notables. Representation also is given to bowling, boxing, hockey, swimming, weightlifting, diving, skating, gymnastics, and wrestling. Biographical narratives are brief but informative, and the work includes a bibliography. Useful appendices enumerate players by sport, position, place of birth, Hall of Fame memberships, women participants, boxers' ring names, and so forth.

Porter's other works include the *Biographical Dictionary of American Sports: Baseball* (Greenwood, 1987), which covers more than 500 personalities, mainly players but also some managers, executives, and umpires. The work includes figures from the Negro leagues but not from the ladies' operations. The *Biographical Dictionary of American Sports: Football* (Greenwood, 1987), treats nearly 525 gridiron personalities of various types. Appendices include both collegiate and professional Hall of Fame members. The *Biographical Dictionary of American Sports: Outdoor Sports* (Greenwood, 1988) covers such competitive ventures as auto racing, golf, lacrosse, horse racing, skiing, soccer, speed skating, tennis, and track and field. About 520 major personalities are covered in brief biographical sketches.

Another recently completed volume serves as a supplement to the preceding efforts: the *Biographical Dictionary of American Sports: Supplement for Baseball, Football, Basketball, and Other Sports* (Greenwood, 1992).

835. College Football Records: Division I-A and the Ivy League, 1869–1984. Jefferson, NC: McFarland, 1987. 198p. ISBN 0-89950-246-6.

This is a useful handbook of team records rather than individual achievements and furnishes listings of won-lost totals (and ties) for each of 111 Division I-A colleges and universities still active in the sport. Arrangement is by conference, under which the schools are listed alphabetically. Entries furnish the schools' nicknames, colors, location, and stadium with seating capacity. Also included are the years in which the football competition began, first year in the conference, and number of conference championships. Overall records are given, as are team versus team totals. Introductory information given at the beginning of the section for each conference includes founding date, charter members, overall records, and conference champions, year by year. Appendices furnish a variety of summary listings, including bowl game records. There is an index of nondivision opponents; knowledge of conference affiliation is a prerequisite for use.

836. **Encyclopedia of American Wrestling.** Mike Chapman. Champaign, IL: Leisure Press, 1990. 533p. ISBN 0-88011-342-1.

Although the ancient sport of wrestling has developed a somewhat less-than-honorable reputation in view of the recent performances of progressional grapplers, Chapman establishes his perspective outside the realm of exhibition and histrionics. His coverage is given primarily to amateur wrestling, which is a truly competitive and taxing sport requiring skill, speed, and strength. The history and development of the sport in this country is revealed in various chapters dealing with U.S. champions in the Olympics, AAU National Freestyle Championships, United States Freestyle Senior Opens, Greco-Roman Nationals, Collegiate Nationals, Midlands Championships, Junior Nationals, and the Junior World Tournaments. Coverage is given to special awards; biographical treatment is given to nearly 80 members of the National Wrestling Hall of Fame. There is a concise bibliography but, unfortunately, no index.

837. **The Encyclopedia of North American Sports History.** Ralph Hickok. New York: Facts on File, 1992. 516p. ISBN 0-8160-2096-5.

Games and sports have been an important part of human civilization since its beginnings. This comprehensive one-volume encyclopedia furnishes over 1,000 entries that include personalities, events, awards, stadiums, organizations, and other subjects pertinent to the history of sports on this continent. The work is of interest to inquirers at all levels; entries tend to be brief but informative, with baseball receiving the most coverage (some 3,000 words). In any one-volume effort of this type, the challenges will generally represent omissions of favorite personalities and scant coverage of favorite pastimes. Most interesting is the treatment given to the history and development of the various sports. There is a bibliography of several pages and many large photographs. There is a subject index to furnish access.

A recent work with a unique format is the *Atlas of American Sport* by John F. Rooney, Jr. and Richard Pillsbury (Macmillan, 1993). The title identifies regional differences in games played by Americans through maps by state, city, and zip code area. It also furnishes essays and photographs and shows both individual and team sports as they reflect American culture.

838. **Play and Playthings: A Reference Guide.** Bernard Mergen. Westport, CT: Greenwood, 1982. 281p. (American Popular Culture). ISBN 0-313-22136-7.

This unique and well-constructed guide is of value to both scholars and students in its thorough coverage of the literature and background of children's play. As an academic, Mergen has successfully chosen and interpreted the aspects of most concern to future research. The work is divided into two parts, the first of which is a 140-page historical monograph covering various topics of historical interest, such as the play of slave children and the impact of toys, along with the influence of playgrounds, motion pictures, and television. Illustrations are included along with the narrative. Part 2 furnishes a 46-page bibliographical essay of relevant sources, which have been carefully selected and organized, followed by a substantial checklist of books and articles alphabetically arranged. Research collections are described, giving the serious inquirer a comprehensive source of information.

839. **The Pro Football Bio-Bibliography.** Myron J. Smith, Jr. West Cornwell, CT: Locust Hill, 1989. 388p. ISBN 0-933951-23-X.

Smith is known primarily as a prolific military bibliographer, particularly for his work on the U.S. Navy, but he changed directions here with his coverage of sports. For this work, he has identified articles from books, magazines, league publications, team yearbooks, and commercially published annuals, treating some 1,400 players, coaches, managers, and officials involved in professional football. Entries are arranged alphabetically by name with brief enumeration of career data (items, positions, years played) rather than personal information. Articles cited will furnish ample data for the researcher and serious inquirer as well as the football fan.

Smith's earlier work, *Baseball: A Comprehensive Bibliography* (McFarland, 1986) is a thorough and expansive effort that lists articles, monographs, government publications, theses and dissertations, yearbooks, and even literary efforts on the national pastime. Reference works are given, as are histories, studies, and so on. Baseball is treated comprehensively, from youth leagues and amateur status to the big leagues. There are author and subject indexes.

840. **The Sports Encyclopedia: Pro Basketball, 1891–1991.** 4th ed. David S. Neft and Richard M. Cohen. New York: St. Martin's, 1990. 607p.

The authors began their association with Grosset and Dunlap in the mid-1970s and have been producing sports guides for St. Martin's since 1985. This basketball issue covers the first 100 years of the sport and is the fourth edition in this series. It represents a useful and handy digest of statistics and records, as well as a brief but informative historical summary. Treatment is given decade by decade, with yearly chronologies included within each decade. With the progression of time, statistical columns for the more recent players have become more detailed. As basketball is one of the major sports covered, we can expect this volume to become more frequently revised and published by St. Martin's.

The Sports Encyclopedia: Baseball (12th ed., St. Martin's, 1992), is the most recent of this annual series, which updates the records and statistics with the inclusion of records from the season just completed. All types of statistics are recorded.

Football is covered through publication of two volumes. *Pro Football, The Early Years: An Encyclopedic History, 1895–1959* (rev. ed., Sports Products, 1987), describes the early years. *The Sports Encyclopedia, Pro Football: The Modern Era, 1960–1990,* (9th ed., St. Martin's, 1991), furnishes annual coverage through the 1990 season.

841. **Sports: A Reference Guide.** Robert J. Higgs. Westport, CT: Greenwood, 1982. 317p. (American Popular Culture). ISBN 0-313-21361-5.

Another of the entries from the Greenwood series on popular culture, this work furnishes a brief history of sports in the United States. Written at the level of the undergraduate student by an academic who has targeted the athlete in previous publications, this reference guide contains 14 essays on various topics relevant to the study of sports. The historian will especially appreciate coverage given to "History of Sports" and "Sources on the History of Sports." Also included are popular culture, traditional arts, education, race and sex, heroes, even philosophy and religion. Essays describe the scholarly and popular literature and provide historical summaries of the topics. Critical interpretation of studies is rendered along with bibliographies. Appendices furnish a useful 20-page chronology from 1618 to mid-1981, as well as a listing of research centers. There is an index of subjects, authors, and titles.

A useful guide for both researchers and fans is *Sports Halls of Fame: A Directory of Over 100 Sports Museums in the United States* by Doug Gelbert (McFarland, 1992). The work is organized into three sections covering national halls, single-sport museums and multi-sport halls, and local attractions. There is a geographic listing and an index to facilitate access.

Chapter 6

Regional History

With the rise of sectionalism in the United States over the first half of the nineteenth century, the burning issues that divided the nation, states' rights and the practice of slavery, were inextricably linked to geography and the resulting economic systems. The growing disaffection and alienation climaxed in the most troubling single event in this nation's history, the war between the states. The Civil War settled the slavery issue once and for all, but sectionalism has remained a political and economic reality for those elected to serve their constituencies.

This chapter is divided into five sections, beginning with coverage of general sources that are not targeted to a single specific geographical region. Included in the general section are materials on historic preservation, local history in general, and place-names. New England and the Midwest are combined in the next segment, followed by separate sections on the South and on the West. Finally, there is a section that covers U.S. territories and possessions.

Two important organizations are the American Association for State and Local History, with its numerous publications (entry 2), and the National Trust for Historic Preservation (entry 9).

GENERAL

This is the largest section of the chapter and includes a variety of tools, each of which treats the United States as a whole or embraces more than one region. Content varies from identification of local history collections to historic preservation, archaeology, and state names.

Library Resources

842.   **United States Local Histories in the Library of Congress: A Bibliography.** Marion J. Kaminkow, ed. Baltimore: Magna Carta, 1975–1976. 5v. ISBN 0-910946-17-5

These volumes furnish condensed cataloging of some 90,000 items held by the Library of Congress relating to local history as of mid-1972. Volumes 1 and 2 cover the Atlantic States, from Maine to New York and from New Jersey to Florida; volume 3 includes items from the Midwest, Alaska, and Hawaii, along with the South and the Southwest; volume 4 targets the West, including the Northwest and the Pacific States; and volume 5 serves as an index to the entire set, adding supplementary listings of local histories received by the library between 1972 and January 1976. Arrangement within volumes is by LC classification system, with regions subdivided by city, county, and so on, then by format of tools. Entries are abbreviated in a standard format and omit most authors' dates, joint authors, numbers of copies, detailed content descriptions, and other information conveyed in the original cataloging effort. There is a supplementary index of places after each section.

Bibliographical Sources

843. **A Bibliography of American County Histories.** P. William Filby, comp. Baltimore: Genealogical Publishing Co., 1985. 449p. ISBN 0-8063-1126-6.

The author's intent was to create a work that was more scholarly, accurate, and comprehensive than the second edition of Clarence Peterson's *Consolidated Bibliography of County Histories in the Fifty States* (Genealogical, 1963) and to furnish access to material not found in the effort by Kaminkow, which was restricted to holdings of the Library of Congress (entry 1). Filby was successful in his attempt: For all intents and purposes, this volume has replaced the Peterson title. Included here are citations to 4,000 county histories derived from the collections of the Library of Congress, the New York Public Library, various state bibliographies, and lists furnished by librarians from every state. Alaska, Hawaii, and Puerto Rico are included in the coverage, with entries arranged chronologically under state, then county, divisions. Standard bibliographic information is furnished in this useful source. No index is given.

844. **Bibliography of Place-Name Literature: United States and Canada.** 3rd ed. Richard B. Sealock, et. al. Chicago: American Library Association, 1982. 435p. ISBN 0-8389-0369-6

The principal author was responsible for the first edition of this bibliography nearly 40 years earlier in 1948. Since then, it was expanded in the second edition, which covered about 3,600 sources in 1967. The most recent edition furnishes a listing of over 4,800 books and journal articles, along with manuscript compilations located in various libraries. The literature of place-names furnishes exposition of origins, meanings, correct spellings, nicknames, and pronunciations of sites, geographical features, regions, and cities located throughout the United States. There has been an increasing interest in such writings on the part of social historians, reporters, and even the general public. As in previous efforts, there are brief notes accompanying some of the entries. Author and subject indexes aid access.

845. **Directory of State and Local History Periodicals.** Milton Crouch and Hans Raum, comps. Chicago: American Library Association, 1977. 124p. ISBN 0-8389-0426-4.

This useful bibliographic directory identifies state and local history magazines issued in the United States. It includes both current offerings and those that have ceased publication but were covered by national indexing services prior to their demise. Nearly 750 periodicals are represented, arranged first by state, then alphabetically by title of magazine. Entries provide the usual bibliographic information: frequency, address, cost, editor, beginning date, and indexing information. The value of this work lies in its capacity to cite obscure and little-known titles, many of which have not been covered in *Ulrich's Periodical Directory* or in Eric Boehm's *Historical Periodicals* (Clio, 1961). Unfortunately, there are no cross-references within the entries, and the index is not as detailed as one might wish.

846. **Historic Preservation: A Guide to Information Sources.** Arnold L. Markowitz. Detroit: Gale, 1980. 279p. (Art and Architecture Information Guide Series, v.13; Gale Information Guide Library). ISBN 0-8103-1460-6.

As part of a series of art guides, this work carries on a fine tradition with its well-developed treatment of historic preservation literature. Organized into 14 chapters, most of which provide thematic coverage, the work is extremely useful and easily targets the topics of interest. Themes include legal issues, which embrace preservation plans and building codes, and renovation and restoration, treating such activity as the refurbishing of old houses. There is a chapter given to listings of periodicals, but no periodical articles are included among the 827 annotated books and pamphlets. These listings emphasize U.S. publications, although a number of foreign citations are included. Materials are of a varied nature and include manuals of practice as well as research reports and site studies. Four indexes are given: author, organization, title, and subject.

847. **Index to Historic Preservation Periodicals.** National Trust for Historic Preservation Library of the University of Maryland. Boston: G. K. Hall, 1988. 354p. ISBN 0-8161-0474-3.

The National Trust for Historic Preservation Library is based in the Architecture Library of the University of Maryland as a special collection. It furnishes monthly listings of articles to National Trust members and staff through an examination of several hundred serials of international, national, regional, state, and local organizations. Also included are pamphlets, newspapers clippings, and brochures. The present work represents a compilation of these listings from 1979 to 1987. It furnishes over 6,000 entries dealing with such topics as architectural law, restoration, real estate, and federal policy. The material represents both scholarly and popular efforts and includes the publications of the historic preservation organizations. Arrangement of entries is classified by subject heading assigned; unfortunately, there is no subject index. It is a unique and distinctive tool in terms of its coverage.

848. **Reference Guides to State History and Research.** New York: Greenwood, 1982–1991. v.1–6. (In progress). ISBN 0-313-22959-7 (v.1).

This important series of bibliographic guides to state histories is published by Greenwood Press. States are covered individually in separately published works that follow a standardized coverage beginning with part I, which contains historical essays divided by chronological periods or themes. These survey the important literature and identify materials of various types. The second part of the work describes archival repositories and sources of information containing state history materials. Six volumes have been issued thus far, beginning in 1983 with *A Guide to the History of Louisiana,* edited by Light Townsend Cummins and Glen Jeansonne. This was followed by *A Guide to the History of Massachusetts,* edited by Martin Kaufman, et. al. (1988); *A Guide to the History of Texas,* edited by Cummins and Alvin R. Bailey, Jr. (1988); *A Guide to the History of Florida,* edited by Paul S. George (1989); *A Guide to the History of California,* edited by Doyce R. Nunis, Jr. and Gloria R. Lothrop (1989); and *A Guide to the History of Illinois,* edited by John Hoffman (1991).

849. **Region and Regionalism in the United States: A Source Book for the Humanities and Social Sciences.** Michael Steiner and Clarence Mondale. New York: Garland, 1988. 495p. (Garland Reference Library of Social Science, v.204). ISBN 0-8240-9048-9.

A unique work that furnishes a framework for the interdisciplinary study of regionalism in the United States, this annotated bibliography of some 1,600 entries includes both books and periodical articles. It is divided into 14 subject areas, each of which contains materials relevant to the study of major thinkers, trends and developments, and schools of thought. Each discipline addresses the concepts of region and regionalism in its own way, and together they form a revealing package for broader understanding. In addition to history and geography, fields included are American studies, anthropology, architecture, art, economics, folk studies, language, literature, philosophy and religion, political service, psychology, and sociology. Annotations are descriptive and range from 150 to 200 words; some entries are repeated in various sections. This is a valuable work for all inquirers; unfortunately, there is only an author index.

850.   **Researcher's Guide to Archives and Regional History Sources.** John C. Larsen, ed. Hamden, CT: Library Professional Publications/Shoe String, 1988. 167p. ISBN 0-20802-144-2.

This guide consists of a collection of 14 essays written by various archivists and dealing with issues important to the utilization of archival and regional history resources. It serves the needs of both beginning researchers and serious inquirers by presenting a cohesive body of information, beginning with the first chapter, which covers the nature of archival research and the various types of materials and techniques. The work offers an interesting blend of general bibliographic awareness and practical information for conducting studies. Specialized types of materials are described in various areas, such as business, religion, and genealogy. There is a notes and bibliography section that furnishes references to more in-depth topical coverage. The work serves as both a manual/textbook and a bibliographic source useful in preparing for archival work with regional materials. Topical treatment is given to ethics, preservation, oral history, and so forth.

851.   **Sources for U.S. History: Nineteenth-Century Communities.** W. B. Stephens. New York: Cambridge University, 1991. 558p. ISBN 0-521-35315-7.

Author Stephens has provided a companion publication to his earlier work targeting sources for the study of England's local history. The present effort surveys the literature to furnish an important source of information for the study of nineteenth-century local, regional, and state history in this country. Various sources, both primary and secondary (manuscripts, records, books), are listed in bibliographic narratives arranged topically by chapter. Chapter headings include demography, ethnicity and race, land use and settlement, religion, education, politics and local government, industry, trade and transportation, and poverty, health, and crime. Entries are treated as footnotes within the bibliographical essays. The focus on nineteenth-century communities reflects a unique perspective. A helpful segment on the use of primary sources is designed to aid the novice. A topical index furnishes access.

852.   **Travels in America from the Voyages of Discovery to the Present: An Annotated Bibliography of Travel Articles in Periodicals, 1950-1980.** Garold Cole. Norman: University of Oklahoma Press, 1984. 291p. ISBN 0-8065-1791-5.

The author is a seasoned bibliographer in historical studies and serves as a reference librarian in history. He has furnished a useful bibliography of travel articles covering a span of time from the age of exploration to the present. There are over 1,025 entries for accounts published in 170 periodicals, most of them state and local history journals. These entries are organized by region, then state, and are placed in chronological order, furnishing a good historical perspective. The accounts were written by a variety of people, including emigrants, explorers, missionaries, men of commerce, and travelers. Annotations are full; bibliographic citations are complete. The work is easily accessible through an index to travelers, places, and subjects and another to authors, editors, and translators. There is a bibliography of periodicals.

Information Sources

853. American Place-Names: A Concise and Selective Dictionary for the Continental United States of America. George R. Stewart. New York: Oxford University, 1970. Repr. 1985. 550p. ISBN 0-19-503725-1.

Since its publication in 1970, this work has been regarded as the standard source on U.S. place-names. As such, it was designed to furnish the general public with a useful reference tool on the derivation and origin of the different names given to various places. This is a reprint of the original work and continues to find ready acceptance not only by the general public but by scholars and students as well. It selectively describes about 12,000 place names; omitted are certain commonplace names, obsolete names, and those of Hawaiian origin. Entries are restricted to places in the continental United States and furnish name derivation, state, and explanation of historical, geographical, and folk influences. The introduction is extensive and describes the difficulties inherent in place-name history and the structure of the work. A bibliography is included.

854. A Historical Guide to the United States. American Association for State and Local History. New York: Norton, 1986. 601p. ISBN 0-393-02383-4.

For the history buff and traveler, this guidebook furnishes well-written, informative historical essays for two or three sites in every state of the union. These essays are then followed by listings of additional sites, each of which is briefly annotated. The essays are well researched and have previously appeared in a series produced by the association. Photographs are included to increase the volume's appeal as a travel book. Historical sites vary from homes of prominent people to battlegrounds to museums with noteworthy collections. As a convenience tool, the work is useful in identifying and describing noteworthy features of various museums located throughout the nation and in enumerating certain historical sites that are less familiar to interested parties. There is a good index of all places included.

*855. National Register of Historic Places, 1966–1988. National Park Service, et al. Washington: National Park Service, 1989. 807p. ISBN 0-942063-03-1.

The *Register of Historic Places* has appeared as a publication of the National Park Service on an irregular basis since 1969. Originally, the landmarks, buildings, bridges, and other places listed were limited to resources of national significance. Succeeding editions updated their predecessors, adding sites through the National Park Service, acts of Congress, executive orders, National Historic Landmark designation, or nomination from federal and state agencies. The present effort furnishes a cumulative listing of 52,000 sites added over a 22-year period to the register, which now includes properties significant to local and state history as well as the history of the nation. Arrangement is alphabetical by state and county. Dates and criteria for inclusion are enumerated.

The work is available in CD-ROM format as *National Register of Historic Places Index* from Buckmaster Publishing of Mineral, VA.

856. The Passionate Amateur's Guide to Archaeology in the United States. Josleen Wilson. New York: Collier, 1980. 464p. ISBN 0-02-098670-X.

A useful guidebook for the amateur historian and archaeology buff is this well-developed directory of prehistoric sites in the United States. It was the intention of the author to include every prehistoric site open to the public and every museum having prehistoric holdings. The work opens with a brief introduction to prehistoric archaeology in this country and describes its history and development in clear and lucid fashion. Following the introduction is the main text, which describes each site and museum. Entries generally include address, phone number, hours, fees, and brief descriptive notes on the points of interest. Sites in progress are included along with those in full operation. There is a brief bibliography of useful readings, along with a directory of organizations. An index is furnished.

857.   **State Names, Seals, Flags, and Symbols: A Historical Guide.** Benjamin F. Shearer and Barbara S. Shearer. New York: Greenwood, 1987. 239p. ISBN 0-313-24559-2.

At the time this work was issued, it had been close to 50 years since a work of this type had been published. Obviously, it was time for another handbook on state names. The Shearers have produced a useful, interesting, and convenient volume for inquirers at all levels who seek basic information regarding state designations. As the title indicates, coverage is given not only to names but also to seals, flags, and symbols for each of the 50 states. Official birds, songs, mottos, flowers, trees, and so forth are included as well. Entries describe the origins of nicknames, as well as names of capital cities and buildings. Arrangement is alphabetical by state under the symbol being described. Color illustrations show flags, flowers, and birds. There is a selective bibliography of state histories; an index is furnished to provide access.

858.   **Worldmark Encyclopedia of the States.** 2nd ed. New York: Worldmark, 1986. 690p. ISBN 0-471-83213-8.

This work was first issued in 1981 as a companion to the established publication *Worldmark Encyclopedia of the Nations*. The second edition is almost identical in form, shape, and even pagination to its predecessor. The information, however, has been updated, and the product is a useful source for all inquirers. Given here is statistical information and summary data of all types for each of the 50 states, U.S. dependencies, and the U.S. as a whole. Maps and charts are furnished; demographic data is developed in careful manner, employing population estimates developed through Donnelly Marketing Services. Bibliographies are furnished for each segment. Although the information can be found in a variety of sources, such as almanacs, encyclopedias, and handbooks, the work does have value as a convenience tool for its users.

NEW ENGLAND AND THE MIDWEST

Because of our resolve not to include histories of specific states, these regions are represented by a total of only three reference sources. In the case of New England, however, it should be noted that entry 859 is a series entry comprising several bibliographic works that treat each state independently. Of all the regions of the country, the Midwest is least documented in terms of a tradition or heritage.

The Society for the Preservation of New England Antiquities, located in Boston, was founded in 1910 and has 3,000 members. It publishes *Historic Houses in New England* annually and issues a quarterly newsletter. The Midwest Archives Conference, based in Evanston, Illinois, has produced *The Midwestern Archivist*, a semiannual journal, since 1976. Founded in 1972, the conference has 1,100 members at present.

859.   **Bibliographies of New England History.** Committee for a New England Bibliography. Hanover, NH: University Press of New England, 1976–1989. v.1–8. (In progress). ISBN 0-8161-1212-6 (v.1).

The Committee for a New England Bibliography was created in 1969 to respond to the need for organization of the wealth of historical material available in the region. It was decided to produce individual state bibliographies as part of a projected seven-volume series. That projection was exceeded with the recent publication of the eighth volume, and others are still to come. Volume 1, *Massachusetts: A Bibliography of Its History*, edited by John Haskell (1976), established the pattern for the series as an alphabetical arrangement of books, periodicals, and articles under geographical units (state, county, or city). Location symbols are given if materials are not in the *National Union Catalog*. The cutoff date for inclusion is 1972. Works span the entire history of the state from its earliest development to the present. Volume 2, *Maine: A Bibliography of Its History* (1977), with a cutoff date of 1975, was also edited by Haskell. Volume 3, *New Hampshire: A Bibliography of Its History*, edited by Haskell and T.D. Seymour Bassett, was issued in 1979, with a cutoff date of 1977. Bassett edited volume 4, *Vermont: A Bibliography of Its History* in 1981, with 1979 as the cutoff date; Roger N. Parks edited the fifth volume, *Rhode Island: A Bibliography of Its History*, in 1983, with the cutoff date being 1981. Volume 6, *Connecticut: A Bibliography of Its History*, was edited by Parks in 1986, with a cutoff date of 1984. Volume 7, *New England: A Bibliography of Its History*, serves to provide materials covering either the entire region or those dealing with more than one state and was edited by Parks in 1989, with a 1987 cutoff date. Volume 8, also edited by Parks in 1989 and using a 1987 cutoff date, contains additions and corrections to the state bibliographies. Further volumes of this type are planned for 1994 and 1995.

860. **The Encyclopedia of New England.** Robert O'Brien and Richard D. Brown, eds. New York: Facts on File, 1985. 613p. ISBN 0-87196-759-6.

From *Facts on File* comes this effort as part of the plan to furnish one-volume encyclopedias targeting the different regions of the country (see also entry 861). Similar in format to the others, this effort furnishes about 2,500 articles alphabetically arranged and covering various events, personalities, and places associated with the six states of the New England region (Connecticut, Maine, Massachusetts, New Hampshire, Rhode Island, and Vermont). Entries tend to be brief rather than giving in-depth coverage to topics; therefore, it is best used by the general public rather than the serious student. Coverage is given to what is considered to be cultural information in describing people's lives, institutions, historical events, demographics, climate, and politics. Definitions are given and geographical information provided, along with cross-references, maps, photographs, a bibliography, and an index.

861. **The Encyclopedia of the Midwest.** Allan Carpenter. New York: Facts on File, 1989. 544p. ISBN 0-8160-1660-7.

Like the entry above, this recent one-volume encyclopedia is part of the publisher's design to cover the various regions of the United States. The strength of this particular work is its uniqueness as a source of information on a region that, plainly, has been ignored by bibliographers, editors, and publishers in the past. Other than that, the title is subject to the same type of criticism lodged against the other Facts on File efforts. Coverage of the 2,500 entries is brief rather than in-depth; the descriptions of personalities, historical events, institutions, climate, and politics are better utilized by the general public than by those with a scholarly or serious interest. The states of Illinois, Indiana, Iowa, Michigan, Minnesota, Missouri, Ohio, and Wisconsin are treated. Cross-references are included, as are photographs; there is a bibliography and a general index.

THE SOUTH

The South continues to draw the attention of historians, writers, and reporters seeking to furnish enlightenment and understanding of its almost mystical way of life. It has been revered and castigated, praised and condemned, serenely described and bitterly rendered by commentators and observers. No section of the country has inspired such polarization. The materials included here treat both the Old South (genteel, romantic, slow-paced, hospitable, but defensive and even violent in its protection of its way of life) and the New South (urban, sophisticated, and politically aware in pursuing its interests).

The Southern Historical Association was founded in 1934 and operates out of the Department of History at the University of Georgia in Athens. The organization has 4,500 members and has published the *Journal of Southern History* on a quarterly basis since 1935.

Library Resources

862. **Bibliography of Southern Appalachia: A Publication of the Appalachian Consortium, Inc.** Charlotte T. Ross, et al. Boone, NC: Appalachian Consortium Press, 1976. 235p.

This bibliography serves as a union list of the holdings of the eleven member libraries of the Appalachian Consortium. The work is comprehensive and furnishes an excellent bibliography of some 13,000 items covering the region. Approximately 50 percent of the publications are from the social sciences; the sciences account for 25 percent, as do the fine arts. Entries date from the early nineteenth century to near the time of publication, the emphasis being on the periods subsequent to 1940. Brief annotations are given for about half the entries. Arrangement is alphabetical by author, with the holdings of consortium members noted. Also included is a filmography of 16mm films and videotapes, with a list of regional distributors. This unique and useful work is indexed by subject.

863. **French and Spanish Records of Louisiana: A Bibliographical Guide to Archive and Manuscript Sources.** Henry P. Beers. Baton Rouge: LSU Press, 1989. 371p. ISBN 0-8071-1444-8.

Early Louisiana was a region composed of the present states of Alabama, Arkansas, Louisiana, Mississippi and Missouri and administered by Spain, England, and France during successive time periods. Historical inquiries have been aided considerably with the publication of this comprehensive bibliographical guide to relevant materials. The author was a noted archivist, historian, and bibliographer and has produced a first-rate tool for scholars and serious students. The area was initially discovered and claimed by Spain and then settled by France, leaving a rich historical tradition in this region. Arrangement of the bibliography is in five chapters, each devoted to a state. The chapters furnish a documentary history and give locations of important collections (including European archives), reproductions, documents, publications, parish/county records, and so on. There are extensive footnotes, plus a detailed bibliography and a good index.

Bibliographical Sources

864. **The American South: A Historical Bibliography.** Jessica S. Brown, ed. ABC-Clio, 1985. 2v. ISBN 0-87436-464-7.

An excellent contribution to scholarly inquiry and sophisticated investigation, this two-volume effort furnishes a comprehensive bibliography of nearly 8,900 periodical articles written over a 10-year period from 1974 to 1984. Over 500 periodical titles have been used, including foreign language journals providing coverage of the American South. Like other works by this publisher, this offering is derived from the great database that produces *America: History and Life* (entry 51). Volume 1 targets Southern history, with divisions by chronological time periods from the colonial era to 1982. Volume 2 concentrates on cultural history and embraces writings on art, education, religion, law, and so forth. Arrangement of entries in both volumes is alphabetical order, under the heading or subheading. Each volume contains indexes by author and subject (ABC-SPIndex).

865. **Index to Southern Periodicals.** Sam G. Riley, comp. Westport, CT: Greenwood, 1986. 456p. (Historical Guides to the World's Periodicals and Newspapers). ISBN 0-313-24515-0
   The compiler is a professor of communication and has furnished a helpful resource tool for the study of magazine history in the South and topical coverage of events treated in the popular periodical literature. The South is defined in terms of the states of the Confederacy (Alabama, Arkansas, Florida, Georgia, Louisiana, Mississippi, North Carolina, South Carolina, Texas, and Kentucky). Maryland is excluded after the onset of the Civil War. Coverage includes about 90 periodicals published over a period of 120 years beginning in 1764 and emphasizes publications with general appeal rather than those considered the most scholarly. Those specific to black interests or to religious interests are excluded. Arrangement of entries is alphabetical; entries furnish a summary of the title's history, editorial policy, and content. Appendices identify titles by founding date and by location; indexing is furnished.

866. **The Old South.** Fletcher M. Green and J. Isaac Copeland. Arlington Heights, IL: AHM, 1980. 173p. (Goldentree Bibliographies in American History). ISBN 0-88295-539-X.
   This bibliographic series was developed to provide students, teachers, and librarians with reliable guides. It is clear that historical bibliographers Green and Copeland succeeded in their attempt to develop a useful bibliography of selective rather than comprehensive nature for use by advanced undergraduate and beginning graduate students. The Old South is defined as those states in the Confederacy as well as Maryland, Kentucky, Missouri, and even to some degree Delaware. Emphasis has been placed on coverage of the period subsequent to 1820 and on social, economic, and cultural history. More than 2,950 entries representing leading books and periodical articles are enumerated. Arrangement of entries is classified within a mix of format and topical categories (bibliography, general works, travel, the colonial period, science, religion, politics). These are subdivided in detailed fashion; an author index furnishes access.

867. **Travels in the New South: A Bibliography.** Thomas D. Clark, ed. Norman: University of Oklahoma Press, 1962. 2v. (American Exploration and Travel Series, no.36).
   As a companion work to general editor Clark's *Travels in the Old South* (entry 868), these two volumes complete the six-volume set, which is recognized as a standard bibliographic effort. Coverage in volume 1, "The Postwar South, 1865–1900," treats Reconstruction and readjustment. Volume 2, "The Twentieth-Century South, 1900–1955," covers the era of change, depression, and emergence. Fletcher M. Green and Clark combined their efforts to produce the first volume, whereas volume 2 was a product of the creative energy of Rupert B. Vance and Lawrence S. Thompson. The efforts were carefully developed and well executed in furnishing an excellent bibliography of both English language and foreign language publications for scholars and serious students. Volume 1 contains 508 entries, and volume 2 identifies 627 titles. Included are various types of works (surveys, promotional literature, guidebooks, directories) for which evaluative annotations and full bibliographic descriptions are provided. Each volume is indexed.

868. **Travels in the Old South: A Bibliography.** Thomas D. Clark, ed. University of Oklahoma, 1956–1959. 3v. (American Exploration and Travel Series, no.19).

Clark and a number of associates compiled this three-volume bibliography, which along with E. M. Coulter's *Travels in the Confederate States* (1948) and Clark's *Travels in the New South* (entry 867) forms a six-volume set within a larger series. The work has become an important standard, furnishing well-chosen publications from the array of travel literature produced over time. Cited accounts have been authored by immigrants, explorers, soldiers, teachers, farmers, and philosophers, both foreign and native-born. Volume 1, "The Formative Years, 1527–1782," covers the period of Spanish exploration to the American Revolution; volume 2, "The Expanding South, 1750–1825," examines the Ohio Valley and cotton frontier; and volume 3, "The Ante-bellum South, 1825–1860," treats the period of cotton, slavery, and increasing tension. Finishing out the coverage is Coulter's work on the Confederacy and the subsequent volumes on the New South. Entries are annotated, and each volume is indexed.

869. **The Urban South: A Bibliography.** Catherine L. Brown. New York: Greenwood, 1989. p.455. (Bibliographies and Indexes in American History, no.12). ISBN 0-313-26514-7.

From Greenwood Press comes this recent bibliographic effort of value to both scholars and students. Targeting urban development and urban life in the South, the work furnishes more than 7,000 entries of various types of materials representing the interests of social, economic, political, and cultural historians of the region. "Southern" is defined along the lines set by the Census Bureau: all states south of Delaware and the Ohio River west to Texas and Oklahoma. "Urban" is broadly interpreted and suggests all types of gatherings or clusters of people and buildings, including Indian settlements and ghost towns. Nearly 4,500 of the entries are articles from 275 different periodicals, followed by just over 2,000 monographs and nearly 900 dissertations; dates range from the mid-nineteenth century to 1987. Arrangement of entries is by format then by subject. Geographic and subject indexes are given.

Information Sources

870. **Encyclopedia of Southern Culture.** Charles R. Wilson and William Ferris, eds. Chapel Hill: University of North Carolina, 1989. 1,634p. ISBN 0-8078-1823-2.

This recent one-volume encyclopedia is considered an excellent survey of Southern tradition and culture prepared by two academicians. Twelve years in the making and the product of the combined efforts of 800 authorities who contributed entries, it is a special work without peer in its breadth of coverage. There are more than 1,300 entries, with bibliographies arranged under 24 topical sections varying in length from 30-odd to 130-odd pages. Topics include agriculture, environment, violence, and women's life. About 250 of the entries cover personalities, both living and dead, who are representative of the topical element being covered. Each section begins with an introductory essay, followed by thematic articles, then by biographical entries. An extensive general index facilitates the search for specific information.

871. **The Encyclopedia of Southern History.** David C. Roller and Robert W. Twyman. Baton Rouge: LSU Press, 1979. 1,421p. ISBN 0-8071-0579-9.

The editors, both history professors, developed this one-volume encyclopedia to furnish answers to the most frequently asked questions about the South. The South is defined as the section of the country that accepted slavery in 1860 and includes Washington, D.C., Delaware, Arkansas, West Virginia, and Missouri, as well as the states of the Confederacy. Designed for the full array of inquirers, from scholars and serious students to the general public, the work consists of 2,900 articles written by the editors and 1,100 contributors, who have signed their entries. Coverage is given to personalities, events, definitions of terms, and places over a period of time from the beginnings to the present day. Most noteworthy are the lengthier treatments given to each of the 16 states and to archival materials with descriptions of state holdings. An index is furnished.

872. **The Encyclopedia of the South.** Robert O'Brien and Harold H. Martin, eds. New York: Facts on File, 1985. 583p. ISBN 0-87196-728-6.

Another of the Facts on File regional one-volume encyclopedias, this, like the others in line, is designed primarily for the relatively unsophisticated user. Therefore, the brief unsigned entries, ranging in length from a paragraph to a full page and providing somewhat scanty coverage of topics, are less useful to scholars and serious students than are other works of this type (entries 870, 871). Nevertheless, there is a place for this effort in its coverage of 15 states (the Confederacy plus Arkansas, Kentucky, Maryland, Missouri, and West Virginia). Entries are alphabetically arranged and treat personalities, institutions, places, events, and products. The intent is to be inclusive and furnish brief information of cultural, geographic, statistical, political, and topical aspects. The work is illustrated with nearly 90 b&w pictures. A detailed index is furnished.

THE WEST

Similar to the South in the romantic and mystical manner in which it has been treated by observers and reporters, the West is the most heavily documented of regions. In the image of the cowboy, the admirable U.S. characteristics of rugged individualism, hardy pioneering spirit, and sense of fair play are represented. Westerners have been perceived as courageous, unassuming, and full of virtue. The lure that the region has had for historians and writers is reflected in the number of bibliographic sources created as reference tools. Most of the coverage is given to the Southwest, with far less concern shown the Pacific Northwest.

The Western History Association was founded in 1962 at the University of New Mexico in Albuquerque and has 2,000 members. It publishes *Western Historical Quarterly*, among other titles.

Library Resources

873. **A Guide to the Manuscript Collections of the Bancroft Library.** Dale L. Morgan and George P. Hammond, eds. University of California, 1963–1972. 2v. (Bancroft Library Publications Bibliographical Series). ISBN 0-520-01991-1

The Bancroft Library was developed by its namesake collector, author, and publisher, who was able to create a superb collection on U.S. West history prior to its sale to the University of California in 1905. Later it was to become the only San Francisco library to escape damage in the great fire of 1906. Organization of manuscripts was by Bancroft's own system, and access was at times elusive. Publication of the two-volume guide in 1964 facilitates the search for materials. Volume 1 covers the West except for California in an area ranging from Alaska to Texas and Hawaii to New Mexico. Volume 2 covers the area of Mexico and Central America. The volumes have been edited by George P. Hammond, director of the library, and they furnish descriptions of thousands of manuscripts ranging from diaries and logbooks to correspondence and papers. Indexes are furnished.

Another important collection is described in *A Catalogue of the Everett D. Graff Collection of Western Americana*, compiled by Colton Storm and published for the Newberry Library through the University of Chicago (1968). Storm, a curator of the Ayer Collections, has described the excellent collection of 4,800 items of the U.S. West and furnished references to other listings.

874. **Spanish and Mexican Records of the American Southwest: A Bibliographical Guide to Archive and Manuscript Sources.** Henry P. Beers. Tucson: University of Arizona, 1979. 493p. ISBN 0-8165-0532-2.

Another of Beers's excellent bibliographic efforts, this narrative describes the development, preservation, and publication of collections of original Spanish and Mexican records relevant to the U.S. Southwest. Documents include administrative papers, judicial records, notarial records, land records, legislative records, and mission registers, as well as military and business papers. The major segments of the work represent the coverage given to New Mexico, Texas, California, and Arizona. In each case, there are chapters on history and government, provincial records, documentary publications, and manuscript collections. The fifth section contains appendices listing repositories, California archives, records of the Office of the U.S. Surveyor General, and so on. The work serves the scholarly interest in furnishing a guide to locations of documents, as well as an extensive bibliography of 70 pages. A comprehensive index furnishes access.

Also available through the University of Arizona is the online database *Documentary Relations of the Southwest*, which indexes and annotates primary and secondary source documents found in libraries in Europe, Mexico, and the United States. The period of coverage is 1520–1820, and documents relate to the study of persons, places, and geographical features pertinent to the U.S. Southwest. A master list is produced in print and in microfiche.

Bibliographical Sources

875. **The American and Canadian West: A Bibliography.** Dwight L. Smith, ed. Santa Barbara, CA: ABC-Clio, 1979. 558p. (Clio Bibliography Series, no.5). ISBN 0-87436-272-5.

Another of the spin-off publications based on the huge database that produces *America: History and Life* (entry 51), this work furnishes an annotated bibliography of over 4,100 articles taken from over 300 periodicals published between 1964 and 1973. Smith is an academic with considerable experience and has organized the material into various categories, such as "Spanish and Mexican Years," "Mining," and "California." Annotations or abstracts vary in size from a few sentences to about 20 lines and are generally well developed. Materials on Native Americans are not included in this expansive coverage of the U.S. and Canadian West because they are treated in a related work by the publisher, *Indians of the United States and Canada* (entry 643). Useful introductory segments are furnished; the publisher's SPIndex, provides access.

876. **Borderline: A Bibliography of the United States-Mexico Borderlands.** Barbara G. Valk, et al. Los Angeles: UCLA Latin American Center, 1988. 711p. ISBN 0-87903-112-3.

One of the more noteworthy recent bibliographical publications is this comprehensive listing of 9,000 books, serials, journal articles, technical reports, government documents, dissertations, maps, and conference proceedings about the borderlands published between 1960 and 1985. These lands are identified as California, Arizona, New Mexico, and Texas, as well as six Mexican states, including Baja, California. The work originated as a database at UCLA formatted in the MARC style of the Library of Congress, from which conversion was made to a print bibliography organized into 26 subject areas with geographical and form divisions. Library locations are given with respect to about 35 major institutions. There is an author index.

The *Borderlands Sourcebook: A Guide to the Literature on Northern Mexico and the American Southwest*, edited by Ellwyn Stoddard, et al. (University of Oklahoma, 1983), is similar in scope and furnishes 60 bibliographic essays covering societal aspects of the region (culture, history, sociology, religion, politics). A composite bibliography is furnished from materials in the essays. Maps and charts are included.

877. A Classified Bibliography of the Periodical Literature of the Trans-Mississippi West (1811–1957). Oscar O. Winther. Bloomington: Indiana University Press, 1961. 626p. (Indiana University Social Science Series, no.19). **Supp.** 1970. 340p. Repr. Westport, CT: Greenwood, 1970–1972. ISBN 0-937-16475-3.

This effort was part of a tradition begun in 1942 with the publication of a bibliography covering the area from 1811–1938. The 1961 edition superseded the initial effort and expanded the coverage another 19 years. Included are nearly 9,250 periodical articles issued over a period of 146 years. Entries are classified by geographical areas—"The Southwest," "The Great Plains," "California,"—and topical headings such as "Agriculture," "Cattle," and "Migrant Groups." Because of the expanse involved, this is a unique attempt to control the literature and has been especially well regarded by both students and scholars. The supplement appeared in 1970 with 4,500 more articles published between 1957 and 1967, demonstrating the increased coverage given to the region. Author indexes furnish access to both efforts.

878. The Frontier Experience: A Reader's Guide to the Life and Literature of the American West. Jon Tuska and Vicki Piekarski, eds. Jefferson, NC: McFarland, 1984. 434p. ISBN 0-89950-118-4.

Editors Tuska and Piekarski, having previously produced a reference work on frontier fiction, continue their scrutiny of the pioneer culture with emphasis on the U.S. West in this guide. The work is divided into major segments representing the life and the literature, each of which comprises numerous chapters. Various historical subjects are treated in the chapters on "The Life," such as missionaries, outlaws, buffalo, and miners and mining. Six other experts assisted the editors in providing coverage of the materials, furnishing introductory essays followed by listings of publications for each topic. Most useful are the in-depth annotations given to the entries in these listings. Suggested fiction and films conclude each of these topical chapters. The second half, "The Literature," covers fiction, poetry, art, and film in similar manner. Name and title indexes conclude the work.

879. Overland on the California Trail, 1846–1859: A Bibliography of Manuscript and Printed Travel Narratives. Marlin L. Heckman. Glendale, CA: A. H. Clark, 1984. 159p. ISBN 0-87062-155-6.

This is a unique work of excellent quality identifying both published and unpublished accounts of the movement to California during a period of 13 years. More than 400 diaries and journals are identified, forming a nucleus of primary source material that is invaluable to historical inquiry in this area. Scholars and serious students benefit most, although the notes and descriptive matter are of interest to the Western history buff as well. Arrangement of entries is alphabetical by name of author, although most names will not be familiar to the general reader. These travel narratives were written in a variety of circumstances and for a variety of reasons. Holdings of libraries and public archival agencies are identified. Entries furnish title, year, places at which the journey began and ended, format, location, and references from sources that identify the items. There is a name and subject index.

880.   **The Plains and the Rockies: A Critical Bibliography of Exploration, Adventure and Travel in the American West, 1800–1865.** 4th ed., rev. and enl. Henry R. Wagner and Charles L. Camp. San Francisco: John Howell Books, 1982. 745p. ISBN 0-910-76011-1.

The original edition of this work was issued in 1921 and was intended to identify original travel narratives of the U.S. West in Wagner's collection and enumerate his "wants." The work was revised in 1937 and again in 1961 by Charles L. Camp, becoming known as the Wagner-Camp title. It has become a standard for librarians, historians, and collectors mainly through the examples set by important dealers and collectors such as Herschel V. Jones and A.S.W. Rosenbach, who used it for purposes of identification of quality works. The fourth edition has been edited by Robert H. Becker and now represents an excellent bibliography describing the various issues and editions of nearly 700 titles. Although selective, it represents the most extensive coverage of its type. It now embraces the trans-Mississippi area; bibliographic description is fuller and much easier to follow. Annotations have been rewritten. Locations are identified. The original numbering scheme is retained.

881.   **Platte River Road Narratives: A Descriptive Bibliography of Travel Over the Great Central Overland Route to Oregon, California, Utah, Colorado, Montana, and Other Western States and Territories, 1812–1866.** Merrill J. Mattes. Urbana: University of Illinois, 1988. 632p. ISBN 0-252-01342-5.

The Platte River Road ran from St. Joseph, Missouri, to Fort Laramie, Wyoming, and from 1812 to 1866 it was this country's greatest trail for Western migration. The author has made a lifelong study of the region and in 1969 furnished an excellent historical study of the road. The recent bibliography contains listings of more than 2,000 travel accounts written on that passage during that time period. The purpose is to include all known overland accounts relating to the Platte River during the 50 years prior to the transcontinental railroad, which eventually caused the demise of wagon travel. Entries are arranged chronologically, then by name of traveler, and furnish author, document type (letter, diary, journal, memoir), library location, route and chronology of the journey, highlights of the trip, and evaluation of the document's importance.

882.   **The Trail West: A Bibliography-Index to Western American Trails, 1841–1869.** John M. Townley. Reno, NV: Jamison Station, 1988. 309p. ISBN 0-913381-05-5.

This work, as its title suggests, is both a bibliography and an index to important trails utilized for Westward migration for a period of nearly 30 years during the nineteenth century. Both published and unpublished sources are listed and include diaries, articles, theses, books, and reminiscenses, many of which are evaluated for their utility. The period of coverage begins with the first wave of settlers bound for California in 1841 and ends with the completion of the transcontinental railroad in 1869. The work is divided into two major parts, the first of which furnishes an alphabetical listing by author. Entries give locations, dates, trails, and a rating of quality. The second part furnishes indexes by chronology, subject, and trail segment. The latter contains descriptions of locations and features. Both researchers and students benefit from this source.

883.   **Six-guns and Saddle Leather: A Bibliography of Books and Pamphlets on Western Outlaws and Gunmen.** New ed., rev. and greatly enl. Ramon F. Adams. Norman: University of Oklahoma Press, 1969. 808p. ISBN 0-939-73806-6.

Adams, through all his extensive bibliographic work during the 1950s and 1960s, considered himself a collector and tailored his effort to the needs of librarians and collectors, hoping it might also be useful for historians. Originally published in 1954, it was revised 15 years later and contains listings for nearly 2,500 titles, more than doubling the coverage of the earlier edition. Bibliographic description is full; evaluative commentary is insightful. Adams attempts to set the record straight historically and does not hesitate to render his thoughts regarding the quality and accuracy of the accounts.

A similar effort is Adams's *Burs Under the Saddle: A Second Look at Books and Histories of the West* (University of Oklahoma, 1964), which was reprinted as a paperback in 1989. This is recognized as an important contribution in its detailed descriptions of over 400 books on gunmen, peace officers, outlaws, and generally notorious individuals. Carefully researched, it, too, sets the record straight.

Information Sources

884. **Atlas of the Lewis and Clark Expedition.** Gary E. Moulton, ed. Lincoln: University of Nebraska, 1983. (The Journals of the Lewis and Clark Expedition, v.1). ISBN 0-8032-2861-9.

Through the efforts and support of President Thomas Jefferson, the Lewis and Clark expedition represented an official activity designed to explore the territory acquired by Jefferson through the Louisiana Purchase. The trip took two and a half years (1804–1806) and traced the Missouri River to its source, then crossed the northern Rockies. The charts, maps, and surveys developed during the expedition are reproduced in this work of historical interest. It represents the first definitive edition, furnishing 134 maps (most of them at their full original size), including 42 that have never been published. Joint sponsorship by the University of Nebraska and the American Philosophical Society made it possible for this important work to be produced.

A more contemporary title is the seventh edition of *Atlas of the Pacific Northwest,* edited by A. Jon Kimmerling and Philip L. Jackson (Oregon State University, 1985). The source is unique in its coverage of the region, which includes Idaho, Oregon, and Washington state. It contains authoritative historical maps among the 167 offered.

885. **The Encyclopedia of the Central West.** Allan Carpenter. New York: Facts on File, 1990. 544p. ISBN 0-8160-1661-5.

Another of the Facts on File efforts to furnish one-volume encyclopedias of the different regions, this is the fourth in the series and covers ten states: Colorado, Kansas, Montana, Nebraska, New Mexico, North Dakota, Oklahoma, South Dakota, Texas, and Wyoming. Like others in the series, the work is intended to meet the needs of the general public rather than those of the scholar or serious student. Of course, serious inquirers will utilize the work for less sophisticated purposes because it offers a convenient package of information. Entries are arranged alphabetically and describe briefly places, events, institutions, and topical material. States receive the most detailed treatment, with entries revealing population, other statistics, archaeology, and history.

The fifth and most recent of the publisher's efforts, also by Carpenter, is *The Encyclopedia of the Far West* (1991). Covered here are nine states; Alaska, Arizona, California, Hawaii, Idaho, Nevada, Oregon, Utah, and Washington, as well as the U.S. Pacific territories.

886. **Historical Atlas of the American West.** Warren A. Beck and Ynez D. Haase. Norman: University of Oklahoma Press, 1989. 156p. ISBN 0-8061-2193-9.

A recent effort from the University of Oklahoma Press, this atlas furnishes nearly 80 maps covering 17 Western states from the 100th meridian westward. Coverage is thorough and furnishes excellent historical perspective, reinforced by narratives accompanying each map. These descriptions provide exposition of major points on the map in some detail and indicate causes and origins of various phenomena. A wide range of information is furnished, along with such elements as World War II prisoner-of-war maps and Great Salt Lake elevations. Most of the maps have a legend to aid in their comprehension. An especially useful feature is the bibliography or list of references used for each map. These are listed near the end under the appropriate map number. A detailed index of names concludes the work.

887. **Maps of Texas and the Southwest, 1513–1900.** James C. Martin and Robert S. Martin. University of New Mexico, for the Amon Carter Museum, 1984. 174p. ISBN 0-8263-0741-8.

This is an attractive, useful atlas of high quality furnishing reproductions of nearly 60 maps developed over a period of nearly 400 years and relating to the Southwestern region. More than a simple atlas, the work furnishes in its first half an interesting and informative historical description of the development of European cartography. The period of exploration and settlement in this country is then interpreted through the examination of maps and reports of regions extending from Florida to California and up to the Canadian borders. The second major segment contains 50 black-and-white and 9 color maps, arranged chronologically and covering the Mexican-U.S. border regions of the West. Reproductions are excellent and together with the expository material make for an important tool. Also furnished are a bibliography and suggested readings, along with an index to provide access.

888. **The Reader's Encyclopedia of the American West.** Howard R. Lamar, ed. Crowell, 1977. 1,305p. ISBN 0-690-00008-1.

This is a comprehensive one-volume encyclopedia furnishing over 2,400 signed entries on the U.S. West, which includes the trans-Mississippi West along with the Far West. Articles cover Indian-white relations, expansion, trapping, mining, and cattle, among other things. Along with Native Americans, such ethnic groups as Basques, Mexicans, Chinese, and Japanese are recognized as important contributors to the region. The articles are written by over 200 contributors, who succeed in providing enlightenment of both the real world and the legend of the West. Cross-references are given to related material and enhance the tool's value for quick and convenient information. Articles range in length from brief specific entries to longer pieces on broader topics. There are numerous illustrations. This title furnishes more thorough coverage than do the Facts on File efforts (entries 885, 885n).

Biographical Sources

889. **Encyclopedia of Frontier Biography.** Dan L. Thrapp. Glendale, CA: A. H. Clark, 1988. 3v. ISBN 0-87062-191-2.

This recent three-volume effort presents biographical sketches of about 4,500 frontiersmen and American Indians. The intent is to cover all people who achieved to a significant degree or who generated interest in the playing out of the drama of the U.S. West. Personalities are varied and include traders, cowboys, scouts, explorers, settlers, politicians, trappers, and outlaws. Excluded are people in the mining industry and those whose mark was made solely through the conduct of wars. Most articles run about one-fourth of a double-columned page and furnish enough detail to describe the person's role and significance. Arrangement is alphabetical by name. There are no illustrations, but a bibliography is given for each biographee. There is a detailed index identifying both topics and names of biographees, as well as personalities associated with them.

TERRITORIES AND DEPENDENCIES

The acquisition and governance of territories, although not specifically granted as a right in the Constitution, has been inferred through other expressed powers, such as the right to make war and conclude treaties. Thus, such activity has always been a cause for debate and sometimes heated emotion, the most recent example being the controversy surrounding the independence accorded the Panama Canal Zone by President Jimmy Carter in planned stages. Alaska and Hawaii most recently shed their territorial status to become states. Others, like the Philippines, have achieved independence. Today, our affiliates are found in both the Atlantic and Pacific, and theoretically include even our nation's capital.

Of the territories past and present, Puerto Rico has received the most attention by publishers, although in recent years there has been more interest in the others. This section reflects that imbalance by giving a subsection to Puerto Rico alone, whereas the other segment embraces the remainder of the territories.

Puerto Rico

Puerto Rico, like Guam and the Philippines, was ceded to the United States by Spain in 1898 and was administered as a territory. In 1952, it was granted independence as a Commonwealth of the United States. For coverage of Puerto Ricans in the Continental U.S., see "The Hispanic Experience," pages 232-233.

890. **Annotated Bibliography of Puerto Rican Bibliographies.** Fay Fowlie-Flores. New York: Greenwood, 1990. 167p. (Bibliographies and Indexes in Ethnic Studies, no.1). ISBN 0-313-26124-5.
This recent effort was the first issue of a new Greenwood series and furnishes a listing of bibliographies that have covered topics important to the study of Puerto Rico. Subject matter varies and includes personalities, broad topics, and specific issues. The compiler, a librarian at the University of Puerto Rico, is an important contributor to Puerto Rican studies, having completed other bibliographic efforts (entry 892). The work opens with an introduction describing the development of bibliographical research on the area. The major part of the text contains an annotated bibliography of bibliographies arranged in classified manner under topics and subjects. Bibliographies contain both Spanish- and English-language publications compiled between 1877 and 1989. Annotations vary in length with the value or complexity of the entry. There are author, title, and subject indexes.

891. **Bibliografia Puertorriquena (1493–1930).** Antonio S. Pedreira. Madrid: Imprenta de la Libreria y Casa Editorial Hernando, 1932. 707p. (Monografias de la Universidad de Puerto Rico. Series A. Estudios Hispanicos, no.1.) Repr. New York: B. Franklin, 1974. ISBN 0-8337-4669-3.
The standard bibliography on Puerto Rico, this work was first issued 60 years ago. It has been reprinted because of its comprehensive nature and value for study and research. Covering more than 400 years, from 1493 to 1930, publications include both monographs and journal

articles. There are approximately 10,000 entries that include works about Puerto Rico and its traditions and works by Puerto Ricans on a variety of topics. Entries are arranged under format (bibliographical sources, general information) or topical categories (natural history, public health, political and administrative history). Of special interest is the section titled "History of Puerto Rico," which lists materials furnishing a broad perspective. The work is designed well as a reference tool, with access facilitated by both a detailed table of contents and author and subject indexes.

892. **Index to Puerto Rican Collective Biography.** Fay Fowlie-Flores, comp. New York: Greenwood, 1987. 214p. (Bibliographies and Indexes in American History, no.5). ISBN 0-313-25193-2.

As part of the Greenwood Press series, this work represents another useful index to published biographies of Puerto Rican people. In all, 146 titles are indexed, 22 of which are in English. These works have all been published prior to 1986 and furnish at least three biographies each. No journal articles are used, but books represent varied types: collective biographies, collections of essays, histories, and anthologies. Entries furnish name, dates, and citation/reference, including volume, page numbers, and presence of illustrations in sources. Personalities are both historical and contemporary, dating from the colonial period to the present.

A complementary source is *Index to Spanish American Collective Biography* by Sara de la Mundo Lo (G. K. Hall, 1981–). Volume 3 of this valuable work was issued in 1983 and covers the Central American and Caribbean countries. This tool is arranged by subject, and indexes 186 biographical works (100 of which are also indexed by the Fowlie-Flores effort). Subjects range from art to religion and medicine. It is well indexed for easy access.

893. **The Puerto Ricans: An Annotated Bibliography.** Paquita Vivo, ed. New York: Bowker, for Puerto Rican Research and Resources Center, 1973. 299p. ISBN 0-8352-0663-7.

This work is considered to be one of the better bibliographic efforts and has succeeded in its purpose, furnishing a source of readily available material useful to a wide variety of inquirers. It represents a selective annotated bibliography that covers Puerto Rican history in comprehensive fashion, touching on all aspects of Puerto Rican existence. There are about 2,600 entries in Spanish and English. Arrangement of entries is within four major format segments: books, pamphlets, and dissertations; government documents; periodical literature; and audio-visual materials. The work was carefully developed and employed the resources of major library collections, among them the Library of Congress, University of Puerto Rico, New York Public Library, Instituto de Cultura Puertorriqueno. An excellent feature is the listing given of the various publishers able to furnish the titles listed. There is both an author/title index and a subject index.

894. **Puerto Rico.** Elena E. Cevallos, comp. and Sheila R. Herstein, ed. Santa Barbara, CA: ABC-Clio, 1985. 193p. (World Bibliographical Series, v.52). ISBN 0-903450-89-5.

This useful bibliography may be used to update or supplement the coverage of the Vivo effort (entry 893). The work consists of over 600 annotated entries of various types of materials relating to Puerto Rico. Included are primarily books and periodical articles, along with some government documents, most of which are in English. Emphasis is given to publications issued since 1970, although certain classic older works are enumerated. Arrangement of entries is under topics, most of which represent social science concerns. There appears to be an emphasis on economics and politics. Annotations are descriptive but include evaluative commentary in many cases. There is a useful and detailed dictionary-type index combining names, authors, titles, and subjects in one sequence. The work is useful for students and the general public.

895. **Puerto Rico: A Political and Cultural History.** Arturo M. Carrion, ed. New York: Norton; Nashville: American Association for State and Local History [1983]. 384p. ISBN 0-393-01740-0.

This is one of the better histories of Puerto Rico. The editor and five other contributors develop a well-structured, cohesive description and interpretation of Puerto Rican tradition and development. All contributors are Puerto Rican and have succeeded in furnishing an accurate perspective of the essence and flavor of Puerto Rico as a distinctive Caribbean entity and a cultural nationality. As a mix of Indian, Hispanic and African ethnic influences merged within a Spanish culture and language, the Puerto Rican experience unfolds from the colonial period through the dependency phase to eventual recognition as a commonwealth; each contributor covers a different stage. Illustrations accompany the text and aid comprehension of the descriptive material. Suggestions for further readings are given that should be helpful; an index furnishes access.

Others

For works on Philippine-U.S. relations, see chapter 3, "Diplomatic History and Foreign Affairs," under "Asia."

896. **Pacific Island Studies: A Survey of the Literature.** Miles M. Jackson, ed. in chief. New York: Greenwood, 1986. (Bibliographies and Indexes in Sociology, no.7). ISBN 0-313-23528-7.

The past few years have seen increased activity in the organization of the literature on the Pacific islands, a result of the growing interest in the region on the part of researchers and writers. The editor is the library school dean at the University of Hawaii and has assembled a useful set of bibliographic essays identifying important English-language monographs and journal articles organized into four major divisions. Polynesia is composed of the Pacific Islands and Hawaii; Micronesia includes the Caroline, Marshall, and Mariana Islands administered by the United States as a trust for the United Nations. Also covered are Melanesia and Australia, with special attention given to the Aborigines and the Torres Straits islanders. A composite author-title-subject index furnishes access to the 2,000 entries.

Similar coverage is given in Gerald Fry's *Pacific Basin and Oceania* (ABC-Clio, 1987), which identifies over 1,175 recent books and articles in the English language, many of which are by natives and residents of the regions covered (Melanesia, Micronesia, and Polynesia). Emphasis is given to the 1975–1985 period in terms of publications; there is a composite index to furnish access.

897. **Panama.** Eleanor D. Langstaff, comp. and Sheila R. Herstein, ed. Santa Barbara, CA: ABC-Clio, 1982. 184p. (World Bibliographical Series, v.14). ISBN 0-903450-26-7.

President Carter's decision to give independent status to the Panama Canal Zone was one of the several political decisions that inspired controversy during his administration. Of the 640 entries in this bibliography, nearly 80 deal with the history and development of the Canal. Historians will find the inclusion of older items, including those examining French involvement, to be useful. Much of the research included among the books, articles, and government documents is of contemporary nature and will be welcomed by both researchers and students in developing an awareness of prevailing conditions during different stages of growth and management. In addition to its history, Panama's geography, environment, recreations, and physical nature are covered in the topical arrangement provided. Annotations are brief but informative. There is an index of authors, titles, and subjects.

898.   **Philippines.** Jim Richardson, comp. Santa Barbara, CA: ABC-Clio, 1989. 372p. (World Bibliographical Series, v.106). ISBN 1-85109-077-0.

Like Puerto Rico and Guam, the Philippines was ceded to the U.S. in 1898 as a result of the Spanish-American War and administered as a territory until 1946, when the country achieved independence as a republic. This bibliography includes over 950 entries, primarily monographs in the English language but also journal articles, census reports, and other varied items. Emphasis is given to contemporary publications, although some older materials are included as well; arrangement is by broad topic. The entries are annotated and furnish informative content description; the work is of value to inquirers at all levels but is especially useful to students. There are author, title, and subject indexes.

The pivotal role of the Philippines during the war is recorded in the entries furnished by Morton J. Netzorg's *The Philippines in World War II and to Independence (December 8, 1941–July 4, 1946): An Annotated Bibliography* (Southeast Asia Program, Department of Asian Studies, Cornell University, 1977). This represents a thorough listing of various materials: books, essays, theses, government documents, and journal articles. Newspaper and periodical files are also identified; publications appeared as late as 1974. Japanese occupation is well documented. No index is provided.

899.   **Samoan Islands Bibliography. Lowell D. Holmes, comp. and ed. Wichita, KS: Poly Concepts, 1984. 329p. ISBN 0-915203-00-6.**

Formerly called the Navigators Islands, Samoa today comprises two segments of islands. Western Samoa is independent, but the eastern segment, American Samoa, is administered as a territory. Most of the islands were ceded to the United States between 1900 and 1904 by their chiefs; Swains Island was annexed in 1925. This comprehensive bibliography enumerates all materials found on the island chain. Included here are books, chapters, articles from periodicals and newspapers, dissertations and theses, films, manuscripts and archives, government documents, and publications of international organizations in various languages. Arrangement of entries is under 44 subject divisions that range from broad to specific in nature. As with any huge project of this type, there are omissions and oversights; most serious in this case is the absence of an index. Scholars and students will need to take the time necessary to access the relevant material.

Chapter 7

Economic History

Behind political, social, and possibly moral convictions, economic self-interest is an important fuel for the engine that drives the actions of the nation and its regions, states, and cities. Most recently, we have seen the power of the economy in the abrupt decline of popularity of President George Bush, who was unable to reverse an economic recession. Liberal or conservative, hawk or dove, Democrat or Republican, every American seems to share the same needs regarding employment, housing, education, and health care.

There are relatively few reference tools that focus on economic history. Sections of this chapter furnish coverage of the major sectors or components of economic life, following the general introductory section.

The Economic History Association, now operating out of the Department of History at George Washington University in Washington, D.C., was founded in 1941 and has 3,300 members. The *Journal of Economic History*, its quarterly publication, has been issued from the organization's beginning.

GENERAL

Tools in this section treat the economy in general rather than targeting any particular component of it. Succeeding sections furnish coverage specific to a sector of the total economy.

900. **American Economic and Business History Information Sources: An Annotated Bibliography of Recent Works Pertaining to Economic, Business, Agricultural, and Labor History and the History of Science and Technology for the United States and Canada.** Robert W. Lovett. Gale, 1971. 323p. (Management Information Guide, v.23).

The author was the curator of manuscripts and archives at the Baker Library of the Harvard business school and was well-qualified to produce a thorough bibliography of general nature. Similar in organization to other titles in this series from Gale Research, the work is divided into six major chapters that treat economic history, business history, agricultural history, labor history, the history of science and technology, and general reference works considered to be of special interest to business and economic historians. Emphasis is placed on recent literature, as the work serves to supplement the earlier effort by Henrietta M. Larson, *Guide to Business History: Materials for the Study of American Business History and Suggestions for Their Use* (Howard University, 1948; repr. Canner, 1964). Lovett's emphasis is on publications between 1948 and 1970, although some earlier classic titles are included. Annotations are brief but informative.

901.   **American Economic History: A Guide to Information Sources.** William Kenneth Hutchinson. Detroit: Gale, 1980. 296p. (Economics Information Guide Series, v.16). ISBN 0-8103-1287-5.

This is a useful and comprehensive bibliographic guide to more than 1,550 books and articles, most published in this country and covering a period from the colonial era to 1960. The entries are organized alphabetically under 10 topical chapters, beginning with an introductory unit on methodology and general works. Subsequent chapters are "Population and the Labor Force," "Land and Agricultural Development," "Technological Change," "Industrial Growth and Structure," "Transportation and Spatial Locations," "Monetary and Financial Development," "International and Inter-regional Growth and Development," "The Role of Government," and "Assessing the Performance of Growth." In each chapter, books and periodical articles are annotated with brief descriptions of the content. These are followed by simple general listings without annotations. Appendices furnish listings of major associations and journals. Author, title, and subject indexes are furnished.

902.   **American Economic History Before 1860.** George R. Taylor, comp. New York: Appleton-Century-Crofts, 1969. (Goldentree Bibliographies in American History). ISBN 0-390-86750-0.

Similar in scope to Thomas Orsagh's *The Economic History of the United States Prior to 1860* (entry 903), this more comprehensive bibliography of books, dissertations, and journal articles covers the period of economic development to 1860. Entries are arranged into time periods (e.g., the colonial period) and topics (land policy). The Goldentree series was developed to furnish students, teachers, and librarians with accurate and convenient guides to U.S. history; it has succeeded in its purpose. The compiler is a historian and former academician familiar with the study of U.S. history and well qualified to provide a useful listing of relevant materials. There is an introductory section on general bibliographies, which should be useful to the beginning researcher. An author index is furnished.

903.   **The Economic History of the United States Prior to 1860: An Annotated Bibliography.** Thomas Orsagh, ed. Santa Barbara, CA: ABC-Clio, 1975. 100p. ISBN 0-87436-205-9.

Less comprehensive than George R. Taylor's *American Economic History Before 1860* (entry 902), this work also deals with the antebellum period. It represents a selective bibliography of nearly 800 books and articles considered useful to a broad spectrum of readers. Excluded are highly specialized items, as well as those that are very general in nature. Arrangement of entries is under different topical categories: income, wealth, capital, labor force, technology, prices, population, and so forth. Annotations are furnished for most but not all entries; these tend to be descriptive. Reviewers gave this tool mixed reviews because of incomplete citations and some imbalance in coverage of various topics. Entries seem to be well chosen, however, and the work should be useful to students for their history or U.S. studies classes. Indexes are furnished.

904.   **Encyclopedia of American Economic History: Studies of the Principal Movements and Ideas.** New York: Scribner's, 1980. 3v. ISBN 0-684-16271-7.

This well-developed reference tool of selective nature furnishes 72 commissioned articles treating the U.S. economy from the nineteenth century to the present. Arrangement is under five major sections: "The Historiography of American Economic History"; "The Chronology of American History"; "The Framework of American Economic Growth"; "The Institutional Framework"; and "The Social Framework." Articles tend to be full in this three-volume effort and furnish in-depth analyses, descriptions, and interpretations of topics. Choice of topics is suspect—witness the inclusion of "socialism" but not "nationalism," or "blacks" but not "American Indians." All entries provide an extensive bibliography useful to the student and to the general public. The value of the work lies in its examination of concepts, themes, trends, and developments germane to economic history but related to political, social, educational, and technological progress. There is a general index in volume 3.

905. **Manuscripts in Baker Library: A Guide to Sources for Business, Economic and Social History.** 4th ed. Robert W. Lovett and Eleanor C. Bishop, comps. Boston: Baker Library, Harvard University, 1978.

The Baker Library of the Harvard University Graduate School of Business Administration published the fourth edition of its guide in 1978 under the direction of its curator of manuscripts (see also entry 900). The library offers 1,400 business collections dating back to the fifteenth century and represents an important resource for researchers and serious students. This guide describes an additional 100 collections acquired since the publication of the third edition in 1969. Records are of varied nature and range from journals of whaling ships to books kept by theater managers. Arrangement is within a classification scheme developed for the library some 50 years earlier. Entries furnish dates, amount of material, name of collection, original location, and clearly written narrative describing types of materials and content. Various indexes furnish access.

BUSINESS, INDUSTRY, AND BANKING

Since Calvin Coolidge's pronouncement that the business of this country is business, we have seen ample evidence of that philosophy in the types of legislation generally pursued by the Republican Party. The country has come through various periods of socioeconomic change, progressing from the Herbert Spencer laissez-faire policies of the late nineteenth century to the adoption of the income tax in 1913 and its attempt to redistribute wealth in line with a growing belief in the virtue of social welfare. In the past two decades, the pendulum has swung back, illustrated by a type of uneasy alliance of the worker with the entrepreneur through profit-sharing and incentive plans. Most recently, there have been troubled times, with the specter of the Japanese and their economic emergence in the face of industrial decline and growing unemployment in this country.

Business and industry (along with labor) have received much attention from publishers of reference books. Certain business sectors or segments, such as the railroads, have received an inordinate share of total publication.

The Business History Conference was founded in 1954 at the College of William and Mary in Williamsburg, Virginia. It presently has 450 members. *Business and Economic History*, its annual journal, has been issued since 1975. Another organization, the American Truck Historical Society, was founded in 1971 and is headquartered in Birmingham, Alabama. It has 12,000 members and has published a bimonthly journal, *Wheels of Time*, since 1980. The Steamship Historical Society of Providence, Rhode Island, was formed in 1935 and has 3,300 members. Its official quarterly journal, *Steamboat Bill*, has been issued since 1940. The National Railway Historical Society was founded in Philadelphia in 1935 and has 19,000 members. The *National Railway Bulletin*, a bimonthly journal, has been produced from the society's beginning.

Library Resources

906. **Directory of Business Archives in the United States and Canada.** 4th ed. Chicago: Society of American Archivists, 1990. 96p.

This directory was started in the late 1960s as a pamphlet of less than 40 pages by the Business Archives Committee of the Society of American Archivists. Through succeeding publications, it has added listings and presently offers a work of nearly 100 pages published under the auspices of the Business Archives Section of the SAA. It remains a highly useful listing of business archival collections in the United States and Canada and is possibly the best source with which to identify holdings of private business organizations and firms. Entries furnish the usual directory-style information, enumerating name, address, and telephone number of the organization, along with the name of the archivist or librarian. Content of the collection is described briefly, as are any restrictions in use.

907. **Trade Catalogs at Winterthur: A Guide to the Literature of Merchandising, 1750–1980.** E. Richard McKinstry, comp. New York: Garland, 1984. 438p. (A Winterthur Book; Garland Reference Library of Social Science, v.241). ISBN 0-8240-8952-9.

The introductory section of this useful catalog of catalogs furnishes a good description of important collections of such publications and will be useful to the business historian. The Winterthur Museum is devoted to the preservation and study not only of the decorative arts and horticulture but also of American material culture and historical objects. Housed here are nearly 1,900 trade catalogs from U.S. firms spanning a period of 230 years beginning in 1750. Arrangement of entries in this catalog is under 30 different subject categories—art supplies, clothing and accessories, food and refrigeration, stoves, paintings and prints, and so on. Entries describe the catalogs, which were generally furnished to retailers and merchandisers and display the company lines. Mail order varieties are also held. Indexes provide chronological, geographical and name access.

Bibliographical Sources

Business Periodicals Index has been issued since 1958 by the H. W. Wilson Company and now appears on a monthly basis. It covers periodical literature at all levels of sophistication and treats all relevant subjects. It is available online through WILSONLINE and on CD-ROM through WILSONDISC.

908. **Banking in the U.S.: An Annotated Bibliography.** Jean Deuss. Metuchen, NJ: Scarecrow, 1990. 164p. ISBN 0-8108-2348-9.

The study of banking and the attitudes of Americans toward the industry remains one of the most interesting areas in economic history. This bibliography was developed by a specialist in business information to illustrate the possible need for restructuring of the industry because of competition from abroad and the impact of automation. Nearly 400 entries are furnished, representing a wide variety of materials, including texts, histories, statistics, abstracts, bibliographies, legislation, serials, and information on the Federal Reserve System. Emphasis is given to recent conditions. The entries represent publications issued between 1984 and 1989. Coverage is given to the management and operation of commercial banks, savings institutions, and investment banking. Annotations are critical in nature. Appendices provide a list of abbreviations, a chronology, and listings of agencies and associations. Author and title indexes furnish access.

909. **The Industrial Belt: An Annotated Bibliography.** Thomas J. Schlereth. New York: Garland, 1987. 256p. (Garland Bibliographies in American Regional Studies, v.1; Garland Reference Library of Social Science, v.272). ISBN 0-8240-8812-3.

This is a much-needed recent bibliography concentrating primarily on books but also listing dissertations and journal articles on the Industrial Belt. The region covers western Pennsylvania, Ohio, Indiana, Michigan, western New York, and northern Illinois. Coverage is given to major cities such as Pittsburgh, Detroit, Cleveland, and Chicago. In general, there is an emphasis on the nineteenth and twentieth centuries, tracing the rise to prominence and subsequent decline of U.S. industrial strength and development. Publications were for the most part issued in the 20 years prior to publication of the bibliography. Entries are organized under 10 sections, most of which are topical: e.g., physical environment, economic activities, social history. Two of the sections identify general sources, including bibliographies and institutions. There are author, geographic, and subject indexes.

910. **Methodology and Method in History: A Bibliography.** Lee D. Parker and O. Finly Graves, eds. New York: Garland, 1989. 246p. (Accounting History and Thought). ISBN 0-8240-3323-X.

This recent work was prepared through the efforts of the Accounting History Research Methodology Committee of the Academy of Accounting Historians. Developed in order to furnish a basis for methodological approaches, the work is organized within a classification schedule of 13 areas. Within these classes, bibliographic references are arranged alphabetically by author. Bibliographic descriptions are full; there is an annotated bibliography of selective nature. The work is a collaborative effort, and selections were made on the basis of a consensus of committee members. The title should be useful to all inquirers professing interest in historical research in accounting and should furnish enlightenment to beginning researchers in the field as well as to scholars from outside the field.

911. **United States Corporation Histories: A Bibliography, 1965–1990.** 2nd ed. Wahib Nasrallah. New York: Garland, 1991. 511p. (Garland Reference Library of Social Science, v.807). ISBN 0-8153-0639-3.

This is a new edition of a bibliography of business identifying some 3,000 business histories of various types. Included here are books, articles from periodicals and newspapers, and dissertations, as well as corporate histories derived from annual reports of the companies. The first edition was published only four years earlier and furnished coverage of publications issued between 1965 and 1985. The present work extends the coverage through 1990. Arrangement of entries is alphabetical by name of corporation; their level of suitability ranges from those of popular general appeal to those of scholarly nature. Included are biographies of prominent executives, who receive varied coverage dependent upon their fame or notoriety. Full bibliographic information is supplied; no annotations are given. The work is indexed by author, chief executive, and industry.

Information Sources

912. **Encyclopedia of American Business History and Biography.** New York: Facts on File, 1988–1992. v.1–9. (Projected 50v). ISBN 0-8160-1371-3 (v.1).

One of the more sophisticated and in-depth offerings from this publisher is the projected 50-volume set covering all aspects of U.S. business. Each of the volumes is edited by a specialist in the field, aided by various historians, who have contributed the signed articles. Entries cover personalities, events, corporations, legislation, and various topics and issues relevant to the theme of each particular volume. The work has been recognized as a valuable contribution, and both students and scholars profit from its excellent coverage. Nine volumes have appeared to date: *Railroads in the Age of Regulation, 1900–1980*, Keith L. Bryant, ed. (1988); *Railroads in the Nineteenth Century*, Robert L. Frey, ed. (1988); *Iron and Steel in the Nineteenth Century*, Paul F. Paskoff, ed. (1989); *The Automobile Industry, 1925–1980*, George S. May, ed. (1989); *Banking and Finance to 1913*, Larry Schweikart, ed. (1990); *The Automobile Industry, 1896–1920*, George S. May, ed. (1990); *Banking and Finance, 1913–1989*, Larry Schweikart, ed. (1990); *Iron and Steel in the Twentieth Century*, Paul F. Paskoff, ed. (1991); and *The Airline Industry*, William M. Leary, ed. (1992).

913. **The Historical Guide to North American Railroads.** George H. Drury, comp. and Bob Hayden, ed. Milwaukee: Kalmbach Books, 1985. 376p. ISBN 0-89024-072-8.

An introductory segment furnishes a historical overview and exposition of railroading. The compiler has served as the librarian for *Train* magazine and during the 1980s published interesting reference books on the topic. This historical guide treats 160 railroads that either vanished or were merged with other lines between 1930 and 1985. These railroads all had lines of track exceeding 50 miles in length and were noteworthy, long-lived, or historically important. This set of criteria eliminates the numerous tiny lines that appeared and disappeared in routine manner. Each entry furnishes a brief history describing the railroad's origin and development, statistics on mileage and rolling stock for 1929 and for its final year, a map for the line in 1930, and a black-and-white photograph. Biographies are given for the owners. There is a glossary of terms and a detailed index.

A companion work by the same author is *The Trainwatcher's Guide to North American Railroads: Significant Facts, Figures, and Features of Over 140 Railroads in the U.S., Canada, and Mexico* (Kalmbach, 1984; repr. 1988). Similar in format to the more recent effort, this also is an alphabetical listing of railroads. Entries furnish descriptions, illustrations, maps, and suggested readings. Glossary and index are supplied.

914. **Manufacturing: A Historiographical and Bibliographical Guide.** David O. Whitten and Bessie E. Whitten, eds. New York: Greenwood, 1990. 503p. (Handbook of American Business History, v.1). ISBN 0-313-25198-3.

The first volume of a new series that eventually will include other business sectors, this work furnishes excellent signed articles by various specialists describing and interpreting manufacturing industries in this country. It is divided into 23 chapters, each furnishing bibliographical and historical essays on one of the various manufacturing industries identified by the Enterprise Standard Industrial Classification Code (ESIC). There is an introductory chapter on business history in the United States in general that describes useful books and articles, followed by the chapters on specific manufacturing segments. Included here is coverage of household appliances and electric lighting, which fall under the electric and electrical equipment sections in the code. Additional coverage includes petroleum, baking products, tobacco, apparel, and leather. The title is useful to graduate students and researchers at all levels; an index is furnished.

915. **Railroad Maps of North America: The First Hundred Years.** Andrew M. Modelski. Washington: Library of Congress, 1984. 186p. ISBN 0-8444-0396-2.

From the Library of Congress comes this important large-size volume of early railroad maps of the United States, Canada, and Mexico, carefully developed and well designed for use by both scholars and students. Included here are over 90 maps taken from the Geography and Map Division of the library, including survey maps, general purpose maps, regional maps, and terminal maps, among others. Although most are in black and white, five are in color; all are fine examples of the mapmaker's art and show cartographic techniques and styles. They are clearly drawn and described in accompanying text. There are nearly 200 illustrations of trains, crews, depots, and even advertising material. An excellent introduction describes the history of railroad cartography. There is a comprehensive index of subjects, places, and persons.

An earlier publication for the Library of Congress is Modelski's *Railroad Maps for the United States: A Selective Annotated Bibliography of Original 19th Century Maps in the Geography and Map Division of the Library of Congress* (1975). This book identifies and describes over 600 maps separately held by the Library of Congress but does not reproduce the maps themselves.

916. **Railroads of North America: A Complete Listing of All North American Railroads, 1827–1986.** Joseph Gross, comp. Spencerport, NY: Joseph Gross, 1986. 275p. ISBN 0-9616476-0-4.

An interesting and well-conceived tool for inquirers at all levels is this alphabetically arranged handbook of railroad companies in North America over a 70-year period. The nineteenth century witnessed the introduction, expansion, and development of the railroad as a major segment of the U.S. economy. This work furnishes brief histories of railroad lines in Canada, Mexico, and Alaska. Included along with common carriers are construction railroads (developed as dummy operations to build the lines but then absorbed by the parent corporation) and private industrial railroads offering some public access. Entries furnish name, reporting marks, maximum mileage, beginning and ending dates, and disposition of assets, when available. There is an index of reporting marks.

A less comprehensive work is *Railroad Names: A Directory of Common Carrier Railroads Operating in the United States 1826–1989* by William D. Edson (Edson, 1989), which is limited to common carrier railroads in the continental United States. Although much of the material is duplicated, there is also much unique information in each title.

917. **Symbols of America.** Hal Morgan. New York: Viking, 1986. 239p. ISBN 0-670-80667-6.

Aimed at the general public as well as students and researchers interested in the advertising business, this entertaining and informative book treats trademarks and logos associated with U.S. products over the years. In the period of business development and merchandising, it was important to develop a symbol that would serve to distinguish a product or service. Hundreds of these are treated, with their origin and development traced; in some cases, one is able to see the changes over the years in well-known symbols (such as that of Morton's salt). There are two major sections: "Visions of America," subdivided by subjects; and "Symbols of Commerce," subdivided by product. Photographs and illustrations in black and white serve to enhance the narrative. There are bibliographic notes and a brand-name index.

918. **United States Business History, 1602–1988: A Chronology.** Richard Robinson, comp. Westport, CT: Greenwood, 1990. 643p. (Garland Reference Library of Social Science, v.807). ISBN 0-313-26095-8.

This is an interesting and informative chronology of U.S. business over a period of nearly 400 years beginning with the arrival of the earliest settlers from Europe. It will be welcomed by inquirers at all levels for its breadth of coverage. It identifies major events on a year-to-year basis, with each year divided into two major sections. "General Events" identifies changes in living conditions and social structure; "Business Events" highlights activities and developments of both general and specific nature in the corporate world. The chronology is a marvel of detail and factual presentation that should prove advantageous to those searching for obscure information. Coverage includes such diverse personalities as Al Capone and Marilyn Monroe; events and organizations also vary considerably. There is a detailed index of names of people and organizations.

Biographical Sources

919. **Biographical Dictionary of American Business Leaders.** John N. Ingham. Westport, CT: Greenwood, 1983. 4v. ISBN 0-313-21362-3.

Greenwood Press commissioned historian John Ingham to produce a large-scale retrospective biographical dictionary. Ingham wrote all the entries himself, unusual for a work of this sort, and submitted them for review by a panel of historians. The intent was to treat historically significant business leaders; therefore, most personalities are deceased. (Lee Iacocca and a few other living persons are included.) Biographical sketches are based on secondary sources but serve adequately to identify and describe the biographees. More than 1,100 personalities are covered, with descriptions ranging from a single paragraph to several pages in length. A bibliography is supplied for each one. Appendices furnish listings by industry, company, birthplace, place of business, religion, ethnicity, birthdate, and gender. Although there are several misrepresentations in the index concerning names of foreign firms, the work is generally accurate.

AGRICULTURE, FORESTRY, AND CONSERVATION

Agriculture has remained an important factor in economic history since the beginning of this nation. There have been major problems requiring resolution: slavery as an institution, state's rights, bank charters, railroad kickbacks, tariffs, and labor and trade unionism, to name only a few. More recently, there is the crisis regarding the foreclosure of family farms.

In addition to works on agriculture, included in this section are tools on conservation, forestry, and reclamation of land. The Nonpartisan League is treated here, but one should consult the next section, "Labor," for treatment of unions, including the United Farm Workers.

The Forest History Society was founded in 1946 in Durham, North Carolina and has 1,750 members. It publishes *Forest History Cruiser* on a quarterly basis. The Agricultural History Society, headquartered in Washington, D.C., was founded in 1919 and has 1,400 members. Its quarterly journal, *Agricultural History*, has been issued since 1927. The Historical Farm Association was founded in 1971 and operates out of Stroudsburg, Pennsylvania. There are 1,200 members; a newsletter is issued.

920. **Agriculture in America, 1622–1860: Printed Works in the Collections of the American Philosophical Society, The Historical Society of Pennsylvania, The Library Company of Philadelphia.** Andrea J Tucher, comp. New York: Garland, 1984, 212p. (Americana to 1860; Four Bibliographies of Printed Works in the Collections of Three Philadelphia Libraries, v.2). ISBN 0-8240-8967-7.

This is the second of four historical bibliographies supported by a grant from the Mellon Foundation and designed to furnish a union list of the holdings of three important Philadelphia libraries. Others cover philanthropy (entry 671), natural history (entry 738), and education (entry 676). The agricultural publications listed here span a 240-year period prior to the Civil

War. The tool serves the interests of scholars and serious students in its emphasis on broadsides, trade catalogs, prospectuses, circular letters, almanacs, printed speeches, and society transactions. The work begins with an introductory history and contains about 2,000 alphabetically arranged entries. The compiler is also responsible for the bibliography on natural history in this series. Like the others, this title furnishes a chronology of the publications and detailed appendices that include an index by subject and institution.

921. **The American Farm Crisis: An Annotated Bibliography with Analytical Intro-duction.** Harold D. Guither and Harold G. Halcrow. Ann Arbor, MI: Pierian, 1988. 164p. ISBN 0-87650-240-0.

This bibliography of recently published materials, most of which date to the mid-1980s, furnishes the historian and student with an excellent historical perspective of today's farming crisis, the causes of which are certain to be studied for the next few years. The work identifies 465 annotated entries covering government documents, journal articles, books, and reports of state agricultural extension agencies. These are arranged into eight chapters that categorize the issues for both understanding and ultimate management. These chapters cover the farm in transition, the scientific and technological revolution, business management, markets and marketing, farms and rural communities, government commodity programs, necessary policy changes, and the use of information and education. Annotations furnish ample descriptions of content. There is a chronology of important dates and a glossary of terms; author and title indexes provide access.

922. **Encyclopedia of American Agricultural History.** Edward L. Schapsmeier and Frederick H. Schapsmeier. Greenwood, 1975. 467p. ISBN 0-8371-7958-0.

As a convenience tool, this work still has value for inquirers at all levels in its alphabetical listing of some 2,500 entries covering agricultural history in a comprehensive manner. The encyclopedia's breadth inspired some negative reactions at the time of publication on the part of reviewers, who felt there were no clearly perceived criteria for inclusion in treating such diverse elements as the Monroe Doctrine and Bob Dylan. Anomalies, such as the inclusion of an entry for Texas but not one for Iowa, are pointed out. Even so, the articles are useful; a number of them have been contributed by historians and furnish perspective of agencies, personalities, legislation, events, and developments, as well as definitions of terms. Arrange-ment is alphabetical, and articles vary from a few lines to a page in length. Cross-references are given, as are brief bibliographies. Numerous topical indexes and a subject/name index give access.

923. **Encyclopedia of American Forest and Conservation History.** Richard C. Davis, ed. Macmillan, 1983. 2v. ISBN 0-02-907350-2.

The lofty goal of this two-volume effort was to produce the standard, authoritative guide and reference to the history of U.S. forestry conservation, forest industries, and related subjects. It contains over 400 articles signed by specialists and covers a broad range of topics, such as biographies of naturalists, national parks, government agencies, legislation, various organizations, related industries, associations, even ecological processes. More than 200 scholars and specialists contributed to the effort, for which the entries are arranged alphabeti-cally by topic. Selection of entries was determined by a panel of experts. The title is useful to inquirers at all levels, because of both its comprehensive nature and its careful execution. Numerous photographs accompany the text. There are five appendices that furnish chronolo-gies and listings and an index to provide access.

924. **Historical Directory of American Agricultural Fairs.** Donald B. Marti. New York: Greenwood, 1986. 300p. ISBN 0-313-24184-0.

Agricultural fairs represent a historical tradition in the study of rural life and have been major gala events for many years. It has been reported that attendance at these fairs today exceeds 125 million people a year. This is a directory of over 2,000 fairs; the most important ones are described in some detail. All types of agricultural fairs are treated, including livestock shows, state fairs, county fairs, 4-H events, and Future Farmers of America-sponsored fairs. The work opens with an introductory narrative describing the nature of fairs and giving the history of U.S. agricultural fairs as well as the role of the Grange. A bibliography is furnished. The 205 major fairs are listed alphabetically and described in terms of origin and history as well as attractions. The appendix lists another 2,000 fairs. There is an index of names and subjects.

925. **The Nonpartisan League, 1915–22: An Annotated Bibliography.** Patrick K. Coleman and Charles R. Lamb, comps. St. Paul, MN: Historical Press, 1985. 86p. ISBN 0-87351-189-1.

The history of the Nonpartisan League is documented in this bibliography of books, manuscript collections, pamphlets, articles, papers, court cases, and government documents available in 18 U.S. and Canadian libraries. Although it can serve as a union list, the title has been developed as a bibliography important to the needs of scholars and serious students in furnishing over 1,000 annotated entries. Also included are black-and-white photographs and political cartoons of the time. The league began in 1915 in North Dakota and was especially influential in the Plains states and the mountain states, where it served as a political party promoting the economic interest of the farmer. This title, recognized as the most complete bibliographic work on the subject, is divided into eight format categories (e.g., books, periodical articles, archival and manuscript collections). It builds on a bibliographic base provided by an earlier history of the league described below.

Robert L. Morlan's *Political Prairie Fire: The Nonpartisan League, 1915–1922* (University of Minnesota, 1955; repr. Minnesota Historical Society, 1985), is a balanced and detailed history of the league and its leader, Arthur Townley. The work is well documented, and prior to publication of the Coleman and Lamb title was considered the top bibliography of the movement.

926. **North American Forest and Conservation History: A Bibliography.** Ronald J. Fahl. Santa Barbara, CA: ABC-Clio, 1977. 408p. ISBN 0-87436-235-0.

Important to the study of U.S. economic history are the forest industries, which, together with conservation policy and practices, inspired much documentation in the United States and Canada. This title, underwritten by various sources and an NEH grant, is a historical bibliography of primary and secondary source material on all aspects of the utilization, exploitation, and appreciation of the forests. More than 8,150 entries are arranged alphabetically. Most are twentieth-century publications, with the cutoff date in mid-1975. The work opens with a well-developed introductory essay on the history of forest bibliography and the manner in which resources may be utilized.

A companion volume born of the same project is Richard C. Davis's *North American Forest History: A Guide to Archives and Manuscripts in the United States and Canada* (ABC-Clio, 1977). It serves as a guide to over 3,800 collections and sets of manuscripts and archives in nearly 360 repositories. Arrangement is by repository under state. A subject index furnishes access.

927. **Reclaiming the American West: A Historiography and Guide.** Lawrence Bacon Lee. Santa Barbara, CA: ABC-Clio, 1980. 131p. ISBN 0-87436-298-9.

This work originated as an article published in the *Pacific Historical Review* two years earlier and was expanded to monographic length with the addition of an introduction by a specialist, along with a bibliography and biographical sketches of important writers and leaders. Also given is a directory of water resource associations and a glossary of terms. Lee defines reclamation historiography as a field of historical literature related to conservation and environmental activity; irrigation agriculture is the key concern. The essay is divided into topical segments covering various aspects of reclamation from the nineteenth century on: the irrigation movement, the Bureau of Reclamation, influence of the engineering profession, the Department of Agriculture, interpretation of historians, and challenges to the Bureau of Reclamation. The essay segments are well-documented, and each is given a bibliography of government documents, articles, books, and dissertations. The work furnishes a useful perspective of reclamation practice and the issues surrounding irrigation. An index provides access.

LABOR

Because of the multifaceted nature of its struggle and emergence, U.S. labor has inspired the curiosity of reporters and the scrutiny of historians more than any other single element or factor of economic history. The labor movement embraces political, social, moral, and humanitarian issues, furnishing incentive for inquiry and documentation on a large scale and from different perspectives. These range from the perception of, on the one hand, a noble struggle waged by a valiant and exploited underdog element striving for social justice to, on the other hand, a selfish and self-serving power wielder determined to control the operations of its employers. The working class, its unions, and its activities are revealed in these reference sources.

Library Resources

928. **American Federation of Labor and Congress of Industrial Organizations Pamphlets, 1889–1955: A Bibliography and Subject Index to the Pamphlets Held in the AFL-CIO Library.** Mark E. Woodbridge, comp. Westport, CT: Greenwood, 1977. 73p. ISBN 0-8371-9686-8.

Prepared as a printed guide to primary source material, this unannotated listing of titles is available at the AFL-CIO Library in Washington, D.C. These pamphlets were created to draw the attention of the general public as well as union members to the major issues and problems of the day, serving as a convenient means by which to publicize union programs. There are more than 750 AFL pamphlets issued between 1889 and 1955 and nearly 300 issued by the CIO between 1935 and 1955, thus offering an excellent perspective on labor history in this country. Arrangement is chronological by year, then alphabetical by title. Entries generally furnish author, title, and pagination, except in cases of reprints of journal articles, for which reference is given to periodical titles and months. Foreign language items are included. A subject index is furnished.

A major effort from Greenwood Press is the actual source material published on 19 microfilm reels as *AFL and CIO Pamphlets, 1889–December 1955: Held in the AFL-CIO Library*. It is useful to labor historians.

929. **A Guide to the Archives of Labor History and Urban Affairs, Wayne State University.** Warner W. Pflug, comp. and ed. Detroit: Wayne State University, 1974. 195p. ISBN 0-8143-1501-1.

The collection at Wayne State University, with the generous support of Walter Ruether and the United Automobile, Aerospace, and Agricultural Implement Workers Union, has achieved national prominence for the study of labor history. By the mid-1970s, the library had acquired over 230 collections of personal papers of important leaders, activists, and government officials. In addition, there are records of prominent labor organizations: the Air Line Pilots Association, the American Federation of Teachers, the Newspaper Guild, the United Auto Workers, the United Farm Workers, the Congress of Industrial Organizations (CIO), and others. The urban affairs materials generally emphasize the Detroit area and represent a more recent collecting specialty. The work is a comprehensive, well-developed guide with lengthy annotations describing the various collections and their creators. There is also a listing of unprocessed materials.

930. **United States Department of Labor Library Catalog, Washington, D.C.** United States Department of Labor. Boston: G. K. Hall, 1975. 38v. ISBN 0-8161-1165-0.

Another of the G. K. Hall catalogs of important library collections is this 38-volume effort enumerating the abundant materials housed at the U.S. Department of Labor in Washington, D.C. All formats are included: books, periodicals, reports, microfilm, microfiche, and cassettes. Union publications such as proceedings, transactions, constitutions, and journals are treated. Of importance to researchers and serious students, the title also features sequential reports from state labor departments. The collection spans the years from 1795 to the time of publication and contains 535,000 items relating to all aspects of labor and working conditions. Such issues as labor history, law, workmen's compensation, strikes and lockouts, and arbitration are treated among the 832,000 catalog cards arranged alphabetically in dictionary fashion. Cross-references are given as well.

Bibliographical Sources

An important online tool is *Laborlaw,* published by the Bureau of National Affairs and available through DIALOG. It is made up of seven subfiles and furnishes summaries of decisions as well as references to determinations regarding labor relations, fair employment, and similar issues. Some of the rulings go back to 1938.

931. **American Labor History and Comparative Labor Movements: A Selected Bibliography.** James C. McBrearty. Tucson, AZ: University of Arizona, 1973. 262p. ISBN 0-8165-0392-3.

The story of U.S. labor is told through the great majority of the nearly 3,200 entries of books and periodical articles, which include both fiction and nonfiction material representing all viewpoints. About 500 of the entries identify labor movements in other countries, creating the comparative aspect mentioned in the title. The author is an academic who headed the Institute of Industrial and Labor Relations at the University of Arizona and is well-qualified to develop this useful tool. Entries on U.S. labor history are listed alphabetically by author under categories identified either chronologically or topically, with foreign labor movements arranged by country. There is a listing of about 200 novels concerning U.S. labor, all of which are described through informative annotations. An author index furnishes access.

932. **American Working Class History: A Representative Bibliography.** Maurice F. Neufeld, et al. New York: Bowker, 1983. 356p. ISBN 0-8352-1752-3.

This updated and expansive revision of a 1964 publication by Neufeld furnishes over 7,250 entries of various types of materials relevant to the history of the U.S. working class. Included here are books, articles, novels, plays, films, dissertations, theses, government documents, union documents, and management publications based on the annual bibliographies compiled by Dorothy Swanson and published in the journal, *Labor History*. Arrangement of entries is in 13 major categories: labor development, legislation, leadership, women, and others. Publications span a period of 175 years from the early 1800s through 1982. The compilers have adhered to their purpose in furnishing a representative bibliography identifying materials that express all viewpoints. An author index is furnished to this tool, which is useful to inquirers at all levels.

933. **Cesar Chavez and the United Farm Workers: A Selective Bibliography.** Beverly Fodell. Detroit: Wayne State University, 1974. 103p. ISBN 0-8143-1502-X.

From the archivist of the important collection at Wayne State University (entry 929) comes this useful, concise bibliography of Caesar Chavez, whose impact on the farm labor movement was monumental. This work represents a revised and expanded edition of the initial publication in 1970 and furnishes an annotated bibliography of books, articles, pamphlets, newspaper pieces, government documents, theses and dissertations, and unpublished source material. Articles are drawn from a variety of periodicals and represent general-interest magazines, scholarly journals, and union, grower, and even church publications. In the mid-1970s, the UFW was much in the news, and inquirers at all levels profit from this effort. Emphasis is given to the organizing efforts of the time. Annotations are descriptive of content and, although brief, are informative.

934. **The Immigrant Labor Press in North America, 1840s–1970s: An Annotated Bibliography.** Dirk Hoerder and Christiane Harzig, eds. New York: Greenwood, 1987. 3v. (Bibliographies and Indexes in American History, no.4, 7–8). ISBN 0-313-24638-6 (v.1).

A relatively recent effort of Greenwood Press is this three-volume annotated bibliography of the immigrant labor press. The set represents an important contribution to researchers at all levels. Volume 1, *Migrants from Northern Europe*, furnishes a listing of labor publications produced in the United States by individuals from the Nordic countries (Iceland, Norway, Denmark, Sweden, and Finland). Volume 2, *Migrants from Eastern and Southeastern Europe*, covers the labor publications of those from Byelorussia, Russia, Lithuania, Latvia, Estonia, Czechoslovakia, Hungary, the Ukraine, Yugoslavia, Bulgaria, Albania, Romania, and Greece, as well as those of Jewish persuasion. Volume 3, *Migrants from Southern and Western Europe*, treats the publications of former Italians, Spaniards, British, Dutch, French, and Germans. Entries in all volumes furnish title, place of publication, duration, languages, first edition and publisher, circulation, dates, frequency, and so forth. Introductory essays open each volume; indexes of titles, places, and dates conclude the efforts.

935. **Labor Education in the US: An Annotated Bibliography.** Richard E. Dwyer. Metuchen, NJ: Scarecrow, 1977. 274p. ISBN 0-8108-1058-1.

The author, an academic in the area of labor studies, opens with a well-developed 26-page introductory history of labor studies in the United States, in which he explains the objectives and describes the operations and clienteles. The comprehensive bibliography is unique in its coverage of this topic and places emphasis on the period beginning with the onset of World War I and progressing to the mid-1970s. Various sources are treated; books, journal articles, ERIC documents, oral history collections and archival repositories. The 1,900 entries are organized into three major sections: "Workers' Education" enumerates the sponsorship of programs independent of unions prior to the 1930s; "Labor Education" identifies union involvement beginning in the 1930s; "Labor Studies" covers the involvement of academe with accredited courses. These sections are subdivided into categories such as "historical and descriptive studies." Author and subject indexes are furnished.

936. **Labor in America: A Historical Bibliography.** Santa Barbara, CA: ABC-Clio, 1985. 307p. (Clio Bibliography Series, no.18.) ISBN 0-87436-397-7.

Another of the convenience tools useful to both researchers and students drawn from the publisher's enormous database, which produces *America: History and Life* (entry 51), this work furnishes nearly 2,900 entries published between 1973 and 1983. The database provided the opportunity to search over 2,000 journals from the fields of history and the social sciences and thus offers an extensive coverage of periodical literature during this time period. Arrangement of entries is within five broad time categories: "Labor in America: Multi-period," "Early American Labor to 1865," "Labor in Post-Bellum America to 1900," "Labor in the New Century, 1900 to 1945," and "Modern Labor, 1945 to 1982." Within these categories are topical subdivisions such as "The Workers" and "The Labor Movement," under which the entries are alphabetically arranged. Author and subject indexes are given.

937. **Labor Relations and Collective Bargaining: A Bibliographic Guide to Doctoral Research.** Milden J. Fox and Patsy C. Howard. Metuchen, NJ: Scarecrow, 1983. 281p. ISBN 0-8108-1632-6.

Another convenience tool useful to scholars and serious students is this well-developed bibliography of doctoral dissertations drawn from over 100 bibliographic sources and dating from 1913 to the present. Most are from U.S. universities, although Canadian and other foreign works are included. More than 2,700 dissertations are identified, making this a comprehensive source of information. Arrangement of entries is alphabetical by author, with detailed subject indexes offering access through geographic and organizational approaches, including industries, trades and professions, and various topics ranging from the narrow and specific to the very broad. Examples of topical treatment include "Turnover/Mobility," "Collective Bargaining," and "Negotiations." An entry furnishes author, title, degree, institution, and date, as well as the bibliographic sources from which it was drawn; order numbers are furnished from *Dissertation Abstracts International* (entry 92).

938. **Worker Benefits: Industrial Welfare in America, 1900–1935: An Annotated Bibliography.** Martha J. Soltow and Susan Gravelle. Metuchen, NJ: Scarecrow, 1983. 230p. ISBN 0-8108-1614-8.

Developed in the midst of the Reagan administration's increasingly laissez-faire agenda, this bibliography furnishes an excellent listing of materials relevant to industrial welfare prior to the Roosevelt administration's New Deal. This is a well-organized bibliography of nearly 700 books, articles, reports, pamphlets and government documents organized into nine chapters. These deal with the development of employer welfare; industrial democracy; descriptive surveys; company and industry programs; employee benefits in mining, railroads, steel, and textile industries; company towns and workers' housing; various specific programs illustrating different benefits; labor's response; as well as biographies of various leaders. This work should reveal areas of needed inquiry to researchers and furnishes excellent suggestions for study to teachers and students. There are two indexes, one by company and one of general nature.

Information Sources

939. First Facts of American Labor: A Comprehensive Collection of Labor Firsts in the United States Arranged by Subject. Philip S. Foner, comp. New York: Holmes & Meier, 1984. ISBN 0-8419-0742-0.

This is a detailed chronology of "firsts" in U.S. labor history, beginning as early as 1526 with a slave revolt in present-day South Carolina and progressing to the signing of a first union contract by the J. P. Stevens Company of North Carolina in 1980. Research for this work entailed the use of union histories, biographical works, and newspapers, as well as monographs on specific topics. Entries are arranged alphabetically under broad subject categories. They vary in length and generally are concise but informative. Access is furnished by a detailed index of names, events, and titles.

Similar in scope is *The Labor Almanac* by Adrian A. Paradis and Grace D. Paradis (Libraries Unlimited, 1983). Important events, aspects, topics, and leaders are rendered along with definitions in an eight-part treatment beginning with a chronology. There are listings of unions, labor leaders, legislation, government agencies, information sources, and activities. A comprehensive index furnishes access.

940. Labor Conflict in the United States: An Encyclopedia. Ronald L. Filippelli, ed. New York: Garland, 1990. 609p. (Garland Reference Library of Social Science, v.697). ISBN 0-8240-7968-X.

This one-volume encyclopedia furnishes comprehensive coverage of events, personalities, and issues relevant to labor conflict in this country over a period of about 330 years from the Virginia indentured servants strike in 1661 to the Eastern Airlines workers strike in 1989. The violence or intensity of the altercations varies considerably from the major struggles involving the Pullman Company, Homestead strikers, and Haymarket "rioters" to milder demonstrations waged by a variety of workers in different industries, crafts, and trades throughout the country at different times. Contributors are varied and include trade unionists, labor historians, and graduate students who have all signed their articles. Entries average two to three pages in length and are arranged alphabetically. There is a chronology of events, table of contents, glossary of terms, bibliography, and an index.

941. Labor Unions. Gary M. Fink, ed. in chief. Westport, CT: Greenwood, 1977. 520p. (The Greenwood Encyclopedia of American Institutions, no.1). ISBN 0-8371-8938-1.

The first volume in the Greenwood series designed to furnish coverage of important U.S. institutions, the work identifies and describes over 200 national labor organizations. These were selected for their importance in terms of longevity, historical impact, size, and influence. Entries are arranged alphabetically by keyword in title and vary in length from two to four pages. The editor, an academician, has been aided by the contributions of various individuals, some of whom have signed their entries. Most useful to researchers at various levels are the suggestions for further research within each entry. There are five appendices that offer listings of chartered unions, a chronology, genealogies, union executives, and membership charts. There is a glossary and an index.

Biographical Sources

942. **Biographical Dictionary of American Labor.** 2nd ed., rev. and exp. Gary M. Fink, ed. in chief. Westport, CT: Greenwood, 1984. 767p. ISBN 0-313-22865-5.

This is a revision and expansion of the editor's initial edition of 1974, which treated 500 figures. The present edition furnishes over 725 biographical sketches of personalities representative of the diversity within the labor movement in this country. There is a conscious effort to include women and minorities; much care has been taken in the revision of previously used entries. The change in emphasis from the "leaders" covered in the first edition to the representative figures of this one has made it possible to include a good percentage of the rank-and-file membership, along with the addition of previously omitted leaders, making it a more comprehensive work for purposes of identification. Appendices furnish listings by union affiliation, religion, birthplace and public office held. The bibliography has been updated; there is a detailed index.

DEPRESSION AND RECESSION

Economic downturns are part of the cycle of a free trade economy and are influenced by certain fundamentals or factors. Severity ranges from the mildest recessions to the Great Depression of the 1920s-1930s. Out of that tragic circumstance came a number of reforms packaged in the New Deal of President Roosevelt. In this section are books relating both to the Great Depression and the reform measures adopted to combat it. Materials on public works can be found in chapter 5 under the heading "Social Welfare and Philanthropy."

943. **The Great Depression: A Historical Bibliography.** Santa Barbara, CA: ABC-Clio, 1984. 260p. (ABC-Clio Research Guides, no.4). ISBN 0-87436-361-6.

Another of the spin-off efforts derived from the great database that produces *America: History and Life* (entry 51), this is a useful convenience tool for both researchers and students. Like others in the series, this title furnishes over 950 entries with abstracts as they appeared in the parent work. Most are periodical articles; all were published between 1973 and 1982. Entries are arranged under five major sections: "The Crash of '29 and Its Economic Aftermath," "The New Democratic Coalition and the Republican Response," "Relief, Reform and Recovery: The New Deal Social Program," "Social Programs, Protest, and Reaction," and "The Culture of the Depression." Selections are drawn from hundreds of periodicals in history and the social sciences. There is an index by author and the publisher's own SPIndex.

944. **The Great Depression: America, 1929–1941.** Robert S. McElvaine. New York: Times Books, 1984. 402p. ISBN 0-8129-1061-3.

This is a historical account furnishing an interesting interpretation of the causes and factors associated with the Great Depression of 1929. Both the scholar and the student will benefit from its scrutiny in developing a better understanding of the phenomenon. In this work, both social and political conditions are examined; interpretations are given of the motives and values of decisionmakers and the common folk. The work is divided into 15 chapters covering such aspects as President Hoover's policies, President Roosevelt's charisma, and the growing militancy of the Congress of Industrial Organizations (CIO), with its demands for a sympathetic government response to the needs of labor. The author sees the major cause of the Depression as the inequity in distribution of income and regards the

Roosevelt administration's support of labor as a political rather than ideological decision. This work appeals to inquirers at all levels.

945. **Historical Dictionary of the New Deal: From Inauguration to Preparation for War.** James S. Olson, ed. Westport, CT: Greenwood, 1985. 611p. ISBN 0-313-23873-1.

Another of Professor Olson's fine historical dictionaries prepared for Greenwood Press, this effort contains about 700 entries covering personalities, laws, agencies, court cases, political groups, and miscellaneous topics, such as "Greenbelt Towns." As in other dictionaries edited by Olson, a number of contributors have aided his effort. Entries vary in length from a half to two pages, depending upon the significance of the topic, and reflect the important aspects of the nation's domestic policy between 1933 and 1940. The title is useful to scholars, students, and the general public because of its comprehensive coverage of relevant concerns and issues, which vary from those of monumental importance to those that are more obscure. Arrangement of entries is alphabetical; four appendices furnish a chronology, a bibliography, and listings of personnel and of acronyms.

946. **New Day/New Deal: A Bibliography of the Great American Depression, 1929–1941.** David E. Kyvig, et al., comps. Westport, CT: Greenwood, 1988. 320p. (Bibliographies and Indexes in American History, no.9). ISBN 0-313-26027-3.

This is an important, relatively recent bibliography of comprehensive nature on the Great Depression. Although the compilers disavow any claim to definitive coverage, one must agree with their perception of the work as the most extensive bibliography of its kind. There are over 4,600 entries, none of them annotated. They are organized into 13 chapters, such as "Overviews and General Histories," "Participant Accounts," "The Hoover Administration," and "The Roosevelt Administration." These are subdivided by topic, then by format. Of the total, 2,500 are articles; there are 1,300 books and 800 dissertations. All works are in English; emphasis is given to publications of the past 25 years. Omission of contemporaneous publications from the 1930s has been noted by reviewers. An author index is provided.

947. **Pickaxe and Pencil: References for the Study of the WPA. Marguerite D. Bloxom. Washington: Library of Congress, 1982; distr. by the Superintendent of Documents, Government Printing Office. 87p. ISBN 0-8444-0384-9.**

The Works Progress Administration was the New Deal agency designed to boost the economy by creating employment through government projects. It became the Works Projects Administration in 1939 and was terminated in 1942. Throughout its brief history, it was most influential in administering funds designated for recovery from the Depression. This bibliography covers the entire history of the operation with almost 400 entries identifying books and articles. There is a separate listing of dissertations. Entries are organized into nine chapters, the first three of which give background information, followed by chapters on individual projects, such as the Federal Writers Project and the Federal Theatre Project. Entries are subdivided into time categories of publication: those prior to 1943, and those from 1943 to 1980. Brief annotations are furnished, and each section is given an introductory narrative. Photographs are included; there is an author index.

Author/Title Index

The numbers in the index generally refer to item entry numbers. Additional sources mentioned in the annotations to the major entries (co-entries and minor entries) are indexed with the designation "n" following the entry number. Also those authors and publications identified or described in the narrative of prefatory and introductory passages rather than within entries are indexed by page numbers preceded by "p." All sources available online or in CD-ROM format are preceded by an asterisk (*).

The following guidelines were used in alphabetizing index entries. Lengthy titles have been shortened in some cases. Arrangement is word by word. Names beginning with Mc or Mac or O' are treated as spelled. Acronyms, initialisms, abbreviations, and hyphenated word phrases employed in titles such as OHA, U.S., and Italian-Americans are treated as single words. Be sure to check listings under both United States and U.S. when in doubt. Numbers (including dates) when part of the title are arranged as though written in word form except when part of a chronological sequence or series. In such cases, the years or dates in the titles are arranged from earliest to latest in terms of coverage and scope.

Subject Index

Access is provided to the different themes, topics, and issues addressed by all entries (major, minor, and co-equal) wherever possible, as well as those covered in the introductory narratives to chapters, sections, and subsections. Specific titles described in those introductions are cited in the Author/Title Index. Numbers generally refer to entry numbers; page number references are preceded by a " p." Entry numbers of co-equal entries and minor entries described within the annotations of major entries are designated by an " n."